Managerial economics

Analysis and cases

Managerial
— economics
Analysis and cases

WILLIAM R. HENRY, Ph.D.
Professor of Business Administration
Georgia State University

W. WARREN HAYNES
Late Dean of Business Administration
State University of New York at Albany

1978   Fourth edition

BUSINESS PUBLICATIONS, INC.
Dallas, Texas   75243

Irwin-Dorsey Limited   Georgetown, Ontario   L7G 4B3

ISBN 0-256-02079-5
Library of Congress Catalog Card No. 77–91316

Printed in the United States of America

1 2 3 4 5 6 7 8 9 0 K 5 4 3 2 1 0 9 8

Preface

This text on managerial economics contains: (1) expositions of theoretical and analytical tools of economics that are useful in managerial decision making; (2) reviews of empirical studies and illustrations of applications of the managerial economics concepts; (3) many short problems and a number of cases involving managerial situations that call for economic analysis; (4) lists of articles in professional journals that are recommended for further reading.

The book reflects several guidelines developed by the author of the first two editions: (1) The exposition of theoretical ideas should flow from simple to complex with considerable repetition of the basic concepts; (2) Each presentation of theoretical analysis should be immediately followed by practical applications to demonstrate relevance and help bridge the gap between theory and practice; (3) An abundance of problems and cases should be provided to let students test their understanding of theoretical concepts and develop the judgment skills required in applications of managerial economics; (4) There should be enough institutional, psychological, and sociological material to give students practice in coping with the influences of complex and shifting environments upon decision processes; (5) The underlying analytical structure from economics should be carefully related to concepts from accounting, finance, production, marketing, personnel, and business policy to help students integrate their professional knowledge.

In preparing this fourth edition, I have been aware that many students add the text to their permanent professional libraries. I have tried to provide adequate expositions over a wide range of topics, so that the book will be satisfactory for future use as a reference by practicing managers and staff economists.

Quantitative approaches to managerial economic analysis have been given a little more emphasis than in earlier editions. However, the assumed mathematical and statistical preparation of students is at the sophomore and junior level. Teachers can easily increase or decrease the quantitative emphasis to suit needs and abilities of particular classes and individual students.

Users of earlier editions will find (in Chapters 6 through 10) a completely reorganized and more carefully developed treatment of the following topics: resource allocation, cost minimization, cost estimation, cost and profitability analysis for continuative production, and cost and profitability analysis for discrete runs of production. Although the remainder of the text is much like the corresponding material in the third edition, close readers will find many small changes. One (not so small) change that deserves attention here is the integration of decision tree analysis. A simple decision tree is explained (in connection with decisions about new products) in Chapter 10. A risk-adjusted tree is discussed (in relation to pricing decisions in oligopoly firms) in Chapter 11. And a sequential decision tree with discounted payoffs is described (in a capital budgeting application) in Chapter 14.

I am very grateful to the following persons:

Louis Ederington of Georgia State University for collaboration in rewriting Chapter 10 (Profitability Analysis: Discrete Runs of Production) and Larry Schroeder of Syracuse University for his help in revising Chapter 4 (Business Conditions Analysis), Chapter 5 (Short-Range Forecasting), and Chapter 15 (Cost Effectiveness and Benefit-Cost Analyses);

Bruce Allen of Michigan State University, Ann Fisher of State University of New York College at Fredonia, and John Crockett of the University of Houston for the large number of constructive suggestions resulting from their close reviews of the manuscript, and copy editor Carol Reitz for her assistance with this edition.

Dean Kenneth Black, Jr. of the College of Business Administration at Georgia State University for urging me to make the book my best effort and giving me a full measure of support in the project.

I shall be grateful for suggestions for improving the fifth edition from teachers and students who use this book.

March 1978   WILLIAM R. HENRY

Contents

PART ONE
INTRODUCTION TO MANAGERIAL ECONOMICS

1. **The scope and method of managerial economics** 3

   Relation to other branches of learning, 4
   Profits: A central concept, 7
   Behavioral theory of the firm, 11
   Models and suboptimization, 12
   Organization of this book, 14
   The usefulness of managerial economics, 15

2. **Five fundamental concepts** 18

   Incremental reasoning, 18
   Opportunity cost, 23
   Contribution, 29
   Time perspective on costs and revenues, 33
   Time value of money, 34
   Some important applications, 37

Cases for part one 44

PART TWO
DEMAND ANALYSIS AND SHORT-RANGE FORECASTING

3. **Demand analysis** 57

   Some basic concepts, 57
   Two common demand models, 68
   Market structure, 73
   Other influences on demand elasticities and demand levels, 75
   Psychological and sociological concepts of consumer behavior, 80

vii

Estimating demand equations, 83
A study of demand for durable goods, 91

4. Business conditions analysis 97

Measuring business conditions, 98
Forecasting without macro models, 101
Forecasting with macro models, 108

5. Short-range forecasting 129

Forecasting industry demand and capacity, 129
Forecasting market demand and the firm's share, 140

Cases for part two 148

PART THREE
RESOURCE ALLOCATION, PRODUCTION ECONOMICS, AND
COST ANALYSIS

6. Resource allocation 167

An overview of production, 167
Decisions about a single input that has constant marginal
productivity, 170
Allocating an input that has decreasing marginal productivity, 185
The product mix problem: Conceptual framework, 196
An introduction to linear programming, 202
Sensitivity analysis, 210
Linear programming and some basic economic concepts, 214

7. Cost minimization 222

Technical substitutability of inputs, 222
Economic substitutability of inputs, 227
Linear programming formulation of least-cost problems, 230
The expansion path, 240
Other forms of input substitutability, 244
Short-run cost functions, 247
Long-run cost functions, 255

8. Estimation of production and cost functions 265

The economic-engineering approach, 265
Statistical estimates of production and cost functions, 277
Using estimated functions, 292

PART FOUR
ANALYSIS OF PROFITABILITY OF CHANGES IN OUTPUT

9. **Profitability analysis: Continuative production** **301**

   Classification approach to cost analysis, 301
   Accounting costs and economic costs, 308
   Break-even charts, 311
   Profit-volume analysis, 319
   Curvilinear functions, 321

10. **Profitability analysis: Discrete production runs** **330**

    Terminating production: Product types (or models) and projects, 330
    Intermittent production: Lots, 354

Cases for part four **382**

PART FIVE
ANALYSIS OF PRICE AND NONPRICE COMPETITION

11. **Price and nonprice competition** **407**

    An overview of price theory, 407
    Theory of pricing with demand taken as given, 409
    Theory of deliberate demand shifting, with price taken as given, 415
    Oligopoly, 420
    Decision tree analysis of an oligopoly firm's marketing
    alternatives, 427
    Appraisal of several shortcuts in pricing, 434
    Incremental reasoning in pricing, 436
    The pricing process, 438

12. **Selected topics in pricing** **454**

    Price discrimination, 454
    Peak-load pricing, 462
    Public utility rate regulation, 470
    Multiple-product pricing, 476
    Transfer pricing, 480

Cases for part five **496**

PART SIX
LONG-RANGE PLANNING

13. **Long-range forecasting and strategy formulation** **539**

    Formulation of corporate strategy, 539
    Social forecasting, 544

Technological forecasting, 550
Resource forecasting, 556
Forecasting joint and derived demands: Input-output analysis, 558
An example of strategy formulation: Radio Corporation
of America, 561
Some examples of long-range forecasting for nonprofit
organizations, 561

14. **Capital budgeting** **568**

Central role of corporate strategy, 568
An overview of capital budgeting, 570
Forecasting cash flow of a project, 571
Measuring project profitability, 573
Costs of capital, 579
Mutually exclusive projects, 583
Risk adjustments, 585
Using decision trees in capital planning, 586
Capital rationing, 592
Empirical studies, 592

Cases for part six **598**

PART SEVEN
APPLICATIONS IN PUBLIC AND NONPROFIT AGENCIES

15. **Cost-effectiveness and benefit-cost analysis** **639**

Role of the public sector in the economy, 640
Estimating demands and evaluating benefits, 642
Production and costs in the public sector, 649
Prices, charges, and subsidies, 651
Benefit-cost and cost-effectiveness analyses, 656
Multiple objectives and group decisions in the public sector, 666

Cases for part seven **671**

Appendix **685**

Index of cases **697**

Index **699**

List of figures

1–1   The two worlds of a decision-maker, 14

2–1   Annual revenues and expenses, widget production, 25

2–2   Expected annual revenues and expenses, gadget production, 25

2–3   Incremental revenue, cost, and profit (change to alternative 2), 26

2–4   Incremental revenue, cost, and profit (change to alternative 3), 26

2–5   Revenue, economic cost, and economic profit (alternative 2), 27

2–6   Revenue, economic cost, and economic profit (alternative 3), 27

2–7   How discounting affects project profitability, 36

3–1   A family of demand curves (hypothetical), 60

3–2   Linear demand curve with varying elasticities and the corresponding total revenue curve (hypothetical), 69

3–3   Constant elasticity demand curves and their log-linear transformations, 72

4–1   Circular flow of national product, 98

4–2   Gross National Product, 101

4–3   Leading, lagging, and coincident indicators, 102

4–4   Condensed flow diagram, 124

5–1   Why cement users are getting squeezed, 139

6–1   A hypothetical production surface for window cleaning (First case: Constant marginal productivity of labor), 171

6–2   Side view of surface, rotated 180°, 172

6–3   Optimum use of input with a rising supply price and constant marginal revenue product, 175

6–4   Constant marginal products of labor in three activities, 176

6–5   Constant marginal revenue products of labor in three activities, 177

6–6   Optimum use of input with falling marginal revenue product and a constant supply price, 180

6–7   Optimum use of an input with falling marginal revenue product and rising marginal resource cost, 182

6–8   Optimum allocation of a limited quantity of an input that has decreasing marginal revenue in multiple uses, 184

6–9   A hypothetical production surface for window cleaning (Second case: Decreasing marginal productivity of labor, 186

6–10   Side view of surface rotated 180°, 187
6–11   Optimum use of an input that has decreasing value of marginal product in a single use, 190
6–12   Graphic method of determining equimarginal allocations of limited quantities of an input among uses in which the input's marginal revenue products are decreasing, 194
6–13   Production possibility curve (heterogeneous inputs), 198
6–14   Production possibility curve (homogeneous inputs), 199
6–15   Production possibility curves (superimposed), 200
6–16   Isocontribution lines: Two outputs, 201
6–17   Optimal combination of two outputs with a given quantity of inputs and a given price of outputs, 202
6–18   Feasible region for a simple LP problem, 207
6–19   Graphic solution for a simple LP problem, 209
7–1   A hypothetical production surface, 223
7–2   Overhead view of production surface: An isoquant map, 224
7–3   Isoquant map with isocost lines superimposed, 228
7–4   Feasible region for nutrient component P, 233
7–5   Feasible region for nutrient component E, 234
7–6   Feasible region for bag weight, 235
7–7   Feasible region with all constraints, 236
7–8   Feasible region with isocost curves, 236
7–9   Least-cost formulation of a poultry ration, 238
7–10   Least-cost formulation of a sausage, 239
7–11   An expansion path, 241
7–12   Incremental reasoning and incremental searching in decisions about input substitution, 243
7–13   Inputs substituting at constant rates, 246
7–14   Inputs that must be combined in fixed proportions, 247
7–15   Total cost of various rates of output under three sets of assumptions about variability of inputs, 248
7–16   Contrasts: Input-output function, scale line, and expansion path, 249
7–17A Total fixed, total variable, and total costs per period at various rates of output in a hypothetical plant, 251
7–17B Marginal, average variable, average fixed, and average total cost at various rates of output in a hypothetical plant, 252
7–18   Short-run cost curves for plants differing in flexibility, 255
7–19   The long-run planning (envelope) curve, 256
7–20   Economies of scale in administration of life insurance companies, 259
8–1   Hypothetical plant process flow diagram, 267
8–2   A long-run cost surface—the engineering view, 270
8–3   Process flow diagram for pear-packing plants, 272
8–4   Five methods of supplying packers with empty boxes, 273
8–5   The relation of costs to rates of output, 278
8–6   Broilers: Economies of scale curve and average cost curves for ten model plants, 279
8–7   Selected transport costs, processing costs and combined costs, for effective production density of 500 birds per square mile per year,

average lengths of haul in miles posted along transport cost curve, 280

8–8   Relationship of processing plant size to combined costs of transportation and processing for different effective production densities, 280

8–9   A multivariate production surface, 282

8–10 Effects of serial correlation upon residuals, 285

8–11 Other methodical disturbances of residuals, 286

8–12 Plant curves and envelope curve, 288

8–13 Seven long-run cost curves statistically estimated from the same set of data for 29 midwestern feed mills, 289

8–14 Economies of scale in banking, 292

9–1   A typical break-even chart, 312

9–2   Break-even chart: Contribution to profit form, 313

9–3   A complex break-even chart, 316

9–4   Estimating the total cost line from a scatter diagram, 317

9–5   Break-even chart with alternative revenue lines for alternative prices, 318

9–6   Profit-contribution chart, 320

9–7   A break-even chart with curvilinear total cost function, 322

9–8   A break-even chart with curvilinear total cost and total revenue functions, 323

10–1 A product's life cycle, 332

10–2 Sales over time—three familiar products, 333

10–3 Life cycles of a series of models, 334

10–4 Hypothetical forecasts for a new plane, 334

10–5 Effects of learning on labor used, 336

10–6 Hypothetical total cost and total revenue for a new plane, 338

10–7 Decision tree for deciding whether to produce a new plane, 339

10–8 Sales and production over product's life cycle, 341

10–9 Changes in output of production runs, 342

10–10 Minimizing economic cost (maximizing profitability) by choosing an optimal rate of production, 347

10–11 Diagram for Project Y, 348

10–12 Network for the NCR project, 350

10–13 Determining optimum time for the NCR project, 352

10–14 Relation of total costs to volume and rate, 353

10–15 Relation of total costs to proportionate changes in rate and volume, 354

10–16 Inventory level under assumptions 1–4, 358

10–17 Effects of order size on inventories and numbers of orders, 359

10–18 Graphical EOQ determination, 362

10–19 Produced goods—inventories under certainty, 367

10–20 Stockout caused by varying lead time, 369

10–21 Stockout caused by varying usage rate, 370

10–22 Inventory with safety stock, 371

10–23 Probability of a stockout at various reorder points, 375

11–1 Pricing and output under pure competition, 410

11–2 Pricing and output under monopoly—short run, 413

11–3 Pricing and output under monopoly—long run, 413

11–4   Pricing and output of a profitable firm under monopolistic competition, 414

11–5   Pricing and output of a marginal firm under monopolistic competition, 415

11–6   Least-cost combinations of promotion and quality improvement for various rates of sales at a given price, 417

11–7A   Optimal total cost and sales at a given price, 419

11–7B   Optimal average and marginal cost and sales at a given price, 419

11–8   Optimal price, 420

11–9   A kinked demand curve, 423

11–10   An oligopolist's decision tree, 429

11–11   A preference curve, 431

11–12   A risk-adjusted decision tree, 433

12–1   Price discrimination—an identical product, two markets, 456

12–2   Load curve for December 19, 1963, 463

12–3   Long-run peak and off-peak pricing: The firm peak case, 464

12–4   Short-run peak-load pricing: The firm peak case, 465

12–5   Peak and off-peak pricing: The shifting peak case, 466

12–6   Cumulative capacity in order of incremental fuel cost, 467

12–7   Alternative levels of public utility rates, 471

12–8   Marginal cost pricing in an increasing-cost industry, 473

12–9   Maximization of profits—two joint products, 477

12–10   Maximization of profits—joint products with destruction of part of one product, 478

12–11   Maximization of profit—alternative products, 479

12–12   Optimum quantity, five products each using one unit of same intermediate product, 483

12–13   False optimum, same five products using common intermediate product, 484

12–14   Imperfect market final product—perfect market intermediate product, 486

12–15   Competing demands—imperfect markets for final product, 487

12–16   Imperfect markets for both final and intermediate product—rising marginal costs, 489

13–1   A set of long-range objectives, 541

13–2   A delphi consensus of scientific breakthroughs, 553

13–3   Trend fitting (s-curves), 554

13–4   History and forecast of industry outputs (history: 1950–1963; forecast: 1964–1975), 559–60

13–5   Projected doctorates awarded and new college teachers required, 564

14–1   Cost of capital, 581

14–2   Comparison of project variability, 586

14–3   Using a sequential decision tree and discounted payoffs, 589

15–1   Consumers' surplus in comparison of programs, 645

15–2   Industrial plant's response to effluent charges, 654

List of tables

2–1 Contributions on five products in a single plant, 30

2–2 Data on five products to be produced in four departments, 31

3–1 Demand schedule, 59

3–2 Income sensitivity of selected consumer expenditures (based on disposable personal income), 79

3–3 Elasticities of demand for oranges (Florida Valencia size 200 and California Valencia size 138), 85

3–4 Income elasticities for food as estimated from cross-section data, 87

3–5 How expenditures on food increase as real income of higher-income families increases, 87

3–6 Demand equations for coffee, 89

4–1 Expenditures on 1975 Gross National Product ($ billions), 100

4–2 National income, 1975, 100

4–3 "Short list" of economic indicators, 103

4–4 Sources and uses of key forecasting information, 115–17

5–1 Interindustry table (in $ millions), 135

5–2 Market area buildup method of estimating a producer's goods' market potential (hypothetical example), 141

6–1 Incremental analysis—how much input to use, where the input has decreasing marginal productivity, 191

6–2 Calculations of marginal revenue products of an input in two of its uses, 193

6–3 Problem information, 203

7–1 Problem information (hypothetical least-cost problem), 231

8–1 Unit labor requirements and production standards for the types of jobs performed in the distribution of empty boxes to the packers, 274

8–2 Equipment requirements for distribution of empty packing boxes with different methods, 275

8–3 Empty box and materials supply—labor, operating, and equipment costs in relation to rates of packed output, 276

8–4 Total variable and fixed costs for a plant of 40,000 pounds per hour capacity, 70 percent packed, and a 200-hour season, 277

8–5 Alternative cost equations derived from identical annual data on total costs, plant volume, and plant capacity, 29 midwestern feed mills, 288

8–6 Long-run average costs in banking, 291

10–1 Hypothetical sales forecasts for a new plane, 335

10–2 Hypothetical average and total costs for a new plane (in $ millions), 338

10–3 Historical production costs—XYZ Construction, 343

10–4 Estimated future costs—XYZ Construction, 344

10–5 NCR century direct-mail campaign, 349

10–6 CPM analysis of NCR century direct-mail campaign, 351

10–7 Determination of EOQ by trial and error, 363

10–8 Usage during reorder periods, 372

10–9 Safety stock analysis, 372

10–10 Probability of a stockout for various reorder points, 374

13–1 Outline for internal appraisal and industry analysis, 543

13–2 Number of companies by industry, using technological forecasting, as related to growth, 556

13–3 Projected 1975 costs per year of undergraduate and graduate education in land grant colleges and universities, 563

14–1 Cash flows from hypothetical project, 573

14–2 Discounted cash flows (10 percent), 575

14–3 Decomposition of cash flows (10 percent), 575

14–4 Discounted cash flows (6 percent), 577

14–5 Decomposition of cash flows (6 percent), 577

14–6 Discounting period by period, with rate changes, 579

14–7 Incremental analysis of mutually exclusive projects, 584

14–8 Expected value of Decision 2, with discounting, 590

14–9 Expected value of Decision 1, with discounting, 591

15–1 Benefits of the proposed Atlanta MARTA system, 660

15–2 Monetary values of the quantifiable benefits of the proposed MARTA system, 661

15–3 Benefit-cost analysis, proposed MARTA system, 662

15–4 Benefits and cost from the individual's viewpoint, 663

15–5 Benefits and costs from society's viewpoint, 664

Part one

Introduction to managerial economics

Chapter 1

The scope and method of managerial economics

Managerial economics is economics applied in decision making. It is a special branch of economics that bridges the gap between abstract theory and managerial practice. It emphasizes the use of economic analysis in clarifying problems, in organizing and evaluating information, and in comparing alternative courses of action. *While managerial economics is sometimes known as business economics, it provides methods and a point of view that are also applicable in managing nonprofit organizations and public agencies.*

Economics is sometimes defined as the study of allocation of scarce social resources among unlimited ends. Managerial economics is the study of allocation of the limited resources available to a firm or other unit of management among the various possible activities of that unit. Thus, *managerial economics is concerned with choice—with selection among alternatives—and it is goal oriented. Managerial economics aims at the maximum achievement of objectives.*

Managerial economics is pragmatic: It is concerned with analytical tools that are useful, that have proven themselves in practice, or that promise to improve decision making in the future. Although it avoids some of the most difficult abstract issues of economic theory, it also faces up to some complications that are ignored in theory, for it must deal with the total situation in which decisions are made.

The relation of managerial economics to economic theory is much like that of engineering to physics, or medicine to biology. It is the relation of an applied field to the more fundamental but more abstract basic disciplines from which it borrows concepts and analytical tools. The fundamental theoretical fields will no doubt in the long run make the greater contribution to the extension of human knowledge. But the applied fields involve the development of skills that are worthy of respect in themselves and that require specialized training. Practicing physicians may not contribute much to the advance of biological theory, but they play an essential role in producing the fruits of progress in theory. Managerial economists stand in a similar relation to economic and management theory, with perhaps the difference that the dichotomy between "pure" and "applied" is less clear in management than it is in medicine.

RELATION TO OTHER BRANCHES
OF LEARNING

Managerial economics has a close connection with microeconomic theory, macroeconomic theory, statistics, decision theory, and operations research. Further, managerial economics draws together and relates ideas from several functional fields of business administration; accounting, production, marketing, finance, and business policy. The fully trained managerial economist uses concepts and methods from all of these disciplines and fields of study.

Microeconomic theory

The main source of concepts and analytical tools for managerial economics is microeconomic theory, also known as the theory of firms and markets, or price theory. This volume contains numerous references to such microeconomic concepts as the elasticity of demand, marginal cost, the short and long runs, and market structures. It also makes use of well-known models in price theory, such as the model for monopoly price, the kinked demand theory, and the model of price discrimination.

In taking a pragmatic point of view, managerial economics neglects some fine points that take up much space in the theoretical literature. For example, managerial economics (at least as developed in this book) makes little use of indifference curves, which are central in the modern theory of demand. Indifference curves have helped clarify some important conceptual issues in economics, such as the separation of the income effects and substitution effects of price change. But so far they have played no part in managerial decisions, since measurement of the variables required in a practical application of indifference analysis is not feasible.

Macroeconomic theory

The chief debt of managerial economics to macroeconomic theory is in the area of forecasting. Since the prospects of an individual firm often depend greatly on business in general, individual firm forecasts depend on general business forecasts. These make use of models derived from theory. The most widely used model in modern forecasting, the gross national product model, is a direct product of theoretical developments in the past 40 years. Although applications bypass some fine points of interest to the theorist, actual use of these models requires an examination of details (inventory in the automobile industry, excess capacity in chemicals, consumer attitudes) that the theory necessarily ignores.

Statistics

Statistics is important to managerial economics in several ways. First, it provides the basis for empirical testing of theory. While deductive reasoning has made a central contribution to economics, the results of that reasoning can never be fully accepted until they are checked against data from the world of reality. This volume presents statistical tests of some of the generalizations most important to managerial economics.

Statistics is important in a second way in providing the individual firm with methods of measuring the functional relationships used in decision making. It is not enough, for example, to state that the firm should base its pricing decisions on considerations of demand and cost. To take such action, the firm needs statistical measurements of the shape and position of the demand and cost functions. As another example, it is not enough to know that linear programming can be used to determine the best product mixes or least-cost input combinations. To apply linear programming, it is necessary to estimate numerous input-output relationships. Statistical approaches are not the only way to obtain estimates of the parameters for decision making. Other sources are accounting, engineering, and subjective managerial estimates. But statistical methods are often helpful.

The theory of decision making

The theory of decision making is a relatively new subject that has significance for managerial economics. Much of economic theory is based on the assumption of a single goal—maximization of utility for the individual or maximization of profit for the firm. It also usually rests on the assumption of certainty—of perfect knowledge. In contrast, the theory of decision making recognizes the multiplicity of goals and the pervasiveness of uncertainty in the real world of management. The theory of decision making often replaces the notion of a single optimum solution with the view of finding solutions that balance conflicting objectives. It probes motivation, the relation of rewards and aspiration levels, and patterns of influence and authority.

The theory of decision making is concerned with the processes by which expectations under conditions of uncertainty are formed. It recognizes the costs of collecting and processing information, the problem of communication, and the need to reconcile diverse objectives of individuals and interests in the organization. It requires consideration of the psychological and sociological influences on human behavior.

Economic theory and the theory of decision making appear to be in conflict, each based on a different set of assumptions. Which theory shall we choose? It is not necessary to make a black-and-white choice. This book is based on the belief that economic analysis is useful in the achievement of better decisions. It does not claim that businesses always can reach the optima indicated by theory, but it does argue that it is useful to have some idea of the direction of such optima. It admits that, while economic theory is easy to apply in simple, slow-moving situations with clear-cut objectives, it is much less able to handle more complex problems with multiple goals and high degrees of uncertainty and where quick decisions are necessary.

One of the main benefits of the case method in managerial economics is that it indicates the strengths and weaknesses of economic analysis in actual decision-making situations. One of the skills to be learned from a book of this type is to evaluate the relevance of particular conceptual tools in dealing with the management problems. The manager must temper the refinements of theory with the requirements of decision making.

Operations research

There is some disagreement about the proper definition of operations research, but in any case it is closely related to managerial economics. Operations research is concerned with *model building*—the construction of theoretical models that aid in decision making. Managerial economics also applies models; economic theorists were constructing models long before that expression became fashionable. Operations research is frequently concerned with optimization; economics has long dealt with the consequences of the maximization of profits or minimization of costs.

Some writers suggest that it is the *team approach* that makes operations research distinctive. Operations research workers have come from the natural sciences, statistics, mathematics, as well as economics. The resultant pooling of diverse talents may be its distinctive feature. Probably more important is the heavy reliance on mathematics. Most of the best-known operations research techniques are quantitative in character, as opposed to the more subjective and qualitative techniques usually used by management. Since economics is now becoming more mathematical, this suggests another parallel development in the two related fields.

The best way to describe operations research is to identify its recurrent techniques and models. The best-known method is linear programming, which is applied to a variety of problems of choice. Operations research workers have also developed inventory models indicating optimum quantities to order and optimum ordering times. Other common techniques are waiting-line (queuing) models, bidding models, and applications of probability theory. Economic analysis involves a logic which is closely related to the logic of these models. For example, the incremental or marginal reasoning used in economics is also applied in inventory models. Economists have also taken a great interest in the relation of linear programming to traditional theories of the firm. Some topics in operations research, such as replacement theory, have developed directly from the work of economists.

It is not important to determine where managerial economics begins and operations research ends. There is a close relationship between the two subjects and each has a contribution to make to the other.

Integrating the functional fields of business

Managerial economics helps business students understand how the managerial process combines and synthesizes ideas and methods from the various functional fields of business administration. The chapters on cost analysis and production economics are rich in concepts and relationships from the fields of accounting and production management. Short-range forecasting, demand, and pricing are closely related to the field of marketing. Chapters dealing with long-range forecasting and capital budgeting contain many topics from finance and business policy. Managerial economics offers opportunity to integrate ideas from the various specialized functions into an overall point of view—the perspective of a general manager.

PROFITS: A CENTRAL CONCEPT

Profit maximization is the central assumption in managerial economics. The reasons for the stress on profits are several. Profits are, after all, the one pervasive objective running through all of business; other objectives are more a matter of personal taste or of social conditioning and are variable from firm to firm, society to society, and time to time. The survival of a firm depends upon its ability to earn profits. Profits are a measure of its success. Further, what is learned about maximizing profits of business firms is also useful in managing nonprofit organizations and public agencies.

Another reason for emphasizing profits has to do with convenience in analysis. It is easy to construct models based on the assumption of profit maximization; it is more difficult to build models based on a multiplicity of goals, especially when those goals are concerned with such unstable and relatively immeasurable factors as the desire to be "fair," the improvement of public relations, the maintenance of satisfactory relations with the community, the wish to perform a service to the community, the desire to increase one's personal influence and power, and so on.

It is therefore usual to proceed in the early analysis as though profits were the only goal. After the consequences of that assumption have been derived, it is possible to bring in other considerations. Economics has developed a systematic and sophisticated system of logic as long as the goal is profits; it becomes more awkward and cumbersome when it incorporates other objectives.

We must be careful about our concept of profit. The amount called "profit" on a firm's profit and loss statement (or "net income" on an income and expense statement) is usually much larger than the *economic profit* of the firm. To determine economic profit, a competitive or "normal" rate of payment for services of capital supplied by the firm must be subtracted from the profit for the period as determined by conventional accounting methods. The capital supplied by the firm is the market value of land, plant, equipment, and working capital, net of amounts borrowed against the physical assets. We shall see later that a "normal" or "going" rate of return on capital supplied by the firm is called the *opportunity cost* of capital and is part of the cost of doing business rather than part of the economic profit.

Theories of profit

One difficulty in defining profit is that no single theory has been able to explain profits in a simple way. Profit is a mixture of a variety of influences. The result is a variety of profit theories. These theories fall into four categories: (1) those emphasizing profit as a reward for taking risks; (2) those stressing the effect of luck, frictions, imperfections, and lags in producing profits; (3) those centering on the monopoly element; and (4) those relating profits to the flow of innovations in the economy.

The first theory of profit explains it as a reward for taking risks and bearing uncertainty. Entrepreneurs are unwilling to assume risks unless a reward compensates them for the chances they take. The greater the risk, the greater the profit incentive required. Thus one would expect a higher rate of profit in unstable and unpredictable industries, such as electronics, than in those with steady, dependable rates of growth, such as electric utilities.

Another theory of profit interprets it as a result of good luck combined with imperfections in the market mechanism. Changes in tastes and preferences, technology, or institutions, not anticipated or initiated by the firm, generate profits for it. In a purely competitive economy without lags, such profits would quickly disappear. Entry of new firms and expansion of existing firms would create a downward pressure on prices and the excess profits would be wiped out. In the real world of imperfections and frictions, the squeezing out of excess profits takes time. Thus, there may be substantial profits that owe their existence to pure luck.

Monopoly because of restricted entry is itself a source of profits. The existence of monopoly permits a curtailment of production and the establishment of prices above the competitive level. Although relative profit in competitive industries is a socially desirable guide for production, since it stimulates expansion in those parts of the economy where expansion is desirable, monopoly profit may be socially undesirable, since it is a reward for curtailing expansion where such expansion would be socially beneficial.

Another theory of profit warns against condemning all monopoly profit too hastily. The innovation theory notes that profits arise from the development of new products, new production techniques, and new modes of marketing. Innovators who develop these new products and methods deserve rewards for their contribution to progress. It is true that they earn excess profits from the monopoly which the superiority of their innovations provides, but this monopoly is temporary. Old innovations are replaced by new ones in a constant process of "creative destruction."[1]

The innovation theory of profit breaks away from the static equilibrium analysis in traditional economic theory. Innovation profits result from change—from the disruption of the equilibrium or status quo. Any theory which ignores innovation neglects the most important function of profits, which is to reward change and to stimulate the replacement of less valuable and productive activities with more vital ones.

Managerial economics and alternative profit theories

One paradox of managerial economics is that, while it makes use of the assumption of profit maximization, it makes little *direct* use of the *theories of profit*. Uncertainty, lags, frictions, and innovations give rise

[1] Joseph Schumpeter, *Theory of Economic Development* (Cambridge, Mass.: Harvard University Press, 1934).

to the alternatives with which managerial economics is concerned. But most of the analysis is in terms of cost, demand, revenues, and market structure rather than directly in terms of profits. Thus we shall be concerned with the measurements of incremental revenues and incremental costs which lie behind incremental profits. We shall consider the contributions to overhead and profits which result from the alternatives under consideration. We shall compute the present value of estimated streams of profit in the future. We shall compare discounted rates of return, which are measures of profitability, with costs of capital. But none of this analysis is a direct application of one theory of profit or another.

Let us consider the risk and uncertainty theory first. Businesses have coped with it in a variety of ways, mostly subjective in character. In recent years, more formal techniques for the analysis of uncertainty have developed under the titles of "decision theory," "decision trees," "Bayesian statistics," "the Monte Carlo method," and "Markov processes." Modern managerial economics has recognized these important ideas and has incorporated them as part of the apparatus required for economic analysis. It is no surprise that a book entitled *Probability and Statistics for Business Decisions* should use the language of economics in many places (incremental cost, incremental gain, marginal utility, opportunity cost, and so on). Nor is it surprising that a book entitled *Economic Analysis for Business Decisions* should be heavily concerned with probability models.

The present volume, however, relegates the topics of risk and uncertainty to a secondary position. There are several reasons for this treatment. One is that the student should become thoroughly familiar with the basic concepts of managerial economics before complicating the analysis with probabilistic models. Some books on the subject tend to displace the important ideas of demand, cost, pricing, and capital budgeting with discussions of normal curves, Bayes' theorem, and Bernoulli processes. This is unfortunate, for the concepts of managerial economics and of statistics are complementary rather than competitive. Both aspects deserve attention. However, since probability is covered in courses in statistics and operations research, it seems appropriate to have a course in managerial economics concentrate on the fundamental economic analysis.

Thus, while we recognize the importance of risk and uncertainty as a source of profits, we shall not make much direct use of this idea, except in a general way, until the last part of the book. The theory of profit as a reward for risk taking is a useful one to keep in mind, but its direct application is better postponed for more advanced work.

We must show similar restraint in relating managerial economics to the innovation theory of profits. Economic analysis cannot produce the innovations; they are dependent upon qualities of imagination and leadership and are influenced by the organizational environments and systems of incentives. Managerial economics does evaluate new alternatives once they are developed. The entire chapter on capital budgeting is concerned with that topic. No analysis of alternatives can produce profits unless some of the alternatives are themselves profitable.

This discussion of profits has enabled us to place managerial economics in its proper perspective. Economics is not and cannot be the source of imaginative ideas for change. It does not provide the tools for determining the appropriate organization for the search for innovations. It is appropriate only for the evaluation of alternatives which have somehow already been discovered. And it does not deal with problems of leadership, communication, and human relations involved in carrying out decisions.

BEHAVIORAL THEORY OF THE FIRM

Behavioral theory of the firm is helpful in understanding processes of decision making with multiple objectives and incomplete information.[2] Only a few highlights of the behavioral theory can be summarized here. The theory views the organization as a coalition of individuals, most of these being further organized into subcoalitions. Goals of the organization are developed through more or less continuous bargaining among potential coalition members.

Organizational goals are stated as aspiration levels (e.g., "increase our market share to 25 percent"; "earn 12 percent after tax on total capital employed"; "spend 8 percent of our budget on research and 2 percent on executive development"). The goals established at any one time may be inconsistent in the sense that it is impossible for all of them to be fully and simultaneously realized.

According to the behavioral theory, organizational decisions and resource allocations are based on information and expectations that usually differ appreciably from reality. The organization cannot and does not attempt to acquire complete information about alternatives that are open to it. Flexibility, the possibility of revoking or modifying decisions, is highly regarded. When there are gaps between aspiration levels and actual results, the firm initiates search procedures to uncover additional alternatives. In many instances, methods of closing the gaps are discovered, and it may even be possible to raise some aspiration levels. In other instances, the aspiration levels must be reduced.

The behavioral theory represents the firm as an adaptive institution. It learns from experience and has a memory. Organizational behavior that works is incorporated into decision rules and standard operating

---

[2] Richard M. Cyert and James G. March, *A Behavioral Theory of The Firm* (Englewood Cliffs, N.J.: Prentice-Hall, 1963).

procedures. These may be modified over the long run as the firm reacts to feedback from experience. However, in the short run, decisions of the organization are dominated by its rules of thumb and standard methods.

The behavioral theory of the firm was developed as a basis for a theory of administrative behavior. However, it is also helpful as a basis for understanding managerial decision processes. It helps us understand how much approximation is involved in the microeconomic theory of the firm with its basic assumptions: a single decision maker, a single objective, and conditions of certainty.

MODELS AND SUBOPTIMIZATION

The real economic world is very complex. A complete description of technological and social factors affecting the outcomes of a firm's decisions would fill a sizable library (if it were possible for all of this information to be known). Only a few characteristics of the environment can be considered in decision making. Even these selected characteristics must be represented approximately rather than exactly. Managers must plan with models, which are simplifications compared to reality, and must settle for local improvement of results, rather than global optimization.

Models

Suppose the quantities of 19-inch color television sets that a particular manufacturer expects to sell in future months are represented by equations relating sales quantities to price, unit cost (which increases as more features are added), per capita incomes, and the manufacturer's expenditures on advertising. Some influences that are difficult to estimate and that will have less effect upon sales are disregarded in the above model: competitors' prices, dealer markups, dealer advertising, changes in official rates of currency exchange with other countries, and so on. Clearly, the manufacturer's view of demand is an approximation.

Models are structures involving relationships among concepts. The concepts are often represented by symbols so that the relationships can be expressed in mathematical form. The mathematical form allows quick determination of expected results of changes in controllable variables. The television set manufacturer of the example above can quickly estimate the effects upon sales of changes in price or advertising outlay with the aid of the demand equation, or model of demand.

Models are abstractions from reality that capture important relationships, allowing the analyst to understand, explain, and predict. The purpose of a model is to represent characteristics of a real system in a way that is simple enough to understand and manipulate, and yet similar enough to the more complicated operating system that satisfactory results are obtained when the model is used in decision making. Thus, the test of whether or not a model is satisfactory cannot be the degree to which it corresponds to the real world. The appropriate test is whether or not it provides successful predictions.

Suboptimization

Few managers actually seek the greatest attainment of a single goal; they settle for partial achievement of a variety of goals, recognizing that furtherance of one objective may mean partial sacrifice of another. Even if the manager could specify a single goal, he or she could not achieve the "true" optimum, for the number of relevant variables and the variety of interrelationships would be too large and complex for any system of thought. Even the most elaborate models are still abstractions from reality. Any model or theory must necessarily simplify. The result is a paradox: Managerial economics often assumes a desire to optimize a given objective, but it then simplifies in ways that assure a failure to fully achieve the optimum.

Throughout this volume are models and principles based on the assumptions of a single objective (profit maximization or, at times, cost minimization for a given output), a single decision maker, and full information. Practitioners must adopt a mixed attitude toward such assumptions. They know that as a description of actual managerial behavior, the assumptions are inaccurate and oversimplified. But they also know that simplifying assumptions are essential if they are to create order out of chaos.

Operations researchers use the term *suboptimization* to describe the process of decision making by abstraction from the total complexity of reality and from the wide variety of goals. They construct models which reflect only part of reality and face up to the bounds of human rationality. Such models indicate optimal positions within the limits or assumptions on which they are constructed. The result may be imperfect but should be superior to decisions based on crude rules of thumb or simple repetitions of past decisions. Rules of thumb and rigid formulas are replaced by the point of view that "it depends."

Learning

A learning process is built into the use of models in day-to-day decision making. Models that do not work in a satisfactory way can be revised. Figure 1–1 illustrates the learning process. The original symbolic model may be one that has worked previously or it may be a new one

Figure 1–1
The two worlds of a decision maker

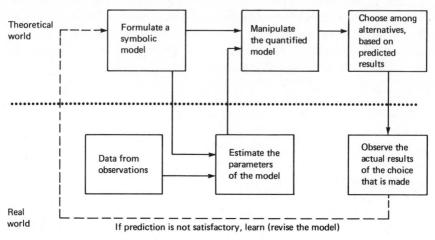

that seems plausible to the user. In any event, the model contains parameters, which are symbols for measurable relationships among the major components of the model. Parameters can be estimated from real-world data, although it is not usually possible to determine their exact values.

By manipulating the quantified model, users obtain quantified predictions of outcomes of alternative lines of action. They choose among these alternatives and observe the actual outcome of their decisions. If the actual experience is not as predicted or within a predicted range, decision makers must revise their theoretical models and reestimate the parameters. This process of testing and revising a theoretical model is what we mean when we talk about "learning from experience."

ORGANIZATION OF THIS BOOK

There are seven main parts of this text. Part one introduces the body of knowledge called *managerial economics*. This first chapter has described the scope and method of the field of study, and Chapter 2 provides five fundamental concepts used through the remainder of the book: incremental reasoning, opportunity cost, contribution, the long-run and short-run perspectives, and the time value of money.

Part two deals with demand and forecasting. Chapter 3 develops the concept of demand as a schedule of alternative price-quantity combinations that may be shifted by a variety of influences. Chapter 4 discusses forecasts of the general business conditions that determine values of the

QUESTIONS

1. "Positive" economics aims at understanding economic processes and systems. "Normative" economics aims at controlling economic processes to achieve objectives. Is managerial economics primarily an application of positive economics or of normative economics? Explain.

2. The intermediate course in microeconomics deals mainly with theories of firms and markets. Is managerial economics simpler or more complex than the microeconomic theory course? How do the objectives of the courses differ?

3. We say that managerial economics helps the business student in his or her effort to tie together or integrate knowledge gained in other courses. How is this integration accomplished?

4. How does an economic model differ from the "reality" to which it is related?

5. Analysis of economic matters with the aid of an economic model could be called "theoretical" analysis. Would it be better to carry out "realistic" analysis in which no simplification or approximation would be permitted?

6. In the behavioral theory of the firm, objectives are stated as "aspiration levels"; in the economic theory of the firm, the objective is stated as profit maximization. Can these theories be reconciled?

FURTHER READING

Alchian, A. A., and Demsetz, H. "Production, Information Costs, and Economic Organization." *American Economic Review* 62, December 1972.

Chang, Emily Chen. "Business Income in Accounting and Economics." *Accounting Review*, October 1962.

Cohan, Avery B. "The Theory of the Firm: A View on Methodology." *Journal of Business* 36, July 1963.

Cyert, Richard M., and Hedrick, Charles L. "Theory of the Firm: Past, Present, and Future." *The Journal of Economic Literature* 10, June 1972.

Machlup, Fritz. "Theories of the Firm: Marginalist, Behavioral, Managerial." *American Economic Review* 57, March 1967.

Morgenstern, Oscar. "Descriptive, Predictive, and Normative Theory." *Kylos* 25 (1972).

Shubik, Martin. "Approaches to the Study of Decision-Making Relevant to the Firm." *Journal of Business*, April 1961.

Simon, Herbert A. "A Behavioral Model of Rational Choice." *Quarterly Journal of Economics* 69 (1955).

Simon, Herbert A. "Theories of Decision-Making in Economics." *American Economic Review* 49, June 1959.*

---

* This article is included in *Reading in Managerial Economics*, rev. ed. (Dallas: Business Publications, Inc., 1977).

Chapter 2

Five fundamental concepts

This chapter introduces some concepts which are basic to all of managerial economics. These concepts may appear elementary—almost self-evident. However, their application requires care.

INCREMENTAL REASONING

Incremental reasoning identifies the impact of decision alternatives (changes in prices, products, inputs, procedures, investments, and so forth) by comparing the resulting change in total revenue with the change in total cost. The net effect of the decision, *the change in net revenue,* is what counts.

A decision is profitable if net revenue is increased. This will be the result if one of the following is true:

1. It increases revenues and reduces costs.
2. It adds to revenues more than to costs.
3. It reduces costs more than revenues.
4. It lowers some costs more than it raises others.
5. It builds up some revenues more than it cuts back others.

A single decision can affect a number of cost items, increasing some and shrinking others. The same decision could step up some revenues while scaling down others. An orderly approach to incremental reasoning is as follows. Let *incremental revenue* be defined as the change in total revenue resulting from the decision; incremental revenue is the algebraic sum of all changes, positive or negative, in individual items of revenue. *Incremental cost* is the change in total cost, or the algebraic sum of all changes in individual items of cost. The impact of the decision upon *net revenue* can then be calculated as incremental revenue minus incremental cost.

An example will show that incremental reasoning deserves attention. Some businesses take the view that to make an overall profit they must make a profit on every job. As a result, they refuse any orders that do not cover full cost (allocated overhead as well as labor and materials) plus a provision for profit. This rule may prevent profit maximization in the short run by leading to rejection of business that will add more to revenue than it adds to cost.

The *relevant cost* is not full cost but rather incremental cost. A simple problem illustrates the point. Suppose a new order will bring in $10,000 additional revenue. Costs of filling the order are estimated as follows:

Labor...	$ 3,000
Materials.......................................	4,000
Overhead (allocated at 120 percent of labor cost).........	3,600
Selling and administrative expense (allocated at 20 percent of labor and materials cost)...................	1,400
Full cost.......................................	$12,000

The above order appears to be unprofitable. But suppose that there is *idle capacity* with which this order could be produced. Suppose that acceptance of the order will add only **$1,000** of overhead (the incremental overhead, limited to the added use of heat, power, and light, the added wear and tear on the machinery, the added costs of supervision, and so on). Suppose also that the order requires no added selling costs, since the only requirement is a signature on the contract, and no added administrative costs. In addition, only part of the above labor cost is incremental with the order, since some idle workers already on the payroll will be put to work without added pay.

It is possible that the *incremental cost* of taking the order will be as follows:

Labor................................	$2,000
Materials............................	4,000
Overhead.............................	1,000
Total incremental cost..............	$7,000

While it at first appeared that the order would result in a loss of $2,000, it now appears that the result is an addition of $3,000 in profit.

Perhaps a brief comment will prevent a common misunderstanding about incremental reasoning. Incremental reasoning does not mean that the firm should price at incremental cost. In fact, charging what the market will bear is consistent with incremental reasoning, which calls for an increase in price if the result is an increase in net revenue. In the example, acceptance of the $10,000 order is advantageous because of idle capacity and the absence of more profitable alternative uses of this capacity. The payoff from incremental reasoning is simply that it focuses attention on effects that are *relevant*, in the sense that they are sensitive to decisions under consideration, while ignoring fixed elements of the situation, which must be taken as given because they are not influenced by available action alternatives.

In connection with the above example, it should be noted that the firm must cover its full costs in order to survive in the long run. This means that charging a price below full cost now will have to be offset by charging a price above full cost at some later time.

Incremental reasoning versus marginal analysis

A reader with some knowledge of economic principles can see that incremental reasoning is closely related to the marginal analysis of economic theory. Similarities and differences of these two approaches should be understood.

1. Marginal analysis deals with *per-unit changes*, whereas incremental reasoning applies to *any changes whatsoever*. For example, marginal cost is extra cost per period, per unit added to the rate of output; incremental cost could be associated with a change of more than one unit in the rate of output, with a change in product quality where there is no change in output level, with a change in method of production, and so forth.

2. Marginal analysis is particularly useful in looking at *trade-offs that are determined by curvilinear relationships*. The graph of a curvilinear relationship is a curved line, rather than a straight one. For example, if total cost rises at an increasing rate as the rate of output is raised, marginal cost increases with rate of output. The concept of marginal analysis calls for comparison of marginal cost with marginal revenue as the rate of output is increased, unit by unit. The best rate of output is found at the point where marginal cost is the same as marginal revenue.

3. Marginal analysis on a unit-by-unit basis as depicted above is a special case of incremental reasoning. However, marginal analysis can also be carried out with methods from algebra and calculus that directly determine optimum conditions. For example, the optimum rate of output

is found by solving a system of equations. Some of these analytic methods are discussed and illustrated in chapters to follow. However, the mathematics involved are well within the grasp of most undergraduates.

4. Incremental reasoning is particularly useful in looking at *trade-offs that are linear*. In such instances, only the end points of a range need to be compared. For example, suppose both total cost and total revenue have a linear relationship to output over the range from zero to the technical capacity of a plant. It is sufficient simply to determine the incremental effect of producing at capacity rather than having zero output.

5. If *discrete alternatives* are to be compared, only incremental reasoning can be used. Suppose the decision is a choice between two technical processes that yield the same rate of output. We cannot compare the processes in terms of marginal cost of changing from one process to the other (remember marginal analysis deals with per-unit changes), but we can determine the incremental cost of using one process rather than the other.

Empirical studies and illustrations

Do managers actually use incremental and marginal reasoning? The answer is that some do and others do not. Managers are not always fully aware of the reasoning behind their own decisions; apparently many of them unconsciously do apply incremental principles. In any case, many of them are inarticulate on their decision-making processes, making it difficult to determine what logic they do apply.

Earley's study of "excellently managed" large firms suggest that progressive corporations do make formal use of incremental analysis, and make use of accounting methods that are consistent with marginalism.[1] Earley finds that most of the 88 firms covered by the study "employ marginal accounting extensively, including segmented variable-fixed cost differentiation and the determination of separable fixed costs. . . . Most of them follow essentially marginal principles, and eschew or subordinate cost allocations and full costing, in their product selection, product investment, and both short- and long-range pricing decisions."[2]

A study of small firms by Haynes makes it clear that the use of incremental accounting methods is far from universal.[3] Of the 100 firms covered by the study, not one used the special accounting methods cited in the previous study. It is true that the managers were often aware of the

---

[1] James S. Earley, "Marginal Policies of 'Excellently Managed' Companies," *American Economic Review* (March 1956), pp. 44–70.

[2] Ibid., p. 61.

[3] Warren W. Haynes, *Pricing Decisions in Small Business* (Lexington: University of Kentucky Press, 1962).

distinction between fixed and variable costs, and it is also true that some of these managers made use of ad hoc cost analyses that helped them apply incremental reasoning. Other managers reached decisions consistent with incrementalism by trial and error or by experimentation. But none of these small firms had a programmed accounting method (a routine method automatically producing data period by period) that provided the kinds of cost figures required for decision making. The item in the accounts that had the greatest impact on decision making was the profit or loss figure on the income statement. If this figure seemed "low" in relation to some predetermined standard, the manager often sought ways of improving the situation. In other words, the accounting results motivated the managers to make decisions but did not provide the information required by those decisions. Accounting performed its stewardship function, supplying data required by the owners, creditors, or tax collectors. It also performed the control function, providing measurements of actual performance that could be compared with earlier experience or with standards. But normally it did not provide incremental data that would be useful for decisions.

The failure of the accounting systems of many firms to supply incremental data is not necessarily a deficiency. In many cases ad hoc analyses are less expensive than programmed accounting systems that must be maintained period after period. Furthermore, what is an incremental cost varies from one decision to another, making it unlikely that a programmed incremental system would always produce the required information. A manager who is experienced in decision making may be able to make the necessary adjustments in the regular accounting data on the back of an envelope in a few minutes. Thus the absence of marginalist accounting methods does not necessarily imply the absence of incremental reasoning.

A few illustrations should help the reader picture the variety of actual practice.

A laundry and dry-cleaning establishment. The managers of this firm rejected an opportunity to make use of idle capacity in the summer months when business was slack. A large motel wished to make a contract that would supply the laundry with business that would not cover "full costs" but that would more than cover incremental costs, leaving a contribution to overhead and profit. Apparently the managers were so certain that the full-cost figure, including allocated overhead, was the correct figure for decision making that they rejected a profitable order. They were unable to give any other reasons for rejecting the order; they did not believe that acceptance of the order would have any effect on their other business either in the present or in the future.

An advertising firm. The managers of a billboard advertising firm paid little attention to their regular financial accounting figures in making decisions on advertising rates. Instead they made up ad hoc income statements for future periods under alternative assumptions about rates. By this method they reached conclusions that appear to be fully in accord with incremental reasoning, even though the managers were unfamiliar with the economic jargon one might use to describe their analysis. Other companies appear to approximate incrementalism by trial and error, learning from experience what policies are likely to be conducive to increased profits.

In a study of small business, most companies appeared to fall between the extremes already discussed. Their managers were concerned with full costs (in retailing they emphasized wholesale costs); they used those costs as a starting point in pricing. But they did not adhere to rigid markups on costs; instead they varied markups on different lines of goods and revised markups over time. Thus the most common pattern was that of *partial incrementalism,* with either full cost or wholesale cost serving as a reference point or resistance point, but with considerable flexibility in adjustments to market conditions.

This review of empirical studies and illustrations supports two conclusions:

1. It is impossible to generalize on the uses of incremental reasoning, actual practice being variable.
2. Some firms could profit by giving more attention to incremental analysis, whether or not they revise their accounts to reflect this analysis.

OPPORTUNITY COST

If a scarce resource (one that is in limited supply to the firm) is put to a particular use, other uses of the resource must be given up. The net revenue that could be produced in the next best use of the resource is called the *opportunity cost* of the resource for the use actually made. The next best use may be inside or outside the firm, depending on the situation. Here are some specific illustrations of the meaning of opportunity cost:

1. Opportunity cost of funds tied up in one's own business is the interest (or profits corrected for differences in risk) that could be earned if these funds were invested in other ventures.
2. Opportunity cost of the time a person puts into his or her own business is the salary that person could earn in other occupations (with a correction for the relative "psychic income" in the two occupations).
3. Opportunity cost of using a machine to produce a particular product

is the sacrifice of earnings that would be possible in using the machine to produce other products.

4. Opportunity cost of using an owned machine that is useless for any other purpose is nil, since the particular use requires no sacrifice of alternatives.

The concept of opportunity cost is closely related to the distinction between explicit and implicit cost. *Explicit costs* are those recognized in the accounts of the firm as a consequence of the firm's transactions, such as payments for materials and labor. *Implicit costs* are those not recognized in the accounts, such as the opportunity cost of capital supplied by owners of the business. More precisely, *implicit cost is the difference, if there is any, between the explicit cost of an item and the opportunity cost of that same item.*

An item may have an explicit cost that is less than its opportunity cost, as in the case of an owner-operator who draws a salary lower than he could earn elsewhere; so there can be positive implicit cost. There may be no explicit cost of an item that has an opportunity cost, as in the case of rent that could be earned by a building that the firm owns and uses in its regular business; so implicit cost can be the full amount of the opportunity cost. And, the explicit cost can be the only relevant cost, as in the case of materials purchased from an abundant supply in the open market; in this case, no *other* use of the materials must be given up in order to have them for the particular use, so the market prices measure the full sacrifices involved in using the materials.

The concept of opportunity cost underlies a distinction between accounting profit and economic profit. *Accounting profit* is the amount called "net profit" on the firm's profit and loss statement; it is obtained by subtracting the explicit expenses of a period from the revenue of that period. To determine whether the firm has an *economic profit*, the accounting profit must be reduced by the amounts of any implicit expenses that the firm had during the same period. Implicit expenses are the differences between the explicit costs of inputs and the opportunity costs of these same inputs as determined in their next best uses outside the firm.

Incremental reasoning versus economic profit calculation

Incremental cost is the difference in cost due to a decision; it is subtracted from incremental revenue in carrying out incremental reasoning to determine whether a change in business activity is profitable. In contrast, *opportunity cost* is the full economic cost of a scarce resource; it is the part of the total cost that is subtracted from total revenue to determine whether a proposed use of the scarce resource is profitable. Incremental reasoning and economic profit calculation are alternative methods of comparing business opportunities where choice among the opportunities is necessary because each requires the same scarce resource.

An example using both approaches. The following example contrasts correct usage of the incremental cost concept and the opportunity cost concept. A firm owns a piece of machinery that has been fully depreciated. The remaining expected life of the machine is one year, at the end of which the machine will have no salvage value. The machine is presently used to produce widgets with revenues and expenses as shown in Figure 2–1.

Figure 2–1
Annual revenues and expenses, widget production

Revenue		
Sale of widgets....................		$5,000
Expenses		
Electricity......................	$ 100	
Materials.......................	1,000	
Labor..........................	2,000	
Total expenses..............		3,100
Accounting profit..................		$1,900

The firm is considering an alternative use of the machine, in which it will be modified and used to produce gadgets. In the alternative use, the annual revenues and expenses would be as shown in Figure 2–2.

Figure 2–2
Expected annual revenues and expenses, gadget production

Revenue		
Sale of gadgets..................		$6,000
Expenses		
Electricity......................	$ 100	
Materials.......................	1,500	
Labor..........................	2,500	
Conversion expense.............	500	
Total expenses..............		$4,600

The firm is also considering outright sale of the machine to another firm that has offered $2,300 for it. There are selling expenses of $100 in this option. Thus, the firm has three alternatives: (1) to continue producing widgets, (2) to convert to gadget production, and (3) to sell the machine. Alternative 1 is the present use of the machine and will be used as a base in illustrating *incremental reasoning*.

Figure 2–3
Incremental revenue, cost, and profit (change to alternative 2)

Total revenue in alternative 2		*Less total revenue in alternative 1*		*Equals incremental revenue*
$6,000	−	$5,000	=	$1,000
Total cost in alternative 2		*Less total cost in alternative 1*		*Equals incremental cost*
Electricity........ $ 100	−	$ 100	=	0
Materials......... 1,500	−	1,000	=	$ 500
Labor........... 2,500	−	2,000	=	500
Conversion........ 500	−	0	=	500
Total incremental cost				$1,500
Incremental revenue		*Less incremental cost*		*Equals incremental profit*
$1,000	−	$1,500	=	−$500

The appropriate calculations for comparing continued widget production (alternative 1) with conversion to gadget production (alternative 2) are shown in Figure 2–3.

Changing to alternative 2 results in an incremental loss of $500 and should not be carried out. Next, compare continued widget production (alternative 1) to sale of the machine (alternative 3). The results are shown in Figure 2–4.

Changing to alternative 3 has an incremental profit of $300 and is the best use of the machine. *Note that the costs used in calculating incremental costs are explicit costs; the concept of opportunity cost is not needed in incremental reasoning.*

Figure 2–4
Incremental revenue, cost, and profit (change to alternative 3)

Total revenue for alternative 3		*Less total revenue in alternative 1*		*Equals incremental revenue*
$2,300	−	$5,000	=	−$2,700
Total cost in alternative 3		*Less total cost in alternative 1*		*Equals incremental cost*
Selling expenses..... $100	−	$ 0	=	$ 100
Electricity.......... 0	−	100	=	− 100
Materials.......... 0	−	1,000	=	− 1,000
Labor............. 0	−	2,000	=	− 2,000
Total incremental cost				−$3,000
Incremental revenue		*Less incremental cost*		*Equals incremental profit*
−$2,700	−	−$3,000	=	$ 300

Another approach to the above decision is based on *economic profit calculation* with the aid of the opportunity cost concept. Consider giving up continued widget production (alternative 1) to make the machine available for conversion to gadget production (alternative 2). Net revenue in alternative 1 is $1,900 (Figure 2–1). If alternative 2 is selected, this net revenue will be sacrificed; it is the opportunity cost of the machine for use in alternative 2. Revenue, economic cost, and economic profit of alternative 2 would be as shown in Figure 2–5. Remember that economic profit is total revenue minus the opportunity cost of all inputs used.

Figure 2–5
Revenue, economic cost, and economic profit (alternative 2)

Revenue....................		$6,000
Economic cost		
Electricity....................	$ 100	
Materials....................	1,500	
Labor....................	2,500	
Conversion....................	500	
Opportunity cost of machine......	1,900	
Total economic cost.........		6,500
Economic profit.................		− $500

Obviously, alternative 2 is not attractive; it has an economic loss of $500 if alternative 1 is given up. Calculations to compare sale of the machine (alternative 3) with continued widget production (alternative 1) are shown in Figure 2–6.

Figure 2–6
Revenue, economic cost, and economic profit (alternative 3)

Revenue........................		$2,300
Economic cost		
Selling expense.................	$ 100	
Opportunity cost of machine......	1,900	
Total economic cost.........		$2,000
Economic profit.................		$ 300

Since the economic profit of alternative 3 is $300, it is the best of the three machine uses considered. *Note that full revenues and full economic costs are used in economic profit calculations. Economic costs are based on opportunity costs rather than on accounting costs if these are different for particular items. The concept of incremental cost is not needed in economic profit calculations.*

Incremental reasoning and economic profit calculations are alternative approaches; they lead to identical final choices among any given set of alternatives.

Empirical studies and illustrations

It is obvious that most managers are continually weighing alternatives, which means that they are at least roughly making subjective evaluations of opportunity costs. Some modern mathematical methods used in larger firms incorporate opportunity cost considerations; this is true of linear programming techniques and replacement models.

Some managers fail to make correct analyses of opportunity costs. Conventional accounting does not accurately reflect opportunity costs. Cost accounting systems that allocate overhead in relation to some basis, such as direct labor cost, overestimate economic costs of activities that use otherwise idle capacity and they underestimate the economic costs of activities that use bottleneck facilities or machines. The following example illustrates some uses of opportunity cost.

Optimal use of water in a hydroelectric system. Electric utilities that own hydroelectric dams also operate steam-generating plants. They face a choice of using hydroelectric power or steam power or some combination of the two. It is relatively easy to measure the cost of generating power in a steam plant, though the correct handling of depreciation may present some difficulty. But the cost of producing hydroelectric power is much more troubling. After all, the dams are already built; their costs of construction are sunk and are irrelevant in making decisions for the future. The same is true of expensive generators, on which wear and tear is probably a small cost relative to the original price of the generators. And water is a "free gift of nature." Why not run the water through the generators as rapidly as possible and minimize the use of the steam plants?

Merely posing the question should suggest the solution to the problem. The use of the water behind a dam is not cost free, for it does require a sacrifice. Water used today cannot be used tomorrow; its use today involves an opportunity cost. Looking at the matter another way, the water behind a dam has value based on its capacity to produce power in the future.

Suppose a utility owns one hydroelectric dam and three steam plants. The three steam plants vary in efficiency, the new plant burning less coal per kilowatt-hour than the old ones. To meet the peak-load requirements, all three plants and the dam must operate near capacity. To meet lower loads it is possible to cut off either the high-cost plants or the hydroelectric dam or both. Running the water through the generators in off-peak periods would run the risk of not having enough stored water for peak periods. The sacrifice (opportunity cost) would be a measure of the loss of revenue and customer dissatisfaction that might result. In addition, the operation of the high-cost steam plants involves a sacrifice in the inefficient burning of fuel. The flow of water should be regulated as to minimize this sacrifice.

If the utility has additional objectives, such as food control or maintenance of navigation (as is true of some public power systems), the analysis becomes more complex but the basic principles are the same. The stored water has value; its use involves an opportunity cost.

CONTRIBUTION

The contribution concept can be used in incremental reasoning and also in economic profit calculations. If the firm has excess capacity, contribution per unit of output is helpful in decisions about accepting orders or shutting down plants. On the other hand, if the firm is operating at capacity of some scarce or bottleneck resource, contribution per unit of the scarce resource is an aid in determining the most profitable use of the resource.

Excess capacity—whether to use or not?

Consider a case in which the price of a product is determined by outside forces—by competition or regulation. Assume this price is $95. Within the firm, total unit cost including allocated overhead is $103. However, incremental cost is only $75. Loss per unit by conventional accounting measurement is $8 per unit. Still, each unit makes a contribution to overhead and a possible profit, and the amount of this contribution is $20. *Contribution per unit of output is incremental revenue per unit less incremental cost per unit.*

The question is whether or not to drop the product. If the company has excess capacity, the decision is easy. This product can be made without reduction in output of other products. The product should not be dropped. *Any contribution is better than none.*

A bottleneck (scarce) resource—how to allocate?

Now suppose the firm has opportunities to make several products, but they all require services of a scarce resource, such as a machine tool. If more of any one product is produced, other outputs must be reduced. Now, the question is how to allocate the limiting resource among its various uses or, from another point of view, which products to produce and how much of each product.

In this situation, the products should be compared on the basis of contributions per unit of scarce resource required rather than contributions per unit of product. And the scarce resource should be allocated first to its best use, then any resource that remains to its next best use, and so on. *More contribution is better than less.*

If a firm has only one production bottleneck, such as machine-hours available, contributions per unit of output can be converted into contributions per unit of machine time, and this conversion can be made for each of the products. Table 2–1 is an example. The firm can produce any of the five products in the table.

Table 2–1
Contributions on five products in a single plant

Product	Price	Incremental cost	Contribution per unit	Machine-minutes requirements
A...........	$15.00	$10.00	$5.00	60 minutes
B...........	14.00	8.00	6.00	90
C...........	13.00	9.00	4.00	40
D...........	12.00	7.50	4.50	30
E...........	6.00	2.50	3.50	15

At first glance Product B appears to be best; it has a contribution per unit of product that is larger than that of the other products. But Product B uses more machine capacity per unit of product. Clearly we must compare the products on the basis of contributions per unit of machine time. For each product, contribution per unit of output can be divided by machine time required per unit of output. The result is contribution per unit of machine time. Results for all five products are as follows:

	Contribution per machine hour
Product A...............................	$ 5
Product B...............................	4
Product C...............................	6
Product D...............................	9
Product E...............................	14

These results indicate that Product E, which at first appeared to be the lowest contributor, is in fact the highest. The product priorities are almost the opposite of those which appear at first glance. If this illustration seems farfetched, it should be stated that in actual practice the order of contributions is frequently quite different from those suggested by casual observation.

Suppose, however, that more than one capacity bottleneck appears. If all five products pass through four processes, each of which can be the bottleneck, it is no longer possible to compute simple contributions in terms of just one of the bottlenecks. The problem becomes one in linear programming. It is discussed briefly in the section below and at more length in Chapter 6.

Empirical studies and illustrations

By introducing the elements of linear programming in bits as the economic aspects are introduced, the reader will be in a better position to study the more comprehensive treatment of linear programming in later chapters. It is important to recognize that linear programming is not a subject completely independent of the concepts of incremental cost, contributions, or opportunity costs, but is in fact a sophisticated way to incorporate those concepts in a mathematical form.

The initial step in linear programming is to set up the fundamental equations of the problem. Let us use the same contributions shown in Table 2–1 but this time assume four bottleneck departments rather than one. These departments are the four constraints. The basic data are shown in Table 2–2.

Table 2–2
Data on five products to be produced in four departments

Product	Contribution per unit	Dept. 1	Dept. 2	Dept. 3	Dept. 4
A........	$5.00	1.00	0.50	1.00	0.50
B........	6.00	1.33	0.60	1.00	1.00
C........	4.00	0.67	0.70	1.00	0.50
D........	4.50	0.50	0.80	1.00	1.00
E........	3.50	0.25	0.90	1.00	0.50

Machine-hours per unit spans Dept. 1–4.

We are now in a position to set up the *objective equation*. If the objective is to maximize contribution to overhead and profits from the products, the objective equation is:

$$Z = 5.00 X_A + 6.00 X_B + 4.00 X_C + 4.50 X_D + 3.50 X_E = \text{Maximum}$$

in which

Z is total contribution.
X_A is output of Product A.
X_B is output of Product B.
X_C is output of Product C.
X_D is output of Product D.
X_E is output of Product E.

Next we set up equations for each of the constraints—for each of the bottleneck departments. Suppose that the capacities in the four departments are:

	Machine hours
Department 1..................	18,000
Department 2..................	15,000
Department 3..................	24,000
Department 4..................	20,000

The number of hours used up by all products in each department cannot exceed the capacity of that department. This condition can be expressed mathematically in the form of four inequalities,

$$1.00X_A + 1.33X_B + 0.67X_C + 0.50X_D + 0.25X_E \leq 18,000$$
$$0.50X_A + 0.60X_B + 0.70X_C + 0.80X_D + 0.90X_E \leq 15,000$$
$$1.00X_A + 1.00X_B + 1.00X_C + 1.00X_D + 1.00X_E \leq 24,000$$
$$0.50X_A + 1.00X_B + 0.50X_C + 1.00X_D + 0.50X_E \leq 20,000$$

Each of these inequalities states that the sum of the machine-hours used up by the five products must be "less than or equal to" the capacity of each department.

It is not necessary here to show how to reach a solution. The task can be turned over to a clerk who is familiar with the simplex method, computer programming, or other methods of solving the problem. The point to note here is that the *objective equation of a linear programming formulation makes use of the contribution concept.*

As has been shown above, the contribution concept is applicable when linear programming is used to solve product mix problems. A friend of Haynes once confessed that he had used linear programming in solving a textile mill's production problems without knowing the difference between full cost and incremental cost. The product profitability estimates he used in setting up the problem were profits above full costs rather than contributions above incremental costs. His solution was wrong. No mathematical technique can overcome incorrect data.

A few years ago the expression "contribution to overhead and profits" was almost unknown, although many managers were actually using the idea without giving it a name. Today the expression has become part of the vocabulary of management; one can say that a manager who does not understand *contributions* is probably not very proficient in cost analysis and decision making. Probably the term is used most widely in product mix and pricing decisions, but it is also applicable to make-or-buy decisions, decisions about product and plant shutdowns, interdivisional arrangements in decentralized companies, and so on.

TIME PERSPECTIVE ON COSTS
AND REVENUES

So widely known are the economic concepts of the long run and short run that they have become part of everyday language. However, economists use these terms with precision that is often missing in ordinary discussion. To the economist, *a decision is viewed in long-run perspective if it affects quantities of all inputs*—if the rate of use of all inputs is variable depending upon the decision. An example would be a decision whether or not to build a new plant at a new location, since all inputs would be affected by such a decision. *Decisions are viewed in short-run perspective if quantities of some inputs remain fixed regardless of the decision* while the quantities of other inputs do depend upon the decision. An example would be a change in the rate of output of an existing plant, since this would require variation in quantities of labor and materials but not in the amount of floor space or the number of machines.

The neat dichotomy between the short- and long-run perspectives breaks down in actual practice. For any one decision, the items of cost that will and will not be affected depend upon the time perspective within which the decision is considered; there are a series of short-run perspectives that can be adopted with more and more items of cost becoming variable as the time perspective is extended. A decision that appears profitable in the short run may have long-run consequences that make it more or less profitable than it appeared in the initial analysis. An example may make this clear.

Consider a firm with temporary idle capacity. A possible order for 10,000 units comes to management's attention. The prospective customer is willing to pay $2 per unit, or $20,000 for the whole lot, but no more. The short-run incremental cost (which includes no fixed cost) is only $1.50 per unit. Therefore, contribution to overhead and profit is $0.50 per unit ($5,000 for the lot).

But long-run effects must be considered. If management can get the order only by agreeing to make a series of future shipments at the same price, some of the so-called fixed costs may eventually become variable with production to fill these orders. For example, it will be necessary to replace some of the machinery and the taxes, insurance, depreciation, and opportunity costs of capital associated with these machines are costs that would be avoidable if the machines were not replaced.

Managerial economists are also concerned with the short-run and long-run effects of decisions on *revenues*. For example, acceptance of an order at a low price might undermine the company image, giving customers a picture of a cutthroat computer rather than that of a stable, dependable supplier. Some present customers may feel that they are being treated unfairly and may transfer to suppliers with firmer policies on pricing.

Decisions should take into account both the short- and long-run effects on costs and revenues. The usual approach is to begin with a short-run analysis and then carry out a series of analyses by extending the time perspective further and further into the future. The evaluation of a decision should encompass all of its outcomes.

Empirical studies and illustrations

The following illustration indicates the rather complex interrelations between the short and long runs on both the cost and demand sides and how such considerations are important in decision making.

A printing company's refusal to price below full cost. A printing company included in a study made by Haynes maintained a policy of never quoting prices below full cost despite the facts that it frequently experienced idle capacity and that the management was aware that the incremental cost was far below full cost. The management had given considerable thought to the problem and had concluded that the long-run repercussions of going below full cost would more than offset any short-run gain. The reduction in rates for some customers might have an undesirable effect on customer goodwill, especially among regular customers who might not benefit from the price reductions. Management also argued that the availability of idle capacity was unpredictable and that by the time the order became firm the situation might change, with an interference of low-price orders with regular-price business. The management wished to avoid the image of a firm that exploited the market when demand was favorable and was willing to negotiate prices downward when demand was unfavorable.

It would be difficult to demonstrate that management's reasoning on pricing was correct, but at least the argument is plausible. On the other hand, there was evidence that the management did not always enforce its policy. It admitted that in special cases it regretfully broke away from its policy. And sometimes it performed special services (such as editing manuscripts) without charge, a practice which amounts to a hidden form of price reduction. Despite these reservations, this illustration does point up the need to consider the long-run as well as the short-run impact of price policy.

TIME VALUE OF MONEY

The time value of money is simply the opportunity cost of money. The opportunity cost is the earning power that the money would have in the best alternative use from which it must be withheld in order to tie it up in a particular use. For example, money tied up in inventories of raw materials could earn interest and dividends if invested outside the firm at comparable risk. *Because of the time value of money, costs and revenues that occur at different times must be adjusted to their equivalent values at some common time before a comparison to determine profitability is made.*

A monetary amount at a given time can be converted to an equivalent greater value at a later time by calculations called *compounding.* A simple illustration will show how compounding works. Suppose you are offered an opportunity to invest $100 today with an assured payoff of $108 two years from now. Probably you will reject this opportunity. The $100 which is in hand today could be increased to a future value greater than $108 if it were put in a savings account so as to accumulate interest over the two years.

Suppose the savings account would earn 5 percent interest, compounded annually. Each year, the initial amount is increased by a factor of 1.05. At the end of one year, you would have $105; at the end of the second year, you would have $110.25. This alternative *future value* of the present outlay is more than the promised future payoff, so the proposal is not profitable.

There is another way of comparing the investment with the payoff. A monetary amount at a given time can be changed to an equivalent smaller amount at an earlier time by a method called *discounting.* This approach asks, "How much money today is equivalent to the $108 two years away? In other words, what smaller present amount, put out at interest, would grow to $108 in two years?"

Again assume that the earning rate of money would be 5 percent. Each year, the initial amount would be $1/1.05$ of the final amount. The $108 final payoff reduces to an equivalent value of $102.86 at the beginning of the second year and this drops to an equivalent value of $97.96 at the beginning of the first year, or at present. Thus, the *present value* of the projected future payoff is less than the required present outlay, and the project cannot be profitable.

It will be necessary to elaborate upon the methods of compounding and discounting in the chapters that deal with investment decisions. For present purposes, it is sufficient to understand the general principle. If a decision affects costs and revenues of future periods, it is necessary to adjust all monetary amounts to their equivalent values at some common point in time. The adjustments are necessary to offset the time value of money and can take the form of compounding (to get greater equivalent values at later points in time) or discounting (to get smaller equivalent values at earlier points in time). Figure 2–7 illustrates the effect of discounting upon the calculated profitability of a project.

The concept of time value of money is related to the concept of time

Figure 2–7
How discounting affects project profitability°

Year	Revenue	Expense
1.....	$ 0 + 925.93 + 1,714.68 + 793.83	$2,500 + 428.67 + 396.91 + 367.51
2.....	1,000	500
3.....	2,000	500
4.....	1,000	500
	$4,000	$3,500

	Undiscounted		Discounted	
Revenue..................	$4,000	Revenue..............	$3,434.44
Expense..................	−3,500	Expense..............	−3,693.09
Apparent profit..........	$ 500	Actual loss.........	−$ 258.65

* All values except the initial outlay of $2,500 are discounted at 8 percent from the end of the period in which they occur.

perspective. Maximization of long-run profit is optimization over a succession of time periods out to a horizon, with appropriate discount factors applied to costs and revenues of future periods.

Empirical studies and illustrations

The practice of discounting is pervasive and observable in everyday business practice. The simplest case of discounting is when one borrows on a note at the bank. If the note is for $1,000, the borrower does not receive the full amount but rather that amount discounted at the appropriate rate of interest. If the discount rate is 6 percent and the note is for one year, the borrower will receive approximately $942. One might say that the present value to the bank of the borrower's promise to pay $1,000 in a year is only $942 at the time of the loan.

Real estate prices reflect the discounting principle, though in a more complicated and less obvious way. The rational way to determine what one will pay for a piece of property is to estimate the future returns expected, which may in the case of a home be primarily subjective in character. One will discount those future returns at the opportunity cost of capital to reflect the sacrifice of alternative earnings. The market value of the real estate is determined by the interaction of such discounted present values set on the property by the various potential buyers and sellers. Even such rules of thumb as "an apartment house should sell at ten times annual rentals" are rough approximations of the discounting principle.

The same principle of discounting should apply to the operations of an individual firm, though considerable uncertainty about the future revenues and appropriate discount rates necessarily exists. If a firm is considering buying a new piece of equipment, it should estimate the discounted value of the added earnings from that equipment. If it is considering the purchase of another firm, or a merger, the same principle of valuation applies.

SOME IMPORTANT APPLICATIONS

This entire volume is devoted to applications of the foregoing analysis to a variety of decisions. It is possible at this point to introduce some elementary but significant applications of the basic concepts: incremental costs, opportunity costs, the long and short runs, and discounting.

Make or buy

Decisions to make or buy are among the most pervasive in industry. The question of purchasing on the outside or producing within the firm requires a direct application of the principles discussed so far, but the issues are complicated by a wide variety of considerations, as we shall see.

The advice that one should make or buy depending on which alternative is cheaper is not very helpful; the term "cheaper" is ambiguous. The costs of making or buying can be measured in a variety of ways: The following are only partial lists of the possible cost measurements.[4]

Cost to make	*Cost to buy*
1. Labor and materials.	1. The purchase price.
2. Labor, materials, and other variable expenses.	2. Purchase price plus delivery expense.
3. Labor, materials, other variable costs, and factory overhead.	3. Purchase price, delivery expense, plus receiving and handling expense.
4. Labor, materials, other variable Costs, factory overhead, and selling expense.	4. Purchase price, delivery expense, receiving and handling expense, plus buying costs.
5. Labor, materials, other variable costs, factory overhead, selling expense, and general overhead.	5. Purchase price, delivery expense, receiving and handling expense, buying costs, plus costs of inspection.

The fact is that some of these measurements are appropriate part of the time and others are needed in different circumstances. The problem is to determine the impact of the decision on costs—the estimation of the incremental costs.

The chief source of confusion in the analysis of costs is in the treatment of burden or overhead. In all probability some of the so-called overhead costs will be affected and others unaffected, creating the necessity of determining which fall into the changing and unchanging cate-

---

[4] James W. Culliton, *Make or Buy* (Cambridge, Massachusetts: Harvard University, Bureau of Business Research, 1942).

gories. To increase the complexity of the problem, some costs may be unaffected in the short run but may increase in the long run. For example, a decision to make a part may absorb short-run excess capacity, but if this capacity is needed for other purposes in the future, restriction of attention to the short run is in error. To put the matter in another way, it is necessary to consider the opportunity costs of each alternative, and the opportunity cost of making instead of buying is the absorption of capacity that may in the future be useful for other products.

The argument that a firm should make parts to fill in the excess capacity created by cyclical or seasonal fluctuations in demand is simply a special application of incremental opportunity cost reasoning. Excess capacity means that the incremental overhead costs of manufacturing are small and that the sacrifices of alternative opportunities are limited. But the effect on supplier goodwill and the resulting difficulties of obtaining supplies in good times must be reckoned with.

Decisions to make or buy should take into account a variety of special considerations which complicate the analysis.

Quality. The firm may be able to achieve greater control over quality by manufacturing the part itself. The result is a reduction in assembly costs or increases in customer goodwill and future sales which should be part of a complete incremental analysis. Alternatively, the firm may not require as high a quality as outsiders are supplying and can bring quality and costs into line by manufacturing itself. On the other hand, the specialized knowledge of outside suppliers may exceed that within the firm, so that the firm cannot match the outside quality.

Assurance of supply. The firm may be able to coordinate the flow of parts more effectively by producing at home. Some suppliers are undependable and others are unable to keep up with demand. If the firm has access to several or many suppliers, this argument for making the part becomes less persuasive. In any case the total impact on costs, including the costs of disrupted production, and the total impact on revenue, including the effect of changed customer goodwill, should be estimated.

Defense against monopoly. A firm may manufacture parts to protect itself against a monopoly in supply. A mere threat to manufacture may in some cases suffice to restrain suppliers from overcharging, but threats must be backed up with demonstrations that the firm is competent to do the job.

Summary. Complete incremental reasoning requires the evaluation of a number of subtle considerations that might at first be overlooked: customer goodwill, supplier goodwill, internal know-how, administrative and technical skills, and the risk that the costs of unimportant sidelines in manufacture might not be controlled satisfactorily. Students of the make-or-buy problem think that there may be a tendency to overlook some of the less measurable advantages of outside supply and to exaggerate the economies of internal manufacture.

Product-line decisions

Most firms produce more than one product. They sometimes face problems of deciding whether to add new products, to drop old products from the product line, to change the relative proportions of products, to farm out part of the production to other firms, and so on. In this discussion we shall deal with the short run, in which capacity is fixed; a longer-run analysis would require a discussion of investment analysis which is postponed to a later chapter. But we must not ignore the longer-run repercussions of the short-run decisions.

The short-run problem itself includes a number of variations. Let us consider first the case in which the firm has excess capacity; its present line of products is not absorbing the capacity. The question is whether to add another product. The first step is to compute the contribution of the new product to overhead and profits. This requires an estimate of the added revenue and the incremental costs of the product. The normal overhead allocations should be avoided in such estimates; instead the estimates should measure the increase in each cost, direct or indirect, resulting from adding the product. If the contribution, the difference between the added revenue and the incremental cost, is positive, the analysis is favorable to adding the product.

A complete analysis, however, must check for other considerations. For example, the management should not introduce the new product if an even better new product is available. A search for all the available opportunities should precede making the final decision. Another way of expressing this idea is to say that the opportunity costs of alternative uses of the excess capacity must be estimated. Another factor is the possible impact of the new product on the products already produced. In some cases it may complement or round out the product line, increasing the sales of the other products. In such a case the contribution to overhead and profits of the new product is greater than the direct contribution of the product itself. In other cases the product may compete with items in the present line, so that the initial contribution estimates must be adjusted downward. Such adjustments in estimates should recognize both immediate and longer-run impacts of the new product. If, for example, the excess capacity is temporary, management must face the question of whether the new product can be abandoned when the demand for the other products recovers, or whether an expansion of facilities will be justified. Often it may be preferable to accept temporary excess capacity rather than to create production bottlenecks when the excess disappears. In addition, management must determine whether it has the know-how to produce and distribute the product.

If the situation is one of full use of capacity, the analysis becomes even more complex. In this case management must not only determine the contribution of each product (and of products that might be introduced into the product mix) but must also determine how much the opportunity cost of increasing the output is in terms of the reduction of the contributions of the other products. The linear programming method of determining which products belong "in the solution" assumes limited capacity and makes use of both contribution estimates and estimates of opportunity costs. A management which does not use linear programming must nevertheless run through analogous estimates if it is going to approximate an optimal use of its resources.

Now we come to an even more complex situation: allocation of resources to a variety of slowly maturing products. An example would be a garden nursery with a fixed acreage of land and a wide variety of planting opportunities. Such a nursery faces the problem of determining which plants to propagate and grow, what ages to assume in such choices, what future prices should be assumed, as well as what prices to charge now on plants which are already mature. In addition, the nursery must determine when to mark down prices on plants tying up land needed for other uses, and when to destroy plant materials that are in the way. The solution to such a problem requires an estimate of the contributions of the various plants over time, which requires in turn estimates of revenues and incremental costs. It also requires the discounting of future revenues, costs, and contributions to arrive at the present value of such contributions at the time decisions on the use of the land are to be made. Estimates of the present value of the contribution for all plants on an acre basis would provide a basis for rational decisions. These estimates would make it possible to compare the contribution from rapidly maturing plants with those from slowly maturing plants.

Such complex models for decision making are open to the criticism that they are impractical; most managers do not have the data or the knowledge to apply the models. The trend, however, is toward a more systematic analysis of product mix problems. And even in firms where decisions continue to be qualitative and subjective, it can do management no harm to think through the logic required for rational decisions on which products to expand, which to contract, and which to abandon.

SUMMARY

Incremental reasoning determines whether a change in business activity would be profitable by comparing the change in revenue with the change in cost. Change in revenue can be $(+)$, $(-)$, or (0); change in cost can be $(+)$, $(-)$, or (0). The net effect of the change in activity is change in revenue minus change in cost, with due regard to the signs of incremental revenue and incremental cost. *Marginal analysis,* a special case of incremental reasoning, focuses upon the results of unit changes in some activity and is particularly useful in considering curvilinear trade-offs.

Opportunity cost is the net revenue that a scarce resource would produce in the best alternative use from which it must be withheld in order to have it for a particular use. If the opportunity cost of an input exceeds its *explicit cost*, the difference is called *implicit cost*. *Accounting* profit must be decreased by implicit expenses in determining *economic* profit. A decision involving a transfer of a scarce resource can be made either by using incremental reasoning or by calculating the economic profitability of the proposed use of the resource.

Contribution of output is the amount contributed toward overhead cost and possible profit. It is calculated as incremental revenue less incremental cost. If the output can be produced without reaching the capacity of any limiting resource, the decision is easy—any contribution is better than none. However, if the firm has an opportunity to produce any of several products where all require services of a bottleneck resource, each product's contribution should be converted to contribution per unit of scarce resource. Then the scarce resource should be allocated first to its best use, then to its next best use, and so on.

A decision is viewed in *long-run* perspective if it affects quantities of all inputs needed in production—if all costs are variable. A decision is viewed in *short-run* perspective if it affects quantities of some inputs but not of others—if some costs are variable but others are fixed. In many decisions, more and more items of cost become variable as the time perspective is extended. Revenue effects of decisions are also likely to change as the time perspective moves further out. The usual approach is to begin with a short-run analysis and then carry out a series of analyses with the time perspective extending further and further until the long-run perspective is reached.

One of the fundamental ideas in economics is the principle that revenues and costs that occur at different times should be adjusted to their equivalent values at a common time before they are compared. For any given monetary amount at a given time, the equivalent value at any later time can be obtained by a process called *compounding*, and the equivalent value at any earlier time can be calculated by a procedure called *discounting*.

QUESTIONS

1. Comment on this statement: "Marginal analysis is always an instance of incremental analysis, but incremental analysis often is not an instance of marginal analysis."

2. For each of the following, which is more appropriate, incremental analysis or marginal analysis: (*a*) deciding whether to drop a product that does not cover its full cost; (*b*) deciding how much of Input A to substitute for Input B, where it is clear that Input A replaces less and less of Input B as more substitution is carried out; (*c*) deciding upon the size of a new plant, given the knowledge that unit cost decreases with greater plant size; (*d*) deciding whether to make a part inside the plant or send it out to be done to order; and (*e*) deciding whether to use Process A or Process B in a new production line to be added to an existing plant.

3. Suppose a student aiming for an MBA degree is taking full load of courses (but works 20 hours per week in a part-time job) and is receiving veteran's educational benefits under the GI Bill. How would you calculate the opportunity costs and full costs of the MBA degree?

4. How do the opportunity costs of a business firm enter into the determination of its taxable income?

5. A controller is attempting to determine the incremental cost of proposed new Product A. In making this product, Machine X, already fully utilized, will be needed. Is the opportunity cost of Machine X part of the incremental cost of new Product A? Explain.

6. In producing a unit of Product A, two units of Input Z will be required. What is the role of the unit price of Input Z in calculating the unit contribution of Product A?

7. The text discusses allocation of available machine-time among several products, all requiring services of the machine, on the basis of contributions per unit of machine-time. It is suggested that machine-time be allocated first to the product with the greatest contribution per unit of machine-time, then to the product with the next greatest contribution, and so forth. How would this allocation process be affected if it were found that prices of each of the products must be decreased as the sales quantity per period is increased?

8. How can you determine whether a given decision is being viewed in long-run or short-run perspective? Can every decision be classified as a short-run or a long-run decision?

PROBLEMS

1. The Port Clinton Downtown Coaches, a booster organization that provides morale and financial support to the football program at the local high school, raises some money by selling programs at home games. They have been selling an average of 1,500 programs per game at a price of 50 cents per program; on the average, sales average one program for every five persons attending a game. The total cost of printing a run of 1,500 programs is $450; the printer has offered to increase the press run to 2,000 copies for a total cost of $575. This year Port Clinton's big game will be against Maumee High School. Tickets for the game are already sold out. Assuming good weather, attendance will be 9,500 persons (2,000 more than average). Should the coaches increase the press run of programs for the Port Clinton–Maumee game to 2,000 copies?

2. William Blackman is considering beginning a one-year MBA program of study at State University. If he does, he will give up a full-time job in which he is earning $10,000 a year and he will have to use $1,000 of savings (now earning

10 percent compounded annually) to pay tuition and fees. He believes he could work part-time, earning $3,000 per year, while he is in the program. Upon completion of his studies, he would expect to get a position with starting pay of $12,000 annually. He projects pay increases of $500 annually for his present job and also for the one he would get after finishing the MBA program. Should he begin the program? How many years will it be before he breaks even?

3. Artnell Company has assigned worker Smith to make Product X and worker Jones to make Product Y. The management is considering reassignment of both workers to make Product Z. Smith is the only available worker who knows how to make Product X and Jones is the only one who knows how to make Product Y. Both workers will be required full-time if the firm makes Product Z. Revenues and costs per period for the three products are as follows:

Product X		*Product Y*		*Product Z*	
Revenue	$850	Revenue	$1,000	Revenue	$2,150
Wages	400	Wages	300	Wages	700
Materials	100	Materials	400	Materials	650
Electricity	50	Electricity	100	Electricity	300

Calculate the economic profit per period from producing Product Z (take into account the opportunity costs of the scarce skilled labor which will be required). Then, apply incremental reasoning to this decision.

4. When his daughter Jane was born, Dr. Robert Elliot bought a life insurance policy to provide money for her college education. The policy paid Dr. Elliot $10,000 on August 15, 1976 (Jane's 18th birthday). Jane planned to begin college on September 1, 1976, at an institution requiring prepayment of the tuition and fees amounting to $2,500 for the first year. Dr. Elliot believes the sophomore year will cost $2,600, the junior year will cost $2,700, and the senior year will cost $3,000. The proceeds of the insurance policy have been deposited in a savings account at 6 percent interest compounded annually. How much additional money will Dr. Elliot need to pay for his daughter's education?

```
┌─────────────────────────────────────────────────────────┐
│                                                           │
│                                                           │
│                                    Cases for part one     │
│                                                           │
│                                                           │
│                                                           │
└─────────────────────────────────────────────────────────┘
```

THE CASE METHOD

The case method provides the most convenient way of acquiring skill in applying managerial economics short of actual decision making itself. Cases reveal the complexity of the environment in which decisions are made. Cases force the student to leave the ivory tower of abstract theory, to face up to the uncertainties of the real world, and to make the simplifications required to create order out of the multitude of facts faced by management.

Many readers of this book will be unfamiliar with the case method. The best way to learn this method is to use it, but a few introductory comments may be helpful.

Procedure in analyzing a case

The steps in analyzing a case may vary from one student to another and from one case to another. It would be wrong to claim that only one procedure is appropriate. The following outline of steps should be taken merely as suggestive of one way of going about the analysis.

Definition of the central issue or issues. *A case may contain a variety of issues from the trivial to the significant. The analyst should focus on the key problems.*

Organization of the evidence. *When the analyst has determined the central issue or issues, he or she can then proceed to organize the facts around topics related to those issues. This requires the separation of the unimportant from the significant and the irrelevant from the relevant. Often it is necessary to organize the facts in a new form: in the form of a break-even chart or flow of funds statement, for example. The construc-*

tion of charts and tables that clarify the situation requires imagination; it is one of the chief tools of orderly decision making.

Determination of the alternatives. *In some cases the alternatives are clear; in others the analyst must invent alternatives appropriate to the situation. The analyst cannot remain content with predetermined alternatives, but must strive for new and better solutions.*

Evaluation of the alternatives. *One of the best ways to organize the facts in a case is to relate them to the alternatives. Some facts become arguments in favor of or against an alternative; some of them suggest the probable consequences of choosing one alternative over another.*

It is necessary, finally, to appraise each alternative—to weigh its strengths and weaknesses. Weak alternatives are discarded in favor of strong ones.

The decision. *Managers must not evade making a final choice of the alternative which seems best to them. They must be decisive. They should be aware of the limitations as well as strengths of their choice, and they should beware of overstating their case. But managers must decide, for inaction itself involves a choice.*

The case method applied in managerial economics

The cases in a managerial economics book have a special character; they are not the same as cases in accounting, finance, or policy. The cases are intended to provide an opportunity to apply the concepts of economics to the problems of management. Rather than being representative of all managerial decisions, they are chosen from those areas of management most amenable to economic analysis.

Nevertheless, these cases should be approached in the same way as other policy cases. The initial effort should go into determining the problems or issues, with secondary regard to whether or not these are economic problems. Some students make the mistake of organizing their case analysis around economic concepts instead of using the concepts as tools where appropriate in the analysis of the case. The objective is not to find out whether the case is one in opportunity costs or demand elasticities or valuation, but rather to determine the issues and then use whatever analysis is appropriate. Some of the cases, however, are intended as simple exercises in the use of economic analysis.

Almost all of the cases in this book are based on actual situations; a few are synthesized from the experience of several firms. Obviously none of the cases supplies all of the facts. Management never has all the facts, though management is in a better position than is the student to search for answers to questions that arise during the decision-making process. Trying to make sense out of a situation without full knowledge may be frustrating, but it is part of the essence of management.

Normally there is no single "correct" solution to a case. Two managers of equal ability might select different alternatives; it is often difficult to say that one alternative is better than the other. It is possible to say, however, that some case analyses and some recommendations are superior to others. The criteria for making this determination are as follows:

1. *The extent to which the analysis and solution show an understanding of the real issues involved.*
2. *The extent to which the analysis is based on the particular facts in the situation.*
3. *The degree to which the solution appears to be workable under the circumstances.*
4. *The extent to which the analyst is able to support his or her position.*

This chapter consists of elementary cases. The fundamental concepts discussed in Chapter 2 should be helpful in making decisions in these cases. The objective should be to size up each situation, to organize and analyze the facts, to evaluate the alternatives, and to reach a solution— and to use economic concepts when they are helpful.

WHAT PRICE PROGRESS?*

Efficiency expert: Joe, you said you put in these peanuts because some people ask for them, but do you realize what this rack of peanuts is *costing* you?

Joe: It ain't gonna cost. 'Sgonna be a profit. Sure, I hadda pay $25 for a fancy rack to holda bags, but the peanuts cost 6 cents a bag and I sell 'em for 10 cents. Figger I sell 50 bags a week to start. It'll take 12½ weeks to cover the cost of the rack. After that I gotta clear profit of 4 cents a bag. The more I sell, the more I make.

Efficiency expert: That is an antiquated and completely unrealistic approach, Joe. Fortunately, modern accounting procedures permit a more accurate picture which reveals the complexities involved.

Joe: Huh?

Efficiency expert: To be precise, those peanuts must be integrated into your entire operation and be allocated their appropriate share of business overhead. They must share a proportionate part of your expenditures for rent, heat, light, equipment depreciation, decorating, salaries for your waitresses, cook . . .

Joe: The *cook?* What's he gotta do wit'a peanuts? He don' even know I got 'em!

Efficiency expert: Look Joe, the cook is in the kitchen, the kitchen prepares the food, the food is what brings people in here, and the people ask to buy

* Reprinted from *Lybrand Journal* (Lybrand Ross Brothers & Montgomery), whose editors note: "We have been unable to locate the source of this paper. If any of our readers can provide us with this information, we shall be delighted to acknowledge our indebtedness."

peanuts. *That's* why you must charge a portion of the cook's wages, as well as a part of your own salary to peanut sales. This sheet contains a carefully calculated cost analysis which indicates the peanut operation should pay exactly $1,278 per year toward these general overhead costs.

Joe: The peanuts? $1,278 a year for overhead? The nuts?

Efficiency expert: It's really a little more than that. You also spend money each week to have the windows washed, to have the place swept out in the mornings, keep soap in the washroom, and provide free cokes to the police. That raises the total to $1,313 per year.

Joe: (*Thoughtfully*) But the peanut salesman said I'd make money . . . put 'em on the end of the counter, he said . . . and get 4 cents a bag profit . . .

Efficiency expert: (*With a sniff*) He's not an accountant. Do you actually know what the portion of the counter occupied by the peanut rack is worth to you?

Joe: Ain't worth nothing . . . no stool there . . . just a dead spot at the end.

Efficiency expert: The modern cost picture permits no dead spots. Your counter contains 60 square feet and your counter business grosses $15,000 a year. Consequently, the square foot of space occupied by the peanut rack is worth $250 per year. Since you have taken that area away from general counter use, you must charge the value of the space to the occupant.

Joe: You mean I gotta add *$250 a year more* to the *peanuts?*

Efficiency expert: Right. That raises their share of the general operating costs to a grand total of $1,563 per year. Now then, if you sell 50 bags of peanuts per week, these allocated costs will amount to 60 cents per bag.

Joe: *What?*

Efficiency expert: Obviously, to that must be added your purchase price of 6 cents per bag, which brings the total to 66 cents. So you see by selling peanuts at 10 cents per bag, you are losing 56 cents on every sale.

Joe: Somethin's crazy!

Efficiency expert: Not at all! Here are the *figures*. They *prove* your peanuts operation cannot stand on its own feet.

Joe: (*Brightening*) Suppose I sell *lotsa* peanuts . . . thousand bags a week 'stead of 50.

Efficiency expert: (*Tolerantly*) Joe, you don't understand the problem. If the volume of peanut sales increases, our operating costs will go up . . . you'll have to handle more bags with more time, more depreciation, more everything. The basic principle of accounting is firm on that subject: "The bigger the operation the more general overhead costs that must be allocated." No, increasing the volume of sales won't help.

Joe: Okay, You so smart, *you* tell *me* what I gotta do.

Efficiency expert: (*Condescendingly*) Well . . . you could first reduce operating expenses.

Joe: How?

Efficiency expert: Move to a building with cheaper rent. Cut salaries. Wash the windows biweekly. Have the floor swept only on Thursday. Remove the soap from washrooms. Decrease the square foot value of your counter. For example, if you can cut your expenses 50 percent, that will reduce the amount allocated to peanuts from $1,563 to $781.50 per year, reducing the cost to 36 cents per bag.

Joe: (*Slowly*) That's better?

Efficiency expert: Much, much better. However, even then you would lose 26 cents per bag if you only charge 10 cents. Therefore, you must also raise your selling price. If you want a net profit of 4 cents per bag you would have to charge 40 cents.

Joe: (*Flabbergasted*) You mean even after I cut operating costs 50 percent I still gotta charge 40 cents for a 10 cent bag of peanuts? Nobody's that nuts about nuts? Who'd buy 'em?

Efficiency expert: That's a secondary consideration. The point is, at 40 cents you'd be selling at a price based upon a true and proper evaluation of your then reduced costs.

Joe: (*Eagerly*) Look! I gotta better idea. Why don't I just throw the nuts out . . . put 'em in a ash can?

Efficiency expert: Can you afford it?

Joe: Sure. All I got is about 50 bags of peanuts . . . cost about three bucks . . . so I lose $25 on the rack, but I'm outa this nutsy business and no more grief.

Efficiency expert: (*Shaking head*) Joe it isn't that simple. You are *in* the peanut business! The minute you throw those peanuts out you are adding $1,563 of annual overhead to the rest of your operation. Joe . . . be realistic . . . *can you afford to do that?*

Joe: (*Completely crushed*) It'sa unbelievable! Last week I was a make money. Now I'm in a trouble . . . just because I think peanuts on a counter is a gonna bring me some extra profit . . . just because I believe 50 bags of peanuts a week is a easy.

Efficiency expert: (*With raised eyebrow*) That is the object of modern cost studies, Joe . . . to dispel those false illusions.

1. What is the incremental cost per bag of peanuts?
2. What is the weekly contribution of the peanut rack?
3. How would the case be changed if there were an alternate use for the space, such as a chewing gum display?
4. Does management need full cost including allocated overhead for some purposes, or can all management decisions be based on contributions above incremental cost?
5. Comment on the efficiency expert's principle that "the bigger the operation the more general overhead costs that must be allocated." Are there better criteria for allocating overhead costs?

NEWVILLE BRANCH OF AJAX CLEANERS
(REVISED)*

B. Fraley was manager of the Newville branch of the Ajax Cleaners. In this position he had considerable autonomy in making decisions affecting the branch. The central office of the company developed the accounting reports for each branch and occasionally made suggestions to the individual managers.

In June 1961 the ratio of wages and salaries of the Newville branch to sales was 46 percent. The company suggested that as a rule of thumb this ratio should never exceed 33⅓ percent. The president of the company recommended that Fraley discontinue the shirt laundry service, a minor adjunct to the dry-cleaning business, in order to bring labor costs into line.

Fraley made an estimate of costs and revenues resulting from the shirt laundry in June. He accumulated data on labor costs and supplies. (He consulted Mr. Frederick, an accountant friend, who suggested the basis for allocating overhead. Exhibit 1 shows the estimate of overhead

Revenue	$740
Full cost	745
Loss	$ 5

costs and direct costs for the shirt laundry department.) The result showed a small loss on the shirt laundry as follows:

Frederick was not certain that the full-cost figure was the appropriate one for Fraley's problem. He had been reading some articles on "incremental income accounting" and suggested that a variation on that approach might be helpful in clarifying the problem at hand as well as future decision-making issues. Obviously such an approach would have to be kept extremely simple and inexpensive to deal with Fraley's small operations.

The steps in establishing a system of incremental income accounting are as follows:

1. Segmentation of the business. Fraley's business might be broken into two segments—dry cleaning and shirt laundry.

2. Segregation of costs between fixed and variable costs. This would require that Fraley make qualitative judgments as to which costs were fixed and which were variable. A more elaborate statistical approach for segregating costs would be too expensive.

* This case was prepared by W. W. Haynes of the Harvard Business School and J. L. Gibson of the University of Kentucky as a basis for class discussion. All names and locations have been disguised. The case is a by-product of research for the Small Business Administration, which agency is in no way responsible for the discussion. The case was revised by W. R. Henry in 1973.

Exhibit 1
Cost computations on the laundry—June 1961 (including overhead allocation bases)

Manager's salary—average time spent in the department	$155
Advertising—sales	22
Telephone—sales	16
Heat, light, power—ratio of departmental heat, light, power costs	5
Employer's payroll tax—ratio of departmental salary costs	9
Rent—floor space	16
Amortization—floor space	23
Insurance—sales	24
	$270

Add direct costs	
Salaries	$200
Supplies	140
Heat, light, power	25
Payroll tax	10
Depreciation	100
	475
Total cost	$745

3. Separation of the fixed costs into assigned fixed costs and unassigned fixed costs. The assigned fixed costs would be those which were fixed for short-period fluctuations in activity but which were avoidable if the segment were permanently discontinued. Examples would be depreciation on specialized equipment and salaries of supervisors in the particu-

Exhibit 2
Chart of accounts—Marginal income analysis

Laundry
1. Sales revenue
2. Variable costs
   a. Salaries
   b. Supplies
   c. Heat, light, power
   d. Employer's payroll tax
   e. Repair and maintenance
   f. Clothes lost and repaired
3. Assigned fixed costs
   a. Depreciation of equipment

Dry cleaning
1. Sales revenue
2. Variable costs
   a. Salaries
   b. Supplies
   c. Heat, light, power
   d. Employer's payroll tax
   e. Repair and maintenance
   f. Clothes lost and repaired
3. Assigned fixed costs
   a. Depreciation of equipment

4. Unassigned fixed costs
   a. Salaries
   b. Advertising
   c. Repairs and maintenance of plant
   d. Taxes
   e. Telephone
   f. Heat, light, power
   g. Employer's payroll tax
   h. Rent
   i. Depreciation of building, fixtures
   j. Amortization of leasehold improvements
   k. Insurance

lar segment. The unassigned fixed costs would be those which did not vary with output and which could not be avoided by discontinuance of the segment.

The result of such an analysis would be a chart of accounts which would appear as in Exhibit 2. Such a system of accounts would break the data into four categories: revenue, variable costs, assigned fixed costs, and unassigned fixed costs. Fraley could easily prepare this report once the system had been established. The report indicated the "contribution" each segment was making to assigned and unassigned fixed costs and to profits.

Some particular expenses might overlap several categories, requiring an allocation. For example, heat, light, and power would fall into both the variable cost and unassigned fixed cost categories. Fraley would have to determine which labor costs would in fact vary with output, which would be fixed as long as the segment was maintained, and which would be attributable only to the total operation. One danger of such a system is that it might not reflect the fact that a cost which had been variable had become fixed, or vice versa.

Frederick offered to assist Fraley without charge in preparing a report for June 1961 based on such a system of accounts because of his interest in the accounting problem it presented. The result is shown in Exhibit 3.

Fraley was then faced with consideration of both the full-cost report and the incremental income report in making his decision about aban-

Exhibit 3
Marginal income analysis report for June 1961

		Dry cleaning		Laundry	
Sales..			$2,800		$740
Variable costs					
Salaries..................................		$ 790		$200	
Supplies..................................		760		140	
Heat, light, power........................		150		25	
Employer's payroll tax....................		43	1,743	10	375
Contribution to assigned and unassigned fixed cost...............................			$1,057		$365
Depreciation.............................			200		100
Contribution to unassigned fixed cost..........		$1,122	$ 857		$265
Unassigned fixed costs					
Salaries.......................	$650				
Advertising...................	88				
Telephone.....................	66				
Heat, light, power.............	35				
Employer's payroll tax.........	36				
Rent..........................	100				
Depreciation..................	183				
Amortization.................	140				
Insurance.....................	95	1,393			
Net loss for the period.............		$ 271			

donment of the shirt laundry. Exhibit 4 presents a summary of the income statement for the entire operation in June.

Exhibit 4
Net income statements for June 1961

Sales..		$3,540
Salaries...	$1,640	
Supplies..	900	
Heat, light, power...............................	210	
Employer's payroll tax...........................	89	
Advertising.....................................	88	
Telephone.......................................	66	
Rent..	100	
Depreciation....................................	483	
Amortization of leasehold improvements...........	140	
Insurance.......................................	95	
Total expenses..................................		$3,811
Net loss..		($ 271)

1. Was the rule of thumb helpful? Why or why not?
2. Was the full-cost estimate helpful? Why or why not?
3. Did the incremental income analysis help in making the decision? Why or why not?
4. What is accomplished by separating fixed costs from variable costs? What is gained by separating assigned from unassigned fixed costs?
5. Are the allocation bases in Exhibit 1 reasonable? Do they contribute to decision making in this firm?
6. Which is relevant in this case: the contribution to the unassigned fixed cost or the contribution to the assigned and unassigned fixed cost? Explain.
7. What is the relation between the variable costs in this case and the incremental cost concept? What is the relation of assigned fixed cost to the concept of time perspective?
8. What considerations result from viewing laundry sales in the light of longer time perspective?
9. What considerations result from thinking about the possible effect on dry-cleaning sales of closing the laundry?
10. What decision was correct in the shirt laundry business?

SELECTED DECISION-MAKING RULES AND PRACTICES

The following examples of practices, policies, and rules of thumb are taken from case studies of actual firms. Some of the examples may be consistent with the principles of managerial economics; others may represent a practical compromise with those principles, while still other are difficult to reconcile with incremental reasoning.

1. Some firms follow the rule that the annual budget for the replacement of equipment should equal the annual depreciation charges on equipment. The vice president of one manufacturing firm, for example, was considering such a policy to accelerate the replacement of equipment which she believed was lagging behind. Many of this company's machines were over 10 years or even 20 years old.

2. The owner-manager of a small printing firm follows the rule: "To make a profit, you must make a profit on every job." By this he means that each job must be priced to cover all the costs, including allocated overhead, and return a profit above those costs.

3. A dry-cleaning and laundry firm considered the possibility of filling in its off-peak excess capacity with laundry service for motels. The company management, however, turned down this opportunity when it learned that the motels would not pay a high enough price to cover the overhead as well as the direct costs.

4. The plant manager of a branch of a large national firm was faced with a decision on making or buying a component. Up to the time of the decision the plant manufactured the part, but a potential supplier was willing to sell at a price below the plant's full cost. In spite of this low price the manager decided to continue manufacture within the plant, because:

a. The overhead presently absorbed by manufacturing the component would have to be reallocated to other parts manufactured within the plant.

b. The reallocation of overhead would result in higher unit costs for other parts.

c. These higher unit costs would require higher prices for the company's products, placing it in a less favorable competitive position.

5. One owner-manager of a furniture company made the following statement: "Overhead must come first." By this he meant that price must cover the overhead costs and then cover as much of the variable costs as possible.

6. A garden nursery and landscaping firm refused to develop plants or trees which took more than eight years to mature. The management reasoned that the high prices of the slower maturing plants didn't compensate for the longer period they tied up the land.

7. Many firms maintain a policy of not buying new equipment or replacing old equipment unless the investment will pay for itself in less than three years (or some other predetermined number of years). This rule is known as the payback criterion.

1. How do the rules and practices of these companies hold up under analysis in terms of the concepts in Chapter 2?

Part two

Demand analysis and short-range forecasting

Chapter 3

Demand analysis

Demand analysis is one of the manager's essential tools in *long-range* planning. Prospective growth of demand in various market areas should be taken into account in choosing sizes and locations of new plants. If demand is expected to fluctuate, plants with flexible design (but higher average unit costs at the most likely rate of output) may be desirable and considerable capital will be needed to carry inventories of finished goods. If demand is sufficiently responsive to advertising, heavy investment in market development may be justified.

Demand considerations also affect *day-to-day* financial, production, and marketing management. Sales forecasts provide some of the key assumptions used in projecting cash flows and net incomes by periods. Sales expectations affect production scheduling and inventory planning. Probable reactions of competitors and customers should be taken into account before changes in prices, advertising, or product design. Managers can make good use of the concepts and techniques of demand analysis.

SOME BASIC CONCEPTS

To the average person, demand usually means *one* quantity sold or to be sold. For example, one often hears an expression such as: "The demand for automobiles may be 7.25 million in the coming year." To the economist, demand is a specific relationship of *various* quantities per period to such variables as price, consumer incomes, prices of substitutes, expected future conditions, season, and availability of credit.

Be aware of this: Demand quantities are *rates*, i.e., amounts per unit of time. Demand relationships can be estimated for whole industries or for single firms. The basic concepts in this section are applicable to either type of demand, industry or firm.

Quantitative expressions of demand

Knowledge about demand can be expressed in several ways. At the most abstract level, the *functional relationship* can be stated:

$$Q = f(X_1, X_2, X_3 \ldots X_n)$$

in which Q is the quantity purchasers are willing to buy, and the X's are the influences on Q. The Q in such an equation represents the quantity per unit of time (such as a week or year) of a particular product (baby shoes, or all shoes) in a particular market (Boston, or the United States), and the Xs represent values of the specified influences (price, advertising, credit availability, and other factors).

For decision making, the manager needs quantified estimates of the relationships of quantity to each of the other variables. A *demand equation* is a convenient way to express quantified relationships. An example is:

$$Q = b_0 - b_1 P + b_2 A + e$$

in which

Q is quantity and is the *dependent* variable.

P and A are independent variables.

b_0, b_1, and b_2 are symbols for the *parameters* to be estimated.

e is error, assumed to be normally and independently distributed with a mean of zero and constant variance.

The above example assumes *linear* relationships of Q to the independent variables. Although the underlying relationships are usually believed to be curvilinear, linear approximations may be satisfactory over the *limited range* of available data and expected future experience.

A frequently used curvilinear model of demand has the form:

$$Q = b_0 P^{b_1} A^{b_2} e$$

in which the variables and parameters are as defined above.

The second equation assumes that the marginal effects of each variable are not constant but rather are dependent upon the value of that variable and of all other influences represented in the demand equation. An equation of the second form has *constant elasticities;* these elasticities are the exponents of the variables. The equation transforms to become *linear in logarithms;* the transformation is

$$\log Q = \log b_0 + b_1 \log P + b_2 \log A + e$$

Quantified demand relationships can also be presented in the form of *demand schedules,* which are tables showing the associated values of quantity and the variables that influence quantity. Table 3–1 is a hypothetical demand schedule that illustrates some assumed relationships of quantities to two variables, price and income. Demand schedules are

Table 3–1
Demand Schedule

Price	Units per month by income (dollars per year)		
	$2,400	*$3,000*	*$3,600*
$10	100	125	150
9	120	150	180
8	150	187	224
7	200	250	300
6	260	325	390
5	340	425	510

specific only at selected points on the demand function, and they become unwieldy if effects of three or more influences upon quantities are to be handled.

The information in Table 3–1 could be represented in the form of a *graph,* a depiction of the relation of quantity to one, or at most two, of the influences, as in Figure 3–1. Graphs are useful when attention is focused upon just one relationship, especially the important relation of quantity to price. Each price-quantity relationship is called a *demand curve* and shows the various quantities that would be demanded at alternative prices, *with other influences held constant.* Figure 3–1 represents the effect of changes in income by shifts in the position of the price-quantity curve.

Demand curves are usually drawn with price on the vertical axis, as if price, rather than quantity, were the dependent variable in the relationship. In some instances, price actually *is* a function of quantity. For example, in wheat growing, the harvest quantity in a given year depends upon weather during the spring and summer as well as upon acreage planted. The harvest must then clear the market at whatever price it will bring.

In other industries, such as automobile manufacturing, it appears that prices are set by producers, leaving quantities to be determined by prices and other market forces. In such cases, quantity is the dependent variable. In statistical estimation of demand, it is of some importance to have the correct variable specified in the dependent position of the demand equation.

Figure 3–1
A family of demand curves (hypothetical)

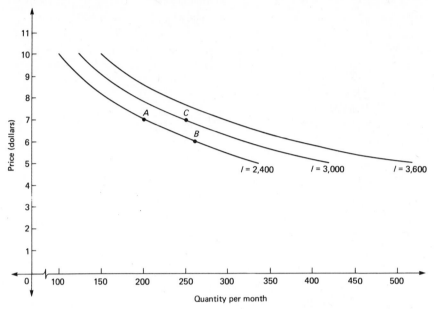

Meaning of "change in demand"

There is an important distinction between quantity change due to price being different and quantity change due to a shift of the demand curve. This distinction is illustrated in Figure 3–1. The quantity increase from Point *A* to Point *B* is entirely the result of a price reduction; it is *movement along a demand curve*. On the other hand, the quantity increase from Point *A* to Point *C* is entirely attributed to the effect of a change in income; it is the result of a *shift in demand*. Influences other than price are conceived as demand curve shifters—forces that move the price-quantity relationship left or right. To us, "changes in demand" will mean such shifts of demand curves.

Price elasticity of demand

Price elasticity of demand is a simple but useful idea. It is a measure of the responsiveness of quantity to price changes (assuming all other influences constant). *Price elasticity is the ratio of percentage change in quantity to percentage change in price.* Elasticity is, roughly, the percentage added to quantity by a 1 percent cut in price.

Elasticity can be calculated as an average value over some range of the demand function, in which case it is called *arc elasticity*, or it can be calculated for a point on the demand function, so as to be called *point elasticity*. To determine arc elasticity, we need price and quantity values corresponding to the end points of the range. Often these end points consist of a present price-quantity combination and an estimate of the quantity that could be sold at a higher or lower price.

Here is the *formula for calculating arc elasticity:*

$$E_p = \frac{\dfrac{\Delta Q}{(Q_1 + Q_2)/2}}{\dfrac{\Delta P}{(P_1 + P_2)/2}} = \frac{\Delta Q}{\Delta P} \cdot \frac{P_1 + P_2}{Q_1 + Q_2} \tag{3-1}$$

in which

E_p is arc elasticity of quantity with respect to price.
P_1 and Q_1 are the original price and quantity.
P_2 and Q_2 are the final price and quantity.
ΔP is the change in price, observing sign of the change.
ΔQ is the change in quantity, observing sign of the change.

Note that the signs of ΔP and ΔQ are usually opposite, so that *the calculated value for elasticity usually has a negative sign.*

The hypothetical demand relationship of Table 3–1 will be used to illustrate how to compute arc price elasticity. Suppose income is constant at $3,000 per year, present price is $10, and present quantity is 125 units per month. At a lower price of $9, a greater quantity of 150 units per month is expected. What is the arc price elasticity over this range of the demand curve? Substituting values into Equation (3–1), we have:

$$E_p = \frac{25}{\$ -1} \cdot \frac{\$10 + \$9}{125 + 150} = -1.73$$

The calculated elasticity coefficient, -1.73, indicates that quantity expands 1.73 percent for each 1 percent of price reduction. The negative sign of the coefficient shows that quantity moves up if price moves down, and vice versa.

Point price elasticity

The responsiveness of quantity to price can be determined for a point on the demand function *if the slope of the function is known.* If the changes in price and quantity are made smaller and smaller, at the limit, $\Delta Q/\Delta P$ becomes $\partial Q/\partial P$, the partial derivative of the demand equation with respect to price.

We can use the above partial derivative to calculate elasticity by the *formula for point elasticity:*

$$e_p = \frac{\partial Q}{\partial P} \cdot \frac{P}{Q} \qquad (3\text{-}2)$$

in which

e_p is point elasticity of quantity with respect to price.
P and Q are price and quantity at any point we choose.

To demonstrate how to work out point elasticity, we shall use an equation relating the number of passengers per year on a rapid-transit system to the fare charged. The equation, from an actual study, is:

$$Q = 2{,}207 - 52.4P \qquad (3\text{-}3)$$

in which

Q is number of passengers per year in millions.
P is fare in cents.

The partial derivative of the function with respect to price is:

$$\frac{dQ}{dP} = -52.4$$

To calculate elasticity at an assumed price of 10 cents, for which the quantity is 1,683 (millions), substitute values into Equation (3-2):

$$e_p = -52.4 \cdot \frac{10}{1{,}683} = -0.3113 \qquad (3\text{-}4)$$

The elasticity coefficient of -0.31 says that passenger traffic would decrease by 0.31 percent for each increase of 1 percent in fares. Here we are dealing with a straight-line demand function and the elasticity would be different at any other point on the function. For example, at an assumed price of 15 cents, for which quantity is 1,421 (millions), we obtain by substituting values into Equation (3-2):

$$e_p = -52.4 \cdot \frac{15}{1{,}421} = -0.5531$$

From the examples above, it should be clear that slope and elasticity are not the same thing. Slope does enter into the determination of elasticity. The ratio dQ/dP is the *reciprocal* of the slope of the demand curve, dP/dQ. However the ratio P/Q also enters the calculation of elasticity as a multiplier, and this ratio falls steadily as we move down and to the right on a straight-line, constant-slope demand curve. Thus, the absolute value of the elasticity coefficient becomes smaller and smaller as price falls, point by point, on a straight-line curve.

Relationship of marginal revenue to price and elasticity

Marginal revenue is, roughly, the addition to revenue by the *last unit* added to sales quantity. In precise terms, *marginal revenue is the ratio of increase in revenue to increase in quantity*, and it has meaning in terms of a point on the demand function as well as in terms of a discrete change in quantity. Managers need to know marginal revenue in making decisions about price and rate of output.

Consider the relation of marginal revenue to price for the case of a demand curve that slopes down and to the right. Price must be reduced as quantity per period is increased. In this circumstance, marginal revenue must be less than revenue received from the last unit added to sales. Revenue received from the last unit is, of course, the price per unit. The explanation of the difference between price and marginal revenue is simple: In adding the last unit to sales quantity Q, the firm accepts a (usually very, very small) reduction in price that applies to all units in sales quantity $Q - 1$.

Marginal revenue can be calculated for a one-unit increase up to quantity Q by the following formula:

$$MR = P - (|\Delta P| \cdot Q - 1) \tag{3-5}$$

in which

MR is marginal revenue.

P is price at quantity Q.

$|\Delta P|$ is the absolute value of the small reduction in price resulting from adding one unit to quantity.

To illustrate the difference between price and marginal revenue, we shall use data points from demand Equation (3–3) and calculate marginal revenue at an assumed price of 10 cents, for which the quantity is 1,683 million passengers annually. The equation, restated in individual quantity units, is:

$$Q = 2{,}207{,}000{,}000 \text{ passengers} - 52{,}400{,}000 \cdot \text{Price in cents}$$

Reduction of price enough to increase Q by one unit would be 1/52,400,000 cent. By substituting values into Equation (3–5), we ascertain:

$$MR \text{ for the one unit increase} = 10¢ - (1/52{,}400{,}000¢ \cdot 1{,}682{,}999{,}999)$$
$$= 10¢ - 32.1¢$$
$$= -22.1¢$$

In the above example, marginal revenue is negative; total revenue would be reduced by 22.1 cents for each passenger added to quantity through price reduction. A price cut as small as the one used in the example would not be feasible. But we know what we need to know. Any price reduction that is made, multiplied times initial quantity, will subtract more from total revenue than the corresponding addition to revenue, the added quantity multiplied by the final price.

The following formula allows calculation of marginal revenue *at a point* if elasticity is known:

$$MR = P\left(1 + \frac{1}{e_p}\right) \qquad (3\text{–}6)$$

With the aid of the above formula, let us again calculate marginal revenue for the transit system at the price of 10 cents, where elasticity was found to be -0.3113 in Equation $(3\text{–}4)$. We obtain:

$$MR \text{ at the point} = 10\cancel{c}\left(1 + \frac{1}{-0.3113}\right) + -22.1\cancel{c}$$

The formula relating marginal revenue to price and elasticity is especially useful if the demand function has a known, constant price elasticity.

Relationships of total revenue to output and elasticity

Values of price elasticity can be in the range 0 to $-\infty$. Values from 0 to $-.1.0^-$ are said to be in the *inelastic* range. In this range, percentage increases in quantity (which work toward elevating revenue) are not as great as the corresponding percentage decreases in price (which work toward lowering revenue). *Total revenue falls as price is reduced.*

Marginal revenues, viewed as the effects of adding one more unit to rate of output, under the assumption that production is sold in the same period, are reckoned for a few elasticities in the inelastic range as follows:

> For $e_p = -0.999$, $MR = P(1 + 1/-0.999) = -0.001 \cdot P$
> For $e_p = -0.5$, $MR = P(1 + 1/-0.5) = -1 \cdot P$
> For $e_p = -0.001$, $MR = P(1 + 1/-0.001) = -999 \cdot P$

In the inelastic range, the effect upon revenue of increasing sales by one unit per period ranges from $-0.001\,P$ at the barely inelastic $e_p = 0.999$ to $-999\,P$ at the highly inelastic $e_p = 0.001$. On the other hand, decreasing the rate of sales by one unit would increase revenue, and it would also cut cost of production. An informed firm facing inelastic demand would not voluntarily decrease price. Instead, it would stand to gain from raising the price and lowering the rate of output. Firms do not knowingly sell at prices where demand is inelastic.

The price elasticity value of -1.0 is called *unitary elasticity*. Percentage change in quantity is equal to percentage change in price in the

opposite direction. *Total revenue is not affected by a small price change.*
Note:

$$\text{For } e_p = -1.0, MR = P\left(1 + \frac{1}{-1.0}\right) = 0 \cdot P = 0$$

Although a firm facing unitary elastic demand would not gain revenue
from a price boost, it would benefit from cost reduction as output fell.
Therefore, a firm facing unitary elastic demand would also wish to move
price up and bring down the rate of output.

Elasticity values in the range of -1.0 to $-\infty$ are said to be *elastic*.
For these values, percentage expansion of quantity is greater than percentage contraction of price. *Total revenue rises if price is reduced.*

The impact upon revenue by reduction of price so as to sell one more
unit per period is shown below for a selection of elasticities in the elastic
range:

$$\text{For } e_p = -1.001, MR = P(1 + 1/-1.001) = 0.001 \cdot P$$
$$\text{For } e_p = -2.0, MR = P(1 + 1/-2.0) = 0.5 \cdot P$$
$$\text{For } e_p = -\infty, MR = P(1 + 1/-\infty) = 1 \cdot P$$

Addition of one more unit to the rate of output increases total revenue by
amounts ranging from 0.001 times price for the barely elastic $e_p = 1.001$
to the full value of price for the completely elastic $e_p = -\infty$ (where no
price reduction is necessary when output is increased). A firm that has
elastic demand may or may not gain from cutting price and increasing
quantity. Increasing output does increase revenue but cost is also
greater. The decision about price and output depends on comparison of
marginal revenue with marginal cost; techniques of making such comparisons are developed in chapters to follow.

What determines elasticity?

Demand tends to be more elastic as goods (1) face a greater number
of close substitutes at similar prices, (2) make up greater percentages of
the total expenditures of purchasers, and (3) are regarded as luxuries
rather than as necessities. Demand for insulin, a compound vital to the
life of diabetics, would be quite inelastic because there are no substitutes,
it comprises a small part of total expenditure of buyers, and it is certainly regarded by the buyers as a necessity.

On the other hand, motor homes would have highly elastic demand
because there are good substitutes at comparable and even lower annual
costs (truck campers, travel trailers, motels and eating out, tents and
camping gear), they comprise a large part of total expenditure for most
prospective buyers, and most of the prospective purchasers regard motor
homes as luxuries. We would expect shoppers in the motor home market
to be very aware of prices of various brands and models and of sub-

stitutes for motor homes. We would also expect sales of motor homes to increase smartly with reductions in their prices.

Relations of total and marginal revenue functions to the average revenue (demand) function

If we have an equation relating price, P and quantity Q, other equations relating total revenue TR and marginal revenue MR to quantity are easy to derive. Observe: If $P = f(Q)$

then

$$TR = P \cdot Q = f(Q) \cdot Q$$

and

$$MR = \frac{\partial TR}{\partial Q}$$

Here is an example. Suppose price is the following function of quantity:

$$P = 42.12\cent - 0.01908\cent \cdot Q \tag{3-7}$$

then

$$TR = P \cdot Q = 42.12\cent \cdot Q - 0.01908\cent \cdot Q^2 \tag{3-8}$$

and

$$MR = \frac{\partial TR}{\partial Q} = 42.12\cent - 0.03816\cent \cdot Q \tag{3-9}$$

Be certain the above procedure is understood. It will be used repeatedly in parts of this book to follow.

Income elasticity of demand

Income elasticity of demand is a measure of the responsiveness of the quantity of purchases to changes in income. Purchases of some commodities respond very little to income changes. Examples are salt and potatoes. Sales of other commodities increase or decrease rapidly with increases or decreases in income. Examples are motor yachts and private aircraft. Industries subject to rapid shifts in demand are known as "feast and famine" industries. In general, durable consumer goods are more responsive to changes in income than are nondurable goods.

Income elasticity of demand for most commodities is positive, indicating higher purchases at higher incomes. Income elasticity for a few commodities is negative; such commodities are known as "inferior goods." Examples are salt pork and dried beans, which increase in popularity in periods of low income, then give way to more expensive foods in more prosperous periods.

The formula for average income elasticity over a discrete change in volume is:

$$e_I = \frac{\dfrac{Q_2 - Q_1}{(Q_2 + Q_1)/2}}{\dfrac{I_2 - I_1}{(I_2 + I_1)/2}} \qquad (3\text{--}10)$$

in which I_2 and I_1 represent the new and old incomes.

The formula for income elasticity at a point is:

$$e_I = \frac{\partial Q}{\partial I} \cdot \frac{I}{Q} \qquad (3\text{--}11)$$

in which

I is income at a given point on the equation relating quantity to changes in income with no change in price or other variables in the demand function.

Q is quantity at the same point.

$\partial Q / \partial I$ is the first derivative of the demand equation with respect to income.

Disposable personal income is the most common measure of income for such purposes, but other measures of income are also in use.

Knowledge of income elasticities is useful in forecasting the effects of changes in business activity on particular industries. If one has made a forecast of national income or disposable personal income, one can then apply income elasticities in estimating the changes in the purchases of individual commodities. Such forecasting is limited by the same difficulties to which the price elasticities are subject: Sales are influenced by other variables not covered by the elasticity measure, and past relationships may not persist in the future.

Cross elasticity of demand

Cross elasticity of demand measures one of the most important demand relationships, the closeness of substitutes or the degree of complementarity of demand. The quantity of sales of one commodity or service is influenced by the prices of substitutes; the lower the prices of substitutes the lower the sales of the commodity under consideration. The formula for cross elasticity is:

$$e_c = \frac{\dfrac{Q_2 - Q_1}{(Q_2 + Q_1)/2}}{\dfrac{P_{o2} - P_{o1}}{(P_o + P_{o1})/2}} \qquad (3\text{--}12)$$

in which P_{o1} and P_{o2} represent the new and old prices of the other commodity.

Point cross elasticity is calculated by the formula:

$$e_c = \frac{\partial Q}{\partial P_o} \cdot \frac{P_o}{Q} \qquad (3\text{–}13)$$

in which

$\partial Q / \partial P_o$ is the first derivative of the demand equation with respect to price of the other good.

P_o is price of the other good.

Q is quantity of the own good.

A *high positive cross elasticity* means that the commodities are close substitutes. Butter and margarine are examples of commodities that are close substitutes. Competing brands of many consumer goods, such as foods and toiletries, are close substitutes. A *cross elasticity of zero* means that the goods are independent of each other in the market. A *negative cross elasticity* means that the goods are *complementary* in the market— a decrease in the price of one stimulates the sales of the other. An example would be the sale of high-fidelity components and the prices of records. Reduced prices of records in recent years have no doubt stimulated the sale of high-fidelity components.

This ends the discussion of demand elasticity concepts. The concept of elasticity is a flexible tool that may be used to measure the influence of changes of any variable on another. The reader probably can work out the formulas for other elasticities that may be useful. Two examples are market share elasticity (responsiveness of the percentage share one firm has of the market to changes in the ratio of its prices to industry prices) and promotional elasticity (responsiveness of sales to changes in advertising or other promotional expenditure).

TWO COMMON DEMAND MODELS

Many forms of equations could be used in estimating demand relationships, but only two of these forms—the arithmetically linear form with varying elasticity and the log-linear form with constant elasticity— are commonly used. These two forms are closely examined in this section.

Arithmetically linear model

If only two variables are involved, the arithmetically linear form is simply an equation for a straight line. An example of a straight-line demand curve is shown in Figure 3–2 along with the corresponding marginal revenue curve. Below these, the total revenue curve is depicted.

Figure 3–2
Linear demand curve with varying elasticities and the corresponding total revenue curve (hypothetical)

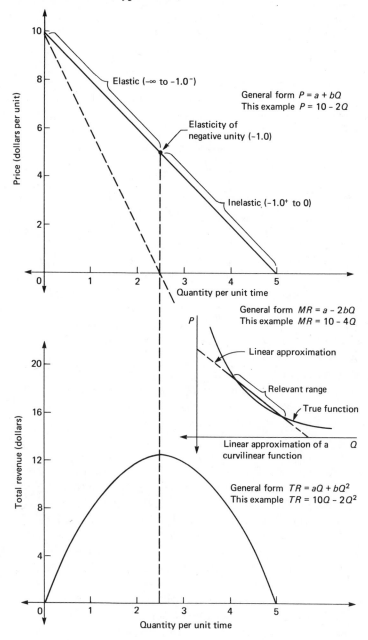

A straight-line demand curve has an equation of general form, $P = a + bQ$. Parameter a is the intercept of the price axis (corresponding to a quantity of zero) and parameter b is the slope that determines how much price change there is for each unit of increase in quantity per period (b nearly always has a negative sign). The quantity axis can be marked off in any convenient units (individual units if desired, but hundreds, thousands, or millions can also be units of quantity).

The slope of any marginal revenue function that corresponds to a straight-line demand function is twice as steep as the slope of the demand function. The intercept of the marginal revenue function is the same as that of the demand function. Given, a demand function, $P = a + bQ$, then total revenue TR is the function

$$TR = P \cdot Q = aQ + bQ^2 \qquad (3\text{-}14)$$

and marginal revenue MR is the function

$$MR = dTR/dQ = a + 2bQ \qquad (3\text{-}15)$$

in which the slope is twice the slope of the corresponding demand equation. The above relationships are depicted in Figure 3–2, where the marginal revenue function has the same intercept as the demand function, $10, but has a slope twice as steep, −$4 compared to −$2 per unit of quantity.

At that price which restricts sales quantity to zero, total revenue is also zero. As quantity increases above zero with reductions in price, there is an initial range in which total revenue grows at a decreasing rate. The explanation of the decreasing rate is this: Total revenue at any given quantity is the summation of marginal revenues for each of the units added to a quantity up to the given rate, and these marginal revenues are steadily falling as quantity increases. Total revenue reaches its maximum at the sales quantity for which marginal revenue is zero. As quantity expands beyond the point that produces maximum revenue, revenue falls off at an increasing rate. The explanation for the increasing rate is that marginal revenues continue to fall steadily, becoming more and more negative in this range. At the point where sales quantity is so great that price is down to zero, total revenue again has a value of zero.

Price elasticities change from −∞ to −1.0 to 0 with movement down and to the right along any straight-line demand curve. The elasticity value of −1.0 corresponds to the quantity for which total revenue is maximum and marginal revenue is zero, and this set of values is always at the midpoint of an arithmetically linear demand curve.

For the example straight-line curve in Figure 3–2, we can calculate elasticities at selected points, using $\partial Q/\partial P = 1/(\partial P/\partial Q) = 1/-\$2 = -\$0.5$ and Equation (3–2), as follows:

At price \$10, quantity 0, $e_p = -\$0.5 \cdot \$10/0 = -\infty$ (perfectly elastic)
At price \$8, quantity 1, $e_p = -\$0.5 \cdot \$8/1 = -4.0$ (elastic)
At price \$5, quantity 2.5, $e_p = -\$0.5 \cdot \$5/2.5 = -1.0$ (unitary)
At price \$2, quantity 4, $e_p = -\$0.5 \cdot \$2/4 = -0.25$ (inelastic)
At price 0, quantity 5, $e_p = -\$0.5 \cdot \$0/5 = 0$ (completely inelastic)

If their entire ranges were depicted, many real demand curves would be curvilinear and convex to the origin, resembling the curve in the inset diagram of Figure 3–2. However, a relatively short range of prices and quantities often includes all the alternatives that are feasible to consider—perhaps all that the firm is likely to face or all those for which data have been obtained. Because it is often a good approximation along the short relevant range, easy to estimate by statistical methods, and easy to use in analytical calculations, the arithmetically linear curve is frequently used by managerial economists as a model of demand.

We have been discussing the form, $P = a + bQ$, which is an equation for a demand curve drawn in conventional position with price as the dependent variable. The same data points could be traced with an equation of form, $Q = c + dP$, with quantity being dependent. In the latter case, parameter c would be the value of Q when price is zero (the intercept of the horizontal axis for a demand curve drawn in conventional position) and parameter d would be $\partial Q/\partial P$ (the reciprocal of the slope, $\partial P/\partial Q$, of a demand curve drawn in conventional position). For example, the following equations trace the same data points:

$$P = 42.12\cancel{c} - 0.01908\cancel{c} \cdot Q$$
$$Q = 2207.5 - 52.4 \cdot P$$

Log-linear model

Several constant-elasticity, log-linear forms of demand equations are shown in Figure 3–3. Curve A, the solid trace, has a constant elasticity of -1.0. It is a rectangular hyperbola—all rectangles with one corner on the function and the opposite corner at the origin have the same area, and this area is $P \cdot Q$, or total revenue. So total revenue is the same at all price-quantity combinations on the function. The marginal revenue function corresponding to Curve A, and to *any* demand curve with constant unitary elasticity, is a straight line at value zero. Observe:

$$MR = P\left(1 + \frac{1}{e_p}\right) = P\left(1 + \frac{1}{-1}\right) = 0$$

Curve B, the dashed trace, has a constant elasticity of -2.0, from the elastic range. Total revenue increases at a decreasing rate as quantity per period increases. Marginal revenues corresponding to constant elasticity demand curves are the product of price times some constant,

Figure 3–3
Constant elasticity demand curves and their log-linear transformations

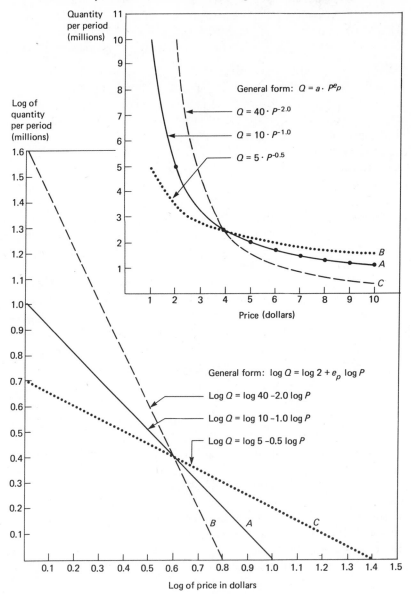

where the constant is a function of elasticity. For Curve B, the marginal revenues are positive and are one half of price:

$$MR = P\left(1 + \frac{1}{e_p}\right) = P\left(1 + \frac{1}{-2}\right) = 0.5P$$

Curve C, the dotted trace, has a constant elasticity of -0.5, from the inelastic range. Total revenue falls at a decreasing rate as sales quantity expands. Marginal revenues are negative for elasticities in the inelastic range, and they are the product of price times some constant, where the constant is a function of elasticity. For Curve C, the marginal revenues are simply the negatives of prices, since:

$$MR = P\left(1 + \frac{1}{e_p}\right) = P\left(1 + \frac{1}{-0.5}\right) = -1 \cdot P$$

Note that constant elasticity demand functions have the general form $Q = a \cdot P^{e_p}$ in which the exponent, e_p, represents elasticity. The Effect of the elasticity exponent is, roughly, to determine the slope and rate of bending of the curve; compare Curves A, B, and C to see that the demand curve bends faster as the absolute value of the elasticity exponent is raised. The effect of the coefficient a is roughly to shift the function farther from the origin as the value of the coefficient is made larger.

Any smooth single-bending curve in the quadrant can be closely tracked by *some* equation of the constant elasticity form. It is necessary to find an appropriate combination of positioning coefficient a and the slope-and-bend exponent e_p. Finding values for these parameters is a task in statistical estimation.

There are no convenient statistical methods for estimating constant elasticity demand equations in their original form. However, constant elasticity curves transform to straight lines if the price and quantity values are replaced by their logarithms. This result is shown in Figure 3–3. Linear regression statistical techniques, with their well-known properties, can be used in estimating the parameters of the log-transformed functions. The transformation works like this:

$$\text{Original form:} \quad Q = a \cdot P^{e_p}$$
$$\text{Log transformation:} \quad \log Q = \log a + e_p \cdot \log P$$
$$\text{Example of original form:} \quad Q = 20 \cdot P^{-1.0}$$
$$\text{Example of transformation:} \quad \log Q = \log 20 - 1.0 \cdot \log P$$

MARKET STRUCTURE

It is time to note the differences between two kinds of demand schedules or curves: the industry (market) demand and the firm's demand. It is possible to compute price elasticities and income elasticities for either kind. In general one would expect price elasticity of an individual firm's demand to be greater than that of industry demand, since the company faces competition from the similar products of rival firms. The firm's demand function could include variables related to prices charged by competitors and their promotional activity; such variables often take the form of a ratio of the firm's price to an industry average price and a ratio of the firm's outlay for promotion to the estimated industry total outlay. The precise relationship between industry demand and the firm's demand depends on the nature of competition within the industry—on the structure of the market.

A classification of markets

Based on the relationship of firm demand to industry demand, there are four categories of market structure:

1. Monopoly.
2. Pure competition.
3. Monopolistic competition.
4. Oligopoly.

The case of *single-firm monopoly* is rare. It is approximated in public utilities, such as electric utilities, which are usually granted a monopoly privilege within a specified market area by government franchises. Even an electric utility faces some competition from substitutes (gas, fuel oil). Thus the concept of monopoly is not a neat one. If a single firm actually controls an entire industry, *the company demand curve and the industry demand curve are the same.*

The case of *pure competition* is equally rare. The conditions for pure competition are: (1) a homogeneous commodity for all firms in the industry; (2) numerous sellers and buyers, so that none has a perceptible influence on the total market; and (3) free entry into and exit from the industry. The theory of pure competition also assumes perfect knowledge of the prevailing price on the part of buyers and sellers. Under these conditions the product of one firm is indistinguishable from that of another. Advertising, patents, brand names, and other features that separate one firm's product from that of another do not exist. While cases which meet all of these requirements are exceptional, some markets approach pure competition closely enough that the theory is a useful approximation. Under such conditions, *the demand for the individual firm's product approaches perfect elasticity.* A perfectly elastic demand implies that the firm can sell all it wishes at the market price. It can sell nothing at a price that is higher, for buyers will transfer to other sellers.

Monopolistic competition refers to markets in which (1) the sellers are numerous and (2) the product of each firm is differentiated from that of the competitors. In such a situation *the firm's demand curve slopes downward to the right, with an elasticity greater than that of the indus-try demand. There is some question whether one may refer to the indus-try demand curve at all in such a case, for the product of each firm is to some degree different from that of the next.* Nevertheless, it is useful to retain the concept of the industry as long as one recognizes its limitations.

Oligopoly refers to markets with small numbers of firms; the Greek base of the word means "few sellers." The markets for steel and cement approximate the conditions of *homogeneous oligopoly*, for most buyers of standardized products care little about who the supplier is but are in-terested in minimizing the cost of an approximately standard product. *Differentiated oligopoly* is more widespread (automobiles, machinery, household appliances). In such conditions products are differentiated physically; advertising, sales practices, trade names, and other devices also distinguished the product of one firm from that of another. It is more difficult to generalize about the shape or elasticity of the demand curve in oligopoly than in the preceding market situations. In fact, *the inter-dependence of the price policies of competing firms in oligopoly may pre-clude drawing a simple demand curve, showing the relationship between a firm's own price and the quantity it sells.*

OTHER INFLUENCES ON DEMAND ELASTICITIES AND DEMAND LEVELS

The preceding section dealt with the influence of market structure on demand. It is now appropriate to review a variety of other influences affecting demand. Most of these affect industry demand, but some op-erate directly on company demand.

Derived demand

Some commodities and services are final goods, ready for direct use by consumers. Others are producer goods: materials, parts, services, or components that are to be used in further production. Demand for pro-ducer goods is *derived from demand for ultimate consumer goods* and thus is known as *derived demand.* Demand for steel is a derived demand; consumers do not buy steel directly, but rather they buy finished products that combine steel with labor and other inputs. Similarly, demand for labor services is usually derived from demand for the final products re-sulting from combining the labor with other inputs.

In general, derived demands are *less* elastic than final demands. The less costly the component in relation to the total cost of the final good, the more likely this is to be the case. For example, demand for glue used in binding books is probably quite inelastic, since a large percentage change in the price of glue will have little effect on the total cost of production. Some labor unions may try to take advantage of this "principle of unimportance" in demanding high wages for special skills that are a small proportion of total cost of products. However, a derived demand can still be subject to competition from close substitutes. If it is easy to replace a certain type of labor with machinery, for example, the elasticity of demand for that labor may be high.

Another factor distinguishes demand for producers' goods from that for consumer goods. Buyers of producers' goods are usually experts, less influenced than lay people by promotional activity and more influenced by a careful evaluation of the characteristics of the commodity. Expert buyers are often sensitive to small price differences.

If the demand for a final good increases, the derived demand for the *durable* producers' goods may rise more rapidly. The reason is that *the demand for increased capacity is likely to be large in proportion to the normal replacement demand.* This effect is called the *acceleration principle*. Operation of the acceleration principle is best explained by an example. Producers of coal by open-pit methods use power shovels that have expected lives of about 20 years. In other words, the annual replacement of shovels amounts to about 5 percent of the total shovels in use. Suppose demand for coal, after having been stable, increases by 5 percent. Now the derived demand for power shovels will consist of replacement demand, 5 percent of the shovels in use, plus expansion demand, another 5 percent of the shovels in use. Thus, a 5 percent increase in demand for final product affects the producer's good as a 100 percent increase in derived demand.

Attitudes and expectations

Demand for a durable good, consumers' or producers', is likely to be more volatile than demand for nondurable goods for two additional reasons: (1) it can be stored, and (2) its replacement can be postponed.

Storability of durable goods makes possible the expansion or contraction of inventories. In the recessions since World War II, the decrease in the size of inventories in billions of dollars has been almost the same magnitude as the decrease in the entire Gross National Product. Those industries dependent upon the buildup of inventories as an important part of total demand suffer disproportionately in recessions. If a producer of durable goods wishes to forecast demand, he or she must give some attention to the probability that inventories of the product will be increased or decreased. This may require an evaluation of the current inventory-sales ratio and of buyers' attitudes toward increases in inventories.

Storability of the commodity also affects the short-run price elasticity of demand. If buyers believe that a reduction of price is temporary, they will tend to build up inventories. A price increase believed to be transitory may have the opposite effect. If, on the other hand, buyers forecast that the price decrease is merely a beginning of a trend, they may wait for even lower prices and use up their inventories, whereas a price increase viewed as the start of a trend would stimulate stocking. Expectations are a central influence on demand for durable goods. Customers buy not for the past or present but for the future and must make predictions of the state of future markets.

Another influence on demand for durable goods is the postponability of replacement. In periods of recession, consumers postpone the replacement of automobiles, furniture, and other durable consumer goods. In the Great Depression of the 1930s, especially in 1932 and 1933, there was little replacement of producers' goods, as is indicated by the fact that the net investment was small or even negative. But in periods of expected shortages, such as the period just after the beginning of the Korean War, replacement demand takes an upward leap.

Long-run and short-run demand

In general, the short-run elasticity of industry demand is less than the long-run elasticity (unless the change in price is considered to be temporary). The reasons for this are:

1. It takes time for buyers to become familiar with the new price and to adjust to it, and to make the required changes in their consumption habits.

2. It may take time to wear out durable items that are not to be replaced. For example, reduced rates for mass transit systems may not have full effects until some private automobiles have worn out.

Product improvements

Changes in the product itself will bring a change in its demand. In many industries, firms are constantly improving products. A large part of research and development activity is devoted to modifying products which already exist.

In the modern world, the constant flow of innovation—the development of new products, new distribution and selling techniques, and new modes of production—has a tendency to create new substitutes for old products. The result is what Schumpeter has called "creative destruction," which includes the destruction of demands for old goods and services. No evaluation of demand is complete until the analyst has examined the possible encroachment of new products on old markets. Since forecasting of technological change may go quite wide of marks, innovation is another factor creating uncertainty in predictions of demand.

Promotional activity

Management does not necessarily take the demand as given. It can act to shift the position and shape of the demand curve. A sales force can promote the product through *personal selling*. *Advertising* can create a greater awareness of a product and its attributes; it may develop tastes which were formerly unknown or unexpressed. Changes in distribution *channels* or in the *service* provided may help shift the demand curve upward.

Managers can sometimes manipulate the closeness of substitutes or degree of differentiation to some extent through advertising and other forms of sales promotion. The objective is to increase the degree of differentiation, with an increase in the monopoly power of the firm. But maximization of differentiation is not, and should not be, the objective of every firm. Many firms indeed profit from imitating competing products. Some furniture firms, for example, send representatives to furniture shows to copy the designs of leading firms. The objective in such cases is to minimize the degree of differentiation so that the imitating firms can take advantage of the resultant high elasticity of demand with somewhat lower prices. In such cases advertising may be aimed at demonstrating similarities to products of competitors, rather than emphasizing differences from these products.

Population changes

Population growth is another important influence on demand. Shifts in the age distribution of population bring about substantial changes in markets for a wide range of products. In most parts of the world the proportion of the population below 20 years of age and over 65 years of age is increasing sharply. The proportion of income under the control of these age groups is increasing even more rapidly. Demography, the study of population, will become increasingly significant in demand studies in the future.

Empirical studies and illustrations

This section will concentrate on studies of the volatility of demand and studies of the acceleration principle.

Studies of demand volatility. The Department of Commerce studied effects of income changes on demands for various commodities. Instead of measuring income elasticity of demand, these studies focus on income sensitivity, a slightly different concept. Income elasticities measure the ratio of percentage changes in quantity demanded to percentage changes in income; indexes of income sensitivity measure the ratio of percentage changes in expenditure (in dollars) to percentage changes in income.

The study covers both prewar and postwar conditions. Some of the main findings are summarized in Table 3–2.

These data support the hypothesis that demand for durable goods is more volatile than demand for nondurables, but differences between durables and nondurables since the war are much less than before. Probably the increased liquidity of consumers and greater stability of business activity account for these changes in sensitivity; consumers are no longer at the mercy of current income in allocating their expenditures.

A few comments on income sensitivity of demand for individual commodities may be of interest. Postwar demand for street railway and bus services has shown a negative income sensitivity, suggesting that these are considered to be inferior services for most consumers; consumers apparently prefer to use more expensive automobile services if their incomes allow. Income sensitivity of demands for gas, electricity, water, and

Table 3–2
Income sensitivity of selected consumer expenditures (based on disposable personal income)

Commodity group	Prewar	Postwar
Total personal consumption expenditures	0.8	1.0
Durable goods	2.1	1.2
Nondurable goods	0.7	0.9
Services	0.5	1.0
Automobiles and parts	2.8	1.1

Source: U.S. Department of Commerce, Office of Business Economics, as published in L. J. Paradiso and M. A. Smith, "Consumer Purchasing and Income Patterns," *Survey of Current Business* (March 1959), pp. 21–28.

telephone services has shown a sharp increase from the prewar to the postwar period (from 0.2 to 1.3 and over), suggesting that public utilities are no longer insulated from the business cycle. Demand for physicians' and dentists' services has shown an increased income sensitivity (from around 0.8 to 1.1 and over), while that for alcohol has declined, perhaps indicating a shift in consumer attitudes on what are luxuries and what are necessities.

Status of the acceleration principle. Do statistical studies support the famous principle of intensified fluctuations in derived demand? The answer depends on how strictly one wishes to interpret that principle. If one expects it to provide precise predictions of demand fluctuations, he is going to be disappointed. Several factors complicate the operation of the principle:

1. If demand for a final good increases, but under conditions of excess capacity, no stimulation of derived demand may take place.

2. If expectations are optimistic, demand for a producers' good may increase even without an increase in final demand.

3. Addition of extra shifts or overtime work makes it possible to increase output without adding to facilities.

4. Technological developments may stimulate purchases of improved producers' goods without any change in ultimate demand; furthermore, technological progress may change the capital-output ratio.

Thus it should be no surprise that empirical support for the acceleration principle is meager. Econometricians have been engaged in testing the principle since the pioneer work of Tinbergen in 1938; their findings have been mostly negative.[1] Recent studies have attempted to verify more flexible interpretations of the acceleration principle, relating investment to changes in output over a series of previous periods and making an allowance for excess capacity.[2] These modifications, plus a recognition of the role of expectations, place the acceleration principle in a more favorable light.

Study of the acceleration principle produces mixed feelings. Despite the failure of most empirical studies to support the principle, it is a matter of common sense that changes in demand for final output must require varying levels of investment. It is also common sense to recognize that in a world of changing technology, shifting expectations, and excess capacity the principle could not work out in a neat, mathematical way. It probably is wise to retain the acceleration principle as a partial prediction of demand for producers' goods; the principle is not satisfactory as a explanation or as a mechanical device for predicting changes in demand.

PSYCHOLOGICAL AND SOCIOLOGICAL CONCEPTS OF CONSUMER BEHAVIOR

Traditional demand analysis takes price, income, and the availability of substitutes as the independent variables, and the quantity purchased as the dependent variable. Economists are aware that human beings are involved in this relationship but they usually give little attention to the psychological and sociological motivations of these human beings.

[1] See J. Tinbergen, "Statistical Evidence on the Acceleration Principle," *Economica* (May 1938), pp. 164–76; T. Hultgren, *American Transportation in Prosperity and Depression* (New York: National Bureau of Economic Research, 1948), pp. 157–69; and J. R. Meyer and E. Kuh, *The Investment Decision* (Cambridge, Mass.: Harvard University Press, 1957).

[2] L. M. Koyck, *Distributed Lags and Investment Analysis* (Amsterdam: North-Holland Publishing Company, 1954), chap. IV; and Robert Eisner, "A Distributed Lag Investment Function," *Econometrica* (January 1960), pp. 1–29.

The question is whether the behavioral sciences are helpful in the analysis of demand. In this book it is possible only to list some major propositions along with some recent findings and some current directions of research.

A few major propositions

1. One of the basic propositions of psychology is that there is much more to human choice than the careful evaluation of alternatives. People make choices for a great variety of reasons, some of which are observable (such as a reaction to a change in price), some of which the individual may not wish to reveal in an interview, and some of which even the decision maker may not realize.

2. Behind patterns of consumer behavior that appear on the surface to be straightforward are deeper causes and motives which are difficult to observe and to measure. Accordingly, research into such behavior is a difficult task, involving techniques that go behind and beyond the simple correlation of prices, incomes, and quantities purchased.

3. Consumer behavior is socially conditioned. Economists themselves have long recognized the inadequacies of the traditional approach of adding together individuals' demand curves to obtain market demand curves. This approach implicitly assumes the independence of each individual's demand for a product. Such an assumption ignores such notions as:

a. Veblen's "conspicuous consumption," which views people as buying not merely to satisfy inner wants but also to impress others.

b. Duesenberry's "demonstration effect," which portrays individuals coming under the influence of the consumption patterns of those with whom they come into contact. A family moving into a wealthy neighborhood is running the risk that the "demonstration" of higher consumption patterns there will set a higher goal of spending. Studies have shown, for example, the major importance of neighborhood influence in the purchase of air conditioners.

c. The notion that commodities serve as status symbols. The drop in automobile sales and the introduction of compact cars in the late 1950s were attributed by some to the reduced prestige value of the automobile. Some observers argued that homes were taking the place of automobiles as status symbols.

4. Interviews may reveal shifts in consumer expectations and attitudes which help explain changing consumption patterns. In particular, it is claimed that optimism or pessimism about the future will determine the level of purchases of durable consumer goods, such as furniture, appliances, and automobiles.

Some current hypotheses

There are at present two competitive approaches to consumer behavior. One approach tries to avoid the rather undefined areas of psychology and sociology by relating purchasing outcomes to relatively measurable variables, such as income or price. The other approach makes a more direct attack on the intervening psychological and sociological variables. The managerial economist takes an interest in these alternative attacks on the problem despite the inconclusive state of present research, for these studies should eventually increase our ability to predict changes in demand.

Earlier sections developed measures (such as income elasticities) that related purchases to the absolute level of income. Two alternatives to the absolute income hypothesis have been proposed: the relative income hypothesis, which stresses the relative position of the consumer on the income scale, and the permanent income hypothesis, which suggests that consumption is related to average income or anticipated income over a number of periods.[3]

The permanent income hypothesis has important implications for the purchase of durable consumer goods. It separates current income into two components: transitory income and permanent income. The *transitory income* includes any fluctuations in short-run income that are not expected to persist in the long run. An increase in transitory income, according to this hypothesis, is more likely to flow into durable goods purchases which are intermittent in character. Transitory income appears to be closely related to the concept of "discretionary" income which has long been used in studies of the demand for durable goods. *Discretionary income* is that part of income left over after deduction of regular, recurrent expenses; it is available for the purchase of durable goods. One weakness in this approach is the difficulty of drawing the dividing line between that part of income which is permanent and that part which is transitory or discretionary. Nevertheless, the permanent income hypothesis promises to lead to a deeper understanding of consumer behavior.

Other studies are attempting to relate consumption to recent changes in income, to increases in household wealth, and to the size of liquid assets. The heavy purchases of durable goods after World War II, for example, are claimed to relate not only to the difficulties of purchasing such goods during the war, but also to the high levels of liquid assets.

Another approach focuses on expectations, attitudes, and other psychological and sociological variables. George Katona has long argued that attitudes such as optimism about the future and the willingness to

---

[3] See Robert Ferber, "Research on Household Behavior," *American Economic Review* (March 1962), pp. 19–63, for an excellent survey of the literature. Much of the present section is based on Ferber's survey.

buy are important determinants of consumer behavior. These changes in attitudes may bring about shifts in consumption patterns long before income and wealth changes take place. Data on attitudes provide an insight into underlying motives and thus lead to a deeper understanding of behavior.

At the same time that Katona and his associates at the Survey Research Center were collecting attitudinal data, they were also surveying consumer intentions to buy, which are on a somewhat different plane from the underlying psychological motives. Close relations between intentions to buy and actual purchases were discovered. Some observers have argued that success of predictions based on intentions to buy makes deeper probing into motives unnecessary, since the data on expectations and attitudes appear to add little to the predictive power of this type of analysis.

Other research workers are focusing attention on consumer decision-making processes. For example, attention is being devoted to the extent to which consumers deliberate on the purchase of durable goods. Deliberation appears to be more frequent among consumers with more education and higher incomes.

Such a wide variety of hypotheses and research approaches is confusing to the practitioner. In time this type of analysis should lead to a deeper understanding of consumer behavior and a higher predictive power in dealing with broad consumption aggregates and with the demand for individual commodities.

ESTIMATING DEMAND EQUATIONS

The *exact* nature of relationships of various influences to the quantity sold per period cannot usually be determined. It is not feasible to set up conditions under which each of the influences is varied, one at a time, as the others are held constant. A manager cannot hold weather constant, keep the selling effort of competitors from changing, increase or decrease prices of competing goods, or change consumer incomes. Information about demand relationships is necessarily limited to *estimates* of the demand equations.

Models

An assumed relationship of quantity per period to price and other variables becomes a *model* when it is expressed in a mathematical form. One example of a model of demand is:

$$FHA = a + bI + cP + dCCF$$

When the parameters of the above model were estimated, the following demand equation was obtained:

$$FHA = 1.63 + 1.15\,I - 0.74\,P - 0.34\,CCF \qquad (3\text{--}16)$$

in which

FHA is the log of the deflated average acquisition cost of FHA-insured new one-family houses (a measure of quantity of housing per purchaser).

I is the log of the deflated effective average income of home buyers.

P is the log of the deflated price for a standardized house.

CCF is the log of the composite credit factor (an index of monthly payments, reflecting changes in average mortgage amounts, interest rates, and lengths of mortgage amortization periods).

The above equation is a constant-elasticity, linear-in-logs form. The equation should be understood to specify that the average acquisition cost of new one-family houses increases by 1.15 percent for each 1 percent increase in average income, decreases by 0.74 percent for each 1 percent increase in deflated price of a standardized house, and decreases by 0.34 percent for each 1 percent increase in the composite credit factor.[4] The equation has some obvious uses in forecasting that might be carried out by home builders and credit agencies.

In order to estimate the parameters of a demand equation, data are necessary. Experiments are one kind of source of data pertaining to demand.

Experiments

Experiments can be carried out either in a laboratory or in the marketplace. Laboratory experiments allow good control over the experimental conditions. Participants in the experiment can be carefully selected to have demographic characteristics of the population of interest. The form of the experiment usually provides a limited amount of money to the participants; they are then allowed to choose between brands of a product, and they get to keep both the product selected and the remainder of the money. The prices of the brands can be deliberately varied to determine the price elasticity of the brand of interest and its cross elasticities with competing brands.

Results of laboratory experiments cannot be extrapolated to provide forecasts for the marketplace unless the participants in the experiment are actually representative of the target population. Further, the experiment must be carried out in such a way that participants do not alter their behavior because of knowledge that they are under observation.

Experiments can also be carried out in actual markets. This is often

---

[4] L. Jay Atkinson, "Factors Affecting the Purchase Value of New Houses," *The Survey of Current Business,* 46, no. 8 (August 1966), pp. 20–34.

done in connection with new products, where there may be interest in consumer responses to different packages and different advertising approaches as well as in effects of price changes. *Test marketing* is experimentation in a few selected market areas with the objective of obtaining estimates of demand relationships for a total market that contains many areas.

An excellent example of market experimentation is a study of demand for fresh oranges by University of Florida researchers in 1962.[5] Grand Rapids, Michigan, believed to be representative of the Midwest market, was the test market. Florida oranges from two areas (Indian River district and Florida interior) in two sizes (200 and 163) were evaluated against California size 138.

Table 3–3
Elasticities of demand for oranges (Florida Valencia size 200 and California Valencia size 138)

| A 1 percent change in the price of: | Produces these percentage changes in quantities of: | | |
	Florida (Indian River)	Florida (interior)	California
Florida Indian River...............	−3.07	+1.56	+0.01
Florida interior...................	+1.16	−3.01	+0.14
California........................	+0.18	−0.09	−2.76

Nine supermarkets cooperated. Prices per dozen were systematically varied plus to minus 16 cents from a base price, in 4-cent increments. The base price was the average retail price of each type prior to the experiment. Thus, each of the types of oranges was offered at nine different price levels. The experiment ran 31 days and involved sales of over 9,250 dozen oranges.

The researchers estimated price elasticities for each type of orange and were also able to estimate cross elasticities between the different types. Several of these estimates are shown in Table 3–3. The numbers on the diagonal in the table are elasticities with respect to own prices and the off-diagonal numbers are cross price elasticities.

Experimentation in actual markets is very expensive. Retailers must be compensated for their cooperation and for any losses that they may have. Many observers are required to make counts of purchases and to relate these to such circumstances as customer traffic, time of day, loca-

---

[5] Marshall B. Godwin, W. Fred Chapman, Jr., and William T. Hanley, *Competition Between Florida and California Valencia Oranges in the Fruit Market,* Bulletin 704, December 1965, Agricultural Experiment Stations, Institute of Food and Agricultural Services, University of Florida, Gainesville, Florida, in cooperation with the U.S. Department of Agriculture and Florida Citrus Commission.

tion, etc. Costs also include possible permanent losses of customers who switch to competing products during the experiment and possible loss of information to competitors who may also monitor the experiment. Furthermore, competitors sometimes sabotage market tests through unusual price changes, sudden changes in advertising, special offers to consumers (coupons), and so forth.

Because of the expense and administrative and logistical problems of running a market test, along with the danger of revealing information to competitors and the vulnerability of the test to competitive sabotage, such experiments are usually carried out only for brief periods of time and only in a few markets. The brevity of the experiments tends to assure constant incomes and unchanging tastes and perferences but it also precludes estimates of long-run effects of changes in price, package, advertising, etc. Only short-run elasticities can be estimated.

Another limitation of market experimentation is that test markets must be selected very carefully to be representative of the whole market. Some cities have been favored for test marketing to the extent that there is concern that their populations have been "over tested"—i.e., subjected to so much experimentation that their reactions to variations in influences on demand are no longer representative of the larger market.

Household consumption surveys

Household consumption surveys provide data that are especially helpful in estimating relationships of incomes and demographic characteristics to the quantities of goods purchased per week. A consumption survey begins with selection of a sample of households that is representative of the population in the market or markets of interest. For example, the national market could be stratified into regions, then into rural and urban populations, and finally into income groups within each degree of urbanization.

A survey is usually designed to determine consumption of a selected set of commodities in a cross section of households during a short period, perhaps one week. Measurement of consumption involves going into the home and making an initial inventory of the amounts of each item that are on hand, obtaining the cooperation of the housewife in keeping a diary of her total purchases during the week, and returning to the home to make a final inventory of quantities on hand at the end of the period.

An excellent example of a household consumption survey is a study by the Institute of Home Economics and the Agricultural Marketing Service in the spring of 1955. This survey obtained detailed data on a week's consumption of about 250 commodities for households in four regions, with three urbanizations within each region, and by income group within each urbanization.

Table 3–4
Income elasticities for food as estimated from cross-section data

Item	All U.S.	Urban	Rural nonfarm	Farm
		Income elasticity		
1. Per person use of purchased farm foods	0.24	0.14	0.26	0.15
2. Value of food marketing services bought with food per person	0.42	0.33	0.46	0.26

Some results from the 1955 Household Consumption Survey are shown in Tables 3–4 and 3–5. These results, as summarized by one of the principal investigators, suggest:

1. The quantity of all food per se, excluding marketing services, consumed per person varies with the level of income within each urbanization but has a quite *low* income elasticity (Item 1, Table 3–4).

2. The value of food marketing *services* per person bought with food per se, both in retail stores and eating places, varies with the level of income two to three times as much as the *quantity* of food per se consumed among families within each urbanization category (Item 2, Table 3–4).

3. Income elasticity of food expenditures is *less* among families with higher real incomes than for lower-income groups (Table 3–5).[6]

Table 3–5
How expenditures on food increase as real income of higher-income families increases

Income above mean (percent)	Expenditures per person (percent)
25	8
50	17
100	22
200	51

Household consumption survey data pertain to a very short period and may not permit adequate estimates for commodities with consumption that varies markedly from season to season. Quantity data cannot be obtained for consumption away from home; this consumption can be measured only by expenditures. If there are regional price differences, it is not usually possible to separate the regional demographic influence

[6] Marguerite C. Burk, "Ramifications of the Relationship between Income and Food," *Journal of Farm Economics* 44, no. 1 (February 1962), p. 115.

from the price effects. (It would be possible if reliable estimates of price elasticities were available, such as those from experiments.) In spite of the above problems, household consumption surveys are the best sources of data for estimates of the influences of income and demographic factors. The principal drawback related to this method is the great expense involved.

Time-series data

Time-series data are observations of economic variables at various points through time. Such observations can be especially useful in estimating the influences of price changes on quantity sold per unit of time. However, great care must be taken in making and using estimates based on time-series data.

An example that illustrates several problems encountered in time-series analysis is a study of U.S. demand for coffee.[7] The demand model was

$$Q = F(Yd, rP)$$

where

Q is the quantity of unroasted coffee beans annually deflated by population.

Yd is aggregate real disposable income deflated by population and consumer price index.

rP is a weighted average of prices of regular and instant deflated by consumer price index.

Estimates of the demand parameters are shown in Table 3–6 for the total populations for 1920–41 and 1947–66.

One problem encountered by the investigator was the postwar introduction of instant coffee. This product uses less green coffee beans per cup than regular coffee because of greater efficiency of extraction, but the price also reflects the cost and the value of extra convenience built into the product. Instant coffee gradually increased its share of the market over the postwar period. The investigator estimated Equation 3 in Table 3–6 with quantities of green beans adjusted to what they would have been if the instant coffee consumed had been regular, but effects of the introduction and gradual acceptance of instant coffee are not clear. The form of the product changed over time. *Change of products* is a major problem in making estimates from data collected over any long period of time.

Another problem facing the investigator was the apparent switch of

---

[7] John J. Hughes, "Note on the U.S. Demand for Coffee," *American Journal of Agricultural Economics* 51, no. 4 (November 1969).

Table 3–6
Demand equations for coffee

Equation*	by†	Ey‡	brp†	Erp‡	R^2	DW
1. 1920–41, total population....	4.21	0.338	−0.084	−0.302	0.758	7.25
2. 1947–66, total population....	−5.05	0.556	−0.030	−0.143	0.74	1.86
3. 1947–66, Q′, total population.	−2.72	0.290	−0.033	−0.150	0.51	2.10

* The means of the Q's for Equations 1 through 3 are: 17.6, 16.1, and 17.0. The Q's are per capita pounds in green (unroasted) beans annually.
   † by and brp are regression coefficients for Yd and rP.
   ‡ Ey and Erp are the elasticities of quantity with respect to income and relative price, respectively, evaluated at the means.

income elasticity from positive in the prewar period to negative in the postwar period. It is possible that coffee became an inferior good as incomes rose and consumption of distilled wines and spirits increased. However, the role of alcoholic beverages in the demand for coffee could not be determined. Their consumption over time is highly collinear with disposable income; as a result, per capita wine and spirit consumption and incomes could not be used as independent variables in the same equation. If the investigator attempted to do so, both of the coefficients relating income to coffee quantity and alcoholic beverage consumption to quantity would be unreliable estimates. The only really satisfactory way of coping with two-variable *multicollinearity* is *to remove the effect of one of the collinear variables.* For example, if the effects of income upon consumption of coffee were already known (through household consumption surveys, for example), these could be removed and there would be no need to have income as a variable in the demand equation. Consumption of alcoholic beverages could then be used as a shift variable in the demand equation, thus picking up the effect of a specific trend in consumer tastes and preferences.

A third problem often encountered in deriving estimates from time-series data is *autocorrelation,* in which the residuals (unexplained variations in the dependent variable) are serially correlated when plotted in the order of occurrence. The effect of autocorrelation is to make the standard errors unreliable. Autocorrelation was apparently not a problem in the study of the demand for coffee, since the tests for autocorrelation with the Durbin-Watson statistic were close to or above 2.0. This value indicates absence of serial correlation in the residuals.

Empirical studies and illustrations

Studies of automobile demand both before and after World War II indicate that its price elasticity is not much more than 1.0, a fact that helps explain the reluctance of automobile manufacturers to reduce price to offset declines in demand.[8] The evidence is overwhelming that the elasticity of demand for cigarettes is extremely low in Western countries; in Great Britain, for example, enormous tax and price increases on cigarettes have done little to curtail the volume of purchases.[9] Both the price elasticity and the income elasticity of demand for public utility services are low, as one might expect. The income elasticity of demand for clothing and furniture is probably slightly greater than unity; the income elasticity of expenditures upon rent is probably less than unity.[10]

The best known of the U.S. demand studies of the 1960s was that of H. S. Houthakker and L. D. Taylor.[11] Their findings are not easily summarized, since they applied a variety of approaches to the different commodities in their study. In most cases they tried to apply a dynamic model which recognizes that current expenditures depend upon preexisting inventories and upon habit formation. The short-term effect of price or income changes is distinguished from the long-term result. For durable commodities for which inventories are maintained, the short-term effect of a change in income will be greater than the long-term effect. For habit-forming commodities, the long-term effect is larger than the short-term effect, and income changes have a smaller effect than they do on durable commodities.

One illustration of the Houthakker-Taylor study is the demand for new cars and net purchases of used cars. The equation reached after considerable experimentation was:

$$f_t = 0.5183\, f_{t-1} + 0.1544\, \Delta\, y_1 + 0.0148\, y_{t-1} - 0.4749\, \Delta\, p_t$$
$$- 0.0457\ p_{t-1} + 14.0725 d_t$$

in which

f_t is per capita personal consumption expenditures on new and used automobiles in the year t (1954 dollars).

y_t is total per capita consumption expenditure in year t.

p_t is relative price in year t of the good in question (1954 = 100).

d_t is dummy variable used to separate post–World War II years from earlier years; takes a value of 0 for 1929–41 and 1 for 1946–61.

---

[8] See, for example, C. F. Roos and V. von Szelski, *The Dynamics of Automobile Demand* (New York: General Motors Corporation, 1939), pp. 21 ff.

[9] A statistical study of the demand for tobacco in 14 countries found low price and income elasticities, but a high response to population growth: A. P. Koutsoyannis, "Demand Functions for Tobacco," *The Manchester School of Economic and Social Studies* (January 1963).

[10] Summaries of studies of the demand elasticities for these and other commodities appear in Aaron W. Warner and Victor R. Fuchs, *Concepts and Cases in Economic Analysis* (New York: Harcourt, Brace & Co., 1958), pp. 144–69.

[11] H. S. Houthakker and L. D. Taylor, *Consumer Demand in the United States, 1929–1970* (Cambridge, Mass.: Harvard University Press, 1966).

According to this equation, the short-run relative price elasticity was −0.9578, while the long-run relative price elasticity was −0.1525. The short-run total expenditure elasticity (somewhat like the income elasticity) was 0.1937, while the long-run total expenditure elasticity was 0.0308. An attempt to include consumer credit as a variable did not improve the equation.

The Houthakker-Taylor study covered 83 commodities. The authors do not claim a high degree of accuracy for many of their equations and suggest some ways in which research methods could be improved. It is clear that the study of consumer demand is still in the developing stages.

These various measurements of demand are all subject to error. Obviously they do not have the degree of precision and accuracy of prediction sometimes achieved in the physical sciences. The difficulty of conducting controlled experiments in which one could test consumer responses to given changes in price or income is a great handicap. Furthermore, statistical methods suited to available data on quantities and prices are still under development. One British study which measured predictive accuracy of demand analysis came to rather negative conclusions on the subject.[12] Future improvements in the statistical methods used in measuring demand will undoubtedly increase the usefulness of demand estimates.

A STUDY OF DEMAND FOR DURABLE GOODS

Durable goods offer an especially difficult challenge to the researcher, since consumers are able to build up or contract their stocks of durables at various rates over time. The problem is one of determining the major influences on rates of change in purchasing. It must be decided at the outset whether one is going to measure the influences on the consumption of the services produced by durable goods or is going to try to measure influences on the goods proper. In addition, the researcher faces the following problems:

1. There are no well-defined units in which the quantity of durable goods can be measured. The quantity of wheat is measured in bushels, but in what units do we measure the quantity of automobiles?

2. Great differences exist in the quality of durables at a given time and quality changes over time, complicating the measurement problem.

3. Related to the preceding problems is the difficulty of obtaining adequate price data for durables. What is the price of an automobile? The problem is compounded by the fact that the published "suggested prices" are not always the prices at which the goods are sold.

---

[12] Mark B. Shupack, "The Predictive Accuracy of Empirical Demand Analysis," *The Economic Journal* (September 1962), pp. 550–75.

4. The existence of a secondhand market for durable goods creates a problem of relating the demand for new units to the demand for old units. It is necessary to consider both the "stock demand" (such as the demand for automobiles both new and old) and the "flow demand" (the demand for new automobiles). But the data on the stocks of durable goods are usually inadequate.

5. The most difficult problem in measuring the stock of existing durable goods is that of depreciation. Only rough approximations of depreciation are possible. The possibility of repairing the durable good means that there is more than one way to increase the stock.

All of these difficulties are illustrated in a study of the demand for household refrigeration.[13] The researcher, M. L. Burstein, attempted to overcome inadequacies of the suggested list prices by constructing a price index based on the Sears Roebuck mail-order catalog data. He considered a variety of depreciation patterns, both of the declining balance and straight-line varieties, with a preference for assuming a depreciation rate of 10 percent per annum.

Burstein used two different measures of income in his analysis: (1) disposable personal income, which is in line with the absolute income hypothesis, and (2) expected income (based on a complicated weighted average of income over a period of eight years), which reflects the permanent income hypothesis. Thirty-eight different equations were fitted to the data, to reflect different income concepts, different treatments of depreciation, different statistical techniques, and so on.

While each of the 38 equations gave somewhat different estimates, Burstein concluded that the price elasticity for refrigeration was between −1.0 and −2.0 and that the income elasticity was between 1.0 and 2.0. It is interesting to note that Burstein made no use of psychological or sociological concepts or data in his analysis, placing his analysis in sharp contrast with the studies discussed earlier in this section. We can expect a continued development of these two kinds of research. While the economist may continue to prefer approaches stressing variables (such as price and income) which can be expressed in monetary units, Burstein's study shows that the measurement of such variables may be every bit as difficult as the measurement of psychological or sociological factors.

SUMMARY

Demand analysis and demand forecasts are needed in both short- and long-run planning. A product's *demand function* explicitly specifies relationships of various quantities per period to values of such variables

---

[13] M. L. Burstein, "The Demand for Household Refrigeration in the United States," in *The Demand for Durable Goods,* ed. Arnold C. Harberger (Chicago: The University of Chicago Press, 1960), pp. 99–145.

as price, incomes, prices of other goods, season, credit availability, promotion, expectations, and perhaps still more influences. A product's *demand curve* is the relation of various quantities per period to various prices, other influences being held constant. A change in some influence other than price can shift the demand curve, whereas a change in price causes a change of quantity along the curve itself.

Price elasticity is the ratio of percentage change in quantity to percentage change in price. *Arc* price elasticity, E_p, is calculated by the formula $E_p = \triangle Q/\triangle P \cdot (P_1 + P_2)/(Q_1 + Q_2)$, in which $\triangle Q$ and $\triangle P$ are the signed changes in quantity and price, respectively; P_1 and P_2 are the initial and final prices, respectively; and Q_1 and Q_2 are the initial and final quantities, respectively.

Marginal revenue, MR, is the ratio of change in total revenue to change in sales quantity. It can be calculated at a point, if elasticity at the point is known, by the formula $MR = P(1 + 1/e_p)$, in which P is price at the point and e_p is the elasticity of demand with respect to price.

Elasticity of 0 to -1.0^- is said to be in the *inelastic* range; in this range marginal revenue is negative and total revenue is decreased by a price reduction. An elasticity of -1.0 is called *unitary elasticity;* marginal revenue is zero and total revenue is not affected by a price reduction. An elasticity of -1.0^+ to -00 is in the *elastic* range; marginal revenue is positive and total revenue is increased by price reduction. A firm facing elastic demand may or may not gain from price reduction; revenue is increased, but so is cost. The net result, obtained by comparing marginal revenue and marginal cost, is what counts.

If $P = f(Q)$, then total revenue $TR = f(Q) \cdot Q$, and $MR = dTR/dQ$. In words, if we have a demand function, we can multiply it by the quantity to get a total revenue function. We can then get the marginal revenue function as the first derivative of the total revenue function with respect to quantity.

Income elasticity is the ratio of percentage change in quantity to percentage change in income; it is positive except for the few commodities known as inferior goods. Knowledge of income elasticity is very helpful in forecasting demand. *Cross elasticity* is the ratio of percentage change in quantity of one good to percentage change in price of another good; it is positive for a substitute good, negative for a complement, and zero for an independent good.

Two forms of demand equations will meet most needs. *Arithmetically linear models* are often good approximations over the limited relevant range. Price elasticities change with movements point to point along a linear demand curve; elasticity of unity and marginal revenue of zero are found at the midpoint. If we have an arithmetically linear demand curve, the corresponding marginal revenue curve has the same intercept on the vertical axis but has a slope twice as steep. A *constant-elasticity, log-linear model* becomes linear if we use logarithms of prices and quantities in place of the original values. This form is theoretically appealing and the constant elasticity feature makes it convenient to use.

The relation of a firm's demand to the industry demand depends upon industry structure. In a *monopoly,* industry demand is the firm's demand. In *pure competition* the industry has a sloping demand curve, but the firm's demand appears to be horizontal at the prevailing price. Demands for monopolistically competitive and differentiated oligopolistic *industries* cannot be rigorously defined, since each firm has a somewhat different product. Demand for the output of a *monopolistically competitive firm* slopes down and to the right but is likely to be quite elastic. Demand for the output of any *oligopolistic firm* can be defined only in conjunction with specification of the reactions of competitors to the firm's price changes.

Derived demand is less elastic than the demand for the final good. Derived demand for a durable producer good is likely to be cyclically volatile because of the *acceleration principle.*

Data for use in estimating demand functions can come from *experiments, household consumption surveys,* or *time series.* In time-series analysis, *multicollinearity* and *autocorrelation* pose problems so serious that this method probably should be used only by econometricians— and only with the greatest care even by these skilled professionals. Demands for *durable* goods are particularly difficult to estimate because of problems in finding a suitable common unit of quantity, changes in the nature of the products over time, inadequacy of available price data, and difficulties in estimating wear-out (which *is* use or consumption) in any given period of time.

QUESTIONS

1. Given that a firm is a monopoly, does this condition guarantee above-average returns on the investment by the firm's owners?

2. Given that a firm is in the market structure of pure competition, does this condition preclude above-average returns on the investment by the firm's owners?

3. Would a knowledgeable firm voluntarily establish a sales rate in the inelastic range of its demand curve? Explain.

4. Long-run price elasticity is greater than short-run elasticity. Explain.

5. What would be the expected sign of the cross elasticity of demand for the following:
   a. Fords relative to the price of Chevrolets?
   b. Auto alarm systems relative to the price of CB radios?
   c. Automobile tires relative to the price of gasoline?

    d. 8-track tape players relative to the price of cassette players?

    e. 8-track tape players relative to the price of 8-track players?

6. Rank the following items in the order of their income elasticities, highest first:

    a. Fresh whole milk.

    b. Insulin for control of diabetes.

    c. Travel for pleasure.

    d. Fresh fruit for home consumption.

    e. Works of original art for interior decoration of homes.

7. What is the difference, exactly, between a demand function and a demand curve? Between a shift in demand and a movement along a demand curve?

8. What is the acceleration principle? How does its operation depend upon the relation of present output to capacity?

9. If you have the equation for a demand function, how can you get the corresponding total and marginal revenue functions? Illustrate by an original example.

10. If you have elasticity at a point on a demand function, how can you calculate marginal revenue at that point? Illustrate by an original example.

PROBLEMS

1. Demand for Spartan Company's industrial chemical product has been estimated as $Q = 360 - 0.8\,P$, in which Q is weekly demand in thousands of tons, and P is price in dollars per ton.

    a. If the firm wished to sell 100,000 tons per week, what price should it set?

    b. At a price of \$300 per ton, how many tons per week will be sold?

    c. Calculate arc price elasticity for a change from a sales quantity of 100,-000 tons per week to a sales quantity of 120,000 tons per week, where the sales increase is entirely due to price reduction.

    d. Derive the equations relating total and marginal revenue to weekly sales.

    e. Calculate marginal revenue at a price of \$300 per ton, using the marginal revenue function just derived.

    f. Calculate point price elasticity at the price of \$300 per ton, and then calculate marginal revenue at the \$300 price by using the formula $MR = P(1 + 1/e_p)$.

    g. Assume that the marginal cost of production is constant at \$100 per ton (in other words, each ton added to the weekly rate of output adds \$100 to the firm's weekly cost). How high should the firm set the weekly rate of production?

2. Consider the following demand equation: $Q = 1.63 I^{1.15} P^{-0.74} C^{-0.34}$, in which Q is quantity of a durable good per customer, I is the average income of buyers, P is the price of a standardized unit of the durable good, and C is an index of cost of credit. Assume that the number of customers per year is constant.

a. What additional information do you need to determine price and income elasticities?

b. Assume Q is 25,000 when P is 20,000 and I is 18,000. If P is expected to increase to 20,400 and I to increase to 18,900, what is the forecast of change in Q?

FURTHER READING

Atkinson, L. Jay. "Factors Affecting Purchase Value of New Houses." *Survey of Current Business*, August 1966.*

Hogarty, Thomas F., and Elzinga, Kenneth G. "The Demand for Beer." *The Review of Economics and Statistics* 54, May 1972.*

Katona, George. "On the Function of Behavioral Theory and Behavioral Research in Economics." *American Economic Review*, March 1968.

Simon, Julian L. "The Price Elasticity of Liquor in the U.S. and a Simple Method of Determination." *Econometrica* 34, January 1966.*

Suits, Daniel B. "The Demand for New Automobiles in the U.S., 1929–1956." *Review of Economics and Statistics* 40, August 1958.*

Working, E. J. "What Do Statistical Demand Curves Show?" *The Quarterly Journal of Economics* 41, February 1927.*

* This article is included in *Readings in Managerial Economics,* rev. ed. (Dallas: Business Publications, Inc., 1977).

Chapter 4

Business Conditions Analysis

Short-range forecasts—approximately one to two years into the future —are essential in planning product mix, pricing, level of output, inventories, financial needs, and net income. This chapter discusses business conditions analysis, which develops outlooks for the general level of business activity and for major sectors of the economy. In the chapter to follow, these business conditions are viewed as influences that may shift demands for particular products.

The objective of this chapter is not to produce a sophisticated general business forecaster. The purpose is more modest: to provide a survey of commonly used forecasting methods that will be helpful in evaluation and application of forecasts made by others. Few businesses make their own general business forecasts. On the other hand, many managers do make forecasts of demands for particular products that are partially based upon business conditions analyses carried out by others.

This chapter begins with a brief description of the ways that general business activity and its major components are measured. It then turns to various methods of forecasting changes in business conditions without using formal models of the economy; these include simple barometric methods, survey methods, and opportunistic forecasts. Then the chapter provides a brief discussion of more sophisticated methods of forecasting using partially or completely specified macroeconomic models.

MEASURING BUSINESS CONDITIONS

The best-known measure of *business activity* is *Gross National Product* (GNP), which measures the total market value of all final goods and services produced within an economy during a time period, usually one year. Note that this definition specifies that *market values* are to be used in computing GNP and also that only *final goods and services* are to be measured. The first provision means that certain forms of activity—for example, homemakers' services—are not measured in the national income accounts.[1] Limitation of the measure to final goods and

Figure 4–1
Circular flow of national product*

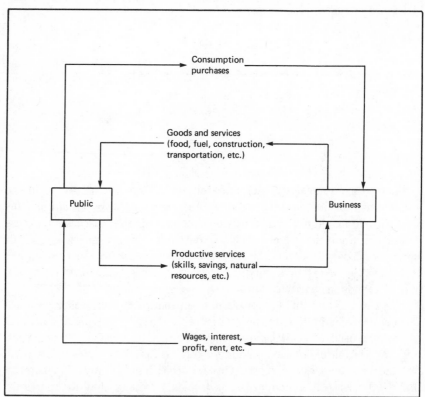

* The national product can be determined by two methods. The upper loop shows the *flow of final goods and services* from the business to the public sector. The total dollar value of these goods and services per year is one measure of the national product. The lower loop shows the *flow of productive services* from the public to the business sector. The total dollar amount that the business sector pays per year for these services is an alternate (and equal) measure of the national product.

---

[1] There have been attempts to quantify such nonmarket output. See, for example, Ismail Abdel-Hamid Sirageldin, *Non-Market Components of National Income* (Ann Arbor: Institute for Social Research, 1969).

services means that intermediate outputs in the production process are not counted separately. This is reasonable, since the value of final output will encompass the value of intermediate goods; to measure both would be double counting of production.

The basic circularity of income-product flows, as illustrated in Figure 4–1, shows that it is possible to measure economic activity from two viewpoints—the total output or the total inputs. *Total output is the sum of the amounts spent on all final goods.* Similarly, *total inputs are measured by the total incomes which accrue to their owners.*

As indicated in Table 4–1, *demand for aggregate production* can be specified as consumption, investment, government, and net exports (the value of exports minus the value of imports). Although personal consumption constitutes the largest component, private investment is the most volatile component and thus the most crucial one in determining the accuracy of forecasts.[2]

On the input side of the ledger, *national income* consists of compensation of employees, proprietors' incomes, rental incomes of persons, corporate profits, and net interest. The factor cost of everything produced in the economy would equal the incomes earned, if it were not for indirect business taxes and capital consumption allowances, i.e., depreciation of equipment used up in the production process. From national income accounts it is quite simple to derive such components as personal income and disposable personal income, as shown in Table 4–2.

If economic activity can be measured either by the sum of amounts spent on all final goods *or* by the total incomes which accrue to resource owners, then one might expect total GNP in Table 4–1 and total national income in Table 4–2 to be equal. But they are not. National income is officially defined as follows: Gross National Product less capital consumption allowance is net national product. Net national product less indirect business taxes and business transfer payments plus subsidies less current surplus of government enterprises is national income. The personal income and disposable personal income concepts are generally more useful than national income. In popular usage, the term *national income* may apply to any measure of aggregate output, but the meaning of the term to economists and forecasters has been more narrowly defined.

Further discussion about national income accounts is beyond the scope of this book. However, it is important to be aware of sources of such income information. Probably most important is the monthly publication by the Commerce Department entitled *The Survey of Current Business.* This publication contains updated income accounts as well as many

---

[2] It is important to keep in mind that for national income purposes, investment means only expenditures on plant and equipment and does not include "investments" in land or the stock market, for these transactions do not involve the actual production of new goods or services but are only transfer transactions.

Table 4–1
Expenditures on 1975 Gross National Product ($ billions)

Personal consumption........................		$ 973.2
Durable goods...........................	$131.7	
Nondurable goods........................	409.1	
Services................................	432.4	
Gross private domestic investment............		183.7
Nonresidential fixed investment............	147.1	
Residential structures.....................	51.2	
Change in business inventories..............	−14.6	
Net exports of goods and services.............		20.5
Exports................................	148.1	
Imports................................	−127.6	
Government purchases of goods and services....		338.9
Federal................................	124.4	
State and local.........................	214.5	
Total GNP.................................		$1,516.3

Table 4–2
National income, 1975

Type	Amount ($ billions)
Compensation of employees.....................................	$ 928.8
Business and professional income................................	65.3
Farm income...	24.9
Rental income..	22.4
Corporate profits and inventory valuation adjustment (IVA)..........	91.6
Net interest...	74.6
Total national income..	1,207.6
Less corporate profits and IVA, contributions for social insurance, wage accruals less disbursements	
Plus government transfers, interest paid by government, dividends, business transfers	
Equals	
Personal income..	1,249.7
Less personal tax and nontax payments	
Equals	
Disposable personal income.....................................	1,080.9

other data concerning the state of the national economy. Statistical supplements to the annual *Economic Report of the President* also contain national income tables. Finally, the *Federal Reserve Bulletin* is another public source of current economic data. The components of national income fluctuate over time, a fact quite visible in Figure 4–2. Forecasting such fluctuations is one objective of business conditions analysis. The next section deals with approaches to business conditions analysis that do not require formal models of the economy.

Figure 4–2
Gross National Product

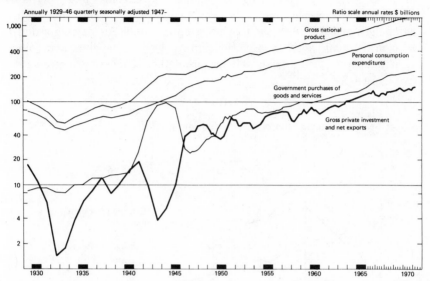

Source: Board of Governors, Federal Reserve System, *Historical Chartbook*, 1972, p. 73.

FORECASTING WITHOUT MACRO MODELS

Indicator forecasts

Just as one can obtain observed levels of GNP or national income over time, many other time series of economic measurements are available. Some of these series have been found to have timing differences in relation to changes in general business activity. There is particular interest in those series with movements that precede (lead) changes in GNP. Search for such series has been a major interest of the National Bureau of Economic Research, especially of Wesley C. Mitchell, Arthur Burns, Geoffrey Moore, and Julius Shiskin.[3]

The basic idea of the indicators approach is that certain types of measured behavior usually begin to slow down *before* the general level of economic activity turns downward. If such a type of behavior also usually speeds up before the level of economic activity turns upward, the data series measuring the behavior is called a *leading indicator*. It

---

[3] The National Bureau of Economic Research is a private nonprofit research organization with the object to "ascertain and to present to the public important economic facts and their interpretation in a scientific and impartial manner." The four individuals mentioned constitute the nucleus of the group at the national bureau which has been studying business cycles over the past 40 years.

reaches a peak before GNP does, and it goes through a trough before GNP turns up. To the extent that such indicators are accurate, they may be useful in forecasting. Economists, politicians, and (perhaps) voters were concerned about the leading indicators during the election campaigns of 1976, when the indicators appear to be forecasting a downturn in economic activity. Relationships of leading, lagging, and coincident indicators to the peak and trough of the business cycle are shown in Figure 4–3.

Figure 4–3
Leading, lagging, and coincident indicators

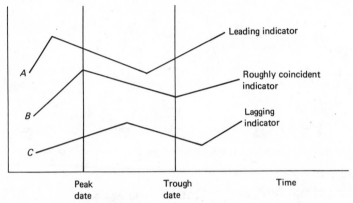

Source: Roger K. Chisholm and Gilbert R. Whitaker, Jr., *Forecasting Methods* (Homewood, Ill.: Richard D. Irwin, Inc., 1971), p. 42.

Economists at the National Bureau of Economic Research (NBER) have devoted much effort to the classification of large numbers of series into these general categories. Further, they have compiled lists of series which are easily accessible to the forecaster. The current "long list" includes 88 U.S. series: 72 monthly and 16 quarterly. Of these, 36 are classified as leading indicators, 25 are roughly coincident, 11 are lagging, and 16 are unclassified by timing.[4] The "short list" is a subset of the long list and includes 25 U.S. series—12 leading, 7 coincident, and 6 lagging. Four of these are quarterly; the remainder are monthly. The

---

[4] In their book, *Indicators of Business Expansions and Contractions,* Geoffrey H. Moore and Julius Shiskin (New York: Columbia University Press for the National Bureau of Economic Research, 1967) briefly review previous efforts in classifying series and note that Mitchell and Burns studied nearly 500 monthly or quarterly series in preparing *Statistical Indicators of Cyclical Revivals,* Bulletin 69 (New York: National Bureau of Economic Research, 1938). They also report that Moore investigated about 800 such series in preparing his book, *Statistical Indicators of Cyclical Revivals and Recessions,* Occasional Paper 31 (New York: National Bureau of Economic Research, 1950).

Table 4–3
"Short list" of economic indicators

Classification and series title	First business cycle turn covered	Median lead (−) or lag (+) in months
Leading indicators (12 series)		
Average work week, production workers, manufacturing....	1921	− 5
Nonagricultural, placements, BES......................	1945	− 3
Index of net business formation.......................	1945	− 7
New orders, durable goods industries..................	1920	− 4
Contracts and orders, plant and equipment.............	1948	− 6
New building permits, private housing units...........	1918	− 6
Change in book value, manufacturing and trade inventories...	1945	− 8
Industrial materials prices...........................	1919	− 2
Stock prices, 500 common stocks......................	1873	− 4
Corporate profits after taxes, Q*.....................	1920	− 2
Ratio, price to unit labor cost, manufacturing.........	1919	− 3
Change in consumer installment debt..................	1929	−10
Roughly coincident indicators (7 series)		
Employees in nonagricultural establishments...........	1929	0
Unemployment rate, total (inverted)...................	1929	0
GNP in constant dollars, expenditures estimate, Q*.....	1921	− 2
Industrial production................................	1919	0
Personal income.....................................	1921	− 1
Manufacturing and trade sales........................	1948	0
Sales of retail stores................................	1919	0
Lagging indicators (6 series)		
Unemployment rate, persons unemployed 15+ weeks (inverted)..	1948	+ 2
Business expenditures plant and equipment, Q*.........	1918	+ 1
Book value, manufacturing and trade inventories.......	1945	+ 2
Labor cost per unit of output, manufacturing..........	1919	+ 8
Commercial and industrial loans outstanding..........	1937	+ 2
Bank rates, short-term business loans, Q*.............	1919	+ 5

* Q means quarterly.
Source: G. H. Moore, and J. Shiskin, *Indicators of Business Expansions and Contractions* (New York: National Bureau of Economic Research, 1967).

short list including median leads (−) or lags (+) in months is shown in Table 4–3.[5]

A set of 36 leading indicators, or even just the short group of 12 leaders, usually contains conflicting signals. A method of summarizing their *net* indication is needed. NBER has developed such a method called the *diffusion index*. The diffusion index is the *percentage* of members of a set

[5] Moore and Shiskin, *Indicators of Business Expansions and Contractions,* p. 34. Note that this book revised the lists of indicators to include new series. It includes an appendix and the 862 series they examined as well as the sources for each.

of series *that is moving upward*. It ranges from zero (when all are moving downward) to 100 (when all series are moving upward).

A diffusion index is an indicator of the extensiveness of an expansion or contraction. Further, it may provide information about forthcoming changes in direction of the set. For example, if during an expansionary period the diffusion index for all leading indicators stands near 90 for several months but then begins to fall, it warns the forecaster that some of the leading series are beginning to turn downward; a general decline in economic activity may be forthcoming.

Individual indicators of economic activity may be of interest not only because they have uses in general economic forecasting but also because they directly provide some information about specific business conditions that can possibly be related to demand shifts for particular goods or services. For *current* information on these indicators, a good source is *Business Conditions Digest* published monthly by the Commerce Department. Data can also be obtained monthly from the Commerce Department's *Survey of Current Business* and the Federal Reserve Board's *Federal Reserve Bulletin*, mentioned previously. Before using these series, especially the various leading indicators, the forecaster may find it helpful to consult the various NBER publications.

Substantive criticisms can be made of the indicators approach. Four weaknesses cited by Lewis are: (1) the indicators give *no indication of the magnitude* of future changes in economic activity; (2) they are *very short range* with probably only six months' advance warning; (3) the *individual series seldom move together,* whereas the diffusion index hides specific series; and (4) for leading series to be useful *there must be no major structural changes in the economy* which might shorten or lengthen their lead time.[6]

Various empirical investigations of predictive accuracy of the indicators approach have been made. Evans sees the NBER approach as providing a good picture of the economy and as a valuable collector and verifier of data, but he concludes that leading indicators cannot be used effectively or accurately as the core of a practical method of forecasting.[7] Nevertheless, economic indicators may be useful in conjunction with other methods.[8]

---

[6] John P. Lewis, "Short-term General Business Conditions Forecasting, Some Comments on Method," *Journal of Business* 35 (October 1962), pp. 347–48.

[7] Michael K. Evans, *Macroeconomic Activity* (New York: Harper & Row, Publishers, 1969), p. 460.

[8] David M. McKinley, Murry G. Lee, and Helene Duffy, *Forecasting Business Conditions* (New York: American Bankers Association, 1965), p. 176; Leonard H. Lempert, "Leading Indicators," in *How Business Economists Forecast,* ed. William F. Butler and Robert A. Kavesh (Englewood Cliffs, N.J.: Prentice-Hall, 1966).

Surveys of attitudes and plans

Among the leading indicators noted in Table 4–3 are new orders in durable goods industries and new building permits for private housing. These orders and permits represent earlier plans and intentions that are in the process of being carried out. Information about *attitudes toward the future* and *plans for the future* may have relatively long leads compared to actual producer or consumer behavior. One method of measuring attitudes and plans simply asks managers or consumers what they expect the future to bring. This is the method of surveys.

This section is limited to a brief review of survey methods. It covers the general approaches used, several sources of this type of forecast, and an overall evaluation of the method. More complete information can be found in Lansing and Morgan's book *Economic Survey Methods* and the many references they cite on specific techniques; these include designing the survey, sampling the population, collecting the data, and analyzing the results.[9] Basically, there are two areas for use of survey methods—producer behavior and consumer behavior; these will be taken up in order. However, first consider a sometimes neglected area of survey forecasting—plans of governments.

Since government expenditures approximate 20–25 percent of GNP, planned activity in this sector must always be considered in business forecasting. *Governments' intentions* are available earlier than reliable information about consumer or producer plans for activities during the corresponding period. For example, in January of 1977 the proposed budget of the United States for the fiscal year October 1, 1977–September 30, 1978 is presented to Congress by the President.[10] Similarly, state governments publish their full-year spending intentions well in advance of the fiscal year. Budgets of governments can be surveyed to determine what the public sector of the economy is planning to do.

Producer expectations regarding investment expenditures, sales, and inventory levels are all subjects of survey research. There are three major surveys of investment anticipations—the Commerce Department–Securities and Exchange Commission (SEC) survey, the McGraw-Hill survey, and the National Industrial Conference Board survey. In the Commerce–SEC survey, firms are queried about their previous quarter's investment and also their anticipated investment during the next quarter. Anticipa-

---

[9] John B. Lansing and James N. Morgan, *Economic Survey Methods* (Ann Arbor: Survey Research Institute, 1971).

[10] The timing and the procedures underlying approval of the budget have been altered by the Congressional Budget Reform and Impoundment Control Act of 1974. For a discussion, see C. William Fischer, "The New Congressional Budget Establishment and Federal Spending: Choices for the Future," *National Tax Journal* 29 (March 1976), pp. 9–14.

tions and realizations can be compared quarter by quarter. The results
of this survey are published the third month of each quarter in the *Survey of Current Business*.

The McGraw-Hill survey appears twice yearly in *Business Week* and
concentrates on *investment plans*, especially of larger firms. The first
survey is taken sometime in October; the results are published early in
November and cover the following year. A resurvey is taken in early
spring and published in April.

The National Industrial Conference Board survey concentrates on
capital appropriations of 1,000 manufacturing firms. Because of the focus
on appropriations, this source of "anticipatory data" is likely to be firmer
than simple expectations, as measured in the two surveys mentioned
above.

In addition to investment anticipations, the Commerce–SEC survey
also obtains *sales* and manufacturing *inventory* expectations. The results
of these surveys appear quarterly in the *Survey of Current Business*.

Predictive accuracy of the yearly Commerce–SEC anticipations results
has been shown to be approximately equal to that of more complex models
(such as those discussed in the section on econometric models below).[11]
However, the McGraw-Hill survey and the quarterly surveys of the
Commerce–SEC were not found to be as accurate as the more complicated forecasting methods.[12] There is still much controversy about the
effectiveness of anticipations data in predicting plant and equipment
expenditures.[13]

Turning to *consumer expectations* surveys, there are several groups
that compile such data. Perhaps the best known of these is the Survey
Research Center at the University of Michigan. The approach taken by
this group is more complicated than simply asking individuals whether
or not they plan to purchase an automobile or appliance sometime during
the next six months, although questions about *buying plans* are a part
of the survey. In addition, there are several queries into the *attitudes*
of consumers, which advocates of this forecasting method believe to be
as important as actual plans. An example of an attitudinal question is:
"Now, about things people buy for their house—I mean furniture, house
furnishings, refrigerator, stove, TV, and things like that—do you think
now is a *good* or *bad* time to buy such large household items?"[14] Answers

[11] Evans, *Macroeconomic Activity*, pp. 468–70.

[12] Ibid., pp. 470–79.

[13] See, for example, Irwin Friend and William Thomas, "A Reevaluation of the
Predictive Ability of Plant and Equipment Anticipations," *Journal of the American
Statistical Association* 65 (June 1970), and the references cited therein.

[14] One of several questions cited in F. Gerard Adams, "Consumer Attitudes, Buying Plans, and Purchases of Durable Goods: A Principal Components, Time Series
Approach," *Review of Economics and Statistics* 46 (November 1964), p. 348.

to questions such as these are then classified as being optimistic, neutral, or pessimistic, and are used in an index of general attitudes. The results of these surveys are reported annually in the Survey Research Center's *Survey of Consumer Finances* and in business news outlets such as *The Wall Street Journal.*

Predictive accuracy of consumer surveys is subject to much dispute. Forecasters directly related to institutions conducting such surveys claim good accuracy and have provided evidence to show the strength of their position.[15] These advocates point out that consumer purchase action requires more than just ability, as might be suggested by a simple relationship of personal consumption to income. In addition, there must be willingness to buy; this is what the surveys purportedly measure.

On the other hand, those who do not agree with the surveying method of forecasting usually argue that directly measurable variables such as credit conditions are the root cause of the behavior. Therefore, in their view surveys add nothing to ordinary econometric models of the economy. Evans notes that attitudinal surveys have not predicted very well nor does their predictive record ". . . appear to have improved in the recent past."[16]

A more moderate view may be advisable. The forecaster may decide that it is better to utilize additional information about attitudes than to ignore it completely. The approach of using all available information is really the cornerstone of the next forecasting method to be discussed.

Opportunistic forecasting

"Opportunistic" is not meant to have a derogatory connotation. Rather, it means that the forecaster takes advantage of all opportunities: he or she will use *all sources of information* which present themselves and is *not restricted to a particular model or technique.* Thus, an opportunistic forecaster might use some basic macroeconomic theory, results of attitudinal surveys, and current changes in the leading indicators. Many business forecasters likely use such an ad hoc approach; the primary source of information regarding the technique is a book by John Lewis and Robert Turner.[17] The discussion of opportunistic forecasting in this section is necessarily brief; only a few high spots are touched.

The opportunistic method requires a certain amount of economic

---

[15] See, for example, Eva Mueller, "Ten Years of Consumer Attitude Surveys: Their Forecasting Record," *Journal of the American Statistical Association* 58 (December 1963); or I. Friend and F. G. Adams, "The Predictive Ability of Consumer Attitudes, Stock Prices and Non-Attitudinal Variables," *Journal of the American Statistical Association* 59 (December 1964).

[16] Evans, *Macroeconomic Activity,* p. 466.

[17] John P. Lewis and Robert C. Turner, *Business Conditions Analysis,* 2d ed. (New York: McGraw-Hill Book Co., 1967).

theory and a working knowledge of the national income accounts. This is because the method of forecasting deals with various sectors of the economy, one at a time, viewing the level of activity in some sectors as given, or *exogenous* (e.g., government spending), and conceiving the level in some other sectors as determined within the system, or *endogenous* (e.g., consumption). The method is iterative, requiring much cross checking and adjustment, with considerations of internal consistency, sector capacities, and so on.

Opportunistic forecasting is a large, catchall category; it excludes only those forecasts made explicitly and solely from survey data, leading indicators, or econometric models. The opportunistic approach is widely used. The so-called consensus forecasts found in various publications (usually near the first of the year) are summaries of forecasts from various sources; most of these individual forecasts fall into the opportunistic classification.

Because of its ad hoc nature, generalized evaluation of opportunistic forecasting is rather difficult. The diversity of the approach is both a strength and a weakness. By using all sorts of information, the method may be able to perform as a predictor "better than" other specific techniques of forecasting. However, the accuracy of the method apparently varies with the intuition and judgment of the particular forecaster. Forecasts prepared by the opportunistic method may be nearly perfect in one year and contain large errors in the following year. Such variance is reduced by using a *partially specified* model such as the GNP model described below.

FORECASTING WITH MACRO MODELS

This section discusses forecasting based on macroeconomic models. It begins with an examination of a partially specified GNP model and goes on to survey business conditions analyses using fully specified, econometrically estimated models.

Opportunistic forecasting with a GNP model

The basic assumption in GNP model building is that demand governs business activity; if total spending increases, business activity increases. The problem of forecasting is thus one of *forecasting components of aggregate demand*.

For this purpose it is desirable to break the GNP into several parts, each of which represents an important segment of total expenditure. Some of these components are much larger than others, as is shown in the data for 1975 in Table 4–1. The time spent on analyzing a component may not be proportional to its dollar magnitude; inventory investment and consumption of durable consumer goods are more volatile than other components and require attention out of proportion to their share of the total.

The problem of consistency. The procedure is to forecast the components of the GNP and to sum. But the components are interdependent, so that *cross checking and adjustment* are required. The level of consumption, for example, depends in large part on the level of the Gross National Product itself. Purchases of plant and equipment depend on many factors, but among them is the rate at which the GNP is increasing and the extent to which demand is exerting pressure on capacity. Inventory investment depends on the rate of current purchases as well as on the accuracy with which this rate has been anticipated. Net foreign investment depends in part on the rate of growth in the domestic Gross National Product as compared with that of foreign national products.

It might be objected that the problem is circular and insoluble. If each component depends on others or on the total, where does one start? Mathematicians would find no difficulty with such a situation; they could construct a series of simultaneous equations to reflect the kinds of interdependence under discussion. In fact, this is exactly what econometricians do. Even without the system of equations, it is possible to make adjustments in one component to bring it in line with a forecast of another, and to make a series of adjustments of this sort until the forecast as a whole appears *consistent*.

Federal government expenditures. The forecaster usually starts with estimates of government expenditures because they are more likely to be independent of other components. While it is true that the government sometimes adjusts some spending according to the level of business activity, most of it must be planned in advance; the forecaster can make use of the budgets, proposed legislation, and presidential messages that indicate the direction of federal spending.

The simplest procedure is to start with the latest figure on federal government expenditures and to concentrate on probable *increases or decreases* from that figure. What are the sources of information about future government spending? The President's budget message and state of the union message early in the year provide information on what he proposes for the next budget period. The Bureau of the Budget publishes more detailed reports on spending plans. Newspapers and weeklies provide information on how the President's program is progressing in Congress and on other changes in expenditure that may emanate from Congress. Commentators try to evaluate the probabilities of certain programs succeeding in getting through the legislative mill and others' failing. Again, it should be stressed that the forecast must be in terms of *spending on current production*. Appropriation of funds by Congress does not assure that those funds will be spent in the period under consideration.

Forecasting federal government spending requires political as well as economic astuteness. One main difficulty is in predicting shifts in military requirements. But, as demonstrated in the Korean War, even under crisis conditions shifts in military spending may be slow. The Department of Commerce publication, *Defense Indicators,* is a useful source of data about military spending.

State and local government expenditures. The task of aggregating the expenditures of thousands of separate state and local governments is beyond the resources of most forecasters. The simplest solution is to deal with probable *changes* in the aggregate. Since World War II, state and local government expenditures have exhibited an upward trend so consistent from year to year that many forecasters simply project the trend into the future. Extrapolation of trends is normally a risky venture; structural forces that accounted for the trend in the past may not endure in the future. In the case of state and local government expenditures, however, continually increasing demands for public programs such as education and police services appear to insure continued annual increments in spending. The increments in state and local spending tend to grow over the years—a trend that should be taken into account in the forecast.

Expenditures on plant and equipment. If one knew nothing about recent levels of spending, forecasting expenditures on new plant and equipment would be extremely hazardous. Again it is simpler to forecast *changes* in the total based on knowledge of current attitudes, plans, and conditions. However, it is well to remember that this category of spending has gone through rather dramatic fluctuations in the past (a fact quite apparent in Figure 4–2). Investment is based on expectations of future sales and profits, and expectations are prone to change sharply. Investment is also sensitive to rates of change in other categories of spending and in current or expected pressures on capacity. Fortunately, several surveys of business plans for investment are available to assist the forecaster. (They are discussed briefly in the section on survey methods above.)

The forecaster of investment must be aware of a wide variety of influences. Current profits and stock prices no doubt influence future expectations. Current monetary conditions partially determine the ability of firms to finance expansions (though heavy reliance on plowed-back earnings blunts this influence). Relationships of production rates to designed capacities (operating ratios) help form expectations of the need for new plant and equipment. The rate of technological change determines obsolescence of old equipment and thus influences the rate of replacement. It is no use pretending that analysis of such diverse influences is easy, and a high degree of accuracy is not to be expected. Fortunately, the supply of data for investment forecasting is constantly increasing. The *Survey of Current Business,* for example, now publishes data on anticipated changes in sales, on manufacturers' evaluations of their capacity, and on the carry-over of plant and equipment projects.

Residential construction. An evaluation of monetary conditions—of the availability of credit, of interest rates, and of the terms on which mortgage loans may be obtained—is more important in forecasting residential construction than in forecasting for any other sector. Changes in financial conditions *lead* changes in construction expenditures. The size of down payments required in purchasing new homes and the length of time for repayment influence the magnitude of construction. Pegged Federal Housing Administration (FHA) and Veterans Administration (VA) interest rates have been major factors in fluctuations in new housing. When those rates are far below current market rates, availability of FHA and VA loans diminishes sharply. Privately financed housing starts have been more stable. Among the other influences are: the level of vacancies in homes and apartments already built; the rate of formation of new families, which depends on the age structure of the population; and consumer attitudes towards future income prospects.

The forecaster of residential construction should give attention to several statistical series. The F. W. Dodge Corporation publishes data on construction contract awards which give an idea of building that is in prospect about five months in the future. Data are also available in the *Survey of Current Business* and elsewhere on housing starts and on construction already under way. Since it takes a number of months to complete buildings that have been started, figures on housing starts provide some insight into the level of construction in the future. The problem of seasonal variations is a handicap in interpretation of data on construction awards and starts. A rise in one of these indexes may merely reflect the usual spring and summer increase in building activity. It is desirable to correct data for seasonal variations, but the methods used for such corrections have difficulty in separating cyclical from seasonal influences.

Inventory investment. Inventory investment is highly volatile, sometimes rising to a positive $20 billion (annual rate) in prosperity and falling to a negative $10 billion in recession. Since World War II no other sector has had a greater influence in determining the pace of expansion or contraction in short-run business activity.

One important influence on inventory investment is the ratio of inventory levels to sales. In short-run forecasting it is reasonable to assume that businesses intend to maintain a certain ratio of stocks to sales, or to production rates in the cases of raw materials and goods in process. Inventories below these levels are inadequate to meet production and customer requirements. Inventories above this level involve unnecessary interest and storage expenditures and risks of obsolescence. Over long periods, technological change and improvements in inventory management may permit changes in these ratios, but in short-run forecasting such trends can be ignored.

The level of inventory investment depends also on expectations of people in business. If they expect sales to increase they will build up inventories, and vice versa. Thus the forecasting of inventory investment must rest on an evaluation of business expectations, which in turn depends on expected changes in the other sectors. *Fortune* magazine and other publications attempt to evaluate inventory-sales ratios and sales expectations and to convert these into estimates of inventory changes.

Some forecasters find it useful to distinguish between voluntary and involuntary inventory investment or disinvestment. Inventories may increase because businesses want them to take care of anticipated improved business. In such a case, a present rise in inventory investment is a favorable indicator of future levels of investment. An increase in inventories may, however, result from a failure of sales to reach anticipated levels, in which case an eventual contraction of the inventory buildup may be expected as firms cut back their orders for replacements. Similarly, inventories may contract because managers planned it so or because of an unexpected increase in sales; the one cause has the opposite significance of the other. It is true that data on inventory investment do not reveal whether the investment or disinvestment is voluntary or not. But it is not difficult in practice to determine whether the present inventory expansion or contraction is one planned by business or instead one that is likely to experience a reversal in the near future.

The big problem in estimating inventory investment is one of timing. One may know that a present expansion of inventories is temporary but may be unable to specify exactly when the reversal will take place. One may be aware that a present inventory disinvestment results from a desire to bring stocks back in line with sales but may not know how long the correction will continue, especially if a continued decline in sales means a continued failure in the restoration of the desired ratio.

The excess of exports over imports. The prospect for the excess of exports over imports is extremely complex, involving an evaluation of both the import and export situations, which requires an investigation of the progress of foreign economies as well as the domestic scene, international comparisons of price and wage changes, revisions in tariffs, and other policies affecting trade, and the study of the markets for particular commodities important in international trade.

Developments such as oil price increases by the Organization of Petroleum Exporting Countries (OPEC) and the opening of trade with the Soviet Union and China have increased the importance of this sector in recent years. An understanding of international economics and of current international affairs would be helpful in analyzing the foreign trade sector.

Consumption. The Keynesian tradition is to consider consumption to be relatively passive. If the main determinant of consumption is income, then the forecast of the other segments should lead to the required forecast of consumption. One need merely apply the multiplier theory, which says that given change in the other segments (investment and government spending) should result in an induced change in consumption because of the changes in income that result. We do not yet have a precise idea of what the magnitude of the multiplier is, though we are quite certain that it is less for decreases in nonconsumption spending than it is for increases in such spending.

One simple rule which provides fairly accurate forecasts of consumption is as follows: In normal recoveries from mild recessions, the increase in consumption is approximately equal to the increase in nonconsumption spending; in mild recessions, consumption remains at the prerecession level or increases slightly. This rule requires modification for more severe recessions or depressions and for inflationary periods or periods when shortages are expected (like the beginning of the Korean War). In any case, the forecaster should modify estimates for special influences on consumption in the period under study. In particular he or she should make a separate study of the demand for durable consumers' goods, which tends to be more volatile and more subject to special influences that will be discussed shortly.

A more sophisticated approach makes the forecast of consumption a part of the solution of at least two simultaneous equations which reflect the relations between disposable personal income and the GNP, between consumption and disposable personal income, and which might treat the increase or decrease in nonconsumption spending as an independent variable. This approach begins to move in the direction of the econometric models to be discussed shortly. These approaches to handling the problem of induced changes in consumption will be developed more fully in a few pages.

No one (and certainly not Keynes himself) ever really believed that forecasting of consumption was a simple matter of estimating income. The forecaster must contend with autonomous as well as induced changes in consumption. There is reason to believe that consumers' attitudes and expectations influence their expenditures. And a multitude of factors help determine spending on particular types of commodities and services.

The forecaster may forecast consumption of durable goods separately, for durable goods more than nondurables are subject to special influences. In fact, the careful forecaster will break durable goods into subcomponents, such as purchases of automobiles, household appliances, furniture, and so on. In the forecasting of the consumption of durable consumer goods, one should take into account the present levels of installment debt; high debt may mean a reluctance of lenders to permit future increases in indebtedness and also a reluctance of consumers to obligate themselves further. One should also evaluate present holdings of consumer durables.

Individual components: Sources and suggestions. The sketch of gross national product model building presented so far provides a framework for the forecaster. Filling in the detail requires a knowledge of sources of information, supported by skills in using that information to the best effect. Table 4–4 lists some of the most important sources of data and indicates their uses.

Some awkward problems. In using the gross national product model, the forecaster must face some difficulties which are mentioned here only briefly. The two most serious problems are those related to price changes and to induced effects of changes in one segment of the economy on other segments.

Forecasting would be much simpler if one could assume stability in prices. But in some years the increase in the Gross National Product in current dollars may be as much a result of inflation as of changes in "real" product. The forecaster should provide separate estimates of changes in production and changes in prices.

One simple procedure is to make an initial forecast, using the framework already described, without any attention to potential price changes, temporarily making the assumption of stable prices. The forecaster can then examine the implications of the initial forecast, making adjustments where necessary. If, for example, the initial forecast is one of a great increase in aggregate demand which will place considerable pressure on capacity, the forecaster may anticipate considerable inflation resulting from the competition for scarce resources. In any case, the forecaster must take care in separating analysis in real terms from that in terms of current dollars. An extrapolation of past increases in state and local government spending which reflects both inflation and increases in volume does not make sense if one is forecasting only the physical increase in output.

As already noted, various segments of the Gross National Product are interdependent. Forecasted changes for one segment may have important implications for another. The econometrician gets around the problem by using simultaneous equations reflecting these interdependencies. The forecaster using the more qualitative model under discussion must somehow make adjustments in the initial forecasts which will perform, at least roughly, the function served by the simultaneous equations. Suits provides a good (and simple) way of dealing with multiplier-accelerator effects.[18]

The two most important kinds of induced effects are (1) effects of

[18] Daniel B. Suits, *Principles of Economics* (New York: Harper, 1970), pp. 193–209.

Table 4-4
Sources and uses of key forecasting information

Component of GNP	Type of information	Source and date	Uses of the information
Federal government spending	President's budget message to Congress.	Newspapers carry summaries in January. Also published by government.	Provides the most important information on federal expenditures for the next fiscal year, starting on July 1. Is subject to revision by Congress.
	Summary of the budget message.	*The Budget in Brief* (government publication in January).	Presents a summary of the budget message.
	Review of the economic situation with emphasis on the federal budget.	President's *Economic Report* (government publication in late January).	Presents an interpretation of the budget and its economic implications.
	Review of the economic situation with emphasis on the federal budget.	*Midyear Budget Review* (government publication in August).	Presents a review of the federal spending program for the current fiscal year, reflecting congressional revisions of the budget.
	Reports on congressional action on presidential spending plans.	Newspapers and weekly magazines throughout the sessions of Congress.	Provides information on the success or failure of the President's program in Congress, as well as predictions of future plans both of the President and Congress.
State and local government spending	Data on the levels of state and local government spending in recent periods.	The national income accounts in the *Survey of Current Business* (monthly).	The usual procedure is to extrapolate the recent trend into the future, with possible revisions based on newspaper reports on expedited programs or on financial difficulties.
Investment in plant and equipment	Surveys of intentions to invest.	McGraw-Hill Book Company (*Business Week* in November); also Department of Commerce and SEC (*Survey of Current Business*, November, March, and other issues).	These surveys provide excellent information in business investment plans for the coming year (or quarter). The past record of these surveys is good for most periods.
	New orders for durable goods.	*Survey of Current Business* (monthly).	Since orders usually lead actual production and sales, this series provides suggestions on future changes in investment.

Table 4–4 (*continued*)

Component of GNP	Type of information	Source and date	Uses of the information
	Nonresidential construction contracts (F. W. Dodge Index).	*Survey of Current Business* (monthly) and *Business Conditions Digest* (monthly).	Since construction awards should normally lead actual construction, this series suggests potential changes in the building of factories, office buildings, stores, etc.
Residential construction	Family formation.	Intermittent projections by the Bureau of the Census.	Provides information of a key segment of the potential market for new housing.
	Residential construction contracts awarded or housing starts.	*Survey of Current Business* (monthly) and *Business Conditions Digest* (monthly).	Provides an indication of potential changes in housing construction before those changes take place.
	Mortgage terms and ease of securing loans (down payments, interest rates, monthly payments).	Newspapers provide intermittent reports. *Federal Reserve Bulletin* (monthly).	Information on the terms of FHA, VA, and regular mortgages indicates the financial restraints on the purchase of new homes.
	Vacancy rate.	Bureau of Labor Statistics.	Indicates the extent of saturation of the housing market.
	Home-building survey.	*Fortune* magazine (monthly).	Indicates developments in residential construction.
Inventory investment	Ratios of inventories to sales on the manufacturing, wholesaling, and retailing levels (requires computations involving series on inventories and series on sales).	*Survey of Current Business* (monthly).	Indicates whether inventories are high or low in relation to a "normal" ratio. Must be interpreted with caution in the light of recent changes in final sales and the attitude of business toward inventories.
	Manufacturers' inventory expectations.	*Survey of Current Business* (monthly).	Indicates extent to which businesses expect to expand or contract inventories.
	Inventory surveys.	*Fortune* magazine (monthly).	On the basis of sales expectations and assumed inventory-sales ratios, estimates amount of inventory change.

Consumer durable goods	Surveys of consumers' intentions to spend and save (including intentions to buy automobiles). Rate of housing construction.	Survey Research Center, University of Michigan and Federal Reserve Board. *Federal Reserve Bulletin* (quarterly). *Survey of Current Business* (monthly).	Indicates intentions to purchase durable goods. There is considerable correlation between these intentions and actual purchases. The building of new houses has an important influence on sales of furniture and appliances.
	Installment credit outstanding (in relation to the disposable personal income).	*Federal Reserve Bulletin* (monthly).	A high level of installment credit already outstanding may mean a lower willingness to incur new debt or a lower willingness to lend.
	Buying-plan surveys.	National Industrial Conference Board *Business Record*.	Suggests potential changes in the purchase of consumer goods.
	Projected consumer outlays on durable goods and housing.	*Consumer Buying Indicators* (quarterly).	Covers surveys of plans of consumers to purchase automobiles, appliances, furniture, and housing.
Nondurable consumer goods and services	Regression lines relating the past consumption of nondurable goods and services to the past disposable personal income.	Past issues of the *Survey of Current Business* provide the necessary data. Special articles in the *Survey of Current Business* review findings on such relationships.	Past relationships to disposable personal income show considerable stability, though the rate of sales to income rises in recession.
Comprehensive collection of indicators	Charts covering most of the best-known indicators.	*Business Conditions Digest* (monthly).	A compact collection of charts covering indicators of income, production, prices, employment, and monetary conditions.

changes in investment and government spending on consumption and (2) effects of the changes in demand for total output on investment. The first is the problem of the *multiplier;* the second the problem of the *acceleration effect*. The present discussion deals only with the multiplier.

The multiplier is the ratio of a change in income to the change in investment or government spending. It may be expressed as:

$$ m = \frac{\Delta Y}{\Delta(I + G)} $$

where $\Delta(I + G)$ is the exogenous cause, the change in investment and government spending, and ΔY is the endogenous effect, the change in income.

The forecaster may proceed as follows. He may initially make an estimate of consumption based on the assumption that disposable personal income remains the same. At this stage he takes into account surveys of consumer attitudes and intentions to buy, financial considerations such as the size of liquid assets and the extent of consumer debt, and any other influences on consumption which he is able to uncover. In later stages of the forecast he drops the assumption of the constancy of income. He examines his estimates of changed nonconsumption spending (investment and government expenditure) to see whether these indicate a rise or fall in incomes which will induce a change in consumption.

The crudest way to handle this problem is to make a rough estimate of the multiplier effect based on past experience and apply it to the data. If the change in nonconsumption spending is positive (an increase), the forecaster may take the multiplier to be approximately 2.0, which would suggest induced increases in consumption approximately equal to the increases in nonconsumption spending. If, instead, the forecast indicates a decline in nonconsumption spending, he will apply a much smaller multiplier, for the evidence is strong that short-run declines in income do not affect consumption as much as increases in income. Consumption is "sticky" in the downward direction; in fact, consumption has declined very little in each of the recessions since World War II, suggesting that the multiplier is closer to 1.0 than 2.0 in such periods. A major decline in investment or government spending would probably have a greater multiplier effect, for consumers would find it more difficult in such circumstances to resist a decline in their standards of living.

A more sophisticated approach involves use of several simultaneous equations which treat the Gross National Product and consumption as unknowns and take investment and government expenditures as exogenous variables. On the basis of past experience one might assume that consumption is 80 percent of disposable personal income and that disposable personal income is 69 percent of the Gross National Product. In such a case the simultaneous equations would appear as follows:

$$GNP = I + G + C$$
$$C = 0.80 \ (0.69 \quad GNP)$$

where

GNP is Gross National Product.
I is investment (including the excess of exports over imports).
G is government spending (including state and local spending).
C is consumption.

These two equations contain two unknowns (both *I* and *G* having been estimated already) and are easy to solve. More advanced approaches would use more complex equations, which might include marginal propensities to consume rather than average propensities, which would separate the effects of increases in nonconsumption spending from the effects of decreases, and which would separate the purchases of durable consumer goods from those of nondurable goods and services.

Checks for consistency. The final step in gross national product model building is to check the various components for consistency. Among the questions that are appropriate are the following:

1. Is the forecast level of government expenditure consistent with the total forecast? If the overall forecast indicates heavy unemployment, a reduction in taxes or an increase in public works might be in prospect. If the overall forecast indicates inflationary pressures, an increase in taxes or curtailment of spending might be imminent.

2. Are the assumptions on the monetary sector consistent with the overall forecast? If the overall forecast indicates heavy unemployment, an easing of money by the Federal Reserve System may be imminent, with possible repercussions on residential construction or other sectors.

3. Are prospective profits consistent with other parts of the forecast? We have not discussed the forecasting of profits, but the thorough forecaster will check to see that prospective profits are in line with estimates of investments.

4. Is the level of personal saving consistent with the rest of the forecast? Again, we have not developed the forecast of personal saving, though it is directly related to the forecast of consumption. A complete forecast would devote special attention to the savings forecast.

5. What magnitude of government surplus or deficit is likely under the conditions indicated? Some forecasters pay particular attention to the prospective deficit or surplus. They believe that deficits or surpluses in the government sector are more important than the simple changes in public expenditures. If government spending is increasing but tax collection is increasing even faster, the stimulating effect of expenditures will be much smaller than would be the case with taxation lagging behind spending.

6. Is the forecast of total output and prices consistent with the available capacity? A strong pressure on capacity might mean that some investment or consumption plans might not materialize and that inflationary pressures will exceed those in the initial forecast.

Recapitulation. The foregoing discussion of gross national product model building has deliberately avoided some of the technical issues the forecaster must face in practice. But an understanding of this approach should be a big help to a decision maker in evaluating published forecasts. The reader should now be aware of the kinds of assumptions that go into such forecasting and, consequently, of the limitations of the forecasts. The following section discusses econometric models. Such models must be *completely* specified.

Econometric models

To begin the discussion of econometric models and to define several terms, consider the following very simple model of the macro economy.

$$
\begin{align}
(1) \quad & Y = C + I + G + X \\
(2) \quad & C = a + bY + dC_{-1} \\
(3) \quad & I = e + fi \\
(4) \quad & G = G' \\
(5) \quad & X = X' \\
(6) \quad & i = i'
\end{align}
$$

where

Y is Gross National Product.

C is consumption expenditures with C_{-1} denoting consumption expenditures in the previous period.

I is investment expenditures.

G is government expenditures.

i is an interest rate.

X is net foreign exports.

$a, b, d, e,$ and f are unknown parameters or constants, i.e., unknown numbers

The above equations are either behavioral equations or identities. The behavioral equations are those which contain unknown parameters (i.e., Equations 2 and 3). The term *behavioral* stems from the fact that these equations specify how economic groups, such as consumers and producers, behave. The remaining equations are identities, either equilibrium conditions (1) or definitional identities (4, 5, and 6). Variables within the set of equations can be classified as endogenous or exogenous. Values of *endogenous* variables are *determined within the system of equations.*

In this example, they include GNP, consumption expenditures, and investment expenditures. Values of *exogenous* variables are *specified from outside the system* by the forecaster. These latter variables include expected government spending, net exports, and interest rate. C_{-1} is a *predetermined* variable.

Steps in forecasting with an econometric model consist of the following. First, a model such as the one indicated above must be *specified*. Economic theory determines the appropriate functional relationships (specification becomes a point of contention when the basic theory differs among forecasters). In the above example, a simple "consumption function" hypothesizes that current consumption depends upon current income and also upon consumption in the previous period. Each equation is an explicit statement of how the forecaster believes some of the sectors of the economy are interrelated; as a group these equations comprise what are believed to be the important behavioral characteristics of the economy, i.e., they "specify the model."

The second step in the forecasting process is *estimation* of the unknown parameters, i.e., the values of *a, b, d, e,* and *f*. This requires two bits of expertise—knowledge of data and their sources and intimate knowledge of statistical estimation methods. The most commonly used form of estimation is some type of regression technique. Of course this technique must take into account the fact that the model is an interdependent one; i.e., consumption is a major portion of income (Y) but is in turn affected by the level of income.

The third step in forecasting is *simulation*. The forecaster "plugs in" values for the exogenous variables to get forecasts of the endogenous ones. For instance, assume that the following behavioral equations had been estimated.

$$C = 44 + 0.35Y + 0.7C_{-1}$$
$$I = 400 - 9{,}620\,i$$

Further assume that the forecaster is willing to assume the following values for the exogenous variables:

$$C_{-1} = 510$$
$$G = 300$$
$$X' = 30$$
$$i' = 0.05$$

The forecaster would then predict the level of Gross National Product to be 1,000.

Note that the structure of the above simple model includes an interperiod feedback effect through lagged consumption that would keep this model going if initial values of G', X', and i' were assumed to hold constant for several periods into the future. Or, a more interesting simulation could be carried out by plugging in expected changes in these "predetermined" variables. Projections more than one period into the future may be of much interest even though these become less and less reliable as the horizon is extended.

In appraising the basic four-step procedure for forecasting—constructing a model, estimating the parameters, choosing values for the exogenous variables, and simulating the future—several possible weak links are obvious. First, there is the *possibility of incorrectly specifying the model.* For example, perhaps interest rates actually have little bearing upon investment expenditures whereas profits of earlier periods are a good predictor of investment. In such a case, predictions will not be very accurate and the forecaster needs to modify the model.

A second possible weakness relates to any attempt to extrapolate into the future based on past experience. *A change in the structure of the economy cannot be measured immediately* even though it may be having important effects on the level of income and employment. This problem can be encountered even in short-run forecasts. Therefore, it would involve really heroic assumptions to project GNP as much as 15 years into the future using a quarterly model of the U.S. economy tested for the period 1945–72.[19]

A third possible weak link in the procedure involves choice of values for exogenous variables. In the more complex models discussed below, these *guesses about the future can be crucial.*

Perhaps the most important positive feature of econometric model forecasting is that it *requires the forecaster to completely specify the assumptions* underlying the forecasts. This allows thorough examination of all aspects of the model and may lead to improvements in the approach.

Another strength of econometric models is their *capability for simulation of a great variety of possible environments.* For example, the impact of a possible major railway strike can be predicted. Such information can possibly lead to more intelligent policy making than would otherwise be possible.

Of course, practical econometric models are much more sophisticated than the naive model presented above. During the past 25 years, econometric model building and forecasting has been a "growth industry." One of the early models of the U.S. economy was constructed and estimated by Lawrence Klein.[20] It was followed by the Klein-Goldberger

---

[19] An analogous procedure would be to "backcast" GNP for 1930 based on the same model and compare predicted with observed values.

[20] *Economic Fluctuations in the United States, 1921–1941* (New York: John Wiley and Sons, 1950).

model, which in turn led to the 32-equation forecasting model used in the early 1960s at the University of Michigan.[21]

Another model constructed during the 1960s was that of the Office of Business Economics of the Department of Commerce.[22] The structure of this model, often called the OBE model, is shown in Figure 4–4. Note the basic relationships and the classification of variables into exogenous, endogenous, and lagged endogenous categories.

In the late 1960s several major econometric models were produced by university and nonprofit organizations. Among these were the very large Brookings Institution model,[23] the Wharton Model at the University of Pennsylvania,[24] and a monetary-oriented model developed jointly by the Board of Governors of the Federal Reserve System and Massachusetts Institute of Technology.[25]

Although there is continuing academic interest in econometric forecasting models, the decade of the 1970s has been notable for model building in the private sector. Reports on the major forecasts produced by the private-sector models are made public from time to time, but the principal work of these organizations, forecasts for particular clients, and the documentation of the models are not available for examination. Among firms producing forecasts from econometric models are: Data Resources Incorporated, Chase Econometrics, Townsend-Greenspan and Company, and several major banks.

The results of numerous econometric and opportunistic forecasts are annually summarized by at least two organizations—The Federal Re-

---

[21] Lawrence R. Klein and Arthur S. Goldberger, *An Econometric Model of the United States, 1929–1952* (Amsterdam: North-Holland Publishing Co., 1955). For a discussion of the University of Michigan model used in the early 1960s as well as a very lucid description of the techniques of forecasting from econometric models, see Daniel Suits, "Forecasting and Analysis with an Econometric Model," *American Economic Review* 52 (March 1962), pp. 104–132. A more up-to-date discussion of the Michigan model is in Michael D. McCarthy, *Wharton Mark III Quarterly Economic Forecasting Model* (Philadelphia: Wharton Series on Quantitative Economics, 1972).

[22] M. Liebenberg, A. H. Hirsch, and J. Popkin, "A Quarterly Econometric Model of the United States: A Progress Report," *Survey of Current Business* (May 1966), pp. 13–20.

[23] James S. Duesenberry, Gary Fromm, Lawrence R. Klein, and Edwin Kuh, *The Brookings Quarterly Econometric Model of the United States* (Chicago: Rand, McNally, 1965). Further results are found in a book edited by the same authors entitled *The Brookings Model: Some Further Results* (Amsterdam: North-Holland Publishing Co., 1969). For critiques of the Brookings Model, see Z. Griliches, "The Brookings Model Volume: A Review Article," *Review of Economics and Statistics* 50 (May 1968), pp. 215–34; or R. J. Gordon, "The Brookings Model in Action: A Review Article," *Journal of Political Economy* 78 (May/June, 1970), pp. 489–525.

[24] Evans, *Macroeconomic Activity*, describes the structure of the original Wharton Model, while McCarthy, *Wharton Mark III Quarterly Economic Forecasting Model*, documents the updated version of this model.

[25] Frank de Leeuw and Edward M. Gramlich, "The Channels of Monetary Policy: A Report on the Federal Reserve–MIT Model," *Journal of Finance* 24 (May 1969), pp. 265–90.

Figure 4-4
Condensed flow diagram

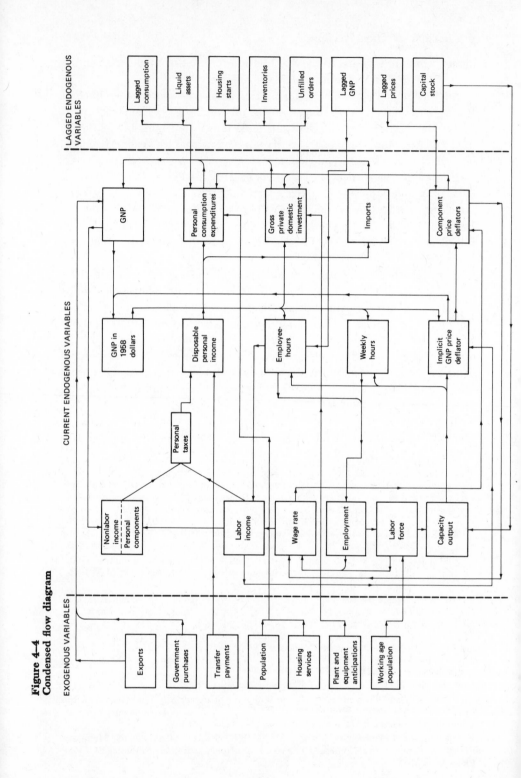

serve Bank of Richmond and of Philadelphia. To gain insight into possible short-run developments in the national economy during the coming year, one would do well to study these summaries along with the leading indicators and then possibly undertake some opportunistic forecasting for oneself. (Additionally, for the producer selling in a regional market, several local or regional econometric models are currently being developed.)

Experience with the forecasting methods

Judging the relative accuracy of econometric forecasts is a difficult task, since the problem is not well defined.[26] For example, should one look at the predictive accuracy of total GNP forecasts or should one also look at the forecasts of the components of GNP? Further, as was indicated above, expected values for exogenous variables must be included whenever a forecast is made. In judging the accuracy of the predictions, should one use the "guesses" of the forecasters (and in a sense rank their abilities to guess what fiscal and monetary policies will be), or should one use actual past values for the exogenous variables and test only the predictive ability of the model as such? In one attempt to test the relative accuracy of the OBE and Wharton models, it was found that using *actual values* of the exogenous variables produced *larger* errors than using the *original forecasting assumptions*.[27]

These findings imply that econometric forecasting is still both an art and a science. Indeed, a major aspect of econometric forecasting involves "fine-tuning" of models, using judgment. The usual method of fine-tuning is to make adjustments in the constant terms of various equations.[28] It appears that there is a certain amount of "opportunism" even in the use of completely specified econometric models. In fact, it may not be correct to regard opportunistic and econometric forecasting as mutually exclusive categories. While econometric forecasters continually fine-tune, opportunistic forecasters often buy services of major private forecasting models and then adjust these forecasts to reflect their own judgments. Thus, although business conditions analysis is becoming more

[26] See Victor Zarnowitz, "How Accurate Have the Forecasts Been?" in *Methods and Techniques of Business Forecasting*, ed. William F. Butler, Robert A. Kavesh, and Robert B. Platt (New York: Prentice-Hall Inc., 1974), pp. 565–96.

[27] See Michael K. Evans, Yoel Haitovsky, and George I. Treqz, "An Analysis of the Forecasting Properties of U.S. Econometric Models," in *Econometric Models of Cyclical Behavior,* ed. Bert G. Hickman (Columbia University Press for the National Bureau of Economic Research, 1972), pp. 949–1139.

[28] Fine-tuning is discussed at length in Michael K. Evans, "Econometric Models," in *Methods and Techniques of Business Forecasting,* ed. Butler, Kavesh, and Platt, pp. 161–89.

and more sophisticated, the judgmental role of the economist-forecaster continues to be important.[29]

SUMMARY

This chapter discussed analysis and short-range forecasting of business conditions—levels of activity for the economy as a whole and for its major sectors. Activity for the economy is commonly measured by *Gross National Product,* which is the market value of all final goods and services. The main components of GNP are consumption, investment, government purchases, and net exports.

Three methods of forecasting business conditions without using structural models of the economy were surveyed. In the *indicators approach,* interest centers on a group of 12 leading indicators and the diffusion index (percent of indicators rising) which summarizes their net indication. *Surveys of attitudes and plans* related to the future may be of particular interest in relation to the outlooks for producer and consumer durables. Neither the indicators approach nor the surveys approach appear to be satisfactory for use as the core of a business forecasting system.

Opportunistic forecasting takes a list of sectors of the economy and forecasts future changes from current values, using all available information. The opportunistic approach appears to be more successful when it is used with *partially specified models* of the economy. In such models, the values of some variables are regarded as functions of others. The values of the independent, or exogenous, variables are forecast first, and the values of the dependent, or endogenous, variables can then be determined. In a partially specified model, particular importance is attached to the *multiplier,* which is the ratio of change in disposable personal income to changes in investment or government purchases.

Over the past two decades, forecasting with *fully specified macro-economic models* has been increasing rapidly and the models used have become more and more sophisticated. This kind of forecasting uses the *econometric approach* in estimating the structural equations of the models. Results from these models, for the economy and its major sectors, are periodically summarized by the Federal Reserve Banks of Richmond and Philadelphia.

---

[29] This point is argued in Otto Eckstein, "Econometric Models and the Formation of Business Expectations," *Challenge* 19, no. 2 (March–April 1976), p. 14. Professor Eckstein is on the faculty of Harvard University and is president of Data Resources Incorporated, one of the principal private econometric forecasting groups.

QUESTIONS

1. In measuring GNP, sales of products or services that will be used as production inputs by another business firm are not included. Why not?

2. How does depreciation enter into the determination of NNP (net national product)?

3. Forecasting with a partially specified GNP model has been called the "lost horse" method. (You go to the place where the horse was last seen and ask yourself where the horse would be likely to go from there.) What are the specific practices used in GNP forecasting that resemble the search for a lost horse as it is described above?

4. What, exactly, is the difference between an endogenous and an exogenous variable? Give several examples of each.

5. What is the multiplier? How does it enter into GNP forecasting?

6. Where could you find current information about the following: government spending, investment, residential construction, inventories, consumer durables, consumption of nondurables?

PROBLEMS

1. A diffusion index is to be calculated for the "short group" of 12 leading indicators. Of this group, eight are moving up and four are moving down. What is the value of the diffusion index?

2. Suppose the value of the multiplier for positive changes is taken to be 2.0. Given that consumption in a recent period was $973 billion, investment was $184 billion, and government purchases were $339 billion, assume investments in the following period were expected to be $193 billion and government purchases were expected to be $359 billion (with the tax collections unchanged). What is the forecast of consumption in the next period?

3. Assume you are using a simple partially specified GNP model as follows:

$$GNP = I + G + C$$
$$C = 0.552\ GNP$$

Using the data for the recent period from Problem 2 above, calculate the forecasts of *GNP* and *C* for the next period.

FURTHER READING

Burch, S. W., and Stebler, H. O. "The Forecasting Accuracy of Consumer Attitude Data." *Journal of the American Statistical Association* 64, December 1969.

Eckstein, Otto. "Econometric Models and the Formation of Business Expectations." *Challenge* 19, March–April 1976.

"Input-Output Structure of the U.S. Economy, 1963." *Survey of Current Business* 49, November 1969.

Katona, George. "Consumer Behavior: Theory and Findings on Expectations and Aspirations." *The American Economic Review* 58, May 1968.

Lewis, John P. "Short Term General Business Conditions Forecasting: Some Comments on Method." *Journal of Business* 35, October 1962.*

McNees, Stephen K. "The Forecasting Performance in the Early 1970's." *New England Economic Review*, July–August 1976.*

Moore, Geoffrey H. "The Analysis of Economic Indicators." *Scientific American* 232, January 1975.*

Okun, Arthur M. "The Predictive Value of Surveys of Business Intentions." *The American Economic Review*, May 1967.

Suits, Daniel B. "Forecasting and Analysis with an Econometric Model." *American Economic Review* 52, March 1962.*

---

* This article is included in *Readings in Managerial Economics,* rev. ed. (Dallas: Business Publications, Inc., 1977).

Chapter 5

Short-Range Forecasting

This chapter views the general business conditions of Chapter 4 as demand and supply shifters. It focuses upon methods of making short-range forecasts of industry demand and capacity and of market demands and the firm's market share. In this chapter, industry, market, and firm demands are defined as follows. *Industry demand* is nationwide demand for a given product or service, including net exports. *Market demands* are a breakdown of national demand into the demands by classes of purchasers or by geographic market areas, or both. A *firm's demand* is the sum of its projected "shares" of the various market demands.

In this chapter's approach to demand forecasting, the firm's pricing is assumed to have some given relationship to an industry average, and the analysis focuses upon prospective future changes from current sales rates. In other words, demand shifts are forecast as changes in quantity per period assuming no change in pricing.

FORECASTING INDUSTRY DEMAND AND CAPACITY

Short-run forecasts of *industry* demand and capacity are important to the *firm* for several reasons. First, it is from industry demand that market demand and the firm's demands can be derived. Second, expected relationships of industry demand to industry capacity are needed in forecasting profit margins. Third, forecasts of demand and capacity in *other* industries are needed in projecting *their* pricing and rates of production; the outlook in other industries is important if these industries supply inputs used by the firm or if they are markets for the firm's products. Fourth, near-term prospects for another industry may be basic considerations in timing an entry into it.

The following discussion provides brief treatments of survey methods of forecasting and of the method of statistical analysis of historical data. It then goes over input-output analysis in some detail. Finally, it explores approaches to capacity forecasting.

Surveys

Surveys used in forecasting industry demand range from informal to sophisticated. A common technique, especially for sales forecasting, is polling of the sales force. Sometimes selected outside consultants are asked for estimates of future industry demand. For some industries, consumer anticipation surveys of the Survey Research Institute or the Census Bureau can be used. For example, a supplier who needs intentions of consumers to build houses during the next three months can simply look at the Census Bureau's *Current Population Reports* "Consumer Buying Indicators" (Series P-65) to obtain an extremely low-cost estimate. Of course, for a firm concerned only with regional markets, this approach may not be sufficient. Finally, there are surveys of consumers or retailers that incorporate random sample designs and pretested, sophisticated questionnaires.

Major problems with sample surveys are their cost plus some conceptual problems in handling nonrespondents and evaluating the true intent of those who do respond. Nevertheless, surveys are and will continue to constitute an important research tool in demand forecasting.

Statistical forecasts

This rather vague heading includes a wide spectrum of somewhat mechanical forecasting methods based upon various statistical techniques. Probably the most naive method of statistical projection is to assume constancy—either no changes, constant absolute changes, or constant rate of change. A stationary-state forecast in period t of the level of the variable X in period $t + 1$, denoted X_{t+1}, would specify

$$X_{t+1} = X_t$$

where X_t denotes the values of X during the forecast period. *Stationary state* means things don't change. Thus, $x_{t+1} = X_t$ means "The value of X in period of $t + 1$ is the same as the value of X in period t."

Constant absolute change can be predicted using the formula

$$X_{t+1} = X_t + (X_t - X_{t-1})$$

That is, the expected next period change in the value of X is equal to the past period's absolute change in this variable. *Constant absolute change* means something changes by the same amount each period. For example, a producer of a food product might observe that sales are rising by 500 boxes each week.

Finally, a *constant relative change* can be forecast as

$$X_{t+1} = \frac{X_t - X_{t-1}}{X_{t-1}} \cdot X_t$$

Thus, if the variable grew at a 5 percent rate during the past period relative to period $t - 1$, this growth rate will continue during the next period.

The above methods of forecasting have one overriding advantage— a low cost. Their weakness is the rigidity in assumptions about the nature of changes over time. Because of this rigidity, they are not capable of predicting turning points in a series of data. However, for certain purposes they may be quite useful.

A more complex forecasting method is *time-series analysis*. "Decomposition of time-series data" is described in many business statistics textbooks and will not be detailed here. Basically it breaks the changes in values of a time series into seasonal movements, cyclical movements, trends, and erratic events. Differences among the various decomposition methods are mainly in the assumption about how the various components interact, e.g., multiplicatively or additively. Chisholm and Whitaker review several of these methods and provide a list of further references which could be studied before choosing any of these methods.[1] The technique called *exponential smoothing* is particularly useful in making sales forecasts for an item based only on its own past history of sales.[2] Finally, some very sophisticated techniques for analysis of time series have recently been developed. These could possibly provide quite useful information in industry demand forecasting.[3]

Still more sophisticated forecasts can be made with the aid of correlation and regression techniques. *Correlation* analysis implies no causal relationship, but specifies the direction and strength of association between two variables. Such a measure can be of use to the forecaster if the

---

[1] Roger K. Chisholm and Gilbert R. Whitaker, Jr., *Forecasting Methods* (Homewood, Ill.: Richard D. Irwin, Inc., 1971), pp. 16–27.

[2] See Robert G. Brown, *Smoothing, Forecasting, and Prediction of Discrete Time Series* (Englewood Cliffs, N.J.: Prentice-Hall, Inc., 1963).

[3] G. E. P. Box and G. M. Jenkins, *Time Series Analysis, Forecasting and Control* (San Francisco: Holden-Day, Inc., 1970); or Charles R. Nelson, *Applied Time Series Analysis for Managerial Forecasting* (San Francisco: Holden-Day, Inc., 1973).

variable of interest is highly correlated with some other variable for which there is a forecast. For example, if demand for building materials is found to be highly correlated with housing starts during the previous quarter and there is a major drop in such starts, it is reasonable to forecast that demand for building materials will fall.

Regression analysis requires more detailed *a priori* assumptions than correlation analysis. In regression analysis, an explicit functional relationship between one or more independent variables and the dependent variable is hypothesized and estimated. Given this estimated relationship and forecasts of values for the independent variables, values of the dependent variable can be projected. For example, assume that the forecaster has specified that the level of total quarterly sales of a particular product in the building materials industry, D, is a linear function of housing starts in the previous quarter, S, and the level of GNP, Y. Using past observations of these variables, the forecaster can estimate the regression coefficients. Assume the following regression equation is estimated:

$$D = 40.35 + 50.13S + 0.000000045Y \qquad R^2 = 0.943$$

The coefficient of determination, R^2, indicates the percent of the total variation in the dependent variable which can be attributed to variations in the independent variables. Thus, in this example, it appears that the two chosen variables account for over 94 percent of the changes in industry demand—an encouraging sign when one wishes to use regression analysis for predictive purposes.[4]

If the forecaster has values of the independent variables for the prediction period, the values are merely "plugged in" to determine a forecast value for the dependent variable. For example, in the regression equation above, if the value of housing starts in the current period were $3,000, and if the predicted value of GNP for the next period were $1,200 billion, then the forecast value of the dependent variable would be $204,430. Two practical points are illustrated in the above example. First, the use of lagged values, when appropriate, makes forecasting easier; observed values from an earlier period do not have to be predicted. Second, if one must use predicted values, it is helpful if these values are already being forecast by others, e.g., GNP.

Success in using regression techniques for prediction depends upon the constancy of the structural relationship between the independent and dependent variables. Also, several assumptions about the nature of the

---

[4] Note that the absolute size of R^2 may *not* be important in other uses of regression analysis. For example, if the primary purpose of the technique were to *test hypotheses* about the theorized relationships between the independent and dependent variables, one would be more concerned with the sizes of the standard errors of the coefficients relative to values of the coefficients themselves. Further discussion of these topics is beyond the scope of this book.

variables must hold for the estimated coefficients to have desirable properties and for the predictions to be accurate. These regression problems are beyond the scope of this book. A user of regression analysis should be aware of them.[5]

One of the real advantages of regression analysis for predictions is that this technique allows a more "scientific" or systematic approach to forecasting. By starting with those variables which theoretically influence the dependent variables, the forecaster is building upon a somewhat more solid foundation than if he or she were simply looking at the situation and making ad hoc prognostications.

Formal econometric models are coming into increasing use in making industry forecasts. *Business Week* recently reported that several major suppliers of machinery and fertilizer and several major demanders of agricultural products are subscribers to agricultural industry forecasts prepared by private forecast services such as Data Resources Incorporated, Wharton, and Chase Econometrics.[6] These forecasts sometimes predict major price changes for agricultural commodities and may thereby alter the behavior of farmers and of demanders of farm products.

Finally, full models have been constructed for several single industries. Examples include the steel industry and the automobile industry.[7] Although such single-industry models are undoubtedly useful, they do not handle interaction among industries in the manner of the next technique to be discussed.

Input-output analysis

The conceptual idea behind input-output analysis is really quite simple. It explicitly recognizes that *industries are interrelated.* For example, the steel industry, rubber industry, electrical power industry, and many others supply inputs used by the automobile industry. Thus, some of the *outputs* of each of the above-listed industries are required as *inputs* to produce automobiles. On the other hand, automobiles are used as inputs by the above-listed industries (automobiles may even be used as inputs

---

[5] A brief review of these problems, including autocorrelation, multicollinearity, etc., are found in Chisholm and Whitaker, *Forecasting Methods.* For even more complete descriptions of the technical nature of these problems, see any basic econometrics book; e.g., J. Johnston, *Econometric Methods,* 2d ed. (New York: McGraw-Hill Book Co., 1972).

[6] "Econometric Forecasting Moves to the Farm," *Business Week,* December 6, 1976, pp. 71–74. The article also notes that congressional agricultural committees are subscribers to the private services even though the U.S. Department of Agriculture has long provided some forecasting of prices and output of farm commodities.

[7] Robert J. Eggert and Jane R. Lockshin, "Forecasting the Automobile Market," and William Hoppe, "Economic Forecasting in the Steel Industry," both in *Methods and Techniques of Business Forecasting,* ed. William F. Butler, Robert A. Kavesh, and Robert B. Platt (New York: Prentice-Hall, Inc., 1974), pp. 421–67.

by the automobile industry). Input-output analysis quantifies interindustry relationships by showing estimated flows of intermediate goods
used in production of final goods and services.[8]

To aid the understanding of input-output analysis, a portion of the
aggregated Input-Output Model for the United States for 1967 has been
reproduced in Table 5-1. The entries in the table are in millions of dollars; flows of inputs are listed down an industry's column and flows of
outputs are shown across an industry's row. For example, reading down
column 7 for coal mining to row 20 for lumber and wood products, except containers, the entry of 22 indicates that a value of $22 million of
output from the lumber and wood products, except containers, industry
was used as input by the coal industry. Note that the diagonal entries
show the value of production by an industry for its own use—for example, the coal industry used $400 million worth of coal.

Other useful tables can be derived from the basic input-output flow
table shown in Table 5-1. For example, an *output distribution table* can
be derived by dividing each entry in the basic table by its corresponding
row total. To illustrate, the $105 million of sales of wooden containers
to the other agricultural products industry turns out to be 19.3 percent
of total demand for wooden containers. An output distribution table
shows the relative importance of various industries as markets for the
output of each industry's intermediate goods.

Direct requirements tables are regularly published along with the
input-output tables. A direct requirements table is derived by dividing
each entry in the basic table by the corresponding *column* total. For
example, inputs from lumber and wood products, except containers (row
20) make up slightly less than 0.7 percent of total inputs to the coal
mining industry (column 7). A direct requirements table shows the
relative importance of various industries as suppliers to each industry.

Looking at the direct requirements entry, one might at first expect
that output of lumber and wood products, except containers, would have
to increase by slightly less than 0.7 cents for each $1 increase in output
of coal mining. However, this is only part of the story. Expansion of coal
mining will require still other industries to expand (for example, construction, mining, and oil field machinery industry) and these other industries will also need inputs from the lumber and wood products, except containers, industry. The *total* requirements from lumber and wood
products for an increase of $1 in coal mining output turns out to be 1.28
cents, nearly twice the direct requirements entry. *Total requirements
tables*, the major achievement of the input-output approach, take these

---

[8] For a more detailed discussion of the basics of input-output analysis, including
its use in forecasting, see William H. Miernyk, *The Elements of Input-Output
Analysis* (New York: Random House, 1965).

Table 5–1
Interindustry table (in $ millions)

(For the distribution of output of an industry, read the row for that industry; for the composition of inputs to an industry, read the column for that industry.)

Industry number		Livestock and livestock products (1)	Other agricultural products (2)	Forestry and fishery products (3)	Agricultural, forestry, and fishery services (4)	Iron and ferroalloy ores mining (5)	Nonferrous metal ores mining (6)	Coal mining (7)	Crude petroleum and natural gas (8)	Stone and clay mining and quarrying (9)
1	Livestock and livestock products	5,610	1,448	96	169	—	—	—	—	—
2	Other agricultural products	8,379	905	105	507	—	—	—	—	—
3	Forestry and fishery products	—	34	34	—	—	—	—	—	—
4	Agricultural, forestry and fishery services	603	1,335	45	—	92	4	(*)	—	—
5	Iron and ferroalloy ores mining	—	—	—	—	33	213	—	—	5
6	Nonferrous metal ores mining	4	1	—	(*)	(*)	1	—	—	6
7	Coal mining	—	—	—	—	—	—	400	(*)	—
8	Crude petroleum and natural gas	—	—	—	—	4	5	1	374	—
9	Stone and clay mining and quarrying	2	119	—	—	5	3	3	—	63
10	Chemical and fertilizer mineral mining	—	12	—	—	—	—	—	—	2
11	New construction	—	—	—	—	—	—	—	—	—
12	Maintenance and repair construction	233	370	—	—	30	16	23	476	18
13	Ordnance and accessories	—	—	—	—	—	—	—	—	—
14	Food and kindred products	3,694	—	24	44	—	—	—	—	—
15	Tobacco manufactures	—	—	—	—	—	—	—	—	—
16	Broad and narrow fabrics, yarn and thread mills	—	9	—	—	1	—	13	—	—
17	Miscellaneous textile goods and floor coverings	10	29	59	46	1	(*)	2	5	2
18	Apparel	(*)	—	—	—	—	—	—	—	—
19	Miscellaneous fabricated textile products	—	43	(*)	5	—	—	—	—	11
20	Lumber and wood products, except containers	3	3	—	—	4	11	3	—	—
21	Wooden containers	—	105	—	13	—	—	22	—	—

Source: Survey of Current Business, February 1974.

feedback effects into account and are derived by matrix operations on the input-output table and the vector of final demands.[9]

The portion of the input-output table reproduced in Table 5–1 was extracted from an 85-industry table published in the *Survey of Current Business.*[10] The 85-industry table is an aggregation from the full 367-industry table published in three volumes by the Department of Commerce. These more complete tables would likely be more useful in short-term industry forecasting.[11]

While firms producing primarily final goods for consumers may not find input-output analysis to be of much use, businesses that produce intermediate goods may find that this approach is extremely helpful in short-range forecasting. For example, in view of the shortage of petroleum-based energy, it is reasonable to expect expansion of coal mining. Although Table 5–1 indicates that apparel are not used as direct inputs into coal production, the corresponding total requirements table shows that each $1 million of increase in coal output will be associated with a $480 increase in output of apparel. The total requirements table shows how expansion of coal mining can be expected to affect each of the other industries.[12]

Another benefit from the input-output approach to forecasting is anticipation of possible bottlenecks in the economy. For example, the analyst may have projected a final bill of goods for consumption and government purchases which calls for increases in output of some intermediate goods that are greater than the analyst considers to be possible. This forecast might suggest buying ahead (before prices begin to rise in the bottleneck industries) and looking around for substitute inputs.

The input-output approach to forecasting contains certain assumptions that should be kept in mind by the user. First, the dollar flows are based on prices in the year of observation; changes in prices over time would cause changes in the dollar flows even if there were no changes in real flows of goods and services. Second, the tables do not reflect the probable changes in interindustry relationships as an industry approaches its own capacity; its relative prices would be expected to rise and the proportions of its output going to various industries would

[9] For a further discussion of these manipulations, see either Chisholm and Whitaker, *Forecasting Methods,* pp. 69–71, or Miernyk, *The Elements of Input-Output Analysis,* pp. 24–28.

[10] "The Input-Output Structure of the U.S. Economy: 1967," *Survey of Current Business* 54 (February 1974), pp. 24–56.

[11] The three volumes are titled: Vol. 1: *Transactions Data for Detailed Industries;* vol. 2: *Direct Requirements for Detailed Industries;* and Vol. 3: *Total Requirements for Detailed Industries.*

[12] For a discussion of forecasting using input-output models, see Robert B. Platt, "Input-Output Forecasting," in *Methods and Techniques of Business Forecasting,* ed. Butler, Kavesh, and Platt, pp. 190–206.

change in line with the differing opportunities for economic substitution of inputs from other sources. Third, the tables contain an implicit assumption that as output of any given industry increases, the inputs used by the industry are maintained in constant proportions; if this assumption does not hold, expansion of the industry may not have the same effects upon other industries as the forecasts from the input-output approach. Finally, even the 367-industry input-output table may not be as detailed as needed for forecasting; many firms have markets that do not correspond very well to the industry groupings that are used in construction of input-output tables.

Note that input-output forecasting techniques can also be used for regional or even local markets. In fact, one of the more active fields within input-output analysis has been the construction of regional models. If the relevant market is really regional in nature, use of the national table may require untenable assumptions about the similarity of the regional and national economies.[13] When used for a single industry, the input-output approach is reasonably simple.[14]

In conclusion, input-output techniques are unique among forecasting methods in that they reflect interindustry relationships, and therefore are really the only form of internally consistent industry forecasting available. Unfortunately, their cost and rigid structural assumptions make them less than the perfect forecasting tool.[15]

Forecasting industry capacity. This section is concerned with the potential rate of real output (capacity) in an industry and how it may be constrained by various factors. Industry capacity forecasts are compared with demand projections to make judgments about an industry's short-term prospects for pricing and profits.

If *labor* is readily available—i.e., there exists a pool of unemployed within the labor market area—it cannot be a constraint on capacity and capital is the relevant restriction. However, in cases of full or nearly full employment in the labor market, increased employment in an industry can occur only via three paths, all of which might increase costs. First, current workers may be employed for longer hours per week. Second,

---

[13] For examples of the use of input-output analysis in state or regional forecasting, see Charles M. Tiebout, "An Empirical Regional Input-Output Projection Model: The State of Washington, 1980," *Review of Economics and Statistics* 60 (August 1969), or William H. Miernyk, "Long Range Forecasting with a Regional Input-Output Model," *Western Economic Journal* 6 (June 1968).

[14] C. Richard Long, "Textiles in Transformation," *Monthly Review,* Federal Reserve Bank of Atlanta 51, no. 5 (May 1966).

[15] Although not a recent contribution to the literature, a set of papers contained in the volume *Input-Output Analysis: An Appraisal* (Princeton University Press, 1955) for the National Bureau of Economic Research provides detailed arguments for and against input-output forecasting. See especially the paper by Carl F. Christ, "A Review of Input-Output Analysis," pp. 137–69, and the comment by Milton Friedman, pp. 169–74.

workers currently employed in other industries may be attracted away from their position. Finally, individuals not in the labor force may be attracted into the labor force. The first two possibilities, of course, involve higher labor costs, either overtime rates or higher wages to attract mobile workers. The third, an increase in labor force participation, requires higher wages and also involves new labor force entrants who are likely to be less productive than the general labor force.

Capital (plant and equipment) is also important in determining an industry's potential output. In the very short run, plant and equipment cannot be increased except in the rare cases in which there are both unoccupied floor space and new equipment available from stocks. Thus, for industries using specialized capital equipment, the forecaster should usually not expect an immediate increase in new capital even if the firms are willing to invest. However, one possibility for short-run increases in capital levels is utilization of previously unemployed capital such as putting into service older machines which had been retired before they were worn out. Of course, the productivity of such machinery is likely to be lower than currently used machines or newly produced machinery, and costs are likely to be higher.

In the slightly longer run where it is physically possible to increase capital through investment, one must consider the *willingness of firms* to add to capital. Expected profitability is the underlying motivation for such expenditures. A final point, closely tied to the concept of capital expansion, is the *ease of entry* into the industry. For certain industries where there are few unique real capital requirements—e.g., management consulting—firms may spring up very rapidly in response to increased demand, thus making capacity constraints very weak. On the other hand, in cases where inputs are unique and require time for production—e.g., the lumber industry—new firms may not find entry easy.[16]

Forecasting of industry capacity will require certain kinds of data. For information about current situations in labor markets, one can consult various documents by the U.S. Department of Labor, especially the publication titled *Employment and Earnings Statistics in the United States and Selected Labor Market Areas*. Current levels of industrial production in various industries are compiled by the Board of Governors of the Federal Reserve System. Also, McGraw-Hill periodically publishes in *Business Week* an index of production compared to capacity in various industries. This index is based on surveys of manufacturers. Finally, a forecaster interested in a particular industry will do well to consult industry trade publications; these often provide valuable insight into

---

[16] For a more specific discussion of the question of industrial capacity, especially the importance of capital expenditures, see Robert C. Yost, "The Capacity Concept and Economic Forecasting," *Mississippi Valley Journal of Business and Economics* (Spring 1968), pp. 16–30.

Figure 5–1
Why cement users are getting squeezed

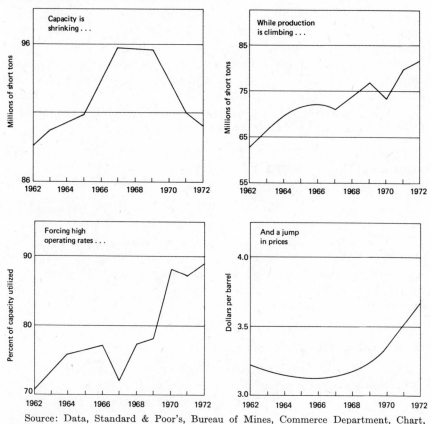

Source: Data, Standard & Poor's, Bureau of Mines, Commerce Department, Chart, *Business Week*.

the current state of the industry, and they may report plans for expansions by individual firms that will substantially change industry capacity.

An example of the impact of capacity upon profitability was observed in the cement industry during the early 1970s. As discussed in *Business Week*,[17] cement producers experienced large demands during the 1950s and responded with large-scale expansions of plant and equipment that increased capacity tremendously. Demand decreased during the 1960s and cement prices also decreased. Low product prices combined with increasing costs decreased profits and resulted in little subsequent expansion of capital within the industry. Because of capacity limitations, cement makers were hard pressed to meet increased demands during the

---

[17] March 10, 1973, pp. 130 a–d.

early 1970s and cement prices rose sharply. These changes are shown graphically in Figure 5–1.

A second interesting aspect of the above example is that cement, like many other goods, is produced for regional markets. In the case of cement, this is due to large transportation costs in its distribution. The *Business Week* article noted that prices were quite different across the nation (ranging from $1.10/100 pounds in Pittsburgh to $1.40 in Atlanta) and that the "shortages" were correspondingly different regionally. Thus, the business forecaster must usually consider the regional markets separately when making capacity forecasts.

FORECASTING MARKET DEMAND AND THE FIRM'S SHARE

We have discussed forecasts for major sectors of the economy and then for particular industries. Attention can now be turned to the individual manager's usual objective in economic forecasting—namely, prediction of demand for his or her own product or products. The discussion begins with estimates of *market potential*, first for producer's goods, then for consumer's goods. Next it moves to forecasts of *market share for an individual firm*.

Market potential for producer's goods

Producer's goods are goods that will be used by other firms in their production process. One common technique of predicting demand for such goods is the "buildup" approach to market potential forecasting.[18] The method includes these steps: (1) determining the industries that purchase the product and the percent of the total market that is attributable to each of these industries; (2) adjusting these percentages to account for changes or trends in market structure; (3) ascertaining the importance of an industry in a particular geographic area relative to that industry nationwide—this involves construction of weights based on published data; and (4) calculating weighted market potentials for specific areas. Such steps are carried out for a hypothetical machine tool manufacturer in Table 5–2.

This method of forecasting market potential can be used for markets defined in ways other than spatially. For example, the buildup approach could be based on types of customers, demographic groups, and types of outlets.

Probably the greatest weaknesses of the method are the importance of judgments in adjusting the weights and the problems with lack of data.

---

[18] This technique and others are discussed in Francis E. Hummel, *Market and Sales Potentials* (New York: The Ronald Press, 1961).

Table 5–2
Market area buildup method of estimating a producer's goods' market potential (hypothetical example)

Industry*	SIC†	SIC weight unadjusted‡	SIC weight adjusted§	Percent SIC‖	Weighted proportion#
Mining machinery	3532	40	30	0.080	2.40
Industrial furnaces and ovens	3567	45	50	0.035	1.75
Truck and bus bodies	3713	15	20	0.60	1.20
			100		5.35

Market potential: 5.35% of national market

* Industries in area which might purchase goods.
† Standard industrial code of industry.
‡ Past relative importance of industries as purchasers of product.
§ Expected relative importance of industries as purchasers.
‖ Relative importance of area in U.S. market. May be found as

(i) $\dfrac{\text{No. production workers in SIC in area}}{\text{No. production workers in SIC in U.S.}}$

(ii) $\dfrac{\text{Value added in SIC in area}}{\text{Value added in SIC in U.S.}}$

or by some other weighing method.
\# SIC weight adjusted *times* percent SIC.

Market potential for consumer's good

Techniques similar to the method discussed above can also be used for forecasting market potential for a consumer's good. One approach to consumer goods market potentials is through the use of consumer "buying power" estimates. Probably the best-known generally available index of buying power is published by *Sales Management* magazine in its "Annual Survey of Buying Power." Indexes of buying power are estimated for all counties and larger cities in the United States. Each index is a weighted average of three factors with the relative weights being 0.5: 0.3: 0.2 for the area's percentage of total national income, percentage of total national retail sales, and percentage of total national population, respectively. The index numbers range from 6.5438 in New York City and 3.9719 in Chicago to levels like 0.0005 in Issaquena County, Mississippi, or 0.0002 in Arthur County, Nebraska. After estimating total national consumer sales potentials for a product, the forecaster would simply multiply this total by a given area's index of buying power to get its market potential.

Market share forecasting. After forecasting market potential for the nation or for a regional market, a firm must estimate what share of this total it will obtain. Probably the most often used approach conceives the firm's market share as depending upon various decision variables such as advertising expenditures, other distribution policies, price, and "effectiveness" of marketing effort. Upon hypothesizing the variables of importance in this process, the forecaster sets up the general behavioral equation $S_i = f(X_1 \ldots X_n)$ which "explains" the ith firm's share. Of course, an explicit functional form with parameters that specify exactly how the X's act to determine S_i is hypothesized. The parameters can then be estimated from market data by statistical methods.

In his *Marketing Decision Making: A Model-Building Approach,* Kotler discusses several different models of market share determination including simple linear models, nonlinear models, and models specifying that the effects or actions occur only with certain time lags.[19] Among the types of explanatory variables mentioned are relative prices, relative advertising expenditures as well as the effectiveness of expenditures, product quality, and levels of service provided. The models as presented provide a systematic yet flexible way of considering various market share determinants.

Another example of forecasting of market shares is provided in the book *Mathematical Models and Marketing Management* by Robert Buzzell.[20] Buzzell discusses use of regression analysis by E. I. du Pont De Nemours and Co., Inc. In forecasting market shares, the basic approach was similar to that used by Weiss; however, the data were obtained from surveys both of households using the product *and* of firms supplying the product. In this way, it was possible to utilize the linear model

$$S_i = a + b_1 AVL + b_2 DP + b_3 ADV$$

where the independent variables are

AVL: a proxy for availability of the product and defined as the proportion of retail outlets stocking the product under investigation.

DP: a proxy for "dealer push" which was measured as the proportion of sales persons specifying the product by name.

ADV: a proxy for advertising thrust measuring the percentage of change in advertising before and during the experiment.

The final variable was included because the experiment was designed primarily to determine the relative effectiveness of different levels of advertising. In some areas a 300 percent increase in advertising was used. The results of the experiment highlighted the importance of availability of the product; increased emphasis upon this factor was planned.

Some useful ideas

A number of interesting ideas which have been applied in actual forecasting for firms or products deserve attention.

---

[19] Philip Kotler, *Marketing Decision Making: A Model-Building Approach* (New York: Holt, Rinehart and Winston, 1971), pp. 92–99.

[20] Boston: Harvard Business School, 1964.

Population changes.   Some demands are closely related to population growth and demographic changes. The producer of baby foods profits from projections of increased birth rates. The publisher of textbooks studies the potential changes in college enrollment in the near future. Real estate investors pay attention to the growing proportion of the population over 65 in age and the special housing needs of this group. Forecasters are using estimates of the rate of family formation to help determine the potential market for residences. Bureau of Census publishes population projections periodically.

Discretionary income.   Some forecasters make use of measurements of discretionary or supernumerary income rather than the usual measures of GNP or disposable personal income. There is evidence that the sale of consumer durables relates more closely to income after the deduction of certain regular expenses than it does to total income. Discretionary income is disposable personal income (personal income after income tax but including transfer payments) less necessary living costs (such as food and clothing) and less fixed commitments (payments on debt). The National Industrial Conference Board has developed a discretionary income series.

Discretionary buying power.   Indexes of discretionary buying power start with discretionary income and add cash balances, near liquid assets, and new consumer credit. Obviously a wide variety of such measurements is possible. (The purist may raise questions about the addition of flows, such as income, to stocks, such as cash, but both stocks and flows are sources of liquidity that may influence consumption.)

Consumer credit outstanding.   A forecaster may wish to consider the status of consumer debt outstanding before estimating the demand for a durable consumer good. A high ratio of outstanding consumer debt to current income may suggest a slowdown of purchases based on new debt for two reasons: lenders will become more cautious about risks, and the consumers themselves will reduce additions to debt. The forecaster may also take into account any changes in the regulation of installment debt by the Federal Reserve Board.

Saturation levels.   Some forecasters give attention to the concept of a limit or saturation level in the particular market. This consideration is especially important for durable consumer goods, such as automobiles or household appliances. As we approach a point at which close to 100 percent of households have refrigerators, the potential market for additional refrigerators becomes limited; the demand becomes mainly a replacement demand (which may be bolstered by planned obsolescence through the use of new designs and colors).

The size and age distribution of existing stocks.   For many consumer durables the size of existing stocks must have a considerable influence on additions to stocks. In a way this repeats the point already made about saturation levels. The age distribution of the outstanding durables may be of particular importance. For example, the automobile market in 1957–58 was depressed by the existence of large numbers of automobiles of recent vintage resulting from the peak sales of 1955–56.

Replacement demand versus new-owner demand. The demand for durables falls into two parts: the demand for replacements by those who already own the item and the demand by entirely new owners. Some forecasters separate these two demands, recognizing that the influences on each are different. New household formation, for example, will have little effect on replacement demand, but may be a major influence on new-owner demand.

More complex patterns of behavior. While it seems that the expectation of price increases should stimulate the purchase of consumer durable goods, such is not always the case. Katona's studies at the University of Michigan show that bad news about the rising cost of living, as in 1966 and 1967, may discourage discretionary purchases.[21] Increases in disposable income resulting from one-time tax cuts are likely to have an impact different from increases that may be expected to be repeated. Katona's studies also suggest that studies of consumer sentiment will improve forecasts of their discretionary expenditures.

An example of demand forecasting for a firm: A bank's demand for loans

This example is based upon a case provided by Data Resources, Inc.[22] Demand at a particular bank for commercial loans was estimated from quarterly time data as:

$$D_c = -21,266.3 + 1,318.6M + 2,763.2S$$
$$(-0.8) \quad (4.5) \quad (3.3)$$
$$+ 9,088.7(CP - BL) + 1,091.8CI$$
$$(2.3) \quad (2.4)$$
$$R^2 = 0.985 \quad DW = 1.736$$

in which

D_c is commercial loan demand in dollars.

M is national money supply.

S is quarter-to-quarter change in sales of the nonelectrical machinery industry (an industry served directly by the bank).

$CP—BL$ is the difference between the commercial paper interest rate and the short-term business loan interest rate (a measure of relative

[21] George Katona, "On the Function of Behavioral Theory and Behavioral Research in Economics," *The American Economic Review* (March 1968), pp. 146–49.

[22] Data Resources, Inc. is an economic information services firm located in Lexington, Massachusetts.

attractiveness of these two sources of funds to commercial borrowers).

CI is total U.S. commercial and industrial loan demand (the bank average "share" is approximately 0.11 percent of the national market).

R^2 is the coefficient of determination (the percent of variation in D_c that is explained by the regression estimate.)

DW is the value of the Durbin-Watson Statistic (a test for autocorrelation.)

The equation was econometrically corrected for first-order autocorrelation.

The bank's demand for mortgage loans was estimated from quarterly time series data as:

$$D_m = 37{,}350.40 + 0.61 M_{-1} - 155.74C$$
$$(3.5) \qquad (5.5) \qquad (-2.8)$$
$$+ 19{,}934.7H - 5{,}354.9U + 5{,}317.61I$$
$$(4.5) \qquad (-3.9) \qquad (2.7)$$
$$R^2 = 0.897 \qquad DW = 1.301$$

in which

D_m is mortgage loan demand in dollars.

M_{-1} is seasonally adjusted mortgage loans outstanding during the previous period.

C is deposits at mutual savings bank and savings and loan associations (competing sources of funds).

H is average housing starts.

U is the state's rate of unemployment (a proxy for ability of residents to buy new homes and for the state's attraction to new residents).

I is the conventional mortgage loan interest rate (entering positively because down payment terms are the rationing mechanism rather than interest rates and because banks can compete more effectively as interest rates rise toward legal ceilings).

The bank's demand for installment loans was estimated from quarterly time series data as:

$$D_i = 19{,}207.3 + 0.85 I_{t-1} - 2{,}899.4U$$
$$(18.3) \qquad (38.3) \qquad (-9.7)$$
$$+ 92.69C + 215.3A$$
$$(4.9) \qquad (3.4)$$
$$R^2 = 0.999 \qquad DW = 1.099$$

in which

D_i is demand for installment loans in dollars.

I_{t-1} is installment loans outstanding during the previous period.

U is the state's unemployment rate.

C is the number of charge cards outstanding.

A is national spending on automobiles and parts.

The above equations, combined with externally developed forecasts of the national, regional, and industry variables, comprise a loan-demand forecasting system for the bank. The forecasts of exogenous variables are provided by Data Resources, Inc. Sensitivity analysis, the simulation of effects of assumed changes in these variables, is perhaps the most useful application of the forecasting system, since it is helpful in making contingency plans in the face of uncertainty. This example shows how the cost of analyzing and using external data can be brought within the reach of medium-size firms by using vendor services.

SUMMARY

The chapter discussed short-range forecasting of industry demands and capacities, market demands, and the firm's shares of the markets it serves. Demand forecasts were viewed as forecasts of changes in quantities per period assuming no changes in relative prices, with the business conditions that were discussed in Chapter 4 being major influences upon the demand shifts.

Two approaches to industry demand forecasting were given brief attention. *Surveys* may be useful in determining attitudes or plans of retailers and consumers, and these may in turn be helpful in forecasting demands for discretionary goods and services. *Statistical forecasts*, in order of increasing sophistication, include: (1) projection and (2) time-series analysis, both being techniques aimed at forecasting a variable using only information about its own past behavior; (3) correlation and (4) regression analysis, both aimed at forecasting one variable on the basis of measured or forecast values of one or more other variables; and (5) econometric models, aimed at forecasting values for a set of endogenous variables based on values of a set of exogenous variables and a structure of relationships specified by an economic model.

A third approach to industry demand forecasting, *input-output analysis*, was discussed at more length. An input-output model specifies flows of intermediate goods and services used in producing final products. *Total requirements tables* are the major achievement of the input-output approach. Each column of a total requirements table shows the increases in outputs of all other industries that would be directly or indirectly required to support a $1 increase in the output of the industry named in the column heading. Total requirements tables are especially useful in deriving forecasts for a particular industry based on forecasts of the bill of final goods and services for consumption and government purchases, where the industry in question is a supplier of producers' goods.

Industry capacity forecasts are needed for comparison with demand forecasts in determining the outlook for industry pricing and profitability. Possible short-range constraints on industry expansion include labor (skilled workers in a full-employment economy) and capital (specialized machines and equipment under order backlog conditions). In a slightly longer-range perspective, constraints may be willingness to expand and ease of entry.

Forecasts of market demand are derived from industry forecasts by using indexes of relative buying power that have been estimated for various market areas and classes of buyers. The market potential for a particular firm is built up by adding the total purchases that have been projected for the various markets served by the firm. Once the forecasts of market potential are in hand, the firm can estimate the share that it will get on the basis of current position and expected effects of its marketing policies—product quality variations, promotion, and pricing.

QUESTIONS

1. Several methods of forecasting do not make use of theoretical models; these methods include simple trend projection, decomposition of time series, exponential smoothing, and simple correlation analysis. Why are such methods widely used? What simple assumption about the structure of the system is implicit in using purely theoretical methods of forecasting?

2. Total requirements tables are described in the text as "the major achievement of the input-output approach." In your own words, what is unique about the information that can be found in a total requirements table?

3. Distinguish clearly among industry demand, market demand, and market share. Use an original example to tell how a business economist might prepare forecasts of each of these and to illustrate how they are related to each other.

FURTHER READING

Leontief, Wassily W. "Input-Output Economics." *Scientific American* 185, October 1951.*

---

* This article is included in *Readings in Managerial Economics,* rev. ed. (Dallas: Business Publications, Inc., 1977).

Cases for part two

This section includes several types of case material. "The State University Press" requires estimation of elasticities of demand and incremental and marginal revenues, in which the concepts of Chapter 3 are paramount, and requires comparisons of marginal revenue with marginal cost to determine profitability. "The Pricing of Automobiles" requires interpretation of demand estimates prepared by others and formation of judgments about the practical implications of these estimates. "An Exercise in Business Conditions Analysis" provides opportunity for practical application of the ideas of Chapter 4. "Bausch and Lomb, Inc." requires use of concepts from Chapter 5; although the case can be studied at a relatively low level, well-prepared students will find that it is complex enough to justify the use of statistical methods.

THE STATE UNIVERSITY PRESS (A)

The State University Press published a work in American history in November 1962. It priced the book at $8.50 and estimated that sales would approximate 1,800 copies. After discounts by distributors, the press expected to receive about $5.70 per copy—barely enough to cover its unit costs.

The manager of a retail store claimed that the price of $8.50 was too high and believed that at a price of $5 the press could expect substantial gift sales of the book, with perhaps a doubling or tripling of volume. The editors of the press believed, however, that sales would be only 50 percent higher at the lower price.

The costs of publishing the book are shown in Exhibit 1. These costs were accumulated after publication but include some estimates. (A pre-

Exhibit 1
Estimated cost of history book (publication date—November 28, 1962) Quantity—1,000 bound copies plus 1,000 unbound sheets

Text
Stock..............................	$ 774.50	
Composition........................	2,305.90	(354.8 hours)
Press..............................	740.40	(106.9 hours)
Ink................................	22.34	
Art................................	40.00	
Cuts...............................	64.66	
Miscellaneous......................	36.50	
Overhead (15% of above)............	597.00	
Total text costs..................		$4,581.30

Jacket
Stock..............................	$ 28.50	
Composition........................	13.00	(2 hours)
Press..............................	58.30	(8.3 hours)
Ink................................	7.26	
Art................................	107.00	
Cuts...............................	39.00	
Overhead (15% of above)............	38.00	
Mailing............................	3.94	
Total jacket costs................		$ 295.00
Binding (1,000 copies).................		724.00
Freight (estimated)....................		120.00
Total cost.....................		$5,725.30

publication forecast of costs had estimated them at $4,881; the higher actual costs resulted from a substantial number of author's changes in the galley proof and page proof stages.)

1. Estimate the elasticity of demand, incremental revenue, and marginal revenue under the following assumptions: (a) a doubling of sales at the lower price; (b) a tripling of sales; (c) a 50 percent increase in sales. (Assume that the proportion of the retail price going to the press is about the same at various prices.)
2. Assuming that the demands can be approximated by straight lines and sales will double at the lower price, estimate the marginal revenue at a number of prices between $8.50 and $5—for example, at $8, $7.50, and $7. Is the assumption of straight-line demands reasonable?
3. Estimate the marginal cost or incremental cost per book for quantities exceeding 1,800. For this purpose assume that the press run would be increased upward from 2,000 to take care of the extra demand at the lower prices. Note that the composition costs are fixed for a single run. Binding costs include a fixed element of, say, $150 per lot, but the remaining binding costs are proportional to volume. Make any other assumptions which seem appropriate. (While a full discussion of costs appears in Chapter 5, the incremental reasoning presented in Chapter 2 should suffice for this purpose.)

4. Would a price of $5 be sound if the press were a private company operated for profit? Discuss.
5. Would a price of $5 be sound for the University Press, recognizing that the objective is not maximum profit but that heavy losses on this book would cut down on funds available for other books?

THE PRICING OF AUTOMOBILES

In 1958, Walter Reuther, the President of the United Automobile Workers, suggested a reduction in the price of automobiles averaging $100 a car. The automobile market was weak in 1958, with resultant unemployment; lower prices would lead to greater sales and would stimulate employment. Mr. Reuther believed that a $100 reduction in prices, about 4 percent, would increase sales by 16 percent.

In testimony before the Senate Subcommittee on Antitrust and Monopoly, Theodore O. Yntema, Vice President of the Ford Motor Company, disagreed with Reuther's estimation.[1] Yntema cited studies which indicated price elasticities ranging from 0.5 to 1.5. Yntema made it clear that he was referring to the elasticity of demand in response to a permanent price change of all manufacturers; he admitted that the elasticity to a temporary price cut might be greater. The studies to which Yntema referred included the well-known prewar volume by Roos and von Szeliski, which found elasticities ranging from 0.65 to 1.53 (Apparently the Roos-Szeliski findings are interpreted in somewhat different ways by various students of automobile demand, but all interpretations fall within the range of 0.65 to 1.53.)

Perhaps more recent studies would be more relevant than that of Roos and Szeliski. A Department of Commerce study of automobile demand resulted in several estimating equations, one of which was

$$Y = 0.0003239 \ X_1^{2.536} \ X_2^{2.291} \ X_3^{-1.359} \ 0.932^{X_4}$$

where

Y is new private passenger car registrations per million households.

X_1 is disposable personal income per household in 1939 dollars.

X_2 is current annual disposable income per household as a percentage of the preceding year in 1939 dollars.

X_3 is the percentage of average retail price of cars to consumer prices measured by consumer price index.

X_4 is average scrappage age in years.[2]

---

[1] Statement before the Subcommittee on Antitrust and Monopoly, Committee on the Judiciary, U.S. Senate, February 4–5, 1958. Extracts from this statement appear in A. W. Warner and V. R. Fuchs, *Concepts and Cases in Economic Analysis* (New York: Harcourt, Brace & Co., 1958), pp. 147–48.

[2] *Survey of Current Business* (April 1952), p. 20. This study is cited in F. E. Nemmers, *Managerial Economics: Text and Cases* (New York: John Wiley & Sons, Inc., 1962), pp. 102–7.

Similar equations based on slightly different assumptions resulted in price elasticities close to the one implied by the above equation, as do studies by Chow.[3]

1. What is the significance of Reuther's demand estimate?
2. What is the significance of Yntema's demand estimate?
3. What is the price elasticity of demand for automobiles according to the Department of Commerce demand estimate?
4. How would the relevant conditions differ between an automobile firm with excess capacity and one with a high ratio of output to capacity?
5. How does long-run demand for automobiles relate to the short-run pricing decision which is the center of controversy in the case?

AN EXERCISE IN BUSINESS CONDITIONS ANALYSIS*

Forecast for 1970: Leading indicators

In late August 1972 the 12 most important leading indicators shown in *Business Conditions Digest* appeared as in Exhibits 1 and 2.

What kind of forecast for 1970 would you make on the basis of movements in these indicators in 1969? How much confidence would you have in this forecast?

GNP forecast for 1970: Mechanical model

PART I

Prepare a forecast of the GNP and its principal components for each quarter through 1970, using the data for 1969, third quarter (*Survey of Current Business*, July 1971) as follows:

---

[3] G. C. Chow, "Statistical Demand Functions for Automobiles and Their Use for Forecasting," in *The Demand for Durable Goods*, ed. A. C. Harberger (Chicago: University of Chicago Press, 1960).

* Note: This case is a modification of one written by Professor John Lintner of the Harvard Graduate School of Business Administration. The case has been influenced greatly by the Duesenberry-Eckstein-Fromm econometric model. This simplified form of the latter material was developed for classroom use to illustrate some of the more fundamental relationships which need to be taken into account in forecasting in the simplest possible way. In itself, it was not intended to provide a model which would be fully adequate for forecasting business conditions in practice.

Exhibit 1
Cyclical indicators: Selected indicators by timing (leading indicators)

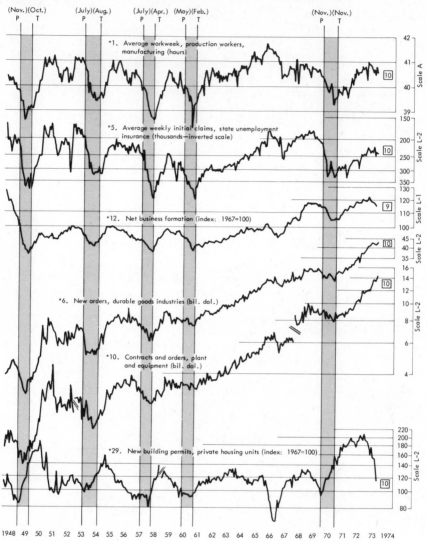

Exhibit 2
Cyclical indicators: Selected indicators by timing

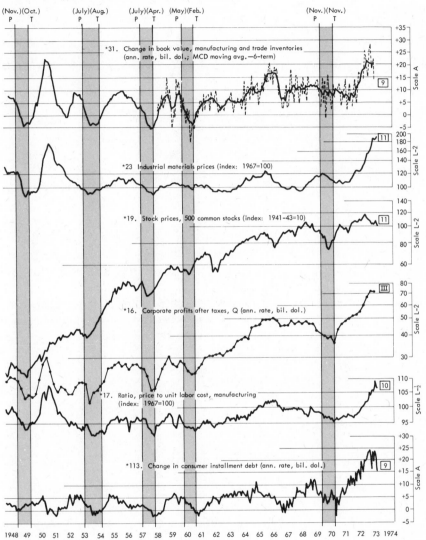

(Nov.)(Oct.) (July)(Aug.) (July)(Apr.) (May)(Feb.) (Nov.)(Nov.)
P   T   P   T   P   T   P   T   P   T

*31. Change in book value, manufacturing and trade inventories
     (ann. rate, bil. dol.; MCD moving avg.—6-term)

*23 Industrial materials prices (index: 1967=100)

*19. Stock prices, 500 common stocks (index: 1941–43=10)

*16. Corporate profits after taxes, Q (ann. rate, bil. dol.)

*17. Ratio, price to unit labor cost, manufacturing
     (index: 1967=100)

*113. Change in consumer installment debt (ann. rate, bil. dol.)

1948 49 50 51 52 53 54 55 56 57 58 59 60 61 62 63 64 65 66 67 68 69 70 71 72 73 1974

	Billions
Gross National Product	$940.2
Change in GNP from previous period	18.4
Personal income	759.3
Disposable personal income	643.2
Personal outlays	600.9
Personal consumption expenditures	584.1
Interest paid by consumers and transfer payments to foreigners	16.8
Change in business inventories	10.4
Corporate profits before tax (adjusted)	78.0
Corporate profits taxes	38.2
Corporate profits after taxes	39.8
Capital consumption allowances (depreciation)	82.1
Indirect business taxes, etc.	87.1
Contributions for social insurance	54.7
Transfer payments, etc.	95.7
Dividends	24.7
Changes in dividends from previous period	0.5

It is important to know the following relationships: Net national product = GNP − Capital consumption allowances. National income = Net national product − Indirect business taxes. Personal income = National income − Corporate profits + Dividends − Contributions for social insurance + Transfer payments. Disposable income = Personal income − Personal income taxes. Gross private domestic investment = Fixed investment + Net change in inventory investment

Assume that the following data are given:

	Annual rates (in $ billions)				
	1969:4	*1970:1*	*1970:2*	*1970:3*	*1970:4*
Government expenditures on goods and services					
Total	$213.0	$217.3	$216.5	$220.1	$223.7
Federal	99.5	100.2	96.8	96.1	95.9
Defense	78.4	78.9	75.1	74.2	73.2
Nondefense	21.2	21.3	21.6	21.9	22.7
State and local	113.5	117.1	119.7	124.0	127.9
Fixed investment	132.3	130.8	132.1	133.5	133.6
Nonresidential investment	102.2	100.8	102.1	104.8	100.8
Residential investment	30.1	30.0	29.9	28.7	32.8
Net exports	2.7	3.5	4.2	4.0	2.7

Source: *Survey of Current Business* (July 1971).

Assume also that:

1. Personal outlays in each quarter are equal to 0.95 of disposable income in the preceding quarter. The portion of personal outlays represented by interest paid by consumers and personal transfer payments by foreigners increases by $0.3 billion in each quarter and the balance

represents consumer expenditures on goods and services. Personal consumption expenditures are personal outlays less such transfers.

2. Examine past inventory behavior and make your own estimates, taking into account what you know, or can find out, about current conditions in the economy.

3. The quarter-to-quarter change in corporate profits before taxes in billions of dollars is equal to:

$$0.4 \ (\Delta GNP)_t + 0.3 \ (\Delta Inv)_t - 0.2 \ (\Delta GNP)_{t-1} - 1.0 \text{ billion}$$

4. The change in corporate profits taxes equals 45 percent of the current change in the corporate profits before taxes.

5. Dividends change by 30 percent of the current change in corporate profits after taxes plus 50 percent of the change in dividends in the previous quarter.

6. The change in contributions to social security (payroll taxes) amounts to 10 percent of the change in GNP.

7. The change in indirect business taxes is equal to 15 percent of the change in GNP.

8. The change in transfer payments by government and certain interest payments increases $1.3 billion per quarter.

9. The change in personal income taxes is equal to 15 percent of the change in personal income.

10. Capital consumption allowances increase by $1.5 billion in each quarter.

PART II

After you have completed mechanical projections based on the above assumptions, consider how reasonable they seem in the light of all the other information you have at your disposal. What assumptions do you believe should be changed? How, how much, and for what reasons? What would be the order of magnitude of the changes induced in your first projection? Has this approach given adequate attention to the multiplier and accelerator? Explain the basis for your conclusion.

PART III

Compare your forecast for 1970 with the actual changes in the GNP and its components during that year. How great was the error in your forecast? What are the apparent reasons for those errors?

(Note: Statistical data will be found in issues of the *Survey of Current Business* and in *Economic Indicators*. Current business literature such as *Business Week, Fortune*, monthly letters of the leading commercial banks and Federal Reserve Banks, the monthly issues of *Economic Indicators*, and the publications of the leading investment services will supply information which may enable you to form an opinion on the reasonableness of the given assumptions and data to be used in the mechanical projections.)

Forecast for the coming year: Mechanical model

The "mechanical" model used in the GNP forecast for 1970 may be adapted for use for any short period in the 1970s. This approach would start with forecasts of federal expenditures quarter by quarter using the sources mentioned in Chapter 4. Next the forecast would move on to state and local government expenditures and to the components of investment. The forecast of inventory investment would proceed as in the 1970 forecast. Then the most tedious task is to forecast consumption using the assumptions listed in the 1970 forecast.

Forecast for the coming year: GNP judgmental model

On the basis of the discussion in Chapter 4, you may forecast the GNP and its principal components for the coming year. In such a forecast you will wish to use many of the sources mentioned in Chapter 4. This exercise is best done as a team effort, with part of the team concentrating on plant and equipment, part on residential construction, part on government expenditure, and so on. After preliminary estimates are made of the investment and governmental components, the team as a whole can cooperate in making estimates of consumption which will take the multiplier into account. Various degrees of mathematical sophistication are possible. The simplest approach is to assume that the induced increase in consumption will be roughly equal to total increase already estimated for all the other components, but as Chapter 4 points out, consumption is stickier in the downward direction and is influenced by factors other than income change.

After this forecast is made, the results may be compared with those in the more subjective approach in the preceding case. The question which then arises is whether the extra work required by the mechanical model produces results in the form of superior forecasts which compensate for the extra effort.

BAUSCH AND LOMB, INC.*

The following excerpts are taken from a brokerage firm's evaluation published in mid-1971:

Bausch & Lomb, one of the oldest and strongest names in the American optical industry now stands on the threshold of one of the most important developments in its corporate life—the introduction of soft contact lenses. These lenses, made

---

* This case was prepared at Georgia State University by Eric Tweedy under William R. Henry. It is based upon hearings of the Senate Select Committee on Small Business in connection with soft contact lenses.

from materials sublicensed under patents originating from work done in Czechoslovakia, are now being gradually introduced to professionals across the country.

B&L is the nation's second largest producer of ophthalmic products, ranking behind the American Optical Division of Warner-Lambert. See our discussion of the "Ophthalmic Industry" for our interpretation of overall industry trends.

B&L has experienced reasonably satisfactory growth from this market, although we believe that it has lost share to American Optical over the last two or three years. The market for frames and lenses increased at least 6.4 percent and 14.3 percent, respectively, in the 1963–70 period; this pattern of growth probably slowed somewhat in the 1967–70 period. However, gains were relatively better maintained in frames than in lenses, reflecting a trend toward higher-priced products, stimulated by a greater emphasis on the fashion aspect of eyeglasses.

We believe that eyeglass sales have been restrained by the poor economy. As the economy turns upward, and particularly as the consumer becomes more interested in discretionary medical spending, B&L should experience a strong surge in its ophthalmic business. The leverage in this operation is believed to be substantial and, on a 10 percent sales move, we estimate that earnings could increase by 25 percent or so.

We believe that the soft lenses, tradenamed Soflens, constitute a significant advance over the traditional hard contact lenses due mainly to a high degree of comfort obtained with the lens even in the initial wearing stages, as well as a closer fit with the eye, reducing the possibility of losing the lens or of having dirt particles lodge under the lens. In addition, and obviously most important, the lenses provide excellent vision correction—fully satisfactory in the substantial majority of patients.

We believe that the lenses are unique and that the market will be relatively uncrowded for some time. Among the significant bars to competition are the following: (i) the lens is covered by both product and process patents; these patents may not guarantee the total absence of competition, but, on the other hand, as the patents are enforced we believe that they will at least hinder the development of alternate products; (ii) B&L has made a number of improvements in both the lens itself and in the manufacturing process; (iii) the lenses have been judged to fall under the Food and Drug Act and, as such, require elaborate premarketing testing procedures and ultimately governmental approval; passage through this process took B&L more than four years, and (iv) the name and reputation of Bausch & Lomb—both at the consumer and professional levels—will support a preference for B&L's products even in a strongly competitive market.

Defense against scientific criticism

The soft contact lenses are open to several criticisms. Of primary concern are the possibilities of infection and poor visual performance. The porous structure of the HEMA polymer is thought by some to provide a breeding place for pathological organisms or fungi tendrils. Dr. Chester Black, past president of the Contact Lens Association of Ophthalmolo-

Extract from Statement of Chester J. Black, M.D.
Before the
Government Regulation Subcommittee
of the
Senate Select Committee on Small Business,
July 7, 1972

Soflens clinical trial results, February 15, 1971—Active patients

Slit-lamp examinations	All investigators	C. J. Black
Total eyes fitted	2,512	250
Less initial visit only	152	11
Eyes with slit-lamp finding on last visit	2,360	239

Slit-lamp findings	Number negative	Percent	Number negative	Percent
Edema	2,191	93	239	100
Vascularization	2,360	100	239	100
Staining	2,304	98	239	100
Injection	2,302	98	232	97
Other complications	2,357	100	239	100

Visual acuities	All investigators	C. J. Black
Total eyes fitted	2,512	250
No acuity reported	34	0
Eyes with acuity reported	2,478	250

Visual acuities	Number	Percent	Number	Percent
20/20 or better	1,311	53	82	33
20/25 or better	2,265	91	243	97
20/30 or better	2,410	97	244	98
Less than 20/30	68	3	6	2

Wearing time	All investigators	C. J. Black
6 months or less	185	25
7 to 12 months	368	50
13 to 18 months	335	21
18 months or more	373	30

gists, appeared in Senate testimony to defend Soflens™ from these
charges. Results of clinical studies were provided that tended to be
favorable toward the efficacy and safety of the Bausch and Lomb lens.
Although Black's testimony was favorable, some other work has indicated problems in both areas, acuity and infection.

Competition

Bausch and Lomb's major competition in the soft contact lens market
comes from Naturalens™, a product of Griffin Laboratories, a subsidiary

of Frigitronics. The Griffin lenses are composed of basically the same material as the Soflens™, but they are more hydrophilic, somewhat harder and thicker, and come in a wider range of fitting parameters. Additionally, the Griffin Naturalens™ has been shown in clinical studies to have better optical properties, to be better suited as a bandage lens and drug dispenser, and to have other valuable therapeutic uses. The Naturalens™ has FDA approval for therapeutic use only.

Extract from a
Statement of Aran Safir, M.D., Mount Sinai School of
Medicine, Department of Ophthalmology, New York City,
Before the Government Regulation Subcommittee of the
Senate Select Committee on Small Business

The B&L lens is easier to fit. There are few choices for the clinician to make. He has little or no control over lens thickness, diameter, and curvature, but can choose from a variety of refractive powers. He can often determine at one sitting whether or not the patient will obtain reasonably good visual acuity. The lenses can then be dispensed directly and the patient scheduled for a re-visit so that his adaptation to the lenses can soon be evaluated.

The Griffin lens is available in a variety of diameters, thicknesses, and curvatures, as well as refractive powers. It has therefore not been possible to keep a stock of lenses that allow for direct dispensing. Considerable time can be spent in trial and error manipulation of these variables. When the prescription is determined, the lens is ordered by mail. One of the greatest difficulties with Griffin lenses has been the lack of predictability of delivery of the lenses ordered. When the lenses have arrived, they have not always performed in the manner expected based on the trial lenses fitted. Precise checking of all the lens variables has not been possible for reasons already given.

However, the Griffin lens has some advantages as a refractive device. Because he can manipulate the lens characteristics, the practitioner can achieve satisfactory vision in a somewhat higher percentage of patients with this lens than he can with the B&L lens. Nevertheless, a significant number (19 percent) of our patients abandoned the Griffin lens because of unsatisfactory acuity.

It is our opinion that the Griffin lens is more comfortable than the B&L lens. We suspect that this is due to the larger diameter of the Griffin lens, because the smallest Griffin lenses feel very much like the B&L lenses. Some patients notice no discomfort with either, but some are aware of mild sensations of a foreign body in the eye, especially with the smaller diameter lenses.

Pricing

Marketing of the B&L product is discussed in this excerpt from the 1971 brokerage study:

Price. The B&L lenses have been priced initially at $65 per pair. This price compares with a typical price from a hard lens manufacturer of $15–$20 per pair. However, the price to the dispenser is a relatively minor portion of the price of the fitted lens to the patient. It appears that the price of the soft lens to the patient, at least at the outset, will be $300 per pair or so, compared with about $200 for the hard lens. In time, we believe that dispensers—particularly optometrists who have been losing share of the contact lens market to ophthalmologists in recent years—will reduce prices to the patient. This will be facilitated by the relative ease with which the soft lens is fitted to the patient, particularly compared to the hard lens, as well as the probability that the time involved in fitting the soft lens will be substantially reduced.

The present price for the Soflens adopted by B&L will, in our opinion, be reduced by perhaps 25 percent over the next three years. This will largely reflect the probable lower cost structure once B&L enters longer production runs but will also reflect the existence of either real or potential competition.

The brokerage firm's study also considers the pipelining of the specialists who will dispense the lenses:

Pipelining and reordering. B&L is selling the lenses to the dispenser in a kit containing 72 lenses, each pair costing $65, five sterilizers, each costing $21, a professional sized sterilizer, and a film projector. The kit is priced at $2,905. The extent of the initial acceptance of the kits will obviously influence the development of sales from B&L to the dispenser for the next year or so. For example, if 20 percent of the nation's 18,000 dispensers—roughly 3,600 dispensers—order kits during 1971, this would result in sales to B&L of about $10.5 million. However, this would also place about 130,000 pairs of soft contact lenses in the hands of the dispenser and act as a brake to additional sales in subsequent months. The extent of this restraint will depend basically on the relationship of the size of the pipeline to the consumer acceptance rate. For example, 130,000 pairs of lenses is equal to only about three months sales if the market for soft lenses reaches 500,000 pairs per year.

Apart from the pipelining consideration, B&L will be shipping lenses to dispensers as they are sold to the consumer. As the dispenser fits each patient, he will reorder the specific lenses used in the fitting, thus maintaining a relatively complete inventory of most popular sizes. In this way, B&L's sales will eventually reach a close relationship to detail demand, but this relationship will be warped initially by the pipelining.

The situation in mid-1972 is detailed in this excerpt from Mr. Dodd's Senate testimony:

The original fitting set offered for sale contained 72 lenses. Some practitioners have adjusted their inventories to meet the specific needs of their practice simply by purchasing additional quantities of lenses or by not re-ordering lenses as they are dispensed. Many practitioners with large contact lens practices carry inventories well above the 72 lenses they received initially, while others stock fewer. A recent survey showed that the average number of lenses in the fitting sets of our accounts was 67.3.

Appendix
Extracts from a Brokerage Firm's Analysis

The following table shows the total number of people, distributed by age groups, wearing corrective lenses, as of June 1966 (000 omitted):

	Persons 3 years	No corrective lenses	With corrective lenses		
			Total	Eyeglasses only	Contact lenses
Total 3+............	178,907	92,693	86,020	84,247	1,773
3–16.................	55,037	46,652	8,263	8,110	153
17–24................	22,393	13,039	9,310	8,474	835
25–44................	45,185	26,250	18,914	18,314	599
45 and over...........	56,292	6,743	49,533	49,348	185
45–54................	21,850	4,112	17,732	17,636	97
55–64................	16,864	1,337	15,526	15,469	57
65+.................	17,578	1,294	16,275	16,244	—

Source: National Center for Health Statistics.

As indicated, the use of corrective lenses increases proportionately with age. Furthermore, the proportion of people wearing contact lenses is centered primarily in the 17–24 age group, where about 10 percent of all corrective lens wearers used contact lenses, and in the 25–44 groups, where 3 percent (of a far larger group) wore contact lenses.

We estimate that the number of people wearing contact lenses in 1970 reached 3.0 million, somewhat less than double the number four years ago. Although not shown in the above table, the usage rate of contact lenses among females is more than twice as frequent as among males (1,242,000 compared with 530,000). The usage of contact lenses, relative to eyeglasses, is relatively heavy in the western part of the United States, among people with incomes over $5,000 per year, and among white-collar workers. These segments of the population are each growing as a percentage of the total. Further, based on Department of Commerce data, as well as trade estimates, we estimate that sales of contact lenses (in pairs) traced the following approximate pattern over the past five years (in millions).

The table below includes both new patients—those purchasing a pair of contact lenses for the first time—and patients reordering a pair of lenses either due to a change in vision or loss of the initial pair. We estimate that the number of different people who have purchased a pair of contact lenses is now approaching 10.0 million. Of these, we believe that about 3.0 million continue to wear the lenses with a high degree of regularity and 7.0 million people either wear them infrequently or not at all.

Year	Contact lenses sold (in pairs)	Eyeglass lenses (in pairs)
1965..............................	0.8	36.0
1966..............................	1.0	37.0
1967..............................	1.2	38.0
1968..............................	1.2	44.0
1969..............................	1.3	45.0
1970..............................	1.0	44.0

Sources: Bureau of the Census, Optical Goods Manufacturers Association and FD&S.

The following discussion is directed at the size of the potential total corrective lens market and, within that, the segment likely to be directed towards contact lens.

According to government data, cited earlier, about 42 percent of all people 17 to 24 years of age wear glasses; similarly, 42 percent of all people 24 to 44 wear glasses. The onset of vision defects is typically at a relatively early age. The following table shows the age at which each segment of the population first obtained corrective lenses (000 omitted):

Present age		Age when first obtained corrective lenses*			
		Under 17	17–24	25–44	45+
All ages	86,020	—	—	—	—
3–16	8,263	8,263	—	—	—
17–24	9,310	6,533	2,531	—	—
25–44	18,914	6,778	4,654	6,571	—
45+	49,533	4,400	4,021	15,550	22,592

* Totals may not add due to small number of people in categories above age 17 who did not recall when they first obtained correction.
Source: National Center for Health Statistics.

As indicated, of the 86 million people wearing glasses at the date of the census, 30 percent of these obtained vision correction before the age of 17 and another 13 percent before the age of 24. The substantial majority of these people were near-sighted, a vision defect well suited to the use of contact lenses. Based on this data, it appears that about one out of seven people under the age of 17 and two out of five people in the 17–24 age category wear some type of corrective lens.

The following table presents the age of the population of the U.S. at the end of 1969 and shows the likely distribution of the population by 1975 and by 1980 (000 omitted):

Year	Total	Under 5	5–14	15–24	25–44	45+
1969	203,216	17,960	41,345	35,054	47,994	60,863
1975*	217,557	19,968	38,565	40,011	53,928	65,086
1980*	232,412	23,245	38,104	41,736	62,302	67,024

* Assumes fertility rate of 2,775 per 1,000 women of childbearing age (known as series C in census projections).

We further assume that contact lens usage has increased modestly as a percentage of all corrective lenses worn over the past four years and, furthermore, that contact lens usage will continue to increase over the next five and ten years. Specifically, we believe the contact lens usage will conform to the following usage rate:

	Percent of all corrective lenses
1966	2.1
1969	2.4
1975	7.2
1980	12.2

(i) As indicated, we believe that 6.0 million people either now wearing eyeglasses or not yet wearing any type of corrective lenses will be converted to contact lenses between 1969 and 1975 and another 5.9 million between 1975 and 1980. Of these, we estimate that the conversion rate to soft lenses will start slowly but build up significantly as the decade proceeds (in millions):

Year	Soft, as percent of total
1971	16.7
1972	50.0
1973	63.3
1974	70.0
1975	73.7
1976	76.3
1977	78.7
1978	81.1
1979	85.8
1980	85.3

The above estimates assume that about 4 million people a year are passing the age of 24, approximately half of whom are wearing some type of corrective lens. Of these, probably half will be attracted to contact lenses, producing a new market of 1 million pairs of contact lenses per year. The balance will be derived from the substantial group of eyeglass wearers attracted to contact lenses for the first time.

(ii) We believe that the conversion of existing contact lens wearers to the soft lenses will probably be relatively minor. The only reasons for switching from a reasonably acceptable product would be either due to the high discomfort associated with dirt and grime lodging under the lens, typically in a city environment, or due to the ability of the wearer to use the soft lens on a less regular schedule, not now available to the hard lens wearer due to the discomfort normally associated with readapting to the lens. The barrier to conversions from hard lenses to soft lenses will be the substantial price of being refitted with soft lenses. We estimate that about 5 percent per year of the existing hard lens population will be attracted to the soft lens—or roughly 150,000 pairs per year. This will build up gradually over the next few years.

(iii) We believe that a substantial number of people who had purchased hard lenses and subsequently dropped out of the market will purchase a pair of soft contact lenses.

The primary reasons for not using the pair of hard lenses, even after spending something in the area of $200, is the high degree of difficulty which most people encounter in adapting to the lens. Many people—probably half—eventually give up this effort and revert to eyeglasses. However, all of these people were motivated at one time to wear contact lenses and, if the adaptation period is eased —as it is with the soft lenses—a significant number may come back to the market. We believe that roughly 5 percent per year of the dropout population, or about 350,000 people, will be attracted back to the market. This will start slowly but build up across the next four years.

1. Using the information from the appendix and whatever other information is available, update for 1975 and 1980 the projected distribution of population by age groups as presented in the Appendix.
2. Using the projection in Question 1, project the usage of corrective lenses by age groups in 1975 and 1980.
3. The appendix contains estimates of the relative usages of contact lenses in 1975 and 1980. These projections were made on the basis of growing discretionary income and improving popularity of the soft lenses. Using whatever information is available, revise these projections. Use the new projections to calculate projected distributions among age groups for usage of contact lenses.
4. The appendix also contains projections of soft lens' share of the market. Revise these estimates and project the share of the total corrective lens market which will belong to soft lenses in 1975 and 1980.
5. On the basis of Question 4 and any other information available, predict the share of the soft lens market which will be enjoyed by Bausch and Lomb in 1975 and 1980.

Note: Good sources of information include the Funk and Scott indexes on corporations and industries, trade and medical journals, Moody's, and other specialized industry or corporate surveys.

Part three

Resource allocation, production economics, and cost analysis

Chapter 6
Resource Allocation

This chapter introduces the theory of production. It shows how to make decisions about the use of *limited resources* and how linear programming can be used in determining an *optimum product mix*.

AN OVERVIEW OF PRODUCTION

Production is any activity that transforms inputs into outputs having greater value. Production is carried out by business firms, public agencies, nonprofit organizations, and households. It embraces a very wide range of things that people do. Consider these examples:

1. Extracting coal and iron ore.
2. Cutting pulp wood that will be used in making paper.
3. Operating a rapid transit system.
4. Storing part of this year's corn crop for some time.
5. Publishing a daily newspaper.
6. Making parts for and assembling a diesel engine.
7. Running a barber shop.
8. Providing telephone service.
9 Repairing automobiles.

10. Picking up garbage.
11. Conducting research on uses of solar energy.
12. Determining consumer reaction to a proposed new product or service.
13. Training first-line supervisors.
14. Cooking a meal or painting a child's bicycle.

The principles of production concern *efficient* uses of inputs in obtaining desired outputs. They are not applicable to only activities that yield *physically tangible goods*, such as construction and manufacturing. They are also relevant to all of the following: enterprises that provide *raw materials*, such as mining and agriculture; operations that make available *personal services*, such as health care and police protection; businesses that provide *services of facilities*, such as storage and equipment leasing; activities related to *financing and risk management*, such as banking and insurance; operations centering on *information and education*, such as publishing and schools; and ventures that provide *entertainment and recreation*, such as concert booking and park operation. Almost all adults need the skills of production economics: resource allocation, cost minimization, and volume-profit analysis.

Production processes

Production processes are integrated sets of activities that *combine and transform inputs* into desired outputs. *Inputs* needed in a typical production process might include *materials* (raw materials, supplies, parts made by others); *labor* (various skills); *services of capital* (consisting partially of the simple presence of capital, as in the cases of land and working capital, and partially of the presence of capital combined with some wear-out and obsolescence, as in the cases of buildings and equipment); and *management* (knowing how, planning, organizing, motivating).

Outputs of production processes are the desired results: *goods and services*. Many examples of these have already been given. Some processes yield more than one output. An example is petroleum refining, which produces a great variety of fuels, oils, greases, and other things. Desirable multiple products emanating from the same process are called *joint products*. It should be noted that some processes have undesirable joint outputs; these may be called *bads*. Some examples of bads are: noise (as from jet airliners), offensive odors (as from some chemical plants), air pollution (from some smelters), water pollution (from some paper mills), solid wastes (from nearly all production), and personal injuries.

A joint product that is undesirable at one time may become desirable at some other time. Pineapple juice was once a problem waste resulting from pineapple slicing, but it later became a marketable joint product that could be sold for substantial revenues. Undesirable joint products, or bads, increase *internal* costs of production to whatever extent producers must compensate persons affected by them, and the costs are imposed on someone regardless of arrangements for compensation.

The *technology* of production determines the *physical relationships of amounts of output to amounts of inputs.* The best technology is that which produces the greatest rate of output from a given combination of rates of inputs. Although inputs can be combined inefficiently, we shall typically assume that firms *are* using the best available technology.

Note that both the outputs and the inputs are to be measured as *rates,* or *quantities per unit of time.* If inputs and the corresponding outputs are to be compared, a common unit of time must be selected. Accounting periods, such as weeks, quarters, or years, are often used as time periods in production analysis. However, shorter periods, such as hours, shifts, or days, are sometimes more appropriate.

Production functions

A specified relationship of various rates of output to the corresponding various combinations of rates of inputs is called a *production function. A production function is a set of alternatives from which a selection may be made.* Such a selection may involve simultaneous choice of a particular rate of output and a particular combination of rates of input— how much to produce and what inputs and techniques to use.

The *short run* is a planning perspective within which the rates of use of some inputs must be taken as given, or fixed. *Fixed rates of use* in the short run means that the presence of these particular inputs and their associated costs must be taken as given, even though the physical rates of utilization may be variable; examples are warehouse space or machine time where the capacity must be taken as given even though the percentage utilization of this capacity can be varied. The set of alternatives is partially restricted by choices that were made in the past and the adjustment time permitted by the time horizon. A short-run production function could be represented as:

$$Q = f(X_1, X_2 | X_3 \ldots X_n)$$

in which Q is the rate of output and the X's are the rates of use of inputs 1 through n; the vertical bar shows that inputs to its right must be taken as given. A short-run function for a particular product might show various rates of output that could be obtained by varying numbers of workers and amounts of materials, with plant and equipment considered fixed. Much of the day-to-day, week-to-week decision making of ongoing firms is concerned with choices among alternatives permitted by short-run production functions.

The *long run* is a planning perspective extending far enough into the future so that the *amounts or capacities and the costs of all inputs become variable*. The horizon provides enough time so that changes can be made in the numbers, sizes, and locations of plants, and even in the nature of the firm's business. In the long run, the set of alternatives is restricted only by available technology. A long-run production function can be expressed symbolically as:

$$Q = f(X_1, X_2, X_3 \ldots X_n)$$

in which the symbols have meanings as stated for the short-run function.

DECISIONS ABOUT A SINGLE INPUT THAT HAS CONSTANT MARGINAL PRODUCTIVITY

This section shows how to allocate a single input that has constant marginal product. By *constant marginal product,* we mean that *increases in output resulting from successive equal increments of input are equal*, regardless of the base rate of input to which the increments are added. Beginning with the simple case of a single input that has constant marginal product allows easy introduction of the basic concepts used in resource allocation. Further, many real-life decisions *do* involve inputs having constant returns within the relevant range.

A production function with constant marginal productivity of one of the inputs

(In this chapter, and in the one to follow, a simple example of a window-cleaning firm has been used to stimulate intuitive understanding of some theoretical concepts that are difficult to grasp in their generalized forms. While the example is trivial, the underlying principles are important and useful.) Figure 6–1 shows a hypothetical production function for a small firm that cleans windows of high-rise office buildings. Total labor per day, measured on the horizontal plane along the axis of 0–80 hours, is varied by changing the length of the workday of a work force held constant at 10 persons. There are various techniques of production, involving successively greater daily expenditures for leased equipment, and the equipment input is measured on the horizontal plane along the axis of 0–$300.

Output per workday, total windows washed, is measured along the vertical axis by the height of the production surface above the horizontal plane. Of the many input-output functions along the production surface, three are traced by solid lines in Figure 6–1. These functions, *AB*, *CD*, and *EF*, correspond to leased equipment inputs fixed at $100, $200, and $300 per day, respectively.

Note that the combination of 70 employee-hours of labor per day with $100 daily expenditure for leased equipment, located at point *P* on the horizontal plane, yields output rate *PQ* (420 windows per work day). The combination of the same 70 employee-hours of labor with a greater $200 daily expenditure for leased equipment, corresponding to point *R*

Figure 6–1
A hypothetical production surface for window cleaning (First case: Constant marginal productivity of labor)

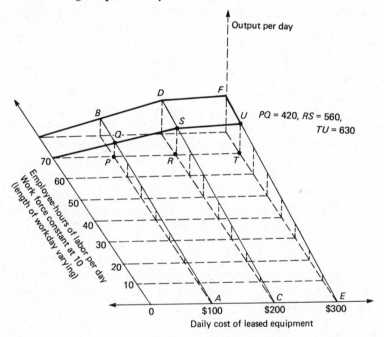

on the horizontal plane, produces the greater output *RS* (560 windows per workday. Combining the same 70 employee-hours with the still greater $300 daily expense of leased equipment, located at point *T* on the horizontal plane, gives the still greater output *TU* (630 windows per workday). Note also that each of the three functions, *AB*, *CD*, and *EF*, is a straight line from its origin.

Now, consider how the three-dimensional surface of Figure 6–1 appears if it is viewed from ground level at some distance from the side on which labor input is measured. Such a side view rotated 180 degrees is depicted in Figure 6–2. Function *AB* from Figure 6–1 is line *OB* in

Figure 6–2
Side view of surface, rotated 180°

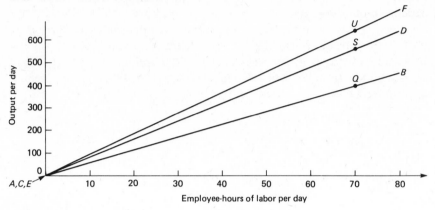

Figure 6–2; Function *CD* becomes line *OD*; Function *EF* appears as line *OF*. Each of these lines is an input-output function—*a relationship of various rates of output to various rates of use of a single input.*

Constant marginal product

The *marginal physical product of an input is roughly the increase in rate of output per unit of added input.* Line *OB* in Figure 6–2 is an example of an input-output function in which the marginal product of the input is constant; marginal product is the same at *all* rates of input within the range of the function. Marginal product can be calculated for a discrete change in input as the ratio of increase in rate of output to increase in rate of input.

Thus, for discrete changes:

$$MPP_x = \frac{\Delta Q}{\Delta X} \qquad (6\text{--}1)$$

where

Q is rate of output.
X is rate of input.
MPP_x is marginal physical product.

For the example of line *OB* in Figure 6–2, in which output increases from 0 to 420 as input increases from 0 to 70:

$$MPP_L = \frac{420}{70} = 6$$

In other words, daily output of cleaned windows increases by six units for each increase of one employee-hour in labor input, holding leased equipment constant. So the marginal product of labor is six windows per employee-hour.

Allocating an input that has constant marginal revenue product and a single use

The marginal physical product of an input is easily converted to an equivalent *monetary* value called *marginal revenue product,* or *MRP.* Since marginal product is a physical quantity of output, we simply multiply this quantity by the output's marginal revenue. In general:

$$MRP_x = MPP_x \cdot MR_y \qquad (6\text{-}2)$$

in which

MRP_x is value of marginal product of input X.
MPP_x is marginal physical product of input X.
MR_y is the output's marginal revenue.

To illustrate, we shall use the constant marginal product of six windows per employee-hour from input-output function OB in Figure 6–2 and an assumption that the firm's output is priced at a constant \$2 per window:

$$MRP_L = 6 \cdot \$2 = \$12$$

In words, the value of labor's marginal product is labor's marginal physical product times the marginal revenue of the output; in the example, each additional hour of labor per day adds \$12 to the value of output.

It is profitable to use additional input if the input's marginal revenue product is *greater* than the input's unit price. Suppose labor in the above example is paid \$10 per hour. Each additional hour of labor adds \$12 to the value of output and only \$10 to the cost of inputs. The difference of \$2 per employee-hour is a contribution toward overhead cost and possible profit, and we want all the contribution we can get.

The firm in the example should use as much labor as it can. Maximum use of the labor input may be constrained by one of the following: availability (willingness) of the labor input (remember that the work force in this example is fixed), labor contracts, availability of supervision and management, physical capacity of available equipment, or the amount of product that can be sold at the given price. *The general principle in determining optimum use of a single input that has a constant supply price and a constant marginal revenue product in a single profitable use is simply to use as much of the input as possible.*

Effect of rising marginal resource cost.   Local supplies of inputs such as labor and raw materials are often limited in the short run. A firm that uses a sizable part of the total local supply may have to offer higher prices, bidding the resource away from other purchasers, if the firm wishes to increase its own rate of use of the input. The input has a rising supply price to the firm as the supply quantity is increased.

Marginal resource cost is, roughly, the amount added to total cost by the last unit of input added to the firm's supply quantity. For the case described above, adding one more unit to increase supply quantity to L requires the firm to accept an increase (usually very, very small) in price, ΔW, that applies to all units in the initial quantity, L-1. Marginal resource cost of labor, MRC_L, can be calculated for a one unit increase up to L, at which W must be paid, as follows:

$$MRC_L = W + \Delta W(L - 1) \qquad (6\text{–}3)$$

From another point of view, $MRC_L = \Delta TSC_L/\Delta L$, in which ΔTSC_L is change in total supply cost of labor, and ΔL is change in total supply quantity. If the change in quantity is made smaller and smaller, at the limit we have:

$$MRC_L = \partial TSC_L \,/\, \partial L$$

in which the second term is the *first derivative* of the input's total supply cost function with respect to quantity. If we have the equation for the input's supply curve to the firm, we can easily derive the total supply cost function and then the first derivative, which gives marginal resource cost as a function of quantity. Although this principle has been explained in terms of the labor input, it would be applicable to any input with a rising supply curve.

To demonstrate, suppose the supply curve of labor to the hypothetical window-cleaning firm has been estimated as $W = \$5.00 + \$0.0125L$, in which W is wage rate in dollars per hour and L is the amount of labor in hours per week. Labor's total supply cost function, TSC_L, is derived as $W \cdot L$, which comes out as $TSC_L = \$5.00_L + \$0.0125_{L^2}$. Labor's marginal resource cost function, MRC_L, is derived as $\partial TSC_L/\partial_L$, yielding $MRC_L = \$5.00 + \$0.0250_L$.

How would this rising marginal resource cost of labor affect the firm's decision about the amount to use, assuming labor's marginal revenue product is constant at \$12? As a general principle, the firm would wish to increase use of the input so long as the input's marginal revenue product is greater than the input's marginal resource cost. Increase in rate of use of the input would be cut off at the point where rising marginal resource cost becomes *equal* to the constant marginal revenue product. For the example we are using, the cutoff, or optimum, quantity of labor is determined by the following equation:

$$MRC_L = MRP_L \tag{6-5}$$

or

$$\$5.00 + \$0.0250L = \$12.00$$
$$L = 280 \text{ employee-hours per week}$$

The nature of the above solution is shown in Figure 6–3. The wage rate corresponding to the optimum quantity is found by substituting this quantity into the firm's supply curve for labor:

$$W = \$5.00 + \$0.0125L = \$5.00 + \$0.0125 \cdot 280 = \$8.50 \text{ per hour}$$

Note that the above solution differs from that of the earlier example in which the wage rate was constant and the firm would use as much labor as it could. In the latter case, rising wages cause a cutoff before the firm reaches any other limit on the use of labor.

Figure 6–3
Optimum use of input with a rising supply price and constant marginal revenue product

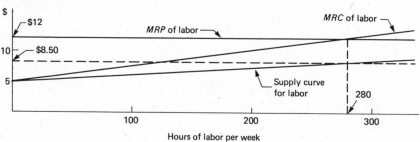

Hours of labor per week

Allocating a limited quantity of an input that has constant marginal revenue products in each of several competing uses

Let us enlarge the scope of activities of the hypothetical firm. Suppose that in addition to cleaning windows, the firm also does sand blast cleaning of exteriors and makes spray applications of protective coatings. Suppose that in both sand blasting and spray application the firm has a constant marginal productivity of labor. Further, suppose that leased equipment expenditure for the ten-person crew is the same $100 per day regardless of the type of work the crew is doing (most of the equipment is the same and the pieces that are different have the same costs per day).

We can represent the marginal product functions of the three activities as shown in Figure 6–4. The function for window cleaning is constant at six windows per employee-hour, as has been discussed in previous sections. For illustration, the function for sand blasting is assumed con-

Figure 6–4
Constant marginal products of labor in three activities

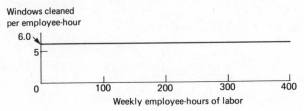

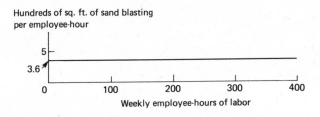

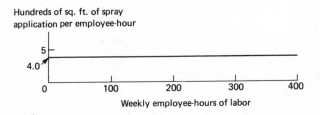

stant at 360 square feet of surface per employee-hour and the function for spray application is constant at 400 square feet of surface per employee-hour.

Now, suppose we are given unit prices of the three outputs:

Window cleaning, per standard window...............	$2.00
Sand blasting, per 100 square feet.....................	4.00
Spray application, per 100 square feet.................	3.25

Labor's marginal revenues products in each of the activities can be calculated (with MR_y being the output's price):

	MPP_L	*Times*	MR_y	*Equals*	$MRPL$
Window cleaning............	6.0	×	$2.00	=	$12.00
Sand blasting...............	3.6	×	4.00	=	14.40
Spray application..........	4.0	×	3.25	=	13.00

These marginal revenue products can be represented as shown in Figure 6–5.

Figure 6–5
Constant marginal revenue products of labor in three activities

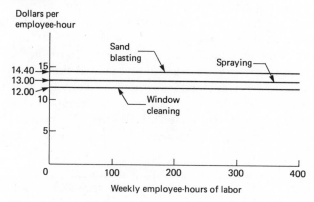

In this illustration, labor's marginal revenue product is greatest in the sand blasting activity. We would use all available labor in this work if we could. However, the amount of sand blasting activity in any given week may be constrained by the amount of this service that can be sold, or perhaps by availability of the specialized equipment required. So we would do as much sand blasting as possible and then allocate labor to the next best use. Labor's next greatest marginal revenue product is in spray application, so this work would get the next priority. Any remaining labor would be allocated to window cleaning.

Let us be certain the allocation procedure is understood. Suppose (1) available labor per week is 400 employee-hours (ten people working 40 hours each), (2) sand blasting equipment is available for up to 80 employee-hours (one workday of 8 hours), and (3) no more than 120 employee-hours of spray application (48,000 square feet) can be sold. The allocation of labor would proceed as follows:

First, 80 employee-hours to sand blasting at constant *MRP*, \$14.40 . . . . \$1,152
Next, 120 employee-hours to spray application at constant *MRP*, \$13.00 1,560
Last, <u>200</u> employee-hours to window cleaning at constant *MRP*, \$12.00 . . . . <u>2,400</u>
     400   \$5,112

The total value of labor's product is \$5,112 with labor in its best allocation. This compares with \$4,800 value of labor's product if used only in the window-cleaning activity.

The principle governing allocation of a limited quantity of an input that has constant marginal revenue products in each of several profitable uses is this: *Allocate the input first to the activity where the input's marginal revenue product is greatest until that activity reaches its limit, then to the activity with next greatest marginal revenue product until the limit is reached, and so on until the input is used up.*

Note this: We have been assuming that there are no variable inputs except labor; *an input's marginal revenue product must be net of the cost of any other variable inputs that are used with it.* For example, suppose the activity of window cleaning required that the firm provide detergent costing 10 cents per window and the activity of sand blasting required that the firm provide nonrecoverable abrasive material worth 25 cents per 100 square feet of surface. Effects of adjusting for costs of these other variable inputs upon labor's marginal revenue product would be as shown here:

	MPP_L	Times	MR_y-VC_o	Equals	MRP_L
Window cleaning	6.0	×	$2.00–$0.10	=	$11.40
Sand blasting	3.6	×	$4.00–$0.25	=	$13.50
Spray application	4.0	×	$3.25	=	$13.00

In the above illustration, VC_o is the *variable cost of other inputs* per unit of product; subtracting this variable cost from the product's marginal revenue, MR_y, leaves labor's marginal contribution earnings per unit of product, and it is the marginal contribution earnings, rather than the raw marginal revenue that should be multiplied by the marginal physical product of the input. Be certain this procedure is understood. It is often needed in practical calculations.

Marginal revenue product

A firm facing a downward sloping demand curve must reduce price as sales quantity per period is expanded. Under this condition, the output's marginal revenue is below its unit price at every rate of output and, like price, drops off as quantity increases. As the output's marginal revenue falls, the monetary value of additional output per unit of added input must also fall, even though the increase in physical output per unit of added input may hold constant. (Some students may benefit from a quick review of the section that deals with marginal revenue in Chapter 3.)

In dealing with constant marginal product and falling marginal revenue, we calculate marginal revenue product as follows:

$$MRP_x = MPP_x \cdot MR_y \qquad MR_y = f(Q_y) \qquad MRP_x = f(Q_y)$$

$$(6\text{–}6)$$

In words, input X's addition to the value of output per additional unit of X used, MRP_x, is obtained by multiplying the marginal physical product of X, MPP_x, times the output's *marginal revenue, MR_y*. Since marginal revenue varies as a function of rate of sales, the input's marginal revenue product is also a function that varies with rate of sales.

Allocating an input that has decreasing marginal revenue product and a single use

Assume that the hypothetical window-cleaning firm offers only the one service and that competitive firms will match any price reduction made. Under this condition, the firm gets its regular share of an increased total volume of business as it cuts price. Suppose the firm's estimated demand curve for window cleaning is:

$$P = \$3 - \$0.0004Q \qquad (6\text{-}7)$$

in which P is price per window and Q is sales quantity in number of windows per week. We can now derive the firm's total revenue function, then the marginal revenue function, and finally labor's marginal revenue product function:

$$TR = P \cdot Q = (\$3 - \$0.0004Q) \cdot Q = \$3Q - \$0.0004Q^2$$

$$MR = \frac{dTR}{dQ} = \$3 - \$0.0008Q$$

$$MRP_L = MPP_L \cdot MR = 6 \cdot (\$3 - \$0.0008Q) = \$18 - \$0.0048Q \qquad (6\text{-}8)$$

In words, total revenue from window cleaning is price times quantity and price is a function of sales quantity, so total revenue is a function of quantity squared. Marginal revenue is the first derivative of total revenue with respect to quantity, therefore marginal revenue is a function of sales quantity. Marginal revenue product of labor is labor's marginal physical product (we used six windows per employee-hour from vector OB of Figure 6–2) times marginal revenue, and is also a function of sales quantity. Labor's marginal revenue product diminishes as sales quantity increases.

It is profitable to increase the rate of using labor so long as labor's marginal revenue product is greater than labor's unit price, or labor's marginal resource cost, if the supply curve is rising. In other words, we want to use more of the input if the addition to value of output is greater than the corresponding addition to cost. Assume that labor is being paid $10 per hour. How much labor should be used?

We are going to use an *analytic* approach. An analytic approach finds an optimum value of a decision variable as the solution of an equation. This is an important concept deserving close attention. We know that labor's marginal revenue product is falling as *sales quantity* is increased, and we have derived Equation (6–8) to show the relation of these variables. We want to expand the use of labor and the resulting *sales quantity,* so long as marginal revenue product of labor is greater than labor's unit price. This implies increasing sales quantity until labor's falling marginal revenue product becomes equal to labor's constant unit price. So we are going to set the expression for labor's marginal revenue product equal to labor's price. We shall solve the resulting equation for *sales quantity*, then derive the implied use of labor. (The nature of this solution is depicted in Figure 6–6.)

$$MRP_L = P_L \qquad (6\text{–}9)$$

Substituting values, we have

$$\$18 - \$0.0048Q = \$10 \qquad (6\text{–}10)$$

Solving for Q, we get $Q = 1,666.67$ windows per week. Dividing Q by labor's constant marginal product of six windows per employee-hour, we get $1,666.67/6 = 277.7$ employee-hours used per week. Price of the product remains to be determined. We can find it by substituting optimum sales quantity into the demand equation. The demand equation is $P = \$3 - \$0.0004Q$, from Equation 6–7. Substituting optimum quantity, we

Figure 6–6
Optimum use of input with falling marginal revenue product and a constant supply price

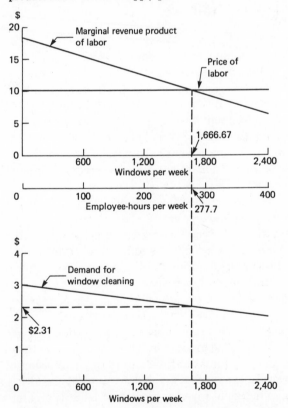

have $P = \$3 - \$0.0004(1,666.67)$. Solving for P, we get $P = \$2.33$ per window (see Figure 6–6).

The principle governing optimum use of an input that has a constant supply price and decreasing marginal revenue product in a single profitable application is this: *Increase rate of use of the input to the point at which the falling marginal revenue product becomes equal to the input's price.*

Now, a reminder of a point previously made. The input's marginal revenue product must be net of cost of any *other* variable input required. To illustrate, suppose the firm's window-cleaning activity required it to furnish detergent chemicals worth 10 cents per window. The effect of this condition upon the calculations made above would be as follows:

1. Demand Equation (6–7) would be shifted down by subtracting the variable cost of other inputs, VC_o, and would become $P - VC_o = (\$3 - \$0.10) - \$0.0004Q$.
2. Labor's marginal revenue product function, Equation (6–8), would become $MRP_L = \$17.40 - \$0.0048Q$.
3. The optimum quantity Equation (6–10) would become $\$17.40 - \$0.0048Q = \$10$.
4. The new solution values would be: $Q = 1,541.67$ windows, labor use is 1,541.67 windows divided by six windows per employee-hour or 256.9 employee-hours, and $P = \$3 - \$0.0004 \cdot 1,541.67 = \$2.38$ per window.

Adjustment for variable cost of other inputs, as in this example, is often necessary in applications of the resource allocation principles.

Effect of rising marginal resource cost. Consider how the decision in the above example would be affected if the firm's labor supply curve were rising—if the firm had to pay higher wages to get more labor. The principle governing use of the input would be to increase the use of it so long as the input's marginal revenue product, *falling* with greater use, is greater than the input's marginal resource cost, *rising* with expanded use. Increase in use would be cut off at the point where rising marginal resource cost becomes equal to falling marginal revenue product.

To illustrate, suppose the marginal revenue product of labor is as given above in Equation (6–8), $MRP_L = \$18 - \$0.0048Q_L$, and the marginal resource cost of labor is as used in a previous example, $MRQ_L = \$5 + \$0.025Q_L$. Optimum use of labor is determined by the following equation:

$$MRC_L = MRP_L \qquad (6\text{--}11)$$
$$\$5 + \$0.025Q_L = \$18 - \$0.0048Q_L$$
$$Q_L = 436.2 \text{ employee-hours per week}$$

The corresponding wage rate is found by substituting the solution quantity of labor into the supply curve for labor, $P_L = \$5 + \$0.0125Q_L$, as show below:

$$P_L = \$5 + \$0.0125(436.2) = \$10.45 \text{ per hour}$$

The solutions in the above example are depicted in Figure 6–7.

Figure 6–7
Optimum use of an input with falling marginal revenue product and rising marginal resource cost

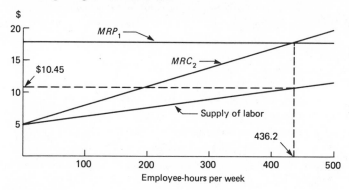

Allocating a limited quantity of an input that has decreasing marginal revenue product in each of several competing uses

The next situation involves one of the most useful ideas in managerial economics; the *equimarginal principle.* In this situation, the total quantity of input will be limited, the input will have constant marginal productivity in each of several uses, and the input's marginal revenue products will be decreasing with each product's rate of output because each product has a sloping demand curve. The situation calls for *equimarginal allocation* of the input—we are going to divide it among competing uses in such a way that the last units assigned to the various uses are adding equal amounts to the firm's net revenue. In other words, the input's marginal revenue product will be pushed down to the same value in each of its uses. We know that this equimarginal condition must exist for an optimum allocation of the limited quantity of input—if it does not exist, the total contribution earned by the input can be increased by shifting the input from one use to another in which the input's marginal revenue product is greater.

Continuing with the hypothetical firm of Figure 6–1, let us assume that the quantity of labor is limited to 400 hours per week (ten persons working 40 hours each). In addition to the window-cleaning service, with its sloping demand curve as given in Equation (6–7), the firm provides sand blasting service, for which the demand curve is also sloping. The problem is how to allocate the available 400 hours of labor between the two services and what prices to set on the two services.

The generalized procedure to solve this kind of problem is as follows:

1. Derive the input's marginal revenue product functions in each of the competing uses. Each of these functions is a relation of the input's marginal revenue product to the rate of sales of one of the outputs.
2. Restate the marginal revenue product functions in terms of *quantity of input used*, so that they have a common quantity dimension.
3. Add quantities (on the restated functions) *horizontally* to obtain an aggregate function showing the total amount of input that can be used in all applications at each value of the input's marginal revenue product.
4. Determine marginal revenue product on the aggregate function at the *maximum available quantity* of the input.
5. Insert the solution value of marginal revenue product into the restated marginal revenue product functions for each of the competing uses, thus obtaining the *amount of input to allocate to each use*.
6. Convert the amounts of inputs used in each of the activities into the corresponding amounts of output; substitute the outputs into the original demand equations to obtain optimum *prices of the products*.

Now, a demonstration of the procedure. We begin by deriving labor's marginal revenue product functions in each of the competing uses (Step 1):

For window cleaning, Q_w, in windows per week:

Demand has been given: $P_w = \$3 - \$0.0004Q_w$
Total revenue, P_wQ_w, is: $TR_w = \$3Q_w - \$0.0004Q_w{}^2$
Marginal revenue, dTR_w/dQ_w, is: $MR_w = \$3 - \$0.0008Q_w$
Marginal product of labor in window cleaning is six windows per employee-hour
Marginal revenue product, $MR_w \cdot MPP_L$, is: $MRP_{L.w} = \$18 - \$0.0048Q_w$

For sand blasting, Q_b, in hundreds of square feet per week:

Assume demand is: $P_b = \$4 - \$0.0005Q_b$
Total revenue, P_bQ_b, is: $TR_b = \$4Q_b - \$0.0005Q_b{}^2$
Marginal revenue, dTR_b/dQ_b, is: $MR_b = \$4 - 0.0010Q_b$
Assume marginal product of labor in sand blasting is 3.6 hundred square feet per employee-hour
Marginal revenue product, $MR_b \cdot MPP_b = MRP_{L.b} = \$14.40 - \$0.0036Q_b$

In the above equations, Q_w is the number of windows per week and Q_b is hundreds of square feet of sand blasting per week. We shall restate the functions so that both are in terms of *quantity of labor per week* (Step 2):

To restate labor's marginal revenue product in window cleaning, we use the relations $Q_w = 6X_L$, in which X_L is the quantity of labor (we produce six windows per employee-hour), and we obtain $MRP_{L.w} = \$18 - \$0.0288X_L$.

To restate labor's marginal revenue product in sand blasting, we use the relation $Q_b = 3.6X_L$ (we produce 3.6 hundred square feet per employee-hour), and we obtain $MRP_{L.b} = \$14.40 - \$0.0130X_L$.

The next step is to aggregate the marginal revenue product functions in the horizontal dimension (Step 3). This step is illustrated by Figure 6–8. In the range of values from \$18.00 down to \$14.40, labor can be used only in the window-cleaning activity and a total of 125 hours can be allocated in driving labor's marginal revenue product down to \$14.40. From \$14.40 on down, labor can be divided between the two activities. To determine the slope of the aggregate function, we can calculate the total amount of labor required to bring marginal revenue product from \$14.40 to zero on each of the functions; the slope of the aggregate function is then \$14.40 divided by the sum of the two quantities of labor.

To bring labor's MRP from \$14.40 to zero in the window-cleaning function requires 500 employee-hours, calculated as \$14.40/\$0.0288 = 500.

To bring labor's MRP from \$14.40 down to zero in the sand-blasting function requires using 1,107.7 employee-hours, calculated as \$14.40/\$0.0130 = 1,107.7.

Figure 6–8
Optimum allocation of a limited quantity of an input that has decreasing marginal revenue in multiple uses

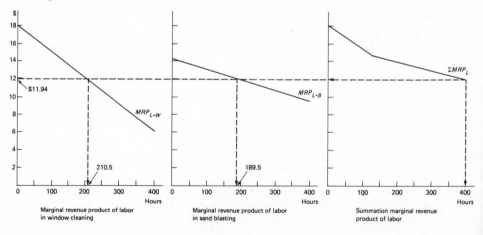

So we see that the aggregate function goes from \$14.40 to 0 with the use of $500 + 1{,}107.7$ employee-hours, or 1,607.7. Thus, the slope of the aggregate function is \$14.40/1,607.7, or \$0.008957, to the right of 125 employee-hours on the quantity axis and below \$14.40 on the value axis.

Now, what is the value of the marginal revenue product on the aggregate function at a total labor quantity of 400 hours (Step 4)? Subtracting the 125 hours in the initial allocation to window cleaning, we have 275 hours remaining to divide between the activities on the aggregate function. Therefore, the value of marginal revenue product at 400 hours is \$11.937, calculated as $\$14.40 - (275 \cdot \$0.008957) = \$11.937$.

Next we insert the solution value of the marginal revenue product into the restated functions for each of the competing uses, obtaining the amount of input that goes to each use (Step 5):

In window cleaning, $\$11.937 = \$18 - \$0.0288X_L$, so $X_L = 210.5$ employee-hours

In sand blasting, $\$11.937 = \$14.40 - \$0.0130X_L$, so $X_L = 189.5$ employee-hours

Finally, we convert the hours of labor input into outputs of the activities and substitute these values into the original demand equations to obtain prices of the outputs (Step 6):

Amount of window cleaning is 210.5 employee-hours times 6 windows per employee-hour or 1,263 windows. Price of window cleaning: $P_w = \$3 - \$0.0004 \cdot 1{,}263 = \$2.495$.

Amount of sand blasting is 189.5 employee-hours times 3.6 hundred square feet per employee-hour, or 682.2 hundred square feet. Price of sand blasting: $P_b = \$4 - \$0.0005 \cdot 682.2 = \$3.659$.

The graphic procedure shown in Figure 6–8 is not simply an illustration. It can be used effectively as *the* method of solution. A sharp pencil and careful plotting will yield solutions that are accurate enough, given the imprecise nature of available planning data. Further, the graphic method can be used in situations involving aggregation of curvilinear functions, where the analytic approach explained above may be intractable except to a highly skilled mathematician.

ALLOCATING AN INPUT THAT HAS DECREASING MARGINAL PRODUCTIVITY

This section discusses decisions about allocations of a single input that has decreasing marginal productivity. By *decreasing marginal productivity* is meant that *increases in physical output resulting from successive equal increments of the input become smaller and smaller as the base rate of use of the input is expanded.* The range in which an input has diminishing marginal productivity may be preceded by a (usually fairly short) range in which it has increasing marginal productivity and then a (usually longer) range in which the marginal productivity is approximately constant. However, if an input does have a range of decreasing marginal productivity in some use that is profitable, the *optimum* allocation of the input to this particular use will be found in this range.

A production function with diminishing returns to the variable inputs

Figure 6–9 shows a hypothetical production function for a firm that cleans windows of office buildings. This figure differs from Figure 6–1 in the way that labor per day is varied. In this illustration, total labor per day, measured on the horizontal plane along the axis of 0–64 hours, is varied by *changing the number of persons in the work force;* length of the workday is held constant at 8 hours. There are various techniques of production, requiring successively greater daily expenses for leased equipment as measured on the horizontal plane along the axis of 0–$300.

Output per workday in total windows cleaned is measured along the vertical axis by the height of the production surface above the horizontal

Figure 6–9
A hypothetical production surface for window cleaning (Second case: Decreasing marginal productivity of labor)

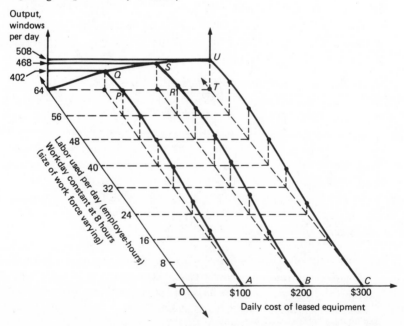

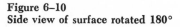

Figure 6–10
Side view of surface rotated 180°

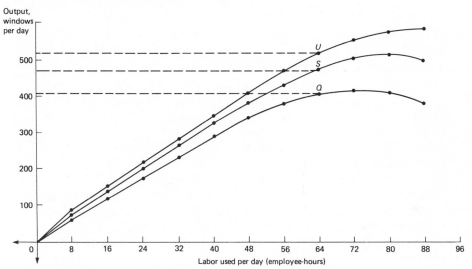

plane. With capital held constant and labor intensity varied, an input-output function is generated. Three such functions, *AQ*, *BS*, and *CU*, corresponding to capital fixed at $100, $200, and $300 per day, respectively, are shown as solid traces across the production surface in Figure 6–9.

It can be seen that the combination of 64 employee-hours of labor with $100 daily cost of leased equipment, found at point *P* on the horizontal plane, produces output *Q* (402 windows per day). The same 64 employee-hours with a $200 daily cost of equipment, corresponding to point *R* on the horizontal plane, yields output *S* (468 windows per day). Finally, the same 64 employee-hours combined with $300 daily equipment cost, point *T* on the horizontal plane, produces the still greater output *U* (508 windows per day). It is clear that increases in capital, with labor held constant, raise the level of output at a decreasing rate. Note also that each of the three input-output functions, showing how output rises as labor is increased with capital held constant, makes a line that curves gently across the production surface. This *curvilinear* relation of total output to total labor is the focus of interest at this time.

By moving to a position at ground level and at some distance from the side on which the labor input is measured, a side view of Figure 6–9 is possible. Such a lateral perspective is depicted in Figure 6–10. Input-output functions *AQ*, *BS*, and *CU* appear as curves *OQ*, *OS*, and *OU*, respectively, in Figure 6–10.

Varying marginal productivity of labor

Although each of the three input-output functions shown in Figure 6–10 does have a short range near the origin in which there is increasing marginal productivity of labor, the input has decreasing marginal productivity over most of the range of the functions. In the range where *marginal productivity is increasing*, there are efficiency gains from *greater specialization of labor* as the size of the work force is increased. Workers spend less time changing tasks and work locations and they develop greater working speeds in the more specialized assignments. However, as the size of the work force grows, *bottlenecks* appear in work processes because of the limited number of pieces of specialized equipment. Workers spend more and more of their time waiting for others to finish using equipment needed in their own next tasks or, alternately, going ahead at the relatively slow rate at which the work can be done without the equipment. When time losses due to equipment bottlenecks become greater than time gains from greater specialization, *diminishing marginal productivity* appears in the relation of total output to total labor input.

The law of variable proportions

Instances of varying marginal productivity of an input are so commonly observed that this relationship has been laid out in a formal statement called "the law of variable proportions." *This law says that if the rate of one input is increased and the rates of other inputs are held constant, the marginal productivity of the one input may increase at first, but it will eventually begin to decrease; it will reach zero at a point of maximum total output, and will thereafter be negative in a range where total output is actually falling.*

Marginal product, the ratio of increase in rate of output to increase in rate of input, has been defined up to this point in incremental terms as: $MPP_x = \Delta Q/\Delta X$, in which MPP_x is marginal product of input X, ΔQ is a discrete change in rate of output, and ΔX is a discrete change in rate of input. By making the changes in input and output smaller and smaller, the ratio $\Delta Q/\Delta X$ can finally be measured at a point on the input-output function, as the slope of a line tangent to the function at that point. Thus, *marginal productivity at a point is $\partial Q/\partial X$, the first derivative of the production function with respect to input X.*

**Allocating an input that has decreasing value
of marginal product in a single use**

If an input has *diminishing* marginal productivity, the input's marginal revenue product calculated as marginal product times the product's price, will *decrease* with greater use of the input even though the product's price is holding *constant*. The use of the input should be increased only so long as the marginal revenue product is greater than the input's price. In other words, use more input only if addition to the value of output is greater than addition to the cost of the input. Expansion of the input's rate of use stops where the falling marginal revenue product becomes *equal* to the input's price. The *optimum* rate of use can be determined analytically.

To demonstrate, suppose employee-hours per day can be increased along Function *OB* of Figure 6–10 in a *continuous* manner (we can hire workers part time, as needed). Further, suppose we have an estimate of the equation for Function *OB:*

$$Q_w = 7X_L + 0.04X_L^2 - 0.0008X_L^3$$

in which Q_w is the number of windows cleaned per day and X_L is employee-hours of labor input per day.

As stated above, the input's marginal product function is the first derivative of the total product function with respect to the input:

$$\frac{dQ}{dX_L} = 7 + 0.08X_L - 0.0024X_L^2$$

And the input's marginal revenue product function is the output's price times the marginal product function (we shall use a constant price of $2 per window):

$$VMP_x = \$2(7 + 0.08X_L - 0.0024X_L^2) = \$14 + \$0.16X_L - \$0.0048X_L^2$$

Set the input's marginal revenue product equal to the input's price (we shall use a price of $10 per employee-hour):

$$\$10 = \$14 + \$0.16X_L - \$0.0048X_L^2$$

Rearrange terms to put the equation in general quadratic form ($0 = ax^2 + bx + c$):

$$0 = -\$0.0048X_L^2 + \$0.16X_L + \$4$$

in which $-\$0.0048$ is the term a, $\$0.16$ is the term b, and $\$4$ is the term c.

Substitute the terms into the solution of the general quadratic form:

$$X_L = \frac{-\$0.16 \pm \sqrt{\$0.0256 - (4)(\$0.0048)(\$4)}}{2(-\$0.0048)}$$

The two roots of the solution are 50 employee-hours per day (the solution we want) and -16.67 (another point where the value of the marginal product is also equal to the input's price). The nature of the above analytic solution is depicted in Figure 6–11.

Figure 6–11
Optimum use of an input that has decreasing value of marginal product in a single use

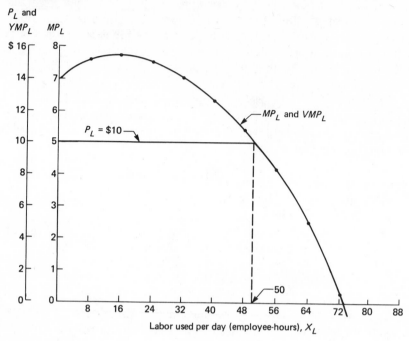

Labor used per day (employee-hours), X_L

Using incremental reasoning in resource allocation

Although a statistical or an engineering estimate of the equation for an input-output function may at times be available, allowing an analytic or graphic solution along the lines of the above example, the manager is often faced with a situation in which information about the input-output relation is very limited. He may know the amount of input he is currently using and the resulting amount of output. Further, he may feel that he can make a pretty good estimate of the effect upon output if he makes an *incremental* change in the input. For example, he may feel that he can make a good estimate of the increase in output if he puts one more person in the work force.

Under circumstances of limited information, the manager can use incremental reasoning. He knows that he should increase the rate of use of the input if the *incremental increase in value of output is greater than the incremental increase in cost of the input.* To illustrate how incremental reasoning applies, Table 6–1 lists values of input and output at selected levels of input for the function *OB* of Figure 6–10. Changes in daily output and the monetary values of these changes are given for successive increases of 8 hours (one employee-day) in labor input. A

Table 6-1
Incremental analysis—how much input to use, where the input has decreasing marginal productivity

Number of persons	Daily labor input (employee-hours)	Daily output (windows)	Increase in daily output	Value of increase in daily output
0....................	0	0	0	$ 0
1....................	8	58.1	58.1	116.20
2....................	16	119.0	60.9	121.80
3....................	24	180.0	61.0	122.00
4....................	32	238.7	58.7	117.40
5....................	40	292.8	54.1	108.20
6....................	48	339.7	46.9	93.80
7....................	56	377.0	37.3	74.60
8....................	64	402.1	25.1	50.20
9....................	72	412.8	10.7	21.40
10....................	80	407.0	−5.8	−11.60

manager, being at one point in this table, could probably make a good estimate of the result of moving down one line. Assume that labor costs $10 per hour, or $80 per employee-day. It can be seen that the increase in value of output is greater than the increase in cost of labor for each successive addition of a person through the sixth person. But it would not be profitable to add the seventh person.

Allocating an input that has decreasing marginal productivity in each of several competing uses

All of the principles and techniques used in allocating a single resource have been provided in sections above. This section demonstrates simultaneous applications of several of the principles. We are going to handle the case of a limited quantity of an input that has decreasing marginal productivity in each of two uses. Both uses are in production of services for which the firm's demand curves slope down to the right. The input's marginal revenue products will be decreasing for two reasons—the input's decreasing marginal productivity as the rate of output expands will be compounded with the effect of the output's decreasing marginal revenue. This situation of decreasing marginal revenue products in each of several uses calls for *equimarginal* allocation. *We want to divide the input between the uses in such a way that the input's marginal revenue products are equalized.*

The analytic method becomes difficult in this example because the equations for the marginal revenue product functions pick up terms having powers higher than the cubic level. So we are going to use only the graphic method. Assume that the hypothetical firm has estimated the following total and marginal product functions in producing the window cleaning service:

$$Q_w = 7X_L + 0.04X_L^2 - 0.0008X_L^3$$
$$MPP_{L \cdot w} = 7 + 0.08X_L - 0.0024X_L^2$$

in which

Q_w is total windows cleaned per work *day*.

$MPP_{L \cdot w}$ is marginal product of labor in window cleaning in windows per employee-hour.

X_L is quantity of labor in employee-hours per *day*.

Assume further that the firm has estimated the following demand and marginal revenue functions for the window-cleaning activity:

$$P_w = \$3 - \$0.0004Q_w$$
$$MR_w = \$3 - 0.0008Q_w$$

in which

P_w is price per window in dollars.

MR_w is marginal revenue in dollars.

Q_w is quantity of windows per *week*.

In the activity of sand blasting, the firm has estimated the total and marginal product functions as follows:

$$Q_b = 4.5X_L + 0.03X_L^2 - 0.0005X_L^3$$
$$MPP_{L \cdot b} = 4.5 + 0.06X_L - 0.0015X_L^2$$

in which

Q_b is total sand blasting per *day* in hundreds of square feet.

$MPP_{L \cdot w}$ is marginal product of labor in sand blasting.

X_L is quantity of labor in employee-hours per *day*.

The firm's demand and marginal revenue functions for sand blasting are:

$$P_b = \$4 - \$0.0005Q_b$$
$$MR_b = \$4 - \$0.0010Q_b$$

in which

P_b is price per hundred square feet in dollars.

MR_b is marginal revenue in dollars.

Q_b is amount of sand blasting per *week* in hundreds of square feet.

The first step in solving the problem is to calculate values of daily and weekly output, marginal revenue, and marginal revenue product for the two activities at several rates of use of labor. Table 6–2 shows the results of such calculations. The second step is to plot marginal revenue products for the individual activities as shown in Figure 6–12A and B. The

Table 6-2
Calculations of marginal revenue products of an input in two of its uses

Daily labor X_L (employee-hours)	Window cleaning*					Sand blasting†					MRC_L‡
	Daily Q_W	Weekly Q_W	MR_W	$MP_{L\cdot W}$	$MRP_{L\cdot W}$	Daily Q_B	Weekly Q_B	MR_B	$MP_{L\cdot S}$	$MRP_{L\cdot B}$	
24	180.0	900.0	2.280	7.54	17.185	125.9	629.5	3.37	5.076	17.10	8.00
32	238.7	1,193.7	2.045	7.10	14.524	158.3	791.7	3.21	4.880	15.66	9.00
40	292.8	1,464.0	1.839	6.36	11.696	196.0	980.0	3.02	4.500	13.59	10.00
48	339.7	1,698.5	1.641	5.31	8.714	229.8	1,149.0	2.85	3.924	11.18	11.00
56	376.9	1,884.5	1.492	3.95	5.893	258.3	1,291.5	2.71	3.156	8.55	12.00

* Daily production
$Q_w = 7X_L + 0.04X_L^2 - 0.0008X_L^3$
Weekly marginal revenue
$MR_w = 3 - 0.0008Q_w$
Daily marginal product
$MP_L = 7 + 0.08X_L - 0.0024X_L^2$
† Daily production
$Q_B = 4.5X_L + 0.03X_L^2 - 0.0005X_L^3$
Weekly marginal revenue
$MR_B = \$4 - 0.0010Q_B$
Daily marginal product
$MP_L = 4.5 + 0.06X_L - 0.0015X_L^2$
‡ Weekly
$MRC_L = \$5 + 0.025Q_L$

Figure 6–12

Graphic method of determining equimarginal allocations of limited quantities of an input among uses in which the input's marginal revenue products are decreasing

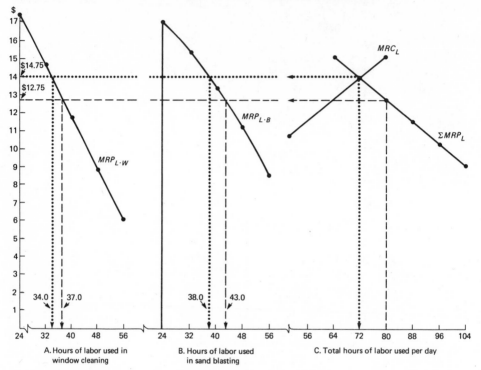

A. Hours of labor used in window cleaning

B. Hours of labor used in sand blasting

C. Total hours of labor used per day

third step is to aggregate the quantities of labor from the several activities at selected values of marginal revenue product to get *some* of the points on the *aggregate* marginal revenue product function in Figure 6–12C. The function is sketched to pass through the points that have been plotted.

Now, assume the quantity of labor available is limited to 80 hours per day. At 80 hours *on the aggregate marginal revenue product function,* MRP_L has a value of approximately $13.75. Reading back along the dashed trace in Figure 6–12 to the value of $13.75 *on the individual marginal revenue product functions,* we find an allocation of 43 hours of labor per day to sand blasting and an allocation of 37 hours per day to window cleaning. This is the (approximately) *optimum allocation of the resource* for the stated conditions.

Outputs and prices of the two services can be found by the following sequence. First, substitute the amount of allocated labor into the total product function to obtain total output per day. Multiply by five (work-

days per week) to get output per week. Then substitute weekly output into the demand function to get price. The results are as follows:
  In window cleaning:

Daily labor input: 37 employee-hours
Daily output: 273.2 windows
Weekly output: 1,366 windows
Price: $2.45 per window
Calculated marginal revenue product: $12.71

In sand blasting:

Daily labor input: 43 employee-hours
Daily output: 211.7 hundred square feet
Weekly output: 1,058.5 hundred square feet
Price: $3.47 per hundred square feet
Calculated marginal revenue product: $12.66

It is gratifying to note that the graphic method comes quite close to equating marginal revenue products. The calculated values in this example differ by less than one half of 1 percent.

Effect of rising marginal resource cost. Suppose all conditions are as described above, except that labor is not limited. Instead, it is available in increasing quantity at an increasing wage rate. Let us assume that the firm has estimated its supply curve and marginal resource cost functions for labor as follows:

$$P_L = \$5 + \$0.0125X_L$$
$$MRC_L = \$5 + \$0.0250X_L$$

in which

P_L is wage rate in dollars per employee-hour.
MRC_L is marginal resource cost in dollars.
X_L is labor in hours per *week*.

  The first step is to plot the marginal resource cost function in Figure 6–12C. Then find the intersection of MRC_L and MRP_L at a value of approximately $14, which corresponds to a labor input of 72 hours per day or 360 hours per week. Reading back along the dotted trace to the individual marginal revenue product functions, we get an allocation of 38 hours per day to sand blasting and 34 hours per day to window cleaning.
  Outputs and prices of the two services can be found by sequential substitutions and are as follows. In window cleaning, daily labor input is 34 employee-hours, daily output is 252.8 windows, weekly output is 1,264 windows, price is $2.49 per window, and calculated marginal revenue product is $13.82. In sand blasting, daily labor input is 38 employee-

hours, daily output is 193.8 hundred square feet, weekly output is 969 hundred square feet, price is $3.51 per hundred square feet, and the calculated marginal revenue product is $13.97. In this example, the marginal revenue products differ by only one percent. The graphic method of solution is accurate enough, considering the character of available planning data.

Remember that the marginal revenue product of an input must be calculated net of the cost of any other variable inputs. The cost of other variable inputs is to be subtracted from the output's price and marginal revenue functions. For example, if window washing required 10 cents worth of detergent material for each window washed, the marginal revenue function in the example above would be shifted down by 10 cents. This adjustment would then carry into the calculation of the input's marginal revenue product. For example, in Table 6–2 at the daily labor input of 24 hours marginal revenue would be reduced from $2.28 to $2.18, and marginal revenue product would be reduced from $17.185 to $16.437.

Methods of resource allocation discussed up to this point are appropriate if decisions about *one* resource are independent of decisions about other resources. The next section takes up the case of *two or more* scarce resources, with simultaneous, interdependent allocation among two or more production activities. This situation poses what is called the *product mix problem*.

THE PRODUCT MIX PROBLEM:
CONCEPTUAL FRAMEWORK

Consider a situation in which a farmer can product two basic crops, corn and soybeans. He also raises cattle. The farmer has 1,000 acres of land available and employs four helpers; each of these works 40 hours per week. The farmer measures his output in bushels of corn, bushels of soybeans, and number of cattle produced and sold at market per year. The farmer may produce one of any number of combinations of products per year. For example, he may produce all corn and no soybeans and no cattle; or he may choose to produce all of any one of the products and none of the others. More realistically, he may choose to produce some of each product (i.e., x bushels of corn, y bushels of soybeans, and z cattle). The number of possible combinations is practically unlimited. How should he go about choosing the best combination to produce; i.e., how many bushels of corn, how many bushels of soybeans, and how many cattle? His choices are many but are limited by his limited resources, land and labor. In view of these limits, a decision to produce one more bushel of corn affects the number of bushels of soybeans that he can produce and the number of cattle, and so on. If the farmer is rational, he will try to produce the optimum mix of products. But how should optimality be defined? What should his objective be?

The general nature of product mix problems

Product mix problems only occur when two or more resources are limited and there are two or more products that require at least one of the limited resources. (If only one resource is limited, it is appropriate to use equimarginal allocation based on marginal revenue product.) A business firm or a nonprofit organization producing goods or services has limited resources in the short run. There are only so many hours of labor available each week; there are only so many units of each required raw material available; only a certain number of hours of use per week are available at each piece of equipment; and so on. Although many different combinations of products may be produced, a decision to produce one unit of any particular product requires the sacrifice of some quantity of at least one of the other products. Any particular combination of products will be called a *product mix*. The basic problem is then: *Within the constraints imposed by the limited resources, select from all possible combinations of product mixes the optimum product mix.* In order to solve this problem it is necessary to develop several additional concepts and to define optimality.

Production possibility curves

Consider again the situation the farmer faces. For simplicity we will assume he is considering only two enterprises: corn and cattle. He has only 1,000 acres of land and a fixed number of hours of labor per week. Figure 6–13 is a hypothetical *production possibility curve*. It shows various combinations of corn (bushels) and cattle (number) that could be produced per year using 1,000 acres of land. A maximum quantity of corn (Y_2) can be grown if there is no raising of cattle (Y_1). By giving up some corn production, land can be made available for use as pasture for cattle. This process substitutes cattle for corn in the product mix.

The production possibility curve in Figure 6–13 is *concave to the origin*. This curvature reflects the assumption of a *diminishing marginal rate of product transformation* of Y_1 for Y_2 for movement from point to point down and to the right. The absolute value of the slope of the curve, $|-\Delta Y_2/\Delta Y_1|$, is increasing. To obtain one more unit of Y_1, more and more Y_2 must be foregone as Y_1 is increased. (As the farmer produces fewer and fewer bushels of corn and more cattle, each *extra* bushel of corn sacrificed yields fewer pounds of additional beef than the bushel before.)

Figure 6–13
Production possibility curve (heterogeneous input)

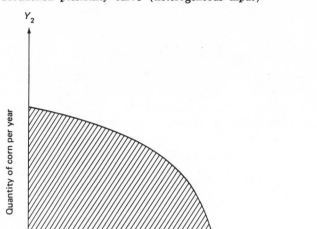

Diminishing marginal rates of product transformation are often observed in practice; they are explained by *heterogeneity* of fixed inputs.
In the example of Figure 6–13, the land is not uniform in quality. It
ranges from rich and level to poor and hilly. All of the land can be
planted in corn or grazed by cattle, or there can be various combinations
of corn and cattle production. As the farmer increases cattle production,
more and more corn must be given up to obtain land for one cow. Increasingly fertile land is being withdrawn from corn production and
reallocated to cattle.

How many product mixes are possible? Each point on the curve represents a *feasible product mix* that will utilize all available land. Each
point in the shaded region of Figure 6–13 also represents a feasible product mix that will leave some land unused, or *redundant*.

A production possibility curve can be drawn for each of the limited
resources. Figure 6–14 is another such curve showing the various combinations of corn and cattle production possible assuming a fixed supply of
labor. This curve is linear if the labor is *homogeneous*. Each point on the
curve and in the shaded region represents a feasible product mix, considering only the limited supply of labor.

Figure 6–15 shows both of the production possibility curves discussed
above. The shaded region is a set of points feasible for both curves. Since

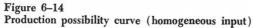

Figure 6–14
Production possibility curve (homogeneous input)

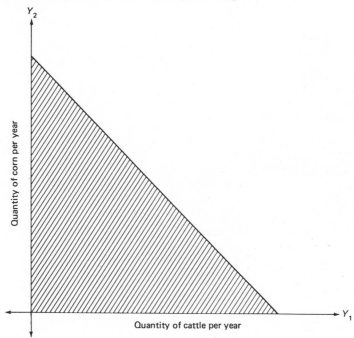

the farmer is limited by *both* resources, land and labor, only those product mixes in the shaded region and along its boundary are feasible.

Now that the set of feasible product mixes has been determined, several other questions must be answered. How much product substitution
is advantageous in such a case? What is the optimum product mix? The
solution depends upon *relative contributions* of the two products. These
contributions are determined by *prices of the products* and by *prices and
necessary amounts of the corresponding variable inputs.*

Isocontribution lines

Changes in product combinations with contributions constant are depicted by the three *isocontribution lines* in Figure 6–16. For example, all
product combinations on isocontribution line $3,000 would contribute
exactly $3,000.

Relative positions of the isocontribution lines are determined by the
absolute amounts of contribution per unit of each product. The slope of
the lines depends upon relative contributions and therefore upon both

Figure 6–15
Production possibility curves (superimposed)

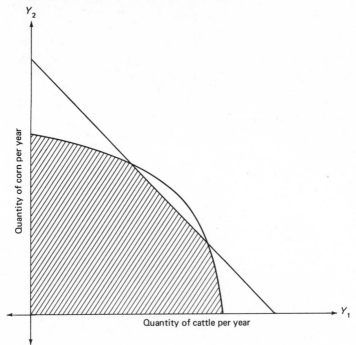

prices and variable costs of both products. Isocontribution line $3,000 is established as follows. First, the contribution per unit of Y_2 (Cy_2) is calculated: It is price less variable unit cost. It should be noted that *if contribution is considered constant, several economic assumptions are implicit.* To assume that price does not change according to the rate of output is to assume that the product has a *horizontal demand curve.* It is also assumed that variable cost per unit is constant. This implies both *constant prices of inputs* and *constant marginal productivity of inputs* over the range considered.

The next step in establishing isocontribution line $3,000 is to calculate the number of units of Y_2 produced alone that would provide a total contribution of $3,000 (e.g., $3,000/$Cy_2$ = number of units of Y_2); the result is the value of the Y_2 intercept. The third step is to calculate the Y_1 intercept using the above procedure and the contribution associated with each unit of Y_1 (Cy_1).

Finally, a straight line connecting the two intercepts completes this particular isocontribution line. Any point on the line segment represents a combination of bushels of corn and number of cattle which would re-

Figure 6–16
Isocontribution lines: Two outputs

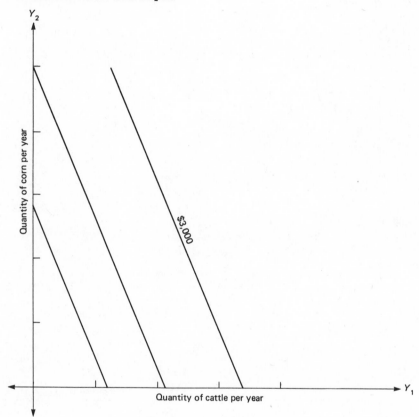

sult in a total contribution of $3,000. Infinitely many other isocontribution lines can be generated in a similar fashion. One such line exists for each value of total contribution.

Optimum product mix

In Figure 6–17 the isocontribution lines from Figure 6–16 have been superimposed on the production possibility curve of Figure 6–15. The objective is to find that combination of products, or that *product mix*, which yields *maximum total contribution*.

Consider Point *A* on the production possibility curve. Is it advantageous to move around the curve to Point *B*? Since the change results in a move to a higher contribution line which implies greater total contribution, the product substitution *is* clearly desirable. However, contribution

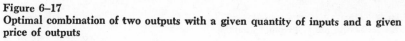

Figure 6–17
Optimal combination of two outputs with a given quantity of inputs and a given price of outputs

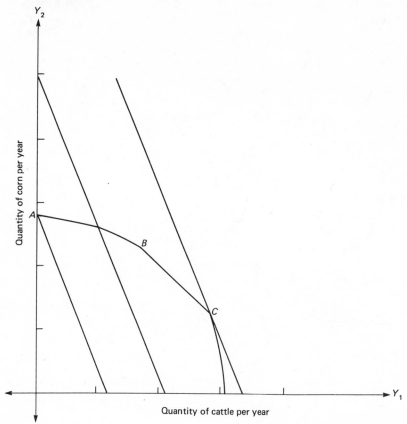

can be increased *still more* by moving around to Point C. In contrast, any move from Point C would result in a product mix falling on a lower isocontribution line and therefore would reduce total contribution. Point C is the optimum product mix in this illustration, because it is the one that produces the greatest total contribution.

AN INTRODUCTION TO LINEAR PROGRAMMING

A particular case of the product mix problem involves the assumptions that *all of the various physical product-substitution possibilities and isocontribution lines are linear*. The advantage of the assumptions of linearity is that they allow the use of powerful mathematical techniques, known as *linear programming,* or LP. If one is going to use these tools, one must be careful that the economic implications of this assumption of linearity are understood. This section considers the formulation of a product mix problem into the LP framework. The necessary assumptions and their implications are discussed as well as the techniques used in solving this class of problems.

An example will be used throughout this section in order to explain the formulation and solution of product mix problems. Assume a manufacturer produces *two products,* desks and bookcases. Both products must be processed through *two work stations.* At work station 1, the wood is sawed and sanded. At work station 2, the products are assembled and stained. Because of a limited amount of labor and a limited number of machines, only 126 hours are available weekly at work station 1. For similar reasons only 96 hours are available at work station 2. Sawing and sanding of desks requires 6 hours; 3 hours are needed for bookcases. Assembling and staining desks and bookcases requires 2 and 4 hours, respectively.

Assuming that contribution per desk is $8 and contribution per bookcase is $6, we wish to determine the optimum number of desks and bookcases to produce and sell. Table 6–3 summarizes the pertinent information.

Table 6–3
Problem information

Work center	Hours required for one unit of product		Total hours available
	Desks	Bookcases	
1. Saw and sand..........................	6	3	126
2. Assemble and stain....................	2	4	96
Contribution per unit......................	$8	$6	

Formulation of an LP problem

1. *The objective of the firm must be stated explicitly as a linear function of the activities.* It is necessary to define explicitly in measurable terms the activities that are competing for the limited resources. In our example the two activities are desk production and bookcase production. We will represent the level of these activities (if a rate, quantity per unit of time) by the number of desks D produced and sold and the number of bookcases B produced and sold.

After the outputs of the competing activities have been explicitly defined, it is necessary to determine the objective the firm wishes to achieve. The rational firm wishes to select and produce that combination of prod-

ucts which will maximize total contribution. In our example then, the
firm wishes to determine that number of desks and that number of bookcases which, if produced and sold, will maximize total contribution.
Mathematically the firm's objective may be stated as:

$$\text{Maximize } 8D + 6B$$

If we let Z represent total contribution, then $Z = 8D + 6B$ is known as
an *objective function.*

Of what significance is it that the objective function must be linear?
For the objective function to be linear requires that the contribution per
unit of each product be constant. In our example, no matter how many
desks are produced, each desk sold returns a contribution of $8. No mat-
ter how many bookcases are produced, each bookcase returns a contribution of $6. Since contribution per unit is defined as the difference between
price and variable cost per unit, both price and per-unit variable cost
must be constant. Constant price implies a horizontal demand curve
which in turn implies pure competition. Strictly interpreted, constant
variable cost per short-run unit implies horizontal supply curves for
inputs and constant marginal productivity of inputs rather than increasing or diminishing marginal productivity.

Constant variable unit cost, although sometimes observed in actual
production, is a special case. Diminishing marginal productivity of variable inputs as output of either product is increased, resulting in increasing marginal cost for that product, would be more generally encountered.
This would make the isocontribution lines *convex* to the origin rather
than straight lines. Although such a change in form of the curves would
not affect the general results of this exposition, it makes determination of
product mix very difficult if there are numerous products to consider.
Constant marginal productivity is often assumed because constant contributions make the problem easier to handle. (If *decreasing* marginal
productivity *must* be taken into account, it can be approximated through
stepwise reductions that allow it to remain constant over successive
ranges of output. If output within each range is then *formally* treated as
a different product, one can still use the approach to product mix determination that is discussed in the following sections.)

2. *The restrictions placed on the firm by limited resources must be
stated explicitly as linear equalities or inequalities.* If these restrictions
did not exist, maximum contribution would be achieved by an "infinite
amount of production." It is only because resources are limited that a
problem exists. These limits constitute the *constraints* of the problem.
For our example there are two constraints, one imposed by a limited
number of hours available at work station 1 and another imposed by the
limited number of hours available at work station 2. Stated mathematically the constraints are:

$$(1) \quad 6D + 3B \leq 126 \quad \text{(work station 1)}$$
$$(2) \quad 2D + 4B \leq 96 \quad \text{(work station 2)}$$

Let us closely examine these two constraints. First consider constraint (1). The coefficient 6 and 3 are *technological coefficients*. Each desk produced requires 6 hours at work station 1. Each bookcase requires 3 hours. There are only 126 hours available. Since D represents the number of desks processed at work station 1, $6D$ represents the total amount of the available time at work station 1 used in producing desks. Similarly, $3B$ represents the total amount of available time at work station 1 that will be used in producing bookcases. It follows that $6D + 3B$ would be the total number of hours used at work station 1 for the production of D desks and B bookcases. Since there are only 126 hours available, then $6D + 3B$ must be less than or equal to ($\leq$) 126. The "less than" is included since we are not required to use all the hours available, but in no case may we use more than 126 hours. Any product mix (D, B) that the firm produces must be determined so that it does not violate $6D + 3B \leq 126$. Constraint (2) may be similarly interpreted.

Of what significance is it that these inequalities must be linear? Linearity implies that the amount of each limited resource required is the same for the nth unit of the activity as it is for the first. Implicit assumptions are that: (1) the resource is homogeneous and (2) the relation of the resource to the output is characterized by constant marginal productivity. Another way of expressing the same thing is to say that constant marginal rates of product substitution are assumed. For example, to process one desk at work station 1 requires 6 hours and one bookcase requires 3 hours. It follows, then, that the marginal rate of substitution between desks and bookcases is 2 (6/3); i.e., the decision to process one more desk at work station 1 requires the sacrifice of processing two bookcases. Similarly, the marginal rate of product transformation at work station 2 would be ½ (2/4). Since each desk requires only 2 hours at work station 2 while each bookcase requires 4 hours, the decision to produce one more desk requires the sacrifice of only ½ bookcase.

3. *Nonnegativity requirements must be recognized.* There is no physical meaning to negative production levels, such as $D = -4$, and so we do not allow production to be negative. We must constrain each unknown production level to be either zero or positive, i.e., to be *nonnegative*, $D \geq 0$ and $B \geq 0$.

An additional assumption inherent in the preceding assumptions is generally referred to as the assumption of *divisibility*. The divisibility assumption simply implies that the activity levels are permitted to assume fractional values as well as integer values. For example, we admit the technological possibility of $D = 2.5$ and $B = 4.41$. (Partial units can be completed in the next time period.)

Now that our problem has been formulated as an LP problem and the necessary assumptions and their implications discussed, it is perhaps appropriate to present the formulation here in its entirety.

$$D = \text{number of desks} \atop B = \text{number of bookcases} \Big\} \text{variables}$$

(1)   Maximize $Z = 8D + 6\}$ objective function

subject to:

(2) $6D + 3B \leq 126$
(3) $2D + 4B \leq 96$ $\Big\}$constraints

and

(4) $D \geq 0$, $B \geq 0\}$ nonnegativity requirements

Management's problem is to find values for D and B that satisfy the relations (2), (3), and (4), and also maximize total contribution (1).

A graphic solution

Graphic methods of linear programming can be used only when there are no more than three variables involved because we can draw in no more than three dimensions. However, the graphic approach is most helpful in demonstrating the underlying logic of LP. In this section, the graphic method of LP is illustrated by use of an example. The basic problem discussed in the preceding section will be solved graphically.

Step 1. Plot the constraints in the problem on a graph. Figure 6–18 is such a graph. The horizontal axis represents the number of desks and the vertical axis represents the number of bookcases. It should be noted that we are concerned only with the first quadrant. This fact is the obvious result of the nonnegativity requirements (4).

The steepest line in the graph represents the constraint imposed on production by the limited number of hours available at work station 1. It was found by plotting the equation

$$6D + 3B = 126$$

Since the actual constraint (2) is an inequality, each point on the line and every point to the left of the line represents a product mix which satisfies this constraint. This line is in fact simply a production possibility curve. The fact that it is linear derives from the assumptions previously discussed.

Similarly, in Figure 6–18 the constraint imposed by work station 2 is plotted. Every point on the line and to the left of the line represents a product mix which satisfies the constraint

$$2D + 4B \leq 96$$

Figure 6–18
Feasible region for a simple LP problem

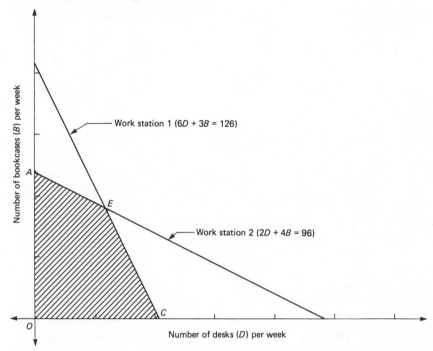

Since both work stations must be used in order to produce a desk or a bookcase, only those product mixes which fall in the shaded area of Figure 6–18 are possible. For a combination to be feasible, the available time at either work station may not be exceeded. The shaded area represents all those product combinations that satisfy both constraints:

$$6D + 3B \leq 126$$
$$2D + 4B \leq 96$$

This area is called the *feasible region* because every point that lies within it or on its boundary represents a combination of values of the variables (the output levels of D and B) which does not violate either constraint. Every point in the feasible region is called a *feasible solution*. Note that each constraint has decreased the size of the area within which solutions may exist. The *solution space* has been reduced from the entire plane to the feasible region as depicted in Figure 6–18.

Step 2.   Calculate all the coordinates of each corner point. A corner point is any point in the feasible region which occurs at the intersection of two or more of the constraints. For example, in Figure 6–18 there are four corner points which are labeled A, E, C, and O. Point A occurs where the nonnegativity requirement $D \geq 0$ and the constraint for work station 2 intersect. C occurs at the intersection of $B = 0$ and the constraint for work station 1. To calculate point E, the following two equations are solved simultaneously:

$$(1) \quad 6D + 3B = 126$$
$$(2) \quad 2D + 4B = 96$$

We multiply the second equation by -3 and add the results to Equation (1).

$$6D + 3B = 126$$
$$\underline{-6D - 12B = -288}$$
$$-9B = -162$$
$$B = 18$$

Substituting $B = 18$ in Equation (1):

$$6D + 3(18) = 126$$
$$6D = 72$$
$$D = 12$$

Point E is then (12, 18). Point O is the origin (0,0), which is always a corner point.

Step 3. With all feasible product mix alternatives delineated, select the one that meets the objective of maximizing contribution. The basic theorem of linear programming tells us that *the optimum solution must always lie at a corner of the feasible region.* Although no attempt will be made to prove this theorem here, the student may intuitively understand the reason for this by studying Figure 6–19. Figure 6–19 is simply the feasible region as depicted in Figure 6–18 with a set of *isocontribution lines* superimposed on it. The line closest to the origin (R) is simply the set of all product mixes which return a total contribution of $120. It was found by plotting the line for the equation

$$8D + 6B = 120$$

Should the firm produce one of the product mixes shown on this line? Before answering, consider the next isocontribution line S. It was found by plotting the equation

$$8D + 6B = 168$$

It should be noted that there are an infinite number of possible isocontribution lines, one for each possible value of total contribution. Since the contribution per unit of each product is unchanging, the isocontribution lines form a series of parallel straight lines. Obviously the firm would be better off to produce a product mix on the second line S because

Figure 6–19
Graphic solution for a simple LP problem

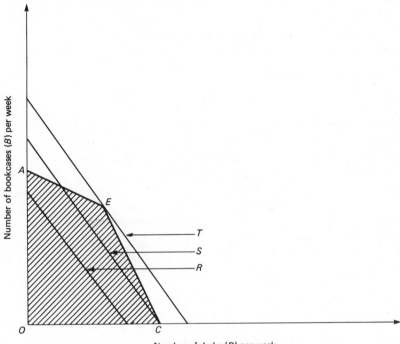

the total contribution is greater for each product mix on this line than it was for line R. In fact the firm should continue to the highest (farthest from origin) line which still has at least one point in common with the feasible region. It should be obvious that this point will always be a corner point as shown by isocontribution line T in Figure 6–19. Any move to a higher isocontribution line results in product mixes which are not feasible. Any move to a lower line results in less than maximum contribution.

For this reason, we need only to compare the value of the total contribution at each corner point. The one resulting in the greatest contribution is the optimum product mix.

Corner point	Computation	Total contribution
O: (0, 0).................	8 (0) + 6 (0)	$ 0
A: (0, 24)................	8 (0) + 6 (24)	$144
C: (21, 0)................	8 (21) + 6 (0)	$168
E: (12, 18)...............	8 (12) + 6 (18)	$204

Thus the optimum product mix is to produce 12 desks and 18 bookcases. Neither the time constraint at work station 1 nor the constraint at work station 2 is violated since:

$$6(12) + 3(18) = 126$$
$$2(12) + 4(18) = 96$$

The resulting contribution is \$204.

Up to this point, we have examined the basic structure of linear programming formulations of product mix problems and we have seen how a simple example can be solved by a graphic method. Practical applications of the product mix formulation usually involve large numbers of production activities and resource restrictions, and the optimum solutions are determined by iterative methods of calculation that are beyond the scope of this book. It is important for managers to understand the economic assumptions that are involved in setting up a linear programming formulation and the economic implications of the solutions that are obtained, but most managers will be able to get assistance from specialists in computer usage when the time comes to calculate solutions to their linear programming problems.

SENSITIVITY ANALYSIS

A user of linear programming should not confine his or her interest to the numerical values of an optimum solution. Since each of the coefficients in the linear programming model is an estimate and thus subject to error and/or change, the user needs to know how much the coefficients can vary without causing changes in a computed optimal solution.

Such an analysis is called *sensitivity analysis* or postoptimality analysis. In some cases, a small variation in one of the coefficients may result in a new optimal solution with a significantly different value for the objective function. In other cases, a large change in a coefficient may result in no change in the optimal product mix and little change in the value of the maximum.

In this section, variations of the three following types will be discussed:

1. Variations in objective function coefficients.
2. Variations in requirements coefficients.
3. Variations in technological coefficients.

Additionally, the effects of the addition or deletion of constraints as well as the addition or deletion of variables can be studied, but these analyses are beyond the scope of this book.

Variations in objective function coefficients

In order to illustrate the use of sensitivity analysis, we will return to the problem discussed in the preceding section. Table 6–3 is a summary of the important data for this problem.

The problem was formulated in the LP framework as:

$$\text{Maximize } Z = 8D + 6B$$

$$Z = 8D + 6B$$

Subject to:

$$6D + 3B \leq 126$$
$$2D + 4B \leq 96$$
$$D, B \leq 0$$

where D represented the number of desks produced and B the number of bookcases; the optimal production schedule was found to be:

$$D = 12$$
$$B = 18$$

This production schedule results in an optimal profit of $204.

Contribution per unit for each of the products is a function of their selling price, cost of materials, direct labor, and other variable costs. Since each of these estimates is subject to error and to future changes, we wish to determine *how much variation each contribution per unit may have in each direction without causing a change in the present optimal solution.*

For example, how much can the contribution per desk vary from $8 without changing the optimal product mix? In answering the question raised above, we may utilize our initial model (designated as I below) as well as our final set of equations (designated as F).

I:	$Z - 8D - 6B$			$= 0$	Row 0
	$6D + 3B$	$+ S_1$		$= 126$	Row 1
	$2D + 2B$		$+ S_2$	$= 96$	Row 2
F:	Z	$+10/9S_1$	$+2/3S_2$	$= 204$	Row 0
	D	$+ 2/9S_1$	$-1/6S_2$	$= 12$	Row 1
	B	$- 1/9S_1$	$+1/3S_2$	$= 18$	Row 2

The first set of equations is the set used at the outset of the process of deriving the algebraic solution. The other set is the final set of equations derived in determining the algebraic solution. In both the first and second set, S_1 is slack time at station 1 and S_2 is slack time at station 2. Addition of these variables allows the inequalities to be replaced by equalities.

In order to answer our question, suppose that **Row 0 of I is changed** such that the contribution of D becomes ($\$8 + \delta$). Row 0 of I becomes

$$Z - (8 + \delta)\, D - 6B = 0 \qquad (6\text{--}12)$$

It can be shown that Row 0 of F would become

$$Z - \delta D + \frac{10S_1}{9} + \frac{2S_2}{3} = 204 \qquad (6\text{--}13)$$

In order to draw any conclusions about the critical range of δ, we must recreate a coefficient equal to 0 for D in Row 0. This may be done by multiplying Row 1 of F by δ and adding it to Equation 6–13 to give

$$Z + \left(\frac{10}{9} + \frac{2}{9\delta}\right)S_1 + \left(\frac{2}{3} - \frac{1}{6\delta}\right)S_2 = 204 + 12\delta \qquad (6\text{--}14)$$

Careful analysis of Equation (6–14) reveals that the current solution is optimal for

$$-5 \le \delta \le 4 \qquad (6\text{--}15)$$

If δ is less than -5, the coefficient of S_1 becomes negative. If δ exceeds 4, the coefficient of S_2 becomes negative. Consequently, as soon as δ falls outside the range in Equation (7–15) the present solution is no longer optimal.

Another way of stating the result is that as long as the contribution of one desk is between \$3 and \$12 *and all other data of the problem remain constant,* the optimal product mix is unchanged. Note that the maximum contribution would change however. For example, if the contribution per desk increased to \$10, we would still produce 12 desks and 18 bookcases. However, the total contribution would increase to \$228 as opposed to \$204. This example serves to illustrate the difference between optimal schedule sensitivity and optimal contribution sensitivity.

Similar analysis shows that if the contribution per bookcase changes by δ where

$$-2 \le \delta \le 10$$

there will be no change in the optimal product mix, provided all other data of the problem remain constant. Monetarily, as long as the contribution per bookcase is between \$4 and \$16, optimal contribution will be attained with the present product mix. This result is interesting in that contribution per unit may *increase* as much as \$10 without changing the optimal product mix. However, a *decrease* of more then \$2 will change the optimal product mix.

The above information would be beneficial to the decision maker in evaluating alternative pricing structures as well as in assessing the impact of changes in costs on production schedules. It also demonstrates that even though the contribution estimates are in fact estimates, the results for the model are not extremely sensitive to relatively large errors.

A word of warning: We considered a change in only one coefficient at a time, assuming that the other coefficient was constant. Coefficients could change simultaneously. Analysis of simultaneous changes in coefficients is called *ranging analysis;* the scope of the book allows no further discussion of this more general case of sensitivity analysis or of the techniques used.

Variations in requirements coefficients

We will now investigate whether the optimal solution is changed if a constant on the right-hand side of the constraints is changed. For example, suppose the number of hours available at work station 1 changes; how far can it vary without affecting our optimal solution? In order to answer this question we must investigate Row 0 of F,

$$Z + \frac{10S_1}{9} + \frac{2S_2}{3} = 204$$

Since, in our final solution, $S_1 = 0$, there was no unused time (slack time) in work station 1. Obviously then, if the number of hours available at work station 1 were decreased, the number of desks and bookcases produced would be affected. The coefficient of S_1, 10/9, represents the decrease in total contribution associated with making one less hour available. Similarly an increase of one additional hour would raise the total contribution by \$10/9. Following the same reasoning, the incremental contribution from one additional hour available at work station 2 is \$2/3.

It is obvious that the optimal product mix as well as the corresponding level of contribution may be quite sensitive to changes in the right-hand constants. It is not possible to change a right-hand constant without affecting the optimal product mix unless the corresponding slack variable is nonnegative.

The increases in contribution by additional hours at each of the work stations can be recognized as the *marginal revenue products* of these limited resources, i.e., the maximum worth of one more unit to the firm, assuming all other data of the problem remain constant.

Variations in technological coefficients

The technological coefficients are the coefficients on the left-hand side of the constraints. They are generally based on work standards. For example, the coefficient of D in Row 1 of I means that production of one desk requires 6 hours of processing time at work station 1. In actual practice a figure such as this would probably be determined by careful analysis of past experience and the application of time and motion studies. Since each such coefficient is an estimate, we would be interested in determining the effect of variations in any one of these coefficients on the optimal solution. For example, the actual number of hours of processing time at work station 1 for a desk could vary considerably from 6 hours because of the skill and experience of the workers, the age and conditions of the machines, or any number of other variables.

We will not make an effort here to discuss methods of assessing the impact of changes in technological coefficients. Such analyses require the development of concepts beyond the scope of this book.

Conclusion

The primary point made in this section on sensitivity analysis is that linear programmers are not finished with their work when they have determined an optimal solution. The linear programming model is commonly referred to as an optimizing model, but it optimizes if and only if one assumes that all relevant variables have been included and that the values of the coefficients are sufficiently accurate. Since decision makers are often faced with uncertainties as to such factors as future demand, prices, costs, technological change, and so forth, no experienced users of LP would be satisfied without carrying out careful sensitivity or post-optimality analyses of the types described above.

LINEAR PROGRAMMING AND SOME BASIC ECONOMIC CONCEPTS

That linear programming has a close relationship to traditional economic analysis should now be apparent. *In a two-product example the boundary of the feasibility area not only looks like a production possibility curve; that is precisely what it is. The isocontribution lines are the same isocontribution lines that appeared before.* The major difference between LP and the traditional analysis is that the curvilinear production possibility curve of traditional analyses is made up of straight-line segments in the LP formulation.

Linear programming relates to traditional economic analysis in other ways:

1. *Linear programming recognizes the irrelevance of fixed costs and focuses attention on the excess of incremental revenue over incremental costs*—and, in particular, on the contribution to overhead and profits. In this way it is consistent with the principles of incremental reasoning introduced in Chapter 2.

2. *Implicitly linear programming takes opportunity costs into account.*

This is quite clear in the simplex method (not described here), in which the procedure is one of comparing the additional revenue resulting from bringing a new product into the solution with the sacrifice of earnings from the products that must be given up.

3. *Linear programming also provides a basis for estimating the marginal revenue products of the inputs required.* It is interesting that this modern mathematical technique, which developed independently of economics, supplies those measures of marginal product which economists all along have insisted provide the correct criterion for decisions on the quantities of inputs to use.

Empirical studies and illustrations

Perhaps the oil industry has gone further than any other in the application of linear programming techniques. The four main categories of the oil business are: (1) exploration, (2) drilling and production, (3) manufacturing, and (4) distribution and marketing. Linear programming has made important contributions to the last three. In production, linear programming is used to find the optimal use of alternative reservoirs available to a company along with the use of crude oil from the outside.[1]

Applications in manufacturing (refining) are more numerous. For example, LP is used to find the optimal combination of products to be produced from given crude oil, to find the optimal blend of crude oils with varying characteristics to produce certain end products, or to solve some combination of these problems. Similarly, linear programming is used to determine the blend of various stocks coming from a refinery which will give the minimum cost of gasoline with required specifications. This blending program is complicated by the fact that the relation between tetraethyl lead content and octane rating is nonlinear, but a method of getting around the problem has been developed.

Oil companies have also used linear programming to minimize transportation costs from refineries to bulk terminals and to determine which refineries and bulk terminals should be expanded. They have also used the method to reduce costs from bulk terminals to service stations.

Similar applications are spreading to other industries, including scheduling of railway freight movements, the allocation of aircraft to alternative routes, and the determination of the optimum mix of products within a given plant. Each application presents its special difficulties, requiring

---

[1] W. W. Garvin, H. W. Grandall, J. B. John, and R. A. Spellman, "Applications of Linear Programming in the Oil Industry," *Management Science* (July 1957), reprinted in E. H. Bowman and R. B. Fetter, *Analyses of Industrial Operations* (Homewood, Ill.: Richard D. Irwin, Inc., 1959), pp. 3–27.

considerable versatility in adapting the general method of linear programming to the specific problems at hand.

SUMMARY

The chapter provided an introduction to the theory of production. It emphasized allocation of resources and determination of an optimum product mix. Production is any activity that transforms inputs into outputs having greater value. Both inputs and outputs are measured as *rates,* or quantities per unit of time. A specified relationship of various rates of output to various combinations of rates of inputs is called a *production function.*

The *marginal physical product* of an input is the ratio of increase in rate of output to increase in rate of input, or, roughly, it is the addition to output per period resulting from adding one unit to the quantity of input used per period. If output per accounting period is varied by changing the hours of running time of a plant or by changing multiples of identical machines and work crews, inputs are combined in constant proportions and their marginal physical products are expected to be *constant,* the same at all rates of output. If an input's marginal physical product, which is a quantity of output, is multiplied by the output's marginal revenue, the result is a monetary amount called the input's *marginal revenue product.*

If an input's marginal product is constant and the output's price is constant, the input's marginal revenue product is also constant. *If an input is not limited and has a constant marginal revenue product that is greater than the input's constant price, it is profitable to use as much of the input as possible.* However, if the input is drawn from local supplies, it may have a rising supply price as the firm attempts to increase the rate of use. *Marginal resource cost* is the ratio of increase in cost of the input per period to increase in use of the input per period; or, roughly, it is the addition to cost resulting from adding one more unit to the rate of use of the input. *If an input has rising marginal resource cost, the best rate of use is found where the rising marginal resource cost becomes equal to the input's marginal revenue product.*

If an input that is in limited supply has constant, but differing, marginal revenue products in each of several competing uses, the priority allocation principle applies: Allocate the input first to the activity in which the input's marginal revenue product is greatest until that activity reaches its limit, then to the activity with the next greatest marginal revenue product until the limit is reached, and so on, until the input is used up.

In cases where the demand curve for a product slopes down and to the right, the product's marginal revenue is below price at every sales rate and drops off as sales rate increases. As the product's marginal revenue falls, monetary value of the input's marginal product also falls even where marginal product is constant; marginal revenue product is the output's falling marginal revenue times the input's constant marginal product. In this situation, *the optimum rate of use of the input is found where falling marginal revenue product becomes equal to the input's price —or to the input's marginal resource cost, if the input has a rising supply curve.*

If an input that is in limited supply has decreasing marginal revenue product in each of several competing uses, the equimarginal principle applies. The input should be allocated among the several uses in such a way that the input's marginal revenue products are equal in the various uses. The *graphic method* of obtaining an *aggregate function* may be useful in applying the equimarginal principle; the method requires determining the value of marginal revenue product on the aggregate function at the limited quantity of the input; this value carried back to the individual functions yields optimum allocations of the input and (implicitly) outputs and pricing of the several products.

When the instantaneous rate of output is varied by changing the intensity of use of one variable input relative to other inputs, the law of variable proportions usually produces a short range of increasing marginal productivity of the input, then a longer range of approximately constant marginal productivity, and finally a range of decreasing marginal productivity. *Marginal product at a point on the production surface is defined by a function which is the first derivative of the production function with respect to the input in question.*

If an input has decreasing marginal productivity, it will have decreasing marginal revenue product even if the product's price is constant. In such a case, optimum use of the input can be derived *analytically* by: (1) multiplying the product's price times the input's marginal product function to obtain the input's marginal revenue product function, and (2) *setting the MRP function equal to the input's price.* If the input has rising marginal resource cost, the MRP function is set to equal the *MRC function.* When quantified estimates of the input-output function are not available, *incremental estimation* and *incremental reasoning* can be used in making resource allocation decisions.

A *product mix problem* occurs when two or more resources are limited and there are two or more products that require at least one of the limited resources. *Production possibility curves* define attainable combinations of products in the light of resource limitations. *Isocontribution lines* define combinations of products that have the same total contributions to overhead and possible profit. *Optimum product* mix is found at that point on a production possibility curve where it just touches the isocontribution line having the greatest value. Many production possibility curves are concave to the origin and can be approximated by linear segments, so that a convex polyhedral production possibility surface is formed. In this case, the optimum product mix is at one of the *corner points* of the surface and can be found by *linear programming* methods.

Sensitivity analysis determines the extent to which each item of data for a linear programming problem could be changed without changing the optimal solution. It also determines the effect upon the value of the solution per unit of change in each of the coefficients of the problem. Sensitivity analysis often provides information having a value similar to that of the solution, and should be a routine procedure when linear programming is used.

An input's marginal revenue product should always be calculated net of the cost of any variable inputs required. In linear programming, each product's contribution is calculated net of cost of any variable inputs that are required.

QUESTIONS

1. At the point of transition from short-run to long-run perspective, what is the change in the relation of inputs to outputs?

2. How does an input-output function differ from a production function?

3. What is meant by "marginal product"? What is meant by "constant marginal product"?

4. The general principle in determining usage of a single input that has a constant supply price and constant marginal revenue product in a single profitable use is simply to use as much of the input as possible. List possible limitations on the rate of use of such an input.

5. Suppose an input has a rising supply price with increases in the rate of procurement. Why and how is the input's marginal resource cost different from its supply price at any given rate of procurement?

6. Suppose other variable inputs are required. How does this requirement for other inputs affect the calculation of a given input's marginal revenue product?

7. What is the equimarginal principle? What conditions make the equimarginal principle applicable?

8. How is a product mix problem different from a situation involving equimarginal allocation of a limited resource among its various uses?

9. What determines whether a production possibility curve is curvilinear or simply a straight line?

10. What conditions must hold if an isocontribution line is to be straight (rather than curvilinear)?

PROBLEMS

1. At Radiology Associates, Dr. Jackson is the only person qualified to carry out a certain specialized procedure. On the average, she can provide this treatment to four patients in two hours.
   a. What is Jackson's marginal product in carrying out the procedure?
   b. Suppose Radiology Associates charges $30 per treatment for this particular procedure. What is Jackson's marginal revenue product?
   c. Assume that Jackson receives a weekly salary of $1,200 for 40 hours work. How much contribution does the firm have per hour of Jackson's time used in the above described procedure?
   d. How much contribution does the firm get per treatment administered?

2. Price of Product X, P_x, must be reduced as sales rate, Q_x, is increased. The following demand curve has been estimated for the product: $P_x = \$5 - \$0.0002Q_x$. Product X is a hand-crafted item with negligible materials cost, and it can be produced at a rate of three units of product for each hour of labor used. Labor is available at a constant price of $9 per employee hour.
   a. Derive the relation of total revenue to sales rate, Q_x.
   b. Derive the relation of marginal revenue to sales rate, Q_x.
   c. Derive the relation of labor's marginal revenue product to sales rate, Q_x, and to quantity of labor per period, Q_L.
   d. How much labor should the firm use? How much output should the firm produce?
   e. Assume that labor in part d above is not available at a constant price. Instead, labor has the following supply curve: $P_L = \$6 + \$0.0004Q_L$. Under the new conditions, how much labor should the firm use? How much output should the firm produce?

3. Appalachian Trading Company buys roots, leaves, bark, and fruits of selected wild plants. These products are brought in by independent gatherers. One particular kind of dried roots is used in blending herbal teas and can be sold to health food manufacturers for 20 cents per pound. The annual supply quantity, Q, in thousands of pounds, of these roots has been found to depend on Appalachian's posted offer price, P, in cents per pound. The estimated supply function is $Q = -200 + 20P$.
   a. How many pounds should Appalachian plan to buy? At what price?
   b. Assume that market conditions have changed. Appalachian must now prepare the roots for resale. Labor and materials used in cleaning the roots and tying them in 100-pound bundles cost $2.50 per bundle. Determine the new optimum annual quantity and the new optimum price to root gatherers.

4. A small firm is limited to no more than $80,000 of new investment during the current period. In subsequent periods, funds are expected to be adequate to support all profitable projects. Each of the following projects has been proposed for funding during the current period:

Project	Amount	Estimated rate of return (percent annually)
Expand inventory of finished product.......	$30,000	8.0%
Expand accounts receivable................	20,000	9.0
Expand raw materials inventory............	10,000	8.0
Market research...........................	30,000	10.0
Product development......................	20,000	9.5
Replace motor truck......................	30,000	8.0
Install coal burner in boiler................	10,000	8.5
Make investments outside the firm.........	Unlimited	7.0

How should the firm allocate the available funds?

5. For the hypothetical window-cleaning firm of Chapter 6, you are given the following:

Demand for window cleaning: $P_w = \$4 - \$0.0005Q_w$, in which P_w is price per standard window and Q is quantity of windows per week.

Demand for sand blasting: $P_b = \$4.50 - \$0.0006Q_b$, in which P_b is price per hundred square feet and Q_b is quantity of blasting in hundreds of square feet per week.

Marginal product of labor in window cleaning: constant at 5 windows per employee-hour.

Marginal product of labor in sand blasting: constant at 3 hundred square feet per employee-hour.

Maximum quantity of labor available: 360 employee-hours per week.

a. Determine the optimum allocation of labor between the two activities.
b. Determine the optimum pricing of the two services.
Hint: Follow the six-step procedure explained in the text.

6. Suppose the rate of production of Product T, Q_T, is related to the amount of labor used per period, X_L, by the following input-output function:

$$Q_T = 6X_L + 0.03X_L{}^2 - 0.0006X_L{}^3$$

Further, suppose Product T's price is a constant $3 and labor's wage is constant at $8 per hour. And assume that the sales rate is the same as the production rate.

a. How much labor should be used?
b. What is the optimum rate of production?

7. A manufacturer produces two types of fasteners. One of the fasteners is sold under the Royal brand name and the other under the Acme brand name. The Royal fasteners sell for $10 per package, while the Acme fasteners sell for $9.50 per package. The variable cost of the Royal fasteners is $5 per package. The Acme fasteners have a variable cost of $5.50 per package. Both the Royal and Acme fasteners must go through the stamping department and the plating and packaging department. The stamping department has 9,600 minutes per day available, and the plating and packaging department has 12,000 minutes per day available for use. Each package of Royal fasteners takes 4 minutes in the stamping department and 2 minutes in the plating and packaging department.

Each package of Acme fasteners takes 2 minutes in the stamping department and 10 minutes in the plating and packaging department.

   a. Solve for the optimum product mix and contribution graphically.

   b. Set this problem up as a linear programming problem.

   c. Determine what would happen if the prices and variable costs changed so that the contribution was $7 per package from the Royal brand and $3 per package from the Acme brand.

   8. The Artistic Ardvark, Inc., manufactures two art statues for sale to the general public. The "Antediluvian" work contributes $8 per unit to overhead and profit, while the "Futuristic" work contributes $6 per unit to overhead and profit. Each type of statue must pass through three departments: mixing, molding, and finishing. The following information has been gathered on the hours each type of statue requires in each department and the capacities of the departments.

Department	Antediluvian	Futuristic	Capacity, hours
Mixing...................	2	4	1,500
Molding.................	5	2	2,000
Finishing................	1	1	500

   a. Determine the optimum product mix and the optimum contribution using the graphic method.

   b. What would be the optimum product mix if the contributions changed to $5 for both types of statues? What would be the optimum contribution in this case? Does this situation violate the rule that an optimum solution will always be found at a corner point?

   c. Formulate the original example as an LP problem.

FURTHER READING

Dorfman, Robert. "Mathematical, or Linear, Programming: A Nonmathematical Approach." *American Economic Review,* December 1953.

Rappaport, Alfred. "Sensitivity Analysis in Decision Making." *Accounting Review,* July 1967.

Chapter 7

Cost minimization

Given a desired rate of production, how can the cost of this output be made as low as possible? This chapter discusses cost minimization by means of input substitutions and changes in plant and equipment. The problem is considered from both the short-run and the long-run points of view. Topics in the chapter include: technical substitutability of inputs, least-cost combinations of inputs as determined by their relative prices, linear programming formulation of cost minimization problems; expansion of the rate of output using least-cost combinations at each rate; cost curves of plants (operating curves) and some of their applications, economies of scale, and envelope curves (planning curves) and some of their managerial applications.

Cost minimization techniques are very useful to managers in all kinds of settings—businesses, nonprofit organizations, government agencies— and society as a whole will benefit from increased efficiency of resource utilization as its managers gain increased understanding of these methods.

TECHNICAL SUBSTITUTABILITY OF INPUTS

For an example of production in which one input can replace another, we shall return to the hypothetical window-cleaning firm. Figure 7–1 is a three-dimensional view of the firm's production surface. Length of the workday is fixed at 8 hours, and the amount of labor per day, as measured against the axis running down the left side of the figure, is varied by changing the size of the work force. There are various techniques of production using successively greater amounts of equipment leased on a day-to-day basis.

We shall assume that *labor per day is continuously variable* by bringing in part-time workers as desired. Further, *daily use of leased equipment is also continuously variable* by changing the amounts and kinds of equipment, day by day, as the manager wishes. Under these conditions,

Figure 7–1
A hypothetical production surface

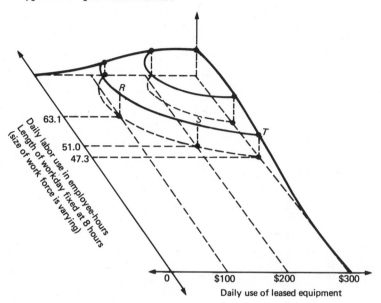

the production surface is like one side of a smoothly rounded hill. The height of the production surface, measured against the vertical axis, is daily output in number of windows washed. As the surface shown in Figure 7–1 is extended further into the quadrant, the hill goes up to a rounded crest and the surface then slopes down out of sight on the other side of the hill. The fact that this surface has a crest representing maximum possible daily output is explained by the limitation imposed by a fixed management input (planning, organizing, controlling, and so forth).

Isoquants

Look at Point R on the production surface in Figure 7–1; this is a daily output of 400 windows using a combination of 63.1 hours of labor and leased equipment costing $100 per day. Considering that the production surface is a smoothly rounded hill, it should be possible to move around the surface from Point R staying always at the same height;

Figure 7–2
Overhead view of production surface: An isoquant map

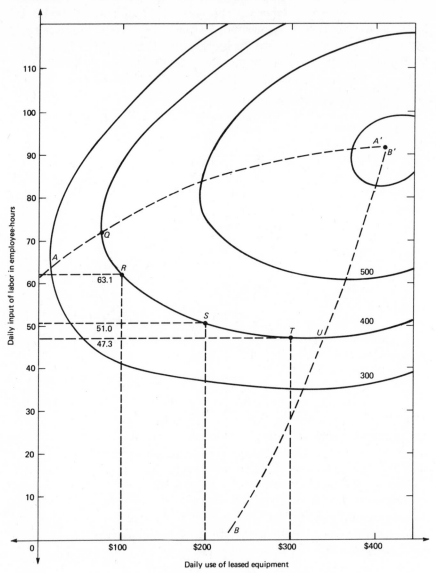

there are apparently many combinations of labor and equipment use that will yield the same daily output of 400 windows cleaned.

Suppose we move around the surface to Point S. In this change, labor is decreased by 12.1 hours to a lower rate of 51 hours per day. On the other hand, leased equipment cost is increased by $100 to a higher rate of

$200 per day. Assume labor is paid $10 per hour. How is total daily out-lay affected by the move from Point R to Point S? Daily labor cost is cut by $121 (12.1 hours times $10 per hour) and daily leased equipment rental is advanced by $100. So the net effect of this input substitution is to *reduce* total outlay by $21 per day.

Consider a move further around the surface at the same height, from Point S to Point T, keeping daily output constant at 400 windows cleaned. This second move decreases daily labor cost by $37 (labor is reduced by 3.7 hours per day to the new lower rate of 47.3 hours) and raises daily cost of leased equipment by $100. So the net effect is to *boost* total cost by $63 per day.

It can be seen that some input substitutions around the line of equal height, RST in Figure 7–1, are advantageous. Others are not. Of the three points considered above, the combination of labor and capital at Point S has the lowest cost. However, one is left with the uneasy feeling that some other points on contour RST may have even lower total cost. We need a method of finding *least-cost* combinations of inputs.

Finding least-cost combinations is easier if we look down on the pro-duction surface from directly overhead. Figure 7–2 is a view of the win-dow-cleaning firm's production surface from above. Curve QRSTU, which maintains a constant height of 400 windows per day in Figure 7–1, ap-pears as a projection to the labor-capital plane in Figure 7–2. QRSTU and the similar curves representing other constant rates of output now look like contour lines on a relief map.

Each *equal-quantity contour*, called an *isoquant*, connects various combinations of inputs that will yield a given rate of output. Only three contours have been drawn in Figure 7–2, but on the smoothly rounded production surface there are countless other contours—there is a contour for each and every feasible rate of output. And the inputs can be substi-tuted, one for another, in moving around each of the contours.

Marginal rates of technical substitution

Let us reexamine the movement from Point R to Point S in Figure 7–2. In this change, capital is substituted for labor while holding output constant at 400. The rate at which capital can replace labor over this range of the output contour is:

$$\frac{\Delta L}{\Delta K} = \frac{-12.1 \text{ hours per day}}{\$100 \text{ per day}} = -0.121 \text{ hours per } \$1$$

A ratio like $\Delta L/\Delta K$ is called a *marginal rate of technical substitution*, *MRTS*. It measures the amount of *reduction in one input* (in the ex-ample, labor) *per unit of increase in the other input* (in the example, capital), *maintaining constant output.* Such a ratio is the slope of a straight line from point to point over the discrete interval corresponding to the substitution of inputs. By making the changes in the inputs smaller and smaller, the *MRTS* ratio approaches the value of the slope of the isoquant *at a point.* We know that a curve like *QRSTU* in Figure 7–2 has an equation. The equation defines the relation of the input on the vertical axis to the input measured on the horizontal axis. Let labor be a function of capital, or $L = f(K)$. Then the marginal technical rate of substitution is $\partial L/\partial K$, the slope of the isoquant at a point, defined by the *first derivative* of the isoquant function with respect to the variable measured on the horizontal axis.

It can be seen in Figure 7–2 that the absolute values of the slopes of the isoquants are decreasing for moves down and to the right. Capital becomes less and less effective in replacing labor as more and more substitution is carried out. The *MRTS*, the rate at which one input will replace another with output held constant, must be somehow related to the marginal productivities of the two inputs. Can we pin down the nature of the relationship?

Again consider the move from Point R to Point S in Figure 7–2. Output is held constant at 400 windows per day. Therefore, the *decrease in production* because of using *less labor* must be exactly offset by the *increase in production* because of using *more capital.* Recall from Chapter 6 that the decrease in output, ΔQ_L, from using less labor must be the marginal product of labor times the reduction in labor in units, ΔL, so: $\Delta Q_L = MPP_L \cdot \Delta L$. Similarly, the increase in rate of output, ΔQ_K, by addition to daily use of capital, ΔK, is the marginal product of capital times the expansion of capital use in units, so: $\Delta Q_K = MPP_K \cdot \Delta K$. With output constant, the decrease in output because of cutting back on labor must be exactly offset by the increase in output through using more capital:

$$|\Delta Q_L| = \Delta Q_K \qquad \text{or} \qquad \Delta Q_L + \Delta Q_K = 0$$

$$|MPP_L \cdot \Delta L| = MPP_K \cdot \Delta K \qquad\qquad (7\text{–}1)$$

Multiplying both sides of Equation (7–1) by $1/\Delta K \cdot MPP_L$, we get:

$$\frac{|\Delta L \cdot MPP_L|}{\Delta K \cdot MPP_L} = \frac{\Delta K \cdot MPP_K}{\Delta K \cdot MPP_L}$$

or

$$\frac{|\Delta L|}{\Delta K} = \frac{MPP_K}{MPP_L} \qquad\qquad (7\text{–}2)$$

In words, Equation (7–2) says that the absolute value of the marginal rate of technical substitution is equal to the ratio of the marginal physical product of the *increasing* input to the marginal physical product of the *decreasing* input. And so we have pinned down the relationship of *MRTS* to the marginal productivities of the inputs. Further in this chapter, the above relationship will be useful.

ECONOMIC SUBSTITUTABILITY OF INPUTS

Diminishing marginal rates and ridge lines

In Figure 7–2, marginal rates of substitution of capital for labor are *diminishing* in absolute value as we move from Point Q down and to the right around Isoquant 400. Capital is a poorer and poorer substitute for labor as more and more substitution is carried out. This is understandable, since the most effective uses of capital are the first ones made as capital is increased, then the next most effective, and so on, whereas the least effective uses of labor are the first ones given up as labor is reduced, then the next least effective, and so on. Note that substitution reaches a *limit* at Point U where Isoquant 400 becomes horizontal. And, moving back up Isoquant 400, substituting labor for capital, we find that this substitution *also* reaches a limit at Point Q where Isoquant 400 becomes vertical.

Combinations of inputs on Isoquant 400 that are *outside* the range from Point Q to Point U could never be economical to use. In going up and to the right beyond Point Q, both labor and capital are being increased merely to maintain output constant (there is not enough management input to get efficient use of the increased quantities of labor and capital). Similarly, in going up and to the right beyond Point U both inputs are being increased with no change in output (again explained by insufficient management input).

By connecting all the points at which various isoquants become vertical in Figure 7–2, we obtain the boundary labeled AA', and by connecting all points at which various isoquants become horizontal we obtain the boundary labeled BB'. These boundaries are called *ridge lines;* they are the tops of the ridges along the production surface of Figure 7–1, as viewed from the origin. A rational manager would not knowingly use input combinations *outside* the ridge lines, since inputs are not free.

Isocost lines

Although input combinations *beyond* the ridge lines are known to be uneconomical and can be eliminated from further consideration, there are many combinations *between* the ridge lines on any one isoquant. One of these combinations has a lower cost than any other. How can the *least-cost combination* be determined?

In finding the least-cost combination, we shall use the concept of *isocost lines.* Any one isocost line connects *all those combinations of inputs that have a given total cost.* Look at Line $300 in Figure 7–3. This line connects all combinations of hours of labor (at $10 per hour) and daily outlay for equipment leasing (in dollars) that have a total cost of $300. The equation for the line is: $\$300 = \$10 \cdot L + \$1 \cdot K$, in which L is labor in hours per day and K is daily outlay for equipment rental in

Figure 7–3
Isoquant map with isocost lines superimposed

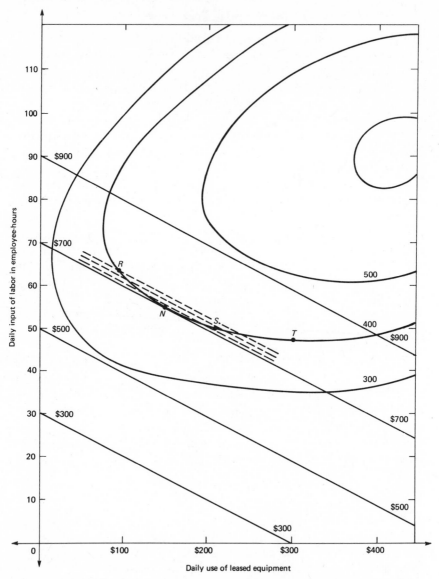

dollars.[1] The equation could be rearranged: $L = (\$300/\$10) - \$1(K/\$10)$, or $L = 30 - 0.1K$.

A *generalized equation* for an isocost line is $C = P_1X_1 + P_2X_2$, *in* which P_1 is the price of the input measured on the vertical axis and X_1

---

[1] In the example used here, capital input is measured in units of dollars of leased equipment expense per period. The price of *one* such unit is $1.

is the quantity of that input, P_2 is the price of the input measured on the horizontal axis and X_2 is the quantity of that input, and C is the given total cost. The generalized equation can be restated in a useful form as: $X_1 = C/P_1 - (P_2/P_1)X_2$. Note that the *slope* of the generalized isocost line is $-P_2/P_1$, the negative ratio of the price of the input measured on the *horizontal* axis to the price of the input measured on the *vertical* axis. Although only four isocost lines have been drawn in Figure 7–3, there are countless others—there is an isocost line for each total cost that one would wish to specify. Of course, "total cost" as used here means total cost of the *variable* inputs, or total variable cost.

Least-cost combinations of inputs

The objective is to find a least-cost combination of inputs for a given rate of output. Consider output rate 400 on Isoquant 400 in Figure 7–3. In moving around the isoquant from Point R to Point T, we move through many isocost lines, but none is lower in total variable cost than Isocost $700 which the isoquant barely touches at Point N. Point N *is* the least-cost combination of labor and capital on Isoquant 400, given the wage rate of $10 per hour and some set of equipment rental rates which is assumed constant for all examples in this chapter.

Let us examine Point N. It is a point of tangency of Isocost $700 and Isoquant 400—a point where the slopes of these two functions are equal. The slope of the *isoquant* is the marginal rate of technical substitution, $\Delta L/\Delta K$, and the slope of the *isocost line* is $-P_K/P_L$, the negative of the ratio of price of *horizontal* axis input to price of *vertical* axis input. At the point of tangency:

$$\frac{\Delta L}{\Delta K} = \frac{-P_K}{P_L} \tag{7–3}$$

By making the increments of labor and capital smaller and smaller, we find that the condition at the point of tangency approaches a limit:

$$\frac{\partial L}{\partial K} = \frac{-P_K}{P_L} \tag{7–4}$$

In words, Equation (7–4) says that, *at the least-cost point* on the isoquant, the marginal rate of technical substitution, which is diminishing in absolute value as we move down and to the right, becomes equal to the negative ratio of the input prices.

The logic of the requirement that the slopes of the functions must be equal is quite simple. Marginal rate of technical substitution, the slope of the particular isoquant, is the *physical* rate at which the inputs can be exchanged, *keeping output* constant. The negative inverse price ratio, *IPR*, the slope of all the isocost lines, is the market rate of substitution, the rate at which the inputs can be exchanged, *keeping cost constant*. If *MRTS* is greater than *IPR*, cost can be reduced by movement down and to the right along the isoquant, cutting through isocost lines of lower and lower value. A location like Point *N* is eventually reached, where the slopes of the functions are equal. This point is the least-cost combination of inputs on the given isoquant.

Finding a least-cost combination by the analytic method

If the equation for an isoquant is known, the least-cost combination of inputs on that isoquant for any given ratio of input prices can be determined analytically. The following steps are used: (1) take the first derivative of the isoquant equation with respect to the horizontal axis input, obtaining a function that is the slope of the isoquant; (2) set the slope function equal to the negative inverse ratio of input prices (the horizontal axis input price is in the numerator of the ratio); (3) solve the resulting equation for the amount of the *horizontal* axis input which is in the least-cost combination; and (4) substitute the value from the preceding step into the isoquant equation to obtain the amount of the *vertical* axis input.

To illustrate, the equation for Isoquant 400 in Figure 7–3 is:

$$L = 83.6 - 0.247K + 0.00042K^2$$

The first derivative of the equation with respect to K is:

$$\frac{\partial L}{\partial K} = -0.247 + 0.00084K$$

Using a wage of \$10 per employee-hour, set the derivative equal to the price ratio and solve:

$$-0.247 + 0.00084K = \frac{-1}{10} \qquad K = \$175$$

Substitute the solution value of K into the isoquant equation, and solve for the value of L:

$$L = 83.6 - 0.247 \cdot 175 + 0.00042 \cdot 175 \cdot 175$$
$$L = 53.24 \text{ employee-hours}$$

LINEAR PROGRAMMING FORMULATION OF LEAST-COST PROBLEMS

Blending and mixing problems are among the most important applications of the concept of least-cost combination of inputs. In these problems, the objective is to find a minimum cost blend or mix of available materials that will meet a set of standards or specifications. Such problems are very important in the petrochemical and animal-feeding industries, for example.

Petroleum refining produces numerous "fractions," each having its own flash point, vapor pressure, viscosity, density, and other measured characteristics. And each has its own opportunity cost—a price at which it could be sold to an outside firm. The objective is to find the minimum-cost blends of basic fractions that will make a finished product, such as a particular kind of gasoline, at least cost. The blending problem in making animal feeds, described in the following section, is formally similar.

Formulation of an animal feed

A hypothetical example illustrates the use of LP in finding least-cost combinations of inputs. The Arion Company manufactures a particular animal feed from a grain and an oilseed meal. The buyers of this feed mix have specified that it must meet at least the following minimal nutritional requirements: It must contain at least 800 units of nutritional component P (protein) and 1,200 units of nutritional component E (energy). The product is sold in 110-pound bags. Ingredient G (a grain) contains 5 units per pound of nutrient P and 15 units per pound of nutrient E. Ingredient OM (an oilseed meal) contains 10 units of nutrient

Table 7–1
Problem information (hypothetical least-cost problem)

	Amount contained		
Nutrient	Ingredient G (grain)	Ingredient OM (oilseed meal)	Minimal requirement
Component P (Protein)...............	5	10	800
Component E (Energy)...............	15	10	1,200
Cost/pound.........................	3¢	4¢	

P and 10 units of nutrient E per pound. The Arion Company must pay 3 cents per pound for ingredient G and 4 cents per pound for ingredient OM. The company wishes to determine the amount of each ingredient it should include in each 110-pound bag in order to meet the nutritional requirements while minimizing their expenditures. Table 7–1 summarizes the pertinent information.

Requirements for LP formulation. The requirements for formulating a least-cost input problem into the LP framework are basically the same as the requirements for product mix problems. They are presented below with only brief discussion since the reader should now be familiar with the basic approach.

1. *The objective function of the firm must be stated as a linear function of the cost of the inputs.* We define our two basic inputs as follows:

G = Number of pounds of grain included in the mixture

OM = Number of pounds of oilseed meal included in the mixture

Since the firm wishes to minimize its total cost for the mixture, the objective function may be stated mathematically as:

$$\text{Minimize } 3\text{\textcent } G + 4\text{\textcent } OM = \text{Total cost}$$

The linear objective function infers constant marginal costs of inputs. This implies constant supply price, thus constant marginal resource costs. No matter how many pounds of G are used in the mixture, the cost per pound is 3¢. The cost per pound of OM is 4¢ regardless of the quantity used.

2. *The restrictions placed on the blend must be stated explicitly as linear equalities or inequalities.* These restrictions again constitute the *constraints* of the problem.

For our example there are three constraints. Two are imposed by the necessary minimum nutritional requirements and one by the requirement that each sack contain at least 110 pounds. Stated mathematically the constraints are:

$$
\begin{aligned}
(1) \quad & 5 && + 10\,OM \geq && 800 \\
(2) \quad & 15 && + 10\,OM \geq && 1{,}200 \\
(3) \quad & G && + \quad OM \geq && 110
\end{aligned}
$$

The first constraint insures that the final mixture will contain at least 800 units of nutrient P. Each pound of G contains 5 units of nutrient P and each pound of OM contains 10 units of nutrient P. Therefore the total number of units of nutrient P is $5\,G + 10\,OM$, which must equal at least 800. The "greater than" ($>$) is used since we could feasibly include more than 800 units of nutrient P. The second constraint may be interpreted similarly for nutrient E. The third constraint ($G + OM \geq 110$) simply states that the total number of pounds in each bag must be at least 110. Readers should take care that they understand the significance of the linearity assumptions built into the constraints.

3. *Nonnegativity requirements must be recognized.* We must constrain each input to be either zero or positive, since a negative level of input has no physical meaning. Therefore we require that:

$$G \geq 0 \quad \text{and} \quad OM \geq 0$$

Additionally, the assumption of divisibility is made; i.e., input levels may assume fractional values.

The entire problem is summarized below and formulated in an LP framework.

G = Number of pounds of ingredient G included
in final mixture

OM = Number of pounds of ingredient OM included
in final mixture

$\left.\right\}$variables

(1) Minimize $C = 3¢\ G + 4¢\ OM$ } objective function

Subject to:

(2) $5\ G + 10\ OM \geq\ \ \ 800$
(3) $15\ G + 10\ OM \geq 1{,}200$ $\left.\right\}$constraints
(4) $\ \ \ \ G +\ \ \ \ OM \geq\ \ \ 110$

and

(5) $G \geq 0,\ OM \geq 0$} nonnegativity requirements

Management's problem is to find values for G and OM that satisfy the relations (2), (3), (4), and (5) and also minimize total cost.

The graphic solution

This problem may be solved algebraically or by the use of the simplex method mentioned earlier. However, since there are only two variables, we will solve it graphically. The basic steps laid out for solving product mix problems are appropriate for the solution of the least-cost combination of input problems also.

Step 1. Plot the constraints in the problem on a graph. Figure 7–4 is

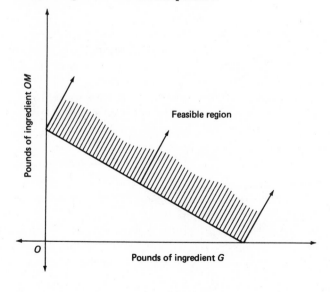

Figure 7–4
Feasible region for nutrient component *P*

such a graph. The horizontal axis represents the number of pounds of feed ingredient G, while the vertical axis represents the number of pounds of feed ingredient OM.

The line in the graph represents the constraint imposed by the minimum requirements for the number of units of nutrient P per bag of the final mixture. It was found by plotting the equation

$$5\,G + 10\,OM = 800$$

Since the actual constraint (2) is an inequality, each point on the line and every point *to the right* of the line represents an input combination which satisfies this constraint.

Figure 7–5
Feasible region for nutrient component *E*

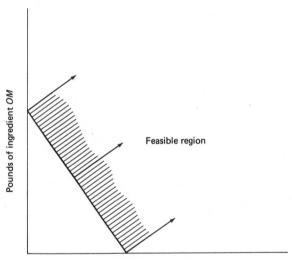

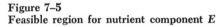

Similarly, in Figure 7–5 the constraint imposed by minimum requirements for nutrient E is plotted. Every point on the line and *to the right* of the line represents an input combination which satisfies the constraint

$$15\,G + 10\,OM \geq 1{,}200$$

Finally, in Figure 7–6 the constraint $G + OM \geq 110$ is plotted. This line is an isoquant showing all possible combinations of both inputs which total to 110 pounds in the final mixture.

In Figure 7–7 all three constraints are plotted on the same graph. Only those points that lie in the shaded area or on its boundary satisfy all three constraints. This set of points then comprises the feasible region.

Figure 7–6
Feasible region for bag weight

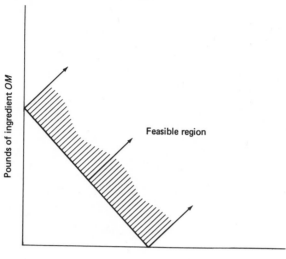

The problem is to select a point from this set of points that minimizes total cost.

Step 2. Calculate the coordinates of each corner point, i.e., each point at which two or more constraints intersect (including the nonnegativity constraints). It is obviously only necessary to calculate the corner points that are feasible. In this example, there are four such points labeled A, B, C, and D on Figure 7–7.

Point	Coordinates
A	(0,120)
B	(20,90)
C	(60,60)
D	(160,0)

Step 3. With all feasible input combinations delineated, the remaining task is to select the one that meets the objective of minimizing cost. The optimum solution must lie at a corner point of the feasible region.

The student may intuitively understand the reason for this by studying Figure 7–8. Figure 7–8 is the feasible region as depicted in Figure 7–7 with a set of isocost lines superimposed on it. Curve ABCD is an *isoquant* for a ration meeting certain requirements. Since the cost of each

Figure 7–7
Feasible region with all constraints

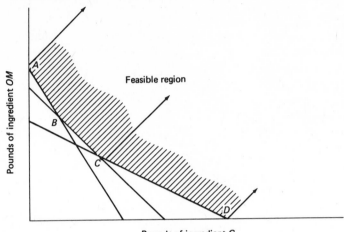

pound of G is 3¢ and each pound of OM costs 4¢, the total cost (TC) of
the mixture is $3\,G + 4\,OM$ (our objective equation). By plotting $3\,G +
4\,OM = TC$ and varying TC, a set of parallel isocost lines is generated.
For example, the line R was formed by plotting the equation

$$3\,G + 4\,OM = \$6$$

All points on this line represent input combinations resulting in a total
cost of $6. The isocost line S was found by plotting the equation

Figure 7–8
Feasible region with isocost curves

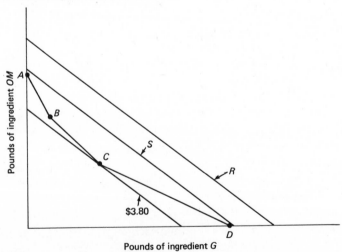

$$3\ G + 4\ OM = \$5$$

All input combinations on this line result in a total cost of \$5. Since the firm is trying to minimize total cost, a shift to the left of the isocost curve is advantageous. The rational firm will use an input combination found by shifting the isocost curve as far to the left as possible. However, since the constraints must be met, the isocost curve must have at least one point in common with the feasible region. It should therefore be obvious that the optimal solution will occur at a corner point of the feasible region.

The total cost for the input combination at each corner point is calculated below.

Corner point	Calculation	Total cost
(0,120)	3 (0) + 4 (120) =	\$4.80
(20,90)	3 (20) + 4 (90) =	\$4.20
(60,50)	3 (60) + 4 (50) =	\$3.80
(160,0)	3 (160) + 4 (0) =	\$4.80

Thus the optimum input combination is 60 pounds of ingredient G and 50 pounds of ingredient OM. The total cost will be \$3.80 for each 110-pound sack of the final mixture. It should be clear to the reader that such a mixture satisfies the minimum nutritional requirements.

Empirical illustration

Computone Systems, Inc., a firm with headquarters in Atlanta, Georgia, provides a service which the firm has named "Instant Linear Programming." This service is used by numerous animal and poultry food companies in formulating rations. A specialized console is provided to the user. At any time, night or day, seven days a week, the feed company nutritionist can quickly set up the ingredient costs and other data of a least-cost linear programming problem by flipping switches on the face of the console. He or she then dials the number of the company's central computer, waits for a tone, and presses a switch to send the problem inputs. Within minutes, the solution to the problem is printed at the feed company's console.

Figure 7–9 is an example of a Computone Systems, Inc. computer formulation for a poultry ration. Note that the printout includes complete nutritional specifications for the ration, the optimal formulation with price ranging for each ingredient, forcing and limiting of ingredients to reflect inventory and nutritional considerations, and the calculation of opportunity prices at which each unused ingredient would enter the for-

Figure 7–9
Least-cost formulation of a poultry ration

LEAST COST FORMULA

①

PLANT............COMPUTONE SYSTEMS, INC. #2
PRODUCT NO. 104
PRODUCT NAME.........BROILER FINISHER
DATE AND TIME.......04/10/73 18.08.21

②

③

AMOUNT	NUM	INGREDIENT NAME	SCALE READING	COST	LOW RANGE	HIGH RANGE	MIN	MAX
1080.94	061	CN GR YL 9.0/12	1080.9	3.20		4.47		
580.81	283	SOYBEAN ML S-49	1621.7	10.00	9.17	16.38		
141.95	072	CN GL ML-80/125	1763.7	13.20	11.79	28.88		
120.91	092	FAT AN&VEG HYDR	1884.6	9.00	3.67	26.35		140.0
43.17	217	PHOS DEFLUOR	1927.8	4.10	.45	18.93		
36.37	098	FEATHER ML HYD	1964.2	6.20	3.91	8.39		80.0
10.95	146	LIMESTONE	1975.1	.80		5.01		
10.00	125	FIXED INGRED	1985.1	18.00			10.0	10.0
6.00	107	FISH ML ANCHOVE	1991.1	19.50		20.73		6.0
2.91	251	SALT	1994.0	1.50		33.06		
2.00	319	VIT PMX BROIL-5	1996.0	48.00			2.0	2.0
1.00	063	COPPER SULFATE	1997.0	3.00			1.0	1.0
1.00	299	TR-MIN BROIL-DM	1998.0	10.10			1.0	1.0
1.00	060	COCCIDIOSTAT	1999.0	100.00			1.0	1.0
.98	310	VIT A 30,000	2000.0	30.00		230.06		

④ $129.14 PER TON

⑤

002	ALFA,DHY 17-516	4.00	1.09	
156	MT&BONE SCRP-50	12.50	8.30	200.00
057	CN GR YL 8.0/12	99.00	3.01	
060	CN GR YL 8.9/12	99.00	0.08	
147	LYSINE-L 50PCT	999.00	84.99	

① FORMULA SPECIFICATIONS
② OPTIMUM FORMULATION
③ INVENTORY RESTRICTIONS
④ FORMULA COST
⑤ OPPORTUNITY PRICES FOR UNUSED INGREDIENTS

computone
SYSTEMS, INC. 361 E Paces Ferry Road, N E. Atlanta, Georgia 30305

⑥

RESTRICTION NAME	MINIMUM	ACTUAL	MAXIMUM	NUTRIENT COST
WEIGHT	1.00	1.00	1.00	4.0367
MET ENERGY POULTRY	1500.00	1500.00	1500.00	.0035
PRODUCTIVE ENERGY		1082.96		
CRUDE PROTEIN	20.50	24.72		
DIGESTABLE PROTEIN		21.65		
ARGININE	1.15	1.55		
LYSINE	1.10	1.10		1.7805
METHIONINE	.45	.45		3.5642
METH & CYSTINE	.84	.84		1.3610
TRYPTOPHANE	.21	.28		
GLYCINE		1.17		
HISTIDINE		.57		
LEUCINE		2.41		
ISOLEUCINE		1.18		
PHENYLALANINE		1.31		
PHENYL & TYROSINE		2.27		
THREONINE		.99		
VALINE		1.28		
CRUDE FAT		8.55		
CRUDE FIBER		2.51		
MOISTURE		8.81		
ASH		5.34		
CALCIUM	1.00	1.00	1.05	.1203
PHOSPHORUS-AVAIL	.55	.55	.57	.2031
PHOSPHORUS-TOTAL		.78		
SALT		.24		
SODIUM	.20	.20	.30	.1403
POTASSIUM		.40.60		
MANGANESE		40.60		
ZINC		31.50		
IRON		118.70		
COPPER		62.61		
IODINE		.12		
XANTHOPHYLL	10.00	15.24		
CAROTENE		1.54		
VITAMIN A	4.00	4.00		.0076
VITAMIN E		2.68		
THIAMIN		1.27		
RIBOFLAVIN		1.98		
NIACIN		18.15		
PANTOTHENIC ACID		5.46		
CHOLINE		524.40		
PYRIDOXINE		2.93		
FOLACIN		.25		
BIOTIN		.06		
VITAMIN B-12		4.21		

PRODUCT PRICING OPTION

PLANT............COMPUTONE SYSTEMS, INC. #2
DATE AND TIME.....04/11/73 11.38.54

		LAST FORMULA	NEW FORM			LAST FORM			TOTAL	
PROD NUM	DATE	ORIG $ TON	ACT $ TON	ACT $ TON	PURCH MARGIN	MARKET $ TON	MARGIN TON	MARKET VALUE TON	CWT	
102	04/04/73	128.33	130.54	130.54	4.61	135.15	10.00	145.15	7.26	
104	04/11/73	129.14	130.20	128.27	6.51	136.71	6.00	142.71	7.14	
112	03/15/73	131.06	122.54	122.54	6.29	128.83	18.00	146.83	7.34	
601	03/28/73	123.03	123.71	123.71	11.18	134.89	32.00	166.89	8.34	
653	03/15/73	83.19	78.67	78.67	1.94	80.61	23.00	103.61	5.18	
664	04/03/73	77.53	81.86	78.09	-1.62	80.24	14.00	94.24	4.71	
803	03/28/73	98.76	93.50	92.95	-1.02	92.48	22.00	114.48	5.72	
822	04/11/73	75.39	76.50	74.25	-.87	75.63	16.00	91.63	4.58	
841	04/11/73	82.31	82.31	82.31	-1.38	80.93	25.00	105.93	5.30	
851	03/02/73	63.25	69.06	66.41	-.22	68.83	20.00	88.83	4.44	

① ② ③ ④ ⑤ ⑥ ⑦

① Least Cost Amount from Last Solution
② Last Solution at Actual Costs
③ New Least-Cost Solution at Actual Costs
④ Column ⑤ minus Column ②
⑤ Last Solution at Market Costs
⑥ Margin Value Previously Stored
⑦ Column ⑤ plus Column ⑥

SIXTY NUTRIENT VALUES FOR EACH INGREDIENT
SOLVES PROBLEMS WITH UP TO
40 INGREDIENTS AND 40 NUTRIENT RESTRICTIONS

For Additional Information Phone: Area Code (404) 261-0070
or write COMPUTERIZED FORMULATION DIVISION
COMPUTONE SYSTEMS, INC.
361 East Paces Ferry Road, N. E.
Atlanta, Georgia 30305

INVENTORY OPTION

PLANT............COMPUTONE SYSTEMS, INC. #2
DATE AND TIME......04/11/73 11.43.46
OPTION.....00 INGREDIENT USAGE REPORT

NUM	NAME	POUNDS	TONS	COST TONS
2	ALFA,DHY 17-516	28481.49	14.2500	1139.
4	ALFA,DHY 20-660	1463.47	.7300	73.
50	COCCIDIOSTAT	199.99	.1000	200.
53	COPPER SULFATE	119.99	.0600	3.
61	CN GR YL 9.0/12	859641.68	429.8200	28368.
69	CORN GLUTEN FD	12000.00	6.0000	540.
72	CN GL ML-80/125	18590.81	9.3000	2463.
79	COTSD ML SOL-44	46087.73	23.0400	3433.
86	DIST DR SOL CN	52221.47	26.1100	2611.
92	FAT AN&VEG HYDR	82593.53	41.3000	7433.
98	FEATHER ML HYD	11645.29	5.8200	722.
107	FISH ML ANCHOVE	720.00	.3600	140.
113	FISH ML MENHADN	11608.09	5.8000	2553.
125	FIXED INGRED	5799.99	2.9000	1044.
138	HOMINY FD YL	4812.17	2.4100	141.
146	LIMESTONE	31770.29	15.8900	190.
160	METH DL-98	590.01	.3000	590.
161	METH-100	313.46	.1600	329.
163	MILO-9	219815.45	109.9100	6374.
172	MOLASSES, CANE	32000.00	16.0000	1020.
201	PH 18.5-20 CA22	1581.14	.7900	69.
217	PHOS DEFLUOR	18585.77	9.2900	762.
231	POUL BY-PROD ML	20000.00	10.0000	3300.
244	RICE MILL FEED	2368.62	1.1800	33.
251	SALT	5480.97	2.7400	82.
283	SOYBEAN ML S-49	286108.76	143.0500	28610.
299	TR-MIN BROIL-DM	119.99	.0600	12.
308	UREA-281 45PCT	11547.83	5.7700	665.
310	VIT A 30,000	623.04	.3100	186.
319	VIT PMX BROIL-5	240.00	.1200	115.
328	VIT PMX SWN 769	353.14	.1800	70.
340	WHEAT MIDDS STD	260014.37	130.0100	9750.
734	DICALCIUM PHOSPHATE	21226.29	10.6100	1252.
961	VIT PX LAY 5.7	1275.00	.6400	255.
	TOTALS	2049999.83	1025.0000	104529.

PROD	POUNDS	TONS	PROD	POUNDS	TONS
102	160000.00	80.00	104	240000.00	120.00
112	400000.00	200.00	601	200000.00	100.00
653	80000.00	40.00	664	60000.00	30.00
803	170000.00	85.00	822	240000.00	120.00
841	240000.00	120.00	851	260000.00	130.00
TOTAL	2050000.00	1025.00			

Figure 7–10
Least-cost formulation of a sausage

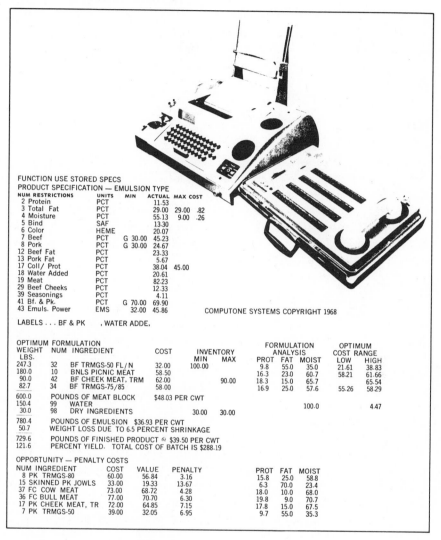

```
FUNCTION USE STORED SPECS
PRODUCT SPECIFICATION — EMULSION TYPE
NUM RESTRICTIONS      UNITS    MIN    ACTUAL  MAX COST
  2 Protein           PCT             11.53
  3 Total  Fat        PCT      29.00  29.00    .82
  4 Moisture          PCT      55.13   9.00    .26
  5 Bind              SAF             13.30
  6 Color             HEME            20.07
  7 Beef              PCT    G 30.00  45.23
  8 Pork              PCT    G 30.00  24.67
 12 Beef Fat          PCT             23.33
 13 Pork Fat          PCT              5.67
 17 Coll/ Prot        PCT             38.04  45.00
 18 Water Added       PCT             20.61
 19 Meat              PCT             82.23
 29 Beef Cheeks       PCT             12.33
 39 Seasonings        PCT              4.11
 41 Bf. & Pk.         PCT    G 70.00  69.90
 43 Emuls. Power      EMS      32.00  45.86      COMPUTONE SYSTEMS COPYRIGHT 1968

LABELS . . . BF & PK    , WATER ADDE.
```

OPTIMUM FORMULATION WEIGHT LBS.	NUM	INGREDIENT	COST	INVENTORY MIN	MAX	FORMULATION ANALYSIS PROT	FAT	MOIST	OPTIMUM COST RANGE LOW	HIGH
247.3	32	BF TRMGS-50 FL/N	32.00	100.00		9.8	55.0	35.0	21.61	38.83
180.0	10	BNLS PICNIC MEAT	58.50			16.3	23.0	60.7	58.21	61.66
90.0	42	BF CHEEK MEAT, TRM	62.00		90.00	18.3	15.0	65.7		65.54
82.7	34	BF TRMGS-75/85	58.00			16.9	25.0	57.6	55.26	58.29
600.0		POUNDS OF MEAT BLOCK $48.03 PER CWT								
150.4	99	WATER						100.0		4.47
30.0	98	DRY INGREDIENTS		30.00	30.00					
780.4		POUNDS OF EMULSION $36.93 PER CWT								
50.7		WEIGHT LOSS DUE TO 6.5 PERCENT SHRINKAGE								
729.6		POUNDS OF FINISHED PRODUCT @ $39.50 PER CWT								
121.6		PERCENT YIELD. TOTAL COST OF BATCH IS $288.19								

OPPORTUNITY — PENALTY COSTS NUM	INGREDIENT	COST	VALUE	PENALTY	PROT	FAT	MOIST
8	PK TRMGS-80	60.00	56.84	3.16	15.8	25.0	58.8
15	SKINNED PK JOWLS	33.00	19.33	13.67	6.3	70.0	23.4
37	FC COW MEAT	73.00	68.72	4.28	18.0	10.0	68.0
36	FC BULL MEAT	77.00	70.70	6.30	19.8	9.0	70.7
17	PK CHEEK MEAT, TR	72.00	64.85	7.15	17.8	15.0	67.5
7	PK TRMGS-50	39.00	32.05	6.95	9.7	55.0	35.3

mulation. Product pricing and perpetual inventory options are also available, as shown in the figure.

Computone Systems, Inc., provides a similar service for meat companies, in which linear programming is used to determine least-cost combinations of ingredients for various sausages. Figure 7–10 shows a Computone "mini-terminal" (it is smaller than the company's standard console) and an example of a least-cost sausage formulation. The printout includes incremental cost for each effective restriction (reduction in cost if the restriction is relaxed by one unit), price ranging for each ingredient included in the least-cost formulation, and opportunity prices for each ingredient that does not enter the formulation.

These are examples of highly sophisticated planning techniques that are economically available to medium and small firms from vendors of management services.

THE EXPANSION PATH

As a firm increases or decreases its rate of production, it is desirable to obtain each successive production rate at its own lowest cost. A curve across the production surface connecting all of the least-cost combinations of inputs for various rates of production is called an *expansion path* —a path of expansion of output at the least cost per period for each rate of output. Figure 7–11 shows an expansion path passing through Points *X*, *Y*, and *Z* on Isoquants 300, 400, and 500, respectively, of the hypothetical window-cleaning firm. The line also passes through least-cost combinations on innumerable isoquants corresponding to other rates of output.

If a manager has equations for some of the isoquants, he or she can determine the least-cost points on these by using the analytic method described in the first part of this chapter. It will be recalled that this method consists of setting the first derivative of the isoquant (with respect to the input measured on the horizontal axis) equal to the *inverse* ratio of input prices (price of the input measured on the *horizontal* axis is in the *numerator* of the price ratio) and solving the equation to obtain the amount of the input used as measured on the horizontal axis. Alternately, if a manager has a set of linear coefficients and restrictions that specify the required characteristics of input combinations at each rate of output, he or she can use a series of linear programming formulations to determine the least-cost points on the expansion path. (The LP method was described in the second part of this chapter.)

A great deal of managerial planning is carried out in terms of analytic calculations or linear programming formulations as described above. However, managers must often make decisions about input substitution under conditions of limited information. Managers typically know the combination of inputs that are currently used and the current rate of output. Further, they may feel that they can make good estimates of the effects upon output of relatively small increases or decreases in either of the inputs. Now managers having no more information than just described might feel that they could not carry out cost-reducing input substitutions. But they would be wrong. They do have enough information to proceed, as shall be shown in the next section.

Figure 7–11
An expansion path

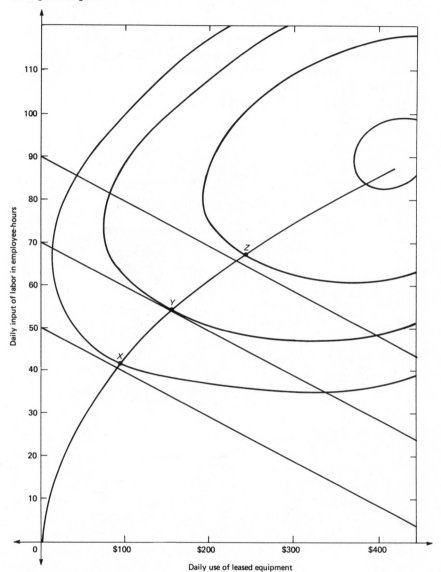

Daily input of labor in employee-hours

Daily use of leased equipment

Using incremental reasoning in decisions about input substitution

In the first part of this chapter, it was demonstrated that the absolute value of the slope of an isoquant *at any given point* is the ratio *there* of the marginal products of the inputs. In equation (7–2), which is reproduced below. we found that:

$$\frac{|\Delta L|}{\Delta K} = \frac{MPP_K}{MPP_L} \tag{7-2}$$

It was also shown that the least-cost combination of inputs is at a point on the isoquant where the absolute value of the isoquant's slope is equal to the inverse ratio of input prices (price of input measured on horizontal axis is in the numerator of the ratio). By substitution of the right side from Equation (7–2), the condition of equality of absolute value of slope to inverse ratio of prices can be stated as follows:

|Isoquant slope| = Ratio of input prices

$$\frac{MPP_K}{MPP_L} = \frac{P_K}{P_L} \tag{7-5}$$

Multiplying both sides of Equation (7–5) by MPP_L/P_K, we get:

$$\frac{MPP_K}{P_K} = \frac{MPP_L}{P_L} \tag{7-6}$$

Equation (7–6) says, roughly, that *at the least-cost point on a labor-capital isoquant, the marginal productivity of the last dollar spent on use of capital is equal to the marginal productivity of the last dollar spent to buy services of labor.*

Consider this. If managers can estimate the effect upon output of a small change in spending on the use of capital, they can certainly then calculate the increase in output *per additional dollar spent.* And if they can estimate the effect upon output of a small change in labor input, they can go on to calculate the increase in output *per additional dollar spent* for labor. If the results per dollar spent are unequal, managers should cut back spending on the input that is least effective per dollar spent and should maintain the rate of output by stepping up spending on the input that is more effective per dollar spent.

Look at an example of the use of incremental reasoning in a decision about input substitution. Suppose a manager is presently at Point *A* on the production surface of Figure 7–12. He is using 60 hours of labor per day with $120 daily cost of leased equipment, and he is getting an output of 400 windows per day. From Point *A* for a move in the direction of Point *B* he estimates that he could increase output 25 windows per day by increasing labor input 8 hours—one employee-day or $80, if $P_L =$ $10 per hour. This result works out to 0.31 windows per $1 spent. On the other hand, from Point *A* in the direction of Point *C* he estimates that an increase of $50 per day in leased equipment cost would increase output by 33 windows per day, or by 0.66 windows per $1 spent.

The manager's calculations indicate that he should *cut back on spend-*

Figure 7–12
Incremental reasoning and incremental searching in decisions about input substitution

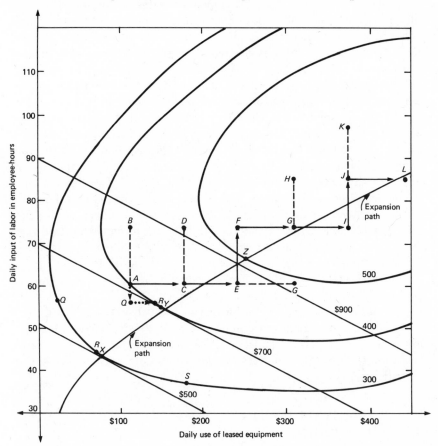

ing for labor and *step up spending on equipment leasing* (since capital gives a greater increase per dollar spent than does labor). Suppose he cuts back outlay for labor by $40 per day, which would reduce output by a little more than 12 windows per day, moving him to Point Q on the production surface. But he increases equipment leasing by $20 per day, which would increase output by a little more than 13 windows per day, moving him from Point Q to Point R just above Isoquant 400. Daily output is a bit more and the input substitution has reduced daily cost by $20. *This kind of estimation and incremental reasoning are within the capabilities of most managers. They require only knowledge of current inputs and output, plus estimates that are not difficult for experienced work supervisors.*

Incremental searching

As managers make substantial changes in rates of output, they typically carry out a "search" process that brings them close to the expansion path and keeps them there. Remember that they do not usually know where the expansion path is located. The search process may not be deliberate—but it works.

Consider the case of a manager at Point A on the production surface of Figure 7–12. She intends to make a sizable increase in rate of production. She has estimated that results per additional dollar spent on equipment leasing are better than results per additional dollar spent on labor. A move toward Point C is better than a move toward Point B, so she does move to Point C, getting all of the first increase in daily output by increasing daily outlay for equipment rental.

The next step in the search process takes place on the next large increase in rate of output. Being at Point C, the manager makes new estimates of productivity per additional dollar spent on each of the variable inputs, and finds capital more productive per dollar than labor. In this way, she decides to move to Point E rather than to Point D.

In further expansions of the firm's production rate, this simple method could select Points F, G, I, and J, successively. It can be seen that the use of common sense in deciding which of the two variable inputs is to be the base of the next increase in output is the driving force in a search process that goes toward and stays near the optimum expansion path. This in spite of the fact that the manager does not *know* the location of the path.

OTHER FORMS OF INPUT SUBSTITUTABILITY

Discrete substitutability at diminishing rates

There are many instances in which production technology and/or institutional arrangements do not permit *continuous* input substitutability at diminishing rates—the kind of substitution to which so much attention has been given up to this point. For example, inputs may be only *discretely* substitutable at diminishing rates. The firm in Figure 7–12 could face a hiring rule requiring that each worker must be given at least a full workday (no part-time hiring allowed). In such a case, Isoquant 300 in the figure would continue to make a continuous technological trace, but the only input combinations *institutionally permitted* to the firm would be points on the isoquant, such as Points Q, R, and S. Or, as is likely, variation in daily equipment leasing might be in terms of discrete changes in the kinds of equipment used and in individual pieces of equipment. In this case, changes in daily outlay for equipment leasing would be *technologically confined* to point-to-point changes across the production surface, and each isoquant would consist of a series of points rather than a continuous trace.

What is the effect of being restricted to *discrete changes* in input combinations? The principles of cost minimization are still the same. It pays to move down and to the right, from point to point, if the marginal rate of substitution is greater than the inverse ratio of input prices. But the decision process takes the following incremental form: Is the absolute value of the *incremental* reduction in cost of the decreased input greater than the *incremental* rise in cost of the increased input? As an example:

$$\text{Is } |\Delta L \cdot P_L| > \Delta K \cdot P_K?$$
$$\text{Is } |-8 \cdot \$10 \text{ per hour}| > \$40 \text{ per day?}$$

If, for either technological or institutional reasons, incremental changes in inputs cannot be matched so as to hold the output rate *constant,* decisions about input substitution may require more careful consideration. Substitution obviously is desirable if cost is reduced as output is increased. In the event that cost is cut but output is *also* curtailed, the foregone value of output lost should be compared with the reduction in cost. On the other hand, if cost is increased and output is also greater, the value of the added production should be compared with the additional cost.

Continuous substitutability at constant rates

Basic materials often substitute at constant, rather than diminishing, rates. Energy sources typically substitute at constant rates. One class or configuration of labor may substitute for another at constant rates. Examples of constant-rate substitution are: aluminum for steel in making parts for auto bodies; rayon for cotton in making textile fabrics; natural gas for fuel oil in firing steam boilers for power generation; concrete for asphalt in surfacing parking areas and driveways; and skilled independent workers in replacing less skilled workers under more supervision.

If one input substitutes for another at a *constant rate*, the isoquants are *straight lines*, as shown in Figure 7–13. If input prices are constant, the isocost functions are also straight lines, as illustrated by the dashed traces for Isocosts $100, $200, and $300 in Figure 7–13. Obviously, the least-cost combination for a given rate of output, such as Output 2,000 in Figure 7–13, will be found at *one of the ends of the isoquant,* depending on the slopes of the isocost lines and thus on the relative prices of the inputs. In general, only one of the inputs will be used. For example, only Input *B* would be used in Figure 7–13.

If the price of Input *B* in Figure 7–13 were increased relative to the price of Input *A,* the isocost lines would all become steeper. At some

Figure 7–13
Inputs substituting at constant rates

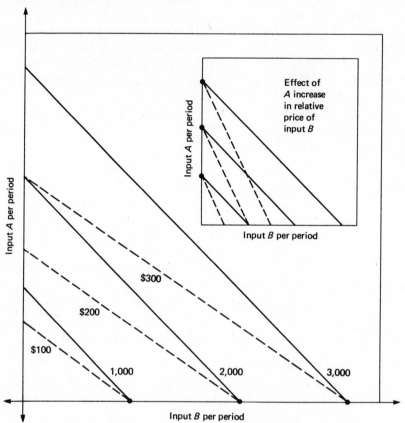

ratio of Input *B*'s price to that of Input *A*, the isocost lines would be parallel to the isoquants and cost would be the same for all input combinations on any given isoquant. If the price of Input *B* should then increase further in relation to the price of Input *A*, all of the least-cost combinations at various rates of output would consist only of amounts of Input *A* and the situation would be as depicted in the inset diagram of Figure 7–13.

Input combination in constant proportions

Some production processes use inputs in proportions specified by formulations or recipes. Examples are: combining sand and cement in making a particular grade of concrete; combining iron ore, lime, and coke in making a particular grade of steel; mixing flour, milk, yeast, and other

Figure 7–14
Inputs that must be combined in fixed proportions

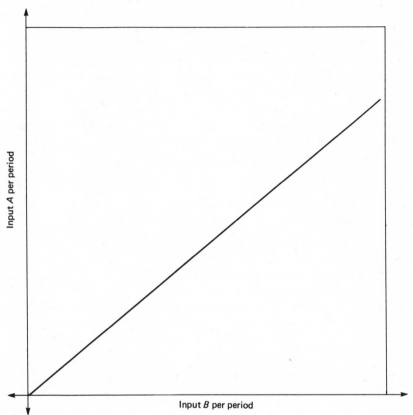

Input *A* per period

Input *B* per period

ingredients in baking a particular kind of bread; and making syrup for a soft drink by mixing sugar, water, and a particular combination of flavorings.

If inputs must be *combined in fixed proportions*, isoquants take the form of *points on a process ray* from the origin as depicted in Figure 7–14. In such cases, there is only one combination of inputs for any given rate of output. Changes in relative prices of inputs, although changing the slopes of isocost lines, do *not* affect the combinations of inputs that are used at various rates of output.

SHORT-RUN COST FUNCTIONS

From here to the end of the chapter we shall deal only with costs of *continuative* production. By "continuative" production, we mean that *production of the particular product or service is expected to continue indefinitely into the future,* so that durable production inputs are to be replaced as they depreciate, the "plant" is to be kept in place indefinitely, and the termination value of the plant at the planning horizon is based on an expectation of continued production of the same product or service. Continuative production contrasts with a *discrete run of production,* in which management has definite plans to terminate production within the planning horizon and must consider costs of amortizing specialized durable inputs that will not be worn out during the production run, start-up costs, learning costs, opportunity costs of delayed completion, and so forth. Note that continuative production is *not* necessarily *continuous* production; a plant that runs one shift per day, or even one season per year, can be analyzed as a continuative case.

Contrasts: Input-output function, scale line, and expansion path

A cost function is a relation of cost of inputs used per period to various rates of output; a *short-run* cost function is one in which cost per period is fixed for one or more of the inputs, regardless of the rate of output; a *short-run total variable cost function* shows the total cost of only the variable inputs used at various rates of production. Figure 7–15 shows the total cost of labor and equipment rental for the hypothetical window-

Figure 7–15
Total cost for various rates of output under three sets of assumptions about variability of inputs

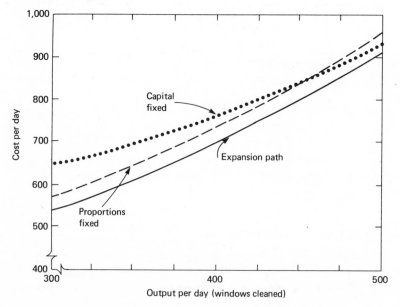

cleaning firm at various rates of output for three sets of assumptions about the variability of inputs.

The three set of assumptions about variation in inputs are depicted in Figure 7–16. The *dotted* line in Figure 7–16 connects all those input combinations found on an *input-output function in which labor input rate is varied but equipment rental is held constant* at $300 per day; and the *dotted* trace in Figure 7–15 is the resulting *total variable cost curve.* Cost rises at an increasing rate on this dotted curve because of the operation of the law of variable proportions in the range of diminishing marginal productivity of the labor input. Any number of other input-output functions could be traced across the production surface, each corresponding to variation in rate of labor input as rented equipment is held constant at some particular rate per day, and each input-output function would generate a total variable cost curve.

Figure 7–16
Contrasts: Input-output function, scale line, and expansion path

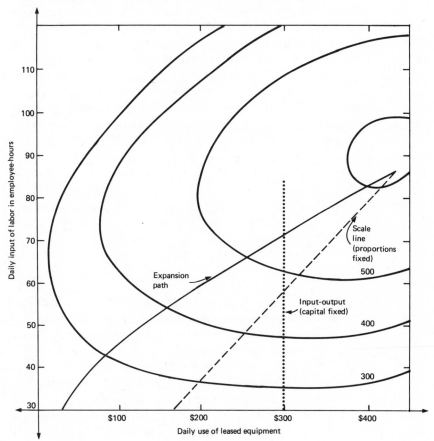

The *dashed* line in Figure 7–16 shows the combinations of inputs used on a *constant-proportions process ray,* or scale line, in which the *ratio of equipment rental to labor input is held constant* at $5 daily rental per employee-hour of labor, and the *dashed* trace in Figure 7–15 is the corresponding *total variable cost curve.* The dashed cost curve rises at an increasing rate as output increases; in this instance, we are looking at a mixture of the scale effect with the law of variable proportions. The scale effect, resulting from increasing both capital and labor in constant proportions, would tend to cause cost to increase at a decreasing rate, but the scale effect is more than offset by the diminishing marginal productivities of capital and labor as they are added to a fixed bundle of management input. Innumerable other constant-proportions process rays could be laid out across the production surface, and each would define a total variable cost curve.

The *solid* trace in Figure 7–16 shows *least-cost combinations of inputs used on the expansion path* for a wage rate of $10 per hour and equipment rental rates as assumed constant for the examples in this chapter, and the *solid* curve in Figure 7–15 is the *total variable cost curve* corresponding to the expansion path. Cost rises at an increasing rate on this curve because the diminishing marginal productivity of the two variable inputs is overcoming the combined effects of scale and input substitutions, both of which would tend to cause cost to increase at a decreasing rate. For the given set of input prices, there is only one expansion path, but variations in the ratio of input prices would generate other paths and each of these would have a corresponding total variable cost curve.

If the management input were being varied along with capital and labor, so as to get least-cost combinations of *all* inputs at each rate of output, we would expect total variable cost to increase at a decreasing rate because of *economies of scale. Economies of scale are a mixture of the scale effect with economies of input substitution as the rate of output is increased.* They can be observed in the long-run cost curves which are discussed in a section to follow.

Total cost curves for a given plant

As shown above, for any given set of input prices there is an expansion path that defines the least-cost combinations of variable inputs and thus specifies the lowest total *variable cost* attainable at each rate of output. The variable cost function derived from the expansion path of Figure 7–16 is depicted in Figure 7–17A. Any total variable cost curve derives its form from the character of the production surface *and* from the possibilities for economic input substitution along the expansion path. Variable cost functions with gentle S shapes similar to the one depicted in Figure 7–17A are often found in practical situations. Near the origin, variable cost is increasing at a decreasing rate, whereas near the point of maximum output, variable cost is increasing at an increasing rate.

By adding fixed costs per period to variable cost, we obtain a function that relates total cost per period to the plant's output. To illustrate, assumed fixed costs of $300 per day have been added to the total variable cost function in Figure 7–17A. The presence of fixed costs per period is explained by inputs that must be treated as fixed. We shall call the bundle of fixed inputs a *plant*. In regarding some inputs as fixed, we are

Figure 7–17A
Total fixed, total variable, and total costs per period at various rates of output in a hypothetical plant

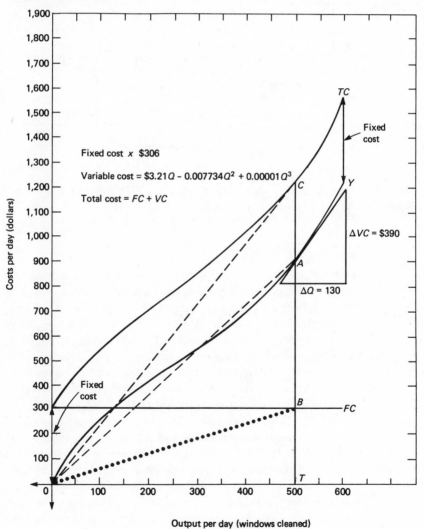

Fixed cost x $306

Variable cost ≈ $3.21Q − 0.007734Q^2 + 0.00001Q^3

Total cost = FC + VC

Output per day (windows cleaned)

Figure 7–17B
Marginal, average variable, average fixed, and average total cost at various rates of
output in a hypothetical plant

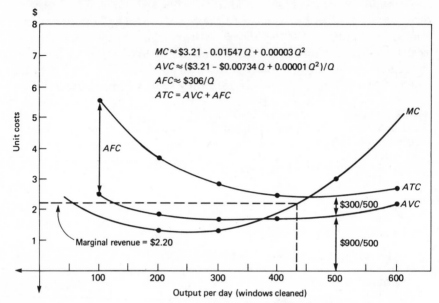

$$MC \approx \$3.21 - 0.01547\,Q + 0.00003\,Q^2$$
$$AVC \approx (\$3.21 - \$0.00734\,Q + 0.00001\,Q^2)/Q$$
$$AFC \approx \$306/Q$$
$$ATC = AVC + AFC$$

viewing production in the short-run perspective. Thus, a cost curve corresponding to a given plant is a *short-run cost curve*.

Unit cost curves for a given plant

Marginal cost at any given rate of output is the ratio of change in cost
per period to change in output per period, or roughly the increase in total
cost per period due to the addition of the last unit to the rate of output.
For example, marginal cost at Point *A* on the total variable cost curve
in Figure 7–17A is approximately the ratio $390/130, or about $3. Marginal cost is the slope of the total cost function, so marginal cost is
specified by the first derivative of the total cost function with respect to
the rate of output. Note that the *slope of the total cost function* in Figure
7–17A at any given rate of output is the *height of the marginal cost function* in Figure 7–17B at that same rate.

Marginal cost is of special interest to the managerial economist because of its possible use in determining the optimum rate of output. It is
profitable to increase the rate so long as marginal revenue exceeds marginal cost, since there is contribution from each unit added, and the
optimum rate is found where the marginal cost function cuts the marginal revenue function from beneath. To demonstrate, assume that the

price of window cleaning is constant at $2.20, so that marginal revenue is also constant at $2.20, as shown in Figure 7–17B. By inspection, the rising marginal cost curve becomes equal to the constant marginal revenue at a production rate of approximately 440 windows per day.

If the equation for the cost function is known, the optimum rate of output can be determined analytically by the approach demonstrated in the following example. By the least-squares estimation technique, a polynomial of third degree was fitted to the total cost and output rate combinations plotted in Figure 7–17A, and the total cost (TC) curve was found to be approximately

$$TC = \$306 + \$3.21Q - \$0.007734Q^2 + \$0.00001Q^3$$

The corresponding marginal cost (MC) function is the first derivative:

$$MC = \frac{\partial TC}{\partial Q} = \$3.21 - \$0.01547Q + \$0.00003Q^2$$

Setting the marginal cost function equal to marginal revenue, we obtain

$$\$3.21 - \$0.01547Q + \$0.00003Q^2 = \$2.20$$

After combining terms and rearranging, the equation is in general quadratic form

$$0 = ax^2 + bx + c \qquad \text{(general quadratic form)}$$
$$0 = -\$0.00003Q^2 + \$0.01547Q - \$1.01 \qquad \text{(our example)}$$

The solution is

$$X = \frac{-b + \sqrt{b^2 - 4ac}}{2a} \qquad \text{(solution for general form)}$$

$$Q = \frac{-\$0.01547 \pm \sqrt{\$0.0002393 - [4 \cdot (-\$0.00003) \cdot (-\$1.01)]}}{2 \cdot (-\$0.00003)} \qquad \text{(our example)}$$

The two values of the solution are

> 438.95, the optimum rate
> 7.67, the *other* rate at which MC also equals MR

Average cost functions. Average variable cost at any given rate of output is total variable cost divided by the rate. For example, at Point A on the variable cost function in Figure 7–17A, average variable cost is $900/500, or $1.80. Average fixed cost at any given rate is fixed cost divided by the rate. To illustrate, at Point B on the fixed cost function in Figure 7–17A, average fixed cost is $300/500, or $0.60. Average total cost at any given rate is the sum of the average variable cost and the average fixed cost. At Point C on the total cost function in Figure 7–17A, average total cost is $1.80 + $0.60, or $2.40.

If the equation for the total cost function is known, equations for the average cost functions are easy to derive. To demonstrate, for the example in Figure 7–17A:

Total cost = Fixed cost + Variable cost
$$TC = \$306 + (\$3.21Q - \$0.007734Q^2 + \$0.00001Q^3$$

Average variable cost, AVC, is VC/Q, so for the above example:

$$AVC = \$3.21 - \$0.007734Q + \$0.00001Q^2$$

Average fixed cost, *AFC*, is *FC/Q*, so

$$AFC = \frac{1}{Q} \cdot \$306$$

Average total cost, *ATC*, is *AVC* + *AFC*, so

$$ATC = \$3.21 - \$0.007734Q + \$0.00001Q^2 + \frac{1}{Q} \cdot \$306$$

How flexibility affects costs

Managers are interested in at least four types of flexibility. The first consists of flexibility to adjust to seasonal and year-to-year changes in sales rates. One way of getting seasonal flexibility is to change hours of operation per day. If the raw materials and the finished products are storable, annual and seasonal flexibility can both be achieved through changes in plant operating time per year. Another way of obtaining annual and seasonal flexibility is to use a number of small identical machines rather than one large unit, although the large unit will usually have a lower cost under conditions of full utilization. Still another approach to annual and seasonal flexibility is to use technology involving relatively large proportions of labor to equipment, for labor can be laid off as sales fall, whereas costs of durable inputs are committed regardless of sales. Several of the approaches listed here may be used in combination.

A second type of flexibility is the ability to adjust to changes in the relative prices of inputs through substitution of one input for another, and a third type of flexibility is the ability to make changes in the nature of the product. These types of flexibility are maintained by using general-purpose rather than specialized machinery and equipment.

A fourth type of flexibility is the ability to quickly and economically expand the designed rate of output of the plant in response to long-term increases in the sales rate. This type of flexibility is achieved by reserving space for expansion, using easily expandable layout and construction, and installing service facilities (utilities, sewer, drives, and so forth) that can handle greater loads than those initially imposed.

Figure 7–18
Short-run cost curves for plants differing in flexibility

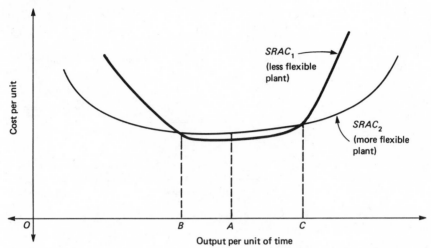

In general, the effect of increased flexibility on costs is as shown in Figure 7–18. The more flexible plant has higher costs than the specialized plant at the specialized plant's design rate, but the more flexible plant may still have lower average costs over a number of periods if there is considerable variation in sales and output rates.

LONG-RUN COST FUNCTIONS

If production planning is viewed in long-run perspective, all inputs can be varied as the rate of production is changed. Machines and equipment can be changed. Methods and processes can be changed as desired. New plants can be built in whatever sizes and locations are advantageous. The firm can even change the business that it is in. Long-run planning reaches to a horizon that is far away.

With no inputs considered fixed in relation to rate of output, there can be no fixed cost per period. Variable cost is also total cost per period. Imagine a least-cost expansion path developed with *all* inputs treated as variable. A team of engineers, accountants, and economists might develop such a path, at least approximately, by careful consideration of all possibilities for input substitution at each of several rates of output. Corresponding to the expansion path there would be a long-run average cost curve such as shown in Figure 7–19. This curve would define the lowest total cost per period and the lowest average cost per unit, respectively, for various rates of output, where each cost is conceived as being established for *continuative* production at *only* the given rate.

Figure 7–19
The long-run planning (envelope) curve

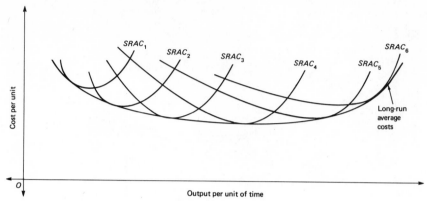

Relation of long-run functions to short-run cost functions

At each point on the long-run curve of Figure 7–19 there is conceptually a *plant*—a bundle of inputs that, once put in place, would be fixed in relation to variations in rate of output. And corresponding to each such plant, there would be short-run total and average cost curves defining the behavior of costs with changes in the rate of output of *that* plant. Of the innumerable short-run cost curves that could be depicted in Figure 7–19, only six have been drawn. These curves correspond to just six of the many, many plant sizes among which management can choose so long as it has the long-run, or planning, perspective.

It can be seen that the long-run curves are envelopes—they "go around" a family of short-run curves. So long as the firm is in a long-range planning posture, it has the full range of possible combinations of cost and rate of output as defined by the long-run curves. Once any one of the plants is actually in place, the firm's range of possible combinations of cost and rate of output will be defined by that plant's short-run curves.

Sources of economies and diseconomies of scale of plants

The shape of the long-run average cost curve—the relation of average cost per unit to the rate of output—is of great interest. It is determined by the technological and institutional economies of scale of the industry. Economies of scale of plants result from combinations of scale effects and economies of input substitution as rate of output is increased with all inputs variable.

Gains from *specialization* of labor and capital equipment are a principal source of reductions in unit cost through increases in plant size. First, consider *labor*. In a very small plant (think of a one-worker automobile repair shop), an employee must carry out many different kinds of activity. He spends much time changing from one task to another (moving to a different location, getting out the tools and parts needed, looking up instructions for the job). And he does not do each task at the speed he might develop if that task were his only work. In contrast, in a large plant (think of an automobile assembly plant), work is divided into small, repetitive operations carried out at relatively high speed on work in process that is moved from one work station to another by a conveyor. Gains in labor efficiency through specialization are very impressive, although there is increased monotony of the work that may require higher wages to be paid.

Gains from specialization of *machines and equipment* as plant size is increased are also impressive. In a small plant (think of a one-worker automotive machine shop), each machine must be flexible—able to take on a great variety of work. For example, a brake lathe, with its accessory jigs and cutting tools, must be able to "turn" almost every kind and size of brake drum or disc, and the lathe may stand idle much of the time. On the other hand, in a large plant (think of a plant that makes components of automobiles) machines can be highly specialized, doing one task over and over again at a relatively rapid cycle rate. For example, stamping machines that form auto body parts from flat steel will process hundreds of parts per minute. Specialization and full-time use of machines greatly decrease the cost of machine use per unit of work completed.

There are further economies of scale of plants that derive from the fact that *costs of specialized machines and equipment do not usually increase in proportion to the capacity for which they are designed*. Making a pipe that will handle 1,000 gallons per minute does not take twice as much material and labor as making a pipe that will handle 500 gallons per minute. Nor does a 100-horsepower motor involve twice as much manufacturing cost as a 50-horsepower motor. Haldi and Whitcomb studied costs of basic industrial equipment using cost relationships of the following form; $C = aX^b$, in which C is cost; X is capacity, or designed rate of output; and b is percentage increase in cost per 1 percent increase in capacity.[2] Any value of b less than 1.0 shows increasing economies of scale. In the category of installed equipment such at that used in chemical and other process industries, 81.5 percent of the equipment had a scale coefficient of 0.8 or less.

---

[2] J. Haldi and D. Whitcomb, "Economics of Scale in Industrial Plants," *Journal of Political Economy* 75, August 1967.

Substitution of capital for labor is another source of economies of scale in plants. Automation—replacement of human services in the transfer and positioning of materials, the control of machine adjustments and cycling, and the inspection of finished work—generally takes the form of complex devices that are capable of high working speeds. Thus, automation is better suited to large plants than to small ones. In general, the larger the plant, the greater the opportunity for cost reduction through automation.

Increases in plant size also open greater opportunities for gains from *vertical integration* of production activities. For example, a large metal-forming plant may be able to integrate a metal smelter and take advantage of continuous-process economies, which include elimination of reheating for further processing. A larger meat-packing plant can integrate economically sized subdivisions that process by-products into valuable finished goods such as leather, glue, and so forth, avoiding transactions and rehandling costs.

Finally, increases in plant size provide more opportunities for *order-size economies* in purchasing and for *economies of car-lot shipping* in transporting incoming and outgoing materials.

If cost reductions were the only effect of increases in plant size, there would tend to be only one plant for each product and every industry would tend to be a monopoly. However, it is commonly observed that many large companies have several plants for each product, and also that many industries are characterized by competition among a number of different firms. So there are diseconomies of plant size in some industries and, at the point where these diseconomies eventually overcome the economies, there is an optimum size of plant—one that gives the lowest cost per unit.

Diseconomies of plant size may result from increasing unit costs of bringing material over longer average hauls from an expanded supply area. Examples of this kind of diseconomies are: costs of hauling logs to lumber mills; costs of assembling cattle and hogs for slaughter plants; and costs of bringing citrus fruit to a juice-concentrating works. Or the diseconomies of plant size may be on the distribution side. There may be increasing unit costs of getting the greater rate of output to customers that are at greater average distances in a larger market area. Examples of this kind of diseconomies are: costs of hauling soft drinks from a bottling plant; costs of transporting finished automobiles from an assembly works; and costs of taking bread away from a bakery.

Economies and diseconomies of size of multiplant firms

A firm that has expanded a plant to optimum size at a given location may still find economies in bringing several plants under a single man-

Figure 7–20
Economies of scale in administration of life insurance companies

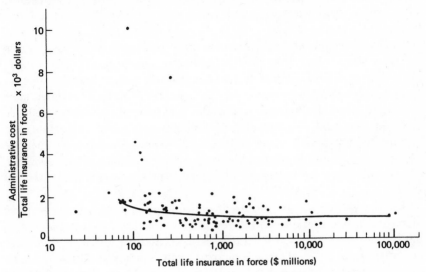

Total life insurance in force ($ millions)

agement. Some economies of size in multiplant firms take the form of reductions in administrative cost per unit of product or service. *Efficiencies of specialization* of labor and equipment in the administrative function are similar to those in production. And a large organization can take advantage of skills of economic forecasters, industrial psychologists, and other highly trained staff members that cannot be efficiently utilized in smaller businesses. Nelson found in a study of life insurance companies that the relation of total administrative cost per $1,000 of insurance in force to the total amount of insurance in force was as shown in Figure 7–20. Note that the output scale in the figure is logarithmic, so that the largest companies are on the order of 1,000 times as large as the smallest. Although there are variations in administrative cost at each size of insurance firm, the underlying economies of size appear to continue to the largest firms in the study.[3]

Multiplant operations can have economies of size in *selling* the output. The Chevrolet Division of General Motors might spend $20 million a year on advertising at a cost of only $20 each on more than 1 million units sold, whereas a similar level of advertising for the American Motors Pacer would cost close to $100 per unit on sales of perhaps 200,000 units. There are also economies of size in *financing* that may benefit multiplant firms. Larger companies may be able to attain blue chip

---

[3] Edward A. Nelson, "Economic Size of Organizations," *California Management Review* 10, Spring 1968.

status, which lowers the cost of equity capital as well as the interest rate on borrowed money. Retailers, Sears, Penney, and many smaller chains, have economies of *purchasing* as a result of their multiplant retail locations.

Finally, *vertical integration* that is not economic even for the largest size of a single-plant firm may be advantageous to a multiplant company. For example, a multiple plant petroleum refiner may be able to integrate the crude oil production function. Or a national retailer may be able to integrate factories that make a variety of consumer goods. A company that publishes a number of daily newspapers in large cities may be able to integrate a paper mill. And automobile assemblers such as General Motors and Ford are able to set up their own divisions to supply components such as batteries, radiators, starters, alternators, and so forth.

Are there *diseconomies* of size of multiple plant firms? Difficulties of management have traditionally been proposed as limits to company size, but the successes of General Motors, Sears, General Electric, and numerous other giant firms show that management is *not* a limiting factor in many industries. Management probably *does* limit the size of firms in those cases where day-to-day operations require the personal attention and creative talent of a particular person. Examples include: manufacture of high-style women's wear; development of urban real estate; production of crops and livestock; operation of fine restaurants; booking of live entertainment; many types of retailing; and provision of professional personal services, such as medical care and legal advice.

SUMMARY

The chapter discussed cost minimization through *optimum combination of inputs*. The problem was considered from both the short-run and the long-run points of view.

An *isoquant* connects all of the various combinations of two inputs that will yield a given rate of output. The slope of an isoquant, called *marginal rate of technical substitution*, *MRTS*, is the ratio of a decrease in vertical axis input to an increase in horizontal axis input, or, roughly, the decrease in vertical axis input per unit of additional horizontal axis input. The absolute value of *MRTS* at any given point on an isoquant is the ratio of the marginal product of the horizontal axis input to the marginal product of the vertical axis input.

An *isocost line* connects all of the various combinations of two inputs that have the same total cost. The slope of an isocost line is the negative ratio of the price of the horizontal axis input to the price of the vertical axis input. The *least-cost combination* of inputs on any given isoquant is at that point where the slope, or marginal rate of technical substitution, is equal to the negative ratio of input prices, which is the *market rate of substitution.*

If an equation for an isoquant is known, the least-cost combination can be found by an *analytic method.* One sets the first derivative of the isoquant, which is a function defining *MRTS*, equal to the negative ratio of input prices, obtaining the optimum quantity of horizontal axis input. This value is then substituted into the original isoquant equation to obtain the optimum quantity of vertical axis input. Least-cost combinations can also be determined by *linear programming methods* for an important class of problems involving blending or mixing.

The *expansion path* connects least-cost combinations of inputs for various rates of output. Location of an expansion path would require a series of analytic calculations or linear programming solutions or engineering studies. However, incremental estimation and reasoning well within the capability of a typical manager will move the firm's activity toward the expansion path.

A short-run total *variable* cost function can be derived from an expansion path by totaling the cost of the combinations of variable inputs at various output rates. The plant's *total* cost function is obtained by adding the plant's fixed cost per period to its variable costs at various rates of production. *Marginal cost* at any given output rate is the ratio of change in cost to change in output rate, or roughly the increase in cost associated with the last unit added to the rate. A marginal cost function is defined by the first derivative of the total cost function, since marginal cost is the slope of the total cost curve. Marginal cost functions can be used in analytic determinations of optimum rate; the method is based on setting the marginal cost function equal to the marginal revenue function and solving for rate of output.

Flexibility can be designed into a plant, so that it will have lower costs in the event of production above or below the expected rate for which it is designed. However, a more flexible plant would ordinarily have higher unit costs at the design rate than would a plant not required to have flexibility.

The long-run average cost curve shows for various rates of production the lowest unit costs attainable at each output rate in a plant designed for continuative production at that rate. Long-run curves tend to be L shaped because of economies of scale; these economies derive from specialization of labor and machines, pure size economies in machine and equipment cost, substitution of capital for labor, economies of vertical integration, and lot-size economies. In some kinds of production, diseconomies of scale arise because of rising costs of raw materials or rising costs of distributing finished products.

QUESTIONS

1. What is measured by the height of an isoquant? By the coordinates?

2. What is meant by "marginal technical rate of substitution" at a point? How is $MRTS$ related to the marginal products of the two inputs?

3. In going around an isoquant, what condition is encountered at the ridge line? Why do we say that input combinations beyond the ridge line can never be economic?

4. What variable holds constant as we move from point to point on an isocost line? What variables change? What is the relation of the slope of an isocost line to the prices of the two inputs?

5. In your own words, tell how to find a least-cost combination by the analytic method.

6. What is an expansion path? What is the relation of the expansion path to the function specifying total cost per period for various rates of output?

7. Contrast continuative production with a discrete run of production?

8. Compare the short-run variable functions corresponding to: (*a*) an input-output function, (*b*) a constant proportions process ray, and (*c*) an expansion path. Which of the three cost functions would have lowest costs at the various rates of output, and why?

9. Contrast the long-run total cost function with the short-run total cost function. How is the long-run function related to a family of short-run functions?

10. What are some principal sources of economies of plant size? What are some principal sources of economies of the firm's size (in the case of multiplant firms)? How could diseconomies of size be explained?

PROBLEMS

1. An engineer made a tentative plan for a small pipeline. In considering possible changes from the initial design, the engineer estimated that pipeline throughput could be increased by 12,000 barrels per 24 hours if the pipe diameter were increased by 2 inches. Or, without increasing pipe size, the flow could be increased by 15,000 barrels per 24 hours if the pumping force applied were made 500 horsepower greater. What is the estimated marginal rate of technical substitution of pipe size for pumping force in making small changes from the original plan?

2. A chemical manufacturer makes a degreaser by blending solvent A with solvent B. Solvent A can be bought at a constant price of $3 per gallon and solvent B can be bought at a constant price of $4 per gallon. Assume that solvent A is to be measured against the vertical axis of an isoquant-isocost diagram. Derive the equation for Isocost line $400.

3. You are given the following equation for Isoquant 400: $L = 83.6 - 0.247K + 0.00042K^2$, in which L is daily labor input in employee-hours and K

is usage of capital in dollars of equipment rental per day. If labor has a wage of $9 per employee-hour, what is the least-cost combination of labor and capital usage?

4. A supervisor has estimated that output of the department can be increased by 4,000 units each 8-hour shift if one more employee is added to the work force. Or, without an increase in the work force, output could be increased by 4,000 units per shift by adding another piece of leased equipment that would cost $250 per week. The plant works one shift each 24 hours, five days per week. The wage rate is $8 per employee-hour.

    a. What is the marginal physical product of labor over the interval described above? What is the increase in output per $1 spent for labor?

    b. What is the marginal physical product of capital over the interval described above? (*Hint:* Capital input can be measured in dollars per shift.) Which input, labor or capital, gives the greatest increase in output per $1 spent on the input?

    c. Assuming output is to be held constant, suggest a substitution of inputs that will reduce cost, and calculate the cost reduction.

5. The Acme Cleaning Chemical Company produces an industrial cleaner for carpets. This chemical is made from a mixture of two other chemicals which both contain cleaning agent A and cleaning agent B along with some inert ingredients. Their product must contain 175 units of agent A, 150 units of B, and weigh at least 100 pounds. Chemical X_1 costs $4 per pound, while chemical X_2 costs $10 per pound. Chemical X_1 contains one unit of agent A, three units of agent B, and some inert ingredients per pound. Chemical X_2 contains seven units of agent A, one unit of agent B, and some inert ingredients per pound.

    a. Determine the least-cost mixture with regard to total weight, the weight of each chemical $(X_1 + X_2)$, and the minimum cost. Do this graphically.

    b. Set this problem up in the LP format.

6. The NP Growright Company manufactures a liquid plant fertilizer from mixing two chemical solutions together. With the exception of two key ingredients, N and P, all of the ingredients are found in two solutions so that regardless of how the solutions are mixed their percentage contents will be satisfactory. The company sells tanks which are guaranteed to contain a minimum of 500 gallons of the fertilizer. Furthermore, in addition to the other ingredients, the fertilizer in the tank units must contain at least 1,000 units of ingredient N and 750 units of ingredient P. Solution X_1 has been found to contain 1 unit of N per gallon and 3 units of P per gallon. Solution X_2 contains 4 units of N per gallon and 1 unit of P per gallon. The costs of solution X_1 and X_2 are $4 and $3 per gallon respectively.

    a. Solve this problem graphically.

    b. Set the problem up in the LP format.

7. Given that total cost per period, TC, for a particular product is related to the product's rate of output, Q, as follows:

$$TC = \$264 = \$3.03Q - \$0.006Q^2 + \$0.00002Q^3$$

    a. How much is the fixed cost per period?

    b. Derive the relation of average fixed cost, AFC, to rate of output, Q.

    c. Derive the relation of marginal cost, MC, to rate of output, Q.
    d. Derive the relation of variable cost, VC, to rate of output, Q.
    e. Derive the relation of average variable cost, AVC, to rate of output, Q.
    f. Derive the relation of average total cost, ATC, to rate of output, Q.

8. In one state, the total cost of operating high schools are found to depend on size of the schools as follows:

$$TC = \$960Q - \$0.402Q^2 + \$0.00012Q^3$$

in which TC is total cost per high school per school year and Q is average number of students attending the school.

    a. Are there economies of scale in high school operation? Diseconomies? What size of school would give the lowest cost per student (minimum AC)?
    b. The solution to part *a* takes into account only the high school's internal costs. Costs of transportation of students to the schools and travel time imposed on students are not considered. Consolidation of schools to take advantage of the internal economies of scale usually increases busing costs and imposes added travel time. How much is the reduction in the high school's internal costs per student when the average number of students attending is increased from 800 to the number that gives the lowest cost per student as determined in part *a* above?
    c. If a school has 1,000 students attending, what is the estimated increase in cost per school year if one more student is added to the student body?

FURTHER READING

Haldi, J., and Whitcomb, D. "Economies of Scale in Industrial Plants." *Journal of Political Economy* 75, August 1967.

McGee, John S. "Economies of Size in Auto Body Manufacture." *Journal of Law and Economics* 16, October 1973.

Maxwell, W. David. "Production Theory and Cost Curves." *Applied Economics* 1 (1969).

Williamson, Oliver E. "Hierarchical Control and Optimum Firm Size." *Journal of Political Economy* 75, April 1967.

Chapter 8

Estimation of production and cost functions

This chapter discusses two approaches to estimation of production and cost functions. The economic-engineering approach consists of design of least-cost combinations of durable and variable inputs in the light of current technology and prices. The statistical approach consists of fitting functions to accounting data by statistical methods. The economic-engineering approach is closest to the long-run perspective on costs, in which *all* inputs and the rate of output are treated as variable, whereas the statistical approach is closest to the short-run perspective, in which *some* inputs and the rate of output are regarded as variable. Principal problems that come up during the applications of these approaches, and the procedures for coping with some of these problems are the focus of this chapter.

THE ECONOMIC-ENGINEERING APPROACH[1]

The economic-engineering approach outlined here is designed for studies that compare the efficiency of alternative technologies, derive

---

[1] This section is based on B. C. French, L. L. Sammet, and R. G. Bressler, "Economic Efficiency in Plant Operations," *Hilgardia* 24, no. 19 (July 1956), pp. 543–721.

short-run cost functions for plants of specific sizes, and derive long-run functions that are envelopes for the cost functions of the individual plants. This section begins with the engineering view of plant costs and long-run costs, then surveys sources of data and procedures used in estimating cost-output relationships, and finishes with an empirical example of an economic-engineering study.

The nature of plant operations

A *stage* consists of all productive services that cooperate in performing a single operation. The meaning of the term "stage" may be made clear by Figure 8–1. The production process begins with receipt of some basic material, either in raw or partially processed form, as in the example of Material *A* in Figure 8–1. Receipt of the material is the first stage in plant operations. The material then moves to a second stage, where it is in some way transformed. *Transformation* can take the form of melting, pulverizing, washing, sorting, milling, stamping, assembling, inspecting, painting, or whatever. The material then moves to another stage where another transformation occurs. In Figure 8–1 a by-product is removed at the third stage and flows in another direction.

At various points, other materials are received, as in the example of Materials *B* and *C* in Figure 8–1, then transformed in various stages, and finally are fed into the main line of flow, where they are combined with the partially completed product. On the other hand, various partially completed products may be "split off" at different stages and given their own individual series of further transformations so as to emerge as final products, as in the example of Product 1 in Figure 8–1.

The various stages are connected by *transportation* links. Between-stage transportation is in a sense a stage itself, in which the only operations performed are to move the product from one place to another. Figure 8–1 also shows the frequent occurrence of temporary storage between the various stages. *Storage* plays an important role in leveling out the flow of materials and products. For example, materials may be received at irregular intervals, but a fairly continuous flow is maintained by feeding materials into, and then withdrawing them from, storage. Storage also compensates for irregularities or differences in rates of activity in the various stages. And in batch-type production, storage is an integral part of the planned production process. Storage is in a sense a stage, too, in which the only operation performed is to hold the product for some period of time.

Variations in rate of output

Technical requirements limit rate variations of some processes. The rate at which a product passes through a stage is very narrowly defined

Figure 8–1 Hypothetical plant process flow diagram

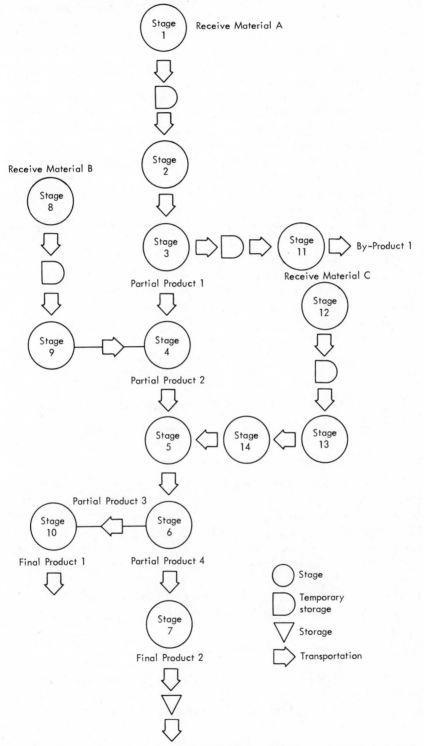

Source: B. C. French, L. L. Sammet, and R. G. Bressler, "Economic Efficiency in Plant Operations," *Hilgardia* 24, no. 19 (July 1956), p. 546.

for such processes as sterilizing, pasteurizing, cooking, baking, drying, freezing, and so forth. Such limitations can be overcome by organizing plants in multiple units—in effect, several plants within a plant. A four-unit plant might operate at instantaneous rates that are one fourth, one half, three fourths, or all of the designed capacity of the plant.

Total plant output within any given period can also be varied by changing hours of operation per day or, for seasonal operations, per season. For example, an automobile plant can produce the year's output in less than a year, shut down for a considerable time to retool for the next model, and continue sales from inventories of finished product. And the retooling period can be shortened or widened as the demand situation may warrant. For some kinds of production, storage possibilities are very limited and production rates must match consumption. For example, electric power must be produced as it is used because there is almost no economic method of storing electricity. But for most production, storage is possible, so that the output used to satisfy a given demand can be produced over a fairly wide time range. In such cases output per year can be varied by changing the number of hours of plant operation.

Of course there are many kinds of production in which the *instantaneous* rate of output can be varied. Such variation requires changes of operating speeds and cycling rates of machines, and repositioning and reassignment of worker tasks. Assembly processes, packaging, order filling, freight handling, and clerical work are some examples of production in which the instantaneous rate of output is varied by changing the intensity of use of variable inputs.

Effects upon marginal cost as output is varied

If *instantaneous rates of plant output are held constant* and total output in a sales or accounting period is varied by *changes in the number of hours worked* per day or per week, the inputs are being combined at constant rates and in a constant proportion despite the changes in output. In this situation, *marginal cost can be expected to be constant* (unless the firm has to pay higher wages for overtime or night work, or fatigue of workers diminishes output per employee-hour). The scale effect, the effect of the law of variable proportions, and the effect of input substitutions cannot enter into the behavior of cost as output is varied.

If total output in a sales or accounting period is varied by *successive additions or subtractions of the services of identical machines and workers performing identical tasks*, the resulting total cost function will be discontinuous, but cost will tend to increase by constant increments as output is increased by constant increments. Thus, marginal cost, calculated discretely as increase in total cost divided by increase in output per period, can be expected to be *constant* in this situation, too.

It is only in the case where output per sales or accounting period is varied by changes in the *instantaneous* rate of production, through changes in the *proportioning* of inputs (in other words, through changes in intensity of use of variable inputs relative to use of services of durable inputs), that marginal cost is expected to change as output is varied.

The long-run cost function

The long-run cost function cannot be determined directly. It must be approached from the short-run perspective by comparing costs of plants of different sizes and technologies, and then combining these into a function showing the least cost of producing at each instantaneous rate of output for various numbers of hours per sales or accounting period. The long-run cost function will appear as an envelope to the many individual plant cost functions. Just as the individual plant functions contain both a rate-of-output element and a time-of-operation element, so will the long-run function.

A model of the long-run cost function is shown in Figure 8–2. The base of the three-dimensional surface (that part below Points *T*, *U*, *V*, and *X*) represents the cost of owning, maintaining, and replacing durable capital goods. (The amount of capital increases with instantaneous rate of output.) The additional elevation of the curving surface above the base represents the costs of those inputs (such as labor and materials) that vary with both the rate of output and the time of operation per sales or accounting period.

An efficient approach to estimation of long-run functions is to select several rates of output, to determine the least-cost method of maintaining each of these rates of output at each of the numerous stages, and to aggregate stage costs into long-run total cost functions.

Cost measurement

Cost measurement should begin at the stage level. Because measurement problems differ somewhat among the major types of inputs, they will be discussed under four headings: labor, materials, other operating inputs, and durable goods.

Labor. Two main sources of data can be used to estimate basic physical and cost relationships of labor to output: (1) plant payroll and output records, and (2) engineering studies of actual operations. Plant payroll records usually show hours of labor per day or week and the pay rates for each worker in the plant. Where these records indicate the na-

Figure 8–2
A long-run cost surface—the engineering view

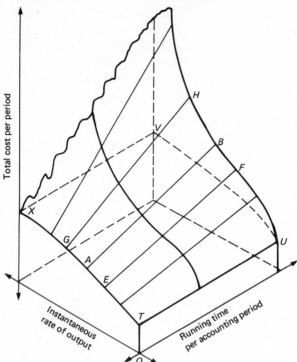
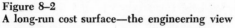

ture of each worker's job, they may be related to the corresponding volumes of products to develop labor input-output functions for most of the plant stages. The disadvantage of payroll records is that they usually reveal little of the specific details of many of the plant jobs, and they may be inaccurate in classifying workers as to actual work performed.

Engineering studies are a means of obtaining labor data that are not readily available from accounting records. These studies consist of detailed descriptions of plant operations (description of each job, number of workers employed in each job classification in each stage of plant operations, and the route and rate of flow of materials through the plant), plus performance standards derived from time studies, work sampling studies, or analysis of standard work data. It is desirable to compare standards based on engineering studies with actual rates of performance to verify that they are the desired "reasonably efficient" values.

The physical performance standards for labor must be transformed into estimates of labor cost, stage by stage, at the selected rates of production. Performance standards determine the number of workers needed at each rate of production, and the number of workers times the wage rate determines the hourly labor cost at each rate of output.

Materials. The costs of materials in the final product are probably the easiest of the inputs to measure for the materials commonly enter in rigidly fixed proportions. Costs of the materials are obtained by simply multiplying the physical quantities by their prices, which may be constant or may be some function of the quantity purchased. Price data usually are readily available from suppliers.

An alternative source of material cost data is plant accounting records. An advantage of data from this source is that they reflect loss due to breakage or damage that may be normal in the course of ordinary handling. A disadvantage is that materials costs from plant records may be based on past purchase prices that are out of line with the prices that should be used in planning future operations.

Other operating inputs. Power, fuel, water, and similar costs may be estimated from accounting records or by engineering studies of production processed. If these costs are a sizable part of the total, engineering studies are desirable. Physical measurements can be made on such components as the power load of each large motor, the fuel use rate required for each heat process, and so on.

Miscellaneous supplies such as office stationery, janitorial materials, and so on are likely to be related to the size of the plant rather than to its rate of operation, and accounting records may be a good basis for estimating these.

Administrative costs are the salaries of managers and executives. Accounting records are the chief source of these. Frequently these accounts are inaccessible to outsiders, and if they are available the salaries may be related to profits in such a way that the figures for a particular year do not indicate long-run levels. Discreet inquiries and careful adjustments may be advisable.

Durable goods. Three main sources of data are: plant accounting records, engineering-architecture estimates of building costs, and data supplied by manufacturers of machines and equipment. Values and period charges found in accounting records will usually be of limited value, since they reflect not future costs of replacement, but past purchase prices at varying dates and price levels. Moreover, book charges for depreciation may be out of line with actual costs. The engineering-architecture approach consists of estimating the physical inputs required to build a plant of a given size and multiplying these requirements by an appropriate set of prices to obtain estimates of replacement costs. Esti-

Figure 8–3
Process flow diagram for pear-packing plants

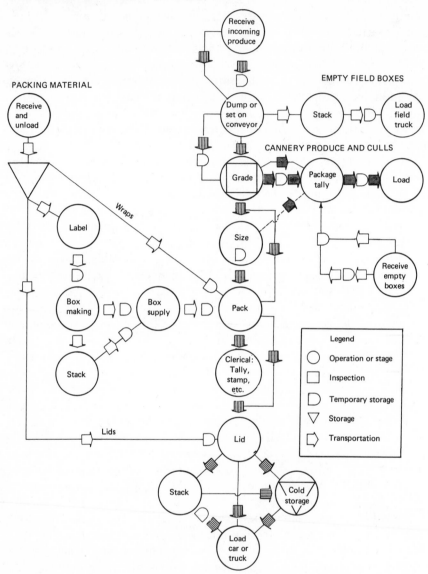

Source: B. C. French, L. L. Sammet, and R. G. Bressler, "Economic Efficiency in Plant Operations," *Hilgardia* 24, no. 19 (July 1956), p. 595.

mates of repair costs and depreciation rates are derived from plant records and engineering judgments. Insurance, taxes, and costs of capital are based on going rates for these items.

Empirical examples

The engineering approach to estimation of cost functions consists of the following steps: (1) selecting the *rates of operation* for which the various *plants* are to be *designed;* (2) breaking the production process flow into *stages* (in each stage the product undergoes some transformation), *transportation links* that move the product from stage to stage, and *temporary storage points;* (3) determining least-cost *combinations* of labor, materials, and equipment *at each stage* for *each of the design rates of output;* (4) synthesizing these optimally designed stages into complete

Figure 8–4
Five methods of supplying packers with empty boxes

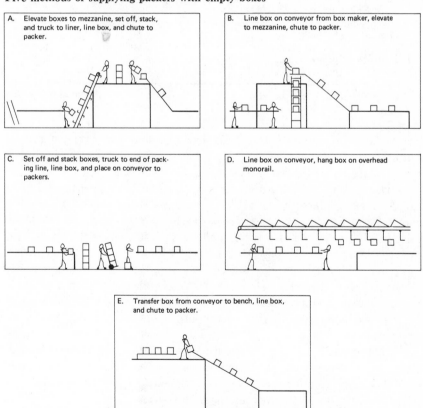

A. Elevate boxes to mezzanine, set off, stack, and truck to liner, line box, and chute to packer.

B. Line box on conveyor from box maker, elevate to mezzanine, chute to packer.

C. Set off and stack boxes, truck to end of packing line, line box, and place on conveyor to packers.

D. Line box on conveyor, hang box on overhead monorail.

E. Transfer box from conveyor to bench, line box, and chute to packer.

Source: B. C. French, L. L. Sammet, and R. G. Bressler, "Economic Efficiency in Plant Operations, *Hilgardia* 24, no. 19 (July 1956), p. 635.

Table 8–1
**Unit labor requirements and production standards for the types of jobs performed
in the distribution of empty boxes to the packers**

Operation	Net unit time, employee-minutes per box	Production standard,* boxes per hour
Bring package of pads and liners from nearby supply point	0.014	3,860
Place bottom pad and side liners		
Fold and place one pair of side liners	0.110	490
Place one pair of side liners (no folding required)	0.036	1,500
Place bottom pad	0.036	1,500
Nest boxes on conveyor, set off, and stack	0.048	1,130
Transfer empty boxes—for example, from conveyor to elevator, conveyor to chute, conveyor to monorail hook, conveyor to bench		
One box per transfer	0.066	820
Two boxes per transfer	0.054	1,000
Four boxes per transfer	0.030	1,800
Truck empty boxes (standard pear boxes)		
Fork truck: distance 30 feet	0.007	7,700
distance 60 feet	0.009	6,000
Hand truck: distance 30 feet	0.022	2,460
distance 60 feet	0.031	1,740

* Based on net time plus allowance for rest and delay of 10 percent of total work time.

plants; and (5) *estimating cost* for each plant at the designed rate of output and at other rates (so as to produce short-run cost curves for each of the plants as well as several points on the long-run cost curve).

A University of California study of costs of pear packing provides excellent insight into the nature of the engineering method.[2] Figure 8–3 shows a process flow diagram for pear packing. The researchers determined the best method of carrying out the work in each of these 20 stages at three rates of processing (15, 40, and 70 thousand pounds per hour).

For example, at the stage labeled "box supply," the five methods depicted in Figure 8–4 were compared. Labor requirements shown in Table 8–1, equipment requirements and costs shown in Table 8–2, and costs of box supply in relation to rate of output as shown in Table 8–3, were estimated.

All 20 stages, optimally designed at each of the three rates of operation, were synthesized into complete plants. Variable and fixed costs were then estimated for each plant at various rates of output; Table 8–4 shows the resulting estimates for the middle-sized plant.

[2] Ibid.

Table 8–2
Equipment requirements for distribution of empty packing boxes with different methods

Item	Method				
	A	B	C	D	E
Work table and box chute per 250 boxes per hour, each.....................	1	—	1*	—	1
Gravity conveyor per 100 boxes per hour, feet.........................	32	32	32	—	32
Hand truck per 100 boxes per hour, each..	0.1	—	0.5	—	—
Box elevator per 2,000 boxes per hour....	1	1	—	—	—
Box mezzanine, floor area per 100 boxes per hour, square feet.................	300	300	—	—	—
Monorail conveyor per 100 boxes per hour, feet..........................	—	—	—	70	—

* Work table only.

Figure 8–5 summarizes the findings of the California study of pear-packing costs. Both the short-run (plant) cost curves and the long-run (envelope) curve are L-shaped.

Advantages of the engineering method are: (1) it standardizes technology, factor prices, plant efficiency, operating ratios, and other factors affecting costs, thus enabling isolation of the effects of changes in rates of output and sizes of plants; and (2) costs can be simulated by use of expected future factor prices and other assumed future conditions, thus possibly generating especially useful information for decision making. The disadvantages of the method include the time required and the great cost if careful estimates are made.

Adding spatial costs to plant costs.   Plant cost curves obtained by the engineering method are usually L-shaped with the lowest unit cost at the design rate of operation. However, there are cases in which plant operating rates can be either increased or decreased from the design rate, but the result of moving in either direction is to increase the unit cost. Figure 8–6, from a New Hampshire study of broiler chicken processing costs, is an example of U-shaped *plant* cost curves derived by the engineering method.[3] However, note that the L shape is still generated for the long-run, or envelope, curve.

The New Hampshire study dealt only with *internal* costs of broiler processing plants. A North Carolina study subsequently showed that the above-described L-shaped long-run cost curves would be U-shaped if costs of *distributing* feed to broiler farms and *assembling* live broilers to

[3] George B. Rogers and E. T. Bardwell, *Economies of Scale in Chicken Processing,* New Hampshire Agricultural Experiment Station Bulletin 459, April 1959.

Table 8–3
Empty box and materials supply—labor, operating, and equipment costs in relation to rates of packed output

Volume range boxes per hour	Number of workers	Labor	Equipment repair and operation	Total	Replacement cost	Annual fixed cost†
		\\\\multicolumn Direct cost* ($ per hour)			Equipment ($)	

Volume range boxes per hour	Number of workers	Labor	Equipment repair and operation	Total	Replacement cost	Annual fixed cost†
Method A						
0–190........	2	$2.10	$0.05	$2.15	$1,060	$130
101–245........	3	3.15	0.05	3.20	1,240	150
490........	4	4.20	0.07	4.27	2,010	240
735........	5	5.25	0.09	5.34	2,780	330
790........	6	6.30	0.09	6.39	2,950	350
820........	7	7.35	0.10	7.45	3,050	360
980........	8	8.40	0.11	8.51	3,620	430
1,225........	9	9.45	0.13	9.58	4,390	520
1,470........	10	10.50	0.15	10.65	5,160	610
1,580........	11	11.55	0.16	11.71	5,510	660
1,640........	12	12.60	0.16	12.76	5,760	690
Method B						
355........	2	2.10	0.06	2.16	1,520	180
625........	3	3.15	0.08	3.23	2,370	280
730........	4	4.20	0.09	4.29	2,700	320
820........	5	5.25	0.10	5.35	2,980	360
1,250........	6	6.30	0.13	6.43	4,340	520
1,460........	7	7.35	0.15	7.50	5,000	590
1,640........	8	8.40	0.16	8.56	5,570	660
Method C						
225........	2	2.10	0.01	2.11	290	40
445........	3	3.15	0.03	3.18	580	80
660........	4	4.20	0.04	4.24	860	110
870........	5	5.25	0.06	5.31	1,130	150
1,075........	6	6.30	0.07	6.37	1,400	180
1,130........	7	7.35	0.08	7.43	1,530	200
1,290........	8	8.40	0.08	8.48	1,690	220
1,505........	9	9.45	0.10	9.55	1,970	260
1,720........	10	10.50	0.12	10.62	2,250	300
Method D						
355........	1	1.05	0.09	1.14	1,450	190
625........	2	2.10	0.14	2.24	2,390	320
820........	3	3.15	0.16	3.31	2,580	340
1,250........	4	4.20	0.21	4.41	3,700	490
1,640........	5	5.25	0.27	5.52	4,830	640
Method E						
245........	1	1.05	0.02	1.07	370	50
490........	2	2.10	0.04	2.14	740	100
735........	3	3.15	0.06	3.21	1,110	150
980........	4	4.20	0.08	4.28	1,470	200
1,225........	5	5.25	0.10	5.35	1,840	250
1,470........	6	6.30	0.12	6.42	2,210	300
1,715........	7	7.35	0.14	7.49	2,580	350

* Direct costs are based on the following: wage rate of $1.05 per hour; power costs $0.03 per motor horsepower per hour; direct repair, 0.5 percent of replacement cost per 100 hours of use.

† Estimated as 13.2 percent of replacement cost.

Table 8–4
Total variable and fixed costs for a plant of 40,000 pounds per hour capacity, 70 percent packed, and a 200-hour season

Stage or cost component	Average annual fixed cost	Rate of total output—1,000 pounds per hour						
		10	15	20	25	30	35	40
		cost per hour—dollars						
1. Dump..........	$641	$1.40	$1.40	$1.40	$1.40	$2.50	$2.50	$2.50
2. Grade..........	280	8.56	9.61	10.66	11.71	13.81	14.86	16.96
3. Pack..........	1,722	22.94	34.58	45.88	57.19	68.82	78.13	91.43
4. Packer tally.....	2	1.05	1.05	1.05	1.05	1.05	1.05	1.05
5. Lid, stamp, etc...	495	2.47	2.47	3.52	3.52	3.52	4.57	5.62
6. Car loading.....	137	1.45	1.45	2.90	2.90	2.90	4.35	4.35
7. Box making and label.........	—	3.65	5.47	7.29	9.12	10.94	12.76	14.59
8. Box supply......	320	1.14	1.14	1.14	2.24	2.24	2.24	2.24
9. Package cannery.	200	1.40	2.60	2.60	3.80	3.80	5.00	6.20
10. Transportation..	320	5.14	6.39	7.65	8.90	11.40	12.66	13.91
11. Supervision and miscellaneous..	—	7.82	10.42	10.42	11.96	11.96	11.96	14.56
12. Miscellaneous equipment....	1,578	—	—	—	—	—	—	—
13. Office and administration......	7,150	—	—	—	—	—	—	—
14. Building costs...	5,488	—	—	—	—	—	—	—
15. Miscellaneous general costs...	659	—	—	—	—	—	—	—
16. Sampling.......	153	1.10	1.65	2.20	2.75	3.30	3.85	4.40
Total.......	19,145	58.12	78.23	96.77	116.54	136.24	155.93	177.81

the plant were added to the processing costs.[4] The amount of transport cost to be added to processing cost depends upon average length of haul, which in turn depends upon both the plant size and the "effective production density" of the broiler-growing area in birds per square mile per year. Figure 8–7 shows combined processing and transport costs for plants of various sizes at one level of effective production density, and Figure 8–8 shows the combined curves at six different levels of production density.

STATISTICAL ESTIMATES OF PRODUCTION AND COST FUNCTIONS

Production and cost functions can be estimated from accounting data by statistical methods. The statistical approach starts with *specification*

[4] William R. Henry and James A. Seagraves, "Economic Aspects of Broiler Production Density," *Journal of Farm Economics* 42, no. 1 (February 1960)

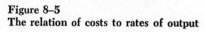

Figure 8–5
The relation of costs to rates of output

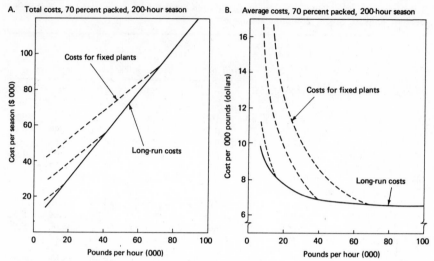

Source: B. C. French, L. L. Sammet, and R. G. Bressler, "Economic Efficiency in Plant Operations," *Hilgardia* 24, no. 19 (July 1956), p. 681.

of a model of production or cost behavior. Careful *adjustment of data* may be necessary where they do not conform to explicit or implicit assumptions of the model. Statistical techniques can then be used to *estimate parameters* of the model and to *establish ranges* above and below each of the estimates that will allow specified levels of confidence.

Data used in statistical estimation may consist of observations on each of the variables in the model *for a single firm across a number of time periods* in which the firm had various rates of production; observations of this type are called *time-series* data. Or the data may come from observations on each variable *across a number of firms during a single time period* in which the firms were producing at various rates; observations of this type are called *cross-section* data.

The objective of statistical analysis may be to estimate an *input-output function* or *production function*—a relation of physical rate of output to physical rates of use of one or more variable inputs. Some studies have an objective of estimating a *short-run cost curve*—the relation of cost to changes in rate of output of a plant designed for some given rate of production. Other studies have an objective of estimating a *long-run cost curve*—the relation of cost to rate of output with each rate being produced in its own plant, a plant designed for least-cost production of that particular rate.

Figure 8–6
Broilers: Economies of scale curve and average cost curves for ten model plants

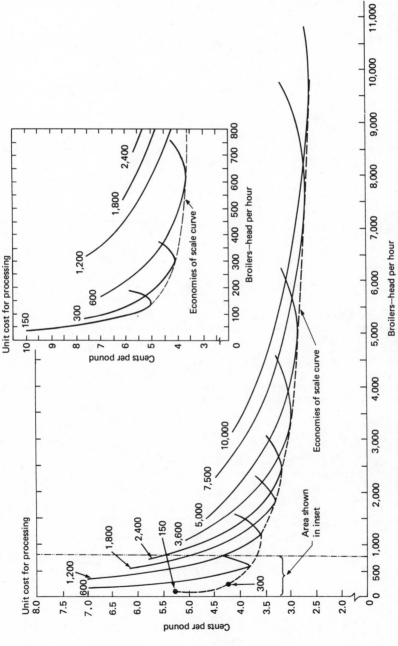

Source: George B. Rogers and E. T. Bardwell, *Economies of Scale in Chicken Processing*, New Hampshire Agricultural Experiment Station Bulletin 459, April 1959.

Figure 8–7
Selected transport costs, processing costs and combined costs, for effective production density of 500 birds per square mile per year, average lengths of haul in miles posted along transport cost curve

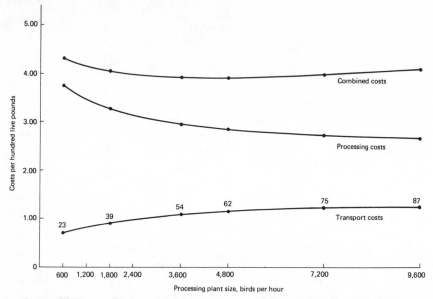

Source: William R. Henry and James A. Seagraves, "Economic Aspects of Broiler Production Density," *Journal of Farm Economics* 42, no. 1 (February 1960), p. 7.

Figure 8–8
Relationship of processing plant size to combined costs of transportation and processing for different effective production densities

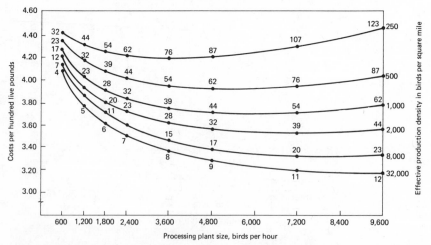

Source: William R. Henry and James A. Seagraves, "Economic Aspects of Broiler Production Density," *Journal of Farm Economics* 42, no. 1 (February 1960), p. 9.

Models of production and cost

Models are approximations of reality, expressed in symbols. Their use is to explain the behavior of a (dependent) variable, where that behavior is believed to depend on the values of some other (independent) variables. Models should be consistent with the economic theory of production and cost and with what is known about technological and institutional influences. However, models are often deliberately simplified out of necessity. Simplification may consist of using linear approximations of functions believed to be slightly curving. Or it may consist of omission of explanatory variables believed to have only slight effects upon the dependent variable. Simplified models may provide a good fit over the limited range of available data.

Linear forms. Linear-form models containing a single explanatory variable are often useful. Here are two examples:

1. An input-output function, $Q_i = b_0 + b_1 L_i + U_i$, in which Q_i is observed output per period in the ith period (time-series data) or in the ith plant (cross-section data), L_i is observed labor input per period in the ith period or plant, U_i is the sum of disturbances (effects of unspecified variables) in the ith period or plant, and the b's are the parameters to be estimated. Output per period is often measured as "value added." This model is appropriate in estimating *input-output functions* like AB, CD, and EF in Figure 6–1.

2. A cost function, $C_i = b_0 + b_1 Q_i + U_i$, in which C_i is observed cost per period in the ith period or plant, Q_i is observed rate of output in the ith period or plant, U_i is the sum of disturbances in the ith period or plant, and the b's are parameters. This model corresponds to *cost functions* like GH, AB, and DF in Figure 8–2.

Linear-form models may contain two or more explanatory variables. Here are two examples of *multivariate* models:

1. An input-output function, $Q_i = b_0 + b_1 L_i + b_2 K_i + b_3 X_{3i} + \cdots + b_n X_{ni} + U_i$, in which Q_i is the observed rate of output in the ith period or plant, L_i is observed rate of labor input in the ith period or plant, K_i is observed amount of capital services used (or available) in the ith period or plant, each of the X's is the observed value of some other input or some other influence in the ith period or plant, U_i is the sum of disturbances in the ith period or plant, and the b's are parameters. This is a model of a *production surface* similar to that depicted in Figure 8–9 (in which capital and labor are the only inputs).

2. A cost function, $C_i = b_0 + b_1 Q_i + b_2 X_{2i} + \cdots + b_n X_{ni} + U_i$, in which C_i is observed cost in the ith period or plant, Q_i is observed rate of output in the ith period or plant, each X is the observed value of some other influence on cost in the ith period or plant, U_i is the sum of disturbances in the ith period or plant, and the b's are parameters. This is

Figure 8–9
A multivariate production surface

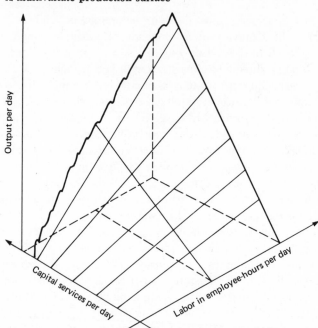

a model of cost based on a *production surface* like that of Figure 8–9 for the two-input case.

Curvilinear additive forms. In all of the linear forms above, marginal productivities of inputs and marginal costs of the output are assumed to be constant. Curvilinear models, allowing changes in marginal productivity and marginal cost with changes in the rate of output, are often desirable. Such changes are accommodated by the quadratic and cubic forms, as in the following examples:

1. A quadratic input-output model, $Q_i = b_0 + b_1 L_i + b_2 L_i^2 + U_i$, in which Q_i is observed output in the ith period or plant, L_i is observed labor use in the ith period or plant, U_i is the sum of disturbances in the ith period or plant, and the b's are parameters. The use of the squared value of an input as one of the variables of the model allows the marginal productivity of the input to increase (or decrease, but not both) as the rate of output goes up. This model and the one following are said to be *additive* because the effects of the various explanatory variables in any given period are algebraically summed to obtain their net effect upon the dependent variable. This model would be used if the input-output relationship were believed to be like that of any one of the functions AB, CD, or EF in Figure 6–9.

2. A cubic model of cost, $C_i = b_0 + b_1 Q_i + b_2 Q_i^2 + b_3 Q_i^3 + U_i$, in which C_i is observed cost in the ith period or plant, Q_i is the observed rate of output in the ith period or plant, U_i is the sum of disturbances in the ith period or plant, and the b's are parameters. Using both the squared and the cubic values of rate of output allows marginal cost first to decrease and then to increase as the rate of output expands. Thus, this form can accommodate scale economies and diseconomies in a cost function, or it can accommodate the effects of the law of variable proportions in an input-output function. It would be useful if the cost is believed to be derived from a production surface like that in Figure 7–1. Note that either the quadratic or cubic form can be made multivariate by adding more variables and the corresponding parameters.

Curvilinear multiplicative form. The following form (often called a "Cobb-Douglas function") has been used in many studies of production: $Q_i = L_i^{b_1} \cdot C_i^{b_2} \cdot U_i$, in which Q_i is observed output in the ith period or plant, L_i is observed labor use in the ith period or plant, C_i is observed use of capital services in the ith period or plant, U_i is the sum of disturbances in the ith period or plant, and the b's are parameters. A sometimes useful characteristic of this form is that the parameters b_1 and b_2 are constant percentage changes in rate of output for each 1 percent of change in labor or capital, respectively. Another sometimes useful characteristic is that the effects of the explanatory variables are multiplicative in terms of their net effect upon the dependent variable. This form allows any input to have increasing, constant, *or* decreasing marginal productivity $(b > 1, b = 1,$ and $b < 1$, respectively), and it allows increasing, constant, *or* decreasing returns to scale $(\Sigma b\text{'s} > 1, \Sigma b\text{'s} = 1,$ and $\Sigma b\text{'s} < 1$, respectively). To allow estimation of this model by multiple regression methods, the data are transformed to their logarithms and the model is stated as: $\log Q_i = \log b_0 + b_1 \log L_i + b_2 \log C_i + \log U_i$. Other inputs could be added to labor and capital in the above model, or inputs other than labor and capital could be used as explanatory variables in the model.

Data problems

Available data often do not conform to the explicit and implicit assumptions of the models that have been specified and the statistical methods that will be used. Careful adjustments of data may be needed prior to estimation of parameters.

General data problems. Measured cost may be above or below actual cost, or it may need movement in time to match it to the corresponding output. *Depreciation* is treated as fixed cost per period in most accounting systems, but the wear-and-tear component does vary with changes in the rate of output. Thus, depreciation in a given period may be either too high or too low as it stands. *Maintenance* in a given period may consist largely of repair of accumulated wear resulting from heavy use in an earlier period, or it may contain costs of preparing for intensive use in a period to follow. *Bonuses,* paid in one period at the end of a fiscal year, may be the result of services during the entire year.

Output may also need adjustment to make it comparable from observation to observation. A product may have changed over time, or it may differ somewhat from plant to plant. And a product mix may have the added problem that proportions of products in the mix are not constant from one observation to another. It may be necessary to measure output in terms of labor content or percent of plant capacity used, or in terms of an index based on these variables.

Time-series data problems. Time-series cost data usually contain effects of *price inflation.* Cost can be restated in constant dollar terms with the aid of a price index. The data may contain effects of *technological change* such as introduction of new materials, new processes, or new machines and equipment. Effects of technological change *during adjustment periods* may be different from *long-run* effects. Cost data can be standardized for technology by adjustments based on engineering estimates, or the adjustment can be made statistically by using dummy variables in the regression equation. The method of dummy variables is explained in an empirical example to follow.

Cross-section problems. Cross-section data usually contain effects of *differences in ages of plants.* Older plants may not be up to date technologically, so some items of cost are higher than they would be in a modern plant. On the other hand, depreciation costs of older plants may be based on original costs that are far below present replacement costs of the same items. Costs may need adjustment to remove effects of *regional differences* in wage rates, prices of raw materials, utilities rates, local property taxes and insurance, and so forth. Also, data may need adjustment to remove effects of *differences in accounting practices;* one firm may use maximum allowable rates for depreciation and amortization, whereas another may use rates closer to actual experience.

Problems revealed during statistical estimation

There are further problems that may become apparent after the process of statistical estimation begins. *Multicollinearity,* a high degree of correlation between two or more of the explanatory variables, may make standard errors of regression coefficients so large relative to values of the coefficients that the estimates are useless. The only satisfactory solution of the multicollinearity problem is to obtain independent estimates of the effects of all except one of the collinear explanatory variables, to adjust the values of the dependent variable so that these effects have been re-

Figure 8–10
Effects of serial correlation upon residuals

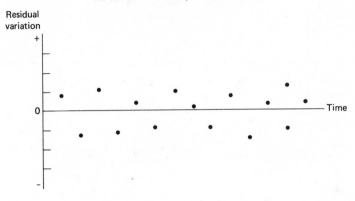

A. Residuals randomly distributed in time

B. Residuals serially correlated

moved, and to leave the collinear explanatory variables out of the model when it is reestimated.

The residuals from time-series analyses should be plotted against *time* to determine whether there is evidence of *serial correlation.* The desired appearance of the residuals is as shown in Figure 8–10A. A pattern like that of Figure 8–10B is due to serial correlation. The effect of serial correlation is to cause standard errors of the regression coefficients to be underestimated.

The residuals should also be plotted against the values of *each of the explanatory variables* to show any evidence of correlation. If there is correlation, the estimates of the regression coefficients will be biased. The desired appearance of residuals in a plot against an explanatory variable is as shown in Figure 8–11A. If the residuals appear as in Figure 8–11B, the explanatory variable has a curvilinear effect that has not been picked up; the model may be improved by adding the square of the variable and reestimating. If the residuals have a pattern like that of Figure 8–11C,

Figure 8-11
Other methodical disturbances of residuals

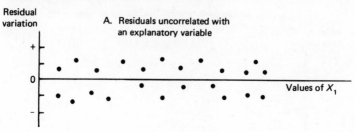

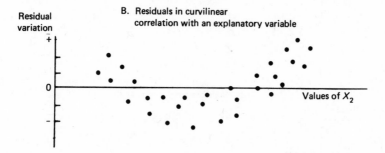

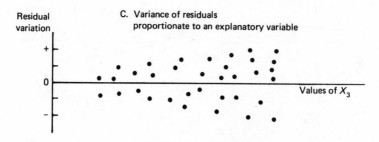

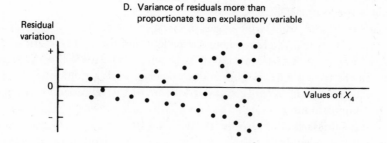

their variance is proportionate to the values of the explanatory variable; the model can be reestimated with the logarithms of the explanatory variable substituted for its original values. If the residuals make a pattern like that of Figure 8–11D, their variance is more than proportionate to the values of the explanatory variable; the model can be reestimated with the square roots of the explanatory variable substituted for its original values.

Empirical examples

Multicollinearity in a study of feed manufacturing costs. Some cross-section statistical cost studies have attempted simultaneous estimates of the relation of cost to variation in output rates (short-run curves) and the relation of cost to variation in designed capacity of plants (long-run curves). A study of animal feed manufacturing costs showed that *multicollinearity* is a serious problem in this approach.[5] The objective of such studies is illustrated by the following cost function which was estimated from observations on 29 feed plants:

$$C = 10{,}018 + 6.8193V + 0.3051K$$

in which

    C is annual cost in dollars.

    V is annual volume in tons of feed.

    K is the designed annual capacity of each mill in tons.

When K of the above equation is 10,000 tons per year, unit cost varies with V as in Curve I of Figure 8–12. When K is 20,000 tons per year, unit cost varies with V as in Curve II. By connecting the low points of the various plant curves, which are at the design capacities of the plants, the long-run (envelope) curve is obtained, as illustrated by the dashed trace in Figure 8–12.

The R^2 statistic for the above estimate was 0.98, which is regarded as a good fit to the data. However, the investigators went on to estimate the parameters of several other cost models, *using the same data* from the 29 feed mills, and obtained the results shown in Table 8–5. All of the estimates were a good fit as measured by the R^2 statistic. However, there was a considerable range of forms among the estimated long-run average cost curves, which are depicted in Figure 8–13. Note that Equations 1f and 1c, very different in form, are about equal in goodness of fit.

This study of feed manufacturing costs illustrates the effects of multicollinearity. Observed values of the independent variables, rate of output V and design capacity K, are highly correlated. Used together in a re-

---

[5] J. F. Stollsteimer, R. G. Bressler, and J. N. Boles, "Cost Functions from Cross-Section Data—Fact or Fantasy?" *Agricultural Economics Research* (July 1961).

Figure 8–12
Plant curves and envelope curve

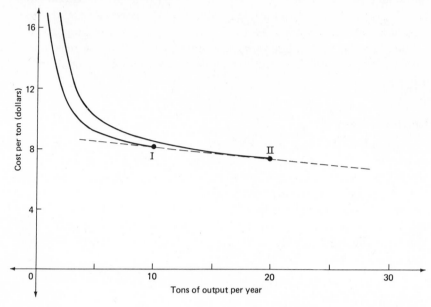

Table 8–5
Alternative cost equations derived from identical annual data on total costs, plant volume, and plant capacity, 29 midwestern feed mills*

Model	Total cost equation†	R^2
1c	$C = 70.042V^{0.8} + 0.30140(K - V)$ $\quad(16.80)$oo $\quad\quad(1.86)$	0.96
1d	$C = 22.702V^{0.9} + 0.30001(K - V)$ $\quad(20.53)$oo $\quad\quad(2.25)$o	0.98
1f	$C = 2.229V^{1.1} + \;\;0.41178(K - V)$ $\quad(18.10)$oo $\quad\quad(2.83)$o	0.97
3a	$C = 10{,}018 + 6.8193V + 0.3051K$ $\quad\quad\quad(15.05)$oo $\;(2.27)$o	0.98
3c	$C = 7.1080V + 0.4458K - 0.00000182VK$ $\quad(15.16)$oo $\;(3.22)$o $\quad\quad\quad(1.75)$	0.98
3d	$C = 5{,}799 + 6.5445V + 0.2578K + 0.00000083K^2$ $\quad\quad\quad(6.22)$oo $\;\;\;(0.43)\quad\quad\quad(0.32)$ $\quad + 0.00000365VK - 0.000000000012VK^2$ $\quad\quad(0.61)\quad\quad\quad\quad\quad(0.73)$	0.98
4a	$C = 0.004122K^{1.4} + 109.3V/(K^{0.27} - 6.01)$	0.94

* Basic data for all models and the results for 1c and 1d were made available by Professor Richard Phillips, Iowa State University, Ames, Iowa.

† In all equations, C represents total mill costs in dollars per year, V represents annual mill volume in tons, and K represents computed annual mill capacity in tons. Figures in parentheses are t ratios: o indicates significance at 5 percent level, while oo indicates significance at the 1 percent level.

Source: J. F. Stollsteimer, R. G. Bressler, and J. N. Boles. "Cost Functions from Cross Section Data—Fact or Fantasy?" *Agricultural Economics Research* (July 1961), p. 84.

Figure 8–13
Seven long-run cost curves statistically estimated from the same set of data for 29 midwestern feed mills

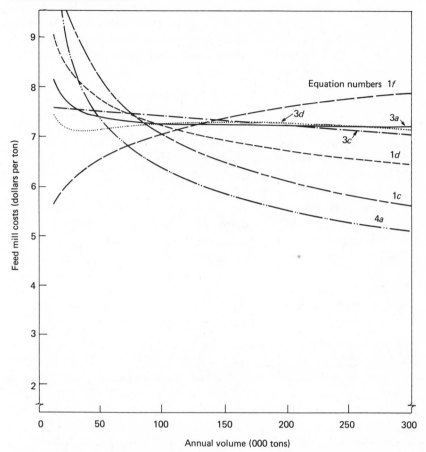

Source: J. F. Stollsteimer, R. G. Bressler, and J. N. Boles, "Cost Functions from Cross Section Data—Fact or Fantasy?" *Agricultural Economics Research* (July 1961), p. 85.

gression equation, the two variables "explain" nearly all of the variation in the dependent variable C. However, the standard errors of the regression estimates of the cost function parameters are quite large compared to the estimates themselves. Thus, the estimated parameters, which are supposed to show the separate effects of each of the independent variables, are useless. The independent variables are so highly correlated with each other that their individual influences cannot be determined.

When there is multicollinearity among explanatory variables, the only satisfactory solution is to obtain independent estimates of the influences of all except one of the collinear variables, to adjust the values of the dependent variable to correspond to standardized values of the collinear variables, and to leave the collinear variables out of the model.

Using dummy variables in a study of banking costs. Discrete influences upon cost can be estimated in statistical cost studies by using dummy variables. In a study of banking costs, dummy variables were used to determine the effects of differences in technology upon economies of scale.[6] The model of cost was as follows:

$$C = b_0 N^{b_1} W^{b_2} S^{b_3} A^{b_4} M^{b_5} O^{b_6}$$

in which

C is annual direct cost of operating the demand deposit function.

N is the number of demand deposit accounts.

W is average annual wage rate.

S is average size of a demand deposit.

A is a weighted index of activity consisting of checks (weight $= 1.0$), deposits (weight $= 1.2576$), and transit items (weight $= 0.6319$).

M is the ratio of regular to total checking accounts.

O is the number of offices operated by the bank.

b_0 is a constant.

b_1 through b_6 are elasticities of cost with respect to the several explanatory variables (each b tells the percentage change in cost for a 1 percent change in the associated explanatory variable).

Observations of cost and each of the explanatory variables were available for a cross section of 956 banks in 1968. Of the total, 610 had used computers more than one year, 78 had used computers less than one year, and 278 had never used computers. In an initial analysis, the parameters of the above model were estimated by using the combined data from all 956 banks. This analysis yielded the set of estimates listed in the fourth column of Table 8–6. All of the regression coefficients are significant and have the expected signs. The coefficient of determination, R^2, is high, indicating a good fit. However the F-test for homoskedasticity of variance does not support the hypothesis of homogeneous variance of the residuals; this result suggests that: (1) an important variable was left out of the model, or (2) the influence of the included variables is not similar for all banks in the sample.

It was decided to test the hypothesis that the three states of technology (computer more than one year, computer less than one year, never used computer) would affect the shape and level of the cost curves of the respective groups. Two sets of dummy variables were added to the model: one to allow shifts in the regression constant b_0 which determines the level of the cost curve, the other to allow for changes in the econo-

---

[6] D. L. Daniel, W. A. Longbrake, and N. B. Murphy, "The Effect of Technology on Bank Economies of Scale for Demand Deposits," *Journal of Finance* 28, March 1973.

Table 8–6
Long-run average costs in banking

Variable	Geometric mean	Standard deviation	R1 All banks	Dummy variable approach R2
Constant			−0.8717	−1.1816
			(0.0798)	(0.1155)
log N	3.8946	0.4526	0.9763	1.0410
			(0.0119)	(0.0209)
log S	3.2300	0.1987	0.3680	0.3718
			(0.0220)	(0.0213)
log A	2.5358	0.1906	0.1837	0.1707
			(0.0211)	(0.0208)
log M	−0.1422	0.1490	−0.1272	−0.1067
			(0.0215)	(0.0212)
log w	1.6957	0.0719	0.4455	0.4894
			(0.0484)	(0.0484)
log ϕ	0.3679	0.4716	0.0463	0.0595
			(0.0101)	(0.0101)
Y				0.4729
				(0.1485)
Z				0.4221
				(0.0832)
Ylog N				−0.1127
				(0.0396)
Zlog N				−0.1046
				(0.0227)
R^2			0.9697	0.9715
S.E.*			0.0929	0.0903
F			5087.7000	3252.4000
n			956	956
d†			1.9258	1.9770
F_H‡			4.3388§	3.0773§

* Standard error of the estimate.
† Durbin-Watson statistic.
‡ F-test for homoskedasticity.
§ The hypothesis that the variance of the residuals is homoskedastic is rejected at the 1 percent level of significance.
Source: D. L. Daniel, W. A. Longbrake, and N. B. Murphy, "The Effect of Technology on Bank Economies of Scale for Demand Deposits," *Journal of Finance* 28, March 1973.

mies of scale parameter b_1. Dummy variable Y was given a value of 1 if the bank had used a computer for less than one year and a value of 0 otherwise. Dummy variable Z was given a value of 1 if the bank had used a computer for more than one year and a value of 0 otherwise.

Reestimation of the model with the dummy variables added yielded the set of estimates listed in the fifth column of Table 8–6. The scale factor showing percentage increase in cost for a 1 percent increase in number of accounts is 1.0410 in banks using conventional technology, indicating slight diseconomies of scale; the same scale factor is 0.9364 (calculated as 1.0410 − 0.1046) for banks that had used computers more than one year, indicating small economies of scale. On the other hand, the scale factor showing the percentage increase in cost for each 1 per-

Figure 8–14
Economies of scale in banking°

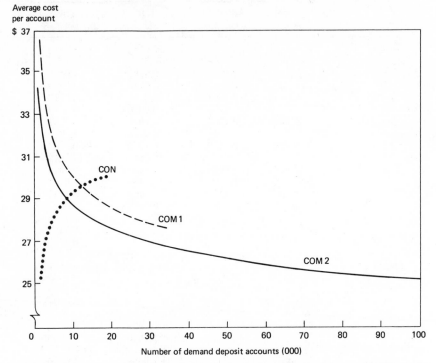

* Average cost of servicing demand deposits for banks without computers (CON), banks
with computers less than one year (COM1), banks with computers more than one year
(COM2), for the dummy variable approach, 1968.
  Source: D. L. Daniel, W. A. Longbrake, and N. B. Murphy, "Bank Economies of Scale for
Demand Deposits," *Journal of Finance* 28, March 1973.

cent increase in average size of demand deposit is 0.3718, as estimated
over all banks, indicating very large economies of scale for size increases
in this dimension.

  Figure 8–14 shows that the average cost curve for banks using computers for less than one year was higher than that for banks using computers for more than one year. This difference is due to start-up costs of
the new technology and it was picked up in this statistical cost study by
using the dummy variable technique.

USING ESTIMATED FUNCTIONS

Managerial uses of empirical cost curves

  Estimates of cost curves enter into many important decisions. These
include short-run choices of rates of output and prices and long-run decisions about numbers, sizes, and locations of plants.

In the case of decisions about rates of output for competitive firms, the optimum rate is the one that makes marginal cost equal to price. Firms with sloping demand curves can choose an optimum combination of price and output at the rate that makes marginal cost equal to marginal revenue. Pricing decisions are discussed in more detail in Chapters 9–12.

Decisions about output and pricing are so important to the firm that reliable estimates of cost functions are worth considerable effort and expense. And managers obviously cannot make these decisions without using some kind of estimates or assumptions about the *short-run* cost functions.

A firm considering plant construction or expansion needs estimates of *long-run* cost functions in determining whether or not to make the investment and what size of plant to build. In a situation with unvarying demand and constant structure of factors affecting cost (factor prices, technology, etc.), the decision rule would be simple: Build the size of plant that makes long-run marginal cost equal to marginal revenue. Under actual conditions, the decision is more complex because demand is usually expected to shift over time, the structure of factors affecting cost may also be expected to shift, and there are construction economies that make it advisable to build or expand plants in substantial increments of capacity. Thus, the plan for expansion of capacity should be optimal through time in the face of dynamic changes; *simulation* of projected results under alternative expansion plans may be the best approach.

Decisions about plant construction or expansion are especially difficult in multiplant firms. A static model that is helpful for such decisions has been developed by Stollsteimer.[7] The problem of simultaneously determining the number, size, and location of plants that minimize the combined transportation and processing costs for raw material produced in varying amounts at scattered production points is handled by the model. The following data are used as input:

1. Estimated or actual amount of raw material to be assembled from each point of origin.
2. Cost of transporting a unit of material between each point of origin and each potential plant site.
3. A plant-cost function which permits determination of the cost of processing any fixed total quantity of material in a varying number of plants.
4. Specification of potential plant locations.

The form of each plant's total cost function is assumed to be linear with respect to total output and to have a positive intercept. Equal factor costs are assumed for all locations. Stollsteimer's procedure determines

[7] John F. Stollsteimer, "A Working Model for Plant Numbers and Locations," *Journal of Farm Economics* 45 (August 1963), pp. 631–45.

approximately optimum numbers, sizes, and locations of plants for the problem described above.

A final caution

It should be kept in mind that production and cost relationships which existed in the *past* may not be relevant to decisions about *future operations* and *future investments* in plant and equipment. Statistical estimates may require further adjustments to reflect changes expected to affect production and costs of future periods. Such changes may involve: relative prices of inputs and thus combinations used, conversions of inputs to output and thus the amounts of inputs used, nature of the product, mix of products, scale of output, scale of plant, and so forth.

SUMMARY

Estimation of production and cost functions is part of the managerial process, since these relationships must be in hand if they are to be used in making decisions. The chapter discussed estimation of functions by both the economic-engineering approach and the statistical approach.

The economic-engineering approach consists of design of least-cost plants for various rates of output on the basis of current technology and prices of inputs. The engineering approach consists of the following steps: (1) selecting *instantaneous* rates of output for which the various plants are to be designed; (2) breaking the production process down into transformation *stages*, transportation *links*, and storage *points;* (3) determining *least-cost* combinations of labor, materials, and equipment for *each* of the design rates of operation in *each* of the stages; (4) combining optimally designed stages into *complete plants* for *each* of the instantaneous rates of output; (5) estimating total and unit costs for each plant at the design rate and at other rates, so as to obtain *short-run cost curves* for each of the plants; and (6) estimating the *long-run total and unit cost curves,* treating costs of the various plants at their design rates as *points* on the long-run curves.

Advantages of the engineering approach are: (1) it standardizes technology, prices of inputs, plant efficiency, operating rates, and other factors affecting costs, so that effects of changes in instantaneous rates and in hours of operation can be isolated; (2) effects of changes in any of the other factors affecting cost can also be estimated; and (3) overall costs under any assumed future conditions can be synthesized. The disadvantages are the large amount of time required and the great cost involved. The engineering approach is the only recourse in the cases involving new products, new processes, or new plants. The engineering and statistical approaches can be combined: The engineering approach can be applied to some of the individual items of cost in adjusting accounting data for use in statistical estimation, or statistical estimation can be applied to some individual items to obtain estimates needed in the engineering approach.

The statistical approach consists of statistically estimating parameters of production or cost models so as to get best (or least-squares) fits of the models to accounting data. The source of the accounting data may be a series of observations on a single firm that operated at different rates over a sequence of time periods (*time-series* data), or it may be a set of observations across a group of firms operating at various rates during the same period of time (*cross-section* data).

Production and cost models should be consistent with economic theory and with what is known of the technology and institutional setting of production, but models are often deliberately simplified. *Linear models* are appropriate where rates of output per sales or accounting period are varied by *changes in hours of operation* or by *changes in multiples of identical machines and work crews*, since these methods tend to result in constant marginal productivities of inputs and constant marginal costs. *Curvilinear models* are appropriate where instantaneous rates of output are varied by *changes in the relative intensities, or proportions*, of various inputs.

Considerable adjustment of accounting data may be advisable prior to statistical estimation. Either the costs or the outputs of a given period may be too high or too low as they stand. Depreciation, maintenance, and bonuses are examples of cost items that may not be matched with the corresponding output. And output may need revision to remove effects of *changes in products* or in the *mix of products* over time, or from plant to plant in cross-section data. In time-series data, effects of *price inflation* and *changes in technology* may need to be removed. In cross-section data, costs may need adjustment to take out the effects of *differences in ages of plants, regional differences in prices of inputs*, and *differences in accounting practices*.

During statistical estimation, certain problems may appear. One is *multicollinearity*, a condition in which there is a high degree of correlation between two or more of the explanatory variables. The condition makes estimates of the model parameters useless. The only really satisfactory method of handling multicollinearity is to *obtain independent estimates* of effects of all except one of the collinear variables, to *adjust values of the dependent variable* to correspond to standardized values of the collinear variables, and to *leave the collinear variables out of the model* when it is reestimated.

Another problem is *serial correlation of the residuals*, which causes underestimation of standard errors of the regression coefficients: it can sometimes be overcome by substituting first differences of the observations in place of the original data. Still another problem is *variance of residuals proportionate or more than proportionate to values of one of the explanatory variables;* either condition causes bias of the estimates of the regression coefficients. The latter problems can sometimes be overcome by *substituting logarithms of the explanatory variable for the original values if variance is proportionate,* and by *substituting square roots of the variable if variance is more than proportionate.*

Most long-run cost curves based on plant costs alone appear to have L shapes with great economies of scale in initial increases of design rate of output and with average and marginal costs becoming nearly constant over the remaining range of design rates. However, addition of spatial costs (assembly of materials and distribution of final products) may produce a U shape in the envelope of combined plant and spatial costs.

QUESTIONS

1. Refer to Figure 8–2. The function that relates *fixed* cost per period to the instantaneous rate of output (the function running from Point T to Point X) increases at a decreasing rate. As a general rule, would such functions be expected to increase at a decreasing rate? Explain.

2. In Figure 8–2, each of the functions that relate *total* cost per period to instantaneous rate of output given any one of the running times (such as Functions TG and UH) increases first at a decreasing rate and then at an increasing rate. How would *output* per period be related to instantaneous rate of output, given any one of the running times? Draw a diagram showing how *total* cost per period is related to rate of output, given any one running time which is then held fixed as rate of output per period is changed. What is the nature of marginal cost in your diagram? What is the explanation of this behavior of marginal cost?

3. Again refer to Figure 8–2. The functions that relate *total* cost per period to running time given any one of the instantaneous rates (such as Functions AB, EF, and GH) increase at constant rates. How would *output* per period be related to running time, given any one of the instantaneous rates? Sketch the relation of total cost per period to output per period, given any one of the instantaneous rates which is then held constant as rate of output per period is changed. What is the nature of marginal cost in this diagram? How can this behavior of marginal cost be explained?

4. In making statistical estimates of cost functions, influences on cost other than changes in the instantaneous rate and the running time must either be removed from the data or be included as variables in the economic model of cost. What would be the best way of handling the following influences on costs appearing in the time-series data for a single plant: (*a*) general price inflation; or (*b*) changes in relative prices of inputs, which may have resulted in input substitutions? What would be the best way of handling the following factors affecting costs in cross-section data for a number of plants: (*a*) variations of the actual operating rates from the designed rates; (*b*) differences in the ages of the plants, which may mean that they were not all designed at the same state of technology; or (c) locational variations in the prices of inputs?

5. In your own words, what is multicollinearity? What statistical problems result from multicollinearity? Table 8–5 and Figure 8–13 are illustrations of multicollinearity in cross-section data and show what happens when annual volume and design capacity, highly correlated with each other, are both used as variables in a model of cost? How could the problems in Table 8–5 be resolved?

FURTHER READING

Benston, George J. "Multiple Regression Analysis of Cost Behavior." *Accounting Review*, October 1966.

Kast, Ronald S., and Walker, David A. "Short Run Cost Functions of a Multi-product Firm." *Journal of Industrial Economics* 18, April 1970.*

Longbrake, William A. "Statistical Cost Analysis." *Financial Management* 2, Spring 1973.*

Stigler, George J. "The Economies of Scale." *The Journal of Law and Economics* 1, October 1958.*

Walters, A. A. "Production and Cost Functions." *Econometrica* 31, January 1963.

---

* This article is reprinted in *Readings in Managerial Economics* (Dallas: Business Publications, Inc., 1977).

Part four

Analysis of profitability of changes in output

Chapter 9

Profitability analysis: Continuative production

Break-even and volume-profit analyses compare costs of output with its expected revenues to determine the profits from alternative products at various rates of production. This chapter deals with these analyses only for cases of *continuative production,* which is *production in a run that is expected to continue indefinitely.* Analyses of finite production runs (models, projects, and batches) are taken up in Chapter 10.

The chapter begins with a discussion of classification of items of cost and the use of accounting data in estimating cost effects of decisions. This discussion is followed by an explanation of conventional break-even and volume-profit analyses and their managerial applications. Finally, volume-profit analysis is extended to the cases of curvilinear cost and revenue functions, and methods of determining optimum rates of output are demonstrated.

CLASSIFICATION APPROACH TO COST ANALYSIS

Cost analysis has the objective of separating costs affected by a decision from those not affected. In other words, we seek to isolate the *incremental* costs of a possible change in business activity. The change

301

in activity may concern rate of output, adding or dropping a product line, doing custom work for others, renting out facilities, leasing additional equipment, or whatever. In isolating relevant costs of a given decision, there must be careful classification of the various items of cost. Classification begins with a distinction between fixed and variable cost.

Fixed and variable costs

Fixed costs are fixed for the time period under consideration *regardless* of the decision, whereas variable costs are those that do depend upon that particular decision. The distinction seems simple and easy to make. Yet one must be on guard against errors and misunderstandings.

1. *The dividing line between fixed costs and variable costs is not the same for all decisions.* Elementary treatments put material costs and direct labor costs in the variable cost category, include depreciation and indirect labor and administrative costs in the fixed cost category, and leave little scope for judgment. Such an approach is far too simple. Take direct labor cost, for example. It makes a difference whether acceptance of an order requires additional overtime or can be filled by working during time that would otherwise be idle. Or take depreciation, often assumed to be a fixed cost that runs on regardless of rate of output. There is a *wear-and-tear* component of depreciation that may be reduced when production is cut back and increased when output expands; only the *obsolescence* component of depreciation is fixed from an economic point of view.

2. *Many individual items of cost are a mixture of a fixed component and a component that varies with activity.* For example, telephone cost is based on a fixed monthly charge plus additional charges for long-distance calls and other optional services used. Salespersons may be paid both a straight salary and commissions based on volume. Supervisors may receive bonuses based on output in addition to their base salaries.

3. *Some costs increase by jumps as output expands.* For example, supervisors' salaries may remain constant as output increases until management adds an additional supervisor, causing costs of supervision to rise to a higher level. Management can smooth some such sudden jumps in cost. It is possible to change the ratio of supervisors to labor or to put supervisors on overtime. But labor efficiency may fall as supervision is spread thinner in relation to the work force.

4. The expression "fixed cost" is open to several interpretations. *We need to distinguish among the following kinds of fixed costs:*

a. Costs that are fixed for the period at the discretion of management. Examples are advertising, research, and management training. These expenses go under the name of *programmed fixed cost.* The category may include a substantial part of the wages and salaries item of cost.

b. Costs that are fixed as long as operations are going on but are escapable if operations are shut down. Salaries of supervisors are an example of such a cost.

c. Costs that run on even if production is halted but are escapable if the company is liquidated. Examples are wages of guards, minimum heating to prevent pipes from freezing, and fire insurance. These outlays may be called *standby fixed costs.*

5. Some students interpret the expression "variable cost" to mean any cost that varies over time. For example, they take the fact that a machine may cost more to replace today than five days ago as evidence that depreciation of machines is a variable cost. This is a complete misinterpretation of what "variable" means. The word does not refer to variations in prices of items over time, but rather to differences in the total cost of the item *within a period* that *depend upon choices among alternative states of business activity* during the period.

6. The difference between "cost" and "expense" is important. *Expense is cost that has been set off against, or matched with, revenue in determining net income of a period. A firm has cost when it has outlay for an input or services of an input.* But costs of inputs and services that flow into inventories (supplies and materials, goods in process, finished goods) do not become expenses until the corresponding output is sold.

Other cost classifications

The fixed/variable classification is inadequate to deal with all of the cost relationships involved in managerial decisions. The following additional classifications will be useful, each classification pointing up a different aspect of decision making.[1]

Incremental costs versus sunk costs. A cost is incremental *if it results from a decision;* costs which do not arise from the particular decision but which run on anyway are excluded from incremental costs. A decision to drive an extra 1,000 miles should take into account the extra fuel costs and wear and tear on tires but can ignore the portion of depreciation which marches on regardless of usage. A decision to buy a second car, in contrast, must reckon with the added depreciation expenses resulting from having two cars aging rather than one. It is necessary to determine which costs are actually incremental for any given decision.

Marginal costs versus incremental costs. Marginal costs are always related to changes in *output;* incremental costs may relate to any decision affecting costs. Marginal costs are always computed for *unit* changes in output; incremental costs are more flexible in that they may relate to

---

[1] This section is heavily influenced by Joel Dean, *Managerial Economics* (New York: Prentice-Hall, Inc., 1951), pp. 257–72.

any change, whether it is a one-unit change in output, a thousand-unit change in output, or a decision that leaves output unaffected but changes costs in other ways.

Opportunity costs versus "costs" requiring no sacrifice. A cost is not *really* a cost from the point of view of economics (or decision making) unless it requires a *sacrifice of alternatives*—unless it is an *opportunity cost*. Determining what an opportunity cost is or, more important, determining the level of opportunity costs requires the measurement of what is given up by foregoing the best alternative use. The use of idle space which has no alternative use is cost-free for a particular purpose, regardless of the amount of depreciation being charged on the space. The use of a machine which has been written off the books completely does involve a cost if its use for the purpose under consideration requires giving up alternative opportunities.

Escapable costs versus inescapable costs (avoidable versus unavoidable costs). A cost is escapable *if the decision frees the enterprise from an outflow of funds that would have been required otherwise*. If cutting back production by 10 percent will free the firm from material costs of $10,000 per month and labor costs of $5,000 per month, those costs are escapable. But if no supervisor can be laid off as a result of this decision, supervisors' salaries do not enter into the escapable costs.

Whether certain costs are escapable varies according to the decision. Some costs that cannot be escaped as a result of reductions in output may be escaped by closing down the department completely. The part of depreciation which relates to wear and tear (the user cost) is escaped by reducing output, but the part which flows on over time regardless of output is escapable only if the machine or building is sold, and even then only if there is a market for such assets. (A fuller discussion of depreciation must be postponed until the next section.)

Common costs versus separable costs. Most firms produce more than one product and thus run into the problem of common costs. Often it is difficult to attribute costs to *particular* products since they result *from the mix of products* rather than from one product taken at a time. In decision making much of the confusion of trying to determine which costs are common and which are traceable to a particular product can be resolved by applying incremental reasoning. It is often easier to determine how much a change in the output of a single product changes a particular cost than it is to determine the product's total "fair share" of that cost.[2] In any case, it is the change in cost rather than the traceability of cost which is relevant.

---

[2] Once the accountant has adopted a routine for allocating overhead costs it may be easy to determine the "full cost" of a product. But the result of this computation is not relevant for most decision making.

Other cost concepts

A few additional terms appear in business literature. Frequently people in business refer to *out-of-pocket costs*. Strictly speaking the term should refer to *cash outlays to outsiders*. Payments for raw materials are an out-of-pocket cost, but depreciation is not. Often managers use the term to mean incremental costs. But the salary of a supervisor requires a cash outlay to outsiders which may not be incremental for a given increase in output. Often the phrase "out-of-pocket" is ambiguous.

A similar confusion surrounds the term *direct cost*. Some accountants apparently define direct costs to be the same as variable costs. One accounting research study states, "Direct costs are those which vary directly with volume (raw material, direct labor, and direct supplies) plus certain costs which vary closely with production and can be allocated to a product or group of products on a reasonably accurate basis."[3] But the expression "direct" seems to refer more to the ease with which a particular expense may be *traced to an individual department or product.*[4] Traceability and variability are not the same thing; the ambiguity on just which is being measured results in confusion. And, as we have seen, even if we restrict direct costs to mean variable costs, its meaning depends on just what decision is being made. A completely programmed system of direct costing cannot provide the exact incremental cost figure required for every kind of decision.

The distinction between *controllable* and *noncontrollable* costs is important in management, which must be concerned with fixing responsibility for keeping costs in line with predetermined standards. This book, however, is less concerned with control than it is with decision making, so that there will be few, if any, references to this dichotomy on the pages which follow.

The term *imputed or implicit costs* refers to costs that are relevant in decision making but are not recorded in the accounts. Implicit cost is the *difference* between opportunity cost and the nominal or explicit cost of an input. Examples of implicit costs are the interest and dividends that could be earned by capital elsewhere, the difference in salary a sole proprietor might earn in an outside position, and the rental that could be earned on property in other undertakings.

The term *differential cost* appears in some accounting literature to mean approximately the same thing as incremental cost in this volume.

---

[3] N.A.A. Research Report no. 37, January 1, 1961, p. 11.

[4] In fact, Gordon Shillinglaw, *Cost Accounting: Analysis and Control* (Homewood, Ill.: Richard D. Irwin, Inc., 1961), p. 102, defines a direct cost as one "that is specifically traceable to a particular costing unit." Some books appear to relate "direct costing" to the collection of variable costs but use "direct costs" to mean traceable costs, a distinction which is confusing to the layperson.

The differential cost may be computed as a total or on a unit-of-output basis.

Recent articles and books on accounting have stressed the need for *relevant costs*—that is, costs that are needed to reach an optimal decision. Relevant costs and revenues are also emphasized in managerial economics.

Empirical illustrations

Uses of fixed and variable costs and the relevance of some of the other cost concepts are illustrated below in an operation familiar to everyone. Even this simple example demonstrates the *need for flexibility* in adapting cost measures to particular problems.

The independent corner grocery store would seem to offer a simple situation for the analyst. However, it presents a number of borderline issues. Let us consider some particular expenses to see whether they fit into the fixed or variable categories.

Cost of goods sold. The sums paid at wholesale for the groceries are the clearest illustrations of variable costs. The greater the volume of sales, the greater these expenses. The complications are relatively insignificant: The firm may benefit from quantity discounts which would keep this cost from being exactly constant per unit of sales; changes in the sales mix, with various commodities selling at different markups, might cause a shift in the cost of goods sold per unit of sales; the sale of an item that has become obsolete and has been sitting on the shelves a long time may involve no real sacrifice, or at least not one equal to the original wholesale cost.

Rental on the building. Rental expense would appear to be the clearest case of a fixed expense, running on without regard to the level of sales. Yet a decision to close down would affect costs in different ways depending on the length of the rental contract and on possible alternative uses of the property. The availability of convenient storage space on the outside might enable the firm to vary warehousing rentals according to volume. If the firm actually owns the store property, the true cost of using it is the sacrifice of opportunities for earnings from alternatives.

Employees' wages. Variability of wages in such a store depends on how short a run one has in mind. If one is looking at the variation within a day, such costs are only partially variable. The store may be able to employ extra help for anticipated rush hours, but may have to keep some help to meet unpredictable peaks in activity. Under contemporary employment conditions, it is doubtful that clerks will work only during peak periods unless they are relatives of the owner. Grocery stores meet this problem in part by shifting clerks from cash registers to stocking tasks;

their ability to transfer workers from jobs that have to be done at particular (but not always predictable) times to fill-in jobs helps control costs. The opportunity to keep employees on overtime also increases the ability to adjust wages to volume but, of course, produces the complication of time and a half for overtime.

Storage costs. Interest on minimum inventories takes on a fixed character. Remaining interest costs, along with associated handling costs and costs of deterioration and obsolescence, might be treated as a variable cost dependent on volume, since the firm can vary the size of inventory with the volume of sales and output. The cost of the storage space, on the other hand, would be included in the rental expense already discussed— usually a fixed cost. One complication is that handling costs, deterioration, and obsolescence depend on the mix of products, which might vary from time to time.

Utilities. The costs of heating, lighting, and water are probably as close to fixed costs as one could find. Even if the charges for electricity include both fixed and variable components (as is true in the case of a two-part tariff), the manager of a grocery store will have little opportunity to relate the total charges to volume; he or she will not turn off the lights simply because the traffic is low. At the same time, they are costs that are escapable if the store is closed down completely, for the utilities can be disconnected.

Depreciation on equipment. Depreciation on refrigerators and other specialized grocery equipment is handled as a fixed expense in usual accounting practice. From the standpoint of short-run decisions it might be ignored, since resale or salvage value of this equipment is probably negligible. No sacrifice is involved in its continued use. In either treatment the cost is excluded from short-run variable costs and from incremental cost.

Advertising expense. Advertising presents a peculiarly difficult conceptual problem in the classification of costs. Suppose management were to adopt the policy of varying advertising with sales volume; it might then appear that advertising is a variable cost, rising and falling directly with sales. But advertising expense is not a result of volume; it is an attempt to manipulate volume. Thus the policy of basing such expenses on volume is arbitrary and usually unsound. Two solutions present themselves: (1) to treat advertising as a fixed expense budgeted by management in advance and thus unrelated to short-run volume, or (2) to leave such expenses out of the fixed-variable classification, placing them in a special category of manipulatable expenses, which we have called "programmed expenses." The literature does not give as much attention to the distinction between such programmed costs and fixed costs as seems warranted.

ACCOUNTING COSTS AND
ECONOMIC COSTS

Accountants did not originally develop their cost concepts for the same purposes that economists have in mind. Differences in purposes have led to differences in definitions. Concepts of cost must serve the purposes at hand.

Limitations of conventional accounting data for decision making

The main function of accounting is *reporting*—telling what has happened to income and wealth during a given period. The profit and loss statement (income statement) attempts to tell how well the firm has done by comparing revenue with expense of a period. Costs used in determining *past* profitability are not those needed in selecting among alternative *future* activities. Another function of accounting is *control*—measuring performance against standards. Classifications of accounts according to areas of responsibility and collections of cost data that are well suited to control purposes may not be appropriate when the purpose is choice among options for the future.

Data from conventional accounting procedures that are quite satisfactory for reporting or control are often deficient for decision making for the following reasons:

1. *Historical cost data may not reflect contemporary opportunity costs of inputs.* Raw materials acquired at $1,000 last month may be worth more today because they could be sold for more. Or, as another illustration, in periods of slack business, opportunity costs of using equipment fall far below the depreciation allocations based on original outlays. On the other hand, in periods of high activity, the sacrifice in giving up one use of equipment so that it can be used for another purpose may have a cost far greater than the depreciation. For some inputs that do have economic (opportunity) costs, the accounts record no costs; an example is the input consisting of use of the firm's cash on hand, which would have earnings if invested elsewhere.

2. *Allocations of overhead cost, which are essential in the accounting objective of determining value of goods produced and placed in inventory, may lead to confusion in decision making.* Accountants often allocate overhead on the basis of direct labor used. Suppose past experience suggests that overhead averages 150 percent of direct labor cost. If management were considering bringing in a labor-saving machine that would cut labor costs by $12,000 per year, there could be an error of projecting a reduction of $18,000 in overhead costs (150 percent of $12,000). Here, the allocation ratio is actually irrelevant to the estimate of what will happen to cost!

3. *Conventional accounting classifications may not isolate the incremental costs that are relevant to the decision at hand.* A cost that is fixed or sunk for one kind of decision may be variable or escapable for another. Classifications used in cost analysis for decision making should be tailor made for the particular decision.

Remember that traditional accounting procedures were developed for purposes other than decision making. Remember also that accounts are the main sources of data for decisions. The manager must learn how to interpret accounting data and how to ask accountants for data and classifications of data that suit particular needs.

The special problem of depreciation

Accepted accounting practice is to base depreciation on original cost and to allocate that original cost over time. The objective is to spread acquisition cost over the time periods in which the asset is to be used. Depreciation in accounting is thus a procedure for spreading the cost of a long-term asset over its useful life in a more or less equitable manner. Many students believe that the accountant's depreciation charge is intended to provide a fund for the replacement of assets, but this is *not* the purpose.

In decision making, we need a depreciation figure which reflects the *sacrifices* in selecting one alternative over another. Measurement of this sacrifice requires considerable judgment (accountants traditionally try to avoid such judgment) and varies according to the decision.

1. Suppose that a machine has broken down completely, beyond any hope of repair. The management wishes to decide whether to buy a new machine or to purchase on the outside the parts that have been produced by the machine. In this case, *reproduction or replacement cost* of the machine is the relevant basis for depreciation—*historical cost* of the old machine is irrelevant.

2. Suppose an old machine appears to have four years of physical life remaining. The issue is whether to sell the machine now and start buying the parts on the outside at once. Original cost of the machine was, let us say, $50,000. Book value net of depreciation is $20,000 and *depreciation for accounting purposes* is $5,000 per annum. However, the measurement of *depreciation needed in the analysis of this problem* is the expected decrease in market value of the machine over future periods. If the machine is worth $7,000 now but is expected to be worth $5,500 a year from now, the sacrifice in retaining it a year is $1,500. Economic depreciation is $1,500 rather than $5,000—it measures the *sacrifice of an opportunity* of selling the machine *now* rather than *later.*

3. Suppose the machine has no market value but still is productive.

The economic depreciation is *nil* regardless of the book value or the accountant's depreciation charge.

4. Now consider a decision to increase output by 50 percent. What is needed is a measure of the increase in depreciation. Managerial economists often assume that this increase is negligible, for obsolescence is unaffected by use and machines or buildings tend to deteriorate over time whether used or not. A more refined approach is to try to measure the *added wear and tear* resulting from use—to measure the user cost. In many cases user cost may be safely ignored, but in others it may be a significant consideration.

Variations on these situations appear in practice, sometimes requiring a complex analysis. Some cases may require a mixture of short-run and long-run considerations. Taxes complicate the issue. But enough has been said to indicate the *opportunity cost* basis for the economist's measurement of depreciation and to indicate that financial accounting is usually concerned with quite a different problem.

Empirical studies and illustrations

Traditional techniques of financial and cost accounting often are at variance with the requirements of economics. But accountants have developed *special approaches for purposes of decision making* which go under various names, such as direct costing, marginal income analysis, differential costing, merchandise management accounting, cost-volume-profit analysis, and contribution accounting.

How extensive are these approaches in actual practice? Chapter 2 cited a study by James S. Earley of a sample of large firms which suggests that differential accounting is becoming widespread. Earley states, "leading cost accountants and management consultants are currently advocating principles of accounting analysis and decision making that are essentially 'marginalist' in character and implications."[5] Earley finds a widespread separation of fixed and variable costs and other procedures moving in the direction of incremental reasoning. It appears doubtful, however, that all of the firms in his sample face up to the full implications of managerial economics. Do they tailor make costs to meet the varying requirements of different decisions? Do they adjust cost estimates to reflect changes in opportunity costs with variations in the use of capacity?

A study of small businesses suggests that their accounting procedures seldom reflect incremental reasoning.[6] Chapter 2 cited cases from the

[5] James S. Earley, "Marginal Policies of 'Excellently Managed' Companies," *The American Economic Review* (March 1956), p. 44.

[6] J. L. Gibson and W. W. Haynes, *Accounting in Small Business Decisions* (Lexington: University of Kentucky Press, 1963).

study in which the accounting systems encouraged the managers to use full costs (including allocated overhead) when incremental costs would have been more appropriate. Many of the managers made little use of accounts in decision making. Most of them resorted to highly subjective ad hoc analyses varying in thoroughness. Some made fairly careful pencil-and-paper calculations which used some accounting data but were mainly based on estimated values.

Actual practice, therefore, appears to vary from situations in which accounting and economics are closely interwoven in providing the information needed for decisions to the opposite extreme in which overhead allocations, past costs, historical depreciation, and similar accounting conventions actually confuse management. Every manager would profit from thinking through the relationships between accounting and economic concepts.

BREAK-EVEN CHARTS

Up to this point we have been looking at cost classification and estimates of the behavior of *particular items of cost in relation to various kinds of changes in business activity*. Our objective was to see how to isolate the incremental, or relevant, costs for any given decision. We now turn our attention to the relation of total cost to rate of output. Our objective is to compare total cost of output with its expected revenue at various rates of production. Such comparisons are commonly carried out with the aid of break-even charts.

Forms of break-even charts

Figure 9–1 illustrates a conventional break-even chart. Rate of output, Q, or perhaps sales quantity, is measured along the horizontal axis. Total revenue, TR, and total cost, TC, are measured along the vertical axis. The total revenue function in the figure is drawn as a straight line through the origin; underlying the use of this linear revenue function is an assumption that price, b_1, is constant regardless of the rate of sales. This assumption is appropriate under conditions of pure competition, in which the firm can sell any rate of output within its capacity at a "going" price determined by forces beyond the firm's control. The assumption of constant price is not appropriate if the firm has a demand curve that slopes down and to the right. Break-even analysis for the case of sloping demand is explained near the end of this chapter.

The total cost function in Figure 9–1 is shown as a straight line from an intercept on the vertical axis. The intercept, b_0, is fixed cost per period, and the slope, b_2, of the cost function is a constant value of variable cost per unit of output or sales. A constant value of variable cost per unit is

Figure 9–1
A typical break-even chart

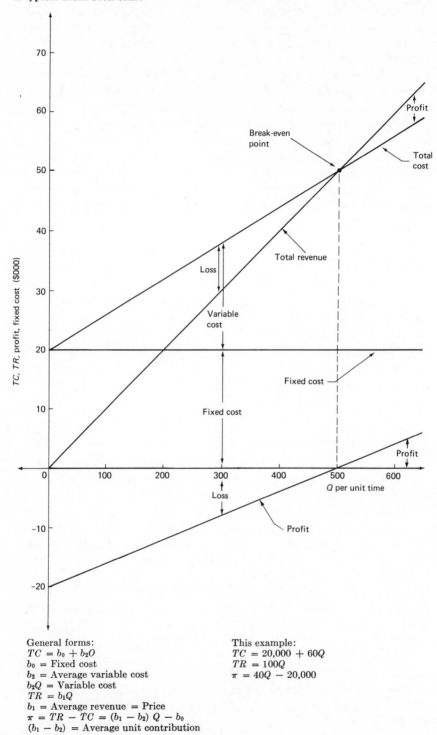

General forms:
$TC = b_0 + b_2 Q$
b_0 = Fixed cost
b_2 = Average variable cost
$b_2 Q$ = Variable cost
$TR = b_1 Q$
b_1 = Average revenue = Price
$\pi = TR - TC = (b_1 - b_2)\, Q - b_0$
$(b_1 - b_2)$ = Average unit contribution

This example:
$TC = 20,000 + 60Q$
$TR = 100Q$
$\pi = 40Q - 20,000$

Figure 9–2
Break-even chart: Contribution to profit form

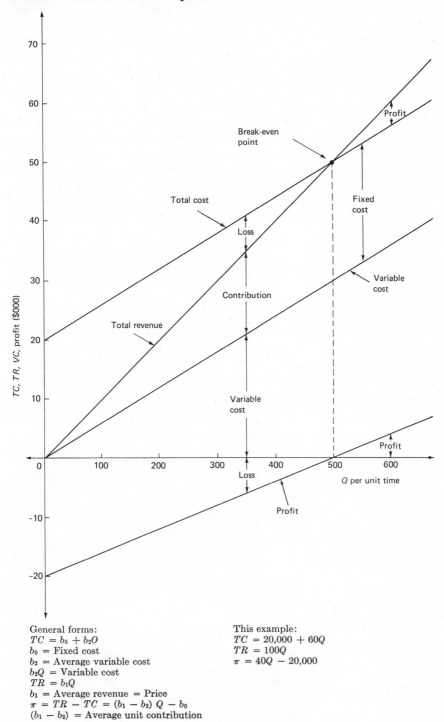

General forms:
$TC = b_0 + b_2 O$
b_0 = Fixed cost
b_2 = Average variable cost
$b_2 Q$ = Variable cost
$TR = b_1 Q$
b_1 = Average revenue = Price
$\pi = TR - TC = (b_1 - b_2) Q - b_0$
$(b_1 - b_2)$ = Average unit contribution

This example:
$TC = 20{,}000 + 60Q$
$TR = 100Q$
$\pi = 40Q - 20{,}000$

based on the following assumptions: (1) variable inputs have constant marginal productivity; (2) input prices do not change with changes in the quantities used; and (3) rates of use of inputs can be changed in a smooth, continuous way—there are no "lumpy" variable inputs. Break-even analysis for cases in which assumption (1) or (2) does not hold is explained near the end of the chapter. Lumpy inputs are discussed below.

The purpose of break-even analysis is not to determine the break-even point—the point at which total revenue equals total cost. This break-even point is of some interest, but the analysis shows something of much greater use to the manager—what happens to profits (or losses) *at various rates of output* greater and less than the break-even quantity. The purpose of break-even analysis is to determine the effects of changes in output and sales upon total costs, total revenue, and profit.[7]

Information contained in a break-even chart can be summed up by a profit function such as the one depicted in the lower portion of Figure 9–1. Profit, π, is $TR - TC$, so it is $b_1 Q - (b_0 + b_2 Q)$, or $(b_1 - b_2)Q - b_0$. In words, profit for the period is the unit contribution (price minus variable cost per unit) times the rate of output or sales, less fixed cost.

Sometimes the information on a break-even chart is presented in an alternative form like the one illustrated in Figure 9–2. In the alternative form, the variable cost function is drawn as a straight line from the origin, and fixed cost is added to obtain a total cost function that parallels variable cost. The contribution to the profit form of break-even analysis has the advantage that contribution to overhead and profit is very easy to see.

Algebraic form of break-even analysis

Algebraic execution of break-even analysis is illustrated by reference to Figure 9–1. The total revenue and total cost functions in this figure are:

General form:	This example:
$TR = b_1 \cdot Q$	$TR = \$100 \cdot Q$
$TC = b_0 + b_2 \cdot Q$	$TC = \$20,000 + \$60 \cdot Q$

where

TR is total revenue per unit of time.
TC is total cost per unit of time.
Q is output per unit of time.

---

[7] The words "total revenue" usually means realized revenue from sales during the production period. However, break-even analysis can also be used in cases where part or all of the production is to go to a deliberate buildup of finished goods inventory. In the latter case, "total revenue" means *value of output as derived from expected revenue of future periods.*

b_1 is price of the product.

b_0 is fixed cost per unit of time.

b_2 is marginal (and average variable) cost per unit of output.

To determine the break-even level of output, set the expression for revenue equal to the expression for total cost, as follows:

General form:

$$b_0 + b_2 \cdot Q = b_1 \cdot Q$$

This example:

$$\$20,000 + \$60 \cdot Q = \$100 \cdot Q$$

The solution is:

General form:

$$Q = \frac{b_0}{b_1 - b_2}$$

This example:

$$Q = 500$$

In words, break-even output is fixed cost divided by unit contribution.

Suppose we wish to calculate profit at some stated level of output, say, 650 units. Profit (π) is total revenue less total cost, as follows:

General form:

$$\pi = (b_1 \cdot Q) - (b_0 + b_2 \cdot Q)$$

This example:

$$\pi = (100 \cdot Q) - (\$20,000 + \$60 \cdot Q)$$

The solution is:

General form:

$$\pi = -b_0 + Q\,(b_1 - b_2)$$

This example:

$$\pi = \$6,000$$

In words, profit is the product of output and unit contribution minus fixed cost.

Construction of break-even charts

Where does one obtain the information used in plotting a break-even chart? There are two common methods of deriving the necessary information from the income statement.

1. One approach, which we shall call the *classification approach,* is to take a *single* income and expense statement and use judgment in classifying items of cost into those that are fixed and those that are variable. Line managers and plant accountants, who have intimate knowledge of the role of each cost item in relation to production, should have little difficulty with such classification. Some careful work may be necessary in separating the fixed and variable components of those items of cost that contain both. If there are lumpy variable inputs, there may be jumps in cost that produce a stairstep effect at each point where input is increased. The slope of the cost function is the sum of the variable costs per unit of output over the various items of cost in this category. The fixed cost is the sum of costs per period over the various items in this category. The final chart might look like Figure 9–3 if there were a lumpy input in the structure of costs.

Figure 9–3
A complex break-even chart

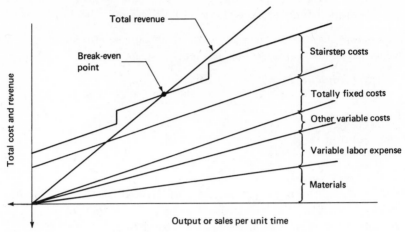

Output or sales per unit time

2. A second approach, which we shall call the *historical approach,* is to compare a *series* of income and expense statements for a sequence of periods in which the management unit had varying levels of output or sales. By plotting the output-cost combinations, the analyst obtains a scatter diagram similar to the one shown in Figure 9–4. Each dot shows the combination of output and total cost *for a particular period.* The dots will not fall exactly on a single line, because influences other than output have also affected costs. Often, however, the dots will have a pattern, so that a line of best fit may be located. *The slope of this line is an estimate of marginal cost* (or average variable cost if the line is straight). *The intercept of the line is an estimate of fixed cost.* More refined methods are possible. For example, one may correct the data for changes over time in prices of materials or other inputs, or for changes over time in labor per unit of output and other conversion ratios. Also, a fit of the cost function to the data can be made by statistical techniques, as explained in Chapter 8.

Scale of the output axis

So far, the discussion has avoided defining precisely what is measured on the horizontal axis of a break-even chart. It is time to deal with this question. If the firm produces *a single standard product,* one simply uses the *amount of physical output* (in pounds, tons, cubic yards, or whatever the appropriate unit may be). The total cost line then provides an estimate of cost at various rates of physical output.

If the output is *heterogeneous,* measurement of output is more complex.

Figure 9–4
Estimating the total cost line from a scatter diagram

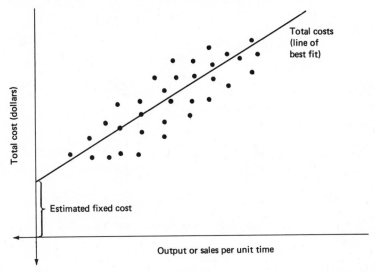

How can one add quantities of refrigerators to quantities of kitchen ranges? One possibility is to assign weights, such as hours of direct labor used, to each of the products; the total output can then be measured as an *index number*. Another possibility is to measure output as a *percent of plant capacity*. A simpler and more widely used method is to measure output in *sales dollars*. Using sales dollars weights the various products by their respective prices. None of these approaches completely overcomes the conceptual problems involved in relating total cost to heterogeneous output. Suppose the labor content of products is used as a weighting factor and labor efficiency changes for one product compared to another; does it follow that the relative costs of the products have changed in the same proportion? Or suppose prices are used as weights and the price of one product changes; has the relative cost of this product changed in the same proportion?

Appraisal of break-even analysis

Break-even analyses are very widely used in decision making and in projecting financial results of business operations. This being so, it is well to consider some of the limitations of the technique.

1. In conventional charts, the price of the output is taken as given. If one wishes to handle a case in which price is a variable that affects sales quantity, one way is to draw a series of total revenue lines on the chart, one for each price to be considered. One can then estimate sales quantity

Figure 9–5
Break-even chart with alternative revenue lines for alternative prices

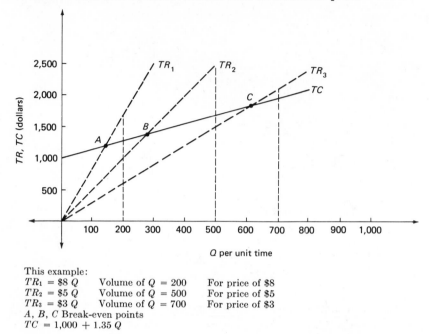

This example:
$TR_1 = \$8\,Q$ Volume of $Q = 200$ For price of \$8
$TR_2 = \$5\,Q$ Volume of $Q = 500$ For price of \$5
$TR_3 = \$3\,Q$ Volume of $Q = 700$ For price of \$3
A, B, C Break-even points
$TC = 1,000 + 1.35\,Q$

at each price, determine profit if that quantity is actually sold, and look at the sensitivity of profit to changes in prices and the corresponding quantities. This approach is illustrated in Figure 9–5.

2. Cost functions developed by the historical approach may be erroneous if there were changes over time in prices of inputs. If production records are available that show physical amounts of inputs used, cost data can be standardized to a specified set of input prices and the error can be avoided.

3. Cost functions developed by the historical approach may be erroneous if there were changes over time in production technology, effectiveness of supervision, legislation and regulation, or other influences on conversions of input to output.

4. When break-even charts are based on accounting data, as they usually are, the cost functions may be in error because of data limitations: omissions of imputed cost, arbitrary estimates of depreciation, and inappropriate allocations of overhead cost.

5. Selling costs are difficult to handle. Selling costs are not so much a result of output as they are a cause of changes in sales quantities. Furthermore, the relationship of selling costs to output is especially unstable over time.

6. Some of the costs of a particular period may not be the result exclusively of output in that period. Maintenance expenses of a given period may be the result of hard use of a past period or preparation for hard use in a future period.

7. Taxes must be considered. One may develop the chart to show part of profit going to the government in taxes. However, if the company has alternating years of profit and loss, with recovery of taxes during loss years, the adjustment for taxes is somewhat difficult to show on the chart.

It is easy to build up a formidable list of limitations of break-even charts. Some writers are skeptical of their usefulness unless they are made much more complex than is usual. At the same time, break-even analysis is simple, easy to understand, and inexpensive.

Usefulness of break-even charts undoubtedly varies from industry to industry. Those industries experiencing frequent changes in input prices, rapid improvements in technology, and many shifts in product mix will profit little from break-even analysis. In other industries, break-even analyses may be quite useful to managers who are familiar with their limitations and simplifications. Management depends heavily on analytic tools that cut through the complexity of reality and focus attention on fundamental relationships.

PROFIT-VOLUME ANALYSIS

Many authors have adapted break-even analysis to the situation of the *multiproduct* firm. They construct break-even charts for the individual product, individual department, or "sector." One variation is what Bergfeld, Earley, and Knobloch call the profit-volume (*P/V*) technique or cost-volume-profit analysis.[8] The main concepts used in the *P/V* technique are:

P/V income = Sector's sales volume in dollars minus sector variable costs.
Profit contribution = *P/V* income minus specific programmed costs.
Specific programmed costs = Cost of selling the output of the sector or other costs of promoting that sector (as opposed to programmed cost for the firm as a whole).
P/V ratio = The ratio between the unit *P/V* income and unit price, i.e., *unit* contribution or *slope* of the *P/V* line.

This variation on the break-even chart is shown in Figure 9–6. The function begins at a *specific programmed cost*, below the zero contribution line. The upward sloping line shows the profit contribution; its *slope*

---

[8] Albert J. Bergfeld, James S. Earley, and William R. Knobloch, *Pricing for Profit and Growth* (New York: McGraw-Hill Book Co., 1957). Modern cost accounting books frequently include a chapter on this type of analysis.

Figure 9–6
Profit-contribution chart

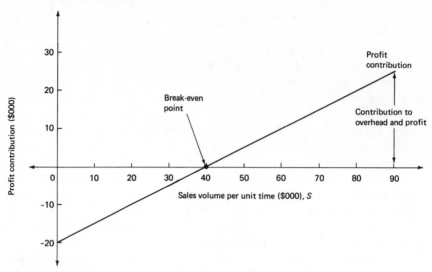

Profit contribution = $0.5 S − $20,000.

is the P/V ratio or *contribution per dollar of sales*. Here, output is heterogeneous and is being measured in sales dollars. One moves along the sloping line to the point representing the expected sales volume. The vertical distance between this point and the zero line is the profit contribution for the sector. Such a chart ignores overheads that cannot be definitely allocated to this sector. It shows whether a product is covering its own variable and programmed costs; it shows what contribution the product is making to overall company overhead and profit. The chart thus permits an evaluation of product profits at varying levels of sales, and also provides information for the comparison of contributions from one product to another.

Algebraic form of profit-volume analysis

Profit-volume analysis by the algebraic technique is explained with the aid of Figure 9–6. The profit-contribution function is determined as follows:

General form:

$$P/V = S - SVC = b_1Q - b_2Q = (b_1 - b_2)Q$$
$$PC = P/V - SPC = \frac{b_1 - b_2}{b_1}S - SPC$$

where

P/V is P/V income.

S is sales volume or total revenue.

SVC is sector's variable cost.

b_1 is product price.

b_2 is sector's average variable cost.

$b_1 - b_2$ is contribution per unit of Q.

$(b_1 - b_2)/b_1$ is contribution per dollar of sales or P/V ratio.

PC is profit contribution.

SPC is specific programmed costs.

To determine the sector's break-even sales volume, set the expression for PC equal to O, as follows:

$$\frac{b_1 - b_2}{b_1} S - SPC = 0$$

The solution is:

$$S = \frac{SPC}{\dfrac{b_1 - b_2}{b_1}}$$

In words, sector break-even volume is obtained by dividing specific programmed costs by sector contribution per dollar of sales. For the example of Figure 9–6: price is \$100, sector's average variable cost is \$50, and SPC is \$20,000;

$$P/V = \frac{100 - 50}{100} S = 0.5S$$
$$PC = 0.5S - 20{,}000$$

Break-even points:

$$0.5S - 20{,}000 = 0$$
$$S = 40{,}000$$

To determine results at any given sales volume, simply substitute that level of sales into the PC equation.

CURVILINEAR FUNCTIONS

Break-even analysis and profit-volume analysis are often concerned with results over relatively short ranges of output. Maximum sales expected at a given price and minimum sales expected at the same price may set the upper and lower limits, respectively, to the relevant range of output. In another setting, sharply rising costs beyond the designed capacity of a plant may set the upper limit to output, and a break-even point that is not far away may set the lower limit. In such cases as these, the assumption that cost and revenue are linear functions of output may be quite close to the true relationships.

Figure 9–7
A break-even chart with curvilinear total cost function

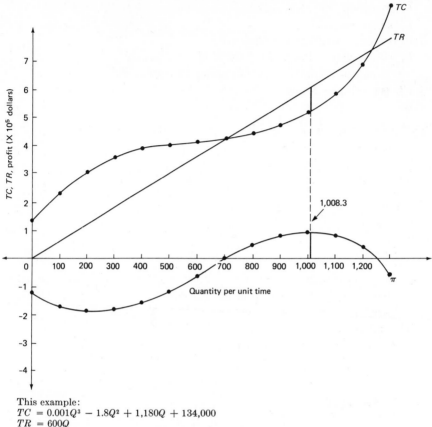

This example:
$TC = 0.001Q^3 - 1.8Q^2 + 1,180Q + 134,000$
$TR = 600Q$
$\pi = -0.001Q^3 + 1.8Q^2 - 580Q - 134,000$

On the other hand, if a relatively wide range of output is to be considered, the total cost function will often be curvilinear. A firm with a curvilinear total cost function would face a linear total revenue function if product price were independent of output of the firm (perfect competition). This situation produces a break-even chart like the one depicted in Figure 9–7. Note that there are two break-even points. Note also that profit is maximum at that particular level of output where the vertical distance between the cost and revenue curves is greatest.

If the firm faces a demand curve that slopes down and to the right (monopoly or monopolistic competition); the total revenue function rises to a peak and then declines (this was discussed in Chapter 3). In this case, both the cost curve and the revenue curve are curvilinear and the break-even chart is similar to Figure 9–8. As before, there are two break-

Figure 9–8
A break-even chart with curvilinear total cost and total revenue functions

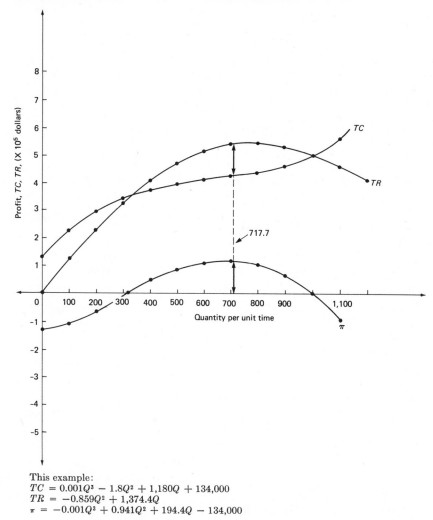

This example:
$$TC = 0.001Q^3 - 1.8Q^2 + 1,180Q + 134,000$$
$$TR = -0.859Q^2 + 1,374.4Q$$
$$\pi = -0.001Q^3 + 0.941Q^2 + 194.4Q - 134,000$$

even points and a particular level of output that produces maximum profit.

Algebraic determination of optimum output

If there is a curvilinear form of the cost function (or of both the cost and the revenue functions), there is a particular level of output that yields maximum profit. This level can be determined analytically by algebraic techniques. The method is explained by reference to Figure 9–8.

The equation for the revenue (R) function in Figure 9–8 is a quadratic form:

$$TR = -0.859Q^2 + 1,374.4Q$$

in which

TR is total revenue per unit of time.

Q is output per unit of time.

The equation for the cost function in the figure is a cubic form:

$$TC = 0.001Q^3 - 1.8Q^2 + 1,180Q + 134,000$$

The equation for profit (π) is the expression for total revenue less the expression for total cost:

$$\pi = -0.859Q^2 + 1,374.4Q - 0.001Q^3 + 1.8Q^2 - 1,180Q - 134,000$$

Combining terms:

$$\pi = -0.001Q^3 + 0.941Q^2 + 194.4Q - 134,000$$

At its maximum point, the slope of the profit function is zero. Since the slope of this function is its first derivative with respect to Q, a general expression for the slope can be found by methods of differential calculus.

$$\frac{d\pi}{dQ} = -0.003Q^2 + 1.882Q + 194.4$$

Let this expression be set equal to 0:

$$0 = -0.003Q^2 + 1.882Q + 194.4$$

The resulting equation can be organized in the general quadratic form:

$$0 = aQ^2 + bQ + c$$

The general quadratic form has two solutions, the two values of Q. These two roots are determined by the general equation:

$$Q = \frac{-b \pm \sqrt{b^2 - 4ac}}{2a}$$

For the example, the equation for the roots of Q and two solution values are:

$$Q = -90.33$$
$$Q = 717.7$$

The negative value cannot be the solution, so the second value is the answer sought.

In words, in the case of a curvilinear cost function, the quantity corresponding to maximum profit can be obtained by:

1. Subtracting the cost function from the revenue function to obtain the profit function.
2. Determining the first derivative of the profit function with respect to Q.
3. Setting the expression for the first derivative equal to zero.
4. Solving the resulting equation for the value of Q.[9]

Although the above procedure pinpoints a particular value for "optimum" output, two cautions should be kept in mind. First, the expected value of profit may not change much over a considerable range of values for output; i.e., profit may not be very sensitive to changes in output in the vicinity of optimum. Second, cost and revenue functions used in analysis are estimates; the true functions may be shaped and positioned somewhat differently.

Either the linear or the curvilinear form could describe the relationship of cost to changes in output over a specified range in a particular firm. However, analyses based on these forms do not have the same results. In the case of curvilinear cost and/or revenue functions, profit reaches a peak at a particular level of output; this output is optimum.

Implications for decision making

We should avoid oversimplified generalizations about the relationship of cost to output in the short run. It appears that short-run cost functions are quite close to linear over the usual range of output in many industries. On the other hand, rising marginal costs are sometimes encountered.

A reasonable way for managers to estimate the effects of alternative actions upon cost is to use their own judgment in determining how the different categories of cost will be affected by these actions. Changes in cost for the various items can then be aggregated to provide cost information that is relevant for the decision. This "flexible" approach can be applied to decisions about product introduction and abandonment, as well as to choices of level of output with plant regarded as given.

Managers should be especially careful not to overlook the possibility of rising marginal costs as output per unit of time is increased. Causes of rising marginal cost can be subtle: gradual declines in labor productivity as work force is increased, creeping managerial inefficiency as the ratio of supervisors to workers falls, and increases in waste of materials and user

---

[9] Determining the maximum value of the profit function (as explained in this chapter) and determining the point at which marginal cost equals marginal revenue (as explained in Chapter 7) are alternative ways of solving the same problem: What is the optimum rate of output/sales?

cost as production presses harder against the designed capacities of machinery and equipment.

SUMMARY

Cost analysis has the objective of *isolating incremental costs* of a possible change in business activities for use in deciding whether to make the change. Incremental, or relevant, costs can be derived from accounting data by the *classification approach*. Classification is founded on a distinction between *fixed costs* (costs that will march on during the period regardless of the decision) and *variable costs* (costs that *do* depend upon the action taken).

Keep in mind: (1) a cost that is fixed in relation to one decision may be variable in relation to another; (2) costs that are fixed in relation to actions that can be taken in the short run do become variable over the longer run of time; and (3) many accounting items of cost contain both fixed and variable components.

Accounting concepts of cost were developed to serve specific purposes: (1) income determination for use in *reporting* what happened to income and wealth during a given period, and (2) measurement of variance from standards to assist management in *control* of performance. When managers are making *decisions about future activities*, data from a conventional accounting system, as it stands, may not be appropriate because: (1) *it may not be in line with contemporary opportunity costs of inputs* —and this limitation is especially applicable to the item of depreciation; (2) *it may contain allocations of overhead costs* that make the data inappropriate for the decision at hand; and (3) *the accounting classifications may not separate incremental costs of the particular decision from the costs that should be regarded as fixed,* or sunk. The manager must learn how to interpret accounting data and how to ask accountants for data and classifications that suit particular needs. Managerial economics and managerial accounting are in close agreement when it comes to analysis for decision making.

Break-even analysis is a technique used in comparing the total cost of output or sales to the corresponding value, at various rates of output or sales. It can be applied in decisions about production for deliberate buildup of inventory or about production matched by sales in the same period. Break-even analysis can reveal the sensitivity of profit to changes in rate of output, prices of inputs or of the product, or input-to-output conversion ratios (such as labor per unit of output). It can be carried out algebraically or by the method of graphing.

Cost functions used in break-even analysis can be estimated from an income and expense statement *for a single period* by using the *classifica-*

tion approach or the functions may be statistically derived from a *series of statements* over various periods in which the firm had differing rates of output. The scale of the output or sales axis may be in *physical units* if the firm has a *single homogeneous product;* if the firm has a *mix of products,* output or sales can be measured in one of the following: an *index* (such as hours of direct labor used), *percent of plant capacity* used in production, or *dollar value of output.*

Profit-volume analysis focuses on *contribution* of a product, department, or sector toward the overhead costs and profit of the firm. The P/V technique can also be used to compare contributions of different products or to compare contributions of the same product at differing prices. The algebraic method of P/V analysis is easy to carry out.

If the firm has a curvilinear total cost curve, faces a sloping demand curve, or both, it has an optimum rate of output that can be determined by two mathematical approaches: (1) determine rate of output at which dTC/dQ, the slope of total cost (which is marginal cost), is equal to dTR/dQ, the slope of total revenue (which is marginal revenue); or (2) determine the rate of output at which dP/dQ, the slope of the profit function, is zero and the function is maximum.

QUESTIONS

1. "The dividing line between fixed and variable cost depends upon the particular decision involved." Explain.

2. Distinguish among outlay, cost, and expense.

3. Why might unit cost, as determined by conventional accounting, differ from the incremental cost per unit, as needed for decision making?

4. What is meant by "the opportunity cost basis" of the economist's concept of depreciation?

5. Could break-even analysis be applied to a case in which all of the output under consideration is to be placed in an inventory of finished goods? Explain.

PROBLEMS

1. A porcelain figurine is made and sold by White Rock Statuary at a variable cost of $500 per unit. The fixed costs per period are $1,000. Each unit is sold at a price of $750.
  a. Draw a break-even chart, labeling all lines, the axes, profit (loss), and the break-even point.
  b. Redraw the graph with a fixed cost of $2,000 per year.

2. Cost and related data are shown below for the Acme and Bettre Corporations:

	Acme	Bettre
Fixed costs...........................	$800,000	$400,000
Discretionary costs................	120,000	240,000
Variable costs/unit................	3	7
Sales price/unit...................	8	10

a. Compute the break-even point for each company.
b. The Acme Company is thinking of increasing advertising expenditures by $100,000. Recompute the break-even point. If the increased expenditure yields 25,000 more units of sales, is it wise?
c. Which company is more susceptible to adverse economic conditions?

3. The Bloom Company has recently purchased a plant to manufacture a new product. The following data pertain to the new operation:

Estimated annual sales....................	24,000 units
Estimated costs:	
Material............................	$4.00/unit
Direct labor.........................	$0.60/unit
Overhead.............................	$24,000 per year
Administrative expenses.................	$28,800 per year
Selling expenses......................	15% of sales

a. If profit per unit is to be $1.02, what will be the selling price?
b. Compute the break-even point, both in dollars and in units.

4. The Arthur Corporation has the following budget for the coming year:

Fixed costs..................................	$40,000
Subcontracting costs (variable).................	$2 per unit
Other variable costs........................	$1 per unit
Sales price....................................	$5
Budgeted production and sales.................	30,000 units

As an alternative to subcontracting, a plant can be leased for the year for $51,200. Total variable cost under this arrangement would be $1.20 per unit.
a. Find the break-even point under the initial budget.
b. Compute the break-even point under the lease arrangement.
c. Should the lease of plant be undertaken?
d. How sensitive is the Arthur Corporation's profit figure to sales volume under each alternative?

5. Pace Company makes an assembly that attaches to an ordinary dump truck and converts the truck into a snow dozer with a hydraulically controlled blade. This product is sold to highway departments and city governments in northern states for use in clearing highways and city streets. The company's sales department has estimated that annual sales Q, in units, will vary with price P, in dollars, as follows: $Q = 15,000 - 1.25P$. Pace Company's accounting department projects annual fixed costs of $6,750,000 and variable production costs at a constant $7,600 per dozer assembly.
a. Derive the function relating the company's annual profit to sales.

   b. Determine optimum production and sales rate, maximum profit, and best price.

   c. Use a graph to illustrate what you have just done.

6. With the data from Problem 5 above, carry out an alternative approach to the determination of optimal output, maximum profit, and best price. This alternative approach is based on marginal cost and marginal revenue.

   a. Derive Pace Company's functions relating marginal cost and marginal revenue to sales.

   b. Determine the sales rate at which marginal cost equals marginal revenue.

   c. How does the optimal sales rate just obtained compare with the rate determined in Problem 5*b* above? What is your conclusion about profit and price as determined by the method of equating marginal cost to marginal revenue?

   d. Use a graph to illustrate the method of equating marginal cost to marginal revenue.

FURTHER READING

Anthony, Robert N. "What Should 'Cost' Mean?" *Harvard Business Review* 48, June 1970.

Coyne, Thomas J. "Commercial Bank Profitability by Function." *Financial Management* 2, Spring 1973.*

Darden, Bill R. "An Operational Approach to Product Pricing." *Journal of Marketing* 32, April 1968.

Reinhardt, J. E. "Break-Even Analysis for Lockheed's Tri-Star: An Application of Financial Theory." *Journal of Finance* 28, September 1973.

Solomons, David. "Economic and Accounting Concepts of Income." *The Accounting Review* 36, July 1961.

---

* This article is reprinted in *Readings in Managerial Economics,* rev. ed. (Dallas: Business Publications, Inc., 1977).

Chapter 10

Profitability analysis: Discrete production runs

This chapter discusses profitability analysis for several types of production involving distinct runs that come to planned ends. Production of product types or models is considered first, and then production that takes the form of projects. Particular attention is given to the effects of learning curves on variable costs, analysis of new product profitability, effects of changes in rates and lengths of production runs, analysis of profitability of model changeover, and the critical path method of estimating project "crashing" cost.

The chapter then moves into an analysis of intermittent purchasing and intermittent production. These activities result from economies of producing at instantaneous rates greatly in excess of sales or usage rates. Thus, inventories are prominent. Attention is paid to economic order quantities, economic lot sizes, and safety stocks.

TERMINATING PRODUCTION: PRODUCT TYPES (OR MODELS) AND PROJECTS

This section deals with production that takes the form of *one* run. The first case considered is that of products, product types, or models that have limited lives. This is followed by an analysis of production that takes the form of projects (construction, system installation, research and development, and others).

Product life cycles

The pattern of a product's sales rates over time is called the *life cycle* of the product. Consider first the total sales of a general product (ice-cooled household refrigerators, kerosene lamps, CB radios, personal calculators). Marketing specialists conceive the life of a successful product as consisting of four recognizable stages, illustrated in Figure 10–1 and defined as follows:

1. *Introduction.* Potential customers are just becoming aware of the product. Demand must be created; the marketing objective is to get some buyers to try the product. Sales rates are low and slowly rising.

2. *Growth.* Customers become generally aware of the product. Acceptance begins to spread rapidly. Sales zoom upward and strain the productive capacities of the industry. More producers enter the industry. The marketing objective is to develop brand preferences.

3. *Maturity.* Most potential customers have made their initial purchases. The market becomes saturated, with demand limited to replacement and population growth. Price and nonprice competition becomes intense.

4. *Decline.* The product begins losing its appeal as life-styles change and other products based on new technologies become available. Excess capacity builds up even though one producer after another drops out of the market.[1]

The life cycle depicted in Figure 10–1 is a generalized pattern; many products do not follow the pattern exactly. Some are failures, abandoned during the introduction stage with heavy losses for the unsuccessful innovator. Others have a slow, prolonged growth stage, rather than the sharp rise in sales rates shown in Figure 10–1. The maturity stage of some products lasts for many years (gelatin desserts, innerspring mattresses, gasoline-powered automobiles), whereas other products may be quickly passing fads (hula hoops, miniskirts, most hit phonograph records). The decline stage may be gradual (black and white television receivers) or abrupt and rapid (mechanical desk calculators). Despite the many deviations from the generalized pattern, the concept of a product life cycle is useful because most general products do pass through these recognizable stages with their wide variations in sales rates. Figure 10–2 shows sales rates for three familiar products that appear to have entered their maturity stages.

---

[1] A more detailed discussion of product life cycles can be found in Theodore Levitt, "Exploit the Product Life Cycle," *Harvard Business Review* (November–December 1965).

Figure 10–1
A product's life cycle

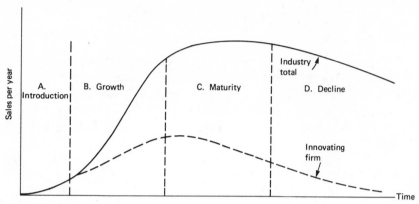

An individual firm's sales over time are that firm's share of the industry's total sales. During the early introduction stage, a firm that is the first innovator may have *all* sales of the product, but the company's output will ordinarily be a steadily decreasing share of the industry total as other firms enter during the growth stage, as illustrated in Figure 10–1. Sales rates *of any given model* may level off, or even begin to decline, long before the onset of the maturity stage of the general product. A producer may be able to lengthen the period of profitable production by introducing a *series* of improved models or product types, as depicted in Figure 10–3. Each such model or type has a life cycle of its own, which may be as short as a single year (1977 Chevrolet Caprice) or may run several years (IBM 7094 computer).

In managing products that have life cycles, special attention must be given to decisions whether or not to introduce new products, alternative strategies for introduction, economic effects of variations in rate of production and lengths of production run, and decisions to shut down production and end the lives of old products. Economic analyses appropriate to these decisions are discussed in the sections to follow.

New product profitability analysis: An overview

In deciding whether and how to introduce a new product, management must estimate profits *over the whole potential life of the product*. Losses may be unavoidable during the introductory stage but may be more than offset by subsequent profits. The firm's planning objective is to maximize the present value of expected future net revenues over a period extending as long as the life of any product under consideration.

Figure 10–2
Sales over time—three familiar products

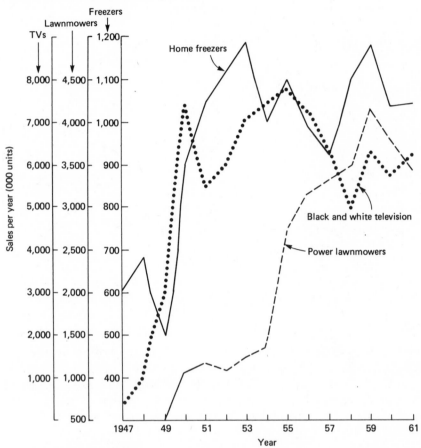

Projecting a new product's sales and revenue. The time path of sales rates for a type or model of a product depends upon (1) the underlying pattern of *total industry sales* for the general product class, and (2) the *firm's share* of industry total, which will depend partially upon the firm's pricing and promotion. Since the company cannot be certain about the success of a new product, it is advisable to make *alternative* forecasts. For example, an aircraft manufacturer might make three forecasts of sales patterns for a new type of plane, as illustrated in Figure 10–4. Management's subjective probability estimates for each of the three sales patterns may be different for alternative pricing strategies, as shown in Table 10–1.

Projecting a new product's costs. In making a new product, there will be a bundle of cost that is *fixed for the production run:* detailed product

Figure 10–3
Life cycles of a series of models

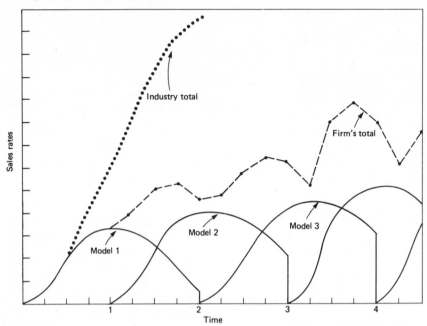

design and styling, construction and testing of a prototype, detailed planning of production processes, purchase of specialized jigs and tools, selection and training of a work force, and cost of positioning and starting up.
As the total volume of the production run is increased, there are more
units to share the fixed cost of the run and *the amount prorated to each
unit is reduced*.

Figure 10–4
Hypothetical forecasts for a new plane

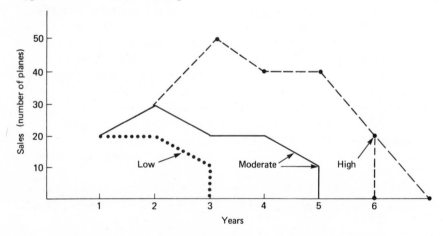

Table 10–1
Hypothetical sales forecasts for a new plane

Degree of success	Total number of planes	Management's subjective probability estimates	
		Price—$10 million	Price—$9.5 million
Low....................	50	.30	.05
Moderate..............	100	.45	.55
High.................	200	.25	.40

Total variable cost of the production run (labor, materials, power, direct overhead) increases with total volume. However, the *additions to variable cost are usually less than proportional to expansion of total production because of a phenomenon called the learning curve.*

Effects of learning curves on variable costs per unit

It has been observed that a labor force working on a new product becomes more efficient as the length of the production run is increased. Skills improve, more specializations are developed, coordination gets better, and innumerable adjustments are found that make the work easier and faster. The resulting patterns of declining labor cost per unit over successive units of output are called *learning curves*. Learning curves are apparent in building a series of similar structures (houses, industrial plants, bridges); in assembling complex products (computers, automated machine tools, naval vessels, aircraft); and in carrying out a series of difficult process startups (metal refining, paper making, chemical synthesis, container manufacturing).[2]

A common form of the learning curve is based on reduction of labor per incremental unit of output by a constant fraction each time the total output to date is *doubled*. For example, suppose that the labor requirement is reduced by 10 percent with each doubling of output. Incremental labor required for the ith unit is 0.9 times the incremental labor needed for the $(i/2)$th unit; the factor 0.9 is called the *learning rate* for the particular work process. The equation for the learning curve in the above example is $L_i = 0.9 \, L_{i/2}$, in which L is incremental labor per unit. If the first unit produced (the prototype) requires 1,000 units of labor, the second is projected to take 900 units, the fourth to need 810 units, the eighth to require 729 units, and so on. On long production runs, learning curves can produce very sizable reductions in labor used per unit, as may be seen in Figure 10–5.

Learning rates vary from one work process to another.[3] The *proportion*

---

[2] Frank Andress, "The Learning Curve as a Production Tool," *Harvard Business Review* (January–February 1954).

[3] Winfred B. Hirschmann, "Profit from the Learning Curve," *Harvard Business Review* (January–February 1964).

Figure 10–5
Effects of learning on labor used

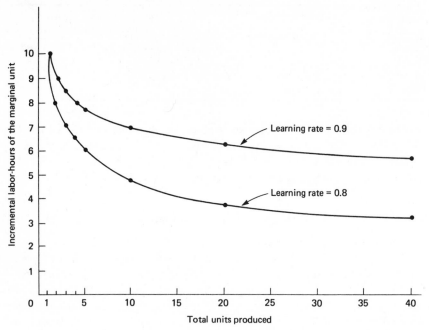

of labor used in tasks that are not machine-paced is an important determinant of the learning rate. Learning curves are particularly impressive in aircraft manufacturing, where most labor is used in manual techniques. The following rules of thumb have been developed for estimating learning rates prior to any experience with a new work process:

If the proportion of direct labor not paced by machines is	*The expected learning rate is*
0.75	0.80
0.50	0.85
0.25	0.90

The rate of improvement in labor efficiency tends to be greater (value of the learning rate coefficient tends to be smaller) than the above values if the product is a completely new design. On the other hand, if the product is a slight modification of one that has already been run by the same work force, the initial unit will have labor costs reflecting some of the learning from the previous production run and subsequent improvement will be smaller (the learning rate coefficient will be larger) than the values above.

The effects of learning curves upon labor costs make it imperative for new product profitability to be analyzed over the whole life cycle of the product. It is often necessary to take losses in early periods, when labor costs are high, in order to reach those points on the learning curve at which labor costs become low enough that profits can be made.

Deciding whether to introduce a new product

A hypothetical example of an aircraft manufacturer's decision on whether to introduce a new plane illustrates the interaction of the learning curve effect upon costs and the pricing effect upon revenue.

Cost analysis. This structure of costs is hypothetical but representative of costs of manufacturing a moderate-sized passenger plane.

1. Variable costs.
   a. Direct labor, primarily assembly labor—a learning rate of 0.8 is assumed.
   b. Materials and components—materials cost per unit stabilize early in the production run and are assumed constant. Components (landing gear, engines, radios, instruments, seats, etc.) are standard items, used in a number of other aircraft, and have a constant cost per unit.
   c. Indirect labor and power—assumed to have a constant cost per unit.
2. Fixed costs for the production run.
   a. Research, engineering, styling.
   b. Purchase of specialized jigs, dies, and tools.
   c. Selling and promotion.

Total and unit costs at various levels of total output are similar to those listed in Table 10–2 and illustrated in Figure 10–6.[4] As total output increases, cost per unit decreases in the fixed cost category because the fixed total cost is prorated over more units, and cost per unit decreases in the variable cost category because of the effect of the learning curve upon direct labor cost per unit.

Profitability analysis, using a decision tree. Profitability analysis requires comparisons of costs and revenues at the various levels of output for which management has made subjective probability estimates. Assume management's sales and probability forecasts for the new plane are the seven-year projections in Table 10–1 and the cost estimates for the plane are those listed in Table 10–2. A decision tree provides an efficient organization of the alternative outcomes of the new product venture and

---

[4] Adapted from S. G. Sturmey, "Cost Curves and Pricing in Aircraft Production," *Economic Journal* (December 1964)

Table 10-2
Hypothetical average and total costs for a new plane (in $ millions)

Output	Direct labor	Other variable costs	Variable cost per unit	Fixed cost per unit	Average total cost per unit	Total cost at this output
10............	$1.54	$6.20	$7.74	$30.00	$37.74	$377.40
20............	1.28	6.20	7.48	15.00	22.48	449.60
30............	1.15	6.20	7.35	10.00	17.35	520.50
40............	1.05	6.20	7.25	7.50	14.75	590.00
50............	0.98	6.20	7.18	6.00	13.18	659.00
100............	0.80	6.20	7.00	3.00	10.00	1,000.00
200............	0.65	6.20	6.85	1.50	8.35	1,670.00

their probabilities, as these depend upon pricing strategies; a tree for this example is shown in Figure 10–7.

A decision tree is comprised of nodes and branches and runs from left to right. At the extreme left, *the square node represents a decision point* from which there are two action branches representing the firm's alternative pricing strategies. The action branches lead to *round nodes standing*

Figure 10–6
Hypothetical total cost and total revenue for a new plane

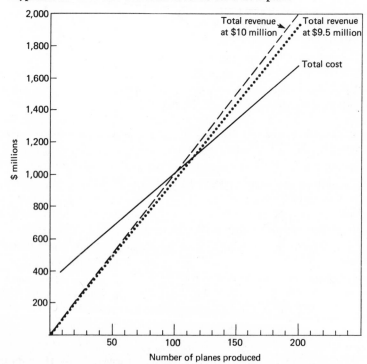

Figure 10–7
Decision tree for deciding whether to produce a new plane

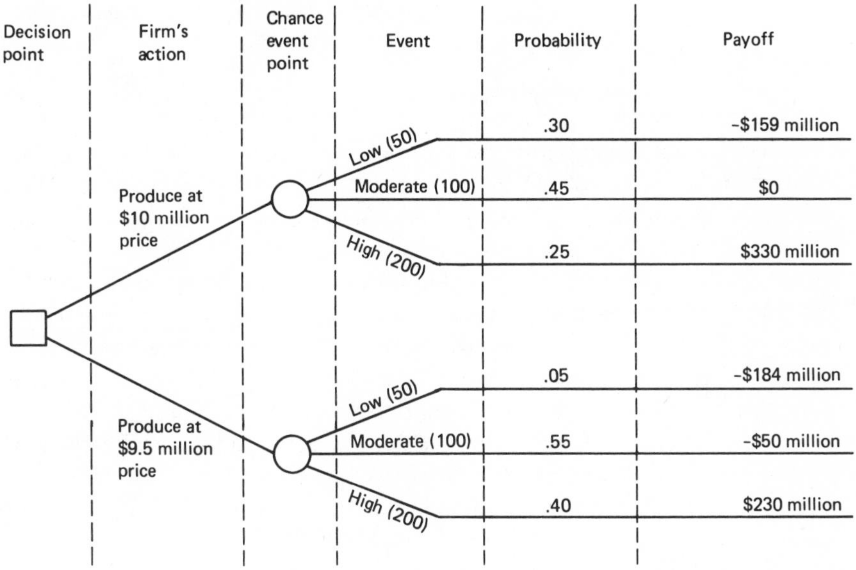

for chance event points. Chance events are alternative states of nature that are beyond the firm's control (here the alternative states of nature are sales volumes that depend upon customer acceptance and actions of competitive firms). On each chance event branch, the estimated probability of the event and the firm's outcome or *payoff* (revenue minus cost), given the event have been posted.

Let us calculate the *mathematical expectation of payoff* for each of the pricing strategies. Calculations begin at the payoffs at the extreme right of the decision tree. The expected value of the strategy of pricing at $10 million per unit, on the top action branch, is the sum of the products of the payoffs times their probabilities and is determined as follows (all values in millions of dollars):

Probability	Times	Payoff	Equals	Expected value
.30	×	−$159	=	−$47.7
.45	×	0	=	0.0
.25	×	330	=	82.5
Expected value of strategy				$34.8

The expected value of the strategy of pricing at $9.5 million per unit can be calculated for the lower action branch as follows:

Probability	Times	Payoff	Equals	Expected value
.05	×	−$184	=	−$ 9.2
.55	×	−$50	=	− 27.5
.40	×	$230	=	92.0
Expected value of strategy				$55.3

Based on expected values, the new product is profitable, and the strategy of pricing at $9.5 million produces a greater expected value than pricing at $10 million per plane. *Note:* The *expected* value of a decision is the *average outcome* that it would have if it could be carried out a great number of times with probabilities of payoffs as estimated by management for the particular decision. The outcome of any one decision will of course be some specific payoff—a payoff that may differ from the decision's expected value. It is reasonable to base *all* decisions on expected values if the firm's total activities and financial base are large enough that the firm's overall value cannot be substantially reduced by the outcome of any one of the decisions. If possible downside variations in outcomes are large in relation to the firm's total income and wealth, management may wish to *adjust payoffs for risk* by substituting the corresponding preference values into the decision tree. A technique for risk adjustment of decision trees is explained in Figure 11–11.

Skimming versus penetration pricing. In the example above, results of alternative constant prices over the product's life cycle were projected. Pricing strategies that involve changes in prices over the life cycle could be more profitable. One such strategy is *skimming*, in which the product is initially offered at a relatively high price and the price is gradually reduced to tap a wider and wider market. The objective is to *maximize total revenue from eventual saturation of the market.* Skimming is most suitable for products that have relatively inelastic demand at the high introductory prices and relatively elastic demand at the subsequently lowered prices. Skimming is often used in introducing a new product that is unique or very much differentiated (Polaroid innovations, personal pocket-sized calculators, electronic wristwatches).

An alternate strategy for new product pricing is *penetration* pricing, in which the price at introduction is lower than the level that will be maintained after the product is established in the market. The objective is *a rapid buildup of sales rate.* Penetration is most suitable for products that have relatively elastic demand at the low introduction prices, economies of scale that give substantial reductions in unit costs at greater rates of output, and a potential for early imitation that makes it advisable to price low to discourage entry of competitors. Penetration has often been used in introducing new food products and toiletries (two packages for the price of one, a coupon worth 50 percent off the regular price). Tang, a man-made substitute for orange juice, and Pringles, chips made from dehydrated potatoes, are examples of products that first appeared as special offers.

Ways of changing a production run that is underway

As a firm observes sales of a product, it can revise its plans for output of the current production run. In decisions about changes in output of a run that is underway, costs already incurred or obligated are treated as sunk. Only *those costs that vary* with changes in production rate or length of the run are relevant.

Although total output must be matched to total sales over the product's life cycle, *output can be greater than sales* in a given period (with a buildup of finished goods inventory) or *sales can exceed production* in a period (with depletion of inventory and/or an accumulation of back orders). Over a product's life, the firm may set up a series of production runs in the manner illustrated in Figure 10–8. If we focus attention on any one production run, we see that its own volume can be varied in four different ways:

1. *With rate of production held constant, total output of the run can be increased (decreased) by adding to (subtracting from) the length of the run,* as depicted in Figure 10–9A. For example, a manufacturer who has a greater sales rate than expected can build up an order backlog, maintain the original planned rate of production, and increase the planned length of the production run.

2. *With planned total output of the run held constant, the length of the run can be cut (or stretched out) by accelerating (or slowing down) the rate of production,* as shown in Figure 10–9B. For example, a manufacturer or contractor may be asked to speed up the delivery rate of an

Figure 10–8
Sales and production over product's life cycle

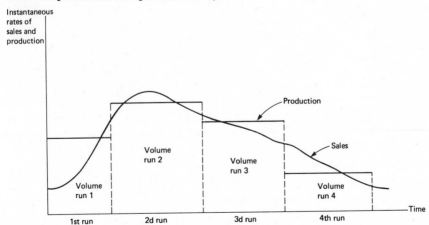

Figure 10–9
Changes in output of production runs

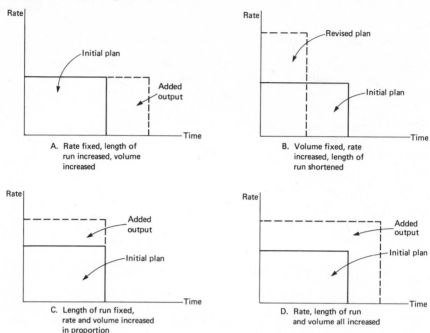

A. Rate fixed, length of
   run increased, volume
   increased

B. Volume fixed, rate
   increased, length of
   run shortened

C. Length of run fixed,
   rate and volume increased
   in proportion

D. Rate, length of run
   and volume all increased

order or the completion date of a contract (for a given number of air-craft of a particular type, for a series of similar structures, for a large building, for an elaborate data processing system, and so on).

3. *With length of the run held constant, the instantaneous rate of production and the planned total volume can be varied in the same proportion* as illustrated in Figure 10–9C. This kind of change in volume is appropriate when a change in sales rate is viewed as permanent, or at least indefinite.

4. *Rate of production, length of run, and planned total output can all be varied simultaneously,* as in Figure 10–9D.

Method 4 is an amalgam of the first three methods. It will not be analyzed as such, since a clearer understanding can be gained by study-ing its components. Method 3, in which instantaneous rate and planned total volume are varied in the same proportion, is simply that change in *rate of output of a continuative production process* that has been analyzed at some length in earlier chapters. It will not be given further attention in this chapter. Thus, we shall analyze only Method 1 (change in length of run with rate constant) and Method 2 (change in rate with total output constant) in the sections to follow.[5]

---

[5] The analysis is based on Jack Hirshleifer, "The Firm's Cost Function: A Suc-cessful Reconstruction?" *Journal of Business* 35 (July 1962), pp. 235–55.

Analyzing profitability of a change in length of run

With a production run underway, is it profitable to accept additional orders and *lengthen the run?* The decision depends on a comparison of incremental costs of the added output with the corresponding incremental revenue. The incremental costs resulting from stretching a production run are of two types: (1) incremental production costs, and (2) opportunity costs of any limited resources required during the stretch, if the use of these resources means foregoing contribution that could be earned from other products or a new model of the same product. Let us first analyze a case in which the firm has *no alternative uses for its fixed inputs,* so that there are *no opportunity costs* associated with the increase in the length of the run.

First example: Opportunity costs are zero. Suppose XYZ Construction Company has built eight identical gasoline service stations and is preparing a bid on four more stations to be built from the same plan. The effect of the learning curve upon incremental unit cost is to be taken into account. The company's records show that its variable costs in building the first, second, fourth, and eighth stations (restated in current, or inflation-corrected, dollars) were as listed in Table 10–3. Al-

Table 10–3
Historical production costs—XYZ Construction

Job	Direct labor	Indirect labor	Materials cost	Total cost
1	$62,200	$4,000	$50,200	$116,400
2	51,800	3,900	49,700	105,400
4	44,000	3,900	49,800	97,700
8	37,300	3,900	49,600	90,800

though costs of materials and indirect labor appear to have stabilized early in the production run, there is evidence of a learning curve in the direct labor column. As a check on this hypothesis, management of XYC Company calculates direct labor costs for several ith units as a percentage of the corresponding $(i/2)$th units, with the following results:

Number of unit (i)	$i/2$	Cost of ith unit/Cost of $i/2$th unit
2	1	0.860
4	2	0.849
8	4	0.849

Based upon the above results, management concludes that the learning rate is approximately 0.85.

To estimate the direct labor cost of the next four units, the following approach is used. The formula for a learning curve of the above type is

$$L_n = L_m \left(\frac{n}{m}\right)^x$$

in which

L_n is direct labor required for the nth unit.

L_m is known labor used in the mth unit.

x is the log of the learning rate coefficient divided by the log of the number 2.

Values of x for selected learning rates are listed below:

Learning rate	Value of x
0.75	−0.4150
0.80	−0.3219
0.85	−0.2345
0.90	−0.1520
0.95	−0.0740

For the estimates that XYZ Company needs, m is 8; n is 9, 10, 11, and 12; x is − 0.2345; and L_m is $37,300.

Direct labor costs of the 9th unit can be estimated as follows:

$$L_9 = \$37,300 \times \left(\frac{9}{8}\right)^{-0.2345}$$

$$= \$37,300 \times \left(\frac{8}{9}\right)^{0.2345}$$

$$= \$36,284$$

Assume materials costs are constant at $49,700 and indirect labor costs are constant at $3,900. Adding in the direct labor cost just estimated, the total incremental production costs of the 9th unit can be projected at $89,884. Incremental costs of the 10th, 11th, and 12th units can be estimated in the manner described above, and the projected costs of all four units are as listed in Table 10–4. The total *incremental production costs* are estimated at $354,616. Any revenue in excess of this amount is expected to be a contribution toward the company's overhead cost and possible profits.

Table 10–4
Estimated future costs—XYZ Construction

Job	Direct labor	Indirect labor and materials	Total cost
9	$36,284	$53,600	$89,884
10	35,399	53,600	88,999
11	34,616	53,600	88,216
12	33,917	53,600	87,517

Second example: Opportunity costs exist. Suppose XYZ Construction Company *does* have alternative uses for its fixed inputs, in which uses the company would earn contributions. These alternative contributions can be viewed as *opportunity costs of the fixed inputs* for the service station construction project; these contributions, which must be sacrificed if the company builds the stations, are costs that should be *added* to incremental production costs.

For example, assume that if the firm did not build the stations, it could take on two smaller jobs—one with an estimated contribution of $15,000 and the other with an estimated contribution of $25,000. In this case, the opportunity costs of the fixed inputs is $40,000, and the total incremental *economic cost* of the service station project is the *incremental production cost* of $354,616 *plus the opportunity cost* of $40,000—or $394,616.

Third example: Analyzing profitability of model changeover. Opportunity costs are particularly important for a firm that is deciding whether to continue production of a current model or to switch to a new model. For example, suppose that a firm is at the end of a third year of production of the current model and is considering whether to make a major styling change or to simply "face lift" by substituting a few bolt-on items. Further, assume that pricing will be the same with or without the major change in the product, but that the new model would be expected to have sales of 500,000 units during the next year compared to 350,000 units that the firm expects to sell if it continues the current model. However, of the 150,000 units of sales foregone by continuing the current model, it is estimated that perhaps 90,000 will be recouped during the subsequent year when the delayed change in styling is finally introduced. So the net loss in sales during the next year is reduced to 60,000 units. *The opportunity cost of delaying the major model changeover is the contribution that the company would expect to earn on the net loss of 60,000 units,* and this opportunity cost should be compared with the *incremental increase in contribution that can be earned on 350,000 units of the current model* (as a result of being far out on the learning curve instead of passing through the first 350,000 units of a new curve for the new model) plus the value of the *income from one year's investment of the postponed fixed cost* associated with a new production run (detailed engineering and styling, purchase of specialized tools and dies, selection and training of the work force, etc.).

Analyzing profitability of a change in rate of production

There is usually a particular instantaneous rate of production that gives the lowest production cost per unit for a given total output that may be desired from a production run. Increasing the rate beyond this point, so as to compress the total volume of output into a shorter time period, increases average cost per unit and total cost of the production run. However, the production cost increase may be more than offset by the greater value that the output has if it becomes available sooner.

Effects of increased rate upon costs. There are several reasons for the greater cost of a given volume when there is a speedup in rate of production. First, total fixed costs of the production run are higher. In aircraft production, for example, increases in rate become more and more difficult within the capacity of a single assembly line, so that it becomes less expensive to get faster output by setting up a second assembly line. There is a corresponding increase in cost of specialized jigs and tools, selection and training of the work force, and setting up and starting up the line.

The second reason for increased costs of a given volume when it is produced in less time is that less benefit is derived from the learning curve. If only a single line is used, with a greater number of workers being stationed on the line, the initial units of the production run cost more because of the greater amounts of lost time and rework; as the run proceeds, the work process comes down on its own learning curve, but the labor requirement per unit is greater for any given unit in the sequence. If a second line is set up, neither work force moves as far along the learning curve as would be the case with only one line; this effect can be appreciated by using the data from Table 10–2 to compare the direct labor cost of producing 100 airplanes on one line with the cost of producing 50 airplanes on each of two lines:

One line—100 units × $800,000 per unit = $80,000,000
Two lines—50 units × $980,000 per unit × 2 = $98,000,000

The difference in direct labor cost in the above example is $18 million for the production run, or $180,000 per unit.

Effects of increased rate upon value of output. *Value of output may be greater if a production run is completed in less time* for several reasons. First, it may be possible to sell more units, or to get a higher average price, or both, so as to earn more contribution from sales of a consumer product that is in the growth phase of its life cycle (for example, an item of high-style clothing that is in fashion). Second, if the product is a durable producer's good that will be useful over a period of years (an office building, an industrial plant, a large data processing system, a fleet of jet planes for passenger service), the stream of services begins *sooner* and may also have *greater total value* if the production run or construction project is completed earlier. Third, there may be an opportunity to use the firm's fixed inputs (plant, general-purpose machines

Figure 10–10
Minimizing economic cost (maximizing profitability) by choosing an optimal rate of production

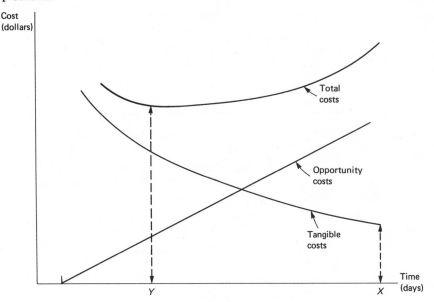

and equipment, management) to earn *contribution on other products* if the run of the first product is completed in less time.

Model for analysis of profitability. A model to analyze the profitability of *increasing the rate of production for a given total volume* can be derived. All of the above increases in value of the firm's output are viewed as *opportunity costs that are reduced* as the production rate is increased. On the other hand, cost of the firm's *tangible production inputs* (labor, materials, power, etc.) *goes up* as the production rate is increased. The model appears as shown in Figure 10–10. If there were no opportunity costs to consider, cost would be minimized by choosing a rate such that the cost of tangible inputs is minimized, illustrated by Point X in Figure 10–10. But where there are opportunity costs, the total cost of the production run is lowest at a saddle point corresponding to a faster production rate, as illustrated by Point Y in Figure 10–10.

Estimating cost of crashing a project:
The critical path method

In production that takes the form of projects (construction, system installation, research and development), the work process consists of a great many different activities and tasks. Some of these must be completed before others can be undertaken. Suppose that construction Project Y consists of the following five tasks:

	Activity	Hours required
a.	Procure materials....................	0.5
b.	Make Part 1.........................	3.0
c.	Make Part 2.........................	2.0
d.	Assemble Part 1 to Part 2............	1.0
e.	Paint the assembly..................	1.0

What is the least time in which Project Y can be completed? Let us prepare a diagram showing the activities that must be performed in sequence and the ones that can be carried out simultaneously. The diagram is to be made up of *arrows* representing each of the activities, plus *nodes* representing points at which one activity must be finished before another activity can be started. The diagram for Project Y is shown in Figure 10–11.

Figure 10–11
Diagram for Project Y

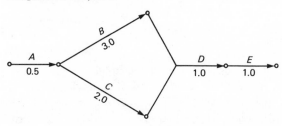

The minimum time for project completion is the greatest total time required to travel any path from the beginning to the end of the project. In Project Y, there are two possible paths: *a-b-d-e,* requiring 5.5 hours, and *a-c-d-e,* requiring 4.5 hours. The first path may be called the *critical path,* since it is the one that determines minimum time. The project could be speeded up by doing task *b* in less time, but there would be no gain from shortening the time for task *c.* In general, a project can be finished earlier *only* by speeding up, or "crashing," the *activities along the critical path.*

The critical path method (CPM) is a technique used to identify the critical and noncritical activities in a large project. Only about 10 percent of all activities will usually be found to be critical. Project completion time can be shortened by carrying out the critical activities at a greater than normal rate—with higher than usual cost. The cost of cutting a day from time required varies from one critical activity to another. There is

Table 10–5
NCR century direct-mail campaign

Activity		Activity duration in days		Activity dollar cost		Rate of cost increase
		Normal	Crash	Normal	Crash	(\$ per day)
A.	Rough copy...............	8	3	\$ 400	\$ 650	\$ 50
B.	Copy for announcement....	2	1	125	225	100
C.	Layout..................	10	5	600	1,200	120
D.	Approval.................	3	3	—	—	—
E.	Research mailing lists......	5	1	100	540	110
F.	Final art.................	12	7	750	1,500	150
G.	Approval—announcement...	2	2	—	—	—
H.	Final copy...............	6	2	250	400	38
I.	Type set.................	3	1	350	525	88
J.	OK mailing lists...........	1	1	—	—	—
K.	Printing—announcement...	4	2	150	400	125
L.	Printing.................	18	12	2,150	3,350	200
M.	Order mailing lists.........	14	6	500	620	15
N.	Deliver to mailing center— announcement..........	1	1	—	—	—
O.	Deliver to mailing center...	2	2	—	—	—
P.	Mail material.............	5	1	1,150	1,650	125

Source: Edward J. Feltz, "The Costs of Crashing," *Journal of Marketing* 34 (July 1970), p. 66.

some point along the critical path at which one day can be cut at the least cost, then another point at which a day can be cut at the next least cost, and so on. Thus, the critical path method can be used to determine the *least-cost ways of cutting successively greater and greater amounts of time*, so as to obtain the function in Figure 10–10 which *relates cost of tangible inputs to project time*.

Illustration of CPM: National Cash Register's direct-mail campaign. Edward Feltz has provided an illustration of use of the critical path method in connection with a direct-mail marketing campaign.[6] The mailing was planned to go to potential buyers of computers and data processing systems. The project was divided into the 16 separate tasks listed .in Table 10–5; as shown in the table, costs and times were estimated on both a *normal* basis and a *crash* basis for each of the tasks. The final column in the table is based on the assumption that for any one activity, the cost per day cut from the time requirement is a constant.

The CPM network for this project is shown in Figure 10–12; the letters correspond to the tasks listed in Table 10–5 and the numbers show the normal and crash times, respectively. There are six possible paths from the start of the project to the finish. The one that takes the longest

---

[6] Edward J. Feltz, "The Costs of Crashing," *Journal of Marketing* 34 (July 1970), pp. 64–67.

Figure 10–12
Network for the NCR project

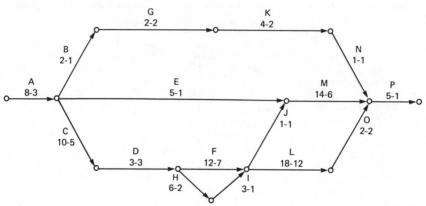

Source: Edward J. Feltz, "The Costs of Crashing," *Journal of Marketing* 34 (July 1970), p. 65.

with all activities carried out on a normal basis is the path *a-c-d-f-l-o-p*, which requires 58 days; this is the *initial* critical path for the project.

Neil Beckwith shows that, in order to reduce project time at least cost, one should start on the initial critical path and crash the activities that add least cost per day cut from completion time. *Eventually, more than one path becomes critical and activities must be crashed simultaneously.* Beckwith carried out the critical path method for the National Cash Register (NCR) direct-mail campaign by steps as shown in Table 10–6, obtaining the relation of direct project cost to project time that is illustrated in Figure 10–13.[7]

What is the optimum completion time for the NCR project in the example above? Well, that depends upon management's estimated opportunity cost per day, where this cost is the contribution unearned because the project has not been finished. If opportunity cost is estimated at $125 per day, total cost is minimized at either 44 or 48 days (cost is the same), as shown in Table 10–6 and Figure 10–13. If opportunity cost is a greater amount per day, $175, the firm's total cost is lowest at 41 days, as shown in Table 10–6 and Figure 10–13.

Potential savings from optimal crashing may seem small in the light of the above example. At the cost of $125 per day for foregone opportunity, total cost is minimized at $13,375 instead of the $13,775 total cost if the project is carried out at normal time for each activity (the reduction is not quite 3 percent). At an opportunity cost of $175 per day, total cost is minimized at $15,500 instead of the $16,675 cost of doing

---

[7] Neil Beckwith, "Cost of Crashing—A Comment," *Journal of Marketing* 35 (October 1971).

Table 10–6
CPM analysis of NCR century direct-mail campaign

Normal time and cost of direct-mail project	*Total rate of cost increase ($ per day)*	*Project duration (days)*	*Project cost (direct)*
Critical path ACDFLOP		58	$6,525
Activity A reduced 5 days @ $50 per day............................	$ 50	53	6,775
Activity C reduced 5 days @ $120 per day........................	120	48	7,375
Activity P reduced 4 days @ $125 per day........................	125	44	7,875
Activity F reduced 3 days @ $150 per day........................	150	41	8,325
Critical paths ACDFLOP and ACDHILOP			
Activity F can be reduced 2 more days @ $150 per day, Activity H can be reduced 4 days @ $38 per day, Activity I can be reduced 2 days @ $88 per day, so these critical paths should be reduced by expediting activities F and H 2 days @ $188 per day...............................	188	39	8,701
Activity L reduced 5 days @ $200 per day........................	200	34	9,701
Critical paths ACDFLOP, ACDHILOP, ACDFJMP, and ACDHIJMP			
Activities L and M reduced 1 day @ $215 per day........................	215	33	9,916

Note: The schedule contains critical path ACDFLOP in which no activity can be expedited so this is the minimum total project duration. The expediting of additional activities would increase total project cost without decreasing the project duration.

Source: Neil Beckwith, "The Cost of Crashing—A Comment, *Journal of Marketing* 35 (October 1971).

the project at normal time (a reduction of a little more than 7 percent).

Although the cost reductions in the above example are small in absolute terms, *they are sizable in percentage terms.* The project in the example is very small and very simple. In practice, the critical path method is being applied to large projects involving thousands of activities and millions of dollars of total cost. Optimal crashing of such projects involves simultaneous crashing along several critical paths. The technique must be carried out by computer-aided methods that are beyond the scope of this book. The objective here is simply to understand that the critical path method is a technique for determining the relationship of direct project cost to time for the economic model which is depicted in Figure 10–10.

Figure 10–13
Determining optimum time for the NCR project

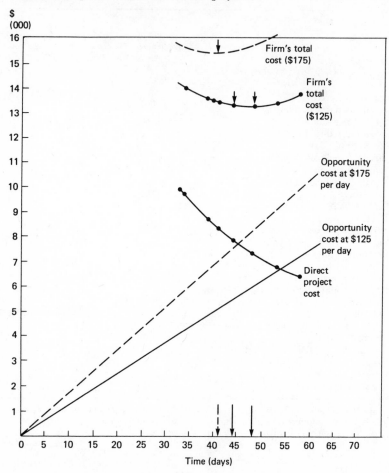

Simultaneous changes in rate and volume

In discussing changes in costs as *output is increased,* one should be careful to specify the exact nature of the increase in output. If one refers to an expansion of total production volume by making a longer production run at the same rate (print 10,000 books rather than 5,000), tangible production cost per unit is expected to be reduced. On the other hand, if by "increase in output" one really means a rise in the instantaneous rate with a proportionate shortening in the production run and with the same total volume (produce 1,000 army tanks in one year rather than in two years), the average tangible production cost per unit is expected to be greater. These two relationships are shown in Figure 10–14; any one

Figure 10–14
Relation of total costs to volume and rate

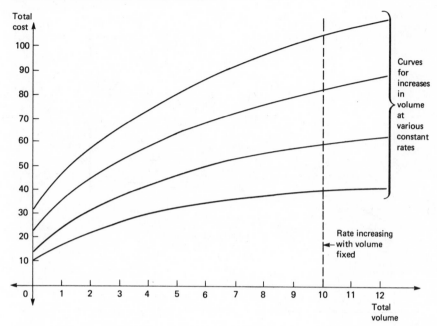

curve in the figure shows how total cost changes as total production volume is increased at some given rate—total costs increase at decreasing rates, so that both marginal and average unit costs are falling. On the other hand, the total cost for any given total volume rises if a higher rate of output is used.

The interplay of the volume and rate effects is illustrated in Figure 10–15. On the dashed trace in the figure, increase in total volume is accompanied by a proportionate increase in rates. At low levels of volume, total cost increases at a decreasing rate because of volume economies (learning and fixed cost spreading) that exceed rate diseconomies (increase in amount of fixed cost and decrease in learning effect). At greater levels of volume, rate diseconomies dominate and total cost increases at an increasing rate.

The behavior of average and marginal costs when production rate and total volume are increased proportionately *in an eventually terminating production run* depends upon relative magnitudes of the economies of the volume increase and the diseconomies of the rate increase. Average costs may either rise or fall. At low levels of total output, the learning effect is strong and the fixed cost of the production run can be spread over a sizable percentage increase in output, as planned total output is increased. In this range, marginal and average costs *can* fall if volume

Figure 10–15
Relation of total costs to proportionate changes in rate and volume

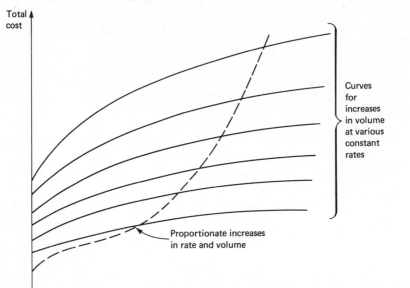

economies dominate rate diseconomies. As planned total output reaches further out, rate diseconomies overcome the volume economies and marginal and average costs rise.

Perhaps the most common type of *increase in output* is the case in which both the rate of production and the total volume of production are increased in the same proportion. This is the case in which an expansion of demand is regarded as permanent by a firm that is in continuative production of a given item. When rate of output is raised for a continuative process, the planned increase in total future volume is directly proportionate to the increase in rate. The total, average, and marginal cost curves in most economics textbooks and in the earlier chapters of this book are based on the implicit assumption that the production process is continuative.

INTERMITTENT PRODUCTION: LOTS

This section deals with production that takes the form of *intermittent* runs. These cases arise when economies of high rates of production are very great, leading to production on general-purpose machines that are switched from one item to another, with production rates that exceed each item's rate of sales or use. Examples are book printing, metal stamping, and manufacture of printed circuits. Inventories are prominent because they are the sources of supplies for sale or use during periods in which there is no production. In these cases, production rates are predetermined, but there are decisions to be made about lengths of production runs and levels of inventories.

Production scheduling and its relation to inventories:
An overview

Production scheduling and inventory planning may be related to either intermediate or final products. We shall consider the two cases in turn.

Intermediate goods.   Many production tasks must be performed in sequence (after other tasks have been done, or before other tasks can be done, or both). Suppose two different tasks that lie in a sequenced process require services of the same limited input, perhaps a particular machine. In an earlier section of this chapter, we looked at a simple production process consisting of the following tasks:

a.   Obtain materials for Product Y.
b.   Make Part 1.
c.   Make Part 2.
d.   Assemble Parts 1 and 2.
e.   Paint the assembly.

In the earlier case, tasks *b* and *c* were treated as simultaneous activities. Suppose the same machine must be used to make both Part 1 and Part 2, making it impossible to carry out tasks *b* and *c* at the same time.

How should the production of Parts 1 and 2 be scheduled? We could produce one unit of Part 1 and then one unit of Part 2 and so forth, or we could produce 100 units of Part 1 and then 100 units of Part 2. The essence of the economic problem is this: There are costs associated with switching production over from Part 1 to Part 2 (perhaps the dies must be changed in a stamping machine), and these costs can be held down by making longer production runs and fewer switches; on the other hand, if the firm schedules only a few long runs per year, larger average inventories of Parts 1 and 2 will be held and the carrying costs of these inventories will be greater. It can be seen that production scheduling is related to inventory management: How large should the inventory of a particular good be allowed to grow, and how low should inventories of alternative goods be allowed to fall, before production is switched from the particular good to the alternate good or goods?

Final goods.   A similar scheduling problem occurs if the firm produces several final products that require services of the same fixed inputs. Efficient production may take place at rates much greater than normal sales rates of the products (as in printing of books), so that the firm produces several final products and switches production from one to another (each book goes through a series of printings over time). Should the firm schedule a few long production runs or many short ones? If it chooses the former, the cost of producing an average unit is incurred further in advance of receiving revenue from sale and average inventory carrying costs are greater; if it chooses to make more but shorter production runs, costs of setting up (switchover) are greater.

Inventory types and functions

The types and functions of inventories used in industry and business are as follows:

1. *Decoupling inventories.* As shown for the intermediate goods above, inventories decouple production processes so that rates of carrying out any given task in a sequence can be independent of the rates at which the other tasks are done. Decoupling allows the given tasks to be done at high speeds on general-purpose machines. The firm in the example can assemble Parts 1 and 2 continuously in spite of the fact that only one of the parts is being made, by drawing the other part from its inventory.

2. *Buffer inventories.* Inventories can also be used to buffer one activity against the uncertainty about the timing or rate of another. Raw materials inventories protect the production process from uncertainties about deliveries of additional materials. Work-in-process inventories buffer the successive stages of production against work disruptions in prior stages. Finished goods inventories insulate the production process from the uncertain demands of customers.

3. *Lot-size inventories.* Consider a situation in which a firm needs only one-half boxcar of an item each month. Because of the higher freight charges for partial car loads, the firm may order a full boxcar load. This larger order size increases the average stock of the item at the plant. The firm is willing to carry the increased stock or inventory in order to reduce transportation costs. Similar situations are encountered when the firm has relatively high costs of setting up machines for production runs of a particular item. The firm may be willing to produce greater amounts in excess of nearby usage or shipments in order to reduce setup costs.

4. *Seasonal or anticipations inventories.* These inventories allow smooth production in the face of highly fluctuating demand, thus decreasing the required capacity of the fixed inputs. For example, toy manufacturers expect the greatest sales rates for their products just before the Christmas season. In anticipation of this seasonal demand, they spread the work over earlier months in which production exceeds current sales. The seasonal buildup of inventories (and inventory-associated

costs) allows smoother annual production schedules with reduced costs of capacity and lower costs of employment (hiring, training, overtime, lay-offs, etc.).

Optimal inventory planning: An overview

The remainder of this section is concerned with choice of the optimal inventory policy for either produced or purchased goods. Within the firm, views on this question will probably differ from one department to another. The marketing department will desire inventories of finished goods large enough to insure that customer's orders can always be filled promptly. Production managers will want large inventories of inter-mediate goods to insure that production is not interrupted by breakdowns or work stoppages earlier in the stages of the work process.

On the other hand, the finance department views inventory as a neces-sary evil. Inventory ties up capital that could be used elsewhere, thus it has an opportunity cost. High levels of inventory also increase costs of such items as storage, taxes, insurance, pilferage, and deterioration. With a view to minimizing the firm's needs for capital, the finance department desires relatively low inventory levels.

The firm must try to devise an inventory policy, or an inventory system, that strikes the best possible balance among the conflicting ob-jectives of the specialized departments. It seeks to minimize *total* in-ventory-associated costs: (1) the costs of carrying the inventories, (2) the costs of running out of stock, and (3) the transactions costs of order-ing or the setup costs of producing. The first item increases with size of inventories, whereas the other two items decrease with size.

We shall examine inventory planning in stages. First, we assume the firm knows the rate at which units will be used or sold from inventory and the timing of deliveries of purchased items or completion of pro-duced items—there is no danger of running out of stock. Under these assumptions of certainty, we first look at stocks of goods purchased from other firms and then at production scheduling and inventory levels of produced goods. Then we recognize that uncertainty does exist and that buffer inventories should be added to protect against variations in delivery or completion time and in sales or usage rates.

Optimal purchased goods inventories under certainty

We begin with the simplest case: *purchased goods under certainty*. The following assumptions are made:

1. Usage is known and constant. The total number of items required for one year is known exactly. The rate of use is uniform over time.

2. Lead time is known and constant. Lead time is the time elapsing between placing an order and receiving delivery.
3. The entire order is received in one delivery at one point in time.
4. The purchase price is constant irrespective of order size. This assumption rules out quantity discounts.

Behavior of inventory under the above assumptions is shown in Figure
10–16. In this figure, Q represents the quantity that is ordered each time
an order is placed. The *optimum* value of Q is called the *economic order
quantity,* or *EOQ*. As items are used, inventory level falls, as depicted by
the solid line in the figure. Since the usage rate is known and constant,
the line is smooth and straight. The firm knows that inventory will fall
to zero at exactly time T, but since a new order will not arrive immediately, an order must be placed prior to T. The lead time is known, allowing order time O (and the corresponding inventory level, called the *reorder point,* or ROP) to be calculated by subtracting lead time from the
time at which stock reaches zero.

Since the inventory level is at Q upon receipt of an order and falls to
zero at a constant rate, the average inventory level is $Q/2$. Any increase
(decrease) in order quantity will raise (lower) average inventory by one
half of the change in quantity. If average inventory is increased, it will

Figure 10–16
Inventory level under assumptions 1–4

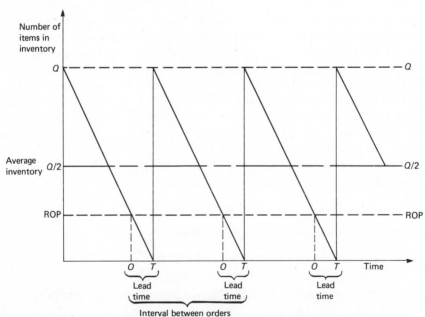

Figure 10–17
Effects of order size on inventories and numbers of orders

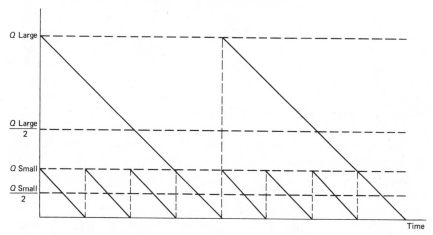

last longer and the firm will reorder less often, as shown in Figure 10–17. There are *costs of carrying inventory* and there are *costs of ordering;* the problem is to *minimize the total* of the costs. Let us examine the nature of the costs involved, beginning with inventory-carrying costs.

Inventory-carrying costs. This classification includes all costs directly incurred by the company because of the level of inventory on hand. As the level of inventory increases, these costs will increase.

1. *Cost of capital.* Some businesses make the mistake of assuming that cash tied up in inventories costs nothing. However, money invested in inventory is not available for other purposes. It has an opportunity cost, and inventory can tie up large amounts of capital. It is not uncommon for a manufacturing firm to have as much as 25 percent of its total capital in the form of inventories.

How does a firm estimate the cost of capital for inventories? Some firms use the bank interest rate to estimate this element of carrying costs. However, very few businesses would be satisfied with uses of the firm's capital which do not earn more than a lender's rate of return. For this reason, many firms use the rate of return which the company expects to realize on the average from its total capital investment. The theoretically correct rate is the firm's *marginal cost of capital,* which is discussed in the capital budgeting chapter of this book. It would usually be somewhat higher than the firm's average rate of return.

This element of carrying cost is often expressed as a percentage of the value of average inventory on hand.

2. *Storage and handling costs.* Inventory must be stored. If storage space is rented or could be used for other productive purposes (opportunity cost) a charge for the storage space should be considered. However,

if storage space is in a state of excess capacity that cannot be used for other productive purposes, such a charge is not justified. In either case, the cost of moving items to and from storage, including damages, wages and equipment expense, should be included.

3. *Costs of obsolescence, deterioration, pilferage.* Any one of these costs may be major or minor depending on the nature of the inventory under consideration. For example, in style goods industries, the problem of obsolescence is acute; because of changing sales patterns and customer desires, some inventory may be no longer salable. Likewise, items such as fresh fruits and vegetables may have extremely high costs due to partial spoilage and deterioration. Other items may get dirty from handling, dry out, get damp, or deteriorate in other ways.

The total of these costs per dollar of inventory value per year can usually be obtained by dividing their actual costs, as determined by cost accounting, by average value of inventory.

4. *Taxes and insurance costs.* Many states and cities have inventory taxes. These may be based on inventory investment at a particular time of the year or on average inventory investment for the entire year. Most companies also carry insurance on their inventories. Tax and insurance charges are usually expressed as a percentage of average inventory investment, and thus require no additional calculations.

It should be evident that *all of the costs under the general heading of inventory-carrying costs vary directly with the size of inventory.* There is no general rule as to how an aggregate figure for carrying cost should be calculated. The specific components which are important in this calculation vary from case to case depending on the nature of the specific inventory under consideration. For example, as has been pointed out, obsolescence as a part of inventory-carrying cost varies widely with time and is not the same for different items in an inventory. The same is true for most of the other costs composing carrying cost. This would perhaps indicate the desirability of calculating a different carrying cost for each item in the stock list. Since this is generally impractical, average figures for all inventory or for broad classes of inventory are usually chosen. For manufacturing companies, annual carrying costs average about 20 percent of average annual inventory investment. For other types of firms, the figure varies from 5 to 65 percent. However, for reasons pointed out above, one must not rely too readily on averages.

Ordering costs. The term *order cost* applies to the expense of issuing an order to an outside supplier. When material is ordered, orders must be written and invoices processed. The lots received must be inspected and delivered to stores or production stations. Order costs include the fixed cost of maintaining an order department and the variable costs of preparing and executing purchase requisitions. Perhaps writing a purchase order does not sound expensive. However, some companies estimate the cost to run from \$5 to \$15 per order. The cost may be hundreds of dollars if bids must be requested and processed. As an estimate, to be used with considerable judgment, the cost of the procurement operation, including overhead charges, divided by the number of orders placed may be used to approximate order cost.

On a per-order basis, ordering costs are independent of order size. Total ordering costs over a period of time vary directly with the number of orders placed. Thus, *total ordering cost varies directly with the usage rate*, taking order size as given, but it *varies inversely with order size and average inventory quantity*, taking usage as given.

Trial and error approach. An example illustrates the trial and error method of determining *EOQ*. Assume that a firm is ordering a basic stock item from an outside supplier. The firm uses 1,000 of these items per year at a price of \$2 per unit. The firm has estimated the cost per order to be \$2.50 and the carrying cost to be 25 percent of the value of average inventory. The firm wishes to determine a quantity to order which will minimize total inventory-associated costs. One order per year (1,000 items) would obviously minimize yearly ordering cost but would also result in maximum carrying costs because of the large resulting average inventory. The average inventory level could be substantially reduced by ordering 50 times a year, but this would result in high annual ordering costs.

The example highlights the basic trade-offs in an economic order quantity problem. In general, carrying costs can be kept low by ordering frequently but the resulting ordering costs will be high. Similarly, ordering costs can be kept low by ordering infrequently but the resulting carrying costs will be high. The determination of economic order quantities requires finding the quantity which results in the lowest *total* cost.

This trade-off is depicted graphically in Figure 10–18. In this figure as the number of units per order increases, carrying cost increases. However, the ordering cost decreases. The total cost for any point is simply the sum of ordering cost and carrying cost at that point. The resulting total cost curve is U shaped. *The objective is to determine the number of units per order that corresponds to the minimum point on this total cost curve.*

Returning to the example, the approximate least-cost order quantity can be determined by trial and error, and is shown in Table 10–7. It should be noted that as carrying costs decline, ordering costs increase. Total costs decrease initially, but then beyond some point begin to increase. Minimum total costs occur when 100 units are ordered each time.

The economic order quantity having been determined, attention turns to the inventory level at which an order should be placed. Such an inventory level is called a *reorder point*, or *ROP*. Assume that there are 50 workweeks in a year and that lead time is two weeks. Since a constant usage rate has been assumed, (1,000 units/year)/(50 weeks/year), or 20

Figure 10–18
Graphical EOQ determination

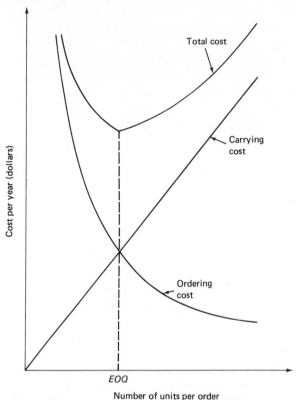

units, are used weekly. Therefore 40 units, 2 weeks × 20 units/week, are used during lead time. The *ROP* is 40 units. The complete decision rule is: When the inventory level drops to 40 units, an order should be placed for 100 units. It should be noted that stockouts will never occur, since lead time is exactly two weeks. During the two weeks of waiting for the order to be received, the 40 units in inventory are used up. At the point when inventory level drops to zero, the new order is received; the inventory level becomes 100 units; and the cycle begins again.

Algebraic-incremental approach. The trial and error approach works fairly well, because total costs are not very sensitive to *small* deviations from the optimum order quantity. Note in Table 10–7 that total costs are fairly low for any order size between 72 and 125 units. Thus, it is not too serious an error if the firm fails to include the economic order quantity in the trials—any number that is close will have a total cost nearly as low as that corresponding to the *EOQ*.

Table 10–7
Determination of EOQ by trial and error

Number of orders	Units per order	Units in average inventory	Value of average inventory	Annual carrying cost	Annual ordering cost	Total cost
1........	1,000	500	$1,000	$250.00	$ 2.50	$252.50
2........	500	250	500	125.00	5.00	130.00
4........	250	125	250	62.50	10.00	72.50
8........	125	62.5	125	31.25	20.00	51.75
10........	100	50	100	25.00	25.00	50.00
12........	84	42	84	21.00	30.00	51.00
14........	72	36	72	18.00	35.00	53.00

Note: Annual usage, 1,000 items; purchase price, $2 per item; cost per order, $2.50; inventory-carrying cost, 25 percent.

An algebraic approach can be used to determine the *exact* least-cost order size. In deriving this approach, the following symbols are used:

Q is economic order quantity in number of units.

R is total annual requirements in number of units.

S is cost of placing one order in dollars.

C is annual carrying cost as a percentage (of value of average inventory).

P is per-unit price of the item in question.

Total annual cost = (Purchase cost of R units)
$$+ \text{(Inventory-carrying costs)} + \text{(Ordering cost)}$$
$$\text{Purchase cost of } R \text{ units} = RP \qquad (10\text{–}1)$$

Inventory-carrying cost = (Average inventory in units)
$$\cdot \text{(Price)} \cdot \text{(Carrying cost \%)}$$
$$= \left(\frac{Q}{2} \right) \cdot P \cdot C, \text{ or } \frac{QCP}{2} \qquad (10\text{–}2)$$

Ordering cost = (Number of orders) · (Cost per order)
$$= \left(\frac{R}{Q} \right) \cdot S, \text{ or } \frac{RS}{Q} \qquad (10\text{–}3)$$

Hence

$$\text{Total annual cost, } TC = RP + \frac{QCP}{2} + \frac{RS}{Q} \qquad (10\text{–}4)$$

In order to minimize total annual cost, take the first derivative of Equation (10–4) with respect to Q:

$$\frac{dTC}{dQ} = \frac{CP}{2} - \frac{RS}{Q^2} \qquad (10\text{–}5)$$

Set the first derivative equal to zero, and solve for Q:

$$\frac{CP}{2} - \frac{RS}{Q^2} = 0$$

$$\frac{CP}{2} = \frac{RS}{Q^2}$$

$$Q^2 CP = 2RS$$

$$Q^2 = \frac{2RS}{CP}$$

$$Q = \sqrt{\frac{2RS}{CP}} \qquad\qquad (10\text{--}6)$$

Equation (10–6) is the classic formula for determining economic order quantity. It may be used for direct calculation of *EOQ* whenever assumptions 1–4 at the beginning of this section are met.

Applying the *EOQ* formula to the example problem above, we have

R = 1,000 units (the annual requirement)
S = \$2.50 per order (cost of one order)
C = 0.25 (25%), (the annual carrying cost as a
           percentage of average inventory)
P = \$2 (per-unit purchase price)

$$Q = \sqrt{\frac{2RS}{CP}}$$

$$= \sqrt{\frac{2(1,000)(\$2.50)}{\$2(0.25)}}$$

$$= \sqrt{\frac{\$5,000}{\$0.50}}$$

$$= \sqrt{10,000}$$

$$= 100$$

Let us look at the economic meaning of the above results. It was shown in Equation (10–6) that total yearly costs are minimized if $CP/2 - RS/Q^2 = 0$, or $CP/2 = RS/Q^2$. The term on the *left side of the latter equation represents the addition to inventory-carrying costs as a result of increasing the order quantity by one unit:* average inventory is increased by 0.5 unit and the value by $P/2$ dollars, so incremental carrying costs are $CP/2$. On the other hand, if the order size is increased, the number of orders per year is reduced; the *right side of the equation is the incremental saving in ordering cost as a result of increasing order quantity by one unit.*

If the left side of the equation is larger, the firm can reduce total cost by cutting the order quantity. If the right side of the equation is larger, the firm can decrease cost by enlarging the order quantity. Therefore, total costs are minimum at the order quantity for which incremental ordering cost and incremental saving in carrying cost are equal.

Sensitivity of EOQ. Let us see how *EOQ* is affected by changes in carrying cost percentage, ordering cost, and annual requirements. First, if the carrying cost percentage in the above example were doubled (from 0.25 to 0.50), *CP* would be increased from \$0.50 to \$1.00. Recalculating *EOQ*, we get

$$Q = \sqrt{\frac{2(1,000)(\$2.50)}{\$1}}$$
$$= 70.7$$

In this example, the *EOQ* is reduced from 100 units to about 71 units, and the number of orders per year is increased from 10 to 1,000/71, or about 14.

Next, if the ordering costs in the above example were doubled (from \$2.50 to \$5), 2*RS* would be increased from \$5,000 to \$10,000. Recalculating *EOQ*, we get

$$Q = \sqrt{\frac{2(1,000)(\$5)}{\$0.50}}$$
$$= 141.4$$

In this case, *EOQ* is raised from 100 units to about 141 and the number of orders per year is cut from 10 to 1,000/141, or about 7.

Finally, if the annual requirements in the above example were doubled (from 1,000 to 2,000 units), 2*RS* would be increased from \$5,000 to \$10,000. It has just been shown that this would raise *EOQ* to 141.4 units. The number of orders per year would be increased from 10 to 2,000/141, or about 14.

Should a quantity discount be taken?

Suppliers often offer price reductions based on size of orders. These price reductions are called *quantity discounts*. Quantity discounts can be appraised in the following manner. First, determine the economic order quantity without considering the discounts. If the resulting amount is smaller than the minimum required to get the first discount, calculate total annual cost based on *EOQ* without discount. Then calculate total annual cost based on an order quantity large enough to get the first discount. If the discounted price and larger order quantity result in a lower annual cost, the total annual cost should next be calculated for the still larger order quantity needed to get the second quantity discount. Such comparisons can be continued until the order quantity resulting in the lowest total annual cost has been found.

Production scheduling and produced goods inventories under certainty

We shall now move to consideration of production scheduling and determination of optimal *produced* goods inventories—either final products or intermediate goods. Assume that the goods will be used or sold at a known constant rate. If production is continuous, at the same rate as sales or use, there will be no need for inventories. Suppose, however, that economic production (production at a competitive unit cost) requires operating at a more rapid rate than the use or sales rate. Book printing and metal stamping are examples of production that takes place at rates greatly exceeding normal rates of sale or use. In such cases, the firm's fixed inputs (printing presses or stamping machines) will be switched from one product to another. Each product will have an inventory that is replenished from intermittent production runs.

Let the annual requirements of a given good be represented by R, in units. The total costs of producing R units per year plus the total costs of inventories held are comprised of the following elements.

Fixed costs. These are the opportunity costs of fixed inputs. They are not affected by choice of lot sizes in production runs.

Variable costs. These are the costs that vary with quantity produced per year, R, but are assumed to be a constant, V, in dollars per unit, irrespective of the lot sizes.

Setup costs. These are costs of switching from production of some other good to production of the given good. They include attachment of special-purpose dies and tools, adjustment of machines, movement of materials into position, clerical costs of planning and scheduling, and opportunity costs of lost time of machine and equipment use during the changeover. The setup costs are assumed to be a fixed amount, S, for each production run.

Inventory-carrying costs. Carrying costs for produced goods are similar to carrying costs of purchased goods. We shall assume that annual carrying costs of the given good are a constant percentage, C, of the average value of inventory. Let the average production cost per unit be P'. Then carrying cost per unit is CP'.

If the R units are produced in one long production run, annual setup costs are low but inventory carrying costs are high. If the goods are produced in a large number of short production runs, average inventory costs are low, but setup costs are high. The optimal size of a production run (lot size) is that quantity at which the incremental increase in carrying costs equals the incremental reduction in setup costs for a one-unit expansion of the lot size. The analysis is like the determination of economic order quantity for purchased goods, with two differences:

1. Setup cost is usually much higher than an ordering cost.
2. Some units are sold or used while the production run is going on.

Figure 10–19
Produced goods—inventories under certainty

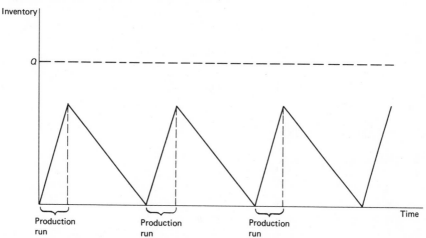

Thus, if the number of units produced in the run is Q, the inventory level never reaches Q; inventory rises and falls as shown in Figure 10–19.

Optimum lot size: Algebraic approach. In deriving the formula for optimum lot size, the following symbols are used:

R is annual requirements in units.

Q is quantity produced in one production run.

S is setup costs, per time.

CP' is inventory-carrying costs per unit per year.

V is variable cost per unit.

F is fixed costs.

B is quantity that would be produced in one year of continuous production.

Using these symbols, the length of a production run as a fraction of a year is Q/B. If production were continued for a whole year, the inventory level at the end of the year would be $B - R$, or total production minus the quantity used or sold. Thus, the inventory level at the end of a single production run is $(B - R) \cdot Q/B$, and the average inventory is $(B - R) \cdot Q/2B$.

In words, the total annual costs of production of R units and holding of inventories is: (Total annual setup costs) + (Annual inventory-carrying costs) + (Variable costs) + (Fixed costs). These *items* of cost, in turn, are as defined below:

Total annual setup costs = (Setup costs per time)

· (Production runs per year)

$$= S\left(\frac{R}{Q}\right) \tag{10–7}$$

Annual inventory-carrying costs = (Carrying cost per unit)

$$\cdot \text{ (Average inventory)}$$

$$= CP' \cdot \frac{(B - R)}{B} \cdot \frac{Q}{2} \qquad (10\text{-}8)$$

Variable costs = (Variable cost per unit) · (Annual requirements)

$$= VR \qquad (10\text{-}9)$$

$$\text{Fixed cost} = F \qquad (10\text{-}10)$$

So

Total annual cost, $TC = \dfrac{SR}{Q} + CP' \cdot \dfrac{(B - R)}{B} \cdot \dfrac{Q}{2} + VR + F$ (10-11)

Taking the first derivative of Equation (10-11), we get

$$\frac{dTC}{dQ} = \frac{(B - R)}{B} \cdot \frac{CP'}{2} - \frac{SR}{Q^2} \qquad (10\text{-}12)$$

The terms in the first derivative are as follows: The incremental addition to annual carrying cost, per unit added to lot size, is $[(B - R)/B] \cdot (CP'/2)$. The incremental reduction in annual setup cost, per unit added to lot size, is SR/Q^2.

Setting the incremental costs equal to each other, which is the same thing as setting the first derivative equal to zero, we have optimum lot size:

$$\frac{(B - R)}{B} \cdot \frac{CP'}{2} = \frac{SR}{Q^2}, \text{ or } Q^2 \frac{(B - R)}{B} \frac{CP'}{2} = SR, \text{ or}$$

$$Q^2 = (SR) \cdot \frac{B}{(B - R)} \cdot \frac{2}{CP'}$$

or, finally,

$$Q = \sqrt{\frac{2SR}{CP'} \cdot \frac{B}{B - R}}$$

To illustrate the use of the optimum lot size formula, suppose the values of the several variables are as follows:

$$R = 4{,}000 \text{ units annually.}$$
$$B = 8{,}000 \text{ units annually.}$$
$$S = \$500 \text{ per setup.}$$
$$V = \$10 \text{ per unit.}$$
$$CP' = \$2 \text{ per year.}$$

Then,

$$Q = \sqrt{\frac{2 \cdot \$500 \cdot 4{,}000}{\$2} \cdot \frac{8{,}000}{8{,}000 - 4{,}000}}$$

$$= 2{,}000$$

Length of production run $= \dfrac{Q}{B} = \dfrac{1}{4}$ year, or 3 months

Average inventory $= \dfrac{Q}{2}\left(\dfrac{B - R}{B}\right) = 500$ units

Summing up, the firm should schedule two production runs a year, of three months each.

Optimal purchased goods inventories under uncertainty

The models discussed above are appropriate for situations in which economies of lot size make it advantageous to build up (and then deplete) inventories under certainty. We assumed that demand was known and constant, or uniform, over time. We also assumed that lead time was known and constant. These assumptions are not always realistic. Lead time may vary because the supplier has run into production difficulty or because of transportation delays. Furthermore, there is often fluctuation in demand or use from period to period.

Stockouts and their causes. When a customer's order cannot be filled immediately or when production must be halted temporarily because supplies of a product are not available, a *stockout* is said to have occurred. A stockout could result from two causes. First, delivery could be delayed. If the lead time on an order is longer than expected, a stockout may result as depicted in Figure 10–20. Note in the figure that lead time in the first period is as expected and there is no stockout. But in the second

Figure 10–20
Stockout caused by varying lead time

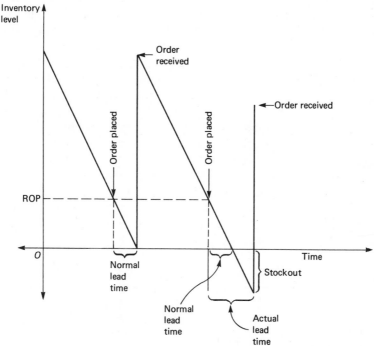

Figure 10–21
Stockout caused by varying usage rate

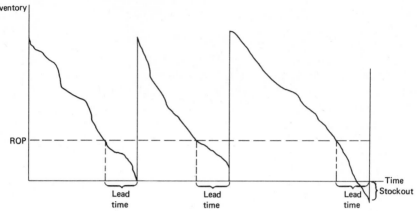

period, lead time is longer than expected and a stockout occurs even though the good is used at a known constant rate.

The second cause of a stockout could be that the product is sold or used at a faster rate than expected, as illustrated in Figure 10–21. Note in the figure that the product is used at uneven rates. If there were no lead time between placing and receiving an order, the fluctuations in usage would not create a problem. The manager could wait until inventory fell to zero—whenever that might occur—and then place the order. The possibility of stockouts results from the facts that lead time is required between placing and receiving orders, and that sales or usage rates *during the time between placing and receipt of the order* may not be exactly as forecast. During the first period in Figure 10–21 the good is sold or used at the expected rate during the lead time and no stockout appears. And during the second period, the good is needed at a slower rate than forecast, so no stockout appears. But during the third period, the good moves faster during the lead time than the forecast of requirements, and a stockout does occur.

Safety stocks. The firm can protect against stockouts due to unforeseen variations in lead times and usage rates by maintaining safety stocks. A *safety stock* is an amount of inventory over and above the quantity normally needed to bridge the time gap between placing and receiving an order. Figure 10–22 shows how the safety stock protects against stockouts.

Determining optimum size of safety stock. Increases in size of a safety stock reduce the probability of stockouts. On the other hand, inventory-carrying costs are increased. To determine the optimum size of safety stock, one must compare the addition to inventory-carrying cost

Figure 10–22
Inventory with safety stock

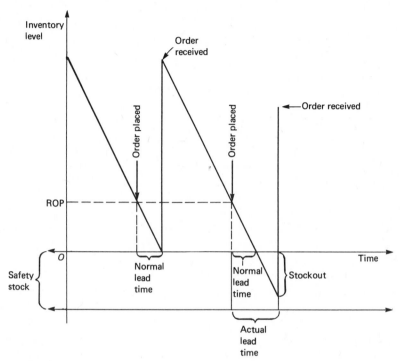

with the incremental savings in stockout costs. If incremental stockout cost savings are greater than incremental inventory-carrying costs, the safety stock should be enlarged. If not, the stock should be cut back.

An example shows how the analysis can be carried out. Through study of its past records, XYZ Company has accumulated information about rates of usage of a particular item during the reorder period—the time between placing and receiving an order—and has tabulated this information as shown in Table 10–8. The last column of the table shows the probabilities that usage will be in the various ranges for which experience has been accumulated; for example, the probability is 0.15 that usage during the reorder period will be between 101 and 150 units. To simplify the analysis, let us approximate the usage that falls within a given range by the midpoint of that range: For example, the range between 101 and 150 units will be represented by a value of 125 units.

The average, or expected, usage over a reorder period can be obtained by calculating the sum of the probability weighted average of the midpoint values in the second column of Table 10–8 (by multiplying each midpoint value by the corresponding probability of usage in the final column). The expected usage is $0.04(25) + 0.08(75) + \ldots + 0.04(375) +$

Table 10–8
Usage during reorder periods

Range of units used during reorder period	Number of times quantity used was in this range	Approximate average use	Probability of this use
0– 50	8	25	0.04
51–100	16	75	0.08
101–150	30	125	0.15
151–200	52	175	0.26
201–250	44	225	0.22
251–300	24	275	0.12
301–350	14	325	0.07
351–400	8	375	0.04
401–450	4	425	0.02

$0.02(425) = 200$. If the firm were to maintain no safety stock, it would place an order whenever stock fell to 200 units. On the average, usage during the reorder period is expected to be 200 units, but it will often be more and it will often be less. If it is more, there will be a stockout, and Table 10–9 shows that the probability of such a stockout is 0.47. (In other words, the probability that more than 200 units will be used is 0.47.)

Consider this question: Should the firm maintain a safety stock by using a reorder point above 200 units? The decision depends on comparison of incremental inventory-carrying costs with expected incremental savings in stockout costs. What are the stockout costs? If the product is a final good, stockout costs are the loss of contribution on sales not made plus any loss of goodwill expressed in terms of loss of contribution on future sales. If the product is an intermediate good, stockout cost is the loss of contribution on products not run because of slowdown or work stoppage. Stockout costs are sometimes difficult to estimate, but the estimates are necessary for rational decision making.

Let us assume that the firm in the example has an estimated stockout cost at $3 per unit out of stock and a cost of carrying one item in in-

Table 10–9
Safety stock analysis

Safety stock	Reorder point	Probability of stockout	Expected stockout cost	Incremental savings in stockout cost	Incremental increase in carrying cost
0	200	0.47	$417		
50	250	0.25	201	$216	$100
100	300	0.13	87	114	100
150	350	0.06	30	57	100
200	400	0.02	6	24	100
250	450	0.00	0	6	100

ventory for one year at $2, and that annual requirements are 1,000 units a year and the economic order quantity is 250 units, with four reorder periods per year.

If the firm maintains no safety stock, but reorders when inventory falls to 200 units, there is a 0.53 probability (see Table 10–8) that no stockout will occur. However, there is a 0.22 probability that approximately 225 units will be needed, so that a stockout of 25 units will occur; there is a 0.12 probability that usage will be about 275 units, so that a stockout of 75 units will occur; there are known probabilities of larger usages and larger stockouts. The expected stockout in units per order period is a probability weighted average of the stockout possibilities:

$$\text{Expected stockout } (ROP \text{ at } 200 \text{ units}) = 0.53(0) + 0.22(25) + 0.12(75) \\ + 0.07(125) + 0.04(175) \\ + 0.02(225) = 34.75$$

To convert the expected stockout per order period to expected annual cost, we multiply it by the number of order periods per year (R/Q) and by cost per unit out of stock:

$$\text{Expected annual stockout costs } (ROP \text{ at } 200 \text{ units}) = 34.74 \cdot 4 \cdot \$3 \\ = \$417$$

If the firm raises its reorder point from 200 to 250 units so as to provide a safety stock of 50 units, the expected stockout and expected stockout cost can be calculated as follows:

$$\text{Expected stockout } (ROP \text{ at } 250 \text{ units}) = 0.75(0) + 0.12(25) + 0.07(75) \\ + 0.04(125) + 0.02(175) \\ = 16.75$$

$$\text{Expected stockout cost } (ROP \text{ at } 250 \text{ units}) = 16.75 \cdot 4 \cdot \$3 = \$201$$

It can be seen that adding 50 units to safety stock results in an incremental savings in expected annual stockout cost that amounts to $216 ($417 − $201). On the other hand, average inventory is increased by 50 units, so annual carrying costs are 50 units times $2 per unit, or $100. Since the incremental savings in expected stockout costs is greater than the incremental inventory-carrying costs, the increase of the reorder point to 250 units reduces costs.

Total stockout costs and incremental savings in stockout costs are shown in Table 10–9 for several reorder points with safety stocks being increased by 50 units between reorder points; incremental increases in carrying costs are $100 for each increment of 50 units in safety stock. Incremental savings in expected annual stockout costs are greater than incremental increases in inventory-carrying costs up to a safety stock of 100 units (reorder point of 300 units). We conclude that XYZ Company should reorder the *EOQ* of 250 units whenever its inventory falls to 300 units.

The *incremental analysis* in the above example illustrates the nature of the decision about the size of safety stock, and is the technique that must be used *if orders are required to be in lots* such as the 50-unit increments used in the example. Suppose orders can be in any desired quantities. In this case, safety stock can be varied unit by unit. If stockout cost per unit is designated as Z, one additional unit added to inventory will lower stockout cost by Z if a stockout does occur. But a stockout may not occur. The expected reduction in stockout cost per order period is $Pr \cdot Z$ where Pr stands for the probability that a stockout will be experienced during the reorder period. The expected annual reduction in stockout costs is $Pr \cdot Z \cdot N$, where N is the number of order periods per year (i.e., $N = R/Q$).

Table 10–10
Probability of a stockout for various reorder points

Reorder point	Probability of a stockout
50	0.96
100	0.88
150	0.73
200	0.47
250	0.25
300	0.13
350	0.06
400	0.02
450	0.00

According to the data in Table 10–8, if the firm were to wait until inventory fell to 50 units before reordering, this quantity would be sufficient to meet usage requirements 0.04 of the time; the probability of stockout would be 0.96. If the firm were to reorder when stock fell to 100 units, the probability that this quantity would be sufficient would be 0.12 (i.e., 0.08 + 0.04), so the probability of stockout would be 0.88. Probabilities of stockout using various reorder points, calculated in like manner, are listed in Table 10–10.

One additional unit added to inventory will increase annual carrying costs by CP'. As safety stock is increased, Pr will fall and so will the expected annual stockout costs. Total costs will be minimized by increasing inventory until incremental increase in carrying cost is equal to the incremental reduction in expected stockout cost. That is:

$$CP' = Pr \cdot Z \cdot N$$

or

$$Pr = \frac{CP'}{Z} \cdot N$$

Figure 10–23
Probability of a stockout at various reorder points

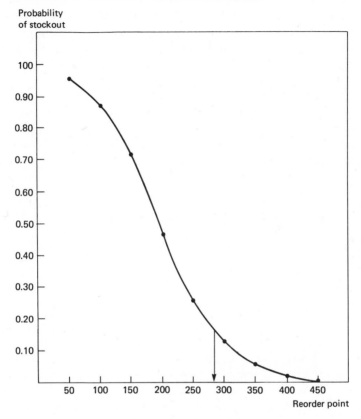

In words, the optimal safety stock is the level at which the probability of a stockout during an order period is equal to the ratio of the annual carrying cost of one unit to the unit cost of a stockout.

For the above example, Z is \$3, N is 4, and CP' is \$2. Therefore, total costs are minimum where Pr is \$2/\$3 · 4, or 0.167. Figure 10–23 shows the probability of stockout at various reorder points (from Table 10–10), and it can be seen that the value of 0.167 corresponds to a reorder point of approximately 285 units.

Production scheduling and produced goods inventories under uncertainty

Analysis of safety or buffer stocks of produced goods is basically identical to the approach used above. The firm must compare incremental inventory-carrying costs with incremental stockout costs. One thing is different—there is no reorder point. The lead time consists of time between the end of one production run for the item and the beginning of the next run, as was shown in Figure 10–19. At the end of a production run, the produced good inventory will stand at $[(B - R)/B] \cdot Q$, where B is production rate on a full year basis, R is expected usage rate per year, and Q is quantity produced on one run, which is also expected usage over the period between runs.

The firm should estimate: (1) the probability that usage will exceed inventory at the end of a run by each of various amounts, and (2) the cost of a stockout. It should then compare incremental stockout costs with incremental carrying costs in the manner explained above.

Unfortunately, analysis may not be completed once the optimal safety stock has been estimated in the above manner. Since the relevant lead time is the time between production runs, this period can be shortened by scheduling more and shorter runs. Start-up costs will be increased, but the need for safety stocks will be reduced. Analysis of the possibility of shorter runs is beyond the scope of this text, but the reader should be aware of it.

SUMMARY

The chapter discussed the profitability analysis of production runs that have planned termination or interruption. The first section was concerned with production that takes the form of *a single run*. The first kind of terminating production considered was production of models or types that pass through *life cycles*. New product profitability analysis should extend over the whole life cycle, since it may be necessary to take early losses in order to get to the profitable range of production at low unit costs. *Learning curves* decrease variable unit cost as more units are added to the total of a run. *Skimming pricing* is sometimes used on new products—the objective is to increase total revenue from the amount of product that eventually saturates the market. *Penetration pricing* is an alternative approach—the objective is to get a rapid buildup of sales and output rates to levels that allow low unit costs.

After a production run is underway, the firm can change either the *length* of the run (and its total output) or the *rate* (leaving total output constant). Changes in length of run were analyzed first. The profitability of such a change can be determined by comparing incremental costs of the additional output with incremental value. Incremental costs include *added costs of tangible production inputs; if* the increase in length of run requires services of the firm's fixed inputs that have alternative uses, incremental costs also include *opportunity costs of the fixed inputs*. In deciding whether or not to make model changeovers, special attention must be given to comparison of: (1) contribution that must be foregone on any net loss in sales if the changeover is not made, with (2) cost reduction on the units produced in a longer production run of the old model, as compared with cost for the same number of units in the first year of a new model.

Profitability of a change in the rate of production for a fixed total output can be analyzed by comparing the resulting increased cost of production with increased value because the result of production is available sooner. A convenient model for determining the optimum rate treats foregone value because of delayed completion as an opportunity cost; the approach is to minimize the sum of tangible production cost (which increases with rate) and opportunity cost (which decreases with rate). The *critical path method* is very useful in making estimates of minimum costs of project completion at various dates.

Effects of simultaneous proportionate changes in rate and volume of terminating production runs were considered. At low levels of rate and total output, learning effects are strong and so are the effects of spreading the fixed costs of the production run. Thus, total costs of the run's total output may increase at a decreasing rate with incremental unit costs and average unit costs falling. As rate and total output get into higher ranges, diseconomies of the rate increase may dominate. If so, total costs of the run's total output will then increase at an increasing rate with incremental unit costs and average unit costs rising.

In *intermittent* runs of production, the instantaneous rates of production are much greater than the rates of sale or use. Thus, inventories are prominent. The problem of the best length of a production run is, from another point of view, a problem of optimum size of inventory. For *purchased* goods under *certainty*, the economic order quantity is determined by the formula: $Q = \sqrt{2RS/CP}$, in which Q is the order quantity, R is total annual requirement in units, S is cost of placing one order in dollars, C is annual carrying cost as a percentage of value of inventory, and P is per-unit price of the item. Whether to take a quantity discount can be determined by comparing total annual costs using *EOQ* without the discount with total annual costs using the order quantity that is required to obtain the discount.

For *produced* goods under *certainty*, the optimum size of a production lot is determined by the formula:

$$Q = \sqrt{\frac{2SR}{CP'} \cdot \frac{B}{B - R}}$$

in which

Q is the lot size.
S is setup cost per production run.
R is annual requirement in units.

CP' is annual carrying costs per unit of average inventory of the item.

B is quantity that would be produced in one year of continued production.

Stockouts may occur if usage during a reorder period is greater than expected or if the reorder period is longer than expected. The probability of stockouts can be reduced by holding safety stocks. Optimum size of a safety stock is determined by the same approach for both purchased and produced goods. The optimum safety stock size is that level at which the probability of a stockout is equal to the ratio of the annual carrying cost of one unit to the unit cost of a stockout.

QUESTIONS

1. What is meant by the "learning rate"? Why do learning rates vary from one process to another?

2. What is a decision point? A chance event point? A payoff? A mathematical expectation of payoff?

3. Under what conditions might it be profitable to use a skimming price for a new product? A penetration price?

4. What are the effects upon costs and revenues when the total volume is increased for a finite production run at a given rate?

5. What are the effects upon costs and revenues when the rate of production is increased for a given volume?

6. What is a critical path? What is crashing?

7. How could the deliberate creation of inventories be explained, if production and sale were being carried out under conditions of certainty?

8. What is an economic order quantity? A reorder point? An optimum safety stock?

PROBLEMS

1. The following table shows labor used at various points in the production run of the Cape Florida Mark III off-shore sport fishing boat.

Unit	Employee-hours used
1	1,200
2	960
4	768
8	615

    a. Estimate the learning rate coefficient.

    b. Estimate the amount of labor that will be required for the 16th unit built.

    c. Estimate the amount of labor that will be required for the 9th unit built.

2. The second unit of the new Sky-Rider sport glider required 245 employee-hours of labor. Only about one tenth of the labor is machine-paced in making this product. Estimate the labor requirement for the third and the fourth units in the production run.

3. How could you change the learning curve formula $L_n = L_m \ (n/m)^X$ so that the linear regression approach could be used in making a statistical estimate of the value of coefficient X? The estimate is to be derived from production data similar to that provided in Problem 1 above.

4. Oceancraft Corporation has designed a jet-powered hydrofoil that will be the fastest craft afloat. Its intended use is in marine pursuit and interception by law enforcement officers. Total sales of the product during the expected five-year life cycle will depend partially upon management's pricing and partially upon the uncertain behavior of competing firms. Unit costs will fall at greater total sales levels because of spreading fixed costs of the production run and the effect of learning upon labor costs.

In considering just two of the possible prices for the hydrofoil, Oceancraft's management made the following estimates of the probabilities of various sales levels and the total unit costs at each of the sales levels.

| | Probabilities | | |
Sales (units)	Price— $1 million	Price— $0.9 million	Unit cost ($ millions)
20.............	0.20	0.10	$1.55
50.............	0.50	0.30	1.00
100.............	0.30	0.60	0.82

    a. Construct a decision tree to assist in the choice of price.
    b. Calculate expected values of the alternative pricing strategies.
    c. Would it be appropriate to base the decision on the expected values, or should some adjustment be made for risk?

5. Refer to Figures 10–12 and 10–13 and Tables 10–5 and 10–6. Assume that the opportunity cost of the NCR project is estimated at $190 per day. List the activities (alphabetical designations may be used) and the planned duration of each activity in days if the project's total cost (direct cost plus opportunity cost) is minimized.

6. The Dudway Company has determined that it utilizes 5,200 units of the Mark 30 Widget each year. The usage rate is approximately constant throughout the year. Studies by the industrial engineering department indicate that it costs $18.50 to place an order. It has been estimated that carrying costs are approximately 20 percent of the average inventory. The price of the Mark 30 Widget is $10 per unit. What should the economic ordering quantity be?

7. Boxkahn, Inc., purchases approximately 50,000 rolls of tape per year from Strongfasten, Inc. This tape is utilized at a constant rate throughout the year. Currently the company estimates that each order to suppliers costs $10 and that its carrying cost are approximately 15 percent. At present, Boxkahn pays

$5 per roll of tape. Strongfasten has offered Boxkahn a 10 percent discount if it will order at least 1,200 rolls at a time. Should Boxkahn accept this offer? If so, how many units should they order?

8. Terry, Inc., is concerned about the cost of stockouts for a consumer goods product which it sells. Because many customers will purchase a similar product elsewhere rather than return, it estimates the cost of a stockout to be $4 per unit. The annual demand for this product is 5,000 units, and it has been determined that the *EOQ* is 500 units per order. The cost for carrying one unit in inventory for one year is estimated to be $2. From past history Terry has found the distribution of sales during the reorder period to be as given below.

Number of units used during reorder period	Number of times this quantity was used	Probability of this usage	$P(d > r)$
0	5	0.05	0.95
25	25	0.25	0.70
50	25	0.25	0.45
75	30	0.30	0.15
100	10	0.10	0.05
125	5	0.05	0.00

a. Determine the *ROP* (reorder point).
b. Determine the expected usage during lead time.
c. Determine the safety stock.

FURTHER READING

Arrow, Kenneth J. "The Economic Implications of Learning by Doing." *Review of Economic Studies* 24, June 1962.

Bass, Frank M. "A New Product Growth Model for Consumer Durables." *Management Science,* January 1969.

Brown, Rex V. "Do Managers Find Decision Theory Useful?" *Harvard Business Review* 48, May–June 1970.*

Hirchman, Winfred B. "Profit from the Learning Curve." *Harvard Business Review* 42, January–February 1964.

Hirsh, W. Z. "Manufacturing Progress Functions." *Review of Economics and Statistics* 34, May 1952.

Hirshliefer, Jack. "The Firm's Cost Function: A Successful Reconstruction?" *Journal of Business* 35, July 1962.

Levy, F. K., et al. "The ABC's of the Critical Path Method." *Harvard Business Review* 41, September–October 1963.

Magee, John F. "Guides to Inventory Policy: 1. Functions and Lot Sizes." *Harvard Business Review,* January–February 1956.

---

* This article is reprinted in *Readings in Managerial Economics,* rev. ed. (Dallas: Business Publications, Inc., 1977).

Magee, John F. "Guides to Inventory Policy: 2. Problems of Uncertainty." *Harvard Business Review,* March–April 1956.

Magee, John F. "Guides to Inventory Policy: 3. Anticipating Future Needs." *Harvard Business Review,* May–June 1956.

Sturmy, S. G. "Cost Curves and Pricing in Aircraft Production." *Economic Journal,* December 1964.

Thomas, C. Hamshaw. "Product Forecasting—The BAC 3-11 Airliner." *Long Range Planning,* June 1970.

Cases for part four

Profitability analysis is an integral part of most problem-solving situations in which a manager becomes involved. This is true regardless of whether the decision maker is a profit-seeking business person or a government agency manager concerned with satisfying certain public needs. The cases in this section focus on cost analysis in making decisions on product mix and on the abandonment or expansion of activities.

The student will have the opportunity to determine the classifications of cost, to use incremental analysis, and to study the use of various accounting systems for managerial decision making. Some of the cases make use of break-even analysis and have information so that break-even charts can be developed using both the statistical method and the engineering method. One case allows the student to visualize the problems and opportunities which are involved because of varying capital investments and varying contributions per dollar of revenue through the use of the profit-volume contribution analysis.

It is not possible to find cases which isolate cost considerations from other economic variables. The cases in this section require some attention to the demand concepts covered in Chapters 3 and 4. Some of the cases foreshadow the discussion of pricing which is treated more formally later in the text. Marketing considerations are important throughout. No attempt is made here to isolate one aspect of the analyses from the rest of the business considerations.

RANDOLPH STONE COMPANY

The Randolph Stone Company was a partnership engaged in stone quarrying and the paving of roads. The company sold primarily to state

Exhibit 1
Profit and loss statement (1956–1961)

	1956	1957	1958	1959	1960	1961
Net sales	$131,758.71	$248,025.45	$404,037.72	$196,432.41	$84,574.65	$433,658.51
Operating expenses						
Salaries and wages	19,186.50	35,196.48	41,484.90	24,543.03	17,379.57	46,598.01
Travel expense	114.00	529.26	308.79	171.96	54.90	204.60
Stationery and office supplies	67.35	126.12	78.18	78.66	0.36	94.14
Auditing and legal	1.89	469.50	226.14	40.50	4.20	4.59
Dues and subscriptions	325.32	1,541.10	2,248.77	582.39	439.92	1,499.46
Repairs of equipment	2,157.24	2,933.19	7,496.79	4,475.01	1,294.83	9,559.05
Freight, in	8,104.29	13,779.39	10,270.02	5,315.64	2,763.69	12,542.07
Hired truck expense	13,513.08	27,204.21	39,039.69	15,553.44	7,897.17	42,546.69
Miscellaneous expense	508.41	424.59	1,621.26	569.10	4.65	606.00
Truck repair expense	207.42	456.24	1,981.56	1,082.22	317.94	1,814.10
Gas, oil, and lubricants	8,127.39	6,222.00	12,842.70	5,502.57	3,135.36	6,805.20
Stone purchased and sand	26,895.42	46,092.93	94,143.48	58,066.53	16,924.95	134,154.18
Oils and asphalt	29,425.35	53,740.89	80,837.55	22,336.02	11,076.18	46,041.87
Rent	514.29	—	6,972.51	6,804.60	2,345.34	3,682.26
Insurance expense	300.27	1,135.08	8,874.36	4,402.89	245.19	1,057.95
Utilities	814.38	1,706.19	2,123.79	464.82	245.55	333.18
License and fees	90.66	471.00	739.14	1,033.71	563.25	766.98
FICA expense	342.54	763.98	1,004.40	670.38	451.05	1,375.62
Kentucky unemployment contributions	344.01	831.39	1,345.29	744.48	452.91	1,249.77
Interest expense	1,592.01	4,795.50	4,852.20	3,533.55	1,863.54	1,350.84
Bonding expense	520.35	1,156.05	256.89	713.64	371.19	2,420.46
Depreciation of equipment	6,075.39	12,144.33	15,988.59	17,354.13	17,221.83	31,498.68
Telephone and postage	—	84.69	36.99	42.42	15.39	6.00
Taxes	—	3.81	33.15	263.55	15.75	315.00
Commissions	—	750.00	—	—	—	—
Advertising	—	—	402.15	440.43	37.50	52.89
Federal unemployment insurance	—	—	74.16	80.94	73.35	91.77
Sales tax	—	—	—	2,260.89	2,319.72	6,926.25
Bad-debt expense	—	—	—	1,042.41	42.18	274.80
Road construction supplies	—	—	—	—	—	911.31
	$119,227.56	$212,557.92	$335,283.45	$178,169.91	$87,557.46	$354,783.72
Net profit (loss)	$ 12,531.15	$ 35,467.53	$ 68,754.27	$ 18,262.50	$(2,982.81)	$ 78,874.79

and local governments; its gravel was purchased for road construction in nearby sections of the state.

The company owned and operated five stone quarries located within 100 miles of each other. In addition, it owned a paving operation in the same vicinity.

The quarries were generally profitable, returning on the average a book profit of from 10 to 20 percent of the book value of the partners' property. Occasionally one of the quarries operated at a loss, though this resulted partly from the fact that special repairs were charged off as a current expense.

The most unstable part of the business was the paving operation. Its instability resulted from the variations in road construction activities of the state government involved. In election years paving activity was high; in other years it tapered off. The result was that the paving activities of the firm fluctuated sharply from high to low profits.

Exhibit 1 covers data on paving revenues and expenses for the years from 1956 through 1961.

1. Classify the expenses into fixed expenses and variable expenses based on the 1961 profit and loss statement. Use judgment in determining whether the expense is fixed or variable. Some expenses, such as advertising and rent, might be classified in a separate category, since they are more in the nature of programmed or manipulatable expenses which are neither fixed nor a result of changes in output.
2. On the basis of your answer to Question 1, construct a break-even chart.
3. Plot a scatter diagram relating total cost to sales. Complete a break-even chart based on this approach.
4. Compare your two break-even charts (the one based on the classification of accounts; the other on a rough "statistical" analysis). Do they provide approximately the same estimate of fixed costs? How do you account for the differences in the two charts?
5. What limitations would a statistician find in the "statistical" chart constructed as an answer to Question 3?
6. Consider possible effects of the following: price changes over time, changes over time in ages of major items of plant and equipment, and changes over time in the ratio of capital to labor.

M AND H COMPANY (B)*

The M and H Company invited a management consultant to advise it on the use of the company's accounts in decision making. The consultant's report is reproduced below:

---

* Editorial changes are made in the original version of the reproduced report in this case for the purpose of classroom discussion and to disguise the original company.

This report presents the accounts of the M and H Company in the form of marginal income accounting—also known as dfferential accounting, cost-volume-profit analysis, or incremental analysis. The method is closely akin to direct costing, but does not require the tie-in with the day-to-day financial accounts or the change in inventory valuation required by direct costing.

Purposes of marginal income accounting

The objective of marginal income accounting is to aid in decision making rather than the reporting of past performance. It supplements the financial reports. If M and H were to adopt a permanent system of marginal income accounting, it would need special analyses of the accounts only twice a year. These could be kept in a form which is relatively inexpensive—the work could be done in the slack periods in the accounting department.

In the case at instance, marginal income accounting would help achieve the following objectives:

1. Separation of the results of the Boonville and Dorchester operations. As we have seen there has already been a tendency to mix the Boonville and Dorchester accounts in such a way that the results are confusing and misleading. It is imperative for a businessman to know how much each operation is contributing to the business.

2. Separation of the results of the poster, paint, and commercial departments. At present one cannot tell whether any of these departments is contributing adequately to the business to justify its existence. Nor can one tell which branches are the most profitable and thus the most appropriate for expansion.

3. Determination of the incremental costs of each activity. While at the present time one has a notion that the variable costs are much less than the fixed costs—and that the incremental costs are perhaps only 30 to 40 percent of the billings—that such is the case has not been determined in a systematic way. The incremental costs vary from one activity to another. In fact, they vary from one type of decision to another. Any system which helps to determine incremental costs should assist the executives in future decisions about the business.

It might be noted here that marginal income accounting tries to avoid arbitrary allocations of overhead. If some costs are common costs of the company as a whole, and are not a result of any particular activity (Boonville or Dorchester) as such, these costs are marked as company overhead. If some other costs are clearly related to Boonville activity or Dorchester activity but cannot be shown to be a result of a particular department (poster, paint, or commercial), such costs are marked as Boonville overhead or as Dorchester overhead. One of the primary objectives of marginal income accounting is to determine how much Boonville and Dorchester are separately contributing to the company's overhead and profits and how much poster, paint, and commercial departments are contributing to local overhead, company overhead, and profits. Thus a central concept throughout is the *contribution to overhead and profits.*

Arrangement of the accounts

I have identified each major account classification in a way which should be almost self-explanatory. The classes are shown in Exhibit 1. A code has been established for each class.

Exhibit 1
Marginal income—classification of accounts

B–PO–1	Boonville income from poster plant
B–PO–2	Boonville variable costs in poster plant
B–PO–3	Boonville poster plant contribution to poster fixed costs, local and company overhead, and profit.
B–PO–4	Boonville poster plant fixed costs
B–PO–4A	(Part of B–PO–4) Boonville poster plant sunk costs.
B–PO–4B	(Part of B–PO–4) Boonville poster plant escapable fixed costs.
B–PO–5	Boonville poster plant contribution to local and company overhead and profit (after deduction of poster plant fixed costs).

B–PA–1
B–PA–2
B–PA–3
B–PA–4   } The same for the Boonville paint plant
B–PA–4A
B–PA–4B
B–PA–5

B–C–1
B–C–2
B–C–3
B–C–4   } The same for the Boonville commercial plant
B–C–4A
B–C–4B
B–C–5

D–PO–1	D–PA–1	D–C–1	
D–PO–2	D–PA–2	D–C–2	
D–PO–3	D–PA–3	D–C–3	The same for the Dorchester poster plant,
D–PO–4	D–PA–4	D–C–4	Dorchester paint plant, and Dorchester commercial plant, respectively.
D–PO–4A	D–PA–4A	D–C–4A	
D–PO–4B	D–PA–4B	D–C–4B	
D–PO–5	D–PA–5	D–C–5	

In addition there are three overhead accounts, two local contribution accounts, and one company profit account.

B–OH	Boonville overhead
D–OH	Dorchester overhead
B–6	Boonville contribution to company overhead and profit
D–6	Dorchester contribution to company overhead and profit
O	Company-wide overhead
P	Company profit

Marginal income analysis for July 1967 through December 1967

The operational results for the six months from July through December 1967 appear in Exhibit 2. These results are based on a close study of each individual expense item to determine whether it is fixed or variable, sunk or escapable, and attributable to Boonville, Dorchester, or the company as a whole.

Break-even charts: Boonville

The results can also be shown in the form of a series of break-even charts. Rather than construct a break-even chart for the company as a whole, it makes

Exhibit 2

B–PO–1	$355,230.92
Less B–PO–2	107,621.19
Equals B–PO–3	247,609.73
Less B–PO–4A	96,155.16
Less B–PO–4B	89,651.49
Equals B–PO–5	61,803.08

B–PA–1	$206,261.48
Less B–PA–2	72,305.19
Equals B–PA–3	133,956.29
Less B–PA–4A	32,343.98
Less B–PA–4B	51,502.33
Equals B–PA–5	50,109.98

B–C–1	$81,361.56
Less B–C–2	54,718.73
Equals B–C–3	26,642.83
Less B–C–4A	—
Less B–C–4B	2,299.83
Less B–C–5	24,343.00

D–PO–1	$99,898.50
Less D–PO–2	40,619.18
Equals D–PO–3	59,279.32
Less D–PO–4A	13,608.73
Less D–PO–4B	15,937.68
Equals D–PO–5	29,732.91

D–PA–1	$23,318.21
Less D–PA–2	3,866.94
Equals D–PA–3	19,451.27
Less D–PA–4A	4,068.32
Less D–PA–4B	5,517.93
Equals D–PA–5	9,865.02

D–C–1	$14,514.51
Less D–C–2	9,883.79
Equals D–C–3	4,630.72
Less D–C–4A	—
Less D–C–4B	591.66
Equals D–C–5	4,039.06

Total Boonville contribution to local and company overhead and profits ($61,803.08 + $50,109.98 + $24,343.00)	$136,256.06
Less B–OH (Boonville overhead)	89,482.10
Equals D–6 Boonville contribution to company overhead and profits)	$ 46,773.96
Total Dorchester contribution to local and company overhead and profits ($29,732.91 + $9,865.02 + $4,039.06)	$ 43,636.99
Less D–OH (Dorchester overhead)	31,011.46
Equals D–6 (Dorchester contribution to company overhead and profits)	$ 12,625.53
Total contribution to company overhead and profits	$ 59,399.49
Less O (company-wide overhead)	100,011.60
Equals company's loss	(40,611.11)

more sense to construct individual charts for each segment of the business separately. An overall break-even chart would add together differing elements, thereby obscuring the outcome of particular operations.

The special break-even chart required to be constructed is known as the profit/volume chart. On it is plotted first of all the fixed costs (both sunk and escapable) resulting from the particular segment. Then is plotted what is called the P/V line (the profit-volume line) which is the incremental income at various volumes of sales. It is, in other words, the added income *minus* the added (variable) costs. The slope of the P/V line is the P/V ratio—the added contribution per unit of sales. Where the P/V line crosses the zero horizontal line is the break-even point. At this point, the income less the variable costs is

Exhibit 3
P/V (break-even) chart, Boonville poster department (July–December 1967)

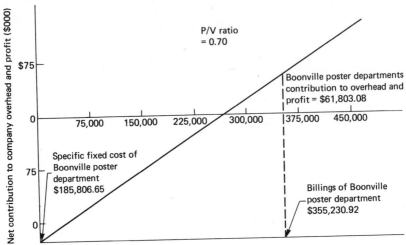

enough to cover the segment's fixed costs. *But* at this point the segment makes *no* contribution to the company's overhead and profits.

Take Exhibit 3, for example. The specific fixed costs of the Boonville poster department amount of $185,806.65. The *P/V* ratio is 0.70, which means that every $1 of Boonville poster sales adds $0.70 more income. It takes billings of $266,580 in each six-month period to break even in the poster plant—that is, to cover the specific fixed costs. Beyond that point the contribution to profit increases rapidly, reaching a level of $61,803.08 at billings of $355,230.92. At billings of $450,000 it would appear that the contribution would be over $127,500.

However, one qualification is necessary. Exhibit 3 probably exaggerates the added profits *beyond* present levels of sales in one respect. Remember that the salesmen's earnings have been treated as a fixed cost and partly as a variable cost. As billings push on beyond present levels and the salesmen become relatively more dependent upon commissions, the proportion of variable costs will rise, with a reduction in the *P/V* ratio line somewhere beyond the present level of sales. This error is probably not serious—it might reduce the ratio from 0.70 to 0.65 beyond the sales level of $420,000 (or something of that magnitude).

Which of the three Boonville departments is the most profitable? The paint department made the largest contribution in ratio to its revenue in the six months under study. (See Exhibit 4.) The contribution of $50,109.98 on sales of $206,261.48 appears to be more favorable than the poster department's contribution of $61,803.08 on revenues of $355,230.92. This comparison is misleading, however. The results for the poster department are for its poorest six months. It will make a much larger contribution in the other six months, while the paint department will remain relatively stable. In addition, the poster department's *P/V* ratio is somewhat higher, which means that its contribution will respond rapidly to sales increases.

Exhibit 4
P/V (break-even) chart, Boonville paint department (July–December 1967)

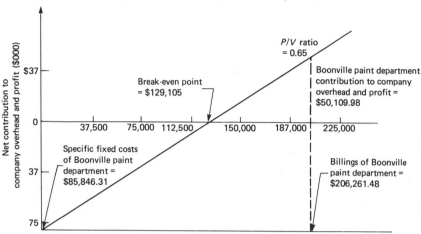

The Boonville commercial department's high ratio of contribution to sales certainly indicates that it is a desirable adjunct of the business. (See Exhibit 5.) Its main advantage is its low proportion of fixed costs. Its main disadvantage is it low *P/V* ratio, which would preclude it from ever making the kind of profit which is possible in the poster department.

The fact appears to be that all three Boonville operations are profitable in every sense of the word—even though the overall company income statement shows a loss for the six months from July through December 1967.

Exhibit 5
P/V (break-even) chart, Boonville commercial department (July–December 1967)

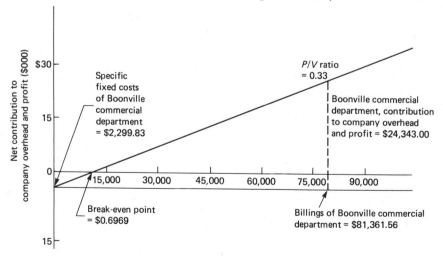

Break-even charts: Dorchester

The analysis for the Dorchester operations runs along similar lines. For some reason the poster department P/V ratio is lower (0.59) in Dorchester than in Boonville—its variable costs are proportionally higher than in Boonville (Exhibit 6). But the billings are high enough to give a high ratio of contribution ($29,732.91) to billings ($99,898.50). Of course, the contribution should be considerably higher in the summer months.

Exhibit 6
P/V (break-even) chart, Dorchester poster department (July–December 1967)

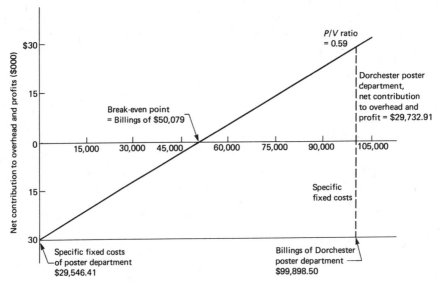

The Dorchester paint department's P/V ratio of 0.83 is extremely high (Exhibit 7). One wonders whether all the variable costs for this segment have been discovered. Perhaps some of the poster department's variable costs should be shifted to the paint department. I have checked over the original worksheets and have found that M and H's accounts show $12,714.21 of labor for the poster department but only $1,181.56 for the paint department. Perhaps this allocation of labor costs should be rechecked.

If the present allocations are correct, the Dorchester paint department is extremely profitable in relation to sales and would be fantastically profitable if volume could be increased.

The Dorchester commercial department also makes a satisfactory contribution to overhead and profit (Exhibit 8). In this case the contribution results from the high volume in relation to fixed costs rather than to the P/V ratio which is relatively low. The low P/V ratio of 0.32 results, of course, from the fact that commercial work takes proportionally more labor and materials (outright sales cost).

Exhibit 7
P/V (break-even) chart, Dorchester paint department (July–December 1967)

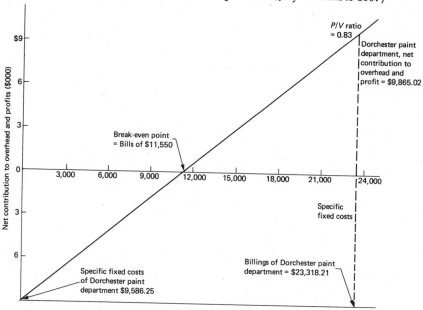

Exhibit 8
P/V (break-even) chart, Dorchester commercial department
(July–December 1967)

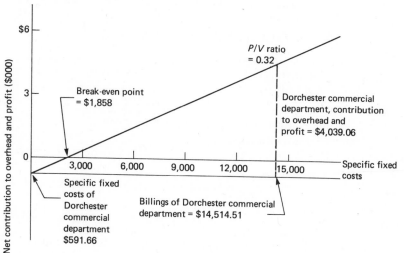

Future marginal income reports

I have tried to think of methods by which the analysis could be simplified so that future marginal income reports could be constructed with less effort. Accountants often use shortcuts which assume all costs of one type are variable and of another type are fixed, and so on. I think that such simplifications would not be appropriate in your business for several reasons:

1. It is desirable to separate specific fixed costs from local overhead and company-wide overhead. It is unlikely that any simple formula will do this exactly.

2. Costs which are fixed in one period may become variable and vice versa. Therefore a periodic review of the classification is desirable.

3. As you change your business—buying new property and perhaps selling off old property—you will need flexibility in changing the classification.

I am returning the original worksheets showing the classification of accounts. It will serve as a useful guide for future marginal income reports. But it will not provide automatic answers to all problems of classification which might arise.

1. What is the purpose of separating sunk fixed costs from escapable fixed costs? What is the meaning of these terms? How is this breakdown relevant?
2. What is the meaning of the term "specific fixed costs" as used in the consultant's report?
3. Would an overall break-even chart for the company as a whole serve the purpose just as well as the individual P/V charts?
4. What are the meaning and significance of the break-even points shown on the P/V charts?
5. Three types of "contribution" are shown in Exhibit 2. What is the significance of each?
6. What purposes could be served by this type of analysis?

THE MINERVA OXYGEN VENT VALVE*

In March 1959, H. R. Deming, president of Dem-A-Lex Dynamics Corporation of Lexington, Massachusetts, called a meeting of the executive committee to consider a proposal which would establish improved quality control over an item produced by Dem-A-Lex as subcontractor for several prime contractors. The item was an oxygen vent valve used in the "Minerva," a rocket-powered missile.

This valve had been adopted by several large missile manufacturing companies during 1958 for use in the recently developed Minerva missile. In early 1959, however, the Department of Defense announced that

* This case was prepared by Andrew McCosh under the direction of Stanley I. Buchin of the Harvard University Graduate School of Business Administration as a basis for classroom discussion rather than to illustrate either effective or ineffective handling of administrative situations. Copyright © 1965 by the President and Fellows of Harvard College. Used by specific permission.

the Minerva missile had ben designated as an operational first-line weapon and that all prime contractors of the Minerva missile were to enter crash production programs. Because of the increased urgency of the program and the importance of the oxygen vent valve to the Minerva's proper functioning, an executive committee meeting had been called to consider a proposal, submitted by Mr. Massey, the company's production manager. Massey's proposal recommended the utilization of a newly introduced piece of testing equipment which would greatly reduce the number of defective vent valves delivered by Dem-A-Lex to the various prime contractors.

Company history

Deming, a graduate electromechanical engineer, had left his position with a large electrical products manufacturing company in 1948 and started a small research service organization in an Army surplus Quonset hut. He stated, "I had always wanted to tinker around with my own ideas and push them to completion, and when I saw the chance to obtain a research grant for the development of a high temperature pressure indicator, I couldn't resist the temptation to apply for the grant. I was completely fed up with all the red tape, required reports, and voluminous records associated with my previous job."

Since 1948, the company had grown rapidly, and net sales in 1958 had exceeded $6 million (see Exhibits 1 and 2). As the company had expanded, Deming, considered by most of his associates as an inventive genius, decided to devote his time and energy to research and development of new products and had turned the actual operating management of the business over to his son, Stephen Deming, a former Air Force jet pilot and a recent graduate of a well-known business school. Deming, Sr., had developed several unique and commercially salable products since 1948, among which were: metal and fabric strain gauges which signaled a condition of overload on the material; special high-pressure intensifiers and pressure transducers; solenoid-triggered butterfly valves; ultralow temperature liquid pumps and flow regulators; high-tension circuit breakers; and most recently the oxygen vent valve. Patents had initially been obtained on each of these items, but, after they had been a few years on the market, similar devices, but different enough to avoid patent infringement, had been developed by the larger manufacturing companies in the industry. Because of their size and volume production methods, these companies could generally produce the item more cheaply than could Dem-A-Lex.

As a result of this, Dem-A-Lex did not attempt to compete on a volume-price basis with the larger firms in the industry, but instead, exploited each product as fully as possible before the larger concerns

Exhibit 1

THE MINERVA OXYGEN VENT VALVE
Balance sheet as of December 31, 1958 (in $000)

Assets

Cash and marketable securities...............................	$378	
Accounts receivable (net).....................................	954	
Inventories..	685	
Notes receivable (employees).................................	126	
Total Current Assets..		$2,143
Land and buildings (net)......................................	$360	
Machinery and equipment (net)...............................	680	
Prepaid expenses...	6	
Other assets..	13	
Total Fixed Assets..		1,059
Total Assets..		$3,202

Liabilities and net worth

Accounts payable...	$250	
Notes payable to bank @ 6%.................................	700	
Dividends payable..	35	
Other accruals...	315	
Total Current Liabilities...................................		$1,300
Mortgage payable on real estate..............................	$120	
Long-term bonds (7% coupon).................................	500	
Common stock (40% owned by Deming, Sr., and his son).........	410	
Earned surplus...	872	
Total Fixed Liabilities and Net Worth......................		1,902
Total Liabilities and Net Worth.........................		$3,202

developed a similar item. After the loss of the high-volume customer to the larger producers, Dem-A-Lex then concentrated its efforts on modification and adaption of the item to the customer with unique or special requirements who could not obtain the special adaptation from the high-volume producer, or whose requirements were too small to interest such a producer.

Flexible production scheduling and the ability of the research department to modify standard production models to meet unusual product specifications have given Dem-A-Lex the ability to capture a specialized portion of the total market for most of its products. H. R. Deming commented, "We are not trying to butt heads with the big boys. Our policy is to sell our real assets—our research and development skills, and our productive flexibility."

Sales of vent valves accounted for nearly 25 percent of Dem-A-Lex's total sales during 1958, while the other 75 percent was made up of the sale of strain gauges, pressure gauges, intensifiers, and transducers, various types of electrically and hydraulically operated valves, regulators, circuit breakers, and other electrical and mechanical devices. Sales revenue from these items had been increasing at an annual rate of 8 percent

Exhibit 2

THE MINERVA OXYGEN VENT VALVE
Statement of profit and loss for year ending December 31, 1958 (in $000)

Gross sales...	$6,193	
Less allowances given for defective valves.....................	143	
Net sales...		$6,050
Cost of goods sold:		
Direct labor..	$1,010	
Materials..	2,030	
Factory burden.......................................	1,362	
Cost of goods sold..................................		4,402
Gross Profit..		$1,648
Operating expenses:		
Selling expense*......................................	332	
Administrative expense*...............................	198	
Research expense*....................................	350	
Interest expense......................................	93	
Total Operating Expenses...........................		$ 973
Net profits before tax.................................		$ 675
Federal taxes (52%)..................................		350
Net income after tax..................................		$ 325
Dividends on common stock............................		30
Net addition to retained earnings......................		$ 295

* See Exhibit 3 for an analysis of this expense.

since 1951. All of these items were manufactured in the general production department with general-purpose equipment, while the vent valve was produced in a separate department on specialized equipment. This specialized equipment had been purchased or built by Deming himself during 1957 and 1958 at a cost of about $525,000. However, Deming commented that if he had to replace all this equipment today by purchase from outside vendors, it would probably cost him over $950,000.

Oxygen vent valve

In November 1956 H. R. Deming had begun work on the development of an improved oxygen vent valve. He had been motivated to experiment with this type of valve because of the high number of failures (nearly 60 percent defective) of valves which were then being used by missile producers. By January 1958 he had designed a valve which was lighter in weight and more resistant to extreme temperature and pressure than any valve then on the market. A new missile designated the Minerva was also introduced in early 1958, and by coincidence Dem-A-Lex's new vent valve met the missile's more rigid technical requirements. Because of this, Dem-A-Lex received subcontracts from

Exhibit 3
Analysis of selling, administrative, and research expenses for year ending December 31, 1958 (in $000)

Selling expense
Advertising.. $ 33
Sales staff's salaries and commissions........................... 251
Traveling expenses... 24
Supplies... 7
Heat, light, and power (allocated on basis of floor space
  utilized by sales department)................................ 2
Samples... 13
Depreciation (allocated on basis of floor space
  utilized by sales department)................................ 2
      Total selling expense................................... $332

Administrative expense
Officers' salaries (included half of Deming, Sr.'s, salary)............. $ 62
Office wages.. 81
Office expenses... 14
Legal and accounting.. 6
Telephone and telegraph..................................... 3
Miscellaneous expenses...................................... 7
Depreciation (allocated on basis of floor space
  utilized by the office. Also included direct depreciation
  computed on various articles of office equipment)............... 4
Bad-debt losses... 16
Heat, light, and power (allocated on basis of
  floor space utilized by the office)........................... 5
      Total administrative expense............................. $198

Research expense*
Officers' salaries (included half of Deming, Sr.'s, salary)............ $ 25
Laboratory supplies and expendable equipment................... 45
Depreciation (allocated on basis of floor space
  utilized by the research laboratory).......................... 4
Heat, light, and power (allocated on basis of floor space
  utilized by the research laboratory).......................... 4
Salaries of research personnel................................. 186
Materials used in development of operational prototypes........... 79
Machinery and equipment depreciation......................... 4
Liability insurance... 3
      Total research expense................................... $350

* During 1958, the research staff spent approximately 75–80 percent of its time on the development and testing of an oxygen vent valve constructed of "Berylitt," a metal alloy recently perfected by Dem-A-Lex.

several missile manufacturers to produce the oxygen vent valve for the Minerva missile.

The oxygen vent valve was a critical component to the proper functioning of any liquid rocket engine. A liquid rocket engine was basically a very simple mechanism. It consisted of a fuel tank, an oxygen tank, a pressure tank, a combustion chamber, and a number of valves for regulating the flow of material from the various tanks into the combustion chamber. Nitrogen gas from the pressure tank was used to force liquid oxygen and a liquid fuel (generally alcohol or kerosene and LOX) through propellent control valves into injector nozzles and thence into the combustion chamber where the mixture was ignited to provide the rocket's thrust.

Most missiles had four vent valves located on either side of the airframe just below the nose cone or warhead; the Minerva missile, however, had eight vent valves. In order to fill the oxygen tank, these vent valves were opened and liquid oxygen at −220°F. was pumped into the oxygen tank through filler valves at the base of the tank until the tank was full. When the tank was completely filled, liquid oxygen spewed out the four vent valves in heavy white streams. These valves then had to be closed before the system could be pressurized. Pressurization was accomplished by pumping nitrogen gas through a second chamber of the oxygen vent valve into the oxygen tank. If the vent valves did not close (because of the very low temperature), all pressure would be lost, and no oxygen could be forced into the combustion chamber.

These valves had to withstand not only temperatures of −220°F.,

Exhibit 4
Analysis of projected factory burden for fiscal 1959 (in $000)

	Budgeted for 1959 assuming no change in production procedures	Budgeted for 1959 assuming plating-polish-ing operation added for 2,000 vent valves	Budgeted for 1959 assuming testing equip-ment rented*
Fringe benefits †.....................	$ 354	$ 358	$ 359
Supervision.........................	213	213	213
Inspection..........................	147	150	149
Purchasing and receiving..............	123	128	128
Repair to tools and equipment.........	99	102	100
Clerical, trucking, and cleanup.........	90	90	90
Maintenance.......................	43	43	48
Valve replacement parts..............	$ 17	$ 0	$ 5
Small tools.........................	41	43	40
Spoiled work.......................	69	65	67
Supplies...........................	83	84	85
Department indirect.................	52	54	54
Heat, light, and power...............	23	26	26
Test machine rental.................			24
Depreciation (allocated on basis of floor space utilized by the production facilities).....................	44	44	44
Total factory burden...........	$1,398	$1,400	$1,432

* These budgeted figures did not include any expected change in overhead costs associated with the addition of the plating-polishing process to the vent valve production operation.

† This item was composed of the cost of unemployment compensation, social security, a company-sponsored health insurance plan, and vacation payments, for all direct and indirect labor. It averaged 20 percent of labor costs annually.

but also those of +500°F. generated by the missile in flight as well as
the great pressure caused by the expansion of nitrogen gas as it was
forced through the valve chamber into the oxygen tank. Deming had
developed an alloy of beryllium and titanium, referred to as "Berylitt,"
which was designed to withstand both extreme temperature and pressure.
Deming felt the vent valves had been quite successful because only 450
vent valves had proved defective out of the total 1958 sale of 1,500
valves. Previous valves had failed, on the average, 60 percent of the
time.

Under the terms of various subcontracts which Dem-A-Lex held,
the prime contractor was permitted to charge Dem-A-Lex $300 for each
vent valve which was found defective. Of this, $250 was the cost of re-
moving the defective valve from the missile and the installation of a new
valve, while $50 was allowed for repairing the defective valve with parts
supplied by Dem-A-Lex. These repair parts had cost Dem-A-Lex an
average of $25 per defective valve in 1958 and had been charged to the
burden account (Exhibit 4) by the accounting department, while the
charge of $300 for each defective valve was recorded as a deduction from
gross sales (Exhibit 2). Thus, each defective valve cost Dem-A-Lex an
additional $325. Because of the urgency of the missile program, the
prime contractor repaired the valves at the missile site, rather than
sending them back to Dem-A-Lex for replacement.

The standard price which Dem-A-Lex received for each oxygen vent
valve was $975. The cost accounting department computed the factory
cost of each vent valve as follows:

Direct materials.................................		$139
Direct labor		
Machining time.............................	$175	
Assembly time..............................	100	
Inspection and packaging time..................	25	
Total direct labor..........................		$300
Overhead: 135% of direct labor....................		405
Total product cost per valve...............		$844

The 135 percent overhead rate was based on the relationship of overhead costs to direct labor costs in 1958 (Exhibit 2). The factory cost
accountant itemized the costs charged to the factory burden account as
shown in Exhibit 4.

Quality control of the oxygen vent valve

Dem-A-Lex, in early 1959, had no way of subjecting its vent valves
to operational temperatures and pressure before the valve was assembled
into the missile. Each component part of the valve was carefully in-

spected for size, required tolerances, and surface before assembly, and the assembled valve was hydraulically tested before shipment to the missile manufacturer, but this did not prevent valve failure when the rocket engine was statically fired at the launching site (a test firing with the missile securely fastened to its launching pad).

One of two types of failure might occur when the engine was statically fired; first, the valve might freeze in the open position because of the frigid temperature of the liquid oxygen, or second, after it was closed, a butterfly valve (inside the vent valve) might freeze in the closed position and as the nitrogen gas was forced into the chamber of the vent valve, pressure would build up until the vent valve ruptured, thus depressurizing the oxygen tank. If either of the above conditions occurred, the valve had to be removed and rebuilt by the replacement of tension springs, the butterfly valve, and various pressure seals and diaphragms. Both types of valve failure were caused by a common factor, the expansion or contraction of the metal components in the valve as it was subjected to operational temperatures. Even the most accurate measurement of specified tolerances could not eliminate these failures, since the internal molecular structure of the metal in each valve was slightly different and thus each valve would be affected differently by the operational temperatures. Stephen Deming stated that it was much cheaper to have the prime contractor repair the defective valve than it was to junk it and that the cost of a valve failure ($300) charged by the prime contractor did not depend upon the type of defect that occurred. The subcontract did not permit the prime contractor to charge Dem-A-Lex $300 for the failure of a valve which had been rebuilt by the prime contractor. Thus, Dem-A-Lex could never be held financially responsible for more than one failure on each valve produced.

Stephen Deming pointed out, however, that the research department had developed a vanadium electroplating and polishing process which, if used, would guarantee that every vent valve would function perfectly. This process would eliminate all defects by reducing the expansion or contraction of any metal surface which had been treated with vanadium. The plating and polishing procedure would require $110 of material and three hours of labor at $3 per hour for each valve produced.

The company currently had excess capacity on the electroplating and polishing equipment located in the general production department and thus would not have to purchase additional equipment to perform this operation. However, there was no excess labor time available in the department, and Deming estimated that two or three new employees would have to be hired to run the plating and polishing equipment. Massey stated that this equipment was currently being used by the general production department about 20 hours per week and that the processing of the vent valves on this equipment would consume another 14 to

15 hours per week, thus loading the equipment to nearly 90 percent of its total capacity. These pieces of machinery occupied approximately 800 square feet of the total factory space of 20,000 square feet and were being depreciated at the rate of $2,100 per year. This equipment would be fully depreciated by December 31, 1963. However, Deming, Sr., commented that he did not feel the additional cost was justified since he thought it was cheaper to "let your customers do your testing for you, and then all you have to do is pay for *just* those valves that have to be repaired. It's nonsense to incur the cost of plating when we don't have to!"

Massey, on the other hand, was in favor of renting a "revolutionary" piece of testing equipment which had just been put on the market. He had recently been approached by the National Machinery and Testing Equipment Co., of Zanesville, Indiana, about newly developed testing equipment which could be used to test each valve before its shipment to the prime contractor. Massey had loaned National Machinery 100 vent valves to test on this new equipment and had been told that 40 of these valves were defective while 60 were operationally perfect. The 60 valves which had tested "good" were especially marked and sent to one of the prime contractors by Dem-A-Lex. Later this prime contractor informed Dem-A-Lex that 12 of the valves which had tested "good" failed to operate and hence had to be rebuilt. The 40 vent valves which tested defective were sent to the general production department for electro-plating and polishing. The National Machinery and Testing Co. stated that they could not guarantee complete accuracy in that a few valves which tested good would prove defective, while some that tested bad would in fact be operationally perfect. However, the equipment was reliable in that it would produce consistent readings on successive tests for any given valve. Massey was very much in favor of renting the testing equipment because he stated "It's obvious that it's going to save us money. By testing the valves we had only 12 rejects in a hundred, while if these same valves had been shipped directly to the prime contractor we would have incurred the cost of making good on about 42 (30 + 12) rejects. Thus, you see, the testing equipment would reduce our number of rejects by 70 percent; this would mean a cash saving of $300 as well as a reduction in the cost of repair parts for each potential reject which would be detected before shipment."

The testing equipment would cost Dem-A-Lex $24,000 a year for rental, and this figure would be a flat rate. There would be no additional installation charge, and the shakedown testing that would be required would be done at the expense of National Machinery. Massey proposed that the testing equipment be installed in a room recently vacated by the office staff. "If we do this," he said "we won't have to charge any overhead to the testing operation, since the space was vacant anyway." The office staff had just recently moved to quarters (2,400 square feet) which rented for $250 per month, across the street from the factory in order that the supplies storeroom could be expanded for the purpose of increasing its operational efficiency. The space which was vacated by the office staff consisted of 2,000 square feet of the total factory area of 20,000 square feet. The valve department occupied approximately 5,000 square feet of the total factory area. However, expansion of the storeroom was not critical and thus could be delayed for an extended period of time. This testing equipment would require the addition of two employees to the payroll who would operate and load the equipment as a team. Because of union regulations these workers would not be permitted to perform any other operation in their slack time. These specially trained employees would be paid $3.50 per hour. The National Machinery and Testing Equipment Co. estimated that the testing equipment could handle 2,500 vent valves annually working a 40-hour week. The machinery was also capable of operating under overtime conditions. The period of the initial rental contract would be one year, though this could be extended at Dem-A-Lex's option. The company also estimated that an annual expense of $3,500 could be expected for normal maintenance of the testing equipment including bimonthly replacement of the freon gas used in the equipment. Massey had also been informed that National Machinery was working on an improved testing machine which would probably be put on the market in 1961 or 1962.

Neither H. R. Deming nor his son, Stephen, was at all convinced of the advisability of renting the special testing machine. H. R. Deming did not feel that the anticipated volume of vent valve production would be enough to justify the rental charge, and further was concerned over the possibility that one of the large manufacturing companies might develop an improved oxygen vent valve which would replace Dem-A-Lex's valve. However, since solid fuel rockets were expected to make their entrance by 1965, at which time the production of liquid fuel rockets would be drastically curtailed, Sears (sales manager) did not feel that any competitor would be interested in spending a lot of time and money developing an improved oxygen vent valve unless specifically requested to do so by a major prime contractor. She did not think that any competitor was working on an oxygen vent valve at that time, and she estimated it would take at least two years and $400,000 for a competitor to develop an improved valve. Sears further pointed out that the increased urgency of the missile program might encourage missile manufacturers to look elsewhere for more reliable vent valves, but she did not think this too likely as long as the number of defective valves did not exceed a "reasonable" level. Dem-A-Lex was well liked by its prime contractors and had built up good rapport with them in past associations. Sears estimated that 2,000 oxygen vent valves would be demanded annually through 1965. Because of the complexity of the vent valve and because of expected increases in labor and material costs, Sears could foresee no reason for the biannually negotiated price of the valve to fall below the current contract price of $975. All of Dem-A-Lex's vent valve two-year subcontracts came up for renewal in January to April 1960.

Stephen Deming was not sure whether the rental of the testing equipment could be justified, but he felt very strongly that all vent valves should be vanadium plated and polished by the newly developed production process. He commented, "Why should we spend $2,000 a month on fancy testing equipment when all we really need to do to solve our problem is to just plate the valves on existing equipment with only a small additional cost per valve?"

After extensive discussion of each of the above points of view, Deming adjourned the executive committee meeting until the afternoon of the following day, when he expected Swen's (the company controller) return from an out-of-town trip. He instructed Stephen Deming to fill Swen in on the discussion which had taken place at the committee meeting and to ask him to be prepared to submit his recommendations relative to quality control of the vent valve to the committee the following afternoon.

1. Calculate the cost of continuing with payments of $300 plus $25 for parts for each failure.
2. Calculate the cost of the vanadium process.
3. Calculate the cost of renting the new equipment.
4. Which of the above alternatives is preferable?

THE STATE UNIVERSITY PRESS (B)

The State University Press is engaged in producing scholarly books and monographs for which the demand is relatively limited. The objective is not profit; if it were, the press would select more popular works with a wider market. The press must operate within the limits of its budget, including subsidies from outside foundations, and must therefore control costs.

One important decision affecting costs is the length of run for each publication. If the first run of a book is too small, the press takes the risk of running out of stock and losing sales. It also must meet the extra setup costs required by a second run. But if the run is too large, the press encounters storage costs and losses from unsold books.

Before publication of each book, one of the press's editors makes an estimate of costs based primarily on past experience with similar books. For example, the cost of publishing 1,000 copies of a monograph in busi-

Exhibit 1
Actual Costs on monograph (publication data—November 15, 1962)

Text		
Stock....................................	$138.00	
Composition..............................	638.00 (98 hours)	
Press...................................	141.40 (20 hours)	
Ink.....................................	3.10	
Miscellaneous............................	10.00	
Overhead (15% of above)...................	140.50	
Total cost of text.......................		$1,071.00
Jacket		
Stock....................................	$ 10.00	
Composition..............................	39.20 (5 hours)	
Press...................................	37.80 (5.4 hours)	
Miscellaneous............................	1.50	
Ink.....................................	2.00	
Overhead (15% of above)...................	13.50	
Total cost of jacket.....................		104.00
Binding......................................		506.83
Freight......................................		40.72
Total actual cost........................		$1,722.55

ness administration planned for November 15, 1962, was $1,300 for composition and printing, $550 for binding, and $50 for freight.

Sometimes the estimates were considerably in error, especially if the author's alterations were numerous. The estimates tended to be on the low side. In the case of the business monograph under discussion, however, the actual costs were close to the estimates, as is shown in Exhibit 1 (many of the figures have been rounded).

The stock cost was a completely variable cost. The composition and press costs were a mixture of direct labor costs and allocations of equipment and space charges.

A second run of 1,000 copies would be considerably cheaper than the first run. A second run of the text would require 11 offset lithographic plates, costing $18 per plate. The stock would cost about $138, as before. The offset press run would take about 11 hours at $9 per hour. The ink would be $3.10. The jacket would require $10 for stock, $2 for ink, $18 for one offset plate, $9 for one offset press run, and $7 for one letterpress run. Binding costs would again be approximately $507. If the second run were smaller than 1,000 copies, the costs would be about the same except for the stock and binding costs. The stock costs would be proportional to the run, but the binding costs include a fixed element of about $100 per run.

Sometimes the press would print extra sheets of a book in the first run, postponing binding the sheets until the first batch of bound copies were sold. On the business monograph under discussion, no extra sheets were printed.

Decisions on the length of run were influenced by the shortage of storage space. No one had made an estimate of storage costs. Probably the rental value of the space used for storage would be $1,000 per annum. The space had a capacity for about 16,000 volumes and was constantly overcrowded. Copies of some old books were stored in a basement room and finally discarded after any hope of further sales had passed.

The retail price of the monograph was set at $3. The press could expect to receive an average of $2.10 per copy after discounts to distributors. The greatest uncertainty concerned the level of sales. One purchaser had guaranteed to buy 500 copies. The press had no previous experience with monographs in the business area and thus had little basis for estimating sales beyond the 500 copies. Sales of monographs in other subject matter areas usually ran below 500, and sometimes as low as 200. The press could make fairly accurate estimates of sales of books on historical subjects and of monographs in archeology and anthropology, because it had published a number of works in those areas, but its estimates on other books were subject to considerable error.

1. Construct a model for the determination of the economic length of run on books.
2. What economic principles are incorporated in your model?
3. Apply your model as best you can to the problem of the business monograph.
4. Did the press make a sound decision is running off 1,000 copies? Explain. Should it have run some extra sheets?
5. Is a formal analysis of uncertainty helpful in this case? Discuss.

Part five

Analysis of price and nonprice competition

Chapter 11

Price and nonprice
competition

This chapter discusses the influences of market structure upon the seller's decisions about pricing, product quality, and promotion. It proceeds from the simple case of pure competition through monopoly and monopolistic competition, including a discussion of nonprice competition, or deliberate demand shifts. Then follows an analysis of some of the possible forms of price and nonprice competition under oligopolistic market structures and an explanation of decision tree approaches to an oligopolistic firm's choices. The chapter concludes with an appraisal of some common pricing practices and a pricing checklist.

AN OVERVIEW OF PRICE THEORY

Conventional theory of the producer's behavior under various market structures was developed for purposes of predicting effects of broad changes in economic forces and evaluating social controls on business activity. Tools designed for the analysis of social and economic issues cannot be expected to provide detailed guidance for management of individual firms. Nevertheless, conventional theory provides a convenient starting point for the discussion of pricing and we shall integrate concepts related to decisions about product quality and promotion.

Basic assumptions

In this chapter, it is assumed that *management wishes to maximize tangible profits* over a period for which the analysis is being made. *Sales and production rates are assumed to be identical,* so that there are no effects of inventory buildup or depletion to be taken into account (some aspects of inventory management are analyzed in Chapter 10). *The firm's structure of cost is based on an assumption of continuative production* (economics of discrete production runs are discussed in Chapter 10). *Costs and revenues of subsequent periods are assumed to be unaffected by pricing and output during the period for which the analysis is being made* (the case of penetration pricing of new products to increase sales of subsequent periods is considered in Chapter 10). *Each firm is assumed to have a single product for which there is a single market* (some decisions involving multiple products and multiple markets are analyzed in Chapter 12). Under the simplifying assumptions listed above, this chapter concentrates upon decisions about pricing, product quality, and promotion under various market structures.

Determinants of market structure

There are two major determinants of market structure. The first is *number of firms in the industry.* We shall say there are *many* firms if any one producer's decisions and activities cannot have perceptible effect upon any other firm's profits; in such instances, competition is diffused and firms pay little or no attention to each other—*any seller can take independent action without appraising the possible reactions of competitors.* We shall say there are *few* firms if one producer's behavior can cause a noticeable change in another company's profits; in these cases, competition becomes personal with adversaries closely watching and reacting to each other—*each firm must consider possible responses of rivals in determining its own actions.* We shall say there is only *one* firm in a monopoly industry; such a seller obviously does not need to weigh possible reactions of *present* competitors, but *potential* competition may be a relevant consideration if the monopoly structure is not permanent.

The second major determinant of market structure is the *extent to which products of the various firms are differentiated.* We shall say the products are *homogeneous* if they are standardized or identical; in such cases, buyers have no reasons to prefer one supplier's product over that of another and *differences in prices cannot be maintained.* We shall say the products of the various firms are *differentiated* if they are perceived by consumers as being different from each other; in such instances, buyers have preferences among the products and *continuing differences among their prices can be maintained.* We shall say that a monopoly firm has a *unique* product with no close substitutes; pricing of a unique product can be changed without noticeable effects upon sales of any other product, and sales of the unique product are not perceptibly affected by changes in the price of any other product.

Principal forms of market structure

From the viewpoint of sellers of products, there are five principal forms of market structure:

1. Monopoly—one seller, unique product.
2. Pure competition—many sellers, homogeneous product.
3. Monopolistic competition—many sellers, differentiated products.
4. Pure oligopoly—few sellers, homogeneous product.
5. Differentiated oligopoly—few sellers, differentiated products.

Behavior of producers within the above market structures may be influenced by the *ease* of entry of new firms. We shall say that entry is *easy* if a new company would have little or no disadvantage compared to established firms; the structures of pure and monopolistic competition permit easy entry. We shall say that there are *barriers to entry* if a new seller would have substantial disadvantages compared to established firms; oligopoly structures typically do have barriers to entry, but the barriers are greater for some oligopolistic industries than for others. Entry of a new firm is *precluded* in a monopoly structure, although some monopolies are temporary.

THEORY OF PRICING WITH DEMAND TAKEN AS GIVEN

This section summarizes the traditional theory of pricing under pure competition, monopoly, and monopolistic competition. In the traditional theory, *demand is taken as given*. Optimum output-sales rates are found at the points where marginal cost and marginal revenue are equal, and optimum prices are found on the demand functions at the best output-sales quantities.

Pure competition

In pure competition there are *many sellers* of a *homogeneous product*. Information about cost, prices, and quality of product is readily available to both buyers and sellers. Any one producer's maximum sales are a small part of the industry total, and variations in any supplier's output and sales have no perceptible effect upon the product's market price. *Entry into the industry is easy.*

Figure 11–1
Pricing and output under pure competition

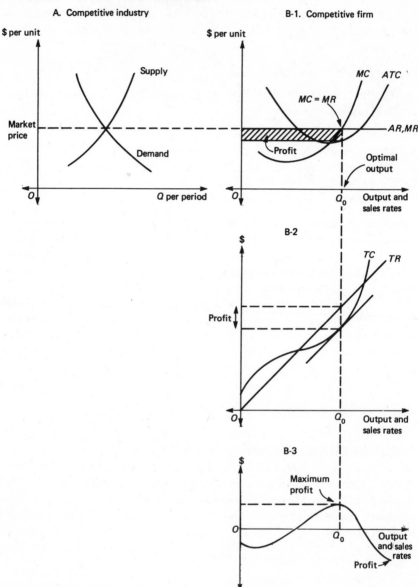

A. Competitive industry

B-1. Competitive firm

B-2

B-3

Note: Figures B–1, B–2, and B–3 are alternative views of *the same thing*, namely the determination of optimum output-sales for a firm under pure competition.

Few industries have a market structure of pure competition. Farmers sell their crops and livestock in markets closely approaching pure competition, and the market in which money is lent to businesses at the "prime rate" is a close approximation. *Each supplying firm in pure competition perceives its demand and marginal revenue functions as horizontal at the market price or rate.* The firm cannot vary product quality, nor can it gain from product promotion. A company in pure competition can produce and sell any quantity up to its capacity at the market price, but at a higher price it can sell nothing. *Thus the competitive firm cannot make a decision about price, but it can choose a rate of output and sales.*

Figure 11–1 illustrates the choice of output and sales rate under pure competition. Optimal rate is at Q_o, the rate at which marginal cost equals marginal revenue. Figure 11–1 depicts marginal cost rising (in the relevant range) with rate of output and sales. Nearly all agricultural production does have rising marginal cost in the short run, and funds allocated to business loans by financial institutions would have rising marginal opportunity costs. Graphic and analytic methods for *quantitative* determination of optimum rates of output under the structure of pure competition are discussed in Chapter 9; see Figure 9–7 and the corresponding explanation.

The average total cost curve in Figure 11–1B includes the opportunity cost of capital provided by the firm's owners; it is conceived as a curve of full economic cost of all outputs used. The price in Figure 11–1B is well above the average total cost at the optimum rate of output and sales, so the firm is earning economic profits. Figure 11–1B would be a short-run condition if all firms in the industry were earning economic profits, because entry of new sellers and expansion of established suppliers would increase total industry output and exert downward pressure on price. In a competitive industry, forces of supply press against demand and push price down in relation to costs of production. We say that a competitive market structure tends to "squeeze out" economic profits as producers adjust capacities over the long run.

It should be noted that a well-managed company in a pure competitive structure may be able to maintain above-average returns on investment in the face of the steady pressure of market forces upon profits. If the industry has developing technology, astute innovation can keep the firm's costs well below those of the industry's marginal producers (the ones that are least profitable).

The theory of pure competition has limited relevance to a discussion of pricing. It does illustrate the role of impersonal market forces in any structure where entry is easy. However, a chapter on pricing and other competitive tactics must emphasize market situations in which firms have some control over price. Such control is present in monopoly, the next structure to be discussed.

Monopoly

In monopoly there is only *one seller* of a *unique product*. No other supplier can provide a close substitute. *At least for the time being, no other firm can enter.* The monopoly producer *is* the industry in which it operates.

Absolute barriers to entry, temporary or more enduring, are the foundations of monopoly structures. Some examples of such barriers include: (1) control of known supplies of low-cost raw materials, such as Alcoa's control of bauxite ores prior to World War II; (2) patents, such as Polaroid's patents on many forms of instant photo devices and materials; (3) franchises, such as the rights granted to single air carriers and single television stations to provide exclusive service to smaller market areas; and (4) economies of scale so great that a single supplier has a notable cost advantage, as in the cases of the electric, gas, and telephone utilities.

A monopoly's demand curve slopes down to the right. The marginal revenue function lies below the demand curve. The firm can choose the most profitable combination of price and output-sales rate. Figure 11–2 illustrates optimal pricing and output for a monopoly in the short run— the cost curves are short-run (operating) curves for a plant which must be taken as given. Figure 11–3 shows optimal pricing and output for a monopoly in the long run—plant size can be changed and the cost curves are long-run (envelope) curves, which may have decreasing costs as in the figure or may have eventually increasing costs. The principle that determines optimal price and output is the same, whether the decision is short run or long run and whether long-run marginal cost is increasing, constant, or decreasing. It pays to increase output and sales if marginal revenue is greater than marginal cost, so the optimum rate is at the point where marginal cost becomes equal to marginal revenue.

Optimal rates are at Q_o in Figures 11–2 and 11–3, and optimal prices are found on the respective demand curves at P_o, corresponding to the optimal rates of output and sales. Graphic and analytic methods for *quantitative* determination of pricing and output that maximize profit for a monopoly are explained in Chapter 9; see Figure 9–8 and the corresponding text.

The long-run perspective on monopoly is actually somewhat more complicated than the view provided in the preceding paragraphs. Both the monopoly firm's demand and its cost structure may be shifting over time, so that the firm's management faces a dynamic optimization problem in making decisions about changes in plant size. Trial and error methods may be used, or the firm may take advantage of computer-assisted enumeration techniques that are beyond the scope of this book.

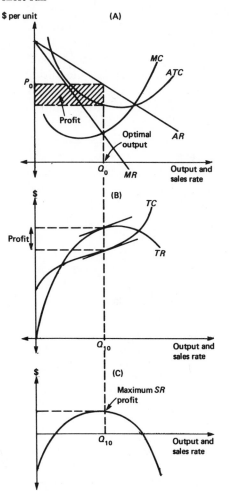

Figure 11–2
Pricing and output under monopoly— short run

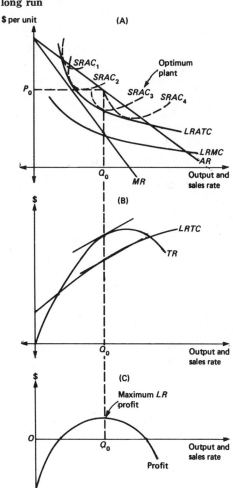

Figure 11–3
Pricing and output under monopoly— long run

Monopolistic competition

In monopolistic competition there are *many sellers* of *differentiated products*. Each product has a downward sloping demand curve. The demand curve does not have a steep slope, because each product faces competition from close substitutes. Further, *entry of new products is easy*. But differentiation gives each seller some scope for price policy, and each producer can make decisions about pricing without considering possible reactions of competitors. Why so? With each supplier small in relation to total industry output and sales, the impact of any one firm's marketing tactics is spread over many competitors and becomes too small to be identified. Thus, no other seller will react with countermeasures.

It is not easy to find industries in which *all* firms can behave as monopolistic competitors. Canned foods, carpets, clothing, and furniture may be examples. Further, the small firms in some differentiated oligopolies do not expect reactions of competitors to their decisions about prices. Banking, insurance, retailing, and some kinds of manufacturing are oligopolistic at the center (which is composed of the larger firms) and monopolistically competitive (among the smaller firms) on the periphery.

A firm in monopolistic competition can determine optimum price and output-sales in the manner of a pure monopoly, as discussed above. The firm selects an output-sales rate that equates marginal cost with marginal revenue and maximizes profit, as depicted in Figure 11–4. Graphic and analytic techniques for quantitative determination, as depicted in Chapter 9 in Figure 9–8, can be used.

The competitive aspect of monopolistic competition enters through long-run adjustments of capacity and output. If the industry is profitable, new producers enter and existing suppliers expand. With each firm facing greater competition from close substitutes, its demand curve is shifted to the left and may be tilted so as to become more elastic. Profits of

Figure 11–4
Pricing and output of a profitable firm under monopolistic competition

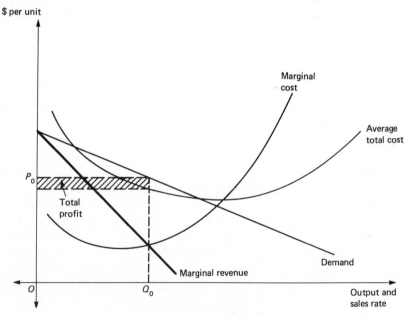

Figure 11–5
Pricing and output of a marginal firm under monopolistic competition

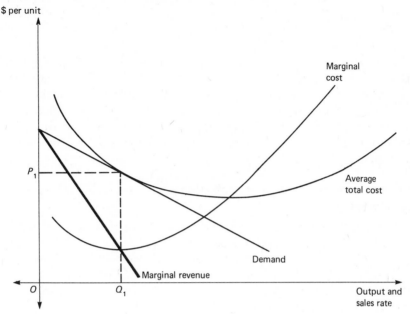

marginal firms are eliminated as their demand curves are pushed back to tangency with the average cost curves, as illustrated in Figure 11–5.

Well-managed companies in monopolistic competition may earn good returns on investment, year after year, despite the steady pressure of competitive forces. Wise choice of new technology can hold costs below those of marginal firms, and skill in nonprice competition (quality improvement and promotion) can push demand to the right, away from the tangency position (and perhaps tilt it so that it becomes less elastic), so that profitability is maintained.

THEORY OF DELIBERATE DEMAND SHIFTING, WITH PRICE TAKEN AS GIVEN

The above section focused on the choice of price and output-sales rate, taking demand as given. But demand can be shifted by the seller's changes in product quality and promotion. The possibility of deliberately shifting the firm's demand curve introduces additional choices and decisions: (1) there is usually some *least-cost combination of inputs for any given promotion activity or for any given improvement in product quality;* (2) there is some least-cost combination of spending on promotion and spending on product quality that will *minimize the total cost of any given shift in demand;* (3) demand becomes less and less responsive as spending for demand shifting is increased, so that *there is some optimum total outlay for nonprice competition at any given price;* and (4) as demand is shifted, the best price may also change—*in the final analysis, pricing, promotion, and product quality are variables to be determined simultaneously.*

This section will not discuss the first complication listed above—the need to minimize cost of carrying out any given promotion activity or achieving any given improvement in product quality. The principles and techniques of production economics—discussed in Chapters 6 and 7—are applicable. This section does take up, in the order listed above, the remaining complications associated with decisions about demand shifting.

Least-cost combinations of promotion and product quality

A family of isoquants is shown in Figure 11–6; each isoquant defines the various combinations of spending on promotion and on product quality per period that will maintain a given rate of sales during that period, *at a given price*. Although only three isoquants are drawn in the figure, there are innumerable others—one for each rate of sales that could be specified.

Figure 11–6 resembles a production function showing the relationships of various combinations of physical inputs to the resulting maximum rates of output, and it will be used to show how cost can be minimized for various rates of sales. However, several cautions are in order. First, outlays for either promotion or product quality during any given period may also affect sales of subsequent periods; the costs of promotion and product quality in Figure 11–6 are net costs after proration of outlays to various periods in proportion to the expected effects upon their sales. Second, costs of quality improvement in Figure 11–6 are the amounts *added* to costs of producing a basic or minimum salable product because of optional quality improvement: design, features, packaging, service, warranties, credit, and so forth. Note that increases in cost due to quality improvement are simple increases in cost per unit so long as we stay on any one isoquant, but they are a compounding of increased cost per unit times increased rate of output if we shift from one isoquant to another that has a greater rate of sales. Third, both promotion and quality improvement ,are measured in Figure 11–6 in terms of the total dollar outlay; there is an implicit assumption that the dollars are being spent as effectively as possible at each level of dollar outlay (costs of improvements in product quality are minimized by input substitutions and costs of promotion are minimized through substitutions among advertising, point-of-sales aids, personal selling, and other dimensions of persuasion).

Figure 11–6
Least-cost combinations of promotion and quality improvement for various rates of sales at a given price

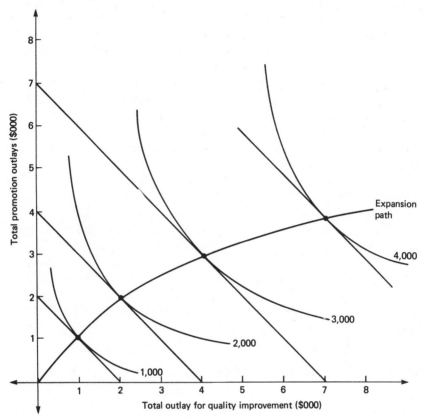

Although quality improvement can be substituted for promotion effort and vice versa, substitution is at a decreasing rate as shown by the curvature of the isoquants in Figure 11–6. And, with additional sales becoming more and more difficult to obtain at the given price, demand shifting has increasing cost, as shown in the figure by the increasing distances between isoquants for equal increments in sales rates. A family of isocost lines is also depicted in Figure 11–6. Each isocost line has a slope of −1, showing that dollars for promotion and dollars for quality can be substituted on a one-for-one basis as total outlay is held constant along the isocost line.

The least-cost combination of promotion and product quality for any given sales rate is found (on the isoquant for that rate) at a point where an isocost line for lowest possible cost is just tangent to the isoquant—or where the isoquant has a slope of -1. At the least-cost point, the increase in sales per dollar spent on promotion is equal to the increase in sales per dollar spent on quality improvement.

In most instances, a firm's information about the relation of sales rates to outlays for promotion and product quality would be approximate and localized; it would be limited to knowledge of current values of the three variables plus rough estimates of the effects of incremental changes in promotion and quality outlays upon the sales rate. Smaller firms may simply rely upon the judgment of experienced managers. Firms that have heavy costs of selling can afford to use sophisticated techniques of market research to obtain more refined and more extended estimates of sales responses to changes in promotion and quality. In either case, if the results per dollar spent on promotion and quality are estimated to be unequal, management should consider cutting back spending in the least effective dimension and maintaining the sales rate by expanding spending in the other direction. For example, suppose the marginal effect of promotion is estimated to be a sales increase of 12 units per additional dollar spent and the marginal effect of quality improvement is estimated to be a sales increase of 9 units per additional dollar spent. In this example, spending on product quality can be cut by 12/9 times any increase in spending on promotion, with sales expected to hold constant. *Caution:* Any estimated marginal rate of substitution at a point on a contoured production surface is applicable only in the vicinity of that point.

Optimal total outlay for demand shifting at a given price

By connecting the least-cost combinations of various isoquants, a sales expansion path would be derived. Such a path is shown in Figure 11–6. The expansion path shows not only the total outlay for demand shifting at each sales level, but also how that outlay is split between promotion and quality improvement.

Management would rarely, if ever, have enough information to make a quantified estimate of its sales expansion path. Fortunately, the incremental choices between increases in promotion and increases in quality (choices that are based on comparisons of estimated effectiveness per dollar spent) carry out a search process that goes toward the expansion path if the firm is far from it and stays near the path if the firm is close. This search process is explained in Chapter 7; see Figure 7–12 and the associated discussion.

Figure 11–7 is derived from the sales expansion path of Figure 11–6. The total revenue function is a straight line because price remains constant as the sales rate is increased. Total cost at various sales rates is the sum of production cost for the basic or minimum salable product

Figure 11–7

A. Optimal total cost and sales at a given price

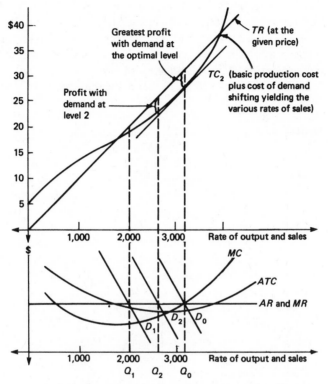

B. Optimal average and marginal cost and sales at a given price

and the cost of demand shifting as determined by the sales expansion path.

The optimum output-sales rate at the given price is found in Figure 11–7A, at the point where total revenue exceeds total cost by the greatest amount. This is the point in Figure 11–7B where marginal cost is equal to marginal revenue (price). Note in Figure 11–7B that demand is depicted as shifting to the right as the total cost increases due to product improvement and greater promotion. The optimum output-sales rate, to which there corresponds some optimum total outlay on product quality and promotion, cannot be determined graphically or analytically unless the firm has knowledge of the sales expansion path. Nevertheless, the concept depicted in Figure 11–7 shows what the firm is *trying* to do as it makes incremental changes in its total outlays for demand shifting—it is trying to get closer to the optimum output-sales rate for the given price

The best combination of product quality, promotion, and price

Imagine for a moment that we have been able to carry out the above described analysis for each of several different prices. Thus, we are able to plot a relationship of profit to price, with the total outlay for demand shifting optimal at each price, and with outlay for any given amount of demand shifting minimized by using least-cost combinations of product quality and promotion. The relationship of profit to price will look like Figure 11–8 with profit maximum at some optimal price.

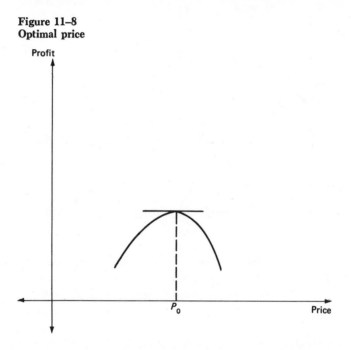

Figure 11–8
Optimal price

Conceptually, the firm has a best combination of price and demand shifting. Product quality and promotion are optimal for the price, and profit is maximum at the price. As a practical matter, this best combination cannot be determined analytically because the firm does not have enough information. But firms are searching toward the best combination as they make incremental changes in their marketing tactics—sometimes in quality, sometimes in promotion, sometimes in price, and sometimes in two or three of these variables concurrently.

OLIGOPOLY

In oligopoly a *few sellers* account for a large part of total industry output. Many economists believe an industry is likely to have oligopoly behavior if the four largest producers have 40 percent or more of total sales. Remaining sales may be divided among a much larger number of relatively small firms; some oligopolies have 100 or more smaller producers.

Any one of the larger firms in an oligopolistic structure can affect market shares and profitability of competitors by its own decisions and actions. Rivals can be expected to attempt to protect their market positions, although their reactions, which can take various forms, may be difficult to predict. Competition among the larger firms is personal and volatile and increases the uncertainty surrounding decision making. *The need to consider possible reactions of competing sellers in making decisions about pricing and other marketing tactics is the distinguishing feature of oligopoly structure.*

Oligopolies are prominent in the U.S. economy. In 1967, 42 percent of value added in manufacturing occurred in industries with four-firm concentration ratios of 40 percent or more.[1] There are two forms of oligopoly. *In pure oligopoly, the various firms sell a standardized product.* Buyers of homogeneous or standardized products care little about who is the supplier, but they are interested in minimizing their procurement costs. They are usually very well informed about available supplies, pricing of recent transactions, and qualities of products. *No supplier can do business at delivered prices higher than those of competitors, and any suppliers who beat competitive prices are deluged with more orders than they can fill.* In most pure oligopolies, the products have large costs of transportation in relation to value; as a result, suppliers have rising costs of delivery over increasing distances from plants. Thus, *sellers in most pure oligopolies tend to develop geographically concentrated shares of the national market;* prices at distant points are usually too low to cover variable costs of supplying. Some examples of pure oligopoly are aluminum, cement, copper, explosives, industrial fuels, red meat in bulk forms, steel, sugar, sulfur, and tin cans.

In differentiated oligopoly, each seller offers a particular combination of design, features, packaging, service, warranties, credit, promotion, and price. *Buyers have preferences among products and there can be continuing differences among prices of various suppliers.* Each product has a market share, given the current prices, and each has a sloping demand curve that is quite elastic and shifts perceptibly with changes in prices or other marketing tactics of any of the larger firms. Some examples of differentiated oligopoly are automobiles, beer, breakfast cereals, canned soups, cigarettes, computers, farm machinery, gasoline, home laundry equipment, household refrigerators, razor blades, soaps and detergents, soft drinks, and television sets.

Entry into oligopolies is usually difficult. These industries usually have economies of scale continuing out to plant sizes that are large in relation

---

[1] F. M. Sherer, *Industrial Pricing* (Chicago: Rand McNally, 1970), p. 3.

to total industry output. A firm attempting to enter a pure oligopoly at a production rate great enough to have costs comparable to those of other firms may increase total industry output so much that prices are driven below costs for a considerable period of time. And a producer attempting entry into a differentiated oligopoly may be at great disadvantage initially because established firms already have a wide distribution of products preferred by buyers. Thus, the new contender has higher unit costs at its lower rates of production and has heavy promotion costs in attempting to gain distribution and acceptance of the new product.

In some industries with differentiated products, there are a few large rivals and a much larger number of smaller firms in any given geographic area. These industries may have an oligopolistic structure from the point of view of the larger firms, although they have a monopolistically competitive structure from the viewpoint of the smaller firms, permitting independent changes in pricing or other marketing tactics without considering reactions by other firms. In these mixed-structure industries, economies of scale and the degree of product differentiation are not great enough to put smaller sellers at a definite disadvantage. Entry into such industries is relatively easy. Examples of industries in which large firms must operate as oligopolies and smaller ones can be monopolistically competitive are banking, insurance, and retailing.

Competitive behavior of firms in oligopolistic market structures can fall into several different patterns, and behavior in a given industry can shift from one pattern to another. No single theory of oligopoly pricing is sufficient. We shall look at several theories, each having some value in this discussion.

"Kinked" demand and "sticky" prices

Suppose management of an oligopoly firm believes *competitors will not follow a price increase but will promptly match any price decrease.* Under these assumptions about reactions of rival firms, the oligopoly firm's demand curve is "kinked," with *an abrupt change in slope at the current price and sales quantity.* Quantity reduction for a small price increase is much greater than the quantity expansion for a comparable cut in price.

A kinky demand curve for an oligopolistic firm with a differentiated product is shown in Figure 11–9. Because of the sharp change at the kink in the response of quantity to a small change in price, the seller's marginal revenue function has two sections. The upper section defines marginal revenues at alternative prices above the current price, and the lower section specifies marginal revenues at alternative prices below the current price. The two sections of the marginal revenue are separated by a vertical gap at the current rate of output and sales.

Figure 11–9
A kinked demand curve

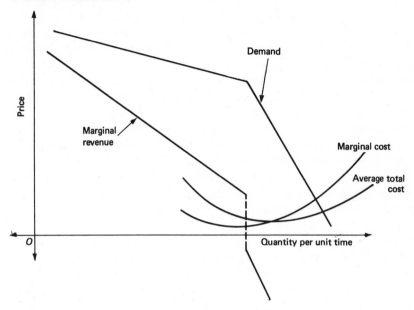

In the example depicted by Figure 11–9, the producer's average and marginal cost functions are positioned in the gap between the upper and lower sections of the firm's marginal revenue function. Thus, marginal revenue is higher than marginal cost at any output and sales rate less than the current level, whereas marginal revenue is lower than marginal cost at any rate more than the current quantity. The firm will be made worse off—contribution will be decreased—by any change in price.

Note in Figure 11–9 that the producer's average and marginal cost functions could shift up or down for a considerable distance before marginal cost would become equal to marginal revenue at some price different from the current value, but shifting costs eventually would make it advantageous for the seller to change price. Note also that the seller's demand curve could make considerable shifts left or right, with the kink remaining at the current price, before the firm would stand to gain from a price change, although shifting demand eventually would lead to price adjustment. And the producer's optimal output and sales quantities would shift with any movements of the demand curve. *Assuming a kinked demand curve, the firm's pricing would be "sticky," holding steady in the face of shifts of cost or demand over considerable ranges; the firm's output would be sticky in the face of cost shifts but would be immediately responsive to demand shifts.*

If an oligopolistic company were selling a *standardized* product, it

could perceive its demand curve as kinked but somewhat different from
the curve in Figure 11–9. If competitors were expected not to follow a
price increase, the firm's demand curve and marginal revenue curve
would be identical and *horizontal at the current price out to the current
sales rate.* If adversaries were expected to promptly match a price reduction, the demand curve would be kinked at the current price and
sales rate, sloping downward through quantities corresponding to the
firm's share of increasing total industry sales. The marginal revenue
curve would have a lower section, separated from the current price and
sales rate by a vertical gap and steeper than the corresponding section
of the demand curve, similar to the lower section of the marginal revenue
function in Figure 11–9. If the producer's average and marginal cost
functions were positioned in the vertical gap between the two sections
of the marginal revenue function, the firm's pricing and output behavior
would be as described above (like that of an oligopoly firm with a *differentiated* product).

The kinked demand theory is a plausible model for an oligopolistic
industry with some excess capacity shared among various producers
more or less proportionately to their sales, with a current price that is
modestly profitable to most or all sellers, and with the larger companies
having similar costs. However, kinked demand theory is a short-run
model. It can explain stickiness of prices at a given level, but it cannot
explain how the industry got to that level or how it may move to another.

If all firms have similar shifts in cost or demand or both, a time may
come when one of the larger producers believes that competitors *would*
follow a price increase. The probability that they will follow is greatest
if both costs and demand have increased, reducing profitability and increasing output until most firms are producing at or close to capacity. If
other competitors *are* expected to follow a price increase, a theory of
price leadership becomes useful.

Price leadership

Suppose management of an oligopoly firm believes its rivals will
promptly follow a price increase within some range. The demand curve
of the firm in question will be seen as smoothly sloping through the
current price and sales quantity, with the quantities at higher or lower
prices being the firm's share of total industry sales. It might at first appear that the seller can act as a monopolist, selecting a price and sales
rate at which its own marginal cost and marginal revenue are equal
and its own profits are maximum. However, other firms may not be
willing to follow a price increase as great as the price leader would like
to make.

A little thought suggests that the price increase by the price leader will not hold unless the other large firms perceive their own demand curves as being rekinked at the new price and also estimate that their marginal cost functions are positioned in the new gap between the two sections of their marginal revenue functions. If the price leader tries to set the price too high, one of the rivals may estimate that its marginal cost function passes through the lower section of the new marginal revenue function. If so, the rival will initiate a price reduction back to the level that it prefers. And other firms will follow the price down.

It appears that an oligopolist wishing to exercise price leadership is more effective if the following tactics are used. First, the leader makes price changes infrequently, foregoing possible gains from small adjustments to avoid risks that the changes will be misinterpreted or opposed. Second, the company announces changes only in response to significant changes in cost and demand that are perceived by all firms in the industry. Third, management prepares rivals for the forthcoming price change by speeches, interviews with the trade press, and general news releases. Fourth, the leader tries to select a new price that compromises conflicts of interest among various rivals; it pays particular attention to the short-run interests of larger producers that have low costs and excess capacity.

If entry into an industry is quite difficult because of economies of scale, there is little differentiation of products, and the industry has a high concentration ratio with few small competitors, a pattern of collusion may replace the price leadership form of industry behavior.

Collusion

Collusion is based on recognition by each firm that both short-run and long-run interests are served by coordinated industry pricing above the level resulting from simple price leadership. Collusion involves secret agreement among rivals on pricing, market sharing, and other aspects of their interdependency. Collusion may be profitable for a time, but it is unwieldy because of the *necessity for secrecy* in setting up the agreements, the considerable *conflicts of interest among the various firms* with respect to market shares and new plant capacity, and the *difficulty of preventing concealed price cuts and other forms of cheating. Collusion also involves considerable personal risk to the participants, because it is illegal in the United States.*

An article in *Fortune* gives insight into methods that were used and difficulties that were encountered in a notorious case of collusion among 29 manufacturers of electrical equipment during the 1950s.[2] At the end of the trial of the conspirators, in February 1961, nearly $2 million in

[2] R. A. Smith, "The Incredible Electrical Conspiracy," *Fortune* (May 1961), p. 224.

fines were levied against the companies involved, seven executives were sent to prison, and 24 managers received suspended sentences. A *Harvard Business Review* article provides some possibly useful advice to a manager considering participation in collusive price fixing and market sharing.[3]

Price wars

In a price war, price reduction by one rival is immediately undercut by another. The price level is driven well below the average cost of even the most efficient producers and may go even below the marginal cost of some firms that continue supplying the market because of long-run benefits from maintaining distribution and product acceptance. A condition of excess capacity combined with a large buildup of product inventory may lead to a price war. A price war eventually makes every firm worse off than it would have been at higher price levels, and all firms become willing to follow a leader in a price increase.

Price wars are usually limited to particular geographic areas. Companies with wide regional or national distribution are very unlikely to undercut a price reduction by a rival, although they will often meet a price cut. If sellers with wide distribution undercut prices of a rival in a local market, without making similar reductions in all of their pricing, they are engaging in price discrimination that may injure a competitor —an action that is illegal. On the other hand, firms that serve only a small area can systematically undercut prices of regional or national companies, because the small suppliers are reducing all of their prices. A price war is usually a mistake on the part of a small producer; it believes that its rivals will stop meeting its price reductions, leaving room for the small firm to earn greater contributions on substantially increased output and sales, utilizing excess capacities and selling burdensome inventories. But the opponents usually continue to match the price cutting of the small contender.

Nonprice competition

In differentiated oligopoly, deliberate demand shifts through quality improvement and increased promotion are likely to receive more emphasis than price reductions as the various producers strive for increased sales. Although competitors sometimes react to an oligopoly firm's changes in product and promotion, their responses may not be immediate and they are unlikely to be head on. Some or all competitors may wait to see the market response to the new tactics. If they do decide to mount a frontal

---

[3] John Q. Lawyer, "How to Conspire to Fix Prices," *Harvard Business Review* 41, no. 2 (May–June 1963), pp. 95–103.

counterattack against product changes or a new sales campaign, it takes time for them to make similar changes in their own products or promotion. On the other hand, they may elect to proceed with their own long-run marketing strategy, rather than setting up a direct challenge to the new activities of the firm in question. Nonprice competition among the major adversaries of an oligopoly industry is not nearly as personal and direct as their price competition.

Under the assumption that there will not be immediate, head-on reaction by competitors, the economic analysis of deliberate demand shifting by an oligopolistic firm is very similar to the analysis for a monopoly. Costs of any product improvement should be minimized by input substitution; costs of any increase in promotion should be minimized through substitutions among selling activities. Costs of demand shifting, to increase sales at a given price, should be minimized by substitution between product quality improvement and increased promotion (see Figure 11–6 and the associated explanation). Optimal total outlay for demand shifting, at a given price, is found at the point where the marginal cost of production plus demand shifting becomes equal to price-marginal revenue (see Figure 11–7 and the corresponding discussion). Demand shifts to the right with a kink maintained at the current price, and the marginal revenue from increased sales is the current price.

DECISION TREE ANALYSIS OF AN OLIGOPOLY FIRM'S MARKETING ALTERNATIVES

At the outset of the discussion of oligopoly structure, it was noted that: (1) the outcome of any change in an oligopoly firm's marketing behavior depends upon the responses of rivals, and (2) these reactions can take various forms and there may be great uncertainty about them. A firm in an oligopolistic industry may benefit from a decision tree approach to its complex choices among marketing tactics. Decision trees provide efficient organization of the firm's estimates of the payoffs or outcomes of various tactics, taking each of the possible response patterns as given, and the firm's subjective estimates of the probability of each of the response patterns.

Constructing a basic decision tree

Suppose a medium-sized firm in a differentiated oligopoly is considering whether or not to follow a price increase which has just been announced by a competitor. Most firms in the industry are modestly profitable and there is some excess capacity. The industry does not have an established pattern of following the company which has just raised its own price. Management of the firm in question is concerned that the

remaining producers in the industry may not follow this particular price
hike.

If the firm in question promptly follows the attempted price leadership of the larger competitor, management believes that there is a 40
percent probability that other sellers will not follow, the price increase
will have to be rescinded, and the firm will have some loss of business
because of its participation in an abortive price increase. On the other
hand, if the firm does not follow the larger company's price action but
rather adopts a "wait and see" posture, management believes there is an
80 percent probability that none of the remaining suppliers will raise
prices.

Outcomes of the firm's decision are as follows. If all firms do match
the price increase of the one large company, the firm in question expects
net earnings of $1.2 million over the relevant planning period. If the firm
in question follows but subsequently rescinds with a loss of business,
management expects net earnings to be $800,000. If the firm waits to see
what others will do and none follows, management projects net earnings
of $1 million.

Figure 11–10 shows how the above problem is specified in a decision
tree. The tree is comprised of a series of nodes and branches, and it runs
from left to right. At the extreme left, a square node represents a *decision
point*—a point at which the firm may choose among alternatives. The
branches leading to the right from the decision point are labeled to correspond to the various action alternatives; the alternatives in the example are "immediately follow" and "wait and see."

At the right end of each branch representing an action alternative,
there is a round node representing a *chance event point*—a point at which
there may be alternative "states of nature" comprised of events that the
firm in question cannot control. In the example, the chance events are
the reactions of the other firms in the industry, and the branches leading
to the right from the chance event points are labeled to show the alternative response patterns; the alternatives in the example are "no other
firms follow" and "all other firms follow."

At the extreme right of the decision tree are the firm's *payoffs*. Each
payoff is an outcome resulting from a combination of a particular posture
of the firm in question with a particular chance event. In the example,
the firm's payoffs are measured in terms of net income. In other applications of decision trees, net cash flow, net worth, discounted present value
of future net cash flows, or some other measure of payoff could be more
appropriate.

Let us calculate the expected values of each of the alternative marketing tactics under consideration. The calculations begin at the payoffs
on the extreme right. For the chance event point at the top of Figure
11–10, there is 40 percent probability of a payoff of $800,000 and a 60

Figure 11–10
An oligopolist's decision tree

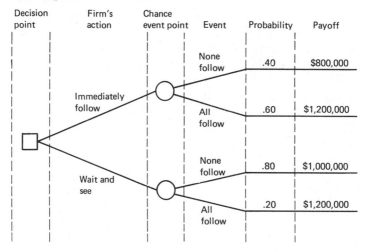

Decision point	Firm's action	Chance event point	Event	Probability	Payoff

percent probability of a payoff of $1.2 million. The expected value of a posture at the upper chance event node is calculated as follows:

$$
\begin{array}{ll}
0.40 \times \$\ \ 800,000 \dots\dots\dots\dots & \$\ \ 320,000 \\
0.60 \times \$1,200,000 \dots\dots\dots\dots & \underline{720,000} \\
& \$1,040,000
\end{array}
$$

Note that the expected value of an action or a decision is the average result that would be expected if this action or decision were carried out *many times under the same conditions.* Obviously, the outcome of *a single trial* of the marketing tactic in the above example would be either $800,000 or $1.2 million.

The expected value of a posture at the lower chance event node can be calculated as

$$
\begin{array}{ll}
0.80 \times \$1,000,000 \dots\dots\dots\dots & \$\ \ 800,000 \\
0.20 \times \$1,200,000 \dots\dots\dots\dots & \underline{240,000} \\
& \$1,040,000
\end{array}
$$

If the firm in the above example is a simple odds player, willing to take its chances on averaging out over the long run, it will be indifferent as to which tactic is chosen. Management can simply flip a coin to determine what the firm will do. However, note that when management acts as an odds player, there are implicit assumptions that: (1) the game will go on and on, and (2) the final outcome of the game will be maximized if every decision is based on the greatest expected value. In other words, the worst possible outcome of any decision cannot stop the game, nor can it change the nature of the game in subsequent plays. In risky decisions that involve only a portion of the activity of a diversified firm, it may be appropriate to approach each decision as a simple odds player. However, the payoffs in the above example comprise the entire operating results of the firm for whole accounting periods, and management may not feel indifferent between one tactic that has a downside potential as low as $800,000 and another tactic that has a minimum outcome of $1 million. Management is probably risk averse. In order to make proper use of the decision tree, the expected values of each posture of the firm at a chance event node should be replaced by a new set of values that reflect management's attitudes toward risk. The next section shows how to measure attitudes toward risk and incorporate them in the decision tree approach.

Risk adjustments

Let us measure management's attitudes toward risk, as of a current date.[4] We begin by setting up the axes of a preference curve, shown in Figure 11–11. The horizontal axis is a scale of monetary value of payoffs. This scale should have a range at least as great as that of the outcomes of any decisions that are to be made. A range of $600,000 to $1.2 million has been set up in this example. The end points of the range of payoffs will be called *reference consequences*. We label the lower end point R_0 and the upper end point R_1.

The vertical axis of the preference curve is used as a scale of relative preferences. We shall assign a preference value of 0 to R_0 and a preference value of 1.0 to R_1. Having established two points on the preference scale by definition, we shall obtain several other points by assessment.

We pose the following questions to management. "Suppose you have placed your firm in a position where there is a 50 percent chance of a $600,000 profit for the next period and a 50 percent chance of a $1.2 million profit. Suppose a very wealthy person comes along and offers to pay you cash for the rights to receive your firm's net earnings during the period. You will have no risk whatsoever. If the person offers you $700,000, will you accept the offer?"

The management immediately replies, in chorus, "No!" It is saying in effect, that a certainty equivalent value of $700,000 is not worth as much as a gamble which has a 50 percent chance of $600,000 and a 50 percent chance of $1.2 million. Expected value of this particular gamble is $900,000.

Next we ask management if it would accept an offer of $800,000. The quick response is "Yes, of course." This answer shows that the management team is risk averse (most are), since it will accept a sure thing of

---

[4] The explanation of risk adjustment in this text is based on John S. Hammond, "Better Decisions with Preference Theory," *Harvard Business Review* 45 (November–December 1967).

Figure 11–11
A preference curve

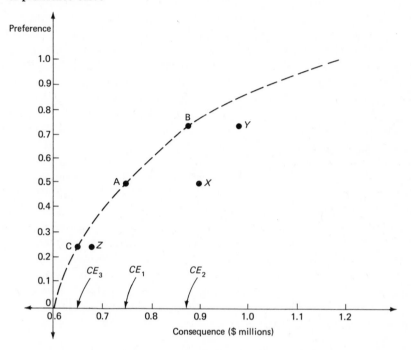

$800,000 in place of a gambling posture which has expected value of $900,000.

We follow by asking management if it will accept $750,000. The query leads to considerable discussion. The group appears to be almost equally divided. After a time, there is consensus on acceptance of the offer. The value of $750,000 can be regarded as a *certainty equivalent* of the assumed gamble. (A certainty equivalent is a value barely acceptable in lieu of a gamble.) Since this is the first certainty equivalent we have obtained by assessment, let us label it CE_1 on the horizontal axis.

To obtain the *preference value* corresponding to the gamble which was assumed above, we use a rule that yields a preference value for any gamble: The preference value for a gamble is *the mathematical expectation of the preferences corresponding to the consequences of the gamble.* In the above example, the assumed gamble had a 50 percent chance of an outcome with an assigned preference value of 0 and a 50 percent chance of an outcome with an assigned preference value of 1.0. Therefore the preference value for the assumed gamble is:

$$
\begin{array}{ll}
0.50 \text{ times } 0 \dots\dots\dots\dots\dots\dots & 0.0 \\
0.50 \text{ times } 1.0 \dots\dots\dots\dots\dots\dots & \underline{0.5} \\
& \overline{0.5}
\end{array}
$$

We now have three points on management's preference curve. The two end points were established by definition, and we have obtained a third point by assessment. The third point is Point A in Figure 11–11.

Note that Point A is $150,000 horizontally to the left of Point X in the figure. Point X is at $900,000, which is the expected value of this gamble that had a preference value of 0.5. The difference between a certainty equivalent value and the expected monetary value of a gamble that has the same preference value is called the *risk premium*. In the above example the risk premium is $900,000 − $750,000, or $150,000.

To obtain another point on management's risk preference curve, we shall set up a hypothetical gamble with a preference value of 0.75. This gamble will have a 50 percent chance of an outcome with a preference value of 0.5 (in the example, $750,000 has just been determined by assessment to have a preference value of 0.5) and a 50 percent chance of an outcome with a preference value of 1.0 (in the example, $1.2 million has been assigned a preference value of 1.0). By a series of questions similar to those used in obtaining the first certainty equivalent, we bracket and then pinpoint a certainty equivalent value that has the same preference value as the hypothetical gamble, eventually obtaining $875,000, shown as Point B in Figure 11–11. This value is labeled CE_2 on the horizontal axis; it is a certainty equivalent of a gamble with an expected value of $975,000 and a preference value of 0.75, as shown in the figure by Point Y.

Next, we set up a hypothetical gamble with a preference value of 0.25. Remember that the preference value of a gamble is the mathematical expectation of the preference values corresponding to the outcomes of the gamble. The next gamble will have a 50 percent chance of an outcome with a preference value of 0 (in the example, $600,000 as initially assigned) and a 50 percent chance of an outcome with a preference value of 0.5 (in the example, $750,000 as determined by assessment). By a series of questions we eventually obtain CE_3, $650,000, as the certainty equivalent of a gamble that has an expected monetary value of $675,000 and a preference value of 0.25, a gamble represented in the figure by Point Z.

Notice what we have done. We began by assigning preference values of 0 and 1.0, respectively, to the outcomes $600,000 and $1.2 million. Then we asked a series of questions to elicit a certainty equivalent value, CE_1, to a gamble with a preference value of 0.5 (that is, a gamble with a 50 percent chance of an outcome with a preference value of 0 and a 50 percent chance of an outcome with a preference value of 1.0). By similar techniques, we obtained certainty equivalent value CE_2 for a gamble with a preference value of 0.75 and certainty equivalent value CE_3 for a gamble with a preference value of 0.25.

The assessment process can be continued to obtain certainty equivalent

Figure 11–12
A risk-adjusted decision tree

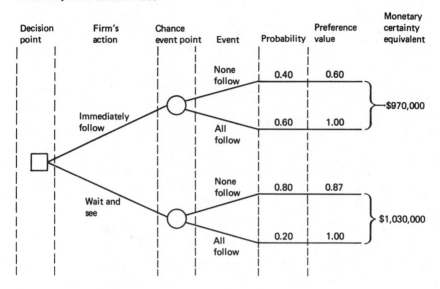

values corresponding to preference values of 0.375, 0.625, 0.875, and so on, until enough points are estimated that a smooth curve can be sketched, as shown in Figure 11–11.

Now, let us see how the preference curve is used in obtaining risk-adjusted values to replace the expected values at the chance event nodes of a decision tree. We begin with the upper chance event node of the decision tree in Figure 11–10. First, replace the payoff of $800,000 by the corresponding preference value of 0.6 from management's preference curve, and replace the payoff of $1.2 million by the corresponding preference value of 1.0. These changes are shown in Figure 11–12. Next, calculate the mathematical expectation of the preferences:

$$
\begin{array}{llr}
0.40 \text{ times } 0.6 & \ldots\ldots\ldots\ldots\ldots & 0.24 \\
0.60 \text{ times } 1.0 & \ldots\ldots\ldots\ldots\ldots & \underline{0.60} \\
& & 0.84
\end{array}
$$

Finally, use the preference curve to find the monetary certainty equivalent of a preference value of 0.84. From the curve in Figure 11–11, this is $970,000. The expected monetary value of the gamble at the upper node of the decision tree is $1,040,000, so there is a risk premium of $70,000 for this particular gamble.

By the method described above, a certainty equivalent value can be determined for the lower chance event node of the decision tree in Figure 11–10. Replace $1 million by the corresponding preference value of 0.87 and replace $1.2 million by the corresponding preference value of 1.0.

These changes have been made in Figure 11–12. Then, calculate the mathematical expectation of preferences for the lower chance event node:

$$
\begin{array}{ll}
0.80 \text{ times } 0.87\ldots\ldots\ldots\ldots & 0.70 \\
0.20 \text{ times } 1.00\ldots\ldots\ldots\ldots & \underline{0.20} \\
 & 0.90
\end{array}
$$

From the preference curve in Figure 11–11, the certainty equivalent corresponding to a preference value of 0.90 is $1,030,000. Since the gamble at the lower chance event node had a expected monetary value of $1,040,000, the risk premium is $10,000.

It can be seen that the certainty equivalent value of the lower chance event node of the decision tree in Figure 11–10 is greater than the certanty equivalent value of the upper chance event node ($1,030,000 is greater than $970,000). So the marketing tactic that places the firm in the posture at the lower node is the best choice.

Other applications of decision trees

Decision trees can be constructed for any decision about marketing tactics that must be made by an oligopoly firm. Decisions about pricing, quality changes, or promotion can be handled, whatever the possible responses of rivals may be. Decisions involving discounting costs and revenues of future periods (to take the time value of money into account) are not difficult. A special strength of the decision tree approach is that decisions involving action–chance event–action chains can be structured. Space allows no further discussion of the technique at this point, but additional explanation can be found in Chapter 14 on capital budgeting.

APPRAISAL OF SEVERAL SHORTCUTS IN PRICING

This section deals with three shortcuts that seem to bypass the difficulties connected with the application of economic analysis to pricing. These shortcuts, in the order in which they will be discussed, are full-cost pricing, the use of suggested prices, and imitative (going-rate) pricing. Each method deserves consideration as a possible way of simplifying the pricing problem, but each has serious limitations.

Full-cost pricing

One difficulty in discussing full-cost pricing is the absence of a generally accepted definition. In this book full-cost pricing means pricing at a level covering total costs, including overhead, plus a predetermined markup. The view that full-cost pricing must assure profitable business operations is widespread. Some writers and trade associations consider the method to be a "scientific approach" to pricing, presumably because it substitutes a formula for subjective judgments. Other writers claim that the method is a reasonable way of dealing with uncertainty and ignorance.

If managers do not know the shape or position of their firms' demand curves, they may find it convenient to adopt a technique that does not require such knowledge. If they are strongly motivated by questions of fairness and justice in pricing, they may adopt a formula that treats all categories of customers alike at all times regardless of conditions of the market. Full-cost pricing may help assure prices that are related to long-run cost in such a way as to discourage the entry of new competition into the industry. Lastly, full-cost pricing may, if adopted by all members of the industry, help protect the firms against price wars and cutthroat price competition, at the same time providing some flexibility in adjusting prices to cost changes.

It might be contended that overhead allocations and profit markups of full-cost pricing help assure that facilities are not allocated to products that fail to carry their share of overhead and produce their share of profit. If firms always operated at full capacity, the logic of this argument would be more appealing. In a world of cyclical change, of seasonality in demand, of varying price elasticities, and of complementary relations in demand, it is difficult to see how full-cost pricing can approach optimal profits.

In addition, it should be noted that full-cost pricing accepts the accountant's definition of costs, with its stress on original costs, its questionable treatment of opportunity costs, and its arbitrary allocations of overhead. It seems unlikely that a price formula based on an inflexible and (for economic purposes) erroneous view of costs can lead to profitable operations.

This discussion of full-cost pricing does not state that the method is entirely without merits. It does suggest, however, that the manager should consider carefully whether it meets the needs of a particular situation before accepting it.

Using suggested prices

Following suggested prices of manufacturers or wholesalers gives the manager time to devote to other decisions. Some managers prefer to minimize the time devoted to pricing and go out of the way to find pre-priced items. The suggested price is probably one that the manufacturer or wholesaler has found feasible under the market conditions and thus permits the retailer to gain the benefit of analysis without having to engage in it. This policy limits flexibility in meeting local conditions, but some sellers prefer to escape the pain of analyzing those conditions.

In the case of resale price maintenance, especially when it is supported by legislation, the choice of the seller is limited. He or she can sell the item only at the price established by the manufacturer. Some small retailers believe that such practices protect them from unfair competition from large outlets. Some manufacturers apparently prefer the control and stability of price that resale price maintenance provides. But in recent years, especially with the advent of discount houses and with court rulings unfavorable to price maintenance, the hold of this pricing practice has diminished.

Imitative ("going-rate") prices

Another approach to pricing is simply to imitate the prices of others. The reasons for such a policy in oligopoly are already familiar to the reader. But the practice appears even when the oligopolistic reasoning is not applicable. Imitation is easy on the decision maker. He or she may get the benefit of another firm's market analysis without worrying about demand elasticities and incremental costs.

The distinction between "price takers" and "price makers" is related to the topic of going-rate pricing. Some sellers—those who operate in highly competitive conditions approaching pure competition—cannot determine prices but must accept those established by relatively impersonal market forces. Such sellers are "price takers"—they must take prices that are given. Examples are sellers of shares in the stock market, farmers selling their crops, or those who sell basic commodities like tin, rubber, or copper in world markets. The sellers with which we are mainly concerned in this chapter are "price makers"—those who have scope for discretion about prices. Since this book is concerned primarily with decision making, it inevitably focuses on enterprises that can make choices. Therefore, the remainder of this chapter will ignore price takers and going-rate pricing.

INCREMENTAL REASONING IN PRICING

Neither the traditional theory of the firm, with its high level of abstraction and generalization, nor the widely known shortcut formulas, with their inflexibility, provide the complete answer to the pricing problem. The present section attempts to provide a general framework within which the manager can formulate a pricing policy. This framework or point of view might best be called *incremental reasoning*. It obviously leans heavily on economic theory, but it reformulates the theory in a form more suitable for decision making.

Incremental reasoning in its most general form states: If a pricing decision leads to a greater increase in revenue than in costs, it is sound; if it leads to a greater reduction in costs than in revenues, it is favorable. What incremental reasoning amounts to, therefore, is the comparison of the impact of decisions on revenues and costs. Such reasoning does not, however, require a restriction of attention to revenues, costs, and profits; it permits, indeed it requires, consideration of the extent to which the decision contributes to or detracts from other goals. Recognition of multiple goals requires weighting of objectives and, at the present state of knowledge, considerable subjective judgment. One way of handling this difficulty is to concentrate first on the impact of the decision on profits and later to adjust for other considerations.

Incremental reasoning requires a full play of the imagination to make certain that all repercussions of the decision are taken into account. The following guides should be helpful.

1. In evaluating the cost of impact of the pricing (and output) decision, *the stress should be on the changes in total revenue and total cost* rather than on average costs. Overhead allocations are irrelevant and should be ignored. Incremental reasoning requires statistical measurement of incremental costs or judgment about which costs are affected and by how much.

2. The method requires *attention to the long-run* as well as the short-run impact of the decision. A decision to increase prices now may increase immediate profits, but it may gradually undermine the firm's reputation for low prices and destroy customer goodwill. Or it may attract new competition.

3. The method requires consideration of *possible complementary relations in demand* between one product and another. The major reason for "loss leaders" in retailing is that they attract customers who will purchase other items. Any time the price decision on one item has an impact on the sale of other items, these additional effects on revenue must be equated.

4. The incremental method takes into account demand elasticities or, more simply, *price-volume relationships*. The decision maker must have some way of determining the impact of price change on volume. Sometimes a statistical or experimental approach to measuring demand may be justified. Other times, the manager may estimate responsiveness of sales to price by evaluating past experience and by considering various factors that might influence demand for this particular product.

5. The method requires attention to *market structure*. In some cases, the closeness of a large number of substitutes may mean that the firm has little control over price. In other cases, differentiation of the product may provide some scope for price policy, though it may require a careful coordination of pricing with sales promotion activity. In still other cases, the possible retaliation of competitors should be taken into account.

6. The method requires some way of dealing with *uncertainty*. The manager never knows the exact consequences of his or her pricing decisions. The degree of uncertainty may vary from one decision to another. No general rules govern optimal behavior in such circumstances, for attitude toward risk varies from one individual to the next. In a large impersonal corporation, individual attitudes toward uncertainty may be ignored; decisions can be based on the aim of maximizing expected profits (average profits). In small firms, the greater willingness of some managers than others to take chances is often a perfectly reasonable reflection of different attitudes toward possible gains or losses. Thus it is impossible to generalize that a manager should always say yes to a decision that offers a .7 probability of adding $100,000 to profits with a .3 probability of losses of $120,000. One manager may be attracted by the fact that this is a better than a fair gamble. Another manager may be concerned that it offers the possibility of complete bankruptcy.

7. Incremental reasoning requires attention to *changing business conditions*. Instead of a mechanical application of formulas through good times and bad, it suggests the possibility of flexibility of prices to meet changing markets. This is not to say that flexibility is always wise, but rather to stress that it is always worthy of consideration.

8. Incremental reasoning implies *individualization of pricing* on the various products of a multiproduct concern. It is true that mechanical formulas simplify pricing decisions. In a firm with thousands of products, such a simplification may cut managerial costs. But demand and competitive conditions facing the products are likely to be diverse; rigid pricing formulas prevent adjustment to that diversity. This is again a question of benefits versus costs. Will the firm gain enough in added profits or in furtherance of its other goals to justify the added management costs?

Note that incremental reasoning implies both cross-sectional flexibility and flexibility over time. By *cross-sectional flexibility* is meant the willingness to adapt prices to the special conditions of demand and cost that face each product. Flexibility over time has to do with the ability to adapt pricing to changing market conditions, to shifts in demand, to changes in price elasticities, and to the availability of excess capacity.

It is more important to develop a way of reasoning about pricing than it is to learn specific rules. Correct reasoning can be tailor made to particular circumstances; rules frequently are applied when they no longer fit.

THE PRICING PROCESS

The pricing process is complex. Many influences and considerations must be taken into account. These are highlighted in the following discussion of parties involved in pricing, a multistage approach in which early decisions simplify subsequent ones, and a pricing checklist that summarizes considerations in pricing decisions.

Parties involved in pricing

The manager responsible for pricing decisions must consider a variety of individuals concerned with price. Oxenfeldt lists seven main parties to the pricing process: those responsible for sales promotion, the ultimate customers for the product, rival sellers, potential rivals, middlemen, suppliers, and the government.[5] Economic theory usually stresses only two of these parties: the buyers and the sellers. The pricing process in practice must take all of them into account, for they all are involved in the pattern of communication and influence which determines the final outcome.

The case of the *middleman* brings out the complexity of the pricing environment. Most manufacturers distribute their products through middlemen rather than directly. The mutual interests of the manufacturer and the middleman are obscure. The manufacturer would like the middleman to carry his product at a minimum markup, but the margin must be large enough to stimulate a desire to carry and "push" the product. The manufacturer would like a variety of middlemen to provide a wide coverage of the market, but middlemen often want to handle products on an exclusive basis. The manufacturer may wish to control prices charged by the middlemen and even the retail price; but the middlemen may wish to expand their sales by cutting price or to obtain a larger margin than the suggested price provides. A reduction of price by the manufacturer may reduce the value of middlemen's inventories, a fact that may lead to resentment unless some adjustment is made. Many of these issues are resolved by reference to trade policies and customs.

The relation of the *government* to pricing decisions is an especially painful one to many businesses. Especially difficult is the problem of avoiding price discrimination of the sort deemed illegal under the Robinson-Patman Act. Most multiproduct firms, especially those with widespread markets, engage in price discrimination in a broad sense. The problem is to determine when such discrimination becomes illegal in the sense of the statutes. The criteria of legality require a determination of whether the pricing practices injure rivals or tend to lessen competition. They also require consideration of whether price differences reflect cost differences—for example, the lower costs made possible by supplying large quantities to certain customers. Similar difficulties arise in the

[5] The following discussion makes considerable use of ideas in Alfred R. Oxenfeldt, *Pricing for Marketing Executives* (Belmont, Calif.: Wadsworth Publishing Co., Inc., 1961).

interpretation of statutes and court decisions governing resale price maintenance, sales below cost, basing point systems of pricing, and a variety of other pricing practices.

A multistage approach

A. R. Oxenfeldt has outlined what he calls a "multistage approach to pricing."[6] This approach breaks the pricing process into a series of successive steps; decisions on the early stages facilitate subsequent decisions. Oxenfeldt outlines six stages, as follows:

Selection of market targets. The firm should determine the character of the market it expects to reach with the product under consideration. It may try to find segments of the market in which it has a special advantage, such as some insulation from competition. It may decide it wishes to sell to a particular income group or to those with special tastes. It may stress winning a larger share of the market. It may wish to develop markets which are complementary to those for the company's existing products. Such a decision requires an evaluation of the firm's capabilities, goals, and resources.

Selection of the firm or brand image. Management should decide what kind of reputation for the firm and brand names it is trying to build up in the public's mind. Some firms establish a reputation for high quality which may justify their high prices. Others may wish to be known as economical outlets for mass-produced commodities. Still others may wish to be known as innovators. The point is that management should make product, packaging, advertising, and pricing decisions which are consistent with the image it is trying to create.

Composition of the marketing mix. Management should coordinate advertising decisions with pricing. For example, if it is trying to increase sales by reducing price, its advertising should aim at increasing the elasticity of demand to such price decreases. Such advertising would stress the price advantage of the company's product. On the other hand, an increase in price might be accompanied by advertising which stresses the quality and distinctiveness of the firm's product. Similarly, decisions on the quality of service, styling, and packaging should relate to the pricing decisions.

Selection of the specific price policy. The firm should next determine an overall price policy within which it can establish individual prices. Some illustrations of such policies are: to follow the price of the leader; to set prices at 10 percent below those of the leader; to determine the best

---

[6] Alfred R. Oxenfeldt, "Multi-Stage Approach to Pricing," *Harvard Business Review* (July–August 1960), pp. 125–33. Oxenfeldt's discussion is similar to Dean's "Steps in Pioneering Pricing" in *Managerial Economics* (Englewood Cliffs, N.J.: Prentice-Hall, Inc., 1951), pp. 413–19.

price for each product individually; to follow the practice of marking up by a predetermined percentage on full cost; to follow the prices suggested by manufacturers or wholesalers; to maintain uniform prices throughout all markets; or to differentiate price according to the characteristics of particular markets.

Selection of a price strategy. The firm should choose current prices that are consistent with its long-term objectives. We have already presented illustrations of such strategies. For example, a penetration price strategy may aim at the creation of familiarity with the product as rapidly as possible, with subsequent dominance of the market. Prices may aim at discouraging the entry of new competition into the market. In other situations the strategy may be one of avoiding "rocking the boat," with restraint in changing prices in a way that will provoke retaliation.

Setting specific prices. The previous steps provide a framework for establishing the prices of individual products. Some of the previous steps reduce this final step to a mere mechanical routine which can be delegated to clerks. But the choice of policies and strategies which call for flexibility will require considerable high-level analysis before prices are determined.

Pricing checklist

The following checklist of considerations in pricing is based on several works which attempt to bridge the gap between abstract theory and needs of the individual firm:

1. Consideration of price-volume relationships (elasticities of demand) to determine what happens to total revenue at various prices.
2. Comparison of those price-volume relationships with incremental costs to determine the most profitable price on each item.
3. Estimation of the contribution to overhead and profits on each product that can be produced with the given facilities.
4. Selection of those products and sale at those prices that will assure the largest contributions to overhead and profits.
5. Investment in new facilities according to the estimated profits in the future of alternative products at optimum prices, taking costs into account.
6. Flexibility of prices over time to meet changing market and cost conditions, unless there are *strong* arguments against flexibility (possible retaliation, high costs of changing decisions, etc.).
7. Consideration of the impact of price changes on the image of the company in the market, on customer goodwill, and on the firm's reputation for fair prices.

8. Consideration of the impact that price changes in one commodity may have on the sales of other items.
9. Experimentation with price changes, when this is not too costly to determine what customer responses are likely to be.
10. Determination of how much customers will benefit from price reductions, for this will give some clues as to the response to price changes.
11. Comparison of the long-range implications of price changes with the immediate impact of those changes.
12. Consideration of the life cycle of the product, with different price strategies for new products than for mature products facing a decline in demand.
13. Consideration of competitors' reactions to price changes.
14. Evaluation of the impact of price changes on the entry or exit of competitive rivals.
15. Coordination of price policies with other marketing policies, so that these are consistent and complementary.
16. Determination of the incremental costs or marginal costs of each product, even when full-cost pricing is applied, in order to evaluate the impact of full-cost pricing from time to time.
17. Avoidance of overestimating how much can be accomplished by pricing alone; it is only one phase of management and cannot guarantee profitable operations.[7]

Empirical studies and illustrations

The major issue in research on pricing has been the extent to which practice has followed mechanical procedures such as full-cost pricing, or, alternatively, has followed the more flexible and more demand-oriented precepts of marginalism. The findings are mixed and still somewhat controversial.

The best-known questionnaire survey on pricing is that of R. L. Hall and C. J. Hitch, who were concerned primarily with oligopoly.[8] They found a great majority of the 38 covered firms applying a full-cost policy. Most of them started with direct cost, added a percentage to cover overhead, and then added another percentage for profit. Hall and Hitch suggest a variety of reasons for adoption of full-cost pricing, among which are considerations of fairness, ignorance of demand, ignorance

[7] This list is based primarily on the following works: Dean, *Managerial Economics*; Oxenfeldt, *Pricing for Marketing Executives;* and W. W. Haynes, *Pricing Decisions in Small Business* (Lexington: University of Kentucky Press, 1962).

[8] R. L. Hall and C. J. Hitch, "Price Theory and Business Behavior," *Oxford Economic Papers,* no. 2 (May 1939), pp. 12, 18–22, 25–27, 29–33; reprinted in T. Wilson and P. W. S. Andrews, *Oxford Studies in the Price Mechanism* (Oxford-Clarendon Press, 1951), pp. 107–38.

of potential reactions of competitors, the belief that the short-run elasticity of market demand is low, the belief that increased prices would encourage new entrants, and the administrative difficulties of a more flexible price policy. Hall and Hitch use the kinked demand analysis to help explain full-cost pricing: This analysis emphasizes the belief that competitors follow a decrease in price, reducing the profitability of such decreases, but do not follow an increase. Hall and Hitch summarize their findings as follows:

1. A large proportion of businesses make no attempt to equate marginal revenue and marginal cost in the sense in which economists have asserted that this is typical behavior.

2. An element of oligopoly is extremely common in markets for manufactured products; most businesses take into account in their pricing the probable reaction of competitors and potential competitors.

3. Where this element of oligopoly is present, and in many cases where it is absent, there is a strong tendency among businesses to fix prices at a level which they regard as "full cost."

4. Prices so fixed have a tendency to be stable. They will be changed if there is a significant change in wage or raw material costs, but not in response to moderate or temporary shifts in demand.

5. There is usually some element in the prices ruling at any time which can only be explained in the light of history of the industry.[9]

The Hall and Hitch conclusions have come under attack. Critics have noted that firms in the study varied margins from product to product; this suggests some attention to market forces. The critics have also suggested that inability to measure marginal revenue and marginal cost precisely does not require abandonment of marginalism, which must be interpreted to include subjective estimates and trial and error approaches to maximum profits.

George J. Stigler's study of price statistics raises doubts about the kinked demand theory.[10] Stigler finds greater price stability in monopoly than in oligopoly, contrary to the implications of the kinked demand theory.

A study in the 1950s by James S. Earley lends support to marginalism.[11] Earley's study covers large firms which are claimed to be "excellently managed," and thus is not necessarily representative of practice in general. Earley finds that these firms are adopting accounting methods that move in the marginalist direction, with breakdowns between fixed

---

[9] Wilson and Andrews, *Oxford Studies in Price Mechanism*, p. 125.

[10] George J. Stigler, "The Kinky Oligopoly Demand Curve and Rigid Prices," *The Journal of Political Economy* (October 1947), pp. 432–49.

[11] James E. Earley, "Marginal Policies of 'Excellently Managed Companies,'" *The American Economic Review* (March 1956), pp. 44–70; and James E. Earley, "Recent Developments in Cost Accounting and the 'Marginal Analysis,'" *The Journal of Political Economy* (June 1955), pp. 227–42.

and variable costs and separation of fixed costs that can be attributed directly to particular segments. He also finds differentiation of margins on different product lines, with attention to competitive pressures and demand elasticities.

The best-known collection of case studies in pricing, that of Kaplan, Dirlam, and Lanzillotti, covers 20 of the largest industrial corporations in the United States.[12] The authors stress these patterns:

1. Considerable concern with "fairness" of prices, with attention to public responsibilities.
2. Establishment of "target returns," stated as percentage returns on investment, consistent with what is considered "fair."
3. Attention to market share, with improvement in the firm's market position a major objective.
4. A preference for stable prices or stable margins.
5. Stress on full costs in the mechanics of pricing, with widespread use of standard costs as the relevant full-cost data.
6. Adjustments of margins on particular commodities to market conditions.
7. Price leadership of both the dominant firm and barometric varieties.
8. Restraint in charging what the market will bear in periods of market shortages.
9. Occasional use of simple and crude rules of thumb in determining price changes, such as doubling the increase in labor costs in a new wage agreement.

Individual cases show considerable diversity in behavior. Some firms, like International Harvester, may give especially strong attention to target returns, but still compute incremental costs when faced with severe competition. Other firms, such as the A&P, may place maintenance or improvement of market share ahead of target returns. The firms vary in willingness to delegate discretion over prices to subordinate officials. One firm follows a policy of pricing to meet competition: The National Steel Corporation follows prices set by U.S. Steel, with stress on control of costs to return a profit at those prices.

Kaplan Dirlam, and Lanzillotti recognize certain limitations in their approach. They have difficulties in evaluating information released by company officials; they cannot be certain, for example, that stated objectives are not sometimes rationalizations rather than descriptions of actual goals. Critics of the study are particularly unconvinced by the authors' dismissal of profit maximization as a useful concept; they doubt

---

[12] A. D. H. Kaplan, Joel B. Dirlam, and Robert F. Lanzillotti, *Pricing in Big Business* (Washington, D.C.: The Brookings Institution, 1958). Also see Robert F. Lanzillotti, "Pricing Objectives in Large Companies," *The American Economic Review* (December 1958), pp. 921–40.

that the firms are as bound by "target returns" as the authors suggest; they note evidence that the "targets" may be estimates of what the traffic will bear, which means that they are subject to market forces.

A study of small firms conducted by Haynes reaches conclusions somewhat different from those already cited.[13]

1. It does not find adherence to full-cost pricing, but rather some flexible attention to costs as resistance or reference points. Small businesses do adjust prices to market forces. They seek, through subjective evaluations of demand and through trial and error, prices that will help them achieve their objectives, one of which is profit maximization.

2. On the other hand, small firms have not adopted the incremental accounting techniques mentioned by Earley. Accounting appears to have a limited role in their pricing decisions, and when it does play a role it leads to stress on full costs and averages, rather than on incremental costs. The extent to which small businesses are marginalists results not from their use of accounting but from their experimentation in the market, their willingness to evaluate demand and costs subjectively, or their imitation of the practices of other firms.

3. Small firms do not appear to give the attention to "target returns" found in big business.

4. Small firms are often concerned with the ethics of pricing and with community relations, as well as with the impact of prices on profits.

A more complete review of the literature would reveal even greater diversity of practice. This is what one would expect when examining decision making in detail, for pricing must be adapted to the structure of the market, the availability of information, the competence of management, and the variety of goals and community pressures. This survey of empirical studies indicates that narrow generalizations about pricing behavior are oversimplified.

SUMMARY

Market structure affects the firm's decisions about pricing, quality improvement, and promotion. *In the structure of pure competition, there are many sellers of a homogeneous product and entry into the industry is easy.* The firm's average and marginal revenue curves are horizontal at the general market price, so the firm must act as a price taker; the firm can choose an output-sales rate. In a pure competitive market structure, long-run expansion of capacity and output pushes prices down and "squeezes out" profits of marginal firms; a well-managed firm may keep costs low enough that it continues to earn good rates of return on capital.

---

[13] Haynes, *Pricing Decisions in Small Business.*

In *monopoly, there is one seller of a unique product and entry into the industry is precluded.* Barriers to entry may be temporary or more enduring; they include restricted access to low-cost raw material, patents, franchises, and economies of scale so great in relation to market demand that a single firm has a decisive cost advantage. In monopoly, the firm's demand and marginal revenue functions slope down and to the right, and it can select a combination of price and output-sales rate that is most profitable.

In *monopolistic competition, there are many sellers of differentiated products and entry is easy.* Monopolistic competition allows the firm to determine short-run pricing and output-sales rate in the manner of a monopoly, but the competitive aspect of the industry enters through long-run capacity and output expansion that pushes each product's demand curve to the left. Profits of marginal firms are eliminated by market forces. Nevertheless, a well-managed firm may be able to keep costs down and demand up, so that it maintains good returns on investment.

Deliberate demand shifting (through quality changes and changes in promotion) can be profitable for firms that have differentiable products. Decisions related to demand shifting include: selecting least-cost combinations of inputs for production of quality changes and increased promotion; determining least-cost combinations of quality and promotion for any given shift of demand; deciding whether additional shifting of demand will be profitable; and determining whether price change is advantageous after a demand shift. Concepts and techniques of production economics can be used in managing demand shifts.

In *oligopoly, a few sellers account for a large part of total industry output.* Products may be either homogeneous or differentiated. Entry into oligopolistic industries is difficult; production at competitive costs requires output that is large in relation to total market demand and must be sold in competition with established firms that have entrenched positions in distribution channels plus, for differentiated products, already developed consumer preferences. The distinguishing characteristics of oligopoly is that actions of one firm may perceptibly affect profits of rivals, leading to immediate and direct reactions as the other firms attempt to protect their market positions; thus, possible reactions of rivals should be taken into account in making decisions about prices, quality, and promotion.

If an oligopolist believes other firms will not follow a price increase but will follow a price reduction, the demand curve is *kinked* at the current price and the marginal revenue function has two sections separated by a vertical gap. If the average and marginal cost functions run through the vertical gap (as is likely), the oligopolist will stand to lose by price change in either direction, and prices will be *sticky* in the face of sizable changes in either cost or demand. Shifts in cost or demand eventually make price changes advantageous. Output is immediately responsive to demand shifts but not to changes in cost unless these lead to price adjustments.

Other patterns of oligopoly pricing behavior include *price leadership* (the leader cannot raise price above the level desired by the lowest-cost firm); *collusion* (this is difficult to maintain because of conflicts of interest about market sharing that lead to cheating, and is illegal in the United States); *price wars* (wars are usually local and short); and *nonprice competition* (the reaction of competitors to demand shifting is not immediate and may not be head on; this is not an alternative for firms in homogeneous oligopolies).

Decision trees may be useful in an oligopoly firm's decisions about marketing tactics. They are comprised of decision points, action branches, chance event points, and event branches for which probabilities and payoffs are specified. If the payoffs are total results for a firm for an operating period, risk adjustment of the decision tree may be advisable. Risk adjustment requires estimates of management's preference function, so that preference values can be substituted in the place of the payoffs on the decision tree.

QUESTIONS

1. What are the unique (or distinguishing) characteristics of each of the following industry structures: (*a*) pure competition, (*b*) pure monopoly, (*c*) monopolistic competition, and (*d*) oligopoly?

2. Why is a decision about price precluded for a firm under pure competition?

3. A monopolistically competitive industry can be regarded as monopolistic from the short-run perspective but competitive from the long-run perspective. Explain.

4. What is meant by the assertion that a monopoly firm *is* the industry in which the firm operates?

5. Explain how the following concepts from Chapters 5 and 6 can be applied in decisions about deliberate demand shifting: (*a*) least-cost combination of inputs, (*b*) least-cost combination of methods of demand shifting, and (*c*) expansion path.

6. Assuming product price is held constant, explain the determination of optimum demand shifting and final rate of sales. What complications arise if the firm attempts to treat pricing and demand shifting as variables to be determined simultaneously?

7. Could full-cost prices be close to optimal prices? Explain.

8. Could a firm that uses full-cost pricing have an operating loss? Explain.

PROBLEMS

1. In a purely competitive industry that produces Product X, the equations for annual market supply and market demand are, respectively:

$$Q \text{ (millions of units)} = 25,000\, P_z + 20\, P_z{}^2$$
$$Q \text{ (millions of units)} = 100,000 - 2,000\, P_z + 6\, P_z{}^2$$

a. Determine the industry's equilibrium price and quantity (P_z is price in dollars).

b. Use a graph to show what you have just done. It should resemble Figure 11–1A.

2. For one small firm in the purely competitive industry of Problem 1, the total cost function can be approximated in the relevant range by the following equation:

$$TC = \$4,800 + \$2.40\, Q_z + \$0.06 Q_z{}^2$$

in which Q_z is the annual output rate in thousands.

a. Use marginal analysis to determine the rate of output that will maximize the firm's profit. Calculate the amount of the profit.

b. Use a graph to illustrate what you have just done. The graph should be similar to Figure 11–1 (B–1).

c. Use the method of maximizing the value of the profit function to determine the firm's optimal rate of output. Compare with the result of part a above.

d. Draw a graph depicting what you have just done. It should resemble Figure 11–1 (B–3).

3. A pure monopoly has estimated the following demand and cost functions:

$$\text{Demand:} \quad Q = 4,000 - 0.8P$$

where P is price in dollars and Q is annual sales in units.

$$\text{Cost:} \quad TC = \$240,000 + \$3,600Q$$

where Q is annual output in units.

a. Using marginal analysis, determine the profit maximizing output-sales rate and price. Calculate the amount of profit.

b. Draw a graph to illustrate what you have just done. It should resemble Figure 11–2A.

c. Employ the technique of maximizing the value of the firm's profit function to determine the firm's optimum output-sales rate. Compare the result with the solution to part a above.

d. Use a graph to depict what you have just done. It should look like Figure 11–2C.

4. Given the short-run curves below, what do $OADq$, $OBCq$, and $ABCD$ represent? What does the area under the MC curve from O to q represent? Is the industry in equilibrium? Explain.

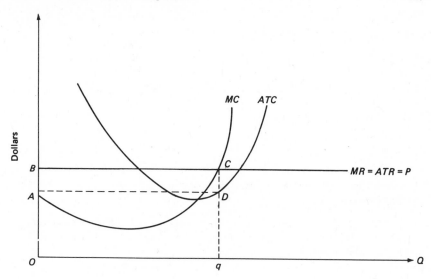

5. Given the short-run curves, what do $OACq$, $OPBq$, $APBC$, and the area under the MR curve from 0 to q represent? Is the industry in equilibrium? Explain.

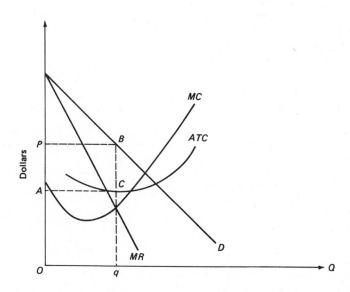

6. The manager of a firm producing rope for a perfectly competitive market is presently having the firm produce 50 units of rope for sale at $50 a unit. He determines the following schedule:

Units of rope	Total cost
48.	$2,395
49.	2,450
50.	2,500
51.	2,545
52.	2,585
53.	2,630
54.	2,680
55.	2,735
56.	2,795

Determine his best production level and draw a graph to show the cost and revenue situation.

7. A monopolist has two separate plants, both capable of producing widgets for sale in a single market. The cost and revenue schedules are as follows. How much does each plant produce and what is the price at which the total output is sold?

P	Q	TC_1	TC_2
$24.	1	$ 50	$ 35
23.	2	55	43
22.	3	59	49
21.	4	62	53
20.	5	64	55
19.	6	65	60
18.	7	67	69
17.	8	77	79
16.	9	92	90
15.	10	110	102
14.	11	130	115
13.	12	151	129
12.	13	173	144
11.	14	196	160

8. An oligopoly firm has estimated the following demand for its single differentiated product:

Above the present price: $P = \$50 - \$0.0025Q$
Below the present price: $P = \$80 - \$0.01Q$

where P is price in dollars and Q is weekly sales in tons. The firm's cost function is:

TC (in dollars per week) = $40,000 = $28Q

a. Determine the firm's optimal rate of output-sales, price, and profit.
b. Draw a graph showing what you have just done.
c. Assume that the firm's variable cost per unit increases $4 per unit because of a new labor contract. Other firms in the industry are not currently facing comparable cost increases. Determine the firm's optimal output-sales, pricing, and profit.

d. Construct a graph depicting what you have just done.
e. Returning to part *c*, assume that *all* firms in the industry are confronted by the same cost increase of $4 per unit, where all firms have a similar construction of costs, revenues, and profits. Now, determine the one firm's optimal output, pricing, and profit.
f. Make a graph illustrating what you have just done.

9. One of the smaller firms in a differentiated oligopoly industry presently has sales of 2,400 units per week at a price of $56 per unit. The firm's cost structure is:

$$\text{TC (per week in dollars)} = \$40{,}000 + \$32Q$$

where Q is weekly output in units. The firm is considering making a change in the quality of its single product. This change would add $3 per unit to the firm's cost. The firm's marketing department has estimated the effect of the quality improvement upon the firm's weekly sales under two assumptions about the reactions of competitors: (1) If competitors do not react, sales can be increased to 3,000 units per week at the current price; (2) if all competitors do react quickly with similar quality improvement and none increases the price, sales can be increased only to 2,500 units per week. Management believes that there is a 0.60 probability that competitors will not react, and a 0.40 probability that all will react quickly.

As a further consideration, management knows that the same quality improvement has been developed by one of the largest firms in the industry (a firm that has traditionally focused on cost cutting and kept its price on the low side). If management of the small firm does not introduce the quality improvement, it believes there is a 0.10 probability that the large firm will do so without a price increase and that all other firms will quickly react with a similar quality improvement, whereas there is a 0.90 probability that the large firm will simply hold the product improvement in reserve for use at some indefinite later time.

a. Construct a decision tree to assist in the decision making of the one smaller firm. Base the payoffs on results of one year's operations.
b. Assume that management increases its estimate of the probability that the large firm will lead the industry in quality improvement without a price increase. The new estimate is 2 chances in 10. Analyze the effect of this change in probability.
c. Is it reasonable to base the smaller firm's decision making on expected values, or should management attempt to substitute preference values into the decision trees? Explain.

FURTHER READING

Adelman, M. A. "The Two Faces of Economic Concentration." *The Public Interest* 21, Fall 1970.

Archibald, G. C. "Chamberlain versus Chicago." *Review of Economic Studies* 29 (1961).

Bain, Joe S. "Price Leaders, Barometers, and Kinks." *The Journal of Business* 33, July 1960.

452 *Managerial economics*

Baron, D. "Limit Pricing, Potential Entry, and Barriers to Entry." *American Economic Review* 63, September 1973.

Bass, Frank M. "A Simultaneous Equation Regression Study of Advertising and Sale of Cigarettes." *Journal of Marketing Research*, August 1969.

Cowling, Keith, and Raynes, A. J. "Price, Quality and Market Share." *Journal of Political Economy* 78, November–December 1970.

Dorfman, R., and Steiner, Peter. "Optimal Advertising and Optimal Quality." *American Economic Review* 44, December 1954.

Douglas, G., and Miller, J. "Quality Competition, Industry Equilibrium, and Efficiency in the Price-Constrained Airline Industry." *American Economic Review* 64, September 1974.

Doyle, P. "Economic Aspects of Advertising: A Survey." *Economic Journal* 78, September 1968.

Drucker, Peter. "The New Markets and The New Capitalism." *The Public Interest* 21, Fall 1970.

Early, James S. "Marginal Policies of Excellently Managed Companies." *American Economic Review* 46, March 1966.*

Hammond, John S. "Better Decisions with Preference Theory." *Harvard Business Review* 45, November–December 1967.

Haynes, W. W. "Pricing Practices in Small Firms." *Southern Economic Journal* 30, April 1964.*

Hirshleifer, Jack. "Where Are We in the Theory of Information." *American Economic Review* 63, May 1973.

Kuhlman, John M. "The Proctor and Gamble Decision." *Quarterly Review of Economics and Business*, Spring 1966.

Lanzilotti, Robert F. "Pricing Objectives in Large Companies." *American Economic Review* 48, December 1958.

Lawyer, John Q. "How to Conspire to Fix Prices." *Harvard Business Review* 41, March–April 1963.

Markham, Jesse W. "Antitrust Trends and New Constraints." *Harvard Business Review*, May–June 1963.

Means, Gardiner C. "The Administered Price Thesis Confirmed." *American Economic Review* 62, June 1972.

Scherer, F. M. "Research and Development Resource Allocation Under Rivalry." *Quarterly Journal of Economics* 81, August 1967.

Schnabel, Morton. "An Oligopoly Model of the Cigarette Industry." *The Southern Economic Journal* 38.

Silberston, Aubrey. "Surveys of Applied Economics: Price Behavior of Firms." *The Economic Journal* 80, September 1970.*

Smith, Stanton D., and Neale Walter C. "The Geometry of Kinky Oligopoly: Marginal Cost, the Gap, and Price Behavior." *Southern Economic Journal* 37, January 1971.

* This article is included in *Readings in Managerial Economics,* rev. ed. (Dallas: Business Publications, Inc., 1977).

Stigler, George J. "The Kinky Demand Curve and Rigid Prices." *Journal of Political Economy* 55, October 1947.

Stigler, George J. "The Economics of Information." *Journal of Political Economy* 69, June 1961.

Stigler, George. "Price and Non-Price Competition." *Journal of Political Economy* 76, January–February 1968.

Swalm, Ralph O. "Utility Theory—Insights into Risk Taking." *Harvard Business Review*, November–December 1966.

Sweezy, Paul M. "Demand Under Conditions of Oligopoly." *Journal of Political Economy* 47, August 1939.

Telser, Richard G. "Advertising and Competition." *Journal of Political Economy* 72, December 1964.

Van Cise, Jerrold G. "How to Live with Antitrust." *Harvard Business Review* 40, November–December 1962.

Weston, J. F., et al. "The Administered Price Thesis Denied: Note." *American Economic Review* 64, March 1974.

Weston, J. Fred. "Pricing Behavior of Large Firms." *Western Economic Journal* 10, March 1972.

Worcester, Dean A. "Why 'Dominant' Firms Decline." *Journal of Political Economy* 65, August 1957.

Chapter 12

Selected topics in pricing

This chapter is concerned with advanced topics in pricing. It begins with a discussion of price discrimination, in which differences in prices of a product in its various markets do not match differences in costs. It then takes up peak-load pricing, in which the price of a nonstorable good is increased and decreased with changes in demand over short periods of time. The next topic is utility rate regulation, in which particular attention is given to the choice between average cost and marginal cost pricing of output of a decreasing cost industry. The chapter moves on to price and output determination for multiple products, i.e., products that are technically interdependent in production. The final topic is interdivisional transfer pricing in large, multiple-product, multiple-process companies.

PRICE DISCRIMINATION

Two definitions of price discrimination are necessary for our purposes. One is a tight, narrow definition, useful for analytic purposes. The other is looser and broader, but closer to the realities of business. The two definitions are:

1. The practice of charging different prices to different segments of the market for the same commodity or service.[1]

---

[1] Joan Robinson's classic definition of price discrimination is "the act of selling the same article, produced under a single control, at different price to different buyers." See *The Economics of Imperfect Competition* (London: Macmillan & Co., Ltd., 1933), p. 179.

2. The practice of charging prices with differences that do not correspond to differences in marginal costs of slightly differentiated goods or services.

The first definition presumes a homogeneous commodity. The second definition recognizes that differentiation of price is likely to accompany differentiation in characteristics of the commodity. *To determine whether price discrimination exists one must compare price differentials with cost differentials.* The absence of price differentials may be discriminatory, as is the case when the same commodity is sold at the same price over a wide territory in which transportation costs vary. The existence of price differentials may, on the other hand, be nondiscriminatory, as would be the case if price differences match differences in transportation costs.

Some writers prefer the term "differential pricing" to "price discrimination," for the latter term may carry unintended connotations. Price discrimination is actually a neutral, technical term describing a particular business practice rather than something that is evil by definition.

Nature of gains from price discrimination

Price discrimination increases net revenue from any given total amount of product. An example demonstrates the nature of the gains from the practice. Suppose a company is selling an identical product in two markets, Market A and Market B, at the same price of $1,000 per unit. It learns that the price elasticity of demand, e_p, is −2.0 in Market A and has the less elastic value of −1.5 in Market B. It calculates the marginal revenue of the product in each of the markets:

$$\text{In any market, } MR = \text{Price}\left(1 + \frac{1}{e_p}\right)$$

$$\text{In Market A, } MR = \$1,000\left(1 + \frac{1}{-2.0}\right) = \$500$$

$$\text{In Market B, } MR = \$1,000\left(1 + \frac{1}{-1.5}\right) = \$334, \text{ approximately}$$

In the example, if one unit of the current total sales rate is reallocated from Market B to Market A, with price being raised in Market B and reduced in Market A by appropriate amounts, the total revenue of the firm is increased by the amount $500–$334, or $166, approximately. Transferring additional units from Market B to Market A would give similar but steadily decreasing gains. With additional transfers, the marginal revenues of the two markets would be coming closer and closer together, falling in Market A and rising in Market B, until the marginal revenues became equal in the two markets. At this point, the potential gains from quantity reallocation and price discrimination would be fully realized.

Choosing pricing and output to maximize profits

The technique for profit maximization under price discrimination will be introduced by the case of an *identical* product that has the same marginal cost for two markets with differing demand elasticities. After this basic problem is understood, the technique can be extended to the case of *differentiated* products with marginal costs that vary among the different markets. A seller facing an opportunity to practice price discrimination needs to know the following things:

1. How much total output and sales?
2. How should total sales quantity be allocated among the various markets?
3. What prices should be charged in each of the markets?

Figure 12–1 shows how answers to the above questions can be obtained. The firm has two market segments, Market 1 and Market 2, each with its own demand and marginal revenue function. The aggregate marginal revenue function, MR_{1+2}, is obtained by *horizontal summation of the quantities* found on MR_1 and MR_2 at each value of marginal revenue (in practice, summation at close intervals may be satisfactory). For example, take the value of $5 for marginal revenue. At this value, how many units can be sold in Market 1? How many in Market 2? It can be seen that the answers are 21 and 22 units, respectively. If the firm always allocates total sales between two markets so as to maximize total revenue, the marginal revenues of the two markets will always be equal and the total sales quantity at any given value of marginal

Figure 12–1
Price discrimination—an identical product, two markets

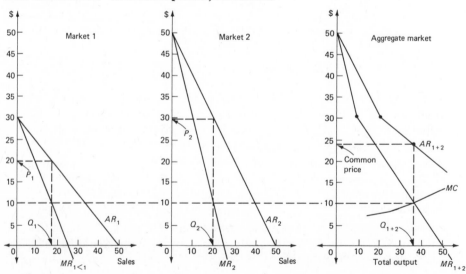

revenue will be the sum of the quantities in the respective markets at that value of marginal revenue. In the above example, the total quantity at a marginal revenue of $5 is 21 plus 22, or 43.

On the cost side of the analysis, only the marginal cost is relevant. In the example of Figure 12–1, there is no difference in cost whether the product sells in Market 1 or Market 2. Therefore, the firm has *one* marginal cost function showing the relation of cost to rate of *total* output.

Optimum total output is found where marginal cost becomes equal to aggregate marginal revenue. In Figure 12–1, this point is found at $10, corresponding to a total output of 36 units. The optimum allocation of output among the markets is found by extending a horizontal line at the optimum value of marginal revenue—a line running back to the individual marginal revenue functions. In the example of Figure 12–1, the horizontal line runs at $10 and intersects Market 2's marginal revenue function at a sales rate, Q_2, of 20 units; the line intersects Market 1's marginal function at a rate, Q_1, of 16 units. Optimum market prices are found by extending vertical lines up to the individual demand curves from the optimal market quantities just determined. In Figure 12–1, Market 1's price, P_1, is $20; the price in Market 2, P_2, is $30.

If the total quantity of 36 units were sold at the same price in both markets, the price that would clear the market is found on the aggregate demand function and is $24. Gains from price discrimination in the example of Figure 12–1 can be calculated as follows:

Revenue per period *with* price discrimination
Market 1, price of $20 times quantity of 16 . . . . $320
Market 2, price of $30 times quantity of 20 600
$920

Revenue per period *without* price discrimination
Market 1, price of $24 times quantity of 10 . . . . $240
Market 2, price of $24 times quantity of 26 624
$864

Price discrimination maximizes total revenue from any given amount of total output by allocating this output among markets in such a way that marginal revenues are equalized in the various markets, and maximizes profit by determining that rate of total output and sales at which aggregate marginal cost is equal to aggregate marginal revenue.

The above-described graphic method of aggregation and solution is not simply an illustration of the principle of price discrimination. It is also a very satisfactory method of determining approximately optimal values in an actual problem. The graphic method is much simpler than analytic approaches requiring derivation of equations for aggregate functions. Careful work on graph paper with a well-sharpened pencil yields solutions that are quite accurate in comparison with the underlying estimates of cost and revenue functions.

Handling marginal costs that differ

Suppose a firm must handle a case involving slightly differentiated products and differing marginal costs of supplying various markets. In this case, the product's marginal costs should be separated into two categories. One is *basic cost*—cost that applies to all output regardless of its market destination. The second category is *market-specific cost*—cost that depends upon the particular market segment. Each market-specific marginal cost, which may be constant or may be a function of sales rate, is substracted from the particular market's marginal revenue function. The (cost-adjusted) aggregate marginal revenue function is then formed by horizontal summation of quantities on the *cost-adjusted* marginal revenue functions at each value of marginal revenue (or at close intervals). Optimum total output is found where aggregate marginal revenue is equal to marginal cost on the product's *basic* marginal cost function. Each market's quantity allocation is found on its adjusted marginal revenue function at the optimum value of marginal revenue determined in the previous step, and each market's price is found on its demand function at the optimum quantity allocation to that market.

Conditions necessary for price discrimination and some examples

Two conditions are necessary for profitable price discrimination:

1. *There must be two or more segments of the overall market that have differences in elasticity of demand at nondiscriminatory prices.*
2. *The seller must be able to prevent arbitrage*—third-party buying in cheap segments and reselling in dear markets—which drives down the price differentials and deprives the seller of the benefits of price discrimination.

How is segmentation of markets maintained? Many methods are used.

1. Railroads can charge more for high-value commodities than for those with low value per unit of volume or weight. A simple inspection of commodities insures that they do not travel at the wrong rate. Airlines charge more for first class than for tourist seats, assigning seats to prevent leakage between the markets.

2. Manufacturers and service companies frequently offer quantity discounts, thus separating large purchasers from small ones. The discounts may exceed the cost differences, favoring the larger purchasers, or they may be less than the corresponding cost differences, with advantages to smaller buyers. Rental charges on office copiers increase with copies made, and incremental charges more than offset increases in maintenance and depreciation costs. On the other hand, many quantity discounts do reflect greater bargaining power of larger buyers.

3. Many sellers charge the same delivered prices even though transportation costs vary from customer to customer according to distances from plant sites. Steel and cement are sold in this manner, as are many consumer products that have nationally advertised prices.

4. Some firms sell approximately the same product under different brand names at widely differing prices. Consumer ignorance of the similarity in quality prevents large-scale transfers of customers from one brand to another. Examples of this form of price discrimination include auto tires, paint, clothing, and many food products.

5. Some producers charge different prices for the same item moving through different trade channels. For example, they may charge more in the replacement market than in the original-equipment market. Replacement demand is likely to be less elastic. Repair parts for automobiles and household appliances are examples.

6. Firms sometimes sell abroad at prices lower than domestic prices, a practice known as "dumping." Tariffs and cost of shipping the product back to the exporting country help maintain segmentation of the market.

7. Special "introductory prices" below those charged to regular customers may be offered to new customers. Record and book clubs use this method, as do many magazine publishers.

8. Theaters usually charge children lower prices even though they occupy just as much space as adults and may actually be somewhat more costly in wear and tear. In most cases it is easy to determine the age category of the customer, but some leakage seems likely on children at ages close to the dividing line.

9. One simple way of segmenting customers, with some leakage, is to offer the product or service at a regular price for most of the year and then reduce the price at times of special sales. Some customers are not patient enough or price conscious enough to wait for the sales; others are bargain hunters and will wait. Such a policy makes it possible to tap both kinds of market. Magnavox has used this method in sales of television receivers, and it is used by the publisher of World Book Encyclopedia.

Personal, or first-degree, discrimination

In one form of price discrimination, the object is to *extract the highest possible price from each individual buyer.* Two examples of personal, or *first-degree,* price discrimination are given below.

1. Charges for some personal services may be adjusted in line with incomes or wealth of purchasers. Medical care, legal advice, architectural and landscaping services, and interior decorating can be priced in this way. The fact that the product is a direct personal service prevents its resale.

2. Some products are sold by bargaining, or haggling every sale. New and used autos, recreational vehicles, pleasure boats, personal aircraft, antiques, and objects of art are often sold in this manner.

Social and legal issues

Price discrimination's social effects are not necessarily harmful. The practice may be beneficial. Although it raises prices to some buyers, it lowers them to others. When price differentiation is used in monopolistically competitive industries and differentiated oligopolies, the *long-run* effect is to increase total output and, if envelope curves are L shaped, to reduce *average* prices as capacity is increased by entry and expansion. On the other hand, price differentiation by a pure monopolist may increase profits that would be excessive even under ordinary pricing. Of course, many pure monopolies are regulated so that average prices are held close to average cost; in such cases, price discrimination allows greater total output and lower *average* prices if the monopoly has decreasing average costs. To sum up, price discrimination may be socially beneficial (on balance, the gains to some outweighing the losses to others), provided it is carried out by regulated monopolies or by firms in monopolistically competitive industries where profits are held in check by entry and expansion.

It is not always possible to determine whether observed price differences are explained by price discrimination. The first difficulty is in determining whether two or more products are really differentiated versions of the same product or, instead, two different products on which price comparisons are inappropriate. A second difficulty is in measuring marginal costs of the various products, which requires some way of dealing with common costs.

The legal status of differential pricing is uncertain. This book avoids the legal intricacies of antitrust and price discrimination legislation and rulings. *In general, the Federal Trade Commission and the courts have permitted price differentials that reflect differences in cost;* our earlier discussion of costs should explain why this criterion has been so troublesome in such cases. The courts tend to rely on average costs rather than marginal costs in measuring cost differentials, with consequent difficulties in the treatment of overhead. The courts have upheld quantity discounts that could be justified in terms of cost differentials. But the courts have ruled against quantity discounts that may injure or suppress competition. *A major criterion of illegality is injury to competitors.*

The position of managers in this area of differential pricing is a complex one. On one hand they are challenged to use imagination in finding more profitable ways of adjusting prices to market conditions. But they may be concerned with their obligations to the public and with avoidance of price differentials that might be considered unfair or harmful to competition. In addition, managers must consider the legal consequences of their pricing behavior, with the possibility, in view of the complexity of the problem, that their ideas of equity may not always conform to those of the Federal Trade Commission or the courts.

Empirical studies and illustrations

Many illustrations of price discrimination could be presented, for it is a widespread practice. To save space, it seems appropriate to restrict attention to price discrimination in the public utilities. The utilities usually sell services that cannot be economically resold by the buyers, and thus they are particularly likely to use price discrimination.

Water supply. An outstanding study of water supply indicates that price discrimination is widely practiced by municipal water companies, both public and private.[2] In New York City some users are unmetered, which means that they pay a flat rate with no extra charge for the heavy use of water. Obviously there is discrimination between such users and those who pay according to volume of consumption. This discrimination encourages the waste of water. In Los Angeles, on the other hand, lower rates are charged for irrigation water than for water in urban use, and the rate differentials are clearly not in proportion to the marginal costs. The result is a subsidy to farm production.

Some of the water rate differentials are in line with cost differences and thus are not discriminatory in the strict definition of price discrimination. For example, most systems charge less per unit for greater volumes, a fact that may reflect the lower cost of delivering and metering the increments in volume. In Los Angeles (and many other cities) a rate differential exists between noninterruptible service and service that the water department may curtail at its convenience. Since the cost of water delivered at peak periods is greater than that delivered at other times, this differential is not necessarily discriminatory—it is a way of charging for the extra load that peak users place on the system.

Gas and electricity. Gas and electricity rates of the Consolidated Gas Electric Light and Power Company of Baltimore have been studied by Davidson.[3] Rate schedules of the Baltimore company are probably representative of those in the gas and electricity industries in general. They incorporate several kinds of price discrimination, all with the approval of the regulatory agencies. One kind of discrimination is called "peak–off-

---

[2] J. Hirshleifer, J. C. DeHaven, and J. W. Milliman, *Water Supply: Economics, Technology and Policy* (Chicago: University of Chicago Press, 1960).

[3] See R. K. Davidson, *Price Discrimination in Selling Gas and Electricity* (Baltimore: The Johns Hopkins Press, 1955), especially chap. 11.

peak discrimination," which involves a failure to relate rates to the differentials in costs between peak and off-peak periods. The simplest form of such discrimination is the charging of the same rate in both peak and off-peak periods. Even when higher rates are charged to peak energy users, the methods of allocating costs often fail to apply as high a proportion of capacity costs to the peak periods as is warranted, resulting in a subsidy of peak production by off-peak sales.

PEAK-LOAD PRICING

The electricity power industry provides one example of a peak-load problem. If electric service is offered at constant prices, hourly sales quantities vary during the day and over seasons of the year due to changes in demand. Electricity cannot be stored economically in significant quantities, and the production-transmission-distribution system fails under sustained overload. Thus, peak hourly sales quantity, or peak load, determines necessary capacity of the system. Figure 12–2 shows an actual hourly load curve for one utility on the date it reached peak load for the particular year.

If the sales peak is high and narrow, capacity adequate to handle peak load may be substantially greater than that needed most of the time. By increasing prices in peak periods, sales quantities (and necessary capacity) can be reduced; at the same time, quantities in off-peak periods can be increased through shifting of demand. *The problem in peak-load pricing is to determine, simultaneously, the best prices in both peak and off-peak periods and "best" capacity.* Similar problems are found in distribution of gas and water and provision of telephone services.

Some general principles

It may be best to confine our attention to electricity for the time being. The electric utilities must have the capacity to meet peak loads. The question is whether they should vary rates from peak to off-peak periods. The answer of almost all economists who have studied the question is that they should charge higher rates at the peaks, since cost of producing for the peak includes cost of some capacity used only during the peak and is clearly greater than the cost for other periods. *Failure to charge higher rates in peak periods causes peak consumption to be higher than it would be otherwise, and the utility must construct extra capacity to meet the peak; cost of extra capacity is then subsidized by necessarily higher rates for off-peak use.* Or, in the absence of such capacity, the utility must engage in "load shedding" (cutting off the electricity supply of some customers), a practice which is arbitrary and inefficient.

Figure 12–2
Load curve for December 19, 1963

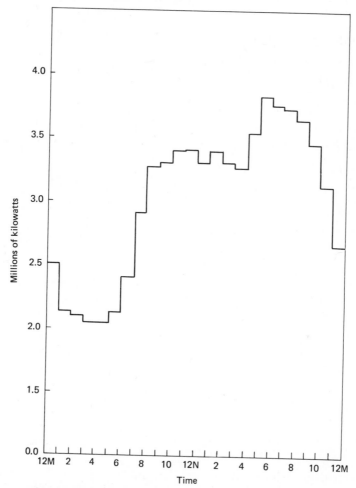

Source: Donald N. DeSalvia, "An Application of Peak Load Pricing," *Journal of Business* (October 1969), p. 460.

Economists who have written on peak-load pricing are in agreement on the following two propositions:

1. Peak prices should be higher than off-peak prices for two purposes: (a) to allocate the limited capacity available at the peaks to those who are willing to pay most for it, and (b) to help cover cost of providing additional capacity required to meet that peak consumption which remains at the higher prices.

2. The only relevant costs in determination of both peak and off-peak

prices are the marginal costs. (Unfortunately, some difference of opinion remains on how to measure the marginal costs.)

A graphic solution: Firm peaks

Economists have developed what appears to be a logical solution to peak-load pricing.[4] *The solution is to equate each period price with its marginal cost.* Figure 12–3 shows the solution for both peak and off-peak periods. This solution is based on an assumption of constant marginal cost. Although a solution for the more realistic case of increasing marginal cost is more complex, it is developed according to the same principles.

Figure 12–3
Long-run peak and off-peak pricing: The firm peak case

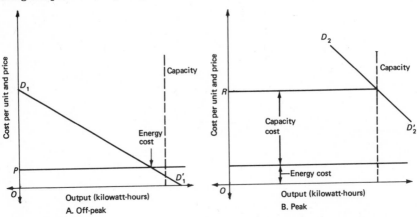

Assume for purposes of simplicity that for half of each day demand is constant at D_1D_1' and the other half constant at D_2D_2'. The kilowatt-hour charge in the low-demand period should include only the energy cost, since there is no need to add to capacity for this period. The kilowatt-hour charge in the high-demand period is equal to the energy cost plus the capacity cost. Capacity cost per kilowatt-hour is total capacity cost per day divided by total kilowatt-hours sold during the peak period. *The capacity cost per kilowatt-hour is part of the marginal cost in the peak period, since capacity must be added to meet this demand.*

The above solution might be called the *long-run* equilibrium solution in which the capacity has already been adjusted to the level of demand. At first, capacity may be short or in excess of this equilibrium, so that

[4] The following discussion is based primarily on P. O. Steiner's "Peak Loads and Efficient Pricing," *Quarterly Journal of Economics* (November 1957), pp. 585–610, and J. Hirshleifer's "Comment" in August 1958 issue of the same journal, pp. 451–62.

Figure 12-4
Short-run peak-load pricing: The firm peak case

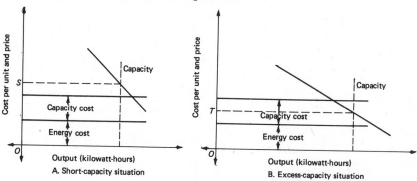

A. Short-capacity situation

B. Excess-capacity situation

the rule must be restated: In the *short-run* the price at the peak should be such as to equate sales quantity with the capacity which is available. If capacity is *in short supply* the price should be set at a level higher than the sum of the per kilowatt-hour capacity and energy costs, to discourage consumption by those who place low marginal values on electricity and to allocate the supply to those with high marginal values. Figure 12-4A illustrates that OS is the appropriate price. In an excess capacity situation the price should be at OT, as shown in Figure 12-4B.

The short-run prices for the peak period are not based on full cost, but they allocate available capacity efficiently. In the first case the utility should add capacity. In the second case it should fail to replace capacity as it wears out. In both cases it should set the rate on off-peak consumption to cover only the energy cost. In the long run, after capacity adjustment, pricing at marginal cost in both periods can be such that it just covers full cost.

A more complete discussion would consider the possibility (some economists would say the inevitability) of curvilinear costs, with rising marginal costs. For such a discussion the reader should refer to Hirshleifer's article.[5]

A graphic solution: Shifting peaks

Increases in peak-period prices flatten the peak and may shift some sales to adjacent periods. Sales in other periods may then equal or even exceed those at the peak. In this case it is necessary to plot both demand curves (the high demand and low demand) on the same graph. Figure 12-5 illustrates. This time we add the two demands vertically to get D_c. *This combined demand curve provides estimates of how much buyers*

---

[5] Hirshleifer, "Comment," p. 455.

Figure 12–5
Peak and off-peak pricing: The shifting peak case

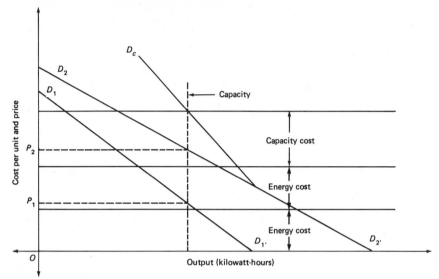

will pay for one unit of off-peak energy plus one unit of peak energy. The utility should expand capacity to the point at which D_c intersects the sum of the capacity cost (as defined in the preceding section) plus twice the energy cost. At this point the prices will cover marginal cost of energy plus marginal capacity cost (the capacity will be fully used in both periods. The prices OP_1 and OP_2 are again set to "clear the market" (use up the capacity). The result is that the capacity is fully utilized in both periods.

This analysis can be generalized to more than two periods and to periods which are unequal in length. The theoretical literature on peak-load pricing has also been extended to cover a wider range of considerations, such as indivisibilities in production and differences in plant costs.[6]

Some practical problems

A number of obstacles stand in the way of actual application of the preceding analysis.

1. Demands in different periods cannot be predicted accurately.

2. Measurement of the marginal energy and capacity costs is no simple problem. Marginal costs of generation are increasing with level of output in a typical power system, due to differences in ages, locations, and

---

[6] O. E. Williamson, "Peak Load Pricing and Optimal Capacity under Indivisibility Constraints," *American Economic Review* (September 1966), pp. 810–27; and M. A. Crews' "Comment" in the March 1968 issue of the same journal, pp. 168–70.

Figure 12–6
Cumulative capacity in order of incremental fuel cost

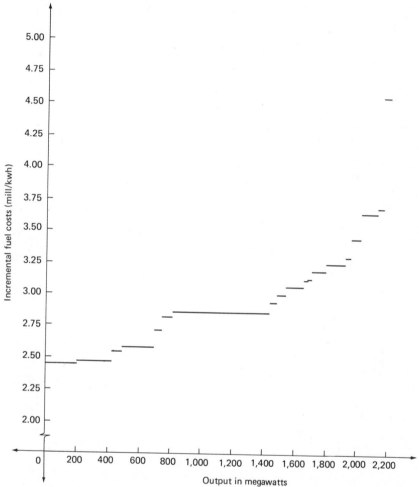

Source: Donald N. DeSalvia, "An Application of Peak-Load Pricing," *Journal of Business* (October 1969).

types of power plants. Figure 12–6 shows DeSalvia's estimates of the relationship of marginal costs to cumulative output of an actual system in 1963.[7] In this figure, the most efficient generation is used first, then the next most efficient, and so on. Off-peak rates equal to marginal or energy costs that increase with cumulative output would make some contribution toward capacity cost, since these rates would exceed energy costs of the most efficient sources.

---

[7] DeSalvia, "An Application of Peak Load Pricing," p. 467.

3. The proposed scheme involves flexible prices over time. This results from the necessity of using trial and error in searching for appropriate prices and from shifts in demand that cannot be exactly matched at all times by shifts in capacity. This poses serious problems for the administration of rate changes—problems that are compounded by the requirement of approval of changes by regulatory commissions. Turvey describes a controlled experiment in England and Wales to determine the effects upon consumption of electricity rate schedules containing peak-load pricing features. The experiment tested three different schedules, using three experimental groups of 890 customers each and a control group of 900 customers, and extended over a five-year period ending in winter, 1971–72.[8]

4. The public would probably react unfavorably to prices which *seem* discriminatory even though they may not be. For example, the public is not likely to understand that high rates for cooking Thanksgiving turkeys are conducive to general welfare.

5. The public would probably also react unfavorably to the instability of prices which the pricing scheme, in an extreme form, would require. They would prefer to know in advance the rates they will pay rather than be subject to sharp shifts in such rates.

6. Some electric companies find that seasonal peaks are more difficult to handle than daily peaks because there is little opportunity to shift demand to a seasonally off-peak period.

The utility managers and public service commissioners are in a difficult position in the sphere of peak-load pricing. If they heed the advice of economists on marginal-cost pricing, they run the risk of public misunderstanding and charges of "unfair" pricing. Furthermore, the construction of rate schedules which meet the theoretical criteria for optimization is no easy task. But if they base their prices on full costs and try to average out rates over peaks and troughs in consumption, they are responsible for a waste of resources. By pricing peak-load consumption at its real cost and thereby deferring some capacity growth, they could reduce resource requirements (primarily investment) by substantial amounts.

Nonprice techniques for improving load factors

The use of pricing for the improvement of utility load factors has been shown to be complex and easily misunderstood. As a result, many companies have shown a preference for marketing and other nonprice techniques which accomplish the same purpose. These consist of increased advertising in off-peak periods and the development of new markets or new products to use facilities in off-peak periods. Electric utilities have engaged in promoting the use of appliances which consume energy in

---

[8] Ralph Turvey, "Peak Load Pricing," *Journal of Political Economy* 76 (February 1968), pp. 101–13.

off-peak periods or at least have a more stable demand. Gas companies have promoted gas-burning air conditioners.

These nonprice devices have the advantage of flexibility. Customers resent frequent changes of price but are tolerant of varying promotional activity. When advertising pushes consumption toward capacity it is easy to diminish the effort, but it is not so easy to take away a low price which has been used to promote a particular type of consumption.

Empirical studies and illustrations

Some public utilities and regulatory commissions have experimented with peak-load pricing over the years. The electric utilities used a peak-responsibility method of pricing in the early 1900s but abandoned it because of difficulties in allocating costs, in predicting when the peaks would come, and in dealing with shifts of sales to off-peak periods which created new peaks.[9] As might be expected from the intricacies of the problem, even the theoretical solution was not understood. It is no wonder that the utilities found it difficult to apply the theory in practice. Nevertheless, the electric utilities have continued to experiment with methods which at least were moving in the right direction. Many electric companies now use rate structure in which rates are higher during the peak season (typically, summer, because of air-conditioning loads).

The gas industry has long charged lower rates to interruptible customers (ones whose consumption can be cut off on short notice when capacity is reached). Other examples of attempts to ease the peak-load problem through pricing are the low early morning fares of the British Railways (the fare for arrival in London before 8:00 A.M. is almost 50 percent below the regular fare) and the persistent experimentation of the airlines with off-season rates. An even more familiar example is the lower prices of motion pictures before 5:00 or 6.00 P.M.

Pricing is, of course, not the only way of dealing with the problem. The use of advertising and other promotional activities to improve load factors is illustrated in many industries. Florida hotels have made a great effort to stimulate occupancy in the off-season period. European countries have advertised the great advantages of travel in the spring and autumn when the tourists are not so much in each other's way. Some universities advertise the advantages of their summer climates in the effort to obtain greater use of their facilities in their off-peak periods.

Peak-load pricing in American utilities

Shepherd surveyed peak-load pricing in American utilities.[10] He reviewed rate schedules of 111 large private and 11 large public systems

---

[9] Davidson, *Price Discrimination in Selling Gas and Electricity,* p. 119.

[10] William G. Shepherd, "Marginal-Cost Pricing in American Utilities," *Southern Economic Journal* 33 (July 1966), pp. 58–70.

accounting altogether for over 85 percent of sales to final consumers in
1963. No true peak-load pricing was found. However, major provisions
favoring off-peak usage were in the schedules of 46 large systems that
had 41.8 percent of total sales in this group (about 35 percent of total
sales in the nation).

Shepherd also surveyed business "message rate" pricing by telephone
systems. Local telephone service usually has a broad daily peak during
office hours. Therefore, office-hour calls are responsible for a large share
of telephone switching capacity. Message rate pricing for business telephones, with a charge for each call in excess of some base, is a step in
the direction of peak-load pricing. All of the largest 8 cities (by population) and 15 of the largest 25 had message rates required for business.
The 8 cities included 25 percent, and the 15 cities included 33 percent,
of all telephones in the United States. Shepherd concludes that some
electric systems and some telephone systems make extensive use of
marginalist pricing, approaching true peak-load pricing, and that much
of the measuring apparatus needed for peak-load pricing is readily available. Institutional and technical barriers can be overcome if utilities
managements and regulatory commissions want to realize the resource
savings of peak-load pricing, and these could be substantial.[11]

PUBLIC UTILITY RATE REGULATION

Pricing (rate making) in the public utilities presents a special problem
in economic analysis. The utilities—electricity, gas, water, telephones,
and public transportation—are "natural monopolies"; in any one locality
a single firm tends to drive out competing firms. These are industries in
which technology of production and distribution results in substantial
economies of scale, which means that one large firm can produce more
economically than can several firms.[12] Legislatures have recognized these
economies of scale and tendencies to monopoly by granting franchises
protecting utility companies from competition and then subjecting them
to rate control by regulatory commissions.

Basic pricing

Three alternative policies for pricing in the public utilities are possible: monopoly pricing, full-cost pricing, and marginal cost pricing. All
are illustrated in Figure 12–7, which depicts a decreasing-cost firm. Price

---

[11] Ibid.

[12] It might seem that the telephone industry is an exception; a telephone company is subject to increasing costs per customer as it expands the number of customers in a given local service area. But if one were to measure cost per callable
number, such increasing costs would no longer appear. In any case, there are obvious
advantages in having a single telephone company in any single locality.

Figure 12–7
Alternative levels of public utility rates

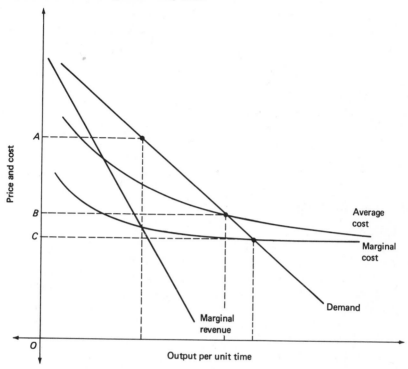

OA is the monopoly price—the price which maximizes profit. Almost all observers agree that this price is intolerable to the public. It provides a monopoly profit to firms at the expense of consumers. It results in a misallocation of resources, since the value to consumers of additional output would exceed the value of resources such additional output would use up.

Price OB is the price sought in the usual utility regulation. It is based on full cost—it covers fixed as well as variable costs and includes a normal return on investment. Price *OB* is set to provide a "fair rate of return" on the investment in the utility. The history of rate regulation is a history of controversy over what rates of returns are fair and conducive to the growth and financial strength of the utilities. It is also a history of controversy over the "rate base"—the value of the property on which the rate of return should be allowed. In periods of inflation the utilities have a strong preference for valuation at reproduction cost. They argue that the original costs, or "book costs," do not reflect the true value of the property and that returns on property valued at such costs are confiscatory. Some regulatory commissions, on the other hand, favor original cost, or a variation of original cost known as "prudent investment," not only because this practice holds down utility rates but also because original cost is easier to determine objectively. Considerable litigation often results from estimates of reproduction cost; accounting conventions reduce the amount of litigation that is possible over original cost.

The issue of original cost, reproduction cost, or other variations, such as "fair value," is still unsettled. The state regulatory commissions have not standardized their practices in establishing the rate bases; a full discussion of this issue must be left to books on public utility economics. It is necessary to note, however, that the exact level of OB, the price at full cost, depends somewhat on the particular regulatory agency which has jurisdiction over the utility.

Marginal cost pricing

Price OC in Figure 12–7 is the price at marginal cost. Much of the literature on welfare economics expresses a preference for this price. The discussion of marginal cost pricing tends to become rather involved, but the argument can be summarized in nontechnical language. It is claimed that the welfare of society is increased if the price is lowered below OB (because the value of the added service exceeds the marginal cost of added output); the recommended price is OC, the point at which the demand curve intersects the marginal cost curve. *At* OC *the value to the marginal user (measured by the price he pays for the last unit, which is also the price he pays for all units) is equal to the value of the resources used up to produce the last unit.* Any higher price and lower consumption, it is argued, means a failure to maximize welfare.

Price OC *has the disadvantage that it does not cover total costs in a decreasing cost firm.* The economists who favor marginal cost pricing recommend that the government pay a subsidy to the utility so that it can cover all costs. Some of them even recommend public ownership on the grounds that the government is not required to cover all costs out of revenues.

If the utility is subject to increasing costs, as may be true of the telephone companies, marginal cost pricing may result in prices which exceed total costs. This result is shown in Figure 12–8. The firm earns excess profits in this case, but not as high as the profits that would be possible without regulation. Special taxes could siphon off a large part of the excess profit.

Marginal cost pricing is objectionable on several grounds. Subsidies mean the loss of the control advantages of rules that revenues must cover costs. Utilities may be distracted from their main business if they have to contend with political agencies for subsidies. Their profits may depend more upon their success in demonstrating the need for subsidies

Figure 12–8
Marginal cost pricing in an increasing-cost industry

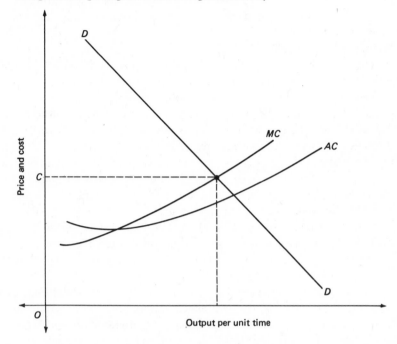

than in controlling costs. A subsidy is often a reasonable method for attaining certain social objectives, but the use of subsidies in the utilities should not be undertaken lightly. It is interesting that most nationalized utilities maintain the rule that revenues must cover costs. Apparently most governments are unwilling to abandon the control advantages of requiring that costs be covered.[13]

Empirical studies and illustrations

The issue of marginal cost pricing has received considerable attention in the electric utilities. Few utilities apply marginal cost pricing on an overall basis, though some of them may approach marginal costs in pricing some special services. The low electricity rates of the Tennessee Valley Authority might be rationalized as moving toward marginal cost pricing, though it does not appear that the literature on the subject was a great influence on TVA rate making. The TVA's low rates result in

---

[13] Nationalized utilities are often subsidized in subtle ways, through reduced taxes or lower interest rates. And some utilities, such as the British Railways, operate with large deficits not as a matter of policy but because they have not been able to bring costs and revenues in line.

large part from such subsidies as low tax rates (the payments in lieu of taxes made to local and state governments are far below the rates private utilities would be required to pay) and low interest rates on funds owed the federal government.

A survey of electricity pricing in Europe suggests that true marginal cost pricing is not widely used there.[14] France and Sweden are the leaders in attention to marginal cost pricing. The Électricité de France, a nationalized concern, has been a pioneer in this respect, though it has used marginal costs more in determining particular prices than in determining the general level of rates. It has even revised particular rates when there is a "deficit between income and expenditures." This suggests that the movement toward marginal cost pricing has been quite cautious. Sweden apparently is more willing to apply the marginal cost principle when marginal cost is above average cost than in the opposite case. In explanation of this position, it is stated that it may be true, theoretically, that electricity rates ought to correspond to marginal costs even when these are lower than average costs. But if this were applied in practice, the losses incurred would have to be borne by some agency other than the electricity undertakings, e.g., the state.[15]

In other countries covered by the survey—Austria, Belgium, Italy, Norway, the Netherlands, the United Kingdom, and Switzerland—average cost pricing (full-cost pricing) appears to predominate, modified by examples of price discrimination in favor of special segments of the market.

Turning now to the United States, all the regulatory agencies, federal and state, follow a full-cost rule for overall pricing. The objective in rate regulation is to allow revenues that will cover all expenses, including depreciation, and leave a fair return on investment. The regulatory agencies vary, however, in the rates of return they allow and in determination of the rate base.

American regulatory commissions consider four major criteria in determining the fair return.[16] The first is the *capital-attraction* criterion. Most commissions are concerned with allowing returns which permit the utilities to attract capital for needed expensions and which contribute to the financial soundness of those utilities. Another criterion is that of *efficiency of management.* Some commissions make it a policy to approve higher returns to utilities which demonstrate outstanding performance in controlling costs and improving services. Such a policy should stimu-

[14] *The Theory of Marginal Cost and Electricity Rates* (Paris: Organisation for European Economics Co-operation, 1958).

[15] Ibid., p. 76.

[16] This discussion is based on J. C. Bonbright, *Principles of Public Utility Rates* (New York: Columbia University Press, 1961).

late greater managerial efficiency. A third criterion is that of *stable rates.* Commissions prefer not to revise rates with each change in demand and costs, on the grounds that constant changes would be inconvenient to both customers and management. The last criterion is that of *fairness to rate payers and investors.* This criterion is perhaps the most nebulous and most difficult to apply in practice. Commissions are not in agreement, for example, on the extent to which public utilities should take part in the general increase in profits earned in competitive industries in periods of inflation. Some of them are quite restrictive in this respect, on the grounds that the owners of the utilities have, like the purchasers of bonds, taken the risk that their earnings might not keep up with prices. Questions of fairness will continue to lead to controversy and litigation in public utility regulation.

Over the history of American public utility regulation, determination of the rate base has been even a greater source of litigation than has determination of the fair rate of return. The problem becomes especially acute in periods of inflation, in which book values (original costs) are below reproduction or replacement costs. The Federal Power Commission and most of the state commissions stress an original cost or prudent investment rate base and give little regard to increasing replacement costs until the utilities actually purchase a new plant at the higher costs. Their preference for original cost is based on administrative convenience. Original costs are readily determined from the accounts and make possible the rapid disposition of rate cases with reduced expenses and more precise results. The supporters of original cost claim that it reduces the costs of regulation and litigation. Another argument for original cost is that it reduces uncertainty and thus is more conducive to credit maintenance.

An important minority of Americans regulatory commissions lean toward what is known as the "fair value" rate base. The definition of "fair value" is rather difficult, in view of the long history of controversy over it since 1898 when the Supreme Court in *Smyth* v. *Ames* made it the law of the land.[17] (The Hope Natural Gas Case[18] of 1944 ended the supremacy of the "fair value" rule and left it to the individual jurisdictions to determine their own principles of rate base valuation.) In general, the fair value rate base is a compromise, incorporating both original cost and reproduction cost and still other considerations. In actual practice, however, some of the commissions which are bound by fair value statutes devote primary attention to original cost, with minor deviations to take other factors into acount.

[17] *Smyth* v. *Ames,* 169 U.S. 468 (1898).

[18] *Federal Power Commission* v. *Hope Natural Gas Company,* 320 U.S. 591 (1944).

According to Bonbright, when it comes to actual practice, *all* of the commissions use versions of original cost, with minor deviations.[19] He claims that the important differences in regulation lie more in different degrees of liberality in rates of return than in determinations of the rate base. This conclusion suggests that regulation should concentrate on the determination of rates of return most appropriate for the growth and financial strength of the utilities and most conducive to the public interest, with a diminished attention to controversies over the valuation of the property. Nevertheless, some authorities would dissent and would argue for a valuation of property more in line with reproduction cost. It may at some time be possible to find an objective technique for determining reproduction cost which will reduce the costs of litigation and delay in administering rate changes.

MULTIPLE-PRODUCT PRICING

Multiple-product price and output determination must cope with product interdependency in production. Interdependency can take the form of joint products, in which one product cannot be produced without the other. Or it can take the form of alternative products, in which output of one product must be decreased to obtain increases in output of another, in the short run.

Joint products in fixed proportions

Figure 12–9 illustrates pricing and output determination for joint products produced in fixed proportions. Only one marginal cost curve is shown, since the costs of the products are indivisible. Two demand curves are shown, one for each of the two products. MR_1 indicates the marginal revenue derived from sales of the first product. MR_2 shows the marginal revenue for the second product. MR_{1+2} is the *vertical* sum of MR_1 and MR_2. The difference between Figures 12–9 and 12–1 (which illustrated price discrimination) is that the marginal revenues are summed vertically rather than horizontally. The reason for this is that *an increase of one unit on the horizontal scale means an increase in units of a package consisting of quantities of each product.* (This package is one unit of product plus some amount of the other product; thus, the quantity axis of Figure 12–9 is denominated in units of the first product. The demand and marginal revenue curves for the other product must be appropriately transformed.) For example, if the horizontal axis measures sides of beef, and D_1 is the demand for sides of beef and D_2 is the demand for whole hides, each one unit of sides (q_1) equals one-half unit of whole hides (q_2). Added revenues results from both products and it is the sum of the

[19] Bonbright, *Principles of Public Utility Rates*, p. 283.

Figure 12–9
Maximization of profits—two joint products

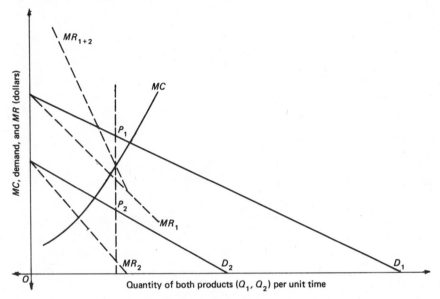

revenues that should be compared with marginal costs. The optimum
is at the point of intersection between marginal cost and the *aggregate*
marginal revenue curve. P_1 and P_2 represent the most profitable prices
for the two commodities.[20]

Figure 12–10 represents a slight alteration in the situation. Here MR_2
becomes negative before MR_{1+2} reaches the marginal cost curve. The
firm will not maximize profits if it keeps on reducing the price on
Product 2 to get rid of it; the negative marginal revenue means a loss
in total revenue. Product 2 will be sold up to the point at which its
marginal revenue is zero, with P_2 the appropriate price. But it is profitable to produce more packages, until MR_1 equals the marginal cost. The
excess units of Product 2 will be destroyed, since their appearance on the
market will depress prices.

Other variations in the situation may be worked out by the reader.
These could include a case in which one of the products is sold in a purely
competitive market or one in which both are sold in such a market. Another interesting variation is the case in which there is a cost of destruction.

---

[20] For a fuller analysis, see M. R. Colberg, "Monopoly Prices under Joint Costs:
Fixed Proportions," *Journal of Political Economy* (February 1941), p. 109. Also see
M. R. Colberg, W. C. Bradford, and R. M. Alt, *Business Economics: Principles and
Cases,* rev. ed. (Homewood, Ill.: Richard D. Irwin, Inc., 1957), pp. 299–302.

Figure 12–10
Maximization of profits—joint products with destruction of part of one product

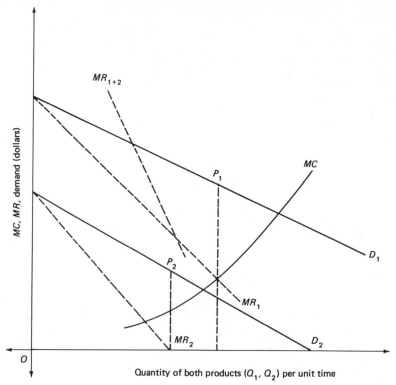

Quantity of both products (Q_1, Q_2) per unit time

Alternative products

Figure 12–11 illustrates output and price determination for alternative products.[21] Both of these products require services of some facility that will be fully utilized. Therefore, output of any one product can be increased only by cutting back output of the other product.

The quantity axis in Figure 12–11 measures total use of the facility, i.e., hours per week. The demand and marginal revenue curves for the several products have been restated in terms of equivalent demand and marginal revenue product curves for hours of facility use per week. The marginal cost curve in Figure 12–11 assumes that variable cost depends only on hours of plant operation and does not change as the plant is switched from product to product. The firm maximizes profit if it selects a product mix such that the marginal revenues (per unit of facility use) are equal across the various products and are also equal to marginal

---

[21] This discussion of multiple-product pricing is adapted from Eli W. Clemens, "Price Discrimination and the Multiple-Product Firm," *Review of Economic Studies* 19 (1950–51), pp. 1–11.

Figure 12–11
Maximization of profit—alternative products

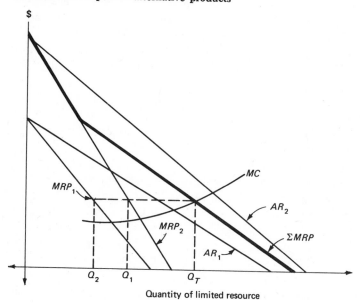

Quantity of limited resource

cost (per unit of facility use) at total output. Amounts of facility use for various products can be converted into equivalent outputs and market prices for the products.

The above analysis can be extended to cases in which variable costs differ from product to product (demands must be net of product-specific variable costs), in which marginal cost is constant up to some limit of plant use (in this latter case, marginal "rents"—the differences between marginal revenues and marginal costs—are equated), and to a special case in which there is excess (economically redundant) plant capacity.

Empirical examples

Decisions on multiple products are relatively unsophisticated in most firms. The construction of models which reflect the important interrelationships is a difficult and costly task. Therefore, most managers rely mainly on experience and trial and error. We would expect that such a rough-and-ready approach will often provide approximations to the theoretical optima.

The classic example of joint costs is that of meat production. The meat packer sells products to both the food chains and the leather tanners. Prices are governed by demand and not by individual product costs. The objective is to set prices at levels that will clear the market for both meat and hides. Output will be at levels that will equate the marginal revenue from both meat and hides to the marginal cost of producing both.

The grocery, in turn, must determine what price to charge for the different cuts of meat it obtains from the carcass. As Holdren states, "the elasticity of demand rather than carcass cost dominates the determination of the relative prices of different cuts of meat.[22] In all of the stores hamburger and chuck roast were sold below the average cost of the carcass. He found that as beef prices rose, the range of prices on different cuts narrowed, with the customer substituting cheaper cuts for more expensive ones. Such substitution relations in demand complicate the determination of the most profitable prices.

Holdren found that the individual store managers tended to keep their prices on chuck, hamburger, and round steak competitive with prices in other stores. They followed the "get rid of" principle in pricing the other cuts. They bought enough carcasses to fill the demand for round steak and chuck roast and altered the prices of other cuts (except hamburger) until the market was cleared. In other words, the stores did not use anything approaching a mathematical model reflecting the demand and cost conditions. They instead followed a series of decision-making rules: Imitate the price of other stores on some cuts; purchase quantities according to the demand for those cuts at the imitative prices; and price the other cuts to get rid of the quantity which results from the previous rules. These rules are rather uninformative on how the prices that are imitated are themselves established, a question which cannot be answered by studying one or a few stores at a time.

TRANSER PRICING

Large, multiple-product, multiple-plant companies develop complex patterns of intracompany transfers of goods. For example, an integrated international petroleum company acquires vast amounts of crude oil from hundreds of sources, allocates the heterogeneous raw material to dozens of refineries that produce industrial goods and consumer products in varying proportions, and routes output through complex marketing channels that include thousands of retail outlets. In any week, a great many decisions must be made within such a firm. These include level of output, product mix, input combinations, pricing, scheduling, routing, and inventory accumulation and depletion; and they must be made at many plants and for many products.

A huge firm such as the one described above must be organized into numerous divisions that are allowed considerable autonomy in day-to-

---

[22] Bob R. Holdren, *The Structure of a Retail Market and the Market Behavior of Retail Units* (Englewood Cliffs, N.J.: Prentice-Hall, Inc., 1960), pp. 121–22.

day decision making. The divisions transfer goods among themselves. The prices at which these goods are transferred affect divisional decision making, and wrong decisions (relative to overall company objectives) can be expected if transfer prices understate or overstate values and costs.

For purposes of decision making, intracompany transfers should be priced at marginal cost. Of course, marginal cost is the market price (opportunity cost) if there is an external market for the good. Otherwise, it is explicit marginal cost as determined within the supplying division.

The simplest case: A specialized intermediate product with excess capacity in the supplying department

Let us consider a hypothetical company with two departments—a supplying department and a using department. The letter S will represent the supplying department and U the using department. P_s will represent the price charged by the supplying department—this is the transfer price. P_u will represent the final price charged by the using department to outside purchasers. In the present example we assume *excess capacity* in S, the supplying department; that is, S can meet all the needs of U for the intermediate product.

This simplest case of transfer pricing requires an additional assumption. The intermediate product is specialized and is used only within the company. All of it is transferred to the using department. None of it is sold on the outside. Another way of stating this assumption is that *no market for the intermediate product exists.*

Under these assumptions, the solution for the transfer price is clear. It is the marginal cost (unit incremental cost) in the supplying department:

$$P_s = MC_s$$

in which MC_s is marginal cost in the supplying department.

This transfer price will motivate the using department to order as many units as it can use and still make a contribution to overhead and profit on each unit, including the last (marginal) unit. *Reminder:* In Chapter 6, it was shown that a variable input should be used up to the point where the marginal revenue product of the input is equal to its marginal supply cost.

Let us consider a hypothetical example. The supplying department, S, produces at a constant marginal cost of $10:

$$MC_s = \$10$$

The using department, U, can produce five different products, each of which makes use of one unit of the same intermediate product. The five products sell at five different prices and incur different marginal costs within the using department, over and above the cost of the intermediate good.

$$P_{u1} = \$25.00 \quad MC_{u1} = \$\ 7.00$$
$$P_{u2} = \$24.00 \quad MC_{u2} = \$\ 7.50$$
$$P_{u3} = \$23.00 \quad MC_{u3} = \$\ 7.50$$
$$P_{u4} = \$22.00 \quad MC_{u4} = \$10.00$$
$$P_{u5} = \$21.00 \quad MC_{u5} = \$13.00$$

It is clear that the company is adding to its profits as long as the final prices exceed the sum of the marginal costs in the using and supplying departments. This is true of the first four products.

$$P_{u1} > MC_{u1} + MC_s \quad \$25.00 > \$\ 7.00 + \$10.00$$
$$P_{u2} > MC_{u2} + MC_s \quad \$24.00 > \$\ 7.50 + \$10.00$$
$$P_{u3} > MC_{u3} + MC_s \quad \$23.00 > \$\ 7.50 + \$10.00$$
$$P_{u4} > MC_{u4} + MC_s \quad \$22.00 > \$10.00 + \$10.00$$

But the final price of the fifth product $(P_{u5} = \$21)$ is less than the sum of the marginal costs.

$$P_{u5} < MC_{u5} + MC_s \quad \$21.00 < \$13.00 + \$10.00$$

The first four products should be accepted and the fifth rejected, assuming of course that there is sufficient capacity in the using department.

Another way of stating this is that the contributions of the first four products are positive and that the contribution of the fifth product is negative.

$$C_1 = \$25.00 - (\$\ 7.00 + \$10.00) = \$8.00$$
$$C_2 = \$24.00 - (\$\ 7.50 + \$10.00) = \$6.50$$
$$C_3 = \$23.00 - (\$\ 7.50 + \$10.00) = \$5.50$$
$$C_4 = \$22.00 - (\$10.00 + \$10.00) = \$2.00$$
$$C_5 = \$21.00 - (\$13.00 + \$10.00) = -\$2.00$$

It should be clear that a transfer price which includes an allocation of the supplying department's overheads or fixed costs will lead to the wrong results. If these allocated overheads were \$6, the transfer price on the intermediate product would become \$16 instead of \$10 and the "contributions" of the third and fourth products as viewed by the using department would be negative rather than positive. The result would be a rejection of the third and fourth products and a loss of contribution on both.

Figure 12–12 is useful in summarizing the discussion up to this point. This graph is unusual in one respect. The quantity (horizontal) axis is measured in units of the *intermediate* product, not the final products. This is because the final products are different and their quantities can-

Figure 12–12

Optimum quantity, five products each using one unit of same intermediate product

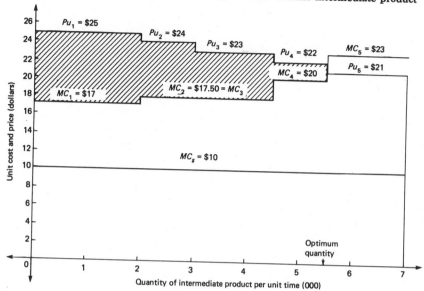

not be measured along a single axis. The intermediate product is homogeneous. We shall assume that the quantities of the sales of the five products could be as high as follows:

Product 1:	2,000 units
Product 2:	1,000 units
Product 3:	1,500 units
Product 4:	1,000 units
Product 5:	1,500 units

The vertical axis is the usual cost and price axis. The prices of the five products are shown. The total marginal cost in both S and U is shown.

If the overheads (fixed costs) amounting to $6 per unit, were included in the marginal costs of the supplying department, the graph would appear as in Figure 12–13.

This graph shows that the apparent optimum would include only Products 1 and 2 and would eliminate the contributions that could be earned from Products 3 and 4.

How could a company make such an error as to select the false optimum in Figure 12–13 in preference to the more profitable set of products shown in Figure 12–12. This error, which in practice must be fairly common, is a result of mixing two functions of accounting: the measurement

Figure 12–13
False optimum, same five products using common intermediate product

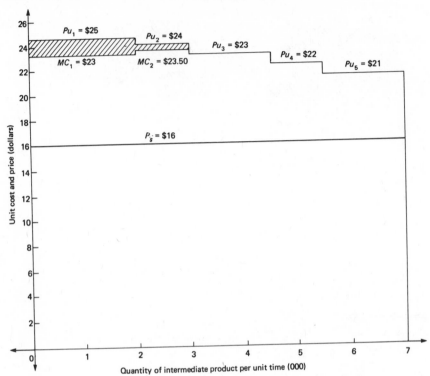

of income and the guidance of decisions. In measuring income it seems reasonable at first glance that the transfer price should be at a level to permit the supplying department to cover its overheads. Therefore, full-cost transfer pricing, including overhead allocation, seems appropriate. At the end of each accounting period a rate of return which reflects the capacity of the department's management to control both variable and fixed costs would seem to measure performance. To allow the supplying department a transfer price which covers only its marginal costs would appear to give all the profit and all the credit to the using department.

This reasoning, attractive as it may at first be, is wrong. The profitability which is important is the company-wide profitability. To allow mere paper allocations of costs to take priority over this company-wide profitability cannot be permitted. The creation of departmental or divisional profit centers, each with its own responsibility for the control of costs, would appear to be consistent with modern ideas on decentralization of responsibility and control. But the purpose of bringing departments together under a single company framework is to achieve the advantages of integration. Decentralization must be interpreted in a way which does not defeat the very purposes of integration.

One way of making the using department contribute to the fixed expenses of the supplying department, even when the transfer price is at the marginal cost, is to require a lump sum payment for the right of access to the supplying department. The lump sum could be determined in advance; the essential point is that it must not depend on the actual volume of purchases from the supplying department.

The case of a marketable intermediate product

The first case we have discussed is that of a specialized intermediate product for which there is no external market. Now let us turn to a case in which *the intermediate product is bought and sold in a competitive market*. Now the opportunity cost concept becomes of paramount importance. In this case, the supplying department, S, should produce all of the units it can as long as it earns contributions to its overhead and profits; this includes units to be sold externally.

If, as we assumed before, the marginal cost to the supplying department is $10 ($MC_s = \$10$), production should be increased up to full capacity as long as the market will take units of the product at prices above that level.

Suppose that the market price is $16. Let us temporarily assume that transportation and outside selling costs are zero. Then the supplying department should expand production to capacity, with the result that a contribution of $6 is earned on every unit.

In this case, the rule for the transfer price is changed. It becomes $16 rather than $10. *The opportunity cost of not being able to sell to the market replaces the internal marginal cost.*

Figure 12–13 now becomes the governing graph. Only Products 1 and 2 should be produced by the using department. Products 3, 4, and 5 require costs which exceed prices. The marginal costs of these products now reflect the opportunity cost of sales on the outside. The supplying department allocates its supply of intermediate product to those uses which can pay the market price, whether these uses are internal departments or external buyers.

Imperfect market for final product—perfect market for intermediate product

Unfortunately, the most significant cases of transfers occur in imperfect markets. Market imperfections complicate the analysis to the point that implementation of theoretical solutions becomes almost unmanageable. It will not be possible to deal with all of the possible varia-

Figure 12–14
Imperfect market final product—perfect market intermediate product

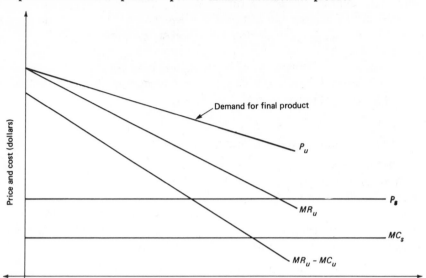

Quantity of intermediate product per unit time

tions here; those who wish to study the subject in greater detail must be referred elsewhere.[23]

Let us start with a one-product firm which sells its final product in an imperfect market but can buy or sell its intermediate product in a competitive market. Figure 12–14 portrays this situation. In this case the demand curve facing the *using* department slopes downward to the right, as indicated by P_u. The marginal revenue curve, MR_u, lies below the demand curve and slopes more steeply for reasons developed in Chapter 3. In this graph it is convenient to subtract the marginal cost within the using department, MC_u, from the marginal revenue to obtain the net marginal revenue, $MR_u - MC_u$.

If there were no market for the intermediate product, the optimum would be where $MR_u - MC_u$ intersects MC_s. On all units up to that point a contribution to company-wide overhead and profits is made. The transfer price should in this case be MC_s. If a perfect market for the intermediate product exists at a price of P_s, the optimum is at the inter-

    [23] The fundamental articles are Jack Hirshleifer's, "On the Economics of Transfer Pricing," *Journal of Business* (July 1956), pp. 172–84; and "Economics of the Divisionalized Firm," *Journal of Business* (April 1957), pp. 96–108. An excellent exposition of the problem, both theoretical and practical, appears in David Solomons' *Divisional Performance: Measurement and Control* (New York: Financial Executives Research Foundation, 1965).

section of $MR_u - MC_u$ and P_s. Although there may be excess capacity in the using department, extra units can be sold in the open market more profitably than they can be sold to the using division. The transfer price should be at the level P_s.

The reader should work out solutions for the case in which the capacity of the supplying department is less than the using department's requirement or the case in which the marginal cost in the supplying department is increasing as output increases.

Competing demands for the intermediate product

The next step is to consider an intermediate product used by several competing using departments, each facing an imperfect market. Figure 12–15 illustrates this case.

Figure 12–15
Competing demands—imperfect markets for final product

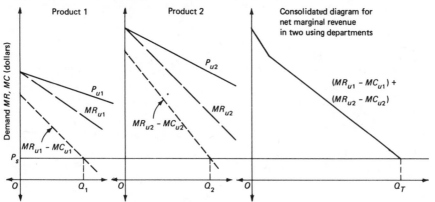

Quantity per unit time of intermediate product

On the consolidated diagram, we sum horizontally the quantities on the $MR_{u1} - MC_{u1}$ and $MR_{u2} - MC_{u2}$ curves. The total quantity of intermediate product, Q_T, is determined where this aggregate curve $(MR_{u1} - MC_{u1}) + (MR_{u2} - MC_{u2})$ cuts P_s. The resultant quantity of intermediate product is then allocated to the two products. This is an application of the equimarginal principle introduced in Chapter 6.

Again the reader can work out solutions when the capacity of the supplying department is limited or when its marginal cost is rising. The marginal cost of the supplying department has been left out of Figure 12–15 for purposes of simplicity. But if MC_s is rising, the analysis is changed slightly and the company may find it profitable to buy part of its supply on the outside.

Imperfect market for the intermediate product

In the preceding section we were saved from having to determine the price of the intermediate product by the fact that a perfect market did that job for us. When the market for intermediate products is imperfect, the problem is complicated by the need to solve a large number of problems simultaneously—the quantity and price of the intermediate product as well as the quantity and price of the final products. The solution requires an application of the concepts introduced in Chapter 2—marginal costs and opportunity costs—and the equimarginal principle from Chapter 6.

It is tempting to leave this problem for more advanced treatises. But the fact appears to be that this case is the most relevant one; to abandon the subject at this point would give a misleading impression of the ease with which transfer prices can in fact be established.

For the present discussion it is desirable to introduce an additional assumption: that the marginal cost of the intermediate product MC_s is rising. A solution to the problem when the marginal cost is constant up to capacity can be introduced later.

Figure 12–16 summarizes the solution to the imperfect market and rising marginal cost case. The net marginal revenues are summed horizontally, but this time the marginal revenue in the outside market is included. The supplying department produces a quantity of the intermediate product where the aggregate net marginal revenue equals the marginal cost. It should be noted that P_s is the transfer price to be charged to the using department; it is *not* the price which should be charged to outside purchasers. The price to outsiders, P_o, will be found on the demand curve directly above the intersection of the transfer price (marginal cost) with MR_o.

Pricing transfers for inventory valuation

Divisional inventories of raw materials, goods in process, and finished goods accumulate and deplete, sometimes by plan and sometimes through errors of judgment. To determine net income and net worth according to conventional accounting standards, inventories should be valued at full cost including allocated overhead. Valuation of inventories at explicit marginal cost would lead to understatement of income and net worth if there were an inventory buildup and to overstatement of these two values if there were inventory depletion. On the other hand, valuation of inventories at opportunity costs (market values greater than full cost) would lead to reporting of net income not yet realized.

Thus intracompany transfers should be priced at *full cost including allocated overhead* for purposes of income and net worth determination. Two sets of transfer prices appear to be necessary. *Marginal costs* are the

Figure 12–16
Imperfect markets for both final and intermediate product—rising marginal costs

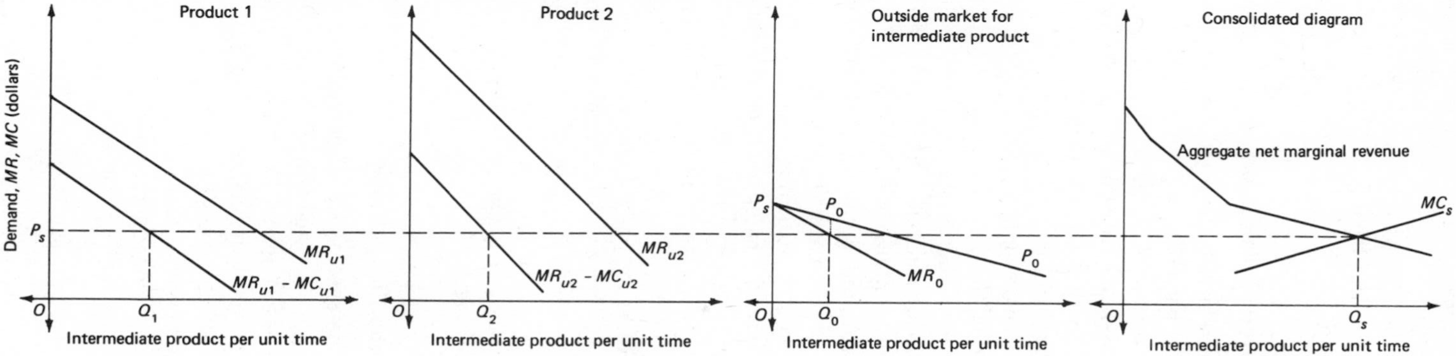

appropriate prices to use as *guides in decentralized decision making*, whereas *full costs* are the proper prices for use in *determining conventional income and net worth* for the whole firm.

Decentralized control without profit centers

Many large firms have attempted to use a management concept in which the various divisions are viewed as "profit centers" and managerial performance is measured in terms of return on investment. If there are substantial interdivisional transfers of goods for which external market prices do not exist, there is no satisfactory basis for establishing transfer prices to support the profit center concept.

Henderson and Dearden have proposed a system for decentralized control without calculating profit or attempting return on investment (ROI) measurement.[24] The system is based on three budgets for each division: a contribution budget, a fixed and managed-cost budget, and a capital budget. The contribution budget is of principal interest here. This budget is negotiated annually between the division manager and his or her superior in the well-known method of management by objectives, and is based on expected revenues less variable costs. If all revenues are from expected sales to other divisions of the same firm using transfer prices based on constant marginal cost, budgeted contribution is zero. (Budget contribution could be above zero if marginal cost were increasing with output.)

Henderson and Dearden show that "variances" from zero-contribution budgets are more satisfactory for control and performance measurement than variances from profit budgets when the "profit" is based on arbitrary transfer prices. Thus, profit centers and ROI measurement are not necessary—indeed, they are not even desirable—for control of decentralized decision making.

Empirical studies and illustrations

Solomons cites the case of an oil company which faced the allocation of the impact of gasoline price wars.[25] A firm transfer price was established between the refining and the marketing departments, roughly at market price less a small deduction per gallon negotiated between the two departments. This meant that the marketing department suffered the impact of price wars. At an earlier date a fixed unit margin was guaranteed the marketing department, which left the production department with the problem of fluctuating prices.

---

[24] Bruce D. Henderson and John Dearden, "New System for Divisional Control," *Harvard Business Review* (September 1966).

[25] Solomons, *Divisional Performance: Measurement and Control*, p. 163.

Another oil company found the problem of transfer pricing so difficult that it treated three departments, refining, marketing, and marine transportation, as a single profit center. In this way it helped make certain that arbitrary transfer prices did not stand in the way of sound decisions.

Another company set transfer prices at the "best price given any outside customer, less (*a*) division selling expense and (*b*) freight, allowances, cash discount, etc., allowed such customer." This rule applied when the product was sold "regularly and in reasonable volume to outside customers." This rule was reasonable, but a similar rule was applied even when the product was not sold on the outside—in this case a deduction from the competitive price was not made for selling expenses. As a result, using divisions might buy on the outside even when internal supplying division costs were lower. An "escape clause," however, permitted the negotiation of lower prices.

Studies of the problem show that determination of the market price is far from simple. For differentiated products no markets in the usual sense may exist. Discounts and terms of payment make comparisons difficult. Apparently the market price solution to the transfer pricing problem can be applied in only a minority of cases. Nevertheless, the marginal cost solution is still relatively unused. This suggests that considerable progress is yet to be made in the area of transfer pricing. Many companies achieve something like marginal cost solutions by encouraging their divisions to negotiate prices between them.

SUMMARY

The chapter discussed several topics in pricing. *Price discrimination* increases revenue from any given amount of product. Profit maximization under price discrimination requires selection of a total output that equates marginal cost with aggregate marginal revenue and allocation of this output among the various markets in such a way that their marginal revenues are equal to aggregate marginal revenue. Prices of the individual products are found on their demand curves at the optimal quantities. The aggregate marginal revenue function is formed by *horizontal* aggregation of quantities at each value of marginal revenue. To engage in profitable price discrimination, the firm must (1) have two or more markets in which price elasticities of demand are different under nondiscriminatory pricing, and (2) have the ability to prevent arbitrage. Price discrimination may be socially beneficial (though some buyers do pay higher prices) if it is carried out by a regulated monopoly or by firms in industries where excess profits are wiped out by long-run entry and expansion. Selective price discrimination that undercuts a competitor's price may be illegal.

Peak-load pricing requires higher prices in peak-load periods and reduced prices in off-peak periods. The long-run solution in the firm-peak case is to set price at marginal cost in both periods, where marginal cost in the off-peak period includes only variable cost, but marginal cost in the peak period also includes an allocation of capacity cost to each unit sold.

Public utility rate regulation requires the regulated firms to charge prices below the monopoly level. The rate structure, or price level, usually sought is at the full-cost level. Some economists argue that social welfare would be increased by regulating rates of natural monopolies down to the marginal cost level, although subsidies to the regulated firms (from general tax revenues) would be necessary.

In *pricing joint products* produced in fixed proportions, marginal revenues from both products are summed *vertically* at each rate of output of one of the products. The optimum rate of output is found where marginal cost is equal to aggregate marginal revenue, and the prices of the two products are found on the individual demand curves at the optimum rate of output. In *pricing alternative products*, the marginal revenue product functions are aggregated *horizontally* with units of the scarce resource or facility being used as measures of rate of production. Optimum total production is found where marginal cost per unit of scarce resource is equal to aggregate marginal revenue product. Individual product uses of the scarce resource are found on their marginal revenue product functions at the solution value, and their prices are found on their demand curves at outputs corresponding to the amounts of scarce resource used.

Transfer pricing requires transfers at marginal cost for purposes of decision making. Marginal cost is the market price (opportunity cost) for an intermediate product that has an external market, or it is the explicit marginal cost of production within the supplying division when this is higher or when the intermediate product has no outside market. For purposes of inventory valuation and income determination only, interdivisional transfers may be made at full cost including allocated overhead.

QUESTIONS

1. What conditions would make it certain that price discrimination is being practiced by a seller? How does price discrimination make the seller better off? What conditions make price discrimination illegal?

2. Show that marginal cost pricing yields some contribution toward a firm's fixed cost if the firm's long-run marginal cost function is rising with increases in the rate of output. Show what happens if the long-run marginal cost is falling with increases in the rate of output.

3. Show that Figure 12–11 is simply an application of the equimarginal principle explained in Chapter 6.

4. For purposes of managerial decision making, a supplying division's transfer price should be quoted to using divisions at the division's internal marginal cost or at the externally determined marginal opoprtunity cost, whichever is greater. What is meant by "the division's internal marginal cost"? By the "externally determined marginal opportunity cost"?

PROBLEMS

1. A firm produces the product q and sells it in a perfectly competitive market for $10 per unit. Its total cost function is $C = q^3 - 9q^2 + 25q + 10$. What should its production be? What is its ATC, MC, MR, and profit at this point?

2. A monopolist sells a homogeneous product in two distinct markets. The estimated demand relations are $P_1 = 300 - 2.5Q_1$ and $P_2 = 500 - 15Q_2$ and the cost relation is $TC = 2,500 + 45Q + 0.5Q^2$. If the monopolist is a profit maximizer, determine the price and quantity in each market and the total profit.

3. Assume that in Problem 2 above the monopolist is forced by law to sell the product at the raw price in each market. What is the price and quantity sold in each market and what is the firm's profit?

4. Overseas Industries serves both a domestic and a European market from New York City. The demand in the two markets differs:

$$P = 500 - 8Q \quad \text{for domestic}$$
$$P = 400 - 5Q \quad \text{for Europe}$$

All sales of Overseas' product are on an f.o.b. New York basis. The total cost function for the company is:

$$TC = \$10,000 + 20Q$$

a. If the markets can be kept segmented, what quantities and prices are applicable to each market?
b. If the markets were not separable, what should the overall quantity be? At what price?
c. Compare the total profit under part a to that under part b. Is price discrimination profitable?

5. Alchemy, Inc., produces two products from a single raw material. Product X is considered to be the byproduct of the manufacture of Product Y. The demand equations of the two products are:

$$Q_y = 500 - 5P_y$$
$$Q_x = 2,500 - 10P_x$$

Three units of X are produced for every unit of Y. Total cost is

$$TC = 200 + Q_y$$

a. What quantity of Y should be produced? At what price should it be offered for sale?

b. What percent of X production will be sold if it is priced appropriately?

c. How would the answer in part *b* change if the production ratio of X to Y were 6 to 1?

d. If the production ratio were flexible, what would be the optimal ratio?

6. Eatmore Foods, Inc., maintains its own farms for the production of cereal grains used in the company's breakfast products. Recently Eatmore was divisionalized by the board of directors in an effort to eliminate coordination problems within the corporation. The problem has arisen, however, as to what prices the Farming Division will charge the Breakfast Foods Division for cereal grains. Wheat, for example, could be sold to the outside market in virtually any quantity for $2.10 a bushel. Assume wheat may also be purchased for $2.10 per bushel. The cost function of the wheat farming operation is:

$$TC = 90,000 + 0.0005Q^2{}_W$$

The Breakfast Foods Division can process wheat into a product which will cost $3.30 per bushel, exclusive of the cost of the wheat. Assume one bushel of wheat goes into each bushel of finished product. The demand equation for this product is:

$$P = 6.50 - 0.0000115Q_P$$

a. What price should the Farming Division charge the Breakfast Foods Division for wheat?

b. How much wheat should Eatmore produce? To whom should it be sold?

c. How much breakfast product should be produced? At what price should it be offered for sale?

7. The Acme Company is divisionalized into the Foundry and the Machine Shop Divisions. The Machine Shop Division produces and sells a patented part for which it needs a custom casting. The demand equation for the final product is:

$$P = 15.40 - 0.0035Q_P$$

Finishing operations on the casting cost $3.10 per unit. The Foundry Division has estimated its cost for producing the casting as:

$$TC = 420 + 0.0015Q^2{}_C$$

a. What quantity of the final product should be produced? At what price?

b. What should the Foundry Division charge for the castings?

8. A firm sells its product in two separate markets. Given the following price and cost structures, what are the prices and quantities it will choose for each market? What is the total quantity produced?

#1		#2			
Q	P	Q	P	Q	TC
1	10	1	15	1	6
2	9.5	2	14	2	7
3	8	3	13	3	9
4	7	4	12	4	18
5	6	5	11	5	28
				6	40

FURTHER READING

Carlin, Alan, and Park, R. E. "Marginal Cost Pricing of Airport Runway Capacity." *American Economic Review,* June 1970.

Dean, Joel. "Decentralization and Intracompany Pricing." *Harvard Business Review* 33, July–August 1955.*

De Salvia, Donald N. "An Application of Peak-Load Pricing." *Journal of Business* 33, April 1960.*

Henderson, Bruce D., and Dearden, John. "New System for Divisional Control." *Harvard Business Review,* September–October 1966.

Hirshleifer, Jack. "Economics of the Divisionalized Firm." *Journal of Business* 30, January 1957.

Hirshleifer, Jack. "On the Economics of Divisionalized Pricing." *Journal of Business* 29, July 1956.

---

* This article is included in *Readings in Managerial Economics,* rev. ed. (Dallas: Business Publications, Inc., 1977).

Cases for part five

Pricing has always been a central interest in managerial economics. Many managers who are engaged in pricing decisions are somewhat baffled by the problem. They find it difficult to organize their thoughts in some kind of pattern. A few managers may refer to the standard works on price theory but find little guidance there in bridging the gap between theory and practice.

The cases in this section provide an opportunity to develop skills in relating economic theory to pricing decisions. It will soon become apparent, however, that traditional economic theory by itself is not sufficient to deal with the complexities of the pricing situation. The cases involve environmental considerations such as antitrust and antidiscrimination legislation. They involve problems of internal organization. In all of them, the pervasiveness of uncertainty about demand, competition, and cost stands in the way of a simple application of theoretical concepts.

CASE CONCRETE PRODUCTS

Case Concrete Products is located in a medium-size city. Prior to June 1956 the firm's principal product was concrete burial vaults. The product line also included lintels, patio stones, and bird baths. The firm enjoyed a local monopoly in the manufacture of these products. There was competition from metal burial vaults; however, the price differential was large enough to reduce the importance of competition.

The basis for the price of burial vaults and other items was full cost plus a markup. The full-cost estimates were determined as follows:

Labor...	$X
Materials...	X
Overhead (10% of labor and materials).................	X
Total cost......................................	$X
Markup (100% of total cost).........................	X
Selling price.......................................	$X

The owner, Mr. Case, spent a great deal of time revising the cost estimates as costs changed. For example, he gave a general hourly wage increase and revised the costs estimates of all products and increased the selling prices.

In order to arrive at the cost estimates, Case ran crude time studies on the workers, recording the time that each spent on a particular product. The overhead rate of 10 percent had been suggested at a trade association meeting which Case attended several years before. He had never verified that overhead was actually 10 percent of direct labor. The firm did not have a job order cost accounting system which would accumulate the cost of each product; rather the cost estimates were checked only periodically against actual costs.

In June 1956 the firm was considering a new product, concrete septic tanks. The manufacture of this product was well suited to the present production scheme. Also there was only one supplier of septic tanks in the city at the time, and Case believed that the building boom was creating a market large enough to support two producers. The molds and a delivery truck would require an investment of $3,700, which would be financed from internal funds. In order to arrive at some estimate of costs, the firm manufactured a pilot model. The cost estimate was:

Materials......................	$26.85
Labor.........................	9.00
Overhead.....................	3.60
	$39.45

Applying the same pricing policy used on the other products would result in a price of $78.90; however, the established producer's price was only $65. Case decided that his initial price should be the same as his competitor's. The competitor did not retaliate by lowering its price; later, however, it did initiate discounts for certain customers. Case did not grant discounts, partly because the volume of sales was "satisfactory" and partly because he feared that if he were too aggressive the competitor might begin producing concrete burial vaults.

1. Does the full cost plus a markup formula make economic sense?
2. Why was the formula not used in pricing septic tanks. Was this wise?
3. Why did not the firm grant discounts on septic tanks? Was this refusal wise?

THOMAS DENTON, CONTRACTOR

Thomas Denton is a small builder. He normally builds six to eight homes in the $20,000 to $30,000 price bracket each year, and gives his personal attention to the details of construction. He subcontracts much of the specialized work, such as plumbing and wiring, but he employs his own carpenters.

Denton classifies his business into two types from the point of view of pricing: (1) a house to be constructed in the future on which he is asked to submit a bid; and (2) a house built "on speculation" to be sold when completed or partially completed. Approximately 70 percent of his business is in the second category. Denton normally charges more for the first type because of the probability that the customer will require many time-consuming changes before the house is complete.

Denton does not follow the practice of some other builders in pricing on a square footage basis. He believes that such pricing does not reflect the variations in materials, fixtures, and his own time required from house to house. Instead he makes a detailed estimate of the labor and materials required in a house, using the form shown as Exhibit 1. Denton does not charge a percentage markup on cost. Instead he adds a sum for his own time, which is indicated at the bottom of Exhibit 1.

Exhibit 1

JOB_____   DATE_____

LOCATION_____

Lot	Towel bars, etc.
Plans	Stone labor
Taxes	Plumbing
Insurance binder	Extras
Comprehensive insurance	Sump pump
Stamps	Wiring
Water	Extras
Gas	Light fixtures
Electricity	Painting
Excavation	Extras
Footings	Caulking
Labor	Sanding floors
Form work	Concrete front porch
Foundation	Steps
Waterproofing	Walk
Drain tile	Concrete back porch
Back fill	Steps
Concrete basement floor	Walk
Steel post	Plastering

Exhibit 1 (*continued*)

Steel basement sash	Lath
Aeroways	Lath labor
Steel girders	Corner rite
Steel bolts	Furnace
Framing lumber	Duct work
¾″ Storm siding	Flashing and gutter work
Rock wool	Linoleum in kitchen
Inside doors	Linoleum in bath
Outside doors	Tile in bath
Windows	Medicine cabinets
Glazing	Kitchen cabinets
Screens	Ironing board
Storm and screen doors	Attic fan
Plywood	Exhaust fan
Kitchen and bath subfloor	Dishwasher
Flooring	Disposal
Building paper	Weatherstripping
Finish lumber	Grading and bulldozer
Carpenter labor	Extra dirt
Extras	Sod
Social security	Shrubs
Nails	Drive
Hardware	Venetian blinds
Roofing	Wallpaper
Garage material	Labor
Garage doors	Cleaning house
Brick chimney	Coach light
Mantle	Fence
Fire brick and tile installation	Freight
Brixment	Hauling expense
Sand	Shutters
Cut stone sills	Flower box
Brick	Advertising
Brick labor	Real estate commission
Angle irons	Miscellaneous
Stone	Contractor's fee
Subtotal $_____	Grand total $_____

Denton's charge for his own time varies from job to job. One consideration is the amount of time required in the construction of the particular house. He will vary this charge somewhat with business conditions. For example, in 1958, when business in this locality was slow, he reduced this charge to speed up the sale of houses already completed. The need to finance the construction of new houses out of the profits from those already built sometimes puts him under pressure to shade prices. In 1958, he had held two houses for over a year before reducing price. Denton is slow in starting new houses until he has sold old ones, largely because he does not like to be heavily in debt and does not like to be under extreme pressure to reduce prices because of a large inventory of unsold houses.

Denton also reduces his bids on houses to be constructed in the winter. He believes that his time is not so valuable in this period of low activity. He also wants to keep his force of carpenters together as much as possible on a full-year basis, since it is difficult to acquire first-grade carpenters. Furthermore he can hire workers at lower rates in the winter. One last consideration in pricing is Denton's estimation of the customer's personality. If he appears to be a person who is demanding of continual changes in the plan and details of the house, Denton will raise his bid.

Denton has never heard of incremental costs, opportunity costs, or demand elasticities. He faces the competition of 10 or 12 builders very much like himself. He is not fearful of retaliation to reductions in his prices from such competitors, for it is difficult to compare houses and most price reductions are secret. One way of reducing price is to offer to do additional work, such as paneling a basement, without charge. Denton does admit, however, that his prices are influenced by the prices he thinks other builders are asking. Denton frequently sells his houses through real estate agents, paying the normal commission on new houses. He sometimes reduces his price for a direct sale to a customer which avoids the real estate commission. The real estate agents claim that this practice is unethical, but they continue to do business with Denton.

1. Does Denton use full-cost pricing? Discuss.
2. Does Denton use going-rate pricing? Discuss.
3. Does Denton use incremental reasoning? Discuss.

SPRAGUE COLLEGE STORE

Sprague College, a small private school, owns a store which competes with several groceries, clothing stores, drugstores, and stores specializing in school supplies. The store has a monopoly on the sale of textbooks in the town of 10,000 in which it is located.

The store management establishes a target return on sales for each of the four departments: books, groceries, clothing, and school supplies. An annual budget estimates the volume of business and the expenses necessary to handle that volume. On the basis of this budget, the management determines what departmental margins are necessary to cover overhead and allow the target return. Each department is given a margin to maintain which should result in the desired margin for the store as a whole. The departments report their achieved margins each week and this serves as an internal control. If a department's volume were to decrease, the average margin required on each item would increase, even though the department might be able to reduce some costs (by reducing the sales force, for example).

In 1960, at the time of the case interviews, the markup on textbooks was 13.6 percent of selling price for both new and used books. The cost of new books is 80 percent of list price, but the store sells below list. The store buys only used books that are to be reused; its markup on such used books is much lower than is usual in college bookstores. The margin in 1960 did not cover the estimated overhead (15.5 percent of revenue). The manager gave this reason for her policy on textbooks: "If I am going to give students a break on anything, why not do it on something they must have?"

Margins on the other merchandise vary considerably. Coffee, for example, is a highly competitive item on which only a 3–5 percent margin is possible; higher prices would result in a transfer of business elsewhere. Higher margins on less competitive goods help compensate for the low margins on coffee and books. The store makes a careful survey of the grocery prices of competitors and tries to keep its prices in line with competition.

The target net profit on sales is approximately 2.5 percent. This results in a return on investment which is higher than the average return on the other college investments. Inventory control, with an emphasis on maintaining the minimum inventory and the highest possible turnover, is essential in attaining the target return. The management maintains detailed inventory records on each item in stock; these records help the control of inventory and serve as a guide in buying.

1. Does the store use full-cost pricing? Discuss.
2. Does the store use going-rate pricing? Discuss.
3. Does the store use target-return pricing? Discuss.
4. Does the store use incremental reasoning in pricing? Discuss.
5. Why does the store give the students a break in textbooks?

INTERNATIONAL HARVESTER COMPANY*

International Harvester has a diversified product line, consisting of agricultural equipment, construction machinery, motor trucks, and mis-

* Based on A. D. H. Kaplan, J. B. Dirlam, and R. I. Lanzillotti, *Pricing in Big Business* (Washington, D.C.: The Brookings Institution, 1958), pp. 69–79, 135–42.

cellaneous equipment. The company wishes to achieve several objectives in pricing these products: (1) a target return on investment of around 10 percent after taxes; (2) maintenance of a reputation for high quality and durable products; and (3) growth, without becoming so dominant that price competition is undermined. The company succeeded in earning the target return in the years immediately after World War II, but more recently has experienced lower profits after taxes.

The company's position of leadership in the market varies from one product to another. In 1947 it led an effort to resist inflation by lowering prices on farm equipment; in other years its increases in farm equipment prices have been followed by competitors. On light trucks International Harvester has followed the product and price policies of the major automobile companies, and has been able to achieve only a low return on investment. On heavy trucks the company is in a stronger position. In 1955 the company abandoned the production of refrigerators and freezers because of an inability to obtain the volume that would provide a profit. The company's traditional emphasis on quality and durability appeared to be inconsistent with the need to cut costs so that the company could compete in the refrigerator and freezer market.

The company's market share of agricultural equipment had steadily declined from 44 percent in 1922 to 23 percent in 1948. Its share varied from about 20 percent on combines and 30 percent on tractors, to 65 percent on cotton pickers. The company wished to maintain a reputation for quality on farm equipment. It also wished to set prices that would permit farmers to earn the initial investment in a satisfactory payback period, which varied from three to ten years, depending upon the product. The company also wished to keep prices on the various models in a reasonable proportion to each other, modified to some extent by the desire to meet competitive conditions in the different markets.

International Harvester's costing practices were similar to those of the large automobile companies. The main stress in pricing was on "normal costs," which are full costs, including current material and labor, plus overhead computed on the basis of "normal" operations. The overhead was prorated on the basis of direct labor costs; sales, service, collection, and administrative costs were allocated in proportion to total sales value. In addition to the normal costs the company estimated the "season's costs," which were the "actual" unit costs accumulated during the season. If the season's costs indicated that the normal costs were unrealistic, the company might revise its prices. The company also measured "specific costs," especially for service parts. Specific costs included only the actual cost of material, direct labor costs, and the direct overhead resulting from the particular item.

The practice in pricing a new product is of interest. The management started with a price based on competitors' prices and the estimated value to the farmer. It then worked back to estimating a "target cost" which, at the given price, would provide the target return on investment. The equipment designers then tried to develop models consistent with such target costs. Exhibit 1 shows the actual experience with three products introduced in 1956.

While the company's profit objective of 10 percent on investment would suggest a target return on sales of about 7 percent (sales are usually about 40 percent higher than invested capital), the company modified the target on particular products according to the competitive situation, the originality of the product, and the value to the farmer. The company recognized the need to maintain a full line, which means carrying some products that do not permit the usual markup. The company also set higher prices when it had an advantage (perhaps because of a superior product) over competition.

As Exhibit 1 suggests, the company modified its introductory prices as it accumulated experience in the actual market. Competition might force it to lower price; costs might exceed the preliminary estimates. When the profit was as low as on Product C in Exhibit 1, the company might redesign the product to reduce costs, increase price, or abandon the line.

Several specific examples will give insight into the company's pricing practices:

1. In May 1957 it raised the retail price on a product from $218 to $228 because of dissatisfaction with the profit. The new price was still in line with competition. The profit position would still be unsatisfactory, but the management doubted the feasibility of even higher prices.

2. In March 1957 the company reduced the price of another product from $525 ($397.17 to the dealer) to $490. The cost to manufacture was $264.34. Management was dissatisfied with the volume on this item and wished to reduce prices to the range charged by two smaller competitors.

3. The company's cotton pickers sold at a price which yielded the target return or better. The product had a high value to potential users. The company was the first to introduce this product; the more recent entrance of competitors had not undermined the company's ability to obtain the target return.

4. The company priced "captive parts" (manufactured only by Harvester) at a price yielding a target return on normal unit costs.

5. The company priced other parts which competed with parts produced by General Motors, Ford, and Mack Truck at prices designed to meet competition. These prices did not show any consistent relationship to unit costs or target returns. The company might continue to produce and sell such parts even though the price covered only the specific costs; such a policy helped the company maintain a full line and spread its overhead burden.

Exhibit 1
Price-cost analysis, representative farm implements introduced in 1956

	Product A			Product B			Product C		
	Target	Intro-ductory	Actual	Target	Intro-ductory	Actual	Target	Intro-ductory	Actual
List price............	$592.60	$592.60	$592.60	$455.85	$455.85	$455.85	$687.40	$691.35	$691.35
Trade discount—23 percent.......	136.30	136.30	136.30	104.85	104.85	104.85	158.10	159.00	159.00
Dealer price...........	$456.30	$456.30	$456.30	$351.00	$351.00	$351.00	$529.30	$532.35	$532.35
Cash discount—2 percent.......	9.13	9.13	9.13	7.02	7.02	7.02	10.60	10.65	10.65
Net from dealer........	$447.17	$447.17	$447.17	$343.98	$343.98	$343.98	$518.70	$521.70	$521.70
Sales and administrative expense*....	67.08	67.08	67.08	51.60	51.60	51.60	77.81	78.26	78.26
Net............	$380.09	$380.09	$380.09	$292.38	$292.38	$292.38	$440.89	$443.44	$443.44
Manufacturing cost†	270.00	274.97	359.43	214.00	217.42	232.62	380.00	395.33	462.38
Profit margin (dollars).....	$110.09	$105.12	$ 20.66	$ 78.38	$ 74.96	$ 59.76	$ 60.89	$ 48.11	($ 18.94)
Profit margin as percent of:									
Manufacturing cost.....	40.8%	38.2%	5.7%	36.6%	34.5%	25.7%	16.0%	12.1%	-4.5%
Total unit (6) + (8)....	32.6	32.5	4.8	29.1	27.9	21.0	13.3	10.2	-3.1
Net from dealer.......	24.6	23.5	4.6	22.3	21.8	17.4	11.7	9.2	-3.6

* Allocated as normal percentages (15 percent) of net from dealer.
† Target and introductory prices based on normal manufacturing cost, including plant overhead.
Source: A. D. H. Kaplan, J. B. Dirlam, and R. F. Lanzillotti, *Pricing in Big Business* (Washington, D.C.: The Brookings Institution, 1958), p. 72.

The company gave the same discount from list prices to all dealers. It also gave volume discounts, which varied from 2.25 to 4 percent. The list price was a suggested price, and some dealers sold at much less.

1. What is the meaning of "normal costs" in this case? Should these costs be the basis of pricing?
2. What is the meaning of "specific costs" in this case? Should they be the basis of pricing?
3. What is "target cost" in this case? How does it relate to pricing?
4. Does International Harvester price to earn a target return? Or is the target return a measure of what the market permits it to earn?
5. Does International Harvester use full-cost pricing, going-rate pricing, target-return pricing, incremental reasoning in pricing, or what? Use Exhibit 1 to prove your point.

SEARS, ROEBUCK AND COMPANY*

The merchandising organization of Sears, Roebuck has the primary responsibility for pricing. The company's 420 buyers initiate prices under the supervision of the merchandise supervisors (in charge of the 50 buying departments) and the vice president in charge of merchandising. The pricing for mail-order selling is more centralized than that for the retail stores. The buyers and merchandise supervisors generally add a predetermined percentage or dollar markup based on the custom of the trade, modified by attention to competitors' prices. The vice president normally approves the price recommendations of the merchandise supervisors, though he does give more attention than they to the prospective return on investment that might result from larger volumes at lower prices or smaller volumes at higher margins.

At the same time, the buyers recommend retail prices for the 35 retail zones in which Sears operates. These prices are suggested retail prices; each store manager may revise prices to fit local conditions and competition. Over 90 percent of the time the store managers follow the recommendations of the parent organization. The central office determines the prices for the regular seasonal and special mail-order sales. The retail store managers determine the time of their sales. On the whole there is considerable centralization of the pricing decisions.

The objectives of the company's price policy are several: (1) to provide the maximum level of sales consistent with a target return on investment of 10 to 15 percent after taxes; (2) to maintain and increase

* Based on Kaplan, Dirlam, and Lanzillotti, *Pricing in Big Business*, pp. 188–98, 237–39.

the company's share of the national market; and (3) to contribute to the company's reputation for low prices.

Pricing and buying are closely interwoven in the Sears organization. The objective of buying is to obtain merchandise at low costs that will permit low retail prices. The company owns about 22 factories, manufacturing commodities such as stoves and plumbing fixtures which at some previous time it could not obtain on satisfactory terms from outside manufacturers. The company also owns part interest in other suppliers. No doubt the company's ability to manufacture itself exerts a downward pressure on costs. Sears' contracts with outside firms normally cover direct costs to the manufacturer and a margin to cover overhead plus a profit comparable to that of Sears. Even so these contracts include a "competitive clause" that permits a transfer to lower-cost suppliers. Sears works closely with the suppliers to help them hold down distribution costs and to aid them in technical and design problems. One objective is to obtain a large volume which will reduce unit costs.

The result of these practices is selling prices ranging from about 15 to 30 percent below the list prices of competitors. These competitors' prices, however, are suggested retail prices and are less rigidly maintained than Sears' suggested prices. In fact, in recent years the differential between Sears' prices and those of competitors has narrowed on many items. Sears tries to meet this competition by emphasis on brand name (the brand name is connected in the consumer's mind with low prices), by attracting customers with low-price "stripped" models and "trading up" to more expensive models providing a higher margin, and by selling last year's models at lower prices.

Sears generally follows customary "price points" on soft goods such as men's shirts and women's garments. Thus shirts sell at $2.95 or $3.95, rather than at some intermediate price such as $3.30, which many customers might interpret as a high price for a $2.95-quality shirt rather than a low price for a $3.95 shirt. The result is an inflexibility in price which may require a variation in quality to meet rising costs.

Sears generally maintains a differential on mail-order prices below retail prices to allow for differences in selling costs, mailing costs, and delays in delivery. Decisions on both retail and mail-order prices are based on knowledge of traditional markups and price points, on estimates of the price differentials needed to obtain volume, expected price changes of competitors, comprehensive reviews of competitive prices, shopping surveys, quality testing, and changes in the company's share of the market for different products. On some lines of merchandise, such as tires, paint, refrigerators, and other large appliances, the company wishes to avoid starting price wars; it avoids price-slashing promotions on these lines.

1. Does the store use full-cost pricing? Discuss.
2. Does the store use going-rate pricing? Discuss.
3. Does the store use incremental reasoning in pricing? Discuss.
4. Would you describe the market structure for Sears as competitive, monopolistic, or oligopolistic? Discuss.
5. What are the arguments for and against decentralization of pricing by Sears?

FULGRAVE PRINTING COMPANY*

Mr. Prescott, President of the Fulgrave Printing Company, believed that few printers had an accurate method of determining the cost of an individual job. He felt that the result was price cutting and deterioration of industry profits, which in 1959 averaged 2.5 percent of sales. The Fulgrave Printing Company had installed a modern cost system which combined forecasted and actual costs and developed data to serve as a basis for pricing. Prescott believed that other firms should adopt a similar system.

Background

The Fulgrave Printing Company, one of over 100 firms in a metropolitan area of over 800,000 population, employed over 300 workers, and was located in a modern air-conditioned plant. Competition was intense, though printers tended to specialize in particular kinds of work. On some kinds of printing the Fulgrave company competed with printers in other cities. The company was a "commercial printer," producing a wide variety of jobs, but avoiding short runs and small volumes that were of interest to smaller firms. Exhibit 1 illustrates the production process of job order print shops and is applicable to the Fulgrave Printing Company.

The company's cost system: Hourly machine rates

The budgeted cost system required the estimation of hourly machine costs for the coming period. The company accountants estimated total labor and overhead costs for the next year; they also estimated the volume of sales and the number of machine-hours required for those sales. These cost and hour estimates became the basis for the hourly machine rate on each machine, group of machines, or other cost centers

---

* This case was prepared by W. W. Haynes and J. L. Gibson of the University of Kentucky as the basis for class discussion. All names and locations have been disguised.

Exhibit 1
Production flow diagram for job order printing

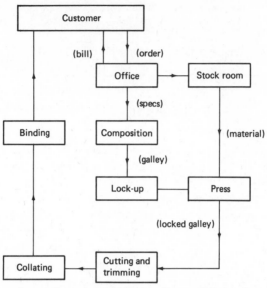

Source: Suggested by William Green, *Wellesley Press,
Inc., Case Study*, Harvard Business School, 1958.

in the plant. The hourly machine rates included overhead costs which
were distributed to the various machines. Exhibit 2 shows how hourly
costs were estimated for one press.

The budgeted cost system required 45 different hourly machine rates.
These rates were sometimes revised during the year to bring them in line
with actual experience. In theory the rates might be revised slightly
every 60 or 90 days. In the 12 months preceding June 1960, however,
only ten rates had been revised. In June 1960, itself, Mr. Green, the
company vice president, revised 14 additional rates. Mr. Green had the
primary responsibility for rate revisions.

In the establishment of the hourly machine rates, seasonal fluctuations in sales were ignored. The objective was to set rates for the year
as a whole. Mr. Green stated that it did not make sense for the company to set higher rates in the low season simply because the fixed costs
had to be distributed over a smaller volume; nor was it reasonable to
compute lower hourly machine rates in the peak seasons.

Costing individual jobs

The hourly machine rates were the chief factors but not the only factor
in pricing individual jobs. In estimating the cost of a job, specialized esti-

Exhibit 2
Determination of hourly cost for vertical press

Investment: $10,000
Floor area: 300 square feet
52 weeks × 40 hours = 1 full-time worker = 2,080 hours to be paid for
52 weeks × 40 hours = 2,080 maximum possible working hours
Less: 10 days vacation = 80 hours (10 days × 8 hours)
Less: 6 days holidays = 48 hours (6 days × 8 hours)
100 percent production = 2,080 hours − 128 hours = 1,952 hours

1. Direct costs

Labor: 2 workers at $1.75 × 2,080 hours	$ 7,280.00
F.O.A.B. unemployment (percent of labor)	254.80
Workmen's compensation	21.84
Power (1,600 K.W.H. at $.04)	64.00
Depreciation (10% of investment)	1,000.00
Repairs (1% of investment)	100.00
Total direct costs	$ 8,720.64

2. Indirect costs

Rent (300 sq. ft. × $3)	$ 900.00
Insurance (½% of investment)	50.00
Taxes (1% of investment)	100.00
Administrative costs (80% of direct costs)	6,976.51
Total indirect costs	$ 8,026.51

3. Total cost for one year (next 12 months) $16,747.15

4. Hourly rates

100% production (1,952 hours)	$ 8.58
80% production (1,562 hours)	10.72
60% production (1,171 hours)	14.30
40% production (781 hours)	21.44
20% production (390 hours)	42.94

mators accumulated the costs on a job for each machine or other cost center through which it would pass. For this purpose time standards were required. In 1960 the company was engaged in estimating time standards on the basis of its own experience. Prior to this time it had relied on time standards or norms published by national agencies. Even when internal time standards were established, the company maintained records showing comparisons with the outside norms to see how its own experience measured up.

Thus the estimated cost in each cost center consisted of the time standard multiplied by the predetermined hourly cost. The full cost of the total job was the sum of such costs on every process used in the production of the order, plus the cost of materials. The charge for materials depended on the quantity used in the individual order. The company usually did not pass on to the customer any savings resulting from consolidating orders in the purchase of materials; quantity discounts were not passed on to the customer unless the order was large enough in itself

Exhibit 3*
Price estimate for an individual job

Materials (including the markup on materials)	
1,000 sheets 17 × 22, 20 lb. white Howard Bond 50 lbs. @ $0.30	$ 15.00
½ lb. Bronze blue ink @ $1.90	0.95
Production	
Composition—2 hours × $7.86 hourly cost	15.72
Lock-up—½ hour × $8.15 hourly cost	4.08
Press, vertical—5 hours × $10.72 hourly cost	53.60
Cutting—1 hour × $5.60 hourly cost	5.60
Total cost	$ 94.95
Markup on total cost (20%)	19.00
Selling price	$113.95

* This exhibit does not represent any actual job priced by the firm on which this case is based.

to result in such a discount. An estimated price for a job is illustrated in Exhibit 3.

Pricing individual jobs

In principle the company followed the practice of pricing on the basis of full cost plus a predetermined markup. A special markup was applied to outside materials before their inclusion in the total cost of the work to which the profit markup was added. However, a certain amount of judgment entered into pricing; it was not merely a mechanical procedure. The authority over pricing was delegated to the sales department, though Green sometimes had an influence over pricing decisions.

The company officials believed firmly in pricing on the basis of full costs. They believed the failure of some companies to adhere to this practice accounted for the severe competition in the industry. In fact, they believed other pricing procedures were unethical and referred to price-cutters as "chiselers."

The predetermined markups varied from one category of business to another. The Fulgrave company divided its business into five categories, each with a different markup percentage as indicated by Exhibit 4.

Company officials did not apply the markups mechanically. They used judgment in modifying the estimates. Sometimes the estimators themselves had an influence over the final price; they might estimate a low machine cost on a particular job because a fast worker would be assigned to it. Green, the vice president, did not approve of this practice, which was based on the estimators' misunderstanding of company policy. He argued that the time standards on any job should be based on average performance, not on the speed of the particular employee

Exhibit 4
Markup schedule*

Type of job	*Markup on cost*
Class #I: The first run of any job requiring speculative creative work. Any job requiring outside purchases of over 60 percent of the final price.	20 percent markup on outside materials plus 20 percent markup on the total cost including outside materials.
Class #II: Reruns of jobs originally in Class #I: First runs of jobs not requiring speculative creativity.	15 percent markup on outside materials plus 20 percent markup on total cost.
Class #III: Reruns of jobs originally in Class #II.	15–15 percent
Class IV: Jobs which are a part of a total program and which will result in additional business.	10–15 percent
Class #V: Magazines and other special publications.	10–10 percent

* Although the job classes are those of Fulgrave Printing Company, the markups are hypothetical.

who might work on a job. He believed that the sales force sometimes put pressure on the estimators to come up with low estimates. In some cases judgment on the part of the estimators was justified. For example, they might know that a particular customer's job would flow expeditiously through the plant and that a reduction in actual cost would result.

Higher markups on brokering

Class #I, with the highest markups, included what is known in the printing business as "brokering." This consisted of jobs which were produced largely on the outside, with only a minority of the work done by the Fulgrave company. Not all printing companies charged a higher markup on such jobs; in fact some companies reduced their markups to get such jobs. Green was certain that the Fulgrave policy was sound, even though the higher markup was applied to the entire job and not merely to the "value added." He gave the following reasons for this position:

1. Since brokering jobs require a relatively small amount of machine time, they absorb only a small amount of overhead. (As noted earlier, the overhead is allocated through the hourly machine rates.) A high markup was needed to assure that the sales commissions were covered.

2. Brokering jobs usually require more work on design and more special contact with the customer.

3. Brokering jobs are frequently speculative; an extra charge would help compensate for the extra risk.

Price competition versus nonprice competition

Green stated that a high proportion of printing costs were fixed for short-run changes in volume. For example, labor costs did not vary greatly in proportion to volume because of the difficulty of retaining printers if they were laid off during the lulls in business. Green estimated that only 45 or 50 percent of the costs were variable. He recognized that the low level of variable costs created a temptation to cut prices; in fact, this was one reason for the cutthroat competition in the industry. Nevertheless, the Fulgrave company resisted pricing below full cost. Green stated several reasons for this policy:

1. Prices below full cost depress the market and result in low industry profits. Such prices are unethical.

2. Regular customers might be offended by special prices on irregular business. They preferred to deal with a company with consistent and stable price policies.

3. While it might seem desirable to get "fill-in" business to make use of idle capacity, there was no assurance that the capacity would in fact be idle when the jobs were ready to be run. Delays in starting jobs were frequent and unpredictable. Low-price jobs might interfere with the flow of regular work.

Green also stated that if the volume of business were down for a considerable period, it would be possible to pare some of the so-called fixed costs. For example, the labor force would be contracted. It was true that other costs such as depreciation would run on anyway, but these were a small percentage of the total. The president of the company, Prescott, admitted that the company might have to adjust to competition if idle capacity became a serious problem. In the period of the 1940s and 1950s, however, there had been no prolonged periods of substantial idle capacity.

The company preferred to rely on nonprice competition to win customers. The company stressed good customer relations. For example, if a customer's order turned out to be for a larger volume than was originally intended, the company would pass on half of the savings in unit costs. Green believed that such a practice helped retain customers. Sometimes the company provided special services to the customer without charge. For example, Green spent part of his evenings doing editorial work on a customer's manuscript.

1. Does the company use full-cost pricing? Discuss.
2. What is the significance of the high proportion of fixed costs in the company's operations?
3. Should the hourly rates be higher, lower, or the same in low seasons? Use Exhibit 2 to prove your points.

4. Would the company be better off to transfer attention from hourly machine rate to incremental costs?
5. Evaluate the reasons for not pricing below full costs.

FALL RIVER NURSERY

The Fall River Nursery was the second largest garden nursery and landscaping firm in its locality, a city of 150,000. The firm was a family concern founded in about 1910, with a continual reputation for quality and service. In 1961 four partners cooperated in managing the firm.

The firm grew most of its own materials on its 500-acre plot, but purchased a few plants from wholesalers. The firm also sold a small fraction of its materials at wholesale; the local climate and soil conditions gave it an advantage on some plant varieties. Most of the sales were at retail at the company's garden center. The mail-order business was relatively small. One of the partners was in charge of the landscaping service as well as service work and spraying, another in charge of growing and propagation, and a third in charge of the garden center.

Pricing policies and practices

The firm did not appear to have a definite policy on pricing. The officials were skeptical of systematic approaches to pricing. They did not maintain a cost accounting system and doubted that it would be useful. In fact one of the partners stated that most experiments in cost accounting in other nurseries had failed and had been abandoned. He claimed that uncertainty about the weather, plant diseases, and soil conditions made it impossible to predict the cost of growing a particular plant variety. The long period it took to produce plants also made it difficult to estimate costs.

The same official stated that the firm's plants are priced "according to the market, just as wheat and corn are priced." The firm's prices were a little higher than prices of nurseries to the south, where labor costs were lower, but lower than prices in the large metropolitan areas. The firm did not maintain systematic records of what other firms were charging, though it did have a file of catalogs of other nurseries. This file was not kept up to date, and it apparently was not used often. In fact the company officials did not appear to know except vaguely what the price differentials from firm to firm were. Thus, if the firm's prices were based on the market, it was on a subjective evaluation of market forces rather than on any kind of statistical analysis.

The officials believed that the firm's prices were slightly on the low side in the local market, if one excluded the prices at some of the large chain groceries. They pointed to some advertisements in the local news-paper showing higher prices at a competitive firm.

Changes in prices

Price changes on plants were infrequent. Prices were established in the summer for the coming year. These prices were published in a cata-log in September. The partners believed that price changes during the year were undesirable; they did not even revise their mimeographed wholesale price during the season. The main exception to this rule was pricing for the end-of-season sale in May, at which time two categories of plants were marked down:

1. Dormant materials that had been dug up the previous fall and winter. These materials including fruit trees, hedges, and shrubs would have to be destroyed if not sold in May.

2. Block clearance items, mostly evergreens. If a few evergreens are occupying a block of land, it is desirable to sell them off at reduced prices to clear the land. Some of these materials may be of lower quality, but usually this is not the case.

From one season to the next the partners revised prices. In 1959, for example, they took into account an increase in labor costs in changing their prices upward.

Round-number pricing and promotional pricing

The company officials have traditionally preferred round numbers in pricing, such as $6 or $7 per plant, though they often used prices such as $6.50 or $8.25. In 1959 they broke away from this policy when they adjusted prices for labor cost changes. For example, they increased one price from $6.75 to $6.95 in the belief that a $7 price would develop customer resistance. In 1960 the firm returned to prices such as $7.25 and $9.25. A plant's price was the same regardless of how the plant was sold —by telephone, by purchase at the garden store, or by mail order.

The partners believed that round-number pricing was consistent with the atmosphere of quality and dignity that the company tried to main-tain. They did not want to be classified with the chain stores and mass mail-order firms which sometimes had a poorer reputation. In 1961, however, the firm experimented with prices of $1.11, $2.22, or $4.44 on distress items in oversupply. In 1961 the partners also experimented with a two-for-one sale which permitted a customer to purchase a second plant for $1 upon purchase of the first plant at the regular price. In addi-tion, bulbs, fertilizers, and other items purchased on the outside were being sold at odd prices in 1961. Expert merchandisers and speakers at trade meetings had convinced the partners that some experimentation with promotional pricing might be desirable in building up volume. But the catalog prices were kept on a round-number basis; the promotional odd prices were the exception rather than the rule.

In 1962, the partners were not yet certain that the experiments with promotional pricing had been successful. They were planning several new "traffic builders," however. For example, they planned to offer to give one popular rose bush free to the purchaser of five rose bushes. The trend appeared to be toward more specials of this sort, but these specials were still the exception.

The pricing of particular plants

The firm did not have control over all of its prices. Some plants were patented; the firm holding the patent set the price and collected a royalty from individual nurseries. The markups on such plants were usually higher than the Fall River Nursery's markups on plants of similar size and variety.

In spite of the general inflation in costs and prices in the 1950s, the prices on some plants were lower than in earlier years. For example, *Juniperus excelsa stricta* (15–18 inches) was selling at $2.50 instead of the $3 of a decade earlier. The reasons for the price decline were the reduction in demand for this variety and the fact that it was more readily available. The company officials were uncertain whether they were making money on this variety at such low prices, but they continued to grow it. One partner, however, stated that the company would not continue to grow a plant that did not return a profit in the long run.

Another plant that had fallen in price was *Taxus cuspidata browni*. This plant was in short supply in 1952–53, but supply had caught up with demand by 1960 and prices had reached a more normal level.

Some of the company's prices were 25 percent or even 50 percent below prices in the large metropolitan markets. The company grew some plants especially adapted to the local climate in large blocks, with resultant economies of scale.

The prices of some plants at first appeared to be out of line with the size of the plant. An example was globe *Taxus*. The officials explained that this plant requires special shearing to give it the desired shape. Thus the labor costs were higher, and it took more years for the plant to grow to a given size. The officials doubted that they were making as great a profit on these plants as on the same variety left unsheared.

Exhibit 1 shows the record of prices of some selected items over the period from 1948 to 1960.

1. How does cost relate to the nursery's pricing?
2. How does demand relate to the nursery's pricing?

Exhibit 1
Prices of selected plants (1948–1960)

Plant and size	1948–49	1950–51	1952–53	1954–55	1956–57	1958–59	1959–60
Juniperus excelsa stricta							
15 to 18 inches............	3.00	N.L.*	N.L.	2.50	2.50	2.50	2.50
18 to 24 inches............	N.L.	3.00	3.00	3.00	3.00	3.00	3.00
2 to 2½ feet..............	N.L.	4.00	4.00	4.00	4.00	4.00	4.00
2½ to 3 feet..............	N.L.	5.50	N.L.	N.L.	N.L.	N.L.	5.00
3 to 3½ feet..............	N.L.	7.00	N.L.	N.L.	N.L.	N.L.	N.L.
Juniperus chinensis glauca							
hetzi							
15 to 18 inches............	N.L.	3.50	3.50	3.00	N.L.	N.L.	N.L.
18 to 24 inches............	N.L.	4.00	4.50	4.00	N.L.	N.L.	N L.
2 to 2½ feet..............	N.L.	N.L.	5.50	5.00	5.50	N.L.	N.L.
2½ to 3 feet..............	N.L.	N.L.	7.00	6.50	7.00	7.00	N.L.
Taxus cuspidata							
15 to 18 inches............	4.00	4.00	4.50	N.L.	N.L.	5.25	5.50
18 to 24 inches............	5.00	5.00	6.00	6.00	6.50	6.95	7.25
2 to 2½ feet..............	6.50	7.00	8.00	8.00	8.50	8.95	9.25
2½ to 3 feet..............	8.00	9.00	11.00	11.00	12.00	12.00	12.50
3 to 3½ feet..............	N.L.	12.00	14.00	14.00	15.00	15.00	16.00
3½ to 4 feet..............	N.L.	N.L.	N.L.	18.00	20.00	20.00	22.50
4 to 4½ feet..............	N.L.	N.L.	N.L.	N.L.	N.L.	25.00	30.00
Taxus baccata repandens							
15 to 18 inches............	N.L.	N.L.	N.L.	5.50	6.00	6.25	N.L.
18 to 24 inches............	N.L.	7.00	N.L.	7.50	N.L.	8.25	8.50
2 to 2½ feet..............	N.L.	N.L.	N.L.	N.L.	10.00	N.L.	9.75
Taxus cuspidata browni							
15 to 18 inches............	N.L.	N.L.	6.00	5.50	5.50	5.25	5.50
18 to 24 inches............	5.00	5.00	6.00	7.00	7.00	6.95	7.25
2 to 2½ feet..............	6.50	8.00	10.00	9.00	9.00	8.95	9.25
2½ to 3 feet..............	8.00	N.L.	N.L.	N.L.	N.L.	N.L.	N.L.
Tsuga hemlock							
2 to 2½ feet..............	3.50	N.L.*	N.L.	N.L.	N.L.	N.L.	N.L.
2 to 3 feet................	N.L.	N.L.	N.L.	N.L.	N.L.	4.00	4.00
2½ to 3 feet..............	4.00	4.00	5.00	5.00	5.00	N.L.	N.L.
3 to 3½ feet..............	4.50	5.00	6.00	6.00	6.00	N.L.	N.L.
3 to 4 feet................	N.L.	N.L.	N.L.	N.L.	N.L.	6.00	6.00
3½ to 4 feet..............	5.00	5.00	7.00	7.00	7.00	N.L.	N.L.
4 to 4½ feet..............	6.00	6.00	8.00	9.00	9.00	N.L.	N.L.
4 to 5 feet................	N.L.	N.L.	N.L.	N.L.	N.L.	8.00	8.00
4½ to 5 feet..............	7.00	7.00	9.00	11.00	11.00	N.L.	N.L.
5 to 6 feet................	8.00	8.00	10.00	N.L.	15.00	11.00	11.00
6 to 7 feet................	10.00	10.00	12.50	N.L.	N.L.	15.00	15.00
7 to 8 feet................	12.00	12.00	16.00	N.L.	N.L.	20.00	20.00
8 to 9 feet................	N.L.	N.L.	20.00	N.L.	N.L.	N.L.	N.L.
11 to 12 feet..............	25.00	N.L.	N.L.	N.L.	N.L.	N.L.	N.L.
Taxus cuspidata capitata							
2 to 2½ feet..............	N.L.*	N.L.	N.L.	N.L.	N.L.	8.00	8.00
2½ to 3 feet..............	7.00	7.00	7.50	7.50	N.L.	9.50	9.50
3 to 3½ feet..............	8.00	8.00	9.00	9.00	10.00	11.00	11.00
3½ to 4 feet..............	10.00	10.00	11.50	10.75	12.00	13.00	13.00
4 to 4½ feet..............	12.50	12.50	13.50	12.75	14.00	15.00	15.00
4½ to 5 feet..............	15.00	15.00	17.00	15.00	17.50	17.50	18.00
5 to 5½ feet..............	17.50	17.50	20.00	18.00	21.00	21.00	22.00
5½ to 6 feet..............	20.00	20.00	23.50	21.00	24.00	24.00	25.00
6 to 7 feet................	25.00	25.00	27.50	25.00	28.00	28.00	30.00
7 to 8 feet................	N.L.	N.L.	N.L.	N.L.	35.00	35.00	40.00

* N.L. is not listed.

3. How does the contribution concept relate to the nursery's pricing?
4. How does the opportunity cost concept relate to the nursery's pricing?
5. What changes in pricing do you recommend?

TELEPHONE CHARGES TO
AUXILIARY ACTIVITIES*

In 1961 the Vice President of Business Administration at the University of Kentucky requested one of his assistants to make a study of telephone charges made to auxiliary activities attached to the university. These activities were not included in the regular university budget but were connected to the central campus PBX. It was desirable that these agencies be charged their share of the total bill paid by the university to the General Telephone Company of Kentucky.

Exhibit 1
Common costs

Central office trunks	$1,466.40
Toll terminals	112.80
Station lines	1,477.00
Attendants' cabinets (positions)	300.00
Other charges	253.45
Total common costs	$3,609.65

The auxiliary agencies included the Campus Bookstore, the Athletics Department (which had a separate budget), the Experiment Station (largely financed out of federal funds), and the various dormitories. In 1960 the university billed each agency at the rate of $10 per month for each main extension (MEX) and $4 per month for each bridged extension (BEX). (A bridged extension is simply a second telephone attached to the same MEX with the same extension number.) In addition, each agency paid any special charges resulting from its operations, such as the cost of installing a telephone, and recurrent monthly charges for buzzer systems, wiring plans, horns, additional listings, and special illumination. The question was whether any revisions of these charges were warranted.

The assistant made a careful analysis of the telephone expenses paid by the university, which amounted to over $13,000 per month. He found that the costs common to the whole PBX system amounted to $3,609.65 per month, as shown in Exhibit 1.

---

* This case was prepared by Bernard Davis under the supervision of W. W. Haynes of the University of Kentucky as a basis for class discussion.

The wages paid the PBX operators directly by the university were another large expense which might be considered a common cost. These wages amounted to $3,647 per month.

In addition, the telephone company charged $1.85 per month for each main extension (MEX) and another $1.85 per month for each bridged extension (BEX). The system included 680 main extensions and 635 bridged extensions. Most of the special charges of $4,010 per month for buzzers, horns, and illumination were not at stake, since everyone agreed that each agency should pay those expenses for which it was directly responsible. The one exception was the substantial charge for "mileage," a charge proportional to the distance of the lines from the PBX to the main extensions. This charge (included in the $4,010) was $734 per month. It would be difficult to allocate this expense to individual extensions because of the difficult bookkeeping problem of recording the lengths of line and keeping up with changes as new extensions were added. Furthermore, it was not clear that an agency should be charged more because it was at a greater distance from the PBX. None of the above figures includes the costs to the university accounting office for recording and distributing these expenses.

The assistant making the study found that a special statistical study would be required to determine the impact of added bridged extensions. Most of the common costs would not be affected by adding more bridged extensions. In fact, the adding of one or ten bridged extensions would result in only the extra charge of $1.85 per phone. But the addition of, let us say, 300 bridged extensions might require an added attendant's cabinet and, more important, additional PBX operators. There were no records to indicate how much bridged extensions added to the total load of telephone calls.

The addition of main extensions would have a clearer impact on costs, requiring added mileage, added attendants' cabinets, and added PBX operators. Again it would make a difference whether a few or a great number of main extensions were contemplated.

Of the total number of telephones in the system, 505 (or 38 percent) were being charged to auxiliary services. Of this total, 322 were main extensions and 183 bridged extensions.

1. Estimate the marginal cost of a main extension and a bridged extension.
2. Estimate the added cost per extension for an increment of 300 extensions and an increment of 300 bridged extensions.
3. How do marginal and full costs relate to pricing in this case?
4. What revisions should the university make in its telephone charges?

STEEL PRICES IN 1962

The most famous pricing decision in recent years was that of the U.S. Steel Company on April 9, 1962, a decision that was rescinded on April 13, 1962. The strong opposition of President John F. Kennedy, along with the refusal of several steel producers to follow the lead of U.S. Steel, resulted in this rapid reversal of price policy.

The publicity at the time of the decision and its reversal stressed cost considerations. The United Steel Workers had signed a contract with the industry in early April which limited wage increases to the estimated rate of annual increase in national productivity. The agreement provided an increase in fringe benefits costing about 10.9 cents an hour, about a 2.5 percent increase in hourly wage costs. The contract was widely hailed as noninflationary and as indicating a growing maturity of union-management relations. President Kennedy praised the agreement as "industrial statesmanship of the highest order" and said that it "should provide a solid base for continued price stability."[1] Steel officials, however, were concerned not merely with the 10.9 cent wage cost increase in 1962, but with the approximate 50 cents per hour increase in employment costs since 1958, the time of the last price increase. Furthermore, they noted that the increase in productivity in the steel industry had been only 1.7 percent per year since 1940, which was lower than the contemplated increase in employment costs. Steel officials were disturbed by their reduced profit position—the low profits resulted in part from the reduced demand in 1960 and 1961 but also from rising costs. The profits of U.S. Steel in 1961 were 36 percent below those in 1958, a recession year. Exhibit 1 presents data on steel output and prices in the years from 1957 to 1961.

The decision of U.S. Steel to increase steel prices by an average of $6 per ton, about 3.5 percent, came as a surprise to many observers, who had assumed that the moderate union demands would mean no increase in prices. No doubt the officials of U.S. Steel tried to take into account not only the rising costs and reduced profits already mentioned, but also the political repercussions and the probable price policies of competitors. It is clear that these officials made an incorrect evaluation of the political repercussions. But some observers would argue that they may also have misjudged the elasticity of demand.

The measurement of the elasticity of the demand for steel is complicated by the fact that steel is not a homogeneous product and that it is sold in a variety of markets at a variety of prices. The fact that steel can be stored means that a distinction must be made between the response

---

[1] In *Business Week*, April 7, 1962, p. 29, Mr. Roger Blough, chairman of the board of U.S. Steel denied that U.S. Steel had made any commitment on prices before, during, or after the wage negotiations. See his article in *Look* magazine, January 29, 1963.

Exhibit 1
Important statistics on the steel industry (1951–1961)

| | U.S. Steel Company ($ millions) | | | | | | | Entire industry | | | |
Year	Products and services sold	Employ- ment costs*	Income Amount	Percent of sales	Dividends Preferred stock	Dividends Common stock	Reinvested in business	Average number of employees	Steel products shipped (net tons)	Ingot production (net tons)	Ingot operating rate
1951	$3,524.1	$1,374.5	$184.3	5.2%	$25.2	$78.3	$80.8	670,700	78,928,950	105,199,848	100.9
1952	3,137.4	1,322.1	143.6	4.6	25.2	78.3	40.1	653,700	68,003,612	93,168,039	85.8
1953	3,861.0	1,569.2	222.1	5.8	25.2	78.3	118.6	682,800	80,151,893	111,609,719	94.9
1954	3,250.4	1,387.0	195.4	6.0	25.2	85.5	84.7	611,000	63,152,726	88,311,652	71.0
1955	4,097.7	1,614.9	370.1	9.0	25.2	122.9	222.0	657,600	84,717,444	117,036,085	93.0
1956	4,228.9	1,681.0	348.1	8.2	25.2	144.9	178.0	653,400	83,251,168	115,216,149	89.8
1957	4,413.8	1,862.0	419.4	9.5	25.2	161.3	232.9	656,700	79,894,577	112,714,996	84.5
1958	3,472.1	1,488.5	301.5	8.7	25.2	161.4	114.9	551,000	59,914,433	85,254,885	60.6
1959	3,643.0	1,576.2	254.5	7.0	25.2	161.8	67.5	538,800	69,377,067	93,446,132	63.3
1960	3,698.5	1,700.0	304.2	8.2	25.2	162.0	117.0	601,600	71,149,218	99,281,601	66.8
1961	3,336.5	1,622.7	190.2	5.7	25.2	162.3	2.7	N/A†	66,125,505	98,014,492	N/A†

* Employment costs include pensions and social security taxes and also payments for insurance and other employee benefits.
† Not available.
Source: United States Steel Corporation, Annual Report 1961; Annual Statistical Reports, American Iron and Steel Institute. The number of employees represents total wage and salaried employees engaged in the production and sale of iron and steel products reported to American Iron and Steel Institute by companies comprising 93 to 97 percent of the steelmaking capacity of the steel industry adjusted to 100 percent of the industry steelmaking capacity.

Exhibit 2
Total world steel trade and U.S. steel exports

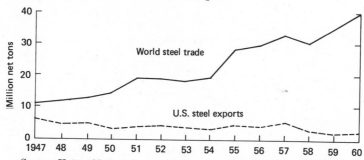

Source: United Nations Economic Commission for Europe and U.S. Department of Commerce as reprinted in American Iron and Steel Institute, *The Competitive Challenge to Steel*, 1961.

to temporary price changes and permanent price changes. Secret price concessions mean that published price data are not always reliable.

Several bits of evidence would suggest that the demand for steel is inelastic. Theodore Yntema's statistical study for the U.S. Steel Corporation presented to the Temporary National Economic Committee (TNEC) in 1938 indicated extremely low demand elasticities.[2] The steel industry used this study to argue that a reduction in steel prices would make little contribution to employment in the depression of the 1930s. One might object to using a depression study in the evaluation of demand in 1962. But the fact that the demand for steel is a derived demand would support the argument that it is inelastic. For example, the price of steel would appear to be a minor factor in determining how much steel is used in the production of automobiles.

On the other hand, the growing competition from steel producers abroad and from substitutes for steel might suggest that the demand for steel produced within the United States was becoming more elastic in the 1960s. In fact, this was one of the arguments used by the steel industry for moderation in wage demands—high domestic costs were hurting the United States' international trade position. In 1956 and 1957 the United States had exported four to five times the steel that it imported. Since 1958 imports had exceeded exports. Competition with Western Europe had become extremely severe, with the disappearance of most of the U.S. exports in Europe but with imports from Europe of over 2 million tons per year.[3] *Business Week* reported that companies in the European Coal and Steel Community were offering products at 10–15 percent below U.S. company prices in European markets. (Exhibits 2, 3, and 4 present data on the export situation.)

---

[2] See United States Steel Corporation, *T.N.E.C. Papers*, vol. 1. pp. 169 ff.

[3] *Business Week*, March 24, 1962, pp. 100–102.

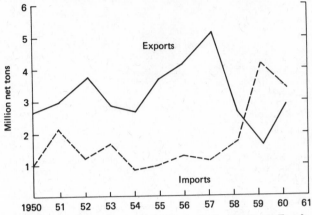

Exhibit 3
Relative importance of direct steel exports and imports

Source: American Iron and Steel Institute, *Foreign Trade Trends*, 1961.

Probably even more important were the inroads that competing metals were making into steel markets. Aluminum had become particularly important as a substitute for steel; no doubt many purchasers made careful comparisons between the cost of aluminum and the cost of steel.

The elasticity of demand facing individual firms such as U.S. Steel was influenced in large part by the extent to which other steel companies followed the price increases of the leader. President Kennedy and other government officials exerted a great effort to prevent an industry-wide increase and thus had an important influence on the elasticity of demand. Two companies, the eighth and ninth in size, announced that they would not increase their prices. Soon thereafter, Bethlehem Steel, the second largest steel company, rescinded its price increase. U.S. Steel followed with restoration of its original prices.

Roger Blough, chairman of the board of U.S. Steel, made these comments on competition.[4]

There was no doubt that a price increase was necessary and we reviewed again all of the competitive factors involved. We did not—and could not—know, of course, whether other major steel producers would also raise their prices if we made the attempt; but from their published annual reports we could assume that they were suffering as we were from steadily rising costs and that they needed, as we did, the profits necessary to pay for the replacement and modernization of worn-out and obsolete facilities.

We were aware, too, that should other companies go along with the price increase, competition with substitute materials and foreign sources of steel

[4] *The U.S. Steel Quarterly,* May 1962, p. 5.

Exhibit 4
U.S. exports and imports of steel-related products

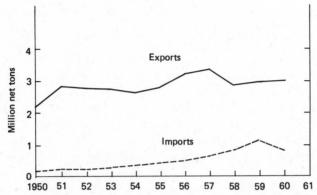

Source: American Iron and Steel Institute, *Foreign Trade Trends,*
1961.

might even add temporarily to our competitive difficulties. But the continued improvement in the economy as well as some improvement in the demand and consumption of steel indicated that a moderate price increase might be competitively possible; and, in view of the need, it was our judgment that we should delay no further in testing the market.

So on Tuesday, April 10, we announced an increase of three tenths of a cent per pound in the general level of our steel prices. This amounted to about 3½ percent and would cover only a little more than half of the 6 percent net increase in over-all costs which had occurred since 1958. Therefore, it would not restore, by any means, the post-price relationship that had existed four years ago; but it would at least assist in meeting the competitive needs of our company, as our president, Mr. Worthington, pointed out in his statement announcing the price action. He said:

"If the products of United States Steel are to compete successfully in the market place, then the plants and facilities which make those products must be as modern and efficient as the low-cost mills which abound abroad, and as the plants which turn out competing products here at home. Only by generating the funds necessary to keep these facilities fully competitive can our company continue to provide its customers with a dependable source of steel, and to provide its employees with dependable jobs. . . .

"The financial resources supporting continuous research and resultant new products as well as those supporting new equipment, are therefore vital in this competitive situation—vital not alone to the company and its employees, but to our international balance of payments, the value of our dollar, and to the strength and security of the nation as well."

In another article Blough commented on competitive pressures at the time of the steel price controversy. He stated that the competitive limitations of the market had restricted U.S. Steel to a 3.5 percent price increase instead of the 6 percent increase in costs. The order by Secretary of Defense Robert S. McNamara to defense contractors to buy steel only from companies which had not raised prices, along with long-distance calls by the President and his associates urging other steel companies not to raise prices, had made it difficult to maintain the 3.5 percent price increase. While eight of the companies had raised prices, the "rest of the steel companies were still selling at $6 lower, and manifold government pressures were being exerted."[5] When Inland Steel and Kaiser Steel announced against price increases, it was obvious that the "eight steel companies that had raised prices would have to lower them in order to survive." Blough also commented that no firm "has yet discovered a way to sell steel in a buyer's market at $6 a ton more than his competition."

Blough believed that one favorable outcome of the steel price controversy was a public awareness "that, in the absence of government intervention, steel prices are determined by the competitive forces of the marketplace—not by the decision of one company. Perhaps the public also realized that the market alone is the infallible arbiter of prices, and if error is made, the market itself will correct it."

The steel controversy involved broad questions about the relationship between government and business. President Kennedy stated that a few steel executives had shown "utter contempt for the interests of 185 million Americans." He apparently believed that the government had the right to intervene to protect the "public interest." Blough, on the other hand, took the position that "it is the duty of government to protect each [individual] . . . in the pursuit of his lawful interests, to insure that force and coercion do not intrude upon those interests, and to guarantee that each individual not intrude upon the lawful interests of others." He therefore denied that it was in the public interest for the President "to substitute his own action for the action of the marketplace by trying to set prices for any competitive products."

1. How do cost considerations affect U.S. Steel's price policy?
2. How do demand considerations affect the company's pricing?
3. Is the steel industry competitive? If so, how is it able to increase prices in the face of low demand and excess capacity? If not, why were the steel companies not able to maintain the 1962 price increases?
4. Which position on the "public interest" is correct: that of President Kennedy or that of the steel companies?
5. Should U.S. Steel have raised prices on April 9, 1962? Should they have rescinded the increase on April 13, 1962?

---

[5] "My Side of the Steel Price Story," *Look* magazine, January 29, 1963, by Roger Blough as told to Eleanor Harris.

UTAH PIE COMPANY v.
CONTINENTAL BAKING CO. (*et al.*)*

This case was argued January 17, 1967; decided April 24, 1967; a re-hearing was denied June 5, 1967. Mr. Justice White delivered the opinion of the Court.

This suit for treble damages and injunction under § § 4 and 16 of the Clayton Act, 38 Stat. 731, 737, 15 U.S.C. § § 15 and 26[1] was brought by petitioner, Utah Pie Company, against respondents, Continental Baking Company, Carnation Company, and Pet Milk Company. The complaint charged a conspiracy under § § 1 and 2 of the Sherman Act, 26 Stat. 209, as amended, 15 U.S.C. § § 1 and 2, and violations by each respondent of § 2(a) of the Clayton Act as amended by the Robinson-Patman Act, 49 Stat. 1526, 15 U.S.C. § 13(a).[2] The jury found for respondents on the conspiracy charge and for petitioner on the price discrimination charge.[3] Judgment was entered for petitioner for damages and attorneys' fees and respondents appealed on several grounds. The Court of Appeals reversed, addressing itself to the single issue of whether the evidence against each of the respondents was sufficient to support a finding of probable injury to competition within the meaning of § 2(a) and holding that it was not. We reverse.

The product involved is frozen dessert pies—apple, cherry, boysenberry, peach, pumpkin, and mince. The period covered by the suit comprised the years 1958, 1959, and 1960 and the first eight months of 1961. Petitioner is a Utah Corporation which for 30 years had been baking pies in its plant in Salt Lake City and selling them in Utah and surrounding states. It entered the frozen

---

* 87 *Supreme Court Reporter* 1327; 386 U.S. 687.

[1] 15 U.S.C. § 15 provides that:

"Any person who shall be injured in his business or property by reason of anything forbidden in the antitrust laws may sue therefor in any district court of the United States in the district in which the defendant resides or is found or has an agent, without respect to the amount in controversy, and shall recover threefold the damages by him sustained, and the cost of suit, including a reasonable attorney's fee."

15 U.S.C. § 26 provides injunctive relief for private parties from violation of the antitrust laws.

[2] The portion of § 2(a) relevant to the issue before the Court provides:

"That it shall be unlawful for any person engaged in commerce, in the course of such commerce, either directly or indirectly, to discriminate in price between different purchasers of commodities of like grade and quality, where either or any of the purchases involved in such discrimination are in commerce * * * where the effect of such discrimination may be substantially to lessen competition or tend to create a monopoly in any line of commerce, or to injure, destroy, or prevent competition with any person who either grants or knowingly receives the benefit of such discrimination, or with customers or either of them . . . ."

[3] Respondent Continental by counterclaim charged petitioner with violation of § 2(a) in respect to certain sales. On this issue the jury found for Continental, and although petitioner failed to move for a directed verdict on the counterclaim before its submission to the jury, the trial judge granted petitioner's motion for judgment notwithstanding the verdict. The Court of Appeals reversed the judgment notwithstanding the verdict on the counterclaim, and remanded the issue for a new trial. No question concerning the counterclaim is before the Court.

pie business in late 1957. It was immediately successful with its new line and
built a new plant in Salt Lake City in 1958. The frozen pie market was a rapidly
expanding one: 57,060 dozen frozen pies were sold in the Salt Lake City market
in 1958, 111,729 dozen in 1959, 184,569 dozen in 1960, and 266,908 dozen in
1961. Utah Pie's share of this market in those years was 66.5 percent, 34.3 percent, 45.5 percent, and 45.3 percent, respectively, its sales volume steadily increasing over the four years. Its financial position also improved. Petitioner is
not, however, a large company. At the time of the trial, petitioner operated with
only 18 employees, nine of whom were members of the Rigby family, which controlled the business. Its net worth increased from $31,651.98 on October 31, 1957,
to $68,802.13 on October 31, 1961. Total sales were $238,000 in the year ending
October 31, 1957, $353,000 in 1958, $430,000 in 1959, $504,000 in 1960, and
$589,000 in 1961. Its net income or loss for these same years was a loss of
$6,461 in 1957, and net income in the remaining years of $7,090, $11,897, $7,636,
and $9,216.

Each of the respondents is a large company and each of them is a major
factor in the frozen pie market in one or more regions of the country. Each
entered the Salt Lake City frozen pie market before petitioner began freezing
dessert pies. None of them had a plant in Utah. By the end of the period involved in this suit Pet had plants in Michigan, Pennsylvania, and California;
Continental in Virginia, Iowa, and California; and Carnation in California. The
Salt Lake City market was supplied by respondents chiefly from their California
operations. They sold primarily on a delivered price basis.

The "Utah" label was petitioner's proprietary brand. Beginning in 1960, it
also sold pies of like grade and quality under the controlled label "Frost 'N'
Flame" to Associated Grocers and in 1961 it began selling to American Food
Stores under the "Mayfresh" label. It also, on a seasonal basis, sold pumpkin
and mince frozen pies to Safeway under Safeway's own "Bel-air" label.

The major competitive weapon in the Utah market was price. The location
of petitioner's plant gave it natural advantages in the Salt Lake City marketing
area and it entered the market at a price below the then going prices for respondents' comparable pies. For most of the period involved here its prices were
the lowest in the Salt Lake City market. It was, however, challenged by each
of the respondents at one time or another and for varying periods. There was
ample evidence to show that each of the respondents contributed to what proved
to be a deteriorating price structure over the period covered by this suit, and
each of the respondents in the course of the ongoing price competition sold
frozen pies in the Salt Lake market at prices lower than it sold pies of like
grade and quality in other markets considerably closer to its plants. Utah Pie,
which entered the market at a price of $4.15 per dozen at the beginning of the
relevant period, was selling "Utah" and "Frost 'N' Flame" pies for $2.75 per
dozen when the instant suit was filed some 44 months later.[4] Pet, which was
offering pies at $4.92 per dozen in February 1958, was offering "Pet-Ritz" and
"Bel-air" pies at $3.56 and $3.46 per dozen respectively in March and April

---

[4] The prices discussed herein refer to those charged for apple pies. The apple
flavor has been used as the standard throughout this case, without objection from
the parties, and we adhere to the practice here.

1961. Carnation's price in early 1958 was $4.82 per dozen but it was selling at $3.46 per dozen at the conclusion of the period, meanwhile having been down as low as $3.30 per dozen. The price range experienced by Continental during the period covered by this suit ran from a 1958 high of over $5 per dozen to a 1961 low of $2.85 per dozen.[5]

We deal first with petitioner's case against the Pet Milk Company. Pet entered the frozen pie business in 1955, acquired plants in Pennsylvania and California and undertook a large advertising campaign to market its "Pet-Ritz" brand of frozen pies. Pet's initial emphasis was on quality, but in the face of competition from regional and local companies and in an expanding market where price proved to be a crucial factor, Pet was forced to take steps to reduce the price of its pies to the ultimate consumer. These developments had consequences in the Salt Lake City market which are the substance of petitioner's case against Pet.

First, Pet successfully concluded an arrangement with Safeway, which is one of the three largest customers for frozen pies in the Salt Lake market, whereby it would sell frozen pies to Safeway under the latter's own "Bel-air" label at a price significantly lower than it was selling its comparable "Pet-Ritz" brand in the same Salt Lake market and elsewhere. The initial price on "Bel-air" pies was slightly lower than Utah's price for its "Utah" brand of pies at the time, and near the end of the period the "Bel-air" price was comparable to the "Utah" price but higher than Utah's "Frost 'N' Flame" brand. Pet's Safeway business amounted to 22.8 percent, 12.3 percent, and 6.3 percent of the entire Salt Lake City market for the years 1959, 1960, and 1961, respectively, and to 64 percent, 44 percent, and 22 percent of Pet's own Salt Lake City sales for those same years. Second, it introduced a 20-ounce economy pie under the "Swiss Miss" label and began selling the new pie in the Salt Lake market in August 1960 at prices ranging from $3.25 to $3.30 for the remainder of the period. This pie was at

---

[5] The Salt Lake City sales volumes and market shares of the parties to this suit as well as of other sellers during the period at issue were as follows:

Company	1958 Volume (in doz.)	Percent of market	Company	1960 Volume (in doz.)	Percent of market
Carnation......	5,863	10.3%	Carnation......	22,371.5	12.1%
Continental....	754	1.3	Continental....	3,350	1.8
Utah Pie.......	37,969.5	66.5	Utah Pie......	83,894	45.5
Pet...........	9,336.5	16.4	Pet...........	51,480	27.9
Others.........	3,137	5.5	Others.........	23,473.5	12.7
Total......	57,060	100.0%	Total......	184,569	100.0%

Company	1959 Volume (in doz.)	Percent of market	Company	1961 Volume (in doz.)	Percent of market
Carnation......	9,625	8.6%	Carnation......	20,067	8.8%
Continental....	3,182	2.9	Continental....	18,799.5	8.3
Utah Pie.......	38,372	34.3	Utah Pie.......	102,690	45.3
Pet...........	39,639	35.5	Pet...........	66,786	29.4
Others.........	20,911	18.7	Others.........	18,565.5	8.2
Total......	111,729	100.0%	Total......	226,908	100.0%

times sold at a lower price in the Salt Lake City market than it was sold in other markets.

Third, Pet became more competitive with respect to the prices for its "Pet-Ritz" proprietary label. For 18 of the relevant 44 months its offering price for "Pet-Ritz" pies was $4 per dozen or lower, and $3.70 or lower for six of these months. According to the Court of Appeals, in seven of the 44 months Pet's prices in Salt Lake were lower than prices charged in the California markets. This was true although selling in Salt Lake involved a 30- to 35-cent freight cost.

The Court of Appeals first concluded that Pet's price differential on sales to Safeway must be put aside in considering injury to competition because in its view of the evidence the differential had been completely cost justified and because Utah would not in any event have been able to enjoy the Safeway custom. Second, it concluded that the remaining discriminations on "Pet-Ritz" and "Swiss Miss" pies were an insufficient predicate on which the jury could have found a reasonably possible injury either to Utah Pie as a competitive force or to competition generally.

We disagree with the Court of Appeals in several respects. First, there was evidence from which the jury could have found considerably more price discrimination by Pet with respect to "Pet-Ritz" and "Swiss Miss" pies than was considered by the Court of Appeals. In addition to the seven months during which Pet's prices in Salt Lake were lower than prices in the California markets, there was evidence from which the jury could reasonably have found that in 10 additional months the Salt Lake City prices for "Pet-Ritz" pies were discriminatory as compared with sales in western markets other than California. Likewise, with respect to "Swiss Miss" pies, there was evidence in the record from which the jury could have found that in five of the 13 months during which the "Swiss Miss" pies were sold prior to the filing of this suit, prices in Salt Lake City were lower than those charged by Pet in either California or some other western market.

Second, with respect to Pet's Safeway business, the burden of proving cost justification was on Pet and, in our view, reasonable men could have found that Pet's lower priced, "Bel-air" sales to Safeway were not cost justified in their entirety. Pet introduced cost data for 1961 indicating a cost saving on the Safeway business greater than the price advantage extended to that customer. These statistics were not particularized for the Salt Lake market, but assuming that they were adequate to justify the 1961 sales, they related to only 24 percent of the Safeway sales over the relevant period. The evidence concerning the remaining 76 percent was at best incomplete and inferential. It was insufficient to take the defense of cost justification from the jury, which reasonably could have found a greater incidence of unjustified price discrimination than that allowed by the Court of Appeals' view of the evidence.[6]

----

[6] The only evidence cited by the Court of Appeals to justify the remaining 76 percent of Pet's sales to Safeway was Safeway's established practice of requiring its sellers to cost justify sales that otherwise would be illegally discriminatory. This practice was incorporated in the Pet-Safeway contract. We are unprepared to hold that a contractual obligation to cost justify price differentials is legally dispositive proof that such differentials are in fact so justified. Pet admitted that its cost-justification figures were drawn from past performance, so even crediting the data accompanying the 1960 contract regarding cost differences, Pet's additional evidence

With respect to whether Utah would have enjoyed Safeway's business absent the Pet contract with Safeway, it seems clear that whatever the fact is in this regard, it is not determinative of the impact of that contract on competitors other than Utah and on competition generally. There were other companies seeking the Safeway business, including Continental and Carnation, whose pies may have been excluded from the Safeway shelves by what the jury could have found to be discriminatory sales to Safeway. What is more, Pet's evidence that Utah's unwillingness to install quality control equipment prevented Utah from enjoying Safeway's private label business is not the only evidence in the record relevant to that question. There was other evidence to the contrary. The jury would not have been compelled to find that Utah Pie could not have gained more of the Safeway business.

Third, the Court of Appeals almost entirely ignored other evidence which provides material support for the jury's conclusion that Pet's behavior satisfied the statutory test regarding competitive injury. This evidence bore on the issue of Pet's predatory intent to injure Utah Pie. As an initial matter, the jury could have concluded that Pet's discriminatory pricing was aimed at Utah Pie; Pet's own management, as early as 1959, identified Utah Pie as an "unfavorable factor," one which "d[u]g holes in our operation" and posed a constant "check" on Pet's performance in the Salt Lake City market. Moreover, Pet candidly admitted that during the period when it was establishing its relationship with Safeway, it sent into Utah Pie's plant an industrial spy to seek information that would be of use to Pet in convincing Safeway that Utah Pie was not worthy of its custom. Pet denied that it ever in fact used what it had learned against Utah Pie in competing for Safeway's business. The parties, however, are not the ultimate judges of credibility. But even giving Pet's view of the incident a measure of weight does not mean the jury was foreclosed from considering the predatory intent underlying Pet's mode of competition. Finally, Pet does not deny that the evidence showed it suffered substantial losses on its frozen pie sales during the greater part of the time involved in this suit, and there was evidence from which the jury could have concluded that the losses Pet sustained in Salt Lake City were greater than those incurred elsewhere. It would not have been an irrational step if the jury concluded that there was a relationship between price and the losses.

It seems clear to us that the jury heard adequate evidence from which it could have concluded that Pet had engaged in predatory tactics in waging competitive warfare in the Salt Lake City market. Coupled with the incidence of price discrimination attributable to Pet, the evidence as a whole established, rather than negated, the reasonable possibility that Pet's behavior produced a lessening of competition proscribed by the Act.

Petitioner's case against Continental is not complicated. Continental was a substantial factor in the market in 1957. But its sales of frozen 22-ounce dessert

---

would bring under the justification umbrella only the 1959 sales. Thus, at the least, the jury was free to consider the 1960 Safeway sales as inadequately cost justified. Those sales accounted for 12.3 percent of the entire Salt Lake City market in that year. In the context of this case, the sales to Safeway are particularly relevant since there was evidence that private label sales influenced the general market, in this case depressing overall market prices.

pies, sold under the "Morton" brand, amounted to only 1.3 percent of the market in 1958, 2.9 percent in 1959, and 1.8 percent in 1960. Its problems were primarily that of cost and in turn that of price, the controlling factor in the market. In late 1960 it worked out a co-packing arrangement in California by which fruit would be processed from the trees into the finished pie without large intermediate packing, storing, and shipping expenses. Having improved its position, it attempted to increase its share of the Salt Lake City market by utilizing a local broker and offering short-term price concessions in varying amounts. Its efforts for seven months were not spectacularly successful. Then in June 1961, it took the steps which are the heart of petitioner's complaint against it. Effective for the last two weeks of June it offered its 22-ounce frozen apple pies in the Utah area at $2.85 per dozen. It was then selling the same pies at substantially higher prices in other markets. The Salt Lake City price was less than its direct cost plus an allocation for overhead. Utah's going price at the time for its 24-ounce "Frost 'N' Flame" apple pie sold to Associated Grocers was $3.10 per dozen, and for its "Utah" brand $3.40 per dozen. At its new prices, Continental sold pies to American Grocers in Pocatello, Idaho, and to American Food Stores in Ogden, Utah. Safeway, one of the major buyers in Salt Lake City, also purchased 6,250 dozen, its requirements for about five weeks. Another purchaser ordered 1,000 dozen. Utah's response was immediate. It reduced its price on all of its apple pies to $2.75 per dozen. Continental refused Safeway's request to match Utah's price, but renewed its offer at the same prices effective July 31 for another two-week period. Utah filed suit on September 8, 1961. Continental's total sales of frozen pies increased from 3,350 dozen in 1960 to 18,800 dozen in 1961. Its market share increased from 1.8 percent in 1960 to 8.3 percent in 1961. The Court of Appeals concluded that Continental's conduct had had only minimal effect, that it had not injured or weakened Utah Pie as a competitor, that it had not substantially lessened competition and that there was no reasonable possibility that it would do so in the future.

We again differ with the Court of Appeals. Its opinion that Utah was not damaged as a competitive force apparently rested on the fact that Utah's sales volume continued to climb in 1961 and on the court's own factual conclusion that Utah was not deprived of any pie business which it otherwise might have had. But this retrospective assessment fails to note that Continental's discriminatory below-cost price caused Utah Pie to reduce its price to $2.75. The jury was entitled to consider the potential impact of Continental's price reduction absent any responsive price cut by Utah Pie. Price was a major factor in the Salt Lake City market. Safeway, which had been buying Utah brand pies, immediately reacted and purchased a five-week supply of frozen pies from Continental, thereby temporarily foreclosing the proprietary brands of Utah and other firms from the Salt Lake City Safeway market. The jury could rationally have concluded that had Utah not lowered its price, Continental, which repeated its offer once, would have continued it, that Safeway would have continued to buy from Continental and that other buyers, large as well as small, would have followed suit. It could also have reasonably concluded that a competitor who is forced to reduce his price to a new all-time low in a market of declining prices will in time feel the financial pinch and will be a less effective competitive force.

Even if the impact on Utah Pie as a competitor was negligible, there remain the consequences to others in the market who had to compete not only with Continental's 22-ounce pie at $2.85 but with Utah's even lower price of $2.75 per dozen for both its proprietary and controlled labels. Petitioner and respondents were not the only sellers in the Salt Lake City market, although they did account for 91.8 percent of the sales in 1961. The evidence was that there were nine other sellers in 1960 who sold 23,473 dozen pies, 12.7 percent of the total market. In 1961 there were eight other sellers who sold less than the year before—18,565 dozen or 8.2 percent of the total—although the total market had expanded from 184,569 dozen to 226,908 dozen. We think there was sufficient evidence from which the jury could find a violation of § 2(a) by Continental.

The Carnation Company entered the frozen dessert pie business in 1955 through the acquisition of "Mrs. Lee's Pies" which was then engaged in manufacturing and selling frozen pies in Utah and elsewhere under the "Simple Simon" label. Carnation also quickly found the market extremely sensitive to price. Carnation decided, however, not to enter an economy product in the market, and during the period covered by this suit it offered only its quality "Simple Simon" brand. Its primary method of meeting competition in its markets was to offer a variety of discounts and other reductions, and the technique was not unsuccessful. In 1958, for example, Carnation enjoyed 10.3 percent of the Salt Lake City market, and although its volume of pies sold in that market increased substantially in the next year, its percentage of the market temporarily slipped to 8.6 percent. However, 1960 was a turnaround year for Carnation in the Salt Lake City market; it more than doubled its volume of sales over the preceding year and thereby gained 12.1 percent of the market. And while the price structure in the market deteriorated rapidly in 1961, Carnation's position remained important.

We need not dwell long upon the case against Carnation, which in some respects is similar to that against Continental and in others more nearly resembles the case against Pet. After Carnation's temporary setback in 1959 it instituted a new pricing policy to regain business in the Salt Lake City market. The new policy involved a slash in price of 60¢ per dozen pies, which brought Carnation's price to a level admittedly well below its costs, and well below the other prices prevailing in the market. The impact of the move was felt immediately, and the two other major sellers in the market reduced their prices. Carnation's banner year, 1960, in the end involved eight months during which the prices in Salt Lake City were lower than prices charged in other markets. The trend continued during the eight months in 1961 that preceded the filing of the complaint in this case. In each of those months the Salt Lake City prices charged by Carnation were well below prices charged in other markets, and in all but August 1961 the Salt Lake City delivered price was 20¢ to 50¢ lower than the prices charged in distant San Francisco. The Court of Appeals held that only the early 1960 prices could be found to have been below cost. That holding, however, simply overlooks evidence from which the jury could have concluded that throughout 1961 Carnation maintained a below-cost price structure and that Carnation's discriminatory pricing, no less than that of Pet and Continental, had an important effect on the Salt Lake City market. We cannot say that the evidence precluded the jury from finding it reasonably possible that Carnation's conduct would injure competition.

Section 2(a) does not forbid price competition which will probably injure or lessen competition by eliminating competitors, discouraging entry into the market, or enhancing the market shares of the dominant sellers. But Congress has established some ground rules for the game. Sellers may not sell like goods to different purchasers at different prices if the result may be to injure competition in either the sellers' or the buyers' market unless such discriminations are justified as permitted by the Act. This case concerns the sellers' market. In this context, the Court of Appeals placed heavy emphasis on the fact that Utah Pie constantly increased its sales volume and continued to make a profit. But we disagree with its apparent view that there is no reasonably possible injury to competition as long as the volume of sales in a particular market is expanding and at least some of the competitors in the market continue to operate at a profit. Nor do we think that the Act only comes into play to regulate the conduct of price discriminators when their discriminatory prices consistently undercut other competitors. It is true that many of the primary line cases that have reached the courts have involved blatant predatory price discriminations employed with the hope of immediate destruction of a particular competitor. On the question of injury to competition such cases present courts with no difficulty, for such pricing is clearly within the heart of the proscription of the Act. Courts and commentators alike have noted that the existence of predatory intent might bear on the likelihood of injury to competition. In this case there was some evidence of predatory intent with respect to each of these respondents. There was also other evidence upon which the jury could rationally find the requisite injury to competition. The frozen pie market in Salt Lake City was highly competitive. At times Utah Pie was a leader in moving the general level of prices down, and at other times each of the respondents also bore responsibility for the downward pressure on the price structure. We believe that the Act reaches price discrimination that erodes competition as much as it does price discrimination that is intended to have immediate destructive impact. In this case, the evidence shows a drastically declining price structure which the jury could rationally attribute to continued or sporadic price discrimination. The jury was entitled to conclude that "the effect of such discrimination," by each of these respondents, "may be substantially to lessen competition . . . or to injure, destroy, or prevent competition with any person who either grants or knowingly receives the benefit of such discrimination. . . ." The statutory test is one that necessarily looks forward on the basis of proven conduct in the past. Proper application of that standard here requires reversal of the judgment of the Court of Appeals.

Since the Court of Appeals held that petitioner had failed to make a prima facie case against each of the respondents, it expressly declined to pass on other grounds for reversal presented by the respondents. 349 F.2d 122, 126. Without intimating any views on the other grounds presented to the Court of Appeals, we reverse its judgment and remand the case to that court for further proceedings. It is so ordered. Reversed and remanded.

The Chief Justice took no part in the decision of this case. Mr. Justice Stewart and Mr. Justice Harlan joined in dissenting:

I would affirm the judgment, agreeing substantially with the reasoning of the Court of Appeals as expressed in the thorough and conscientious opinion of Judge Phillips.

There is only one issue in this case in its present posture: Whether the respondents engaged in price discrimination "where the effect of such discrimination may be substantially to lessen competition or tend to create a monopoly in any line of commerce, or to injure, destroy, or prevent competition with any person who either grants or knowingly receives the benefit of such discrimination. . . ."[7] Phrased more simply, did the respondents' actions have the anticompetitive effect required by the statute as an element of a cause of action?

The Court's own description of the Salt Lake City frozen pie market from 1958 through 1961, shows that the answer to that question must be no. In 1958 Utah Pie had a quasi-monopolistic 66.5 percent of the market. In 1961—after the alleged predations of the respondents—Utah Pie still had a commanding 45.3 percent, Pet had 29.4 percent, and the remainder of the market was divided almost equally between Continental, Carnation, and other, small local bakers. Unless we disregard the lessons so laboriously learned in scores of Sherman and Clayton Act cases, the 1961 situation has to be considered more competitive than that of 1958. Thus, if we assume that the price discrimination proven against the respondents had any effect on competition, that effect must have been beneficient.

That the Court has fallen into the error of reading the Robinson-Patman Act as protecting competitors, instead of competition, can be seen from its unsuccessful attempt to distinguish cases relied upon by the respondents. Those cases are said to be inapposite because they involved "no general decline in price structure," and no "lasting impact upon prices." But lower prices are the hallmark of intensified competition.

The Court of Appeals squarely identified the fallacy which the Court today embraces:

> ". . . a contention that Utah Pie was entitled to hold the extraordinary market share percentage of 66.5, attained in 1958, falls of its own dead weight. To approve such a contention would be to hold that Utah Pie was entitled to maintain a position which approached, if it did not in fact amount to a monopoly, and could not exist in the face of proper and healthy competition."

I cannot hold that Utah Pie's monopolistic position was protected by the federal antitrust laws from effective price competition, and I therefore respectfuly dissent.

1. Did the competitors engage in price discrimination? Were these practices illegal? Should they be considered illegal?
2. Does the fact that Utah Pie Company is a small independent firm, facing large competitors, influence your appraisal of the case?

---

[7] Section 2(a) of the Clayton Act as amended by the Robinson-Patman Act, 15 U.S.C. § 13(a).

3. Is the market structure competitive, monopolistically competitive, or oligopolistic?
4. Did the ruling in the case reduce competition or protect it?

BIRCH PAPER COMPANY*

"If I were to price these boxes any lower than $480 a thousand," said James Brunner, manager of Birch Paper Company's Thompson division, "I'd be countermanding my order of last month for our salespeople to stop shaving their bids and to bid full-cost quotations. I've been trying for weeks to improve the quality of our business, and if I turn around now and accept this job at $430 or $450 or something less than $480, I'll be tearing down this program I've been working so hard to build up. The division can't very well show a profit by putting in bids which don't even cover a fair share of overhead costs, let alone give us a profit."

Birch Paper Company was a medium-size, partly integrated paper company, producing white and kraft papers and paperboard. A portion of its paperboard output was converted into corrugated boxes by the Thompson division, which also printed and colored the outside surface of the boxes. Including Thompson, the company had four producing divisions and a timberland division, which supplied part of the company's pulp requirements.

For several years each division had been judged independently on the basis of its profit and return on investment. Top management had been working to gain effective results from a policy of decentralizing responsibility and authority for all decisions but those relating to overall company policy. The company's top officials believed that in the past few years the concept of decentralization had been successfully applied and that the company's profits and competitive position had definitely improved.

Early in 1957 the Northern division designed a special display box for one of its papers in conjunction with the Thompson division, which was equipped to make the box. Thompson's staff for package design and development spent several months perfecting the design, production methods, and materials that were to be used; because of the unusual color and shape, these were far from standard. According to an agreement between the two divisions, the Thompson division was reimbursed by the Northern division for the cost of its design and development work.

---

* This case was prepared by William Rotch under the direction of Neil E. Harlan of the Harvard University Graduate School of Business Administration as a basis for classroom discussion rather than to illustrate either effective or ineffective handling of administrative situations. Copyright © 1956 by the President and Fellows of Harvard College. Used by specific permission.

When the specifications were all prepared, the Northern division asked for bids on the box from Thompson division and from two outside companies. Each division manager was normally free to buy from whatever supplier he or she wished; and even on sales within the company, divisions were expected to meet the going market price if they wanted the business.

In 1957 the profit margins of converters such as the Thompson division were being squeezed. Thompson, as did many other similar converters, bought its paperboard and its function was to print, cut, and shape it into boxes. Although it bought most of its materials from other Birch divisions, most of Thompson's sales were made to outside customers. If Thompson got the order from Northern, it probably would buy its linerboard and corrugating medium from the Southern division of Birch. The walls of a corrugated box consist of outside and inside sheets of linerboard sandwiching the fluted corrugating medium. About 70 percent of Thompson's out-of-pocket cost of $400 for the order represented the cost of linerboard and corrugating medium. Though Southern had been running below capacity and had excess inventory, it quoted the market price, which had not noticeably weakened as a result of the oversupply. Its out-of-pocket costs on both liner and corrugating medium were about 60 percent of the selling price.

The Northern division received bids on the boxes of $480 a thousand from the Thompson division, $430 a thousand from West Paper Company, and $432 a thousand from Eire Papers, Ltd. Eire Papers offered to buy from Birch the outside linerboard with the special printing already on it, but would supply its own inside liner and corrugating medium. The outside liner would be supplied by the Southern division at a price equivalent of $90 a thousand boxes, and would be printed for $30 a thousand by the Thompson division. Of the $30, about $25 would be out-of-pocket costs.

Since this situation appeared to be a little unusual, William Kenton, manager of the Northern division, discussed the wide discrepancy of bids with Birch's commercial vice president. He told the vice president, "We sell in a very competitive market, where higher costs cannot be passed on. How can we be expected to show a decent profit and return on investment if we have to buy our supplies at more than 10 percent over the going market?"

Knowing that Brunner had on occasion in the past few months been unable to operate the Thompson division at capacity, it seemed odd to the vice president that Brunner would add the full 20 percent overhead and profit charge to his out-of-pocket costs. When asked about this, Brunner's answer was the remark that appears at the beginning of the case. He went on to say that having done the developmental work on the box, and having received no profit on that, he felt entitled to a good markup on the production of the box itself.

The vice president explored further the cost structures of the various divisions. He remembered a comment that the controller had made at a meeting the week before to the effect that costs that for one division were variable, could be largely fixed for the company as a whole. He knew that in the absence of specific orders from top management, Kenton would accept the lowest bid, which was that of the West Paper Company for $430. However, it would be possible for top management to order the acceptance of another bid if the situation warranted such action. And though the volume represented by the transactions in question was less than 5 percent of the volume of any of the divisions involved, other transactions could conceivably raise similar problems later.

1. How does the theory of transfer pricing relate to this case?
2. Is there a conflict in the case between the needs of decisions on pricing and the needs of profit determination? Explain.
3. What price should be set on the special display boxes? Discuss.

Part six

Long-range planning

Chapter 13

Long-range forecasting and strategy formulation

This chapter discusses forecasting for strategic planning. Strategy has a long-run time perspective, since it extends beyond the expected useful life of much of the firm's plant and equipment. Strategic planning selects a future "business to be in," specified in terms of product mix, markets in which the products will be sold, and competitive advantages that the firm expects to achieve.

The chapter begins with a brief description of a process of formulating strategy. This gives an overview of uses of long-range forecasts in strategic planning. The chapter then discusses social forecasting, technological forecasting, and resource forecasting. It concludes with examples of economic analyses in strategic planning by business and nonprofit organizations.

FORMULATION OF CORPORATE STRATEGY

The game of chess provides an example of a need for strategy. Success —i.e., winning—requires planning ahead for at least a few plays. One chess player may have an offensive strategy requiring concentration of powerful pieces for a thrust down the middle of the board. Another may have a defensive strategy requiring early "castling" with a buildup of a deep defense in front of the king's castle. Strategy suggests most of the early moves of each player. Further, every move, even an opportunistic play, is evaluated in terms of its contribution toward the player's overall strategy.

Businesses are formulating strategy when they make decisions about the general direction and scope of their desired growth. Delineation of a future "business to be in" suggests priorities for present resource allocations to technological research, market development, management recruiting and training, plant and equipment expenditures, and mergers and acquisitions. Many contemporary decisions of line managers and staff specialists are partially formed by their relationships to the firm's long-term strategy.

The ongoing, never-ending process of strategy formulation includes specification of objectives, evaluation of the firm's strengths and weaknesses, a forecast of trends in the environment, delineation of economic threats and opportunities, and a search for synergy (economic complementarity among potential activities of the firm).[1]

Objectives and goals

Conventional microeconomic theory asserts that a business firm always acts in such a way that it maximizes profits. Some writers have suggested that firms attempt to maximize sales rather than profits.[2] Others have hypothesized that firms simply attempt to "satisfice"—i.e., reach some "satisfactory" level of profits and sales.[3] Still others have hypothesized that the primary objective of the firm is survival,[4] or that the firm is primarily interested in growth in order to survive.[5] The assumption in this chapter is that firms do attempt to maximize profits over the long run.

A broadly stated goal such as long-run profit maximization is not very helpful in the strategy formulation process. Goals must be more specific. For example, a firm may establish some target rate of *return on total assets used* over the next three to ten years. Ansoff says that even this specific goal must be decomposed into a set of subsidiary objectives

[1] The concept of strategy follows the concept of H. Igor Ansoff, *Corporate Strategy* (New York: McGraw-Hill, 1965). Ansoff's book contains many important concepts and techniques not mentioned here.

[2] William J. Baumol, *Economic Theory and Operations Analysis,* 3d ed. (Englewood Cliffs, N.J.: Prentice-Hall, 1972), p. 320.

[3] Richard M. Cyert and James G. March, *A Behavioral Theory of the Firm* (Englewood Cliffs, N.J.: Prentice-Hall, 1963).

[4] Peter Drucker, "Business Objectives and Survival Needs: Notes on a Discipline of Business Enterprise," *Journal of Business* 31 (1958), pp. 81–90.

[5] John Kenneth Galbraith, *The New Industrial State,* 2d ed. (Boston: Houghton-Mifflin Company, 1971), pp. 171–72.

Figure 13–1
A set of long-range objectives

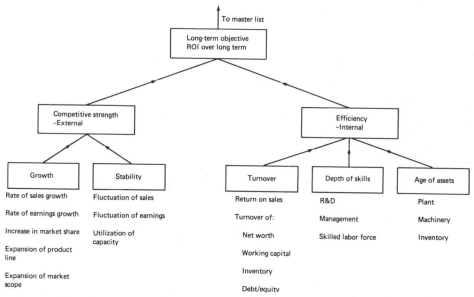

Source: H. Igor Ansoff, *Corporate Strategy* (New York: McGraw-Hill, 1965), p. 53.

relating to external competitive strengths and internal operating efficiency. Figure 13–1 illustrates an operationally useful set of long-range objectives. Note that all of these goals are quantifiable, so that the firm can measure the extent to which its aspirations are being met.

In addition to those objectives related to return on assets used, the firm has a set of objectives related to flexibility. *Internal flexibility is provided by liquidity; external flexibility is attained through diversification.*[6] Both methods help ensure that the business will not be overcome by a single adversity. A business with reserve bororwing power can meet the threat of an unexpected product improvement by a competitor. A firm that is diversified across several product lines is not dependent upon the buying power of any one group of customers.

The objectives of profitability and flexibility are typically conflicting, so that trading off less of one for more of the other is necessary. For example, a reduction in plant and equipment expenditure will allow an increase in assets that are quickly convertible to cash. Furthermore, both objectives are subject to self-imposed responsibilities and institutional constraints. For example, management may feel responsible for provision of steady employment and job security to long-time employees. As another example, a large firm such as General Motors will not likely

---

[6] Ansoff, *Corporate Strategy*, pp. 50–53.

pursue growth within a single product line to the point that competition is wiped out and countervailing actions by the Antitrust Division of the Justice Department are stimulated.

Selecting the "business to be in"

The firm selects an evolving product mix and a corresponding set of markets that appear to offer the best prospects for achieving its objectives. It compares *various possible deployments of its limited* (but possibly in part *unique*) *set of resources* and *organizational competences.* Strategy formulation requires appraisal of the firm's strengths and weaknesses, determination of the particular business competences that are essential for success in various avenues of expansion, and forecasts of the results of successful operation in each line of activity.

The firm's *relative strengths and weaknesses* can be appraised by (1) an examination of past performance to locate patterns of success or failure, and (2) direct comparison of the firm's skills and capacities with those of major competitors. In the words of Quinn, "The purposes of such exercises should be: to identify and exploit the comparative weaknesses of competitors, to marshal sufficient resources into specific subareas of the company's operations to dominate them, to recognize where competitive strengths allow the company wider latitude in pricing or product policies than competitors, and to pinpoint the company's own weaknesses for more aggressive action or purposeful withdrawal."[7] Appraisal of the firm's strengths and weaknesses should cover all of the resources and competences required in its present business, plus any other capabilities that it has or can reasonably expect to acquire. Table 13–1 lists a few examples of the kinds of organizational characteristics that are considered.

Requirements for business success in various industries are determined through (1) listing the technological, marketing, financial, and management capabilities required by the nature of each industry, and (2) developing "competitive profiles" of the most successful firms in each industry. Then, in Ansoff's words, "Superposition of our firm's competence profile with the competitive profiles measures the 'fit' with each new industry and hence the chances of a successful entry."[8]

Forecasts of results of successful business operations in the various industries are obviously needed in choosing a "portfolio" of "businesses to be in." The firm needs estimates of growth prospects, return on assets

---

[7] John B. Quinn, "Technological Strategies for Industrial Companies," in *Technological Forecasting and Corporate Strategy,* ed. Gordon Wills, David Ashton, and Bernard Taylor (New York: American Elsevier Publishing Company, 1969), p. 58.

[8] Ansoff, *Corporate Strategy,* p. 101.

Table 13–1
Outline for internal appraisal and industry analysis

1. Product-market structure
   a. Products and their characteristics
   b. Product missions
   c. Customers
2. Growth and profitability
   a. History
   b. Forecasts
   c. Relation to life cycle
   d. Basic determinants of demand
   e. Averages and norms typical of the industry
3. Technology
   a. Basic technologies
   b. History of innovation
   c. Technological trends—threats and opportunities
   d. Role of technology in success
4. Investment
   a. Cost of entry and exit-critical mass
   b. Typical asset patterns in firms.
   c. Rate and type of obsolescence of assets
   d. Role of capital investment in success
5. Marketing
   a. Means and methods of selling
   b. Role of service and field support
   c. Roles and means of advertising and sales promotion
   d. What makes a product competitive
   e. Role of marketing in success
6. Competition
   a. Market shares, concentration, dominance
   b. Characteristics of outstanding firms, of poor firms
   c. Trends in competitive patterns
7. Strategic perspective
   a. Trends in demand
   b. Trends in product-market structure
   c. Trends in technology
   d. Key ingredients in success

Source: H. Igor Ansoff, *Corporate Strategy* (New York: McGraw-Hill, 1965), p. 146.

used, and year-to-year variability in sales and income, assuming a competent organization, in each line of business. Such estimates cannot be made without projections and analysis of trends affecting demand for products and services, competition, the institutional and legal environment, timing and nature of technological changes, availability and relative cost of resources, and increases in industry capacity.

An overview of long-range forecasting

Long-range forecasting is still a primitive art. It deals with dimly perceived forces that interact in complex ways. For example, changing cultural values could lower birth rates; reduced birth rates diminish prospective future demands for goods and services used in the public schools; in the more distant future, the reduced number of new workers entering the labor market may tend to lift wages and thus increase the demand for capital goods. On the other hand, changing cultural values could eventually reduce the institutional pressure for complete retirement at age 65; the increase in older workers continuing part-time employment could tend to depress wages and thus decrease the demand for capital goods.

There are no adequate formal models around which the whole process of long-range forecasting can be organized. However, the forecasting process can be broken into phases and carried out in a logical sequence:

1. *Projecting, extrapolating, or constructing trends and potential break-throughs and developments in the principal environmental influences, one at a time.*
2. Assessing the potentials for interaction (reinforcement or inter-ference) among the various trends and *adjusting the forecasts to take interactions into account.*
3. *Considering the probable ecological ramifications* of simultaneous environmental changes resulting from the adjusted trends.
4. *Appraising potential social feedback* upon progress of the trends and control of their ecological ramifications.
5. *Developing the apparent range of alternative states of the future business environment.*[9]

SOCIAL FORECASTING

Three areas have been selected for attention in this section. Boundaries of these areas are not well defined, but using them facilitates discussion and allows emphasis of some key interrelationships among the areas. These areas, or groupings, are: cultural trends, political trends, and demographic trends.

Cultural trends

Culture consists of beliefs, values, customs, and attitudes exhibited by members of a society. Culture is learned by these members. Over time, culture changes and so does the behavior of the people, both as consumers

---

[9] Adapted from the statement by Otis D. Duncan "Social Forecasting—the State of the Art," *The Public Interest* 17 (Fall 1969), p. 115.

of goods and services and as suppliers of personal services and capital needed by businesses. Thus, changes in culture can have profound effects upon the demands for products and suppliers of inputs. Some discernible trends in American culture and their implications for long-range planning are discussed below.

The easy life. Puritan and frontier virtues—hard work, thrift, and individualism—are on the decline. In Philip Kotler's apt phrases, Americans want the "soft life," the "sweet life," the "social life," and the "safe life."[10] Thus, demands can be expected to burgeon for products that increase convenience and leisure time (example: convenience foods), provide luxury and recreation (example: motor homes), mark the user as a person of "good taste" and conventional opinions (example: memberships in social clubs), and increase confidence and security (example: variable annuity forms of life insurance). Simultaneously, workers are becoming less and less willing to endure jobs that are dirty, noisy, dangerous, monotonous, and physically arduous.

A secular, this-world, here-and-now attitude. Americans are placing less and less relative value on deferred satisfactions. Even the religious concept of eternal life is receiving decreased emphasis in most denominations. Thus, a sales appeal which reminds consumers that they "only go around once in life," and therefore should make the most of it (with the assistance of a particular product) has been effective. Many consumers are willing to build up heavy loads of debt rather than defer purchases until they can pay cash.

Broader perspective—living in a "larger world." Faster transportation and better communication broaden the perspective of the relevant world.[11] Consider how quickly Concorde crosses the Atlantic, and think of the millions of Americans watching the live broadcasts of the moon walks. Simultaneously, there is increasing interdependence and competition among people and their activities. Effects of an individual firm's actions upon the environment of other firms and persons (external effects) are becoming more important and better understood. Thus, there is an increasing tendency to look to government agencies for protection of the environment and of the interests of various groups through regulation of privately owned businesses and through directly providing some goods and services. Kotler lists several problem areas that make high-growth markets for direct sales to state and local governments (examples were provided by the present author): population growth (example: contraceptives); poverty (example: subsidized housing); urbanization (example: law enforcement equipment); air and water pollution (exam-

[10] Philip Kotler, *Marketing Management: Analysis, Planning & Control* (Englewood Cliffs, N.J.: Prentice-Hall, Inc., 1967), pp. 82–87.
[11] Daniel Bell, "The Study of the Future," *The Public Interest* 1 (Fall 1965), pp. 120–21.

ple: pollution measurement devices) ; congested transportation (example: rapid transit systems); and agriculture (example: supplies for disease and pest eradication programs).[12]

Decreased importance of values associated with the traditional concept of "family." There is a decline in the relative authority and influence of parents compared to children, an increasingly permissive attitude toward sexual interests and activities, and decreased delineation of male and female roles. These trends bring greater emphasis upon products designed for young people or to make consumers look or feel younger. Large markets for pornographic materials have been opened. There is a move toward "unisex" looks in men's and women's clothing. In the labor market, sexual rigidity is breaking down; there are now female airline pilots and male telephone operators.

Cultural values of individuals affect their behavior as consumers, producers, and voters. Thus, changing cultural values propel and shape the trends in political institutions. These trends are discussed in the next section of this chapter.

Political trends

Futuristic books like George Orwell's *1984*[13] or Aldous Huxley's *Brave New World*[14] use the increasing importance of the role of government in daily life of the population as a major theme. General trends in the role of government include: (1) the increased absolute size of governmental budgets and employment; (2) increased use of public planning and regulation; (3) increased emphasis on income redistribution; and (4) increasing importance of international affairs.

Size and composition of budgets. In 1972, expenditures by federal, state, and local governments in the United States amounted to 372 billion dollars, or *32.1 percent of the gross national product.*[15] Changes in the composition of these expenditures can cause large shifts in demand and in the cost of various inputs. For example, the decision to build the interstate highway system had enormous impact upon builders of earthmoving equipment, such as Caterpillar, and upon producers of cement. A future political decision to subsidize large-scale expansion of rapid transit would have similar impact upon a different set of suppliers.

Planning and regulation. So far, the United States has not used public economic planning as much as have France and some other Euro-

---

[12] Kotler, *Marketing Management: Analysis, Planning & Control,* pp. 146–49.

[13] George Orwell, *1984* (New American Library, 1971).

[14] Aldous Huxley, *Brave New World and Brave New World, Revisited* (New York: Harper & Row, 1958).

[15] From preliminary data published in the *Economic Report of the President* (Washington: U.S. Government Printing Office, 1972).

pean countries.[16] However, there has been increasing use of such powers as stockpiling of materials for later resale to stabilize prices. Antitrust and labor legislation and the manners of their enforcement have important bearings upon the nature and result of business behavior. Consumer and environmental protection legislation also affect business practices and opportunities.

Income redistribution. Programs designed to provide minimum incomes, or even those intended to provide minimum requirements for food and health care, affect private firms on the demand side through consumption changes and on the production cost side through their effects on work attitudes.

International affairs. Government policy concerning international trade and finance have tremendous effects upon firms with substantial participation in importing or exporting. Diplomatic recognition of the Federal Republic of China and the opening of trade with the Soviet Union allow American firms some opportunity to compete for product exporting and importing and raw material purchases in two large economies that have enormous potential for the future. Tariffs, quotas, subsidies, rates of exchange, and loan guarantees are examples of government policies and activities that determine the potential for exporting and the intensity of competition from imports.

Demographic trends

Demography is the study of changes in population, its composition by age groups and various other classifications, and the spatial distribution of population groupings. Demography is concerned with changes in such factors as death rates, birth rates, marriage rates, and geographic mobility. Demographic forecasts are helpful in projecting demand for products and availability of labor.

After individuals are born, their progress through the schools and into the labor force can be projected with considerable confidence. For example, the United States currently has over 4 million people per year who are reaching age 18. These are the babies born after World War II. Their needs for jobs, housing, automobiles, and other durable goods are among the most probable forecasts that can be made in business planning.

Estimates of the numbers of people who will be born in future years are subject to wider errors. "Zero population growth" may become a widely accepted objective. A fall in birth rate would be felt by manufacturers of children's clothing and school equipment, by textbook publishers, by teachers, and by educational institutions. Then would come the successive impacts upon producers of teenage goods, the residential

---

[16] See Andrew Schonfield, *Modern Capitalism* (New York: Oxford University Press, 1965).

construction industry, and producers of durable goods needed after family formation.

Projected locations of population groups are of much interest in business planning. In any given year, about one fifth of the population moves. In general, the population is becoming increasingly concentrated in large urban areas. It is estimated that by 1980 the 100 largest metropolitan areas will contain 57 percent of the total population and more than 60 percent of the total purchasing power.[17] However, metropolitan areas are growing at different rates and this increases the usefulness of demographic studies in projecting sales by product mixes and markets and in planning plant sizes and locations.

An example of social forecasting:
General Electric Company

"If . . . sociopolitical forecasting is done comprehensively and successfully, on both a short- and long-term basis, a business is not so likely to be taken by surprise by shifting public needs, changing aspirations of employees or customers and legislative or administrative action by government." These words are from a sociopolitical forecast originally prepared for the General Electric Company.[18] The methodology of this study includes: (1) interviews with more than 60 prominent educators and representatives of business, research administrators, press, and government; (2) a review of a considerable amount of futurist literature; and (3) a synthesis which takes into account at least part of the interactions among the individual ideas and predictions.

The General Electric study forecast that social change in the United States during the 1970s would result from interaction of eight forces:

Increasing affluence. Real income would double from 1965 to 1980. Increasing percentages of income would be spent on travel, leisure, culture, and self-improvement. The authors forecast developing public impatience with circumstances leading to individual hardships—poverty, unemployment, expenses of sickness and accidents, meager income after retirement, and strikes. Money, they thought, would be more and more taken for granted and less and less useful as a motivator.

Economic stabilization. The authors expected that the swing in unemployment during the 1970s would be kept in the range 3.0–4.5 percent and that recession cutbacks in industrial production would be no greater than 5 percent. The greater stability was expected from more use of contracyclical monetary and fiscal policy and certain structural changes in the economy.

---

[17] Kotler, *Marketing Management: Analysis, Planning & Control,* p. 106.

[18] Earl B. Dunckel, William K. Reed, and Ian H. Wilson, *The Business Environment of the Seventies* (New York: McGraw-Hill, 1970).

Rising tide of education. The forecasters expected spending on education to increase from about 6 percent of 1970 GNP to about 10 percent of the greater 1980 GNP. Two or three years of college, provided free to the student, would become the norm. Content of education would shift in the direction of preparation to accept change. The better-educated population would become less tolerant of authoritarianism and develop higher expectations of what it wants out of its work experience.

Changing attitudes toward work and leisure. The authors thought the character of work would be changing (from manufacturing to services, from blue-collar to white-collar, from tools to automation) and that the structure of work would also be changing (more work/study programs, more sabbaticals, more part-time work). They suggested the opportunity for an increase in modular work scheduling allowing employees greater flexibility in selecting the number of hours to work.

Growing interdependence of institutions. The United States is becoming a national, rather than a regional, economy and society. Local problems have national importance because of communication that brings them to the attention of people in other places. There is an expansion of the government role and greater meshing of all levels of government activity because of the awareness of these problems. At the same time, there is increasing willingness to use private enterprise in solving social problems. Traditional boundaries between the public and the private sector are becoming blurred.

Emergence of the postindustrial society. More and more of GNP will be produced in education, professions such as law and medicine, governments, and nonprofit institutions. With the relative decline in profit-making, consumer-oriented operations, new measures of social output will be needed.

Pluralism and individualism. There is growing realization that the federal government cannot by itself cope with such problems as poverty and pollution. The authors forecast a strengthening of local and state governments, along with growth of regional authorities to deal with such problems as rapid transit and metropolitan zoning. They thought that social and organizational patterns would be shaped in the 1970s by a wave of individualism that would emphasize equality, personal worth, and the supremacy of individual rights over those of the organization.

The urban-minority problem. The authors expected urban minorities to press for power over their own services and institutions. Particular targets would be schools, welfare, police and fire services, sanitation, recreation, banks, supermarkets, and lending agencies.

The study goes on to project effects of the above trends upon institutions in the socioeconomic-political system and upon the value system of the population. With respect to the effects upon business, they forecast the following:

1. Increased concern for continuing education and development of employees.
2. Increased expectations of safety and other qualities of products.
3. Increased insistence that business pay more of the social cost of problems it helps create (pollution, congestion).
4. Increased expectations that business will have long-range goals that are consistent with the national interest.
5. Increased opposition to conglomerate forms of business.
6. Increased pressure for "consumer protection," extending to packaging and advertising and possibly to quality and utility of products.
7. Increased governmental regulation of plant location.
8. Increased governmental regulation of hiring, testing, and training, to promote national manpower policies.
9. Stricter control of mergers by large companies.
10. Increased involvement of private business in the social needs markets, with business and government cooperating in organizational patterns similar to those of National Aeronautics and Space Agency and Atomic Energy Commission.
11. Increased use of project task force organization in business.
12. Increased participation in effective decision-making in business by professional and technical experts.
13. Increasing difficulty in motivating individuals toward organizational goals.
14. Increasing emphasis on autonomy, creativity, and inherently gratifying work.[19]

Future social trends will be propelled and formed partially by technological changes. For example, present attitudes toward sexual behavior have been deeply affected by availability of "the pill," which provides effective and inexpensive contraception. On the other hand, many future technological changes will be brought into place in response to changing private and social needs. For example, food needs will likely lead to a technology of ocean farming. Thus, social forecasting and technological forecasting, the subject of the section which follows, are closely related.

TECHNOLOGICAL FORECASTING

Although technological forecasting must have been attempted throughout the industrial era, formal methods of forecasting have been developed only very recently. Most of the techniques have been introduced since the early 1960s. This section describes some ways of forecasting technological change and appraises their present use and limitations.

---

[19] Dunckel, Reed, and Wilson, *The Business Environment of the Seventies*, pp. 75–79.

General approaches to technological forecasting

There are two views of technological change. The *ontological* view sees inventions as coming on the scene independently of external circumstances or needs. The view leads to *exploratory* forecasting, in which one begins with existing technology, projects potential future progress, and then considers how these changes may affect the nontechnical business environment. In other words, exploratory forecasting is started by *mapping technological possibilities out toward their limits.*

The contrasting *teleological* view of technological change sees it as a response to external social forces that create new demands. This view leads to *normative* forecasting in which forecasters start by predicting the future needs and objectives of society. They then work back to the current state of technology to *determine the gaps that must be closed to permit meeting social aspirations.*[20]

Normative forecasts have been criticized on the basis that even widely recognized needs do not necessarily call forth an invention, but they extend further into the future than exploratory methods. On the other hand, exploratory forecasts have been criticized for their refusal to take into account the probable future desires of society, but they are simpler and do focus on technological issues. The most reasonable approach appears to be a combination of the two methods.[21] Jantsch says, "A complete technological forecasting exercise . . . always constitutes an interactive process between exploratory and normative forecasts . . . it constitutes a feedback cycle in which both opportunities and objectives are treated as adaptive inputs."[22]

Specific techniques for technological forecasting

The purpose of technological forecasting is not to predict specific forms that technology will take at some exact date in the future. Instead, the primary interest is in determining the probability that selected end results will be achieved and to evaluate their significance. Quinn points out that technology is knowledge systematically applied; this knowledge improves in small increments and what appears to be a "breakthrough" is often simply an accumulation of small advances that add up to a significant change.[23] It should also be kept in mind that there may be several technologies that can accomplish a given mission.

[20] These concepts are taken from Robert V. Ayres, *Technological Forecasting and Long-Range Planning* (New York: McGraw-Hill Book Company, 1969).

[21] John P. Dory and Robert J. Lord, "Does TF Really Work?" *Harvard Business Review* (November–December 1970), p. 20.

[22] E. Jantsch, "Technological Forecasting in Corporate Planning" in *Technological Forecasting and Corporate-Strategy*, ed. Wills, Ashton, and Taylor, p. 21.

[23] John B. Quinn, "Technological Forecasting," *Harvard Business Review* (March–April 1967), p. 99.

Intuitive forecasting techniques include the Delphi method and scenario writing. *Delphi method* was developed by Olaf Helmer at Rand Corporation.[24] It develops forecasts based on a consensus of experts without permitting personal interactions. "Bandwagon" effects, "halo" effects, and ego involvements with publicly expressed positions are reduced. At the outset, several experts respond to a written questionnaire. Summaries of the forecasts are returned to the experts with a request to modify or defend deviating forecasts. Modifications and defenses are fed back to the panel iteratively until a relative consensus develops or the issues causing disagreement are clearly defined. Figure 13–2 illustrates a Delphi consensus on the timing of selected technological end results.

Scenario writing produces narrative, time-ordered, logical sequences of events. Each such scenario is a description of a possible evolving future environment. Scenarios can be used as inputs to a forecasting technique or as vehicles for communication among forecasters. Scenarios are, strictly speaking, predictions rather than forecasts, since each scenario takes the form, "If (some set of things), then (some other set)." Among the prominent practitioners of scenario writing are Herman Kahn and his associates at Hudson Institute.[25]

More analytic techniques of technological forecasting include morphological analyses, several forms of trend fitting (s curves, envelope forecasting, correlations), and system approaches. *Morphological analysis* is an attempt at identification and enumeration of all possible means of arriving at a given objective. The analyst tries to find new and feasible methods that do not violate scientific principles. For example, given the objective "propel a vehicle," Ayres enumerates possible energy sources ranging from kinetic to nuclear with numerous intermediate steps in energy conversion.[26] Since the purpose of morphological analysis is to find previously overlooked solutions to problems, it is not, strictly speaking, a forecasting device but rather a method of generating inputs for the forecasting process.

Trend fitting is especially suited to forecasting future capabilities, such as the human ability to transmit information or rate of travel. Several kinds of curves may be used; perhaps most common are "s curves." These show slow growth until the potential of a technology is recognized, rapid growth as this potential is exploited, and then deceleration of growth as the curve approaches a limiting value for the particular technology.

Envelope forecasting is based on a smooth curve drawn tangential to a

---

[24] Olaf Helmer, *Social Technology* (New York: Basic Books, 1966).

[25] Herman Kahn and A. J. Weiner, "The Next Thirty-Three Years: A Framework for Speculation," in *Business Strategy*, ed. H. Igor Ansoff (Middlesex, England: Penguin Books Ltd., 1969), pp. 75–106. Also by the same authors, *The Year 2,000* (New York: Macmillan, 1967).

[26] Ayres, *Technological Forecasting and Long-Range Planning*, pp. 75–77.

Figure 13–2
A delphi consensus of scientific breakthroughs

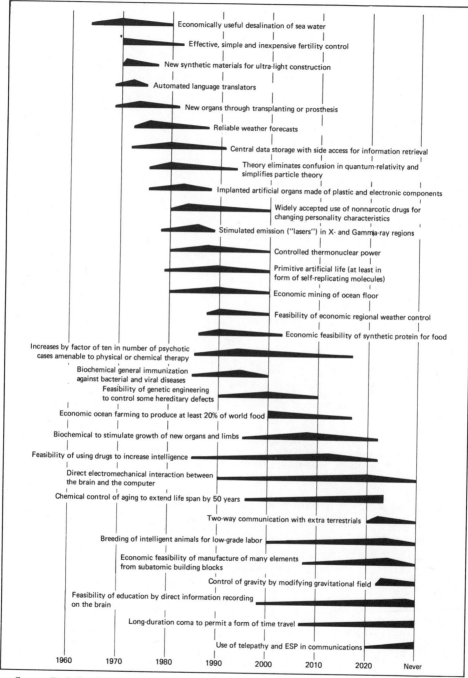

Source: R. J. Gordon and O. Helmer, *Report on a Long-Range Study*, Report P–2982, Rand Corporation, September 1964.

Figure 13–3
Trend fitting (s-curves)

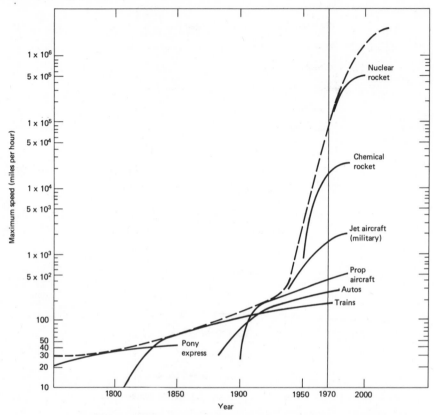

Source: Robert V. Ayres, *Technological Forecasting and Long-Range Planning* (New York: McGraw-Hill Book Company, 1969); reprinted in Arthur Gerstenfeld, "Technological Forecasting," *Journal of Business* 44, no. 1 (1971), pp. 10–18.

family of s curves, as illustrated in Figure 13–3. The implicit assumption of the envelope method is that some new technology will allow the technological trend to continue until some absolute limit, such as speed of sound or speed of light, is approached.

Correlation relates a trend in one technical parameter to a trend or trends in one or more other variables. For example, the speed of commercial air transport tends to increase (with a time lag) as speeds of military aircraft are increased, since research and development for the military sector spill over into the design of commercial equipment. Thus, one trend leads and forecasts the other.

Systems analyses put entire operating systems under scrutiny to pinpoint weaknesses in present technology. For example, an analysis of railroad passenger travel revealed, among other problems, that the rail cars weighed 2,000 pounds per passenger and that passengers were uncomfortable in high-speed turns. Existing technology could be used to lighten cars to 600 pounds per passenger and to bank the cars in turns. Another form of systems analysis assumes new technology and asks what would be its affect on present systems. For example, what would be the effect of a time-shared computer system with 200 terminals, 20,000-character program capacity, virtually unlimited memory, and $300 per hour total user cost? Some consequences: Small businesses could handle all accounting and tax reporting for $100 per week; all interested students in five major institutions could be provided relatively unlimited access to the computer; and many present data processing installations would be obsolete.[27]

Acceptance and some limitations of formal technological forecasting

A survey by Gerstenfeld, summarized in Table 13–2, showed that substantial percentages of firms responding to the questionnaire were using at least one specific method of technological forecasting and that the mean of their forecast horizons was approximately seven years into the future.[28] Although corporate planners must use some form of technological forecasting, they should avoid engaging in science fiction fantasies that involve technological developments beyond the relevant planning horizon. Furthermore, it should be kept in mind that there are unavoidable pitfalls in forecasting. Quinn lists: (1) unexpected interactions of several coincidental and apparently unrelated advances; (2) unprecedented demands, such as the "need" for atomic energy for military purposes; (3) major discoveries of entirely new phenomena, such as lasers; and (4) inadequate data concerning scientific resources committed to various lines of research and development.[29]

Technological developments are sensitive to changes in relative prices of natural resources. If some resources begin rising in price because of relative scarcity, a search for *substitutes* and for other methods of reducing requirements for the scarce inputs is set in motion. If other resources begin to have falling prices because of abundance, a search for *new technological uses* of the plentiful inputs is undertaken. Thus, resource forecasting, the subject of the section to follow, is complementary to technological forecasting.

---

[27] Examples are from Quinn, "Technological Strategies for Industrial Companies," p. 94.

[28] Arthur Gerstenfeld, "Technological Forecasting," *Journal of Business* 44, no. 1 (1971), pp. 10–18.

[29] Quinn, "Technological Strategies for Industrial Companies," pp. 101–3.

Table 13–2
Number of companies, by industry, using technological forecasting, as related to growth

Industry	Number of company respondents per industry	Companies using at least one specific forecasting method		Industry growth rate*	Mean number of years into the future
		Number	Percent of industry		
Transportation equipment...	13	8	61.5%	5.0%	7.15 $(N = 8)$
Chemicals and allied products.	27	18	66.6	8.3	6.52 $(N = 17)$
Electrical machinery, equipment, and supplies........	21	15	71.5	6.4	7.75 $(N = 15)$
Fabricated metals..........	10	7	70.0	4.7	5.50 $(N = 7)$
Primary metals............	7	1	14.3	3.6	5.00 $(N = 1)$
Food and kindred products...	27	14	52.0	3.2	7.15 $(N = 13)$
Paper and allied products....	8	5	62.5	4.9	7.00 $(N = 5)$
Scientific instruments........	5	4	80.0	5.5	5.25 $(N = 4)$
Machinery, except electrical..	18	11	61.0	5.8	7.69 $(N = 11)$
Petroleum refining and related industries..........	14	7	50.0	3.2	10.00 $(N = 7)$
Stone, clay, and glass........	4	2	50.0	3.5	7.50 $(N = 2)$
Textile mill products........	8	3	37.5	3.5	5.00 $(N = 3)$
Total..................	162	95			7.06†$(N = 93)$

* 1957–60 to 1960–65 (annual percent). Growth rates based on Federal Reserve Production Indexes for Industries, U.S. Department of Commerce, Bureau of the Census.
† Average years.
Source: Bureau of the Census, U.S. Department of Commerce, *Long-Term Economic Growth* Washington, D.C.: Government Printing Office, October 1966); reprinted in Arthur Gerstenfeld, "Technological Forecasting," *Journal of Business* 44, no. 1 (1971), p. 16.

RESOURCE FORECASTING

In resource forecasting, it is necessary to consider both "needs" and "availabilities" or, in economic terms, "demands" and "supplies." These are the forces that will determine the relative prices of inputs and thereby affect choices of production techniques and relative prices of products. For example, costs of many products include substantial proportions of energy. Expected future availability and relative prices of oil, coal, gas, electricity, and nuclear energy at various places will affect choices of plant locations, production techniques, and product mixes.

Only the largest business firms will make original studies of resource prospects, since these investigations are complex and expensive. Most firms will adapt projections from outside sources to fit their own needs and circumstances. This section describes one of the generally available resource forecasts and discusses some considerations in evaluating and adapting the results of the study.

"Resources in America's Future": Methods and findings

Resources in America's Future and other publications by the organization called Resources for the Future, Inc., are the products of a large-scale, continuing study of economic growth of the United States with emphasis on the role of natural resources.[30] *Resources in America's Future* contains projections of demand and supply of natural resources to the year 2000 for the United States.

The authors of *Resources in America's Future* emphasize that their numerical results are *projections* rather than forecasts. These projections are based on a set of *assumptions;* most of these are carefully specified. Some of the principal methods are: (1) *trends in consumption are extrapolated* with some modification to reflect informed judgment—these changes usually have the effect of flattening the consumption growth curves; (2) substitutions among materials and more efficient utilization of materials through *expected technological changes were incorporated* if the implications of such changes could be quantified; (3) *sector interrelationships*, along the lines emphasized in the discussion of input-output, *were taken into acount to some extent,* although input-output analysis as such was not used; (4) *three projections were usually made—* these included a probable or medium level plus a low projection and a high projection.

The forecasts were also based on an implicit assumption that the future cultural-political environment would be similar to that of the early 1960s. The book includes virtually no consideration of possible future concerns about pollution. There were explicit assumptions about advances in technology, world trade, and public policy affecting the search for and the use and conservation of natural resources.

The outcome of the study was "the prospect of sustained economic growth supported by an adequacy of resource materials." Although no general shortage of materials was expected, some particular resources were projected to become relatively scarce. This would imply relatively higher prices for these resources as the years pass, although the book does not get into the outlook for prices.

Evaluating and adapting resource forecasts

A user of the resource projections in *Resources in America's Future* could begin by examining the explicit and implicit assumptions about

---

[30] Hans H. Landsberg, Leonard L. Fischman, and Joseph L. Fisher, *Resources in America's Future* (Baltimore: Johns Hopkins Press, 1963). Other RFF publications include: Sam H. Schurr, et al., *Energy in the American Economy 1850–1955;* Marion Clawson, et al., *Land for the Future;* Harold J. Barnett and Chandler Morse, *Scarcity and Growth: The Economics of National Resource Availability;* Harvey S. Perloff, et al., *Regions, Resources, and Economic Growth.*

future technological change, future world trade conditions, and future social and political trends. His or her own assumptions might be different and these differences could suggest modifications in the resource forecasts. Note that business planners could be especially interested in forecasts of *changes in relative prices of inputs:* The task of price forecasting is left for the user of the book.

The user of resource forecasts should be conscious of the pitfalls inherent in projections. For example, in 1963, Resources for the Future projected probable use of 19.3 trillion cubic feet of natural gas in 1970 with proved reserves of 301 trillion cubic feet.[31] Industry testimony before a congressional committee in 1972 includes estimates that actual use in 1970 was 21.8 trillion cubic feet (a little under the "high" projection of the RFF study) and that actual 1970 year-end reserves were 260 trillion cubic feet.[32]

Resource forecasting requires consideration of sector interrelationships. To illustrate, as the demand for automobiles increases, demand for steel (thus for ore and heat) will obviously increase. Less obvious, there will be an impact upon demand for power from such sources as hydroelectric generation, coal, or nuclear energy; steel production requires large amounts of power. However, the relative impact of increased demand upon each of the several sources will depend upon their relative prices, and these will be largely determined by other demands for the same resources. Intersector relationships would be of particular interest to most users of resource forecasts, since most firms must look to other sectors for product demands and supplies of inputs.

FORECASTING JOINT AND DERIVED DEMANDS: INPUT-OUTPUT ANALYSIS

Social forecasting is concerned with long-range trends affecting demands for final products and supplies of labor and capital. Technological forecasting focuses on trends and potential breakthroughs in conversion of inputs into products, and upon the technical possibilities for entirely new products. Resource forecasting concentrates upon trends in resource discovery, use, conservation, and scarcity, and upon technical possibilities for resource substitution. All of these forecasts yield projections for broad sectors of the socio-political-economic system. Further work is required to relate changes in the broad sectors to prospects for the smaller aggregations or subsectors that are of interest to particular firms.

Input-output analysis, discussed in some detail in Chapter 5, can be

---

[31] Landsberg, et al., *Resources in America's Future,* p. 408.

[32] "Natural Gas Policy Issues", *Hearings before the Committee on Interior and Insular Affairs—U.S. Senate,* 92d. Congress, 2d. Session, February 25 and 29 and March 2, 1972.

a useful tool in making long-range forecasts for particular subsectors, or industries. This section reviews such an analysis.

"The American Economy to 1975": Methods and findings

In 1966, Clopper Almon, Jr., published a forecast titled *The American Economy to 1975* which was derived with the aid of input-output techniques.[33] The approach involved constructing an input-output table for the forecast year. The table was based on projections of labor force size and the composition of final demand in 1975, and upon projected input-output coefficients in 1975. Trends in work habits, consumption, and technology were incorporated in these projections.

By comparing projected industry outputs in 1975 with those estimated for 1963 (the most recent data available at the time of the study), Almon obtained projected growth rates for the various industries. Some of these results are shown in Figure 13–4.

Figure 13–4
History and forecast of industry outputs (history: 1950–1963; forecast: 1964–1975)

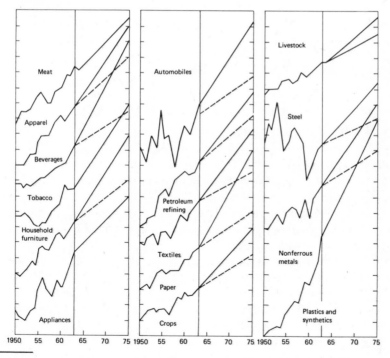

[33] Clopper Almon, Jr., *The American Economy to 1975* (New York: Harper & Row, 1966).

Figure 13–4 (*continued*)

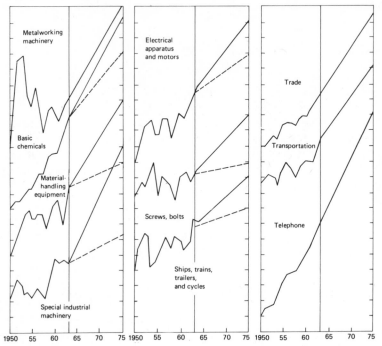

Note: In the vertical scale one division equals 10 percent of 1963 output; dashed line is historical trend; solid line is projection.

Source: Clopper Almon, Jr., *The American Economy to 1975* (New York: Harper & Row, 1966), pp. 10–11.

Evaluation and adaptation of input-output forecasting

Estimates of the level and composition of final demand are crucial assumptions in long-range forecasting by the input-output technique. For example, Almon assumed that defense procurement would decline about 1 percent a year from 1963 to 1975. Subsequent involvement of the United States in Southeast Asia during the 1965–73 period caused defense procurement to be much greater than Almon had assumed. Assumptions about future technology, including future productivity of labor, are also crucial in input-output analysis.

Input-output technique has the virtues of requiring explicit assumptions and of taking intersector relationships into account in a methodical way. It has the disadvantages that much effort and expense are involved and that final results are still in terms of industry sectors that are usually much larger than the markets and sources of supply of a particular firm. Furthermore, such a forecast may contain little or no regional detail, although individual firms usually need to beak down prospects for sales growth into market outlook by areas.

AN EXAMPLE OF STRATEGY FORMULATION:
RADIO CORPORATION OF AMERICA

Radio Corporation of America (RCA) began developing electronic data processing equipment for the U.S. Army in the mid-1950s, and was producing a fairly broad line of data equipment that had finally begun producing a profit by 1964. In December 1964 RCA announced a new line of computer equipment—the Spectra 70. The history of this product illustrates one firm's formulation of strategy as it entered and subsequently exited from the computer industry.

The computer industry, dominated by IBM Corporation, is characterized by high technology, capital intensity, extensive user services, and technical assistance. There are high risks and long waits for payoffs.[34] RCA's entry into the computer industry was intended to offset declining profits from color televisions. The specific goal was to capture 10 percent of the market and stand second in the industry after IBM. The Spectra would be compatible with IBM equipment but lower priced, and improved marketing was expected to move RCA into second place.[35]

By 1970, RCA did have 7.5 percent of the market, but the computer line was still losing money. A major defect in RCA's strategy was the failure to anticipate how competitors would react to RCA's marketing tactics. IBM countered with new technological breakthroughs and reduced prices on peripheral equipment just as RCA was increasing prices on similar machinery.

In 1971, RCA reshaped its corporate strategy. Massive investments with long waits for payoff were to be avoided. The computer line was dropped. However, the business base was to be broadened through other avenues of diversification, and research and development were to be brought more closely in line with marketing objectives.

RCA's new strategy was designed to take advantage of its existing strong marketing position in home entertainment products, to smooth the cyclical results of durable goods industries by diversifying into such activities as automobile rentals and frozen foods, and to move with expected major cultural and social changes.

SOME EXAMPLES OF LONG-RANGE FORECASTING
FOR NONPROFIT ORGANIZATIONS

This chapter closes with an examination of the ways that various techniques have been used and could be used in appraising the future of a particular "industry," higher education. Although this industry does

---

[34] William F. Sharpe, *The Economics of Computers* (New York: Columbia University Press, 1969).

[35] Allan T. Demarce, "RCA After the Bath," *Fortune* (September 1972).

not have goals identical with private enterprise, it does share the long-run objective of survival.

In the case of the state universities, survival depends upon behavior that is acceptable to the state legislators. The state legislatures are facing many urgent and increasing needs for funds and can be expected to keep a closer and closer watch on university budgets. In particular, they can be expected to pay attention to costs and benefits of the relatively expensive graduate programs. Thus, university administrators need to consider projections of costs of producing Ph.D.s and of prospective demands for these graduates.

Trends in costs of producing Ph.D.s

Trends from 1956–57 to 1962–63 in costs of educating various categories of students in land grant colleges and universities were studied by Southwick in an article published in 1969.[36] Southwick classified the output of these institutions as undergraduate students, graduate students, and research (measured in dollars). He then estimated the relationships of changes in each of the above outputs to changes in inputs: numbers of administrators, amount of capital, number of librarians, number of senior teaching faculty, number of junior teaching faculty (i.e., teaching assistants), and number of researchers. The general result was a finding that higher education is becoming more labor intensive; no substantial steps are being undertaken to reduce the ratio of teachers, librarians, and administrators to students.

Southwick then examined trends in unit costs of the various inputs and projected these to 1975. Examples: He expected cost per librarian (including acquisitions of materials and cost in materials handling) to rise to $54,000; and he projected a 1975 cost of $18,200 per member of the senior teaching staff.

The final phase of Southwick's study involved projecting the 1975 unit cost of a year of undergraduate education and a year of graduate education. He did this by multiplying projected required amounts of each input by their unit costs and summing. Results are shown in Table 13–3.

In appraising Southwick's study, two comments are in order. First, although there was no decrease from 1956–57 to 1962–63 in the ratio of 0.09 professional person per undergraduate, there are unexploited technological possibilities in higher education for economic substitution of capital for labor (audiovisual aids, programmed instruction, computer-assisted instruction, etc.). This kind of substitution could be expected to increase if legislatures tightened the appropriations of the universities.

---

[36] Lawrence Southwick, Jr., "Cost Trends in Land Grant Colleges and Universities," *Applied Economics* 1, no. 3, pp. 167–72.

Table 13–3
Projected 1975 costs per year of undergraduate and graduate education in land grant colleges and universities

	Inputs					
Outputs	*Adminis-tration*	*Capital*	*Library*	*Teaching*	*Research*	*Total*
Per undergraduate....	$544	$185	$216	$1,225	$0	$ 2,180
Per graduate.........	340	440	0	2,840	12,500	16,170

Source: Lawrence Southwick, Jr., "Cost Trends in Land Grant Colleges and Universities," *Applied Economics* 1, no. 3, pp. 178–79.

Second, graduate education is a joint product; it produces both graduates and completed research. The graduate cannot be produced without research, but research could be produced without the graduates (if it were done by full-time research personnel instead of the students). There is no way to know whether legislatures would want the same amount of research if graduate education were decreased. Assuming that they would, the projected 1975 net cost (to the state governments) of graduate education is $3,670 per year, and assuming that the average Ph.D. requires three years of graduate education beyond the baccalaureate, the projected 1975 cost (to the state) of producing a Ph.D. is about $11,000.

Trends in demand for Ph.D.s and output of Ph.D.s

In a study published in 1972, Cartter projected the demand for Ph.D.s and the output of Ph.D.s by years through 1990.[37]

Demand for Ph.D.s in academia. Demographic data were used in projecting the demand for Ph.D.s in academic employments. The first step was to project the numbers of persons in the 18 to 21 age group by years (these peak in 1978 and then decline to a 1988 low which is under the 1970 level), the percentages of youths graduating from high school (Cartter assumed an increase from 80 percent in 1972 to 90 percent in 1982), and the percentage of high school graduates entering college (Cartter assumed an increase from 61 percent in 1972 to 70 percent in 1982).

It was necessary to make assumptions about future student/faculty ratios and the future proportions of faculty for which the Ph.D. degree will be required. Cartter assumed a continuation of a 20 to 1 ratio for students to faculty and calculated results for faculty proportions holding the Ph.D. that ranged from the 1972 level of 44 percent to a maximum of 75 percent.

---

[37] Allan M. Cartter, "Faculty Needs and Resources in American Higher Education," *Annals of American Academy of Political and Social Science,* vol. 404 (November 1972), pp. 71–87.

Figure 13–5
Projected doctorates awarded and new college teachers required

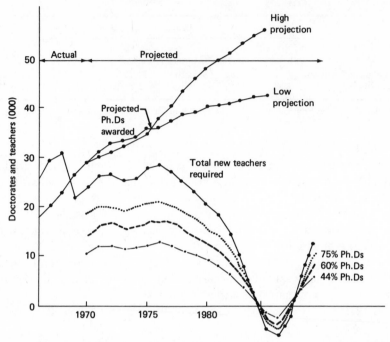

Source: Alan M. Cartter, "Faculty Needs and Resources in American Higher Education," *Annals of American Academy of Political Social Science*, vol. 404 (November 1972), p. 82.

Supply of Ph.D.s. Cartter projected the annual supplies of Ph.D.s as consisting of the initial stock, less retirements and deaths, plus new additions. Because of the rapid buildup of college and university enrollments and faculties in the 1960s, faculty age distributions are heavily weighted in the lower ages. Thus, projected annual depletions due to retirement and death are small percentages of total faculty during the 1970s (about 1.8 percent in 1970, for example).

New additions to the stock of Ph.D.s in future years were hard to project, since some socioeconomic forces would support continued increases in annual output (from 29,436 in 1970 to 56,700 in 1985) and others would taper the rate of growth (to a level of 43,000 in 1985). Cartter made projections using both the higher and the lower rates of growth in output.

Cartter's projected annual production of Ph.D.s is compared to his projected annual requirements for new Ph.D.s in Figure 13–5. The rapidly widening gap after 1975 leads to his statement that "after 1975 it seems unlikely, even under the most optimistic assumption of high employment standards, that anywhere close to half of new doctorates will find teaching positions in higher education."[38]

Nonacademic demand for Ph.D.s. Cartter does not make a detailed study of prospective growth in nonacademic demand for holders of the doctorate. However, he cites Department of Labor projections of annual increases in private industry averaging 4.2 percent (or about 1,600 Ph.D.s per year). This rate would absorb only a tiny fraction of the projected excess of output compared to the academic requirements.

Appraisal. In appraising Cartter's study, the relevance of sociopolitical forecasts should be noted. The so-called counterculture, which rejects many values associated with higher education, will decrease the demand for college teachers (to the extent that it grows). Increasing social concerns on the part of young people will also affect the composition of demand for higher education, with greater emphasis on the humanities and social sciences and perhaps less emphasis upon engineering and physical sciences.

Political trends affect the total funding of research and, through this, the demands for college and university faculty members. Similarly, political trends affect the composition of this demand, since one administration may emphasize development of advanced hardware for military and space efforts and another may place more priority on solutions of domestic social problems.

Changing relative prestige of occupations, a sociological phenomenon, affects the composition of the demand for higher education. For example, if the prestige of a businessperson is falling relative to that of a government employee, there will be some shifting of demand away from business administration courses and into the public administration curriculum.

Input-output techniques could be very helpful in projecting future demand for college and university faculty. Various sectors of the economy require differing compositions of specializations at the baccalaureate level and have differing growth rates. Thus, input-output methods could be used to derive the projected *composition* of the total demand for faculty, by years.

From a larger view, the examples of the Southwick and Cartter studies show that the forecast techniques used in long-range business planning can also be applied in planning for nonprofit organizations.

SUMMARY

The chapter discussed long-range forecasting for strategic planning. Strategic planning selects a product or product mix and a market or a set of markets, establishes specific profitability objectives related to com-

---

[38] Cartter, "Faculty Needs and Resources in American Higher Education," p. 82.

petitive strength and operating efficiency, and determines the degrees of liquidity and diversification to provide flexibility. The company's strategic plan is an attempt to make the best possible match of the firm's competences with the opportunities projected for the future. Long-range forecasting aids strategic planning by providing the outlook for profitability of a well-managed firm in each of the industries that are to be considered.

Although long-range forecasting is more of an art than a science, it can be carried out in a logical sequence: (1) projecting trends and major developments in the principal environmental influences, taking these one at a time; (2) assessing the potentials for interaction among the various trends and developments and adjusting the forecasts to accommodate the interactions; (3) considering the ecological ramifications of the adjusted trends as they evolve simultaneously; (4) appraising potential social feedback aimed at controlling the ecological consequences of the various trends and developments; and (5) developing the range of alternative states of the future business environment.

Social forecasting is concerned with cultural, political, and demographic influences upon the future environment of business firms. Technological forecasting focuses upon future possibilities for conversions of inputs into desired goods and services. Resource forecasting looks at prospects for future changes in supplies and requirements of land, minerals, and energy and pays particular attention to possible changes in the relative prices of resources.

After forecasts have been made for the economy's broad aggregates, such as demands for final products, changes in input-output conversion rates, and available supplies of resources, input-output analyses may be useful in estimating derived demands for intermediate goods.

QUESTIONS

1. What, exactly, is the relation of long-range forecasting to the formulation of a firm's strategy?

2. Appraise the accuracy of the General Electric forecast of social change (1970). What subsequent developments caused deviations of actual subsequent experience from this forecast? How might these developments have been anticipated?

3. Appraise the accuracy of the Rand Corporation Delphi consensus of timing scientific breakthroughs (1964). List several *other* major breakthroughs since 1964. How would you have forecast the timing of the latter group?

4. Obtain recent forecasts of the future energy reserves of the United States prepared by independent agencies and published at approximately the same time. Contrast the forecasts. How can the differences be explained?

FURTHER READING

Day, Lawrence H. "Long Range Planning in Bell Canada." *Long Range Planning,* September 1973.

Lanford, H. W., and Imundo, L. V. "Approaches to Technological Forecasting as a Planning Tool." *Long Range Planning,* August 1974.

Leontief, Wassily W. "Input-Output Economics." *Scientific American* 185, October 1951.*

Mansfield, Edwin. "The Speed of Response of Firms to New Techniques." *Quarterly Journal of Economics* 77, May 1963.

Miernyk, W. H. "Long-Range Forecasting with a Regional Input-Output Model." *Western Economic Journal* 6, June 1968.

Rosen, Stephen. "The Future from the Top: Presidential Perspectives on Planning." *Long Range Planning,* August 1974.

Smalter, Donald J. "Anatomy of a Long-Range Plan." *Long Range Planning,* March 1969.

Taylor, Bernard. "Strategic Planning for Resources." *Long Range Planning,* August 1974.

---

* This article is included in *Readings in Managerial Economics,* rev. ed. (Dallas: Business Publications, Inc., 1977).

Chapter 14

Capital budgeting

Capital budgeting (capital-expenditure planning) is allocation of capital among alternative investment opportunities. Capital budgeting has profound effects upon the competitive position of the firm, the rewards it can provide, and the managerial responsibilities it imposes. Capital-expenditure planning is regarded as one of the important functions of general management.

The capital budgeting process also requires knowledge, skills, and judgment of people in various functional occupations, such as engineering, production, marketing, personnel, finance, accounting, risk, transportation, and real estate. Thus, these specialists should also understand how business investment planning is done. Indeed, anyone intending to make a managerial career in business or in nonprofit organizations needs competence in capital budgeting.

Capital budgeting incorporates many concepts introduced in earlier chapters. Demand, cost, and pricing concepts are essential tools in forecasting investment results. Incremental reasoning is used in separating projected cash flows that would be associated with each of the various opportunities. Finally, investment in a project is justified only if it provides a return equal to or greater than the opportunity cost of the capital.

CENTRAL ROLE OF CORPORATE STRATEGY

Many investment opportunities are uncovered in the ordinary course of business. Needs to replace machinery that is wearing out and to expand departments that are overworked seem obvious and urgent. Numerous suggestions for using capital can be expected to come from operating levels of the firm. Without deliberate effort, most firms discover more capital expenditure proposals than can be accepted. Indeed, there is usually a backlog of apparently worthy projects.

An entrepreneurial management is not content simply to select among investment proposals arising in the spontaneous manner described above. Instead, it stimulates, directs, and coordinates capital budgeting by formulating an explicit statement of the corporate strategy. Corporate strategy includes delineation of the business(es) in which the firm intends to engage, a statement of its attitudes toward business and financial risks, and a plan for achieving competitive advantages. Strategy is not frozen; as time passes and circumstances change, strategy evolves. Ansoff has provided a particularly useful framework for strategy formulation along with partial development of a theory embedding capital budgeting in the larger planning process.[1]

At any given time, strategy is management's concept of the best future use(s) of the firm's resources and competences in the light of opportunities and hazards expected to result from general economic, social, and political trends. Strategy delineates the set of "businesses to be in" in terms of various product-market specializations. For each of these, it lists specific objectives by periods out to the planning horizon. The objectives include numbers and kinds of customers, product mix, market share, product development, rate of growth, flexibility of production and marketing posture, level and stability of return on capital, and nature of intended competitive advantages.

Corporate strategy is also an implicit statement of "businesses that the firms will *not* be in." By foregoing allocations of capital and management to projects that are incompatible with strategy, the firm concentrates its capital and know-how into *critical masses.* Scale of effort and depth of resources are kept sufficient to carry the firm across the thresholds of business success: It is able to develop products, penetrate markets, endure start-up costs, and so forth.

For present purposes, the following relationships of corporate strategy to capital budgeting should be kept in mind.

1. Although many opportunities for investment are uncovered in the ordinary course of business, this spontaneous discovery process has no *sense of direction;* in contrast, corporate strategy stimulates a deliberate search for opportunities and directs the growth of the firm along a desired set of *expansion vectors.*

2. Projects that are clearly not compatible with corporate strategy are rejected, and projects that are clearly essential in implementing the strategy receive priority; decisions about these two groups of projects do not require forecasts of profitability of the individual projects.

---

[1] H. Igor Ansoff, *Corporate Strategy* (New York: McGraw-Hill, 1965).

3. Many other projects will be proposed that are compatible with strategy but not essential to it; capital budgeting is concerned with choices among projects in this group, and these decisions do require forecasts of individual project costs and returns.

AN OVERVIEW OF CAPITAL BUDGETING

Capital budgeting can be conceived as planning for profit maximization over several periods—from the present to some planning horizon—over all activities of a firm, subject to restraints imposed by the availability and cost of capital and the firm's corporate strategy. From this point of view, in which capital is a resource that needs to be allocated among alternative uses, useful insight about the nature of capital budgeting can be gained by considering how the principles of resource allocation explained in Chapter 6 might be applied.

Any given amount of capital should be allocated among alternative uses (that is, among programs and among projects within programs) according to the priority principle: Allocate capital first to that use in which it has the greatest marginal revenue productivity, then to the next best use, and so on, until all of the given amount of capital is used. The firm should expand the total amount of capital in use so long as capital's marginal revenue product is greater than the firm's marginal resource cost of capital.

Capital's marginal revenue product in any given program (receivables, inventories, plants, research and development, expansion of markets, and so forth) is the addition to the firm's future cash flows (future excess of incremental income over incremental expense) per unit of capital used at the margin of that program (that is, in the worst project). Capital's marginal resource cost is the addition to the firm's future performance for capital suppliers (interest payments, dividend distributions, current earnings retentions on behalf of stockholders) that is made necessary at the margin of capital acquisition (by the last increments added to the firm's capital base) per unit of capital obtained.

Capital's marginal revenue product and capital's marginal resource cost are consequences of the presence of capital over some period of time. Both can be expressed as rates: monetary amounts per dollar of capital per year of its presence. Annualized returns and costs of capital are decimal fractions of a dollar, and it is convenient to express them as percentages of the dollar. For example, we might say "the marginal cost of capital is 8 percent" or "the marginal project has a 10 percent rate of return."

A somewhat different point of view must be established in order to understand the specific techniques used in capital budgeting. The alternative perspective is as follows. Each of the possible uses of capital (projects) has incremental effects on the firm's revenues and costs over a series of future periods. From the incremental net revenue of any given project in any given period, subtract the corresponding incremental net cost—the result (which may be positive or negative) is called the project's *cash flow* in that particular period. Most projects produce a multiperiod series of cash flows.

A project's cash flow *in any given period* can be discounted period by period from the time of receipt back to the present, obtaining the present value of *that period's* cash flow. The discount factor to be used over any one of the intervening periods corresponds to that period's marginal cost of capital expressed as an annual percentage rate. Summing the discounted cash flows of *all* future periods for any one project yields the present value of all future incremental effects of that project; the sum may be called the *present value* of the project.

If the initial outlay on a project (the outlay at the outset) is subtracted from the project's present value, the result is called *net present value* of the project. Net present value may be positive or negative; if it is positive, the project is shown to be profitable. Roughly, the net present value method of testing a project for profitability is a method of determining whether the project's rate of return is greater than the corresponding marginal cost of capital. If the firm accepts *all* profitable projects, the method simultaneously determines the total amount of capital that the firm will use and the allocation of this capital among projects.

Clearly, a plan for profit maximization over all of the firm's activities from the present to some planning horizon, subject to restraints imposed by the availability and cost of capital and the firm's strategy, is also a plan for maximizing both the firm's terminal value (that is, the value at the planning horizon) and its present value.

FORECASTING CASH FLOW OF A PROJECT

Incremental revenues and costs are the relevant values in comparing investment proposals. Engineering methods can be used to forecast technical input-output relationships. These technical estimates can be combined with economic forecasts of input and product prices to obtain expected incremental impacts of the project upon the firm's future expenses and revenues. Careful analysis is needed to overcome effects of arbitrary factors for overhead allocations and historical asset valuations upon any accounting data used in capital-expenditure planning.

Keep in mind that a project's cash flow is the amount by which the project's incremental effect on revenues exceeds the project's incremental effect on costs. Cash flow is calculated for each project, period by period.

It is useful to distinguish between two types of investments. The first type consists of *cost-reducing* projects. An example is replacement of one machine by another more productive machine that decreases required labor. Cash flow produced by such a project consists of expected net reductions in operating expenses of future periods.

Another type of investment includes *revenue-increasing* projects. An example is an increase in advertising expected to allow a price increase. Cash flow resulting from such a project would be the expected net increases in revenues of future periods. Some projects combine elements of cost reduction and revenue expansion. An example would be simultaneous modernization and expansion of a plant, expected to yield future reductions in unit cost as well as allowing increased rate of output.

Depreciation is *not* subtracted from revenue in estimating cash flow for a project. The objective is to estimate net cash inflow in each period subsequent to the initial outlay at the outset of the project. Note that if a project should provide total cash inflow just equal to total depreciation, we would say that the project provides a return *of* the initial outlay over a period of years, but that it provides no return *on* capital while it is tied up in the project.

A numerical example will help clarify the process of estimating cash flow. Suppose we are considering a labor-saving machine. The machine is priced to us at $23,000 and there will be a $2,000 installation cost; the initial outlay totals $25,000. Suppose the machine will also provide a higher-quality product on which price can be increased, so that annual revenue is expected to increase $1,500. The machine is expected to reduce annual direct labor expenses by $5,500 a year, but maintenance labor expenses will be increased by $500.

Suppose that in its cost accounting the firm normally estimates indirect labor at 30 percent of direct labor and overhead at 110 percent of direct labor. In the case of the new machine, direct labor will be reduced but indirect labor and overhead will not be affected. Therefore, the factors normally used for overhead allocation must be disregarded. Straight-line depreciation on the machine over a five-year period amounts to $5,000 per year. However, depreciation is not a cash expense and will *not* be deducted in projecting pretax cash flow.

There are tax considerations. Assume taxes are 50 percent of profits. The new machine will increase profits and thus increase taxes; the increase in taxes must be deducted in determining incremental cash flow. Depreciation *will* be subtracted from pretax net cash flow in determining taxable income and the amount of taxes.

Suppose the machine is expected to last for seven years and to have no salvage value. A disposal cost of $1,160 (remove and haul away) is projected. The cash flows of the seven years would be projected as shown in Table 14–1.

The estimated project results are a net posttax cash inflow of $5,750

Table 14-1
Cash flows from hypothetical project

Year 1:
Incremental revenue..............................	$1,500
Net labor savings.................................	5,000
Pretax net cash inflow.........................	$6,500
Less: Taxes at 50% ($6,500 − $5,000)...............	750
Posttax net cash inflow........................	$5,750

Years 2, 3, 4, and 5:
Same as Year 1

Year 6:
Incremental revenue..............................	$1,500
Net labor savings.................................	5,000
Pretax net cash inflow.........................	$6,500
Less: Taxes at 50% ($6,500)......................	3,250
Posttax net cash inflow........................	$3,250

Year 7:
Incremental revenue..............................	$1,500
Net labor savings.................................	5,000
	$6,500
Less: Disposal cost..............................	1,160
Pretax net cash inflow.........................	$5,340
Less: Taxes at 50%...............................	2,670
Posttax net cash inflow........................	$2,670

in each of the first five years, $3,250 in the sixth, and $2,670 in the seventh year. Total estimated cash inflow is $34,670, which is more than the initial outlay of $25,000. Clearly, there is some *return on* capital tied up in the project as well as a *recovery of* the entire initial outlay. However, the total cash inflow is not directly comparable with the initial outlay. As they stand, these numbers ignore the time value (opportunity cost) of money. This opportunity cost must be taken into account in determining whether it is desirable to exchange the initial outlay for an expectation of receiving back a larger total amount in installments distributed over a period of seven years. The technique of measuring profitability of multiperiod projects, with proper consideration given to capital's opportunity costs, is explained in the section to follow.

MEASURING PROJECT PROFITABILITY

Present value of the entire future cash flow expected from an investment—or present value of the project—can be determined by summing *discounted* cash flows of the individual periods. *Profitability* of the project can then be measured by comparing its present value with the required initial outlay. Various present values can be calculated for any given project, depending on the rate or rates used in discounting. Opportunity costs of capital are the appropriate discount rates, since the objective is to determine whether the project has returns to capital that are equal to or greater than the capital's cost. Cost of capital is discussed later in this chapter.

Discounting cash flows

The formula for determining present value of a stream of cash flow is:

$$V = \frac{R_1}{(1+i)} + \frac{R_2}{(1+i)^2} + \cdots + \frac{R_N}{(1+i)^N} + \frac{S}{(1+i)^N}$$

in which

V is present value.
i is interest rate or, more generally, cost of capital expressed as an annual rate.
$R_1, R_2 \ldots R_N$ are after-tax cash flows in years $1, 2 \ldots N$.
N is project duration (conventionally tied to life of asset).
S is salvage value of the asset in year N.

For the illustration given in Table 14–1, computations would be set up as follows, assuming a constant 6 percent discount rate:

$$V = \frac{\$5,750}{(1.06)} + \frac{\$5,750}{(1.06)^2} + \frac{\$5,750}{(1.06)^3} + \frac{\$5,750}{(1.06)^4} + \frac{\$5,750}{(1.06)^5} + \frac{\$3,250}{(1.06)^6} + \frac{\$2,670}{(1.06)^7}$$
$$= \$28,288$$

The arithmetic involved in the above calculations would be simple in principle but time-consuming. Fortunately, discount tables (compound interest tables) can be used to simplify the calculations. Discount tables are widely available in banks and other lending institutions, and a partial set of tables is provided in the appendix at the back of this book. Use of discount tables is explained below.

Internal rate of return

Let us discount the cash flows of Table 14–1 at a 10 percent rate. The factors for present value of $1 received at the end of various future periods can be found in the 10 percent discount table in the appendix. For example, the project's cash flow of $5,750 in Year 1 is discounted to present value by multiplying the cash flow by the present value factor of 0.90909, found in Column (1) on the line corresponding to Period 1. Present value (rounded to the nearest whole dollar) is found to be $5,227.

Results for cash flows of the various periods and for the project as a whole are summarized in Table 14–2. Note that the total present value

Table 14–2
Discounted cash flows (10 percent)

Year	Cash flow	Times	Factor for present value	Equals	Present value
1..................	$5,750	×	0.90909	=	$ 5,227
2..................	5,750	×	0.82645	=	4,752
3..................	5,750	×	0.75131	=	4,320
4..................	5,750	×	0.68301	=	3,927
5..................	5,750	×	0.62092	=	3,570
6..................	3,250	×	0.56447	=	1,834
7..................	2,670	×	0.51316	=	1,370
					$25,000

of the project's cash flows is $25,000, an amount *just equal to* the project's required initial outlay. If discounted at 10 percent, the project has no *net* present value, where net present value is defined as present value *minus* initial outlay. A discount rate that produces zero net present value (by making present value *equal to* initial outlay) is called the project's *internal rate of return.* Each project has its own internal rate. The nature of internal rate of return is displayed below by decomposition of the hypothetical project's cash flows.

Cash flow decomposition at the internal rate. Table 14–3 shows the separation of each period's cash flow into two parts: (1) *returns on the project balance* at 10 percent, and (2) *partial recovery of initial outlay.* The project balance is defined as initial outlay less cumulative recovery. It is helpful to think of a positive project balance as an amount that the company's treasury has lent to the project. During Year 1 there is an amount of $25,000 tied up in the project. Cash flow is $5,750, of which $2,500 is required to provide a 10 percent return on the project balance; the remaining $3,250 can be viewed as a partial return of the treasury's initial outlay, or a reduction of the project balance. Thus, the new project balance is $21,750.

Table 14–3
Decomposition of cash flows (10 percent)

Year	Project balance	Cash flow	Interest at 10 percent	Partial return of initial outlay	New project balance
1..........	$25,000	$5,750	$2,500	$3,250	$21,750
2..........	21,750	5,750	2,175	3,575	18,175
3..........	18,175	5,750	1,818	3,932	14,243
4..........	14,243	5,750	1,424	4,326	9,917
5..........	9,917	5,750	992	4,758	5,159
6..........	5,159	3,250	516	2,734	2,425
7..........	2,425	2,670	242	2,428	−3

By similar reasoning, cash flows of Years 2–6 can be decomposed into interest (returns *on* capital still tied up) and partial returns of initial outlay (reductions of project balance). By the end of Year 7, the project balance has finally been reduced to zero (except for the small rounding error). The initial outlay has been fully recovered, and the project has provided a 10 percent rate of return on capital tied up in the project. Note that the column in Table 14–3 titled "Partial return of initial outlay" divides the initial outlay into seven parts. The amount of $3,250 at the top of the column is tied up in the project for only one year, the amount of $3,575 in the second row is invested for two years, and so on. The amount of $2,428 at the bottom of the column is the only part of initial outlay that is invested in the project over the whole seven-year period.

Note again that present value equals initial outlay (net present value is zero) if the cash flows of a project are discounted at the project's internal rate of return. To calculate a project's internal rate when it is unknown, a trial and error approach can be used. In the first step, a guess at the rate is used in discounting. If the resulting present value is greater than initial outlay, the project's internal rate is higher than the rate that has been used in discounting, so another trial should be made with a higher rate. If present value is less than initial outlay, the internal rate is lower than the rate used in discounting, so another trial can be made with a lower rate. The trial and error process can be continued until a rate is found that makes present value very close to initial outlay; such a rate is a close approximation of the project's internal rate of return. The trial and error process can be speeded by interpolation. Most computer centers have programs for rapid determination of internal rates of return.

Net present value

If a project's internal rate of return is above the firm's cost of capital, the project is profitable. A test of profitability can be made by discounting the project's cash flows at expected cost of capital rates over the relevant periods. To illustrate such tests of profitability, assume that cost of capital is expected to be at a constant rate of 6 percent over the next seven years. The following example, based on the hypothetical project of Table 14–1, shows how the present values of the project's cash flows and of the project as a whole can be calculated.

Refer to the table for 6 percent rate of interest in the appendix. The cash flow of $5,750 in Year 1 is discounted to present value by multiplying it by the present-value factor of 0.94340, which is found in Column (1) of the 6 percent discount table, opposite Period 1. The result, rounded to the nearest dollar, is $5,425. Results for all seven years are summarized in Table 14–4.

Table 14–4
Discounted cash flows (6 percent)

Year	Cash flow	Times	Factor for present value	Equals	Present value
1.................	$ 5,750	×	0.94340	=	$ 5,424
2.................	5,750	×	0.89000	=	5,117
3.................	5,750	×	0.83962	=	4,828
4.................	5,750	×	0.79209	=	4,555
5.................	5,750	×	0.74726	=	4,297
6.................	3,250	×	0.70496	=	2,291
7.................	2,670	×	0.66506	=	1,776
	$34,670				$28,288

Note that the total present value of the project's cash flows is $28,288, much less than their total of $34,670 before discounting. However the reduced amount of $28,288 *is* greater than the initial outlay. Subtracting the $25,000 of initial outlay from the $28,288 present value of the project, we obtain $3,288, the project's *net* present value. The nature of net present value can be clarified by decomposition of a project's cash flows at the rate (or rates) used in discounting.

Decomposition of cash flows at the discount rate. Assume the firm's opportunity cost of capital is a constant 6 percent. This is the rate which the firm can earn on funds invested outside the project in question, either in other projects inside the firm or in outside investments. The cash flow results of the hypothetical project can be decomposed as shown in Table 14–5.

During Year 1, the project balance is $25,000. Again, think of a positive project balance as the amount that the company treasury has lent to the project. The first year's cash flow is $5,750; subtracting $1,500 for interest (cost of capital) leaves $4,250 which can be viewed as a partial return of the treasury's initial outlay, or a reduction of the project balance. Thus, the new project balance is $20,750.

By similar reasoning, cash flows of Years 2–6 can be decomposed into interest (cost of capital) and reductions of project balances by partial

Table 14–5
Decomposition of cash flows (6 percent)

Year	Project balance	Cash flow	Interest at 6 percent	Partial return of capital	New project balance
1..........	$25,000	$5,750	$1,500	$4,250	$20,750
2..........	20,750	5,750	1,245	4,405	16,245
3..........	16,245	5,750	975	4,775	11,470
4..........	11,470	5,750	688	5,062	6,408
5..........	6,408	5,750	385	5,365	1,043
6..........	1,043	3,250	63	3,187	−2,144
7..........	−2,144	2,670	−129	2,799	−4,943

returns of initial outlay. At the end of Year 6, the project balance is −$2,144; the project has returned $2,144 over and above the initial outlay. It is helpful to think of a negative project balance as a deposit which the project has made into the company treasury.

In Year 7, the negative project balance is put to other uses so as to yield a return of 6 percent or annual earnings of $129; this amount can be credited to the project as an additional deposit in the company treasury. The $2,670 cash flow in Year 7 is also an additional deposit, so the project balance is −$4,943 at the end of Year 7 and the end of the project. The final project balance, discounted at 6 percent, has a net *present* value of $3,287 as viewed from the outset of the project. This amount is (except for rounding error) identical with the net present value of $3,288 calculated by subtracting the initial outlay of $25,000 from the project's present value of $28,288.

Why does the project have *net* present value? The answer is simple. It has net present value because it has an internal rate of return greater than the cost of capital that was used in discounting. Thus, it can pay cost of capital on the project balance, and can return more than the initial outlay to the company treasury. In the example above, we could say that a decision to go into the project increases the present value of the firm by approximately $3,288. This gain in present value is one measure of the project's profitability.

Profitability index (PI).   The ratio of present value to initial outlay, called *profitability index* (or benefit-cost ratio), is sometimes used as a measure of relative profitability of projects. For the example in Table 14–4, the profitability index is $28,288/$25,000, or 1.13. The profitability index measures results per dollar of initial outlay, which is desirable in comparing projects of different sizes. For the example used here, the profitability index says that there is a gain of 13 cents in present value for each dollar that goes into the project at the outset.

Discounting period by period, with rates varying.   Cost of capital may vary from period to period. If it is expected to vary over the life of a project, the project's cash flows should be discounted period by period, using the appropriate rate in each period. To illustrate, again using the cash flows from Table 14–1, assume that management has estimated the firm's cost of capital over the next few periods as follows:

Year 1	12%
Year 2	10
Years 3 and 4	8
Years 5, 6, and 7	6

Table 14–6 shows how present values should be calculated for the cash flows of various periods and for the project as a whole.

Table 14–6
Discounting period by period, with rate changes

Period received (at end)	Present value (dollars)	Period discounted—(rate of discount used)*						
		1–(12%)	2–(10%)	3–(8%)	4–(8%)	5–(6%)	6–(6%)	7–(6%)
1..........	$ 5,134	$5,750						
2..........	4,667	5,227	$5,750					
3..........	4,321	4,840	5,324	$5,750				
4..........	4,002	4,482	4,930	5,324	$5,750			
5..........	3,775	4,228	4,651	5,023	5,425	$5,750		
6..........	2,012	2,254	2,480	2,678	2,892	3,066	$3,250	
7..........	1,560	1,747	1,922	2,076	2,242	2,376	2,519	$2,670
	$25,471							

Net present value = $25,471 − $25,000 = $471
Profitability index (benefit-cost ratio) = $25,471/$25,000 = 1.02

* Values in body of table are dollars at ends of periods.

For example, the amount of $2,670 estimated for Year 7 is assumed to be received at the end of the year, so it is discounted back to the beginning of Period 7 (or the end of Period 6) at Period 7's 6 percent cost of capital by multiplying by 0.9434 (the discount factor for 1 year at 6 percent), yielding the value of $2,519. This value of $2,519 is discounted back to the end of Period 5 at Period 6's percent cost of capital, resulting in $2,376, and so on, until the present value of $1,560 is finally obtained for the 7th year's cash flow. Cash flows of earlier years are discounted in a similar manner.

COSTS OF CAPITAL

Costs of capital, as annual rates, are needed in discounting cash flows to test a project's profitability. This section explains what is meant by "cost of capital" and how cost of capital may vary from period to period. In this section, it is assumed that management has selected a ratio of debt to equity which is expected to minimize the total cost of capital and that this ratio is to be held constant as the firm makes changes in total capital employed.[2]

Cost of debt

Average cost of capital for use in any given year is a weighted average of the percentage annual cost of funds obtained by borrowing and the

---

[2] The theoretical relationship of average cost of capital to debt-equity ratio is somewhat controversial, and empirical determination of optimal capital structure of firms of a given risk class appears to be very difficult. Average cost of capital probably varies only slightly with gradual changes in the debt-equity ratio over a fairly wide range.

percentage annual cost of equity (funds obtained by retaining earnings or by selling additional shares of common stock). We shall first examine the cost of borrowed funds. The before-tax cost of debt is simply the nominal interest rate, and if the firm has long-term and short-term debt at differing interest rates, the pretax cost of debt is the weighted average of these rates. After-tax cost of the firm's debt is reduced by the deductibility of interest payments as expenses when the firm's taxable income is being calculated. Thus, after-tax cost of debt is the nominal interest rate times one minus the firm's marginal tax rate expressed as a decimal. For example, if the firm's before-tax interest rate is 8 percent and the firm's marginal tax rate is 50 percent, the after-tax cost of debt is $8 \times (1 - 0.50)$, or 4 percent. It is appropriate to put the cost of capital on an after-tax basis, since this cost is to be compared with internal rates of return that are derived from after-tax cash flows of projects. In other words, both the returns on capital and the costs of capital are on an after-tax basis. Note that the relevant cost of capital is the expected future marginal cost, period by period.

Cost of equity

Cost of equity is the percentage that expected earnings per share must be of the stock's current price in order to maintain the current stock price unchanged. This value is derived from management's estimate of earnings per share required to provide the combination of dividends and capital gains expected by marginal holders of the common stock. Marginal shareholders are those persons just willing to hold the stock at its current price in the light of their expectations of dividends and capital gains.

An approximation of cost of equity which may be useful in some instances can be calculated by adding the stock's current percentage yield to the projected average annual percentage increase in earnings per share and stock price over the next two or three years. (In using this approach, it is assumed that the marginal stockholders and management have similar information and are projecting similar rates of growth.) For example, if the stock's current price is $50 per share, the current dividend is $3 per share, and the projected rate of gain in earnings per share and stock price is 8 percent annually, the cost of equity is $3/$50 + 0.08, or 0.14, or 14 percent.

Weighted average of debt cost and equity cost

Cost of capital for a given period is the weighted average of the cost of debt and the cost of equity, where the debt and equity are sources of funds for new investment in that period. For example, assume that: (1) the firm is maintaining a ratio of 40 percent debt to 60 percent equity; (2) after-tax cost of marginal debt is 4 percent annually; and (3) cost of marginal equity is estimated to be 14 percent annually. The weighted average cost of capital would be 0.40 × 0.04 + 60 × 0.14, or 0.096, or 9.6 percent. *Caution:* Keep in mind that it is the firm's marginal cost of capital that is relevant; the firm's marginal cost of capital is a weighted average of marginal cost of debt and marginal cost of equity.

Marginal cost of capital

It is reasonable to assume that the marginal cost of capital eventually rises with increases in the firm's planned total new investment in the current period. Curve *ACC* in Figure 14–1 shows a theoretical relationship of average cost of capital to amount of investment. Increments of capital are positioned along the curve from left to right in order of ascending cost. Increment *OB* is that portion of the firm's total cash

Figure 14–1
Cost of capital

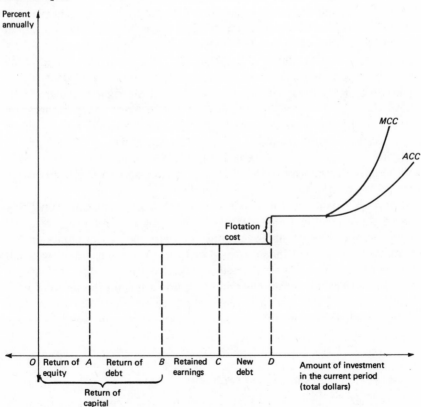

flow from old projects, which can be called *return of capital;* amount OB is approximately equal to the accounting valuation of total depreciation. Although the stream of funds corresponding to partial recovery of initial outlay in old projects could be used for reduction of debt and distributions to owners (thereby returning the capital to its original sources and cutting down the firm's capital base), it is usually retained and invested in new projects. Cost of capital over the range OB is a weighted average opportunity cost; in retaining these funds, the firm foregoes opportunities to reduce debt (thus decreasing required interest payments) and to reduce equity (thus cutting back the earnings "required" to support expected dividends and capital gains per share).

The second increment of capital, amount BD in Figure 14–1, is the sum of the current period's retained earnings plus the proceeds of new borrowing that keeps debt and equity in the desired ratio. Increment BD is an expansion of the firm's capital base. Cost of capital over the range BD is also a weighted average opportunity cost, since the firm is foregoing opportunities to avoid borrowing (which would decrease interest cost) and to distribute some current earnings (which would cut back the needed rate of growth in earnings per share and in stock price).

If management so decides, the firm can acquire any of the various amounts of capital along function ACC to the right of increment BD in Figure 14–1. However, these further increments can only be obtained by going to the capital market to sell additional shares of common stock and to engage in new borrowing that maintains the selected debt-equity ratio. Cost of the first increments of capital to the right of range BD is above the cost in range BD because of transactions charges (flotation costs) on the new common stock. If the firm does sell new common stock, cost of capital (as annual percentage rates) will be quite high unless the funds are to be retained and reinvested over several periods and perhaps all the way to the planning horizon, so that the transactions charges can be prorated over several periods.

Curve ACC is a schedule of alternatives. Management can choose any one of these combinations of total investment and average cost, but the choice for the current period must be *only one* of the points on the curve. As management increases planned total investment, the marginal cost of capital would be expected eventually to rise; the increase in marginal cost would reflect emerging risk premiums on the parts of both stockholders and lenders. In that range where average cost of capital is rising, marginal cost would be above average cost and would be rising more steeply.

Year-to-year changes in costs of capital

Curves ACC and MCC in Figure 14–1 depict the costs of one period's use of capital in various amounts. In future periods, the firm will have cash flow and will be able to choose among reductions of the capital base, maintaining the base, or expansions. Thus, cost of capital over the range *OD* can easily be viewed as the annual percentage rate of cost for using it during the current period. Furthermore, cost of capital to the right of range *OD* can also be regarded as cost of one period's use, provided we keep in mind that the firm would not enter this range unless it expected the prorated stock flotation cost to be justified (which may involve planning to use the capital over several future periods as well as during the current one.)

In future periods, the firm's average and marginal cost of capital schedules will be similar to the one shown in Figure 14–1, but the positions and the shapes of the schedules will likely change from period to period. The height of the range *OD* along the *ACC* curve shifts from period to period with changes in supply and demand conditions in the general money market, and the length of range *OD* in any particular period depends upon the amount of cash flow produced by old projects during that period. The shape of the *ACC* and *MCC* curves to the right of range *OD* depend upon lender and stockholder attitudes toward the firm's riskiness and probable success in expanding at various rates, and these attitudes could change from period to period.

In any given period, the amount of investment (and that period's average and marginal costs of capital) depends upon the nature of that period's set of investment opportunities, the height and form of that period's cost of capital schedules, and management's estimates of marginal costs of capital in future periods. The nature of investment opportunities changes from period to period with the outlook for general economic conditions, competitive conditions, and the firm's success in product and market development. Clearly, a firm's marginal cost of capital can be expected to vary from period to period.

The theoretically correct way to test the profitability of a project is to discount its cash flows, period by period, at varying rates, as illustrated in Table 14–6. The rates to be used for discounting are forecasts of marginal costs of capital in future periods and, for the first period only, the estimated marginal cost of capital in the current period. Although most managers have difficulty in estimating future marginal costs of capital, assumptions about these rates are necessary. Much of the present literature of corporate finance takes it for granted that management is willing to assume that capital's marginal cost will be constant over future periods at the current period's value. More attention should be given to the managerial implications of costs that vary from period to period.

MUTUALLY EXCLUSIVE PROJECTS

It is sometimes necessary to choose between two mutually exclusive projects. In such cases, it is possible for the larger of the two projects to be the best choice even though it has a slightly lower internal rate of return. The larger project can be regarded as the equivalent of the smaller one plus an incremental project. If both the smaller project and the incremental project are profitable, then the larger project should be selected.

An example of mutually exclusive projects is the case in which management can choose between two technologies and two sets of machines and equipment to be used in carrying out a given production process. Since production must be done one way or the other, the investment proposals are mutually exclusive. The following example shows how such a case can be analyzed.

Table 14–7 compares two mutually exclusive projects. The smaller project, Project A, is already familiar to readers of this chapter because of its use in earlier examples. Project B is larger, has longer life, and has a different pattern of cash flows. Project B-A is the incremental

Table 14–7
Incremental analysis of mutually exclusive projects

Period	Cash flows		
	Project A	*Project B*	*Project B-A*
1.	$ 5,750	$ 2,000	$ −3,750
2.	5,750	4,000	−1,750
3.	5,750	12,000	6,250
4.	5,750	16,000	10,250
5.	5,750	14,000	8,250
6.	3,250	12,000	8,750
7.	2,670	10,000	7,330
8.	0	8,000	8,000
9.	0	4,000	4,000
Initial outlay....................	$25,000	$55,000	$ 30,000

Present value of Project B-A:

Period received (at end)	Present value (dollars)	Period discounted—(rate of discount used)*		
		1–(10%)	*2–(8%)*	*All others—(6%)*
1.	$ −3,409	$ −3,750		
2.	−1,473	−1,620	$ −1,750	
3.	4,963	5,449	5,896	$ 6,250 at end of Period 3
4.	7,678	8,446	9,122	10,250 at end of Period 4
5.	5,831	6,414	6,927	8,250 at end of Period 5
6.	5,834	6,418	6,931	8,750 at end of Period 6
7.	4,610	5,071	5,477	7,330 at end of Period 7
8.	4,747	5,222	5,640	8,000 at end of Period 8
9.	2,239	2,463	2,660	4,000 at end of Period 9
	$ 31,020			

Net present value = $31,020 − $30,000 = $1,020
Profitability index (benefit-cost ratio) = $31,020/$30,000 = 1.034

* Values in body of table are dollars at ends of periods.

project, with initial outlay and each cash flow calculated as the amount for Project B less the corresponding amount for Project A. The incremental initial outlay is Project B's $55,000 less Project A's $25,000, or $30,000. Similarly, the incremental first year's cash flow is Project B's $2,000 less Project A's $5,750, or −$3,750.

Assume that marginal costs of capital over future periods have been forecast as follows: year 1, 10 percent; year 2, 8 percent; all subsequent years, 6 percent. Present-value calculations for Project A and Project B-A, after discounting period by period, are shown in Table 14–7. It can be seen that Project A is profitable with a net present value of $1,758. However, Project B-A is also profitable with a net present value of $1,020. Therefore, Project B, which is equivalent to a combination of the smaller project and the incremental project, should be selected.

RISK ADJUSTMENTS

To this point, the discussion of capital budgeting has treated the cash flows of projects as if they were certain. However, each projected cash flow is actually the *mean* of the *expected values* in a *subjective probability distribution*. If these subjective distributions take the *normal* form, variability of project results can be quantified by calculating *coefficients of variation*, where each such coefficient is the *ratio* of the *standard deviation* of expected cash flows to the *mean* of these expectations. The greater the coefficient of variation, the greater the riskiness of the project.

The possibility of *differences in riskiness* among projects must now be dealt with. An example of a comparison of project variability is shown in Figure 14–2, in which two projects have the same means of the probability distributions of expected internal rates of return but the distribution of expected results for Project B has a larger standard deviation than that of Project A. Since most stockholders are risk averse (i.e., prefer less risk to more risk, other things being equal), management should choose Project A over Project B. In this example, it is easy to see that some kind of *risk adjustment* is being made in comparing the results of Project B with those of Project A.

For most managers, the easiest approach to risk adjustment is to increase or decrease costs of capital to be used in discounting, depending on how risky the project looks. If the project appears to have higher risk than average, something can be added to costs of capital as a risk premium. On the other hand, if the project is thought to have lower risk than average, something can be subtracted from costs of capital.

Some companies establish classes of risk and develop a managerial consensus as to the cost of capital adjustments that are appropriate for each class. Risk classification of projects can be assisted by sensitivity

Figure 14–2
Comparison of project variability

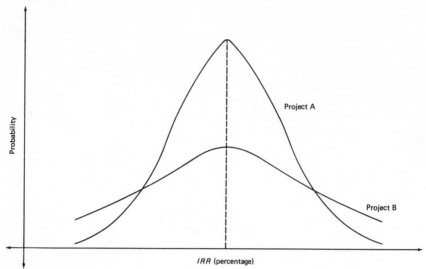

Probability

Project A

Project B

IRR (percentage)

analysis using optimistic, most likely, and pessimistic assumptions about such planning data as equipment life, prices of inputs and products, and rates of output and sales.

Note that the risk evaluation for any given project should be in terms of how that project, *as an addition to the firm's total activity,* could affect the firm's *overall* profitability. A project that has a large variance of expected outcome may not be classified as a high-risk project if the initial outlay is small compared to the firm's total capital base. On the other hand, a project that has moderate variance of expected outcome may be regarded as high risk if it requires an initial outlay that is large in relation to total capital used.

USING DECISION TREES IN CAPITAL PLANNING

Capital planning often involves decision-event-decision chains. The nature of such chains is illustrated by the following hypothetical example.[3] A company has developed a new product that cannot be manufactured in present facilities. Management must decide whether to build

---

[3] The example used and the discussion in this section are adapted from John F. Magee, "Decision Trees for Decision Making," *Harvard Business Review* (July–August 1964), pp. 126–38.

a small plant or a large one. There is uncertainty about future demand for the product.

If the company builds a large plant, it must live with it whatever the size of market demand. If it builds a small plant, the plant can be expanded if demand is found to be high during the introductory period. However, total investment and cost of operating an expanded plant will be greater than the outlay and cost of production for a plant built for large-scale operation at the outset.

Demand may be low initially and continue low for the expected 10-year life of the product. There is a small chance that demand will be high initially and then fall back to a low level after many initial users find the product unsatisfactory. Or demand may be high initially and continue high for the product's expected life.

Here is the decision-event-decision chain: If the firm decides to build a small plant initially, it can observe the first chance event—the size of initial demand—and then make a second decision on whether or not to expand the plant. On the other hand, if the firm decides to build a large plant initially, the flexibility of a subsequent decision about expansion is precluded. But if demand is high initially and continues high, building a large plant at the outset results in greater cash flow during the first years and less total investment.

Suppose the following estimates of demand have been made:

Nature of demand	Probability
High initial demand, high subsequent demand.................	0.60⎫ 0.70
High initial demand, low subsequent demand..................	0.10⎭
Low initial demand, low subsequent demand..................	0.30
Low initial demand, high subsequent demand.................	0.00

If demand *is* high initially, the chance that it will *continue* high is 0.86, calculated as the ratio of 0.60 to 0.70, where 0.70 is the total probability that initial demand will be high. If demand is high initially, the chance that it will be low subsequently is 0.14, calculated as the ratio of 0.10 to 0.70. And, if demand is low initially, the chance that it will continue low is 1.00, calculated as the ratio of 0.30 to 0.30. Comparing 0.86 to 0.60, it is clear that knowledge of high initial demand increases the probability that subsequent demand will be high. Similarly, comparing 1.00 to 0.40, it can be seen that knowledge of low initial demand increases the probability that subsequent demand will be low. Uncertainty about subsequent demand is decreased by knowledge of initial demand.

Assume that management has made the following estimates of annual cash flow under various conditions:

Plant size	Demand	Annual cash flow	Explanation
Large...........	High	$1,000,000	Capacity matched to demand and no room for competitors
Large...........	Low	100,000	High fixed cost, low sales
Small...........	Low	200,000	Small capacity matched to low demand, no room for competitors
Small...........	High	400,000 initially 300,000 thereafter	After two years, competition would become keen
Expanded........	High	700,000	Capacity matched to demand, but not as efficient as plant designed for large volume from the outset
Expanded........	Low	50,000	Highest fixed cost, low sales

Assume, finally, that a large plant would require $3.0 million of initial outlay, a small plant would require $1.3 million, and expansion of a small plant would cost an additional $2.2 million.

A decision tree that organizes the hypothetical firm's alternatives, the chance events and their probabilities, and the firm's outcomes (or payoffs) is shown in Figure 14–3. The tree structure is helpful in determining which of the current alternatives (large plant or small plant) has the greatest expectation of payoff.

Analysis of the tree begins at the second decision point in Figure 14–3. We must determine a monetary value—called the *position value*—for this decision. The position value of a decision is simply the expected value of the decision, or the mathematical expectation of monetary outcome for the preferred action branch of that decision. An expected value is the average result that would be obtained if the decision could be repeated a great number of times under the same conditions.

The position value of the second decision can be calculated as shown in Table 14–8. In discounting the cash flows, a constant marginal cost of capital at 10 percent is assumed for simplicity (in a real problem, it would likely be desirable to discount period by period, at varying rates). The cash flows are treated as if received at the end of the various years, and Table 14–8A shows their present values as of the time that Decision 2 must be made. Table 14–8B shows how the position value of Decision 2 is determined. The expected discounted value of a decision to expand is $3,248,954; subtracting the $2.2 million of additional outlay for plant leaves a net expected value (as of the time Decision 2 is made) of $1,048,954. On the other hand, the expected discounted value of a decision not to expand is $1,525,781. Therefore, if the firm were in the position of Decision 2, having observed high initial demand, the *preferred* action branch would be *not* to expand. The expected discounted value of the preferred action, which is the position value of Decision 2, is $1,525,781.

Figure 14-3
Using a sequential decision tree and discounted payoffs

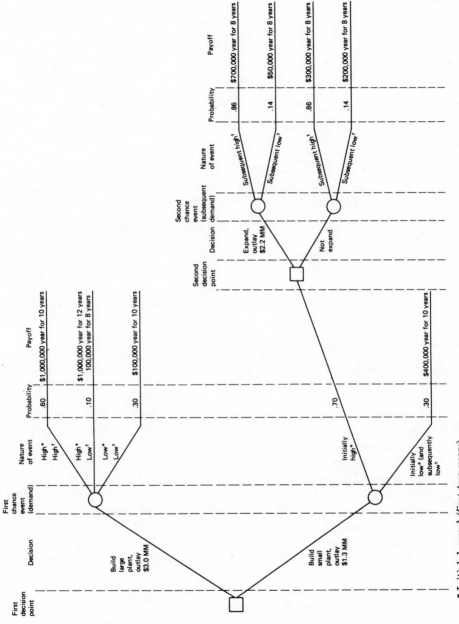

* Initial demand (first two years).
† Subsequent demand (next eight years).

Table 14–8
Expected value of Decision 2, with discounting (Decision 2 is not effective until beginning of year 3)

A. Present values of cash flows

Decision	Chance event	Outcome (cash flow)	Present value (at time of Decision 2)
Expansion	High subsequent demand	$700,000 for 8 years	$3,734,430
	Low subsequent demand	$ 50,000 for 8 years	266,745
No expansion	High subsequent demand	$300,000 for 8 years	1,600,470
	Low subsequent demand	$200,000 for 8 years	1,066,980

B. Expected discounted values of the alternatives

Decision	Chance event	Probability of event × Present value of outcome = Expected value of decision	
Expansion	High subsequent demand	0.86 × $3,734,430 = $3,211,610	
	Low subsequent demand	0.14 × $ 266,745 = 37,344	
			$3,248,954
		Less initial outlay	2,200,000
		Expected net present value	$1,048,954
No expansion	High subsequent demand	0.86 × $1,600,470 = $1,376,404	
	Low subsequent demand	0.14 × $1,066,980 = 149,377	
		Expected net present value	$1,525,781

The preferred action at the time of Decision 1 can now be determined as shown in Table 14–9. Table 14–9A lists the present values of the cash flow outcomes as of the time Decision 1 must be made, and Table 14–9B provides the comparison that allows the preferred action to be selected. The expected discounted value of the outcome of building a large plant is $4,088,744; subtracting the initial outlay leaves an expected net present value of $1,089,744. On the other hand, the expected discounted value of the outcome of building a small plant is $1,798,046; subtracting the initial outlay of $1,300,000 leaves an expected net present value of $498,046. Thus, the preferred action alternative, for a management basing all decisions on comparisons of expected values, is to build the large plant at the outset, before initial demand is known.

Note that the decision to build a large plant has a 30 percent probability of low initial and low subsequent demand, resulting in an outcome with a net present value of −$2,385,540 (present value of $614,460 less the initial outlay of $3 million). On the other hand, the decision to build a small plant has an outcome with a net present value of −$71,080

Table 14–9
Expected value of decision 1, with discounting

A. Present values of cash flows

Decision	Chance event	Outcome (cash flow)	Present value (at time of Decision 1)
Large plant	High initial and high subsequent demand	$1 million for 10 years	$6,144,600
	High initial and low subsequent demand	$1 million for 2 years and $100,000 for 8 years	$1,735,500 440,910 2,176,410
	Low initial and low subsequent demand	$100,000 for 10 years	$ 614,460
Small plant	High initial demand	$450,000 for 2 years plus the Decision 2 position value of $1,525,781	$ 780,975 1,260,982 2,041,957
	Low initial demand	$200,000 for 10 years	$1,228,920

B. Expected discounted values of alternatives

Decision	Chance event	Probability × Present value = Expected value of event of outcome		
Large plant	High initial and high subsequent demand	0.60 × $6,144,600 = $3,686,760		
	High initial and low subsequent demand	0.10 × $2,176,403 = 217,640		
	Low initial and low subsequent demand	0.30 × $ 614,460 = 184,338		
				$4,088,738
		Less initial outlay		3,000,000
		Net present value		$1,089,738
Small plant	High initial demand	0.70 × $2,041,957 = $1,429,370		
	Low initial demand	0.30 × $1,228,920 = $ 368,676		
				$1,798,046
		Less initial outlay		1,300,000
		Net present value		$ 498,046

(present value of $1,228,920 less the initial outlay of $1.3 million), not nearly so bad an outcome for this condition of low initial and low subsequent demand. If the new plant involves a sizable part of the firm's total capital, the outcome of the decision may have a very noticeable effect upon the firm's overall profitability and value. In such a case, management might wish to make risk adjustments in the manner explained in

Chapter 11, pp. 430–434. Equivalent preference values corresponding to *whole-firm* present values would be substituted for the *project* present values in Tables 14–8A and 14–9A, and the preferred action would be selected on the basis of maximizing the expected preference value of the whole-firm outcome. In making risk adjustments, a project should be treated as an addition to the firm's other activities and risk should be viewed in the light of the project's possible effects upon the whole-firm outcome.

CAPITAL RATIONING

Capital rationing is a condition in which management sets an upper limit, which may be zero, on the amount of funds to be brought into the firm by new stock sales and additional borrowing during the current period. This limit is not to be exceeded even if the firm must forego some projects that are profitable by the net present value test with discounting at marginal market costs of capital. Limits on new capital acquisition may be imposed by cautious managers or by owners unwilling to share control of the firm with others.

Under the capital rationing condition, capital becomes a limited resource and develops a marginal opportunity cost. The marginal internal opportunity cost of capital is the annual rate of return that could be earned on additional funds if they were available. If the marginal internal opportunity costs of capital of future periods *were* available, they could be used in discounting projects to test profitability by the net present value method. Accepted projects would be an optimal mix and would not exceed the funds available for initial outlay. Unfortunately, the internal opportunity costs of capital cannot be determined in the absence of an optimal investment plan. Although they are very difficult to estimate by the judgmental method, such estimates are needed if management is to attempt a rational approach to budgeting under capital rationing.

A mathematical programming approach to capital expenditure planning under capital rationing is in development. Already conceived, this approach awaits further improvements in computer techniques for integer programming and in forecasting of future opportunities. Practical applications may be possible in a few years.

EMPIRICAL STUDIES

Do firms actually use the capital budgeting techniques discussed in this chapter? The answer is that few small firms use them but that these techniques are now widely used in larger firms. A 1963 study covering approximately 60 small firms uncovered no instances of the use of present-value or discounted-rate-of-return formulations, and only one manager who was even aware of such methods.[4] On the other hand, a 1960 study of 127 "well-managed" firms showed that 38 of these used discounted cash flow in making investment decisions.[5]

A 1970 study of 369 larger firms (each making at least $1 million of investment annually) showed that 57 percent of the firms were making some uses of discounted cash flow techniques in 1970, whereas only 38 percent had used these in 1964 and only 19 percent had used them in 1959.[6] Of course, one would expect larger firms to have more management personnel with understanding of the more sophisticated methods and to be considering larger projects that are more likely to justify the expense of detailed demand and cost forecasting.

SUMMARY

Capital budgeting is allocation of capital among alternative investment opportunities and determination of the total amount of investment in the current period. Capital budgeting is concerned with choices among projects that are compatible with corporate strategy but not clearly essential to it. Corporate strategy is a delineation of the businesses in which the firm is to be engaged, a statement of attitudes toward business and financial risks, and a plan for achieving competitive advantages.

A project's cash flows must be estimated as the first step in testing or measuring the project's profitability. Cash flows of a cost-reducing project are the expected net reductions in costs of future periods, and cash flows of a revenue-increasing project are the net increases in revenues of future periods. Depreciation, a cost that is in effect prepaid at the time of the initial outlay for the project, is not a cash cost in subsequent periods and is not subtracted from revenue in estimating cash flows. However, depreciation is subtracted from the pretax cash flow in determining taxable income and the amount of taxes that are to be subtracted to put the project's cash flows on an after-tax basis.

A project's profitability can be tested by comparing its present value with the initial outlay. Any excess of present value over initial outlay is called *net present value* and is a measure of profitability. A project's present value is the sum of future cash flows discounted back to the

---

[4] Martin B. Solomon, Jr., *Investment Decisions in Small Business: Theory and Practice* (Lexington: University of Kentucky Press, 1963).

[5] James H. Miller, "A Glimpse at Practice in Calculating and Using Return on Investment," *N.A.A. Bulletin* (June 1960).

[6] Thomas Klammer, "Empirical Evidence of the Adoption of Sophisticated Capital Budgeting Techniques," *Journal of Business* 45 (July 1972), pp. 387–97.

594 *Managerial economics*

present at rates corresponding to costs of capital over the various periods.

A project can have net present value only if the project's internal rate of return is greater than the project's marginal cost of capital. Internal rate of return is that constant rate of discount which makes the project's present value just equal to the initial outlay. Each project has its own internal rate of return.

Costs of capital may vary from period to period. In such instances, each project's cash flows should be discounted period by period, at varying rates. Costs of capital in any given period are weighted averages of the after-tax cost of debt and the cost of equity. Cost of equity is the expected rate of return (an annual percentage rate) that makes marginal (most reluctant) stockholders just willing to hold the common stock at its current price.

It is sometimes necessary to choose between two mutually exclusive projects where the larger of the projects could be the best choice even though the smaller has a somewhat higher internal rate of return. To analyze mutually exclusive projects, the larger project is treated as the equivalent of the smaller one plus an incremental project. The profitabilities of the smaller project and the incremental project are tested by the net present value approach; if both projects are profitable, the larger project (which is the equivalent of the two projects combined) is selected.

Risk adjustment is largely subjective and varies from one management to another. Risk evaluation for any given project should take into account the possible effects upon the firm's overall profitability and value of the possible variations in that project's outcome. Some companies establish classes of project risk and a consensus as to the risk premiums and discounts that should be applied to the costs of capital used in discounting each class of project.

Capital projects may involve decision-event-decision chains. In such instances, decision trees are useful in organizing the relevant information and selecting the preferred initial action. If there are wide variations in the project's possible outcomes and the project is a substantial part of the total capital base, it may be desirable to adjust for risk by substituting preference values for the monetary outcomes in the decision tree.

QUESTIONS

1. Why is an explicit statement of corporate strategy needed in carrying out capital expenditure planning?

2. What is the appropriate test of profitability for a proposed project?

3. What is a project balance?

4. Is a project's net present value the same as the present value of the project's terminal value? Explain.

5. Why might a firm's marginal costs of capital vary from period to period? How does period-to-period variation in capital's marginal cost affect the techniques used in testing the profitability of proposed projects?

6. If a firm's marginal cost of capital is increasing with expansion of investment in a given period, what problem is thereby introduced into capital expenditure planning?

7. If a firm is operating under capital rationing (it will not go outside for funds even though these could be profitably used), what is the nature of the resulting difficulty in carrying out rational capital allocation?

8. "In adjusting for a project's risk, the manager should consider possible effects of the project on the firm's overall profitability rather than just the variance of the expected outcome of the project as such." Explain.

9. "Although only one project will actually be the marginal project accepted during the current period, each project must be tested *as if it were* the marginal project by discounting its cash flows at marginal cost of capital rates." Explain.

PROBLEMS

1. A firm is considering installing a new conveyor for materials handling in a warehouse. The conveyor will have an initial cost of $75,000 and an installation cost of $7,200. Expected benefits of the conveyor are: (*a*) annual labor cost will be reduced by $17,200, and (*b*) breakage and other damages from handling will be reduced by $400 per month. Some of the firm's costs are expected to increase as follows: (*a*) electricity cost will rise by $100 per month, and (*b*) annual repair and maintenance of the conveyor will amount to $900. Assume that the firm uses five-year, straight-line depreciation, the conveyor has an expected useful life of eight years and a projected salvage value of $5,000, and the firm expects marginal income to be taxed at a 48 percent rate.

   a. Estimate future cash flows for the proposed project.
   b. Determine the project's internal rate of return.
   c. Decompose the project's cash flows by using the internal rate of return as cost of capital. Your work should resemble Table 14–3.

2. Assume the following expected marginal costs of capital in future periods for the firm in Problem 1 above:

Period	Marginal cost (percent annually)
1	20%
2	15
3	12
4–8	10

  a. Determine the project's net present value.
  b. Decompose the project's cash flow using the costs of capital listed above. Your work should resemble Table 14–5. (Assume reinvestment of negative project balances at the firm's marginal cost of capital.)
  c. Calculate the benefit-cost ratio for the project.

3. Assume that the engineering department of the firm in Problems 1 and 2 has developed an alternate design for a conveyor. The alternate design has lower initial cost, but it will not save as much labor and there are other minor differences. The initial cost would be $60,000 and the annual reduction in labor cost would be approximately $13,000. Reduction in damage in material handling would be $400 per month and electricity cost would be increased $100 per month (both amounts are in comparison to present conditions, with *no* conveyor). Annual maintenance and repair are projected at $750 for the alternate-design conveyor; it is expected to have a useful life of six years; and the salvage value is estimated to be $1,000.
  a. Determine the cash flows for use in an incremental analysis to aid the choice between the $75,000 conveyor and the $50,000 conveyor.
  b. Using the marginal costs of capital listed in Problem 2, carry out the incremental analysis by calculating the net present value of the incremental project and its benefit-cost ratio. What would you recommend that the firm do?

FURTHER READING

Brigham, Eugene, and Pappas, James L. "Rates of Return on Common Stock." *Journal of Business,* July 1969.

Dean, Joel. "Measuring the Productivity of Investment in Persuasion." *Journal of Industrial Economics* 15, April 1967.*

Haynes, W. W., and Solomon, Martin B., Jr. "A Misplaced Emphasis in Capital Budgeting." *The Quarterly Review of Economics and Business* 2, February 1962.*

Hertz, David B. "Risk Analysis in Capital Investment." *Harvard Business Review,* January–February 1964.

Hirshleifer, Jack. "On the Theory of Optimal Investment Decision." *Journal of Political Economy* 66, August 1958.

Magee, John F. "How to Use Decision Trees in Capital Budgeting." *Harvard Business Review,* September–October 1964.

---

* This article is included in *Readings in Managerial Economics,* rev. ed. (Dallas: Business Publications, Inc., 1977).

Mao, James C. T. "Survey of Capital Budgeting: Theory and Practice." *Journal of Finance* 25, May 1970.*

Solomon, Martin B., Jr. "Uncertainty and its Effect on Capital Investment Analysis." *Management Science* 12, April 1966.*

Weingartner, H. Martin. "Capital Budgeting of Interrelated Projects: Survey and Synthesis." *Management Science* 12, March 1966.

Cases for part six

The cases in this section focus attention on long-range forecasting and capital budgeting. Analysis of actual capital investment problems provides insights which no text discussion can give. In the abstract it is easy to determine the appropriate type of analysis; in practice one must compromise with theory to make it applicable to the complexities and uncertainties of reality; one frequently does not have all the data needed.

Topics covered by the cases in this section range from relatively simple problems such as the determination of the present value of an income stream to a very complicated case involving a new type of business which involves long-range forecasting and capital budgeting in a relatively uncertain environment. Other cases involve determining such things as a fair rate of return, the cost of capital, and accounting and economic profit.

FINCH PRINTING COMPANY

In December 1954 William Welch agreed to become a director of the Finch Printing Company, located in an eastern city with a population of over 300,000. He was a cousin of three majority stockholders in the company—Mabel Finch, the company vice president, and her sister and brother, both of whom were inactive. He understood that one of his responsibilities was to represent the interests of these stockholders.

Background

The Finch Printing Company was founded in 1901 by Jacob Finch, father of the three major stockholders just mentioned. The company engaged in job printing of a high quality. The company had a city-wide reputation for fine workmanship, dependability, and strong managerial ethics. The firm did considerable printing for religious organizations, but its main customers were commercial firms. It printed several journals or trade magazines with a wide geographic circulation, but most of its business was local. The firm never reached a large size; maximum employment was 50.

Jacob Finch maintained several policies which undoubtedly limited the profits of the firm. He refused to do any printing for liquor firms even though opportunities to print for them were numerous. He tried to maintain employment for most of his employees during the depression of the 1930s despite the low level of business, a fact that weakened the financial structure of the company in that period.

Upon Jacob Finch's death in 1941, his daughter, Mabel Finch, took over the management of the company as president. It was not her intention to remain in that position, but she was unable to find a successor until 1953. The company was not particularly profitable during her presidency, despite the general improvement in business activity during World War II and the years that followed. Wartime restrictions limited the ability of the company to make profits.

In October 1953 Mabel Finch succeeded in employing a new president, Arthur Yount, who was thoroughly familiar with the printing industry. Yount received a salary and was to share in the company profits on a prearranged basis. One of Yount's first acts was to sign a contract with a correspondence school, resulting in a 40–50 percent increase in sales (see Exhibit 1).

In 1954, when William Welch became a director, the firm was still located in an antiquated four-story building not entirely suited to modern printing techniques. The building had been largely written off; most of the balance sheet item "Building and building improvements" represented land and a new elevator installed in conformance with safety requirements. The building was located near the center of the city and undoubtedly was worth over $40,000 because of that location.

Developments in 1954, 1955, and 1956

In spite of the improvement in profits from 1953 to 1954 (see Exhibit 1), the company prospects did not appear favorable to Welch. He found that a serious difference had arisen between Yount, the president, and the vice president, Mabel Finch. Finch believed that Yount was not living up to certain agreements made orally when he was employed and that he was not carrying out some of the long-standing policies of the firm. Furthermore, she believed that he was limiting her authority to much narrower confines than was originally intended. Yount apparently believed that Finch was interfering with his management of the

Exhibit 1.   Comparative profit and loss statement for the fiscal years ended September 30, 1953, 1954, 1955, 1956

	1953		1954		1955		For the 6 months ended March 31, 1956	
	Amount	Percent to net sales	Amount	Percent to net sales	Amount	Percent to net sales	Amount	Percent to net sales
Net sales								
Correspondence school	$ 0	0%	$ 64,712	27.55%	$100,058	36.60%	$ 25,530	20.08%
Other	174,625	100.00	170,141	72.45	173,306	63.40	101,594	79.92
Total net sales	$174,625	100.00%	$234,853	100.00%	$273,364	100.00%	$127,124	100.00%
Cost of sales								
Materials cost	$ 72,228	41.36%	$ 87,591	37.30%	$102,677	37.56%	$ 50,867	40.01%
Change in work in process	(508)	(0.29)	(735)	(0.31)	46	0.02	(1,039)	(0.82)
Direct department expenses	2,030	1.16	4,552	1.94	4,618	1.69	2,664	2.10
Wages—direct	44,970	25.75	61,823	26.32	64,866	23.73	32,074	25.23
Wages—indirect	15,266	8.74	14,244	6.07	15,383	5.63	7,454	5.86
Wages—maintenance	3,449	1.98	3,234	1.37	3,469	1.27	1,878	1.48
Spoilage	1,155	0.66	2,409	1.03	1,794	0.66	720	0.57
Payroll taxes	1,594	0.91	2,043	0.86	2,356	0.86	895	0.70
Power and light	1,256	0.72	1,108	0.47	1,141	0.42	624	0.49
Insurance—general	699	0.40	765	0.33	278	0.10	—	—
Water	81	0.05	130	0.06	105	0.04	36	0.03
Fuel	747	0.43	1,097	0.47	991	0.36	870	0.68
Building maintenance	460	0.26	1,377	0.59	833	0.30	147	0.12
Depreciation—building	655	0.38	655	0.28	655	0.24	480	0.38
Depreciation—machinery	5,015	2.87	5,256	2.23	6,124	2.23	3,045	2.40
Cost of sales	$149,097	85.38%	$185,550	79.01%	$205,336	75.11%	$100,715	79.23%
Gross profit	$ 25,528	14.62%	$ 49,303	20.99%	$ 68,028	24.89%	$ 26,409	20.77%
Expenses								
Administrative, general	$ 22,339	19.84%	$ 25,896	16.48%	$ 31,382	18.64%	$ 13,388	19.54%
Selling and delivery	12,295		12,807		19,570		11,450	
Operating profit (loss)	$ (9,106)	(5.22)	$ 10,600	4.51	$ 17,075	6.25	$ 1,571	1.23
Other income	1,640	0.94	8,999	3.83	1,377	0.50	533	0.42
Total	$ (7,466)	(4.28)	$ 19,599	8.34	$ 18,452	6.75	$ 2,104	1.65
Other deductions	+1,748	+1.00	-2,071	-0.88	-2,068	-0.75	-913	-0.71
Profit (loss) before provision for taxes on income	$ (9,214)	(5.28)	$ 17,528	7.46	$ 16,384	6.00	$ 1,191	0.94
Provision for taxes—estimated	0	0	-2,561	-1.09	-5,356	-1.96	-389	-0.31
Net profit (loss)	$ (9,214)	(5.28)%	$ 14,966	6.37%	$ 11,028	4.04%	$ 802	0.63%

business and that she was cutting across organizational channels. There was evidence of the formation of factions at lower levels in the firm.

The board of directors met once a month. In 1955 and 1956 it consisted of five members: Yount (the president), Welch, two members who represented the Bettsville Industrial Foundation which held mortgage bonds in the company, and Oswald (a minority stockholder). Mabel Finch preferred not to hold a position as a director, but she attended meetings as secretary of the board. The majority of the directors appeared to be satisfied with the new presidency, partly because of the improved profit position which offered greater protection to the creditors.

The approximate division of the common stock in the company was as follows:

Mabel Finch	25%
Her sister	18
Her brother	17
Yount	10
Oswald	20
Others	10

The company had paid no dividends to the stockholders for over ten years up to late 1955, when the board voted a dividend of $1 per share. Welch had at first favored a larger dividend but was convinced that this would be unwise after examining a cash budget for the near future. The payments due on the mortgage, the accrued taxes, the bonus due the president, and other obligations seemed to preclude a larger dividend at that time.

Finch had always worked at a low salary, both as president and vice president. In 1956 the board approved an increase in her salary from $3,500 to $5,000. She had felt an obligation to her family to keep her father's business going. She also felt the same responsibility to the company employees that her father had exhibited in earlier years.

The situation in 1956

Welch became increasingly concerned with the company's situation as the years passed. The profit position deteriorated after 1954. The company appeared to be too dependent on a single customer, the correspondence school, and sales to that customer showed evidence of declining in 1956 (see Exhibit 1). The tension between the president and vice president continued, and disharmony spread through the company. For example, the plant superintendent spoke rudely to Finch and refused to let her "interfere" in his department even when it seemed necessary to her to check on the progress of some orders for which she was responsible. Several employees resigned, including one who showed considerable promise as a manager.

Welch was concerned about several risks facing the company: the risk of losing the correspondence business, with a resultant loss of profits; the risk of declines in "other sales"; the risk of the president's resignation with a probable loss of the correspondence business; and the risk that the internal friction would result in greater inefficiency and higher costs. Welch believed that most of the stockholders had long before assumed that their stock was almost worthless, and there was a possibility that Yount (who owned about 10 percent of the stock) might eventually be able to buy up a majority interest at low prices.

Several alternatives occurred to Welch as he thought about the problems of the company:

1. The company might lower prices to get fuller use of its idle capacity and labor force. Welch suspected that a high proportion of the costs were fixed, especially wage costs. Printing firms did not normally hire and fire printers as business increased and decreased; they found it necessary to maintain the work force during the lulls, with resultant idle labor during a substantial part of the year.

2. The company might raise prices to improve its margins, though Welch noted that there were at least 50 competitors in the city, some of which might win customers away if prices were raised.

3. The company might invest in improved equipment in order to cut costs. Welch knew little about printing equipment. The only proposal for new equipment that he could recall during his period on the board was one for a press like one the company owned. When Finch pointed out to the directors that the existent press was idle a good part of the time, this proposal was abandoned.

4. The company might build or lease a new one-floor plant which would result in lower handling costs. Welch did not know what this would cost, but he learned from an acquaintance in the printing business that simply moving and rewiring the equipment might cost $60,000.

5. The company might add to its sales force, which consisted in 1956 of the part-time efforts of the president, the vice president, plus the sales manager, and one additional salesperson. The sales manager and salesperson were paid a 10 percent commission on sales.

Welch was not completely satisfied with any of these alternatives. But he believed that inaction could result in complete failure for the company.

Exhibit 2 presents a comparative balance sheet for the years 1954 through 1956.

1. Do the profit and loss statements in Exhibit 1 show the economic profits of the firm? Do they reflect the full opportunity costs? Explain.
2. Break the expenses in Exhibit 1 into fixed and variable categories. (It may

Exhibit 2

FINCH PRINTING COMPANY
Comparative Balance Sheet

	Year ending March 31		
Assets	*1954*	*1955*	*1956*
Current			
Cash..	$ 15,028	$ 19,073	$ 4,152
Accounts receivable...........................	16,188	18,467	29,995
Inventories			
Raw materials.............................	10,598	10,361	9,682
Finished goods.............................	329	537	189
Supplies...................................	2,038	1,041	1,962
Work in process...........................	4,329	4,284	5,322
Total Current Assets....................	$ 48,511	$ 54,662	$ 51,302
Other			
Cash surrender value—life insurance (pledged)....	$ 4,518	$ 4,750	$ 4,750
Accounts receivable—officers and employees......	119	739	44
Claim for refund of federal income taxes..........	—	892	892
Property, plant and equipment—(mortgaged)			
Building and building improvements.............	23,637	24,291	24,291
Machinery and equipment......................	121,285	118,916	119,168
Delivery equipment............................	53	53	53
Office furniture and fixtures....................	6,544	6,667	6,707
Total Depreciable Assets.................	$151,517	$149,927	$150,219
Less reserve for depreciation.....................	104,818	111,491	115,161
	$ 46,699	$ 38,436	$ 35,059
Land...	9,115	9,115	9,115
Deferred charges..............................	2,623	1,561	1,643
	$111,586	$110,155	$102,805

Liabilities and capital			
Current			
Notes payable (due within one year)			
Bettsville Industrial Foundation...............	$ 3,000	$ 3,000	$ 3,000
For equipment purchased.....................	7,400	3,125	2,192
Accounts payable.............................	21,310	20,534	21,062
Accrued expenses.............................	1,084	1,363	1,861
Provision for taxes on income—estimated.........	2,688	5,523	401
Provision for bonuses—estimated................	—	—	433
Total Current Liabilities.................	$ 35,482	$ 33,545	$ 28,950
Deferred indebtedness			
Mortgage notes payable maturing subsequent to September 30, 1954			
Bettsville Industrial Foundation.................	$ 17,000	$ 12,750	$ 10,500
For equipment purchased......................	3,200	—	—
American Type Founders, Inc...................	—	806	—
Capital stock and surplus			
Common stock authorized and issued (500 shares—no par value)..................	$ 48,480	$ 48,480	$ 48,480
Surplus......................................	7,423	14,573	14,875
	$111,586	$110,155	$102,805

604

Managerial economics

be necessary to split some categories. It will be necessary to use rough judgments in some of the separation of costs.)

3. What is the ratio of incremental cost to revenue (sales) according to your fixed-variable cost breakdown? What is the significance of this fact?
4. Does the capital stock and surplus category on the balance sheet show the economic worth of the firm? Explain.
5. What is the major issue in this case? (Beware of ignoring issues which are not listed in the case.)
6. Mabel Finch continued to insist on the policy of refusing liquor business. Was she correct in this insistence? Was she rational? Was she ethical?
7. What action should Welch recommend?

WHITE CASTLE TRUCKING CO.*

"I'm sorry I can't agree with you Jim. I still believe we should pay for the trucks we have before we go out on a limb and overextend ourselves by committing most of our revenue to meeting time payments." George Pike and his brother, Jim, thus continued their argument over the expansion policy of the White Castle Trucking Company.

This company had come into existence in the spring of 1958 as the result of a casual remark made by the owner of a ready-mix concrete company: "I surely could use some extra 12-yard dump trucks this summer."

Following this remark, George and Jim Pike made a study of the costs and revenues involved in the dump-truck leasing business with the following results:

1. New 12-yard 10-wheel dump trucks cost between $15,000 and $22,000 each. Used trucks in fair operating condition could be purchased for between $3,500 and $10,000 depending upon their age and condition. Many methods were used to depreciate used trucks. The most common method was to depreciate them on an eight-year basis from January 1 of the model year (i.e., a 1953 truck purchased on April 1, 1957, would be depreciated over three and three-fourth years from April 1, 1957).

2. State license fees and insurance would amount to about $625 per truck per year.

3. As each truck had ten wheels, tire repair and replacement costs would be a major consideration. Trucks were used over rough ground and the experiences of other truck-leasing companies indicated that about half of the tires had to be replaced each year. Some of the tires could be recapped which would reduce replacement costs. New tires cost about $225 each. It was estimated that with careful driver maintenance

---

* This case was prepared by Professor Frederic A. Brett of the University of Alabama as a basis for class discussion.

it would cost approximately $800 a year for tires on a per-truck basis.

4. At current prices, the cost of gasoline and oil to operate a truck on an eight-hour basis amounted to between $15 and $18.

5. There were no general figures available for repair and maintenance costs except that a complete overhaul of a truck engine would cost between $1,000 and $1,300. Other truck-leasing companies had found a direct relationship between repair costs and the care given to trucks by drivers. Some companies found it necessary to completely overhaul each truck on an annual basis. Other companies, using a wage incentive plan, had reduced the annual repair and maintenance costs to as little as 40 percent of the cost of a complete overhaul.

6. Truck-with-driver lease rates were $8.50 to $9.50 per hour depending upon location (county) and road surface conditions. Road construction companies usually paid $75 per truck on a daily lease basis. It was common practice for ready-mix concrete companies to lease truck with driver for $60 per day when gasoline and oil were supplied by the lessee.

7. In order to lease trucks to most companies in the area, it was necessary to employ only union drivers. The going rate for drivers was $3.12½ per hour or $25 for an eight-hour day. However, because of competition for jobs, many union drivers worked for a flat $20 per day. These "cut-rate" drivers were considered a risk by many of the companies, which found that repair costs mounted when these drivers were used.

The Pike brothers discussed their findings and decided to start a dump-truck leasing business if they could get a firm contract from one of the concrete ready-mix companies. They contacted Carl Manning who had given them the idea of starting the business by his casual remark earlier in the year. Manning agreed to give them a contract for five trucks at $60 per truck per day (five days a week) for the period May 15 to October 15 and that he would supply gasoline and oil for the trucks. It was further agreed that if a truck started work on a particular day and, at the option of the lessee, worked less than four hours it would be paid on the basis of one-half day; if it worked more than four hours, it would be considered as having worked a full day. If a truck broke down due to mechanical trouble, it would be docked on an hourly rate ($7.50) until repaired and put back in service. Time required for tire changes or minor repairs would not be charged against the truck unless down time ran over one hour, at which time the $7.50 deduction rate would go into effect.

On May 7, 1958, four used trucks were bought from Eastern Mack Trucks, Inc., a local truck dealer, for $16,500. Terms of the purchase contract called for a down payment of $4,000 and monthly payments of $754 for 18 months. A used three-quarter-ton pickup truck was also purchased for $500 cash. This vehicle was to be outfitted and used as a service truck. State license plates for the four trucks amounted to $960 and one-year premiums for liability and property damage insurance cost $1,527.84. The license plate for the pickup cost $24.50 and the insurance premium amounted to $151.70.

On May 10, a fifth truck was purchased for $7,500. Time payments of $388 per month for 18 months and a down payment of $1,000 was the best deal they could make. The annual insurance premium for this truck amounted to $381.96 and the license plate cost $240.

Drivers were hired for four of the trucks and Jim decided to give up his job an an automotive parts salesman and drive the fifth truck as well as manage the company. George would devote only part of his time to the new business. The drivers agreed to work for $20 a day until the new firm got on its feet, at which time they would expect to receive union wages. Jim decided to drive a 1954 International which was in pretty poor condition with the hope that he could "baby it along" until the cash account was improved and funds were available for needed repairs.

All five trucks reported for work on Wednesday, May 14. During the next month and a half, total revenue amounted to $8,160 of which $240 was receivable in accordance with the practice of making lease payments on Saturday of each week. During this same period, cash payments amounted to $6,458, of which $1,142 went for time payments on the trucks, $2,720 for driver's pay, $1,230 for tire repair and replacement, and $816 for truck repairs.

Analyzing the operations for the first six weeks, George and Jim came to the following conclusions:

1. Trucks had operated at only 83 percent efficiency because of down time for repairs. On a total basis, this had resulted in the loss of 29 truck-days at $40 per day or $1,160 ($60 rental less $20 driver pay).

2. The calculated risk of buying the cheaper trucks which were in rather poor operating condition had resulted in high repair costs as well as reducing potential revenue. This condition would have a reverse trend as soon as trucks were overhauled.

3. The high cost of tire repair and replacement would not continue once all worn tires had been replaced.

4. One driver had quit because he lost too much time while his truck was being repaired. The other drivers were not too happy about losing time when their trucks broke down. They felt that as long as they were working for less than union wages they should have full-time trucks to drive.

After a lengthy discussion, George and Jim decided on a new operating policy as follows:

1. Drivers would be hired at $20 a day on a five-day week basis. If their trucks were out of service due to mechanical breakdown, they would

be paid at half-rate to assist in the repair work. It was believed that this policy would encourage drivers to take better care of their trucks in order to earn full pay. Another benefit would be that driver morale would be higher because of the minimum $10 per day wage rate.

2. Repair costs had been high, and it was thought that if a suitable location could be had at a reasonable price, it would be cheaper in the long run to employ a full-time mechanic to work on the trucks at a company-owned garage.

George surveyed the area and on August 1 a service station, located near the edge of town on a little-traveled road, was leased for one year. The station was equipped with a grease rack and a wash shed which could be used as an enclosed repair shop. The station was on a large lot which could park about 50 vehicles. It was thought some revenue could be earned through leasing parking space to independent truckers and thus reduce the overhead for the operation.

On September 30, 1958, the following financial data were taken from the books of the company:

Truck rental income.................................		$23,688
Operating expenses:		
Drivers' wages*...........................	$8,460	
Tire repair and replacement..................	2,389	
Truck repair†.............................	2,178	
Insurance‡.................................	2,337	
Interest and bank charges...................	363	
Gasoline and oil, etc.§......................	274	
Taxes‖.....................................	1,998	
Other cash expenses........................	966	
Total expenses before depreciation.............		18,965
Profit before depreciation.....................		$ 4,723

* Includes regular driver pay for Jim.
† Includes rent on service station and mechanic's pay.
‡ Includes annual insurance premiums on trucks.
§ Supplied for special jobs worked on Saturdays.
‖ Includes annual truck license fees and social security taxes.

Jim was elated over the $4,723 profit the company had made since it was formed in May. George, however, was a bit worried when he realized that the cash account had increased only $501 because of the principal payments on the trucks of $4,222 ($4,568 less $346 interest included in above statement). George was also concerned about the contract's running out on October 15 with no assured work for the trucks during the winter months.

The weather during October and the early part of November was favorable for work and White Castle was able to work 32 days after October 1 before Manning closed down operations for the winter. During this period, $8,060 was collected for truck rentals. The remainder of the winter was a very trying time for the new company. On an overall average, only one truck was kept busy from November 17 until May 4, 1959, resulting in rental income of only $6,420. Operating expenses before depreciation charges for the period October 1, 1958, to May 4, 1959, were:

Drivers' wages*............................	$ 4,880
Tire repair and replacement................	737
Truck repairs†............................	3,160
Taxes‡....................................	1,682
Other cash expenses§.....................	1,442
Total cash expenses.......................	$11,901

* Drivers hired on a daily basis during winter months.
† The winter months were used to overhaul trucks. Other independent truckers used repair shop and receipts from these jobs were used to offset repair costs.
‡ Includes truck license fees due January 1 of each year.
§ Includes interest payments of $641.

The company had been in a very poor cash condition during the winter months and George had had to borrow a total of $1,500 from a local bank to make the March and April payments on the trucks. George was further concerned about the insurance premiums of $2,061.50 and time payments of $1,142 due in May.

On May 4, 1959, all five trucks were leased out to Manning at the same rates as the previous year. Manning stated that he could use twice as many trucks and Jim thought it would be a good idea to refinance the old trucks, which were in good operating condition after the winter repair work was completed, and buy several more trucks for the 1959 season. He reasoned that with only six more payments to be made on the trucks, they could cut the payments to a point where three or four new trucks would not be any more of a burden than the five trucks had been the previous year. In addition, the added revenue from the additional trucks would ease the entire cash position of the company.

George was very much against the idea and voiced his opinion that the old trucks should be paid for before any new time payment commitments were made. If no new obligations were undertaken, the old trucks would be paid for before the slack winter season set in and they wouldn't have to worry about the heavy drain on cash during the winter months.

Jim believed that this conservative approach would stunt the growth of the company and favored a policy of rapid expansion for the new company. To prove his point of view, Jim had their accountant project their cash position for the period June 1, 1959 to May 31, 1960, using the following assumptions:

1. Three additional trucks would be purchased for a total of $15,000. The down payment would amount to $3,000 and monthly payments of $776 for 18 months would complete the contract.

2. The five old trucks would be refinanced for a total of $412 per month for 18 months.

3. Trucks would rent for $60 a day (gasoline and oil to be supplied by lessee) and drivers would be paid on the same basis as last year.

4. Truck repair expense, which would include net service station operations, would not cost more than an estimated $300 per month.

5. Tire repair and replacement would not run more than $500 per truck per year. This lower-than-average estimate was based on the fact that trucks were used on hard surface roads about 90 percent of the time.

6. An additional $2,500 would be used during the winter months to overhaul the new trucks. This amount was in addition to repair costs considered under Assumption 4.

7. All trucks would operate at 85 percent efficiency between June 1 and September 30. Two trucks would be kept busy for the other months on a five-day week basis. This estimate was based upon last year's experience and a snow removal and sanding contract which Jim was assured of for the coming winter.

Jim considered these estimates very conservative, since revenue was being understated for May and October when the company had a good chance of operating above 25 percent efficiency.

1. Was the original investment in the company a sound one? Discuss. What criteria are relevant in evaluating this question?
2. Would the company have been better off to have invested in new rather than secondhand trucks? Discuss.
3. Estimate the economic profit for the company in the period up to September 30, 1958. Estimate the economic profit for the period up to May 4, 1959.
4. Should the company have purchased additional trucks in May 1959?
5. Develop a cash budget based on the assumption listed at the end of the case. Is this budget useful in making the decision on the purchase of additional trucks?
6. Would it be useful to compute the present value or discounted rate of return in this case? What cost of capital would be relevant?

WALDO, SMITH, AND MAXEY

Fred Waldo, Alice Smith, and Thomas Maxey were partners in a sign business. Each had other business interests; the sign firm was a sideline for all of them. In 1946 they started buying up small sign companies in towns of populations under 15,000. This venture had proved highly successful, as shown in Exhibit 1. A comparison of Exhibits 1 and 2 indicates an extremely high return on the original investment (most of the capital consisted of plowed-back earnings). Exhibits 3 and 4 provide additional information on company operations.

Exhibit 1

Comparative statement of income and expense (years ended December 31, 1954–1959)

	1959	1958	1957	1956	1955
Income					
Gross sales...............	$109,790	$114,163	$104,212	$79,124	$68,675
Other income..............	3,068	742	340	0	1,139
Capital gains..............	396	5,046	2,210	658	0
Total income..........	$113,254	$119,951	$106,762	$79,782	$69,814
Operating expenses					
Cost of material............	$ 4,385	$ 2,698	$ 4,264	$ 4,066	$ 4,329
Wages and salaries.........	20,043	25,698	19,878	13,467	12,142
Agency commissions........	12,830	13,591	11,060	10,106	9,042
Transportation expenses....	4,823	5,050	5,433	4,059	3,806
Insurance.................	7,049	1,719	1,306	915	934
Depreciation..............	13,237	14,223	10,148	8,309	7,920
Rent......................	6,240	4,894	4,509	2,827	2,268
Office supplies.............	2,338	2,066	918	834	849
Maintenance..............	1,442	2,116	2,429	1,919	1,890
Taxes and licenses.........	2,960	2,275	1,814	1,202	901
Professional services.......	366	6,123	804	200	249
Travel expenses............	346	303	6,316	3,036	2,546
Other expenses.............	8,360	13,446	12,093	6,532	2,893
Total material cost and expense.........	$ 84,419	$ 94,202	$ 80,972	$57,472	$49,769
Net profit before manager's salary.........	28,835	25,749	25,790	22,310	20,045
Manager's salary...........	4,800	4,800	4,213	4,160	4,160
Net profit.................	$ 24,035	$ 20,949	$ 21,577	$18,150	$15,885

In 1959 and 1960 several major decisions were required of the partners. One concerned the purchase of additional sign companies located in several towns scattered in nearby states. The partners knew that such companies were available at prices of from five to six times earnings. On the basis of past experience the partners had established a rule of thumb that they would not pay more than five times earnings. They had never paid more than this amount in the past.

The partners knew of one small company which was available at a price of five times earnings. The company had allowed its equipment to run down, so that considerable repairs might be necessary. Waldo believed that the profits could be increased by raising rentals from the existing level by 20 percent immediately and by another 20 percent at a later date. For example, the company might raise the rate on a medium-size sign from $10 per month to $12 per month and eventually to $15 per month. The firm's experience in the past was that improved service would permit increased rates.

In establishing rates the company was influenced somewhat by the rates in other small towns. The prevailing rate on the size sign already

Exhibit 2
Balance sheets, 1955–1959 (March 31)

	1959	1958	1957	1956	1955
Assets					
Cash......................	$ 4,756	$ 4,630	$ 2,182	$ 3,337	$ 1,626
Accounts receivable...........	11,384	8,446	12,366	6,150	7,419
Notes receivable.............	824	0	0	0	0
Inventories..................	2,450	2,711	3,349	3,359	2,698
Total current assets...........	$19,414	$15,787	$ 17,897	$12,846	$11,743
Fixed assets................	77,819	77,546	88,334	45,854	43,084
Other assets................	1,333	1,995	1,748	1,257	477
Total assets............	$98,566	$95,328	$107,978	$59,957	$55,304
Liabilities and capital					
Current liabilities					
Notes payable.............	$14,293	$14,088	$ 20,800	$ 5,000	$10,000
Accounts payable..........	2,718	3,382	3,730	1,692	474
Accrued expenses...........	780	989	1,162	178	142
Federal tax withheld........	311	311	264	130	154
Other....................	45	21	827	12	155
Total current liabilities.....	$18,147	$18,791	$ 26,777	$ 7,012	$10,925
Long-term notes...........	4,400	8,800	17,688	0	0
Total liabilities.............	$22,547	$27,591	$ 44,465	$ 7,012	$10,925
Capital					
Maxey....................	$25,340	$22,579	$ 21,171	$17,648	$14,793
Waldo....................	25,339	22,579	21,171	17,648	14,793
Smith.....................	25,339	22,579	21,171	17,648	14,793
Total capital...............	$76,018	$67,737	$ 63,514	$52,945	$44,378
Total liabilities and capital...............	$98,566	$95,328	$107,978	$59,957	$55,304

discussed was $15 per panel, though some rates went as low as $12. Rates were almost double in cities of 50,000 population or above.

Before purchasing a new sign company, the partners did research into its potential volume and costs. Outside organizations supplied traffic data which could be used to establish average daily circulation. It was necessary to obtain cost and profit data from the potential seller or from an analysis of Waldo, Smith, and Maxey's own experience.

Exhibit 3
Additions to fixed assets

	1958–59	1957–58	1956–57	1955–56
Land............................	$ 0	$ 0	$ 3,800	$ 0
Signs...........................	12,800	10,860	48,608	9,770
Trucks..........................	902	820	1,720	1,142
Buildings........................	0	101	142	214
Machinery.......................	356	0	1,039	302
Office equipment..................	97	337	558	118
Total additions................	$14,154	$12,118	$55,867	$11,546

Exhibit 4
Fixed assets and reserves for depreciation

	Balance 4-1-58	Additions	Retirements	Balance 3-31-59
Assets				
Land......................	$ 6,193	$ 0	$ 0	$ 6,193
Signs.....................	104,182	12,800	10,148	106,834
Autos and trucks...........	8,281	902	2,400	6,783
Buildings..................	8,316	0	0	8,316
Machinery and equipment....	2,338	356	0	2,694
Office equipment............	2,155	97	62	2,190
Totals.................	$131,465	$14,155	$12,610	$133,010
Reserves for depreciation				
Signs.....................	$ 43,274	$11,273	$ 9,620	$ 44,926
Autos and trucks...........	6,149	713	2,300	4,563
Buildings..................	2,023	438	0	2,461
Machinery and equipment....	1,325	538	0	1,863
Office equipment............	1,148	274	46	1,376
Totals.................	$ 53,919	$13,236	$11,966	$ 55,189

Waldo expressed the view that six times earnings was too much to pay for sign companies in small towns. He knew of some companies that might be available at that price but wasn't much interested in following up on such opportunities.

In 1960 another issue arose. Maxey wished to sell his interest in the firm to the other partners. The partners wished to set a price that was fair and that recognized Maxey's one-third financial contribution to the firm.

1. Is the rule of buying companies at five times earnings but not at six times earnings a reasonable one? Discuss.
2. The partners were able to borrow large sums of money for new ventures at 6 percent. Assuming this to be the cost of capital and assuming a 15-year life of a sign business beyond the time of the case, estimate the present value of the Waldo, Smith, and Maxey firm. Compare this value with a price of five times earnings.
3. The partners had access to investment opportunities which in recent years had returned more than 20 percent profit (before taxes). Assuming the opportunity cost of capital to be 20 percent, estimate the present value of the firm. Compare this value with a price of five times earnings.
4. Which cost of capital estimate (6 percent or 20 percent) is appropriate? Discuss.
5. Discuss the way in which you handled depreciation in your computation.
6. Should Waldo, Smith, and Maxey buy the small sign company mentioned in the case? Discuss.
7. What would be a fair price to pay Maxey for his one-third interest in the company?

AVELLA, INC.*

Avella, Inc., was a well-established company engaged in the manufacture of various rubber and plastic goods. The products were generally inexpensive, and a high volume of sales had to be maintained to enable the company to recover its fixed costs. The management consciously avoided taking on any products which could be characterized as novelties or fads likely to have a relatively brief period of prosperity. Avella had been fortunate in maintaining a stable pattern of sales over the years and had developed a strong customer loyalty. The company had gained a reputation through its production of a relatively complete line of quality products. There was some competition from the producers of specialties, but no other business in the industry offered competition with such a complete line.

Edgar A. Gordon, who had recently retired as chairman of the board, was firmly convinced that the company should maintain a strong working capital position and finance its resources primarily with equity capital. This policy, he believed, would place the company in a favorable position to exploit opportunities when they arose and would have the further advantage of providing protection during prolonged periods of general economic decline.

This policy was being carefully reviewed. Many of the officers and directors believed that a restrictive policy had checked the growth of the company and had resulted in the loss of many favorable opportunities for profitable investment. There was no desire, however, to make rapid changes. The position of the firm and its policies and procedures were being currently examined.

The company had maintained a minimum cash balance of approximately $1.5 million at all times. Throughout the year, cash needs were carefully budgeted and plotted on a broken-line graph as shown in Exhibit 1.

Any cash flow in excess of what was required in order to finance current operations was invested in short-term government securities. This investment was adjusted up or down according to the seasonal needs for cash. Careful budgeting had resulted in stabilizing the cash balance at about the desired level.

During 19—, Avella, Inc., increased its working capital by $1,310,000.

The statement of financial position at December 31, 19—, and the condensed operating statement for the year 19—, as given in Exhibit 2,

* This case was prepared by Professor Carl L. Moore of Lehigh University as a basis for class discussion. This case is not designed to present illustrations of either correct or incorrect handling of administrative decisions. Copyright 1959 by Carl L. Moore.

Exhibit 1

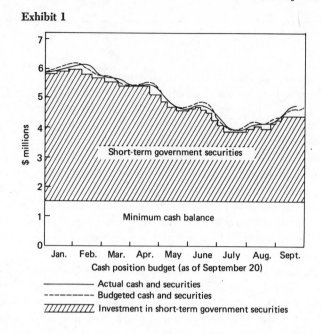

Cash position budget (as of September 20)

——————— Actual cash and securities
- - - - - - - Budgeted cash and securities
/////////// Investment in short-term government securities

were considered by the controller to be typical. The gross cost of the plant and equipment at the end of the fiscal year was $24,362,130. After deducting the accumulated depreciation of $16,740,630, there was a remaining net book value of $7,621,500.

The controller of the company, Charles A. Penberthy, was in the process of reviewing the way in which business investment opportunities were evaluated to determine their economic feasibility. Penberthy was well acquainted with the various activities of the company through his long years of service in production, sales, and financial administration.

Investment proposals were initiated by a new products committee which worked closely with the director of research. Possible projects were carefully screened as to market potential, their relationship to existing product lines, and production possibilities. The controller and his staff assisted in this screening process. As a general rule, a project was not accepted unless analysis revealed that the project would probably

Source of net working capital
   Net income before depreciation charges of $1,302,994.................. $3,510,050
Uses of net working capital
   Dividend payments... $1,250,100
   Fixed asset additions..   959,950
     Total... $2,200,050
Net increase in working capital....................................... $1,310,000

Exhibit 2

AVELLA, INC.

Statement of Financial Position

(December 31, 19—)

Current assets

Cash	$ 1,707,269
U.S. government securities at cost including accrued interest	3,111,398
Accounts receivable	7,818,592
Inventories	8,616,133
Prepaid expenses	309,380
Total Current Assets	$21,562,772

Current liabilities

Accounts payable	$ 1,141,834
Accrued taxes, wages, and miscellaneous expenses	1,788,636
Estimated federal income tax liability less U.S. Treasury notes of $1,080,000	183,301
Total Current Liabilities	$ 3,113,771

Net working capital	$18,449,001

Other assets

Miscellaneous investments	$ 590,417
Real estate, machinery, and equipment at cost less depreciation	8,420,152
Net assets	$27,459,570

Capital

Common stock	$ 7,413,480
Capital in excess of par value	2,527,242
Reinvested earnings	17,518,848
	$27,459,570

Statement of Earnings

(for the year ended December 31, 19—)

Sales and other income	$48,654,260

Cost and expenses

Cost of products sold	$30,232,458
Selling, administrative and general expenses	13,535,720
Federal income tax, estimated	2,479,017
Total costs and expenses	$46,447,204
Net earnings	$ 2,207,056

yield a rate of return upon investment of at least 30 percent before taxes. The 30 percent rate of return had been established as a guide on the basis that the company had been earning approximately that rate on its investment in machinery and equipment over the years. For example, the company earned $4,686,073 before taxes during 19—. The total cost of the machinery and equipment (without allowance for depreciation) at the end of the year was $15,654,257. Relatively insignificant acquisitions or replacements and obvious cost-saving possibilities did not go through such a rigorous screening process.

After the project had been accepted by the new products committee, it was reviewed by the marketing committee of the board of directors.

$$\frac{\text{Net dollar advantage before taxes}}{\text{Average annual investment}} = \text{Rate of return}$$

Both the net additional revenue and the direct cost savings to be derived from the project were considered in arriving at the net dollar advantage before taxes. The net additional revenue was the gross revenue anticipated from the project as reduced by the cost of goods sold and estimated selling and administrative expenses. The cost of goods sold was computed in the conventional manner, including the cost of direct materials, direct labor, and manufacturing overhead. Manufacturing overhead, including depreciation, was applied to the products on a pre-determined rate basis as a percentage of direct labor cost. An allowance of 17 percent of the estimated gross revenue was deducted for selling and administrative expenses. This percentage had been established from past experience studies which showed that the selling and administrative expenses which should be identified with a product were approximately 17 percent of sales. Finally, depreciation computed on a straight-line basis on the facility cost and on what was called the capital corollary was deducted to arrive at the net dollar advantage before taxes, as shown below:

1. Direct cost savings before depreciation..................... $
2. Increased revenue
   Sales... $
   Cost of goods sold....................................   _____
   Gross profit... $
   17 percent allowance for selling and administrative expenses _____
   Net revenue addition.................................   _____
3. Gross dollar advantage [(1) + (2)]....................... $
4. Less depreciation of facility cost and capital corollary......   _____
5. Net dollar advantage before taxes [(3) − (4)]............. $

The capital corollary represented the allocated investment in floor space used. Penberthy maintained that each machine had to absorb a portion of the cost of space used. If the allocated plant costs such as depreciation, taxes, and insurance were not considered, the building expansion required to accommodate additional equipment would be unfairly charged against the last piece added, when in reality all additional pieces helped bring about the need for building expansion. The corollary investment was estimated to amount to 70 percent of the cost of the equipment. Some time in the past a study was made over a period of time to determine the relationship between plant costs and investment. As a result of this study, it was found that the allocated plant costs would amount to about 70 percent of the investment in equipment.

The total average annual investment was then computed. The cost of the equipment itself was divided in half to arrive at an average. The capital corollary cost amounting to 70 percent of the equipment cost was similarly averaged. Furthermore, a provision was made for the increase in working capital which would be required to support the project.

A study had been made showing that approximately 9 percent of the estimated gross revenue was held as accounts receivable, 21 percent of the estimated cost of goods sold was invested in inventories, and 5 percent of the estimated cost of goods sold was held as a minimum cash balance.

Accordingly, these percentages were applied to the expected gross revenue and cost of goods sold resulting from the project to arrive at the additional investment held in the form of working capital.

> One-half facility estimated cost.................... $
> One-half capital corollary.........................
> Total working capital............................. ————
>   Total average annual investment.............. $

As an example, an evaluation of a proposal to manufacture a certain type of air mattress to be used in swimming pools is given in Exhibit 3.

Projects which were accepted were subject to a postcompletion audit. If the results did not come close to expectations, a decision was reached as to whether or not an additional audit was to be made. In certain cases it was believed that if more time were allowed, the project would eventually meet the requirements. On the other hand, some projects might show that there was little opportunity for improvement and that additional audits would not be justified. An unsuccessful project might be liquidated, or it might be continued as a sort of necessary evil which had to be tolerated. For example, a project might be maintained, which did not justify itself, in order to round out the product line.

Penberthy and his staff were actively investigating the possibility of improving the method by which business investment proposals were evaluated. Both Penberthy and his staff had been reading current literature on the subject and had attended various conferences dealing with this topic.

1. Evaluate the capital budgeting procedures of the Avella Company, including the following specific considerations:
   a. The amount of working capital on hand.
   b. The cutoff rate.
   c. The cost of capital to the company.
   d. The formula for computing the rate of return.
   e. The treatment of overhead in the computations.
   f. The treatment of depreciation in the computations.
   g. The use of the capital corollary concept.
   h. The provision for working capital.

Exhibit 3
Economic evaluation of facility acquisition proposal (net dollar advantages before taxes)

Increased revenue		
Sales..	$793,278	
Cost of goods sold.......................................	558,774	
Gross profit...	$234,504	
17% allowance for selling and administrative expenses.........	134,857	
Net revenue increase.....................................		$ 99,647
Gross dollar advantage..		$ 99,647
Less depreciation of facility cost and capital corollary...........		25,730
Net dollar advantage before taxes............................		$ 73,917

Investment		
One-half facility estimated cost..............................		$ 75,675
Capital corollary		
One-half other fixed assets...............................	52,973	
Total working capital....................................	216,677	
Total average annual investment............................		$345,325

$$\frac{\text{Net dollar advantage before taxes—\$73,917}}{\text{Total average annual investment—\$345,325}} = 21.4\% \text{ rate of return}$$

Explanatory notes		
Total facility cost..	$151,350	
(est. life of 10 years, no residual salvage value)		
Capital corollary (70% of $151,350).......................	$105,945	
Sales..	$793,278	
Cost of goods sold.......................................	$558,774	
Selling and administrative expenses (17% of $793,278)........		$134,857
Total working capital		
Accounts receivable (9% of $793,278)......................	$ 71,395	
Inventories (21% of $558,774)............................	117,343	
Cash (5% of $558,774)...................................	27,939	
Total working capital................................		216,677
Depreciation [10% of ($151,350 + $105,995)].................		25,730

2. Would the capital budgeting procedures described in this case be equally applicable to replacement investments and to investments in entirely new facilities? Discuss.

AIR-INDIA (E)*

Purchase of Boeing 707s

    In early 1956 the Chairman of Air-India, J. R. D. Tata, visited the United States to discuss the purchase of jet aircraft with the Douglas

---

* Copyright 1964 by the Indian Institute of Management, Ahmedabad.

Aircraft Co. and the Boeing Co. Up to that time, Air-India had also been considering turbo-propeller aircraft but had determined that they were uneconomical and less acceptable to the traveling public compared to the jets. The management had also investigated the Comet IV type jet, but had found that it did not have the range required for the Bombay–Cairo or Atlantic sectors. Tata found that most of the international airlines of the world were placing orders for either the DC–8 or the Boeing 707 for delivery in the period from 1959 to 1961 (see Exhibit 1).

Exhibit 1
Orders booked as of end of April 1956

Customer	No.	Option		Model	Delivery date
Boeing 707					
Pan American......	23		(6)	120	December 1958 to
			(17)	320	November 1959
American Airlines...	30	5		120	From March 1959
Braniff...........	5			120	From October 1959
Continental.......	4	1		120	1959
Air France........	10	7		320	November 1959 to
					November 1960
Sabena...........	4			320	From December 1959
TWA............	8	22		120	From April 1959
Lufthansa........	4	4		320	Spring 1960
Total.........	88 +	39 options			
Douglas DC–8					
Pan American......	21			J–57	From December 1959
				& J–75	
United Airlines.....	30		(15)	J–57	From May 1959
			(15)	J–75	
National..........	6			J–57	Midsummer 1959
K.L.M............	8	4		J–75	From March 1960
Eastern Airlines....	18	8	(6)	J–57	May 1959
			(12)	J–75	March 1960
JAL.............	4			J–75	1960
SAS.............	7			J–75	1960
Panagra..........	4			J–75	Early 1960
Swissair..........	2			J–75	Spring 1960
Delta Airlines......	6			J–57	June 1959
TCA.............	6			RR–505	
Total.........	112 +	12 options			

Tata discussed the jet purchase proposal at the board meetings on March 5 and May 25, 1956. He noted that the carrying capacity of the jets would be equivalent to three or three-and-a-half Super-Constellations, the type of aircraft which the airline was using in 1954. They would cruise at about 500 miles per hour. Tata noted that introduction of the new aircraft would raise a number of difficult operational and economic problems, but nevertheless came out strongly for the purchase stating:

If the corporation was to remain in business in competition with the other carriers on its routes, it would seem to be left with no option but to place an order for one of these two makes in the very near future in order to have a reasonable place in the queue. If orders were placed within the next three months or so, the corporation would be able to get its aircraft in the second half of 1960 at approximately the same time as other carriers who had already placed their orders.

Tata also remarked that the minimum number of jets which should be purchased was three, which would be the equivalent to ten of the existing Super-Constellations. The total cost including spare engines would be about Rs. 120 million. The corporation could give consideration to the sale of some of its present fleet.

The Second Five-Year Plan made provision for Rs. 100 million for new aircraft. Of this amount over Rs. 20 million were committed to Super-Constellations on order. Thus, not enough was left to finance the purchase of three jets. Tata believed that the problem could be met by deferred payments or by a loan from the Import-Export Bank, the World Bank, or some other financial institution. Furthermore, delivery of even the first of the jets would come near the end of the Second Five-Year Plan period.

There appeared to be little to choose technically between the DC–8 and the Boeing 707. It would be difficult, however, to get delivery of a DC–8 before 1961. The Boeing Company had three positions open for delivery in 1960. Other airlines were in the market for these three, but Air-India could secure the three positions if it acted rapidly.

As of May 25, 1956, Air-India was one of the few international lines not to have placed an order. Tata stated that the issue was urgent since the only alternatives were to go out of business or to give up first- and tourist-class traffic and concentrate on third-class or coach traffic.

On June 6, 1956, company officials circulated a formal memorandum on purchase of the jets, most of which appears below.

Proposal for the purchase of jet aircraft— Boeing 707 intercontinental model

1. Ever since its inception in 1947, and with the approval of the Government of India both before and after nationalization, Air-India International have followed the consistent policy of equipping their fleet with the latest and most competitive type of aircraft available. The original Constellation 749's were changed within three years for 749A's. This was followed by the purchase of 1049 Super-Constellations, culminating with the order for three 1049G's and

for two Mark III Comets (subsequently cancelled). This policy has enabled Air-India International to be from the start and to remain fully competitive with much larger, older, and better-known carriers. In the view of the management, such a policy is essential to the success of any small international airline operating in a highly competitive market. In pursuance of this policy, the development of commercial jet aircraft has been closely watched by the Corporation and its predecessor ever since the early 1950s when the de Havilland Comet first came on the scene.

2. During the [preceding] nine months or so, two much larger types of American jet aircraft, almost identical in design, price, and technical characteristics, have been announced for delivery from 1959 onwards. One is the Douglas DC–8 and the other is the Boeing 707. In carrying capacity and all-up weight, these American jets will be approximately twice the size of the Mark IV Comet and approach a take-off weight of 300,000 pounds. Their four engines will total over 60,000 pounds of thrust as against about 40,000 for the Comet. Their range will be such as to enable pay-loads in excess of 30,000 pounds to be carried on nonstop services over such extreme sections as the Atlantic. They will be capable of carrying up to 140 passengers although the number will be restricted to about 118 in the mixed configuration (28 standard and 90 tourist) of the aircraft proposed to be ordered by the Corporation.

3. Since October 1955, when the first orders were announced by Pan American Airways, practically every major airline in the world has ordered one or the other of these two types and a total of well over 200 has been ordered up to now with correspondingly lengthening deliveries.

4. The advent of this new generation of great jet airplanes offers to the air transport industry immense potentialities for profitable expansion and, at the same time, poses some serious problems. Substantial increases in cruising speed in air transport have in the past invariably generated new strata of air traffic which did not exist before and these increases in traffic have been achieved without any decrease in surface transport. There is every reason to expect that this greatest of all jumps in cruising speeds—from about 300 to 500 mph—will have the same effect. The fact that the increased speed will be coupled with the elimination of intermediate landings on extra long sections will still further accelerate travel from the passengers' point of view. Other features which will attract passengers will be the extraordinarily smooth conditions of flying at extreme altitudes and the freedom from vibration inherent in turbine engines.

5. From the operational point of view, the higher speeds will produce important economies in flight personnel, out-station expenses, and overhead expenses, while the elimination on the one hand of propellers, with their heavy gearing, complicated controls, and feathering devices, and on the other of vibration, which is one of the principal causes of wear and tear, will result in considerable simplification and lower maintenance costs. As against these favorable factors are admittedly some unfavorable ones, amongst which are (*a*) heavy capital cost, (*b*) high fuel consumption at low altitudes, and (*c*) need for long runways for takeoff at high all-up weights.

6. While the cost of these aircraft is high, the capital cost per unit of transportation produced will actually be lower than in the case of Super-Constellation or DC–7 aircraft. In annual ton-miles of capacity, one of these jet aircraft will

be equivalent to approximately 3.75 Super-Constellations, whereas its capital cost is only 2.5 times that of the Super-Constellation.

7. Although fuel consumption per mile is undoubtedly high at low altitudes, jet aircraft spend very little time at such altitudes while the combination of high cruising speed and low turbine fuel prices results in fuel cost per seat-mile or ton-mile being lower than that of piston-engined, propeller-driven airplanes. It is true that potentially the propeller-driven turbine engine (Turbo-prop) aircraft have a fuel consumption considerably below that of the pure jets under almost all comparable flight conditions, but no long-range turbo propeller aircraft, competitive with the coming big jets, is available.

8. The need for long runways for takeoffs at high all-up weight, particularly in the Tropics where conditions of high temperature and humidity prevail, places some financial burden on Government, but this is a problem which every country must eventually face. In the case of India, the additional expenditure will be heavy only at Bombay, where a good deal of cutting, filling, and culvert construction will be required. The only other cities at which relatively small expenditure will be required are Delhi and Calcutta. The Director-General of Civil Aviation and his experts have been informed of the requirements, and estimates of cost are under preparation. It is respectfully submitted that with the whole world entering the Jet Age in civil aviation, India cannot possibly remain out of it on the ground of the extra expenditure of 20 or 30 million rupees on aerodrome.

9. With the general background, the main features of the project may now be specifically discussed. On the main principle of jet operation, there is today no choice before Air-India International. The matter was generally discussed at the two last meetings of the Board and it was agreed in principle that the Corporation must enter the field of jet operations if it is to remain in business at all. The possible alternative of giving up first- and tourist-class traffic on the Corporation's main routes and concentrating exclusively on coach or third-class traffic is not considered either a practical proposition or a financially prudent one, as coach operations are likely to be extremely marginal. Assuming therefore, that Government accept the view recommended by the Corporation that jet aircraft must be ordered, the main points to be decided are (*a*) the number of aircraft to be ordered, (*b*) the type to be purchased, (*c*) the type of engines to be fitted, (*d*) deliveries, and (*e*) financial arrangements.

10. *Number of aircraft:* The minimum number of aircraft in a fleet which it is practical to operate on long routes is three, four being a more satisfactory figure. In view of the heavy cost of these aeroplanes and their high work capacity, it is proposed to limit the initial fleet to three.

11. *Type of aircraft:* The technical personnel of the Corporation, assisted by a Government of India expert, have recently undertaken a fairly detailed comparative study of both the Douglas DC–8 and the Boeing 707 on the basis of specifications and explanations furnished by representatives of the two manufacturers. Simultaneously, confidential enquiries were made with a number of other international airlines which have ordered jets. From the Corporation's own studies and the confidential reports received from other airlines, it is clear that there is, to all intents and purposes, nothing to choose between the two types on technical grounds and that either will be suitable for operation on the Cor-

poration's main present and future routes. There is also nothing to choose in price as the price of both the types is almost identical. The choice of engines in both cases is also the same. Consequently, it has become clear that the ultimate choice must depend on other than technical or financial considerations, such as the reputation and experience of the manufacturer and delivery.

12. *Comparison of Douglas and Boeing Companies:* The Douglas Aircraft Company, one of the world's three giants in aircraft production, has an unequalled reputation in the civil transport field, having since 1934 brought out a series of transports, beginning with the DC–2 and ending with the DC–7, all of which have proved an operational and commercial success. On the other hand, they have never produced a large jet aircraft of their own although they have built a large number of Boeing Jet bombers under license. Their immense technical and other resources, however, are such that no doubt is entertained as regards the technical and operational soundness of the DC–8 when built.

13. The Boeing Company is also one of the largest aircraft manufacturers in the world. While they have produced only three multi-engined transport types in their history, including the Stratocruiser, which is still in use on intercontinental routes, they have for years been one of the largest producers of heavy military aircraft—bombers, tankers, and freighters—and are today the only producers of heavy and super-heavy jet bombers. They have built themselves over a thousand B–47 jet bombers, the all-up weight of which approximates or exceeds that of the proposed transports, and are today in full production of the B–52 bomber which is a considerably bigger and heavier aircraft than the 707 jet transport. Their unique experience in the heavy jet field is, in the management's opinion, more than adequate to compensate for their small experience in the civil aircraft field.

14. *Delivery:* As the reputation and experience of both manufacturers are found equally satisfactory, the final choice would seem to boil down to considerations of delivery, and here there is a considerable difference between the two. While DC–8 aircraft will be available for delivery only in the winter of 1960–61, three Boeing 707 aircraft, equipped with Rolls Royce Conway engines, are today offered, subject to prior sale, for delivery in the first quarter of 1960. A reference to engine types will be made later in this memorandum.

15. As in the past, the Corporation is anxious to initiate operations with an entirely new type at the beginning of summer and not in the winter when flying conditions are more difficult and traffic less abundant. Delivery in early 1960 would, therefore, enable the Corporation to inaugurate jet operations a whole year sooner than originally thought possible. The advantages of the time gained would be enormous as the Corporation would have virtually no competition on its U.K. route for at least a year, during which it would be able to establish a strong position while securing highly profitable payloads from the start. The only drawback to the early delivery offered is that, being subject to prior sale and having been offered also to other airlines, like BOAC and Qantas, it necessitates an almost immediate decision on the part of the Corporation and Government if the three open positions in January, February, and March 1960, are to be secured. Because the advantages of the earlier delivery are so great, while the risks involved are so small, the management of Air-India International and the undersigned have no hesitation in recommending to the

Board and to Government the grant of the earliest possible sanction to the issue to the Boeing Company of a Letter of Intent for the purchase of three Boeing 707/420 aircraft for delivery in the months mentioned above. The reason why an immediate decision is considered to involve no risk whatsoever is that in the unlikely event that within the next two or three years the Corporation or Government were to change their mind in regard to jet operations in general or to the purchase of these aircraft in particular, there would be no difficulty in disposing of the order to some other airlines not only at no loss but, in view of the past experiences, with the probability of a considerable profit.

16. *Choice of engines:* Both the manufacturers have offered their aircraft with a choice of two engines—the American Pratt & Whitney J–75 and the British Rolls Royce Conway. Both the engines have about the same thrust rating of about 16,000 pounds. In favor of the Conway are the facts that (*a*) it is about 1,400 pounds lighter in weight, (*b*) it has a specific fuel consumption lower by 2 to 4 percent, (*c*) it is paid for in sterling, and (*d*) it is available earlier. In favor of the J–75 is the fact that the large majority of the airlines which have ordered Boeing and Douglas jet transports have preferred it to the Conway. The main reason for this is attributed to the fact that the bulk of the orders are from American operators who naturally prefer an American engine. The J–75 will, however, not be available with full thrust for delivery in time for the Corporation to begin operations during the summer of 1960. Up to now, Trans-Canada Airlines alone have ordered the Conway engine but it is considered certain that when BOAC and Qantas finalize their orders for one or the other of these jet transports, they will specify the Conway engine.

17. While the Corporation is anxious to start operations with jets in 1960 rather than 1961, it attaches great importance to the engine chosen for its aircraft being in use in sufficiently large numbers to ensure that the resale value of its aircraft is not adversely affected and also to ensure the maximum of future improvement and development. It is recommended, therefore, that the Conway engine be ordered on the condition, if Boeing and Rolls Royce can be induced to accept it, that it will, within a period of one year, have the right to switch its order to the Pratt & Whitney J–75 at the cost of delayed delivery if necessary. Such a condition would give sufficient time to the Corporation to satisfy itself thoroughly about the Conway engine and about its adoption by other airlines.

18. *Terms of payment and finance:* The Second Five-Year Plan, as approved by Government in Parliament, has made a provision of Rs. 100 million for purchase by Air-India International of new aircraft during the period of the Plan. Out of this amount, a sum of about Rs. 25 million will be utilized for meeting a part of the cost of two 1049G's on order.

19. The total cost of the Boeing jet project will be a little over Rs. 110 million, as detailed in Exhibit 2. This exceeds capital funds available for the Second Five-Year Plan period by about Rs. 35 million. About two thirds of the total expenditure will actually be incurred during the last year of the Plan period and the aircraft will be used throughout the Third Five-Year Plan period. If the Government finds it impossible to make the additional amount available prior to the Third Five-Year Plan period, it is considered that there would be no difficulty in arranging for short- to medium-term credit facilities, either in India

Exhibit 2
Estimates of capital cost for Boeing 707 and DC–8

Particulars	Boeing 707		DC–8	
	$	Rs.	$	Rs.
Cost of aircraft................	15,450,000	73,388,000	15,750,000	74,812,000
Cost of 9 spare engines @ $225,000 each........................	2,025,000	9,619,000	2,025,000	9,619,000
Radio, galley, etc..............	200,000	950,000	200,000	950,000
Cost of special equipment including engine overhaul facilities and test cell................	1,800,000	8,550,000	1,800,000	8,550,000
Cost of simulator..............	1,000,000	4,750,000	1,000,000	4,750,000
Initial provisioning for rotational units and other spares for a one period..................	2,000,000	9,500,000	2,000,000	9,500,000
	22,475,000	106,757,000	22,775,000	108,181,000
Import duty @ 2.5% (preferential rates of duty as applicable to aircraft and engines have been assumed)....................	562,000	2,669,000	569,000	2,704,000
Flight and ground training expenses....................	239,000	1,135,000	239,000	1,135,000
Delivery charges of 3 aircraft @ $26,300 or Rs. 125,000 per aircraft....................	79,000	375,000	79,000	375,000
Total capital cost........	23,355,000	110,936,000	23,662,000	112,395,000

or abroad, for the amount of Rs. 35 million to Rs. 40 million. Such a loan could, for instance, be obtained from the Export-Import Bank, the amount being repayable over a period of three to five years. Such an arrangement would in effect carry over the project into the Third Five-Year Plan period.

20. *Profitability:* As will be seen from the summarized data and estimates covering the projects appended to this memorandum (see Exhibits 2, 3, and 4), a net profit, subject only to taxes and interest on capital, of about Rs. 9.51 million per year is expected to be made from the operation of three aircraft proposed to be purchased. These estimates have been prepared on a conservative basis. For instance, the estimated cost of fuel, which forms the biggest single item of operating expenditure, has been increased by a safe margin for tolerances and increased consumption and, in addition, 20 percent has been added to the existing price per gallon of this type of fuel. Similarly, the estimated cost of stores, materials, and labor per hour of operation has been increased by about 20 percent. On the revenue side, estimates have been based on an average passenger load of 15 first class and 49 tourists, as against 28 first class and 90 tourist seats available, equivalent to a passenger load factor of 55 percent. With the estimates for mail and cargo calculated on the basis of what we actually expect to carry in the light of our existing experience, the overall load factor has been estimated at only 49 percent. Considering the very large carrying capacity and revenue earning potentiality of these big jets during peak seasons, the

Exhibit 3
Estimates of operating cost of the Boeing 707

A. Operational summary

1. Frequencies: 6 times weekly Bombay/London/Bombay and 2 times weekly London/New York/London *during season* (once weekly during off-season)
2. Hours: 8,135
3. Miles: 3,687,000
4. Cargo ton-miles: 61,400,000

B. Summary of operating cost

	Total cost Rs.	Cost per hour Rs.	Cost per mile Rs.
1. Crew	1,857,000	228.27	0.504
2. Fuel and oil	19,386,000	2,383.04	5.258
3. Engineering labor for maintenance and overhaul of aircraft and engines	4,653,000	572.00	1.262
4. Materials and spares for maintenance of aircraft and engines	10,331,000	1,270.00	2.802
5. Landing fees	1,592,000	195.70	0.432
6. Depreciation and obsolescence	9,990,000	1,228.03	2.710
7. Insurance of aircraft	3,869,000	475.60	1.049
8. Route diversions, practice, and test flights	1,050,000	129.07	0.285
9. Total direct operating cost	52,728,000	6,481.71	14.302
10. Indirect cost at 100% of the direct operating cost excluding fuel and oil item 2. (This percentage is generally applied in preparing cost estimates. In case of 1049 operations the indirect cost ratio is 82.5%)	33,342,000	4,098.59	9.043
11. Total operating cost	86,070,000	10,580.30	23.345
Revenue (see Exhibit 4)	95,580,000	11,749.23	25.924
Estimated profit	9,510,000	1,168.93	2.579
Comparative unit cost for Super-Constellation 1049s		3,775	14.953

management believes that the estimated financial results will be improved upon in practice.

21. The annual turnover of the jet fleet of three Boeings, shown in the estimates at Rs. 95 million, is higher than the total turnover of the Corporation in the current year, estimated at Rs. 80 million with a fleet of five Super-Constellations and three Constellations. With the addition of the 1049G to replace the Constellation lost in the China Sea, and the possible retention of one of the two 1049Cs, for the replacement of which two 1049Gs have been ordered, the estimated revenues for 1957–58 will probably be about Rs. 100 to 105 million. Thus the addition of the three jets in 1960 will require doubling the Corporation's turnover. While this may at first appear optimistic, no serious difficulty is expected in reaching such a target for the following reasons:

   a. Unless there is a significant change in the existing traffic trends, which

Exhibit 4
Estimates of revenue for operation of jet aircraft Boeing 707 or DC–8

		Millions of Rs.	*Millions of Rs.*
Passenger revenue*			
1. Bombay/London			
15 Std. passengers × Rs. 4,080 × 312 flights.....		19.09	
49 Tourist passengers × Rs. 2,834 × 312 flights...	43.33		
Less off-season fare differential on tourist revenue for 5 months, est. Rs.			
18,050,000 @ 15%........................	2.71	40.62	
2. London/New York			
15 Std. passengers × Rs. 3,564 × 78 flights.......	4.17		
49 Tourist passengers × Rs. 2,348 × 78 flights....	8.97		
	13.14		
Less off-season differential on total revenue for 5 months or a pro rata revenue of			
Rs. 550,000 @ 7.5%.....................	0.41		12.73
Mails			
1. Bombay/London 3,000 lbs. × Rs. 12.5 ×			
312 flights..................................		11.70	
2. London/New York 1,000 lbs. × Rs. 7.5 ×			
78 flights...................................			0.59
Cargo			
1. Bombay/London 8,000 lbs. × Rs. 4.10 ×			
312 flights..................................		10.23	
2. London/New York 3,200 × Rs. 2.46 ×			
78 flights...................................			0.61
Total Bombay/London revenue.........		81.65	
Total London/New York revenue.......			13.93
Total revenue......................		81.65	+ 13.93
		= 95.58	

* Passenger fares: single fares less 15% to cover round-trip rebate, concessional fares, etc. Double the amount is taken for a round-trip fare.

have lasted for many years, the normal growth of traffic may be expected to account for an increase of 50 percent to 60 percent in the next four years.

b. The rapid development of tourist passengers and the introduction of a third-class or "coach" fare on main routes in the next year or two are expected to create an additional demand. By the time the big jets come into operation it is anticipated that the pattern of international air transport will be that first-class and tourist services on main trunk routes will be operated with jets, while "coach" traffic and traffic on secondary routes will be operated with turbo-propeller and piston-engined aircraft.

c. The Corporation intends, before 1960, to open some new routes, including the Atlantic.

If, however, the Corporation's expectations were not to materialize to the full extent and the Corporation finds that it could not economically use the whole of its piston-engined fleet with the addition of the jets, there should be no difficulty in the disposal, at prices well above their then value in the Corporation's books, of some of its Constellations or Super-Constellations.

22. In conclusion, the Government is requested kindly to grant urgent approval to the following proposals:

a. General approval to the project for the purchase of three 707/420s equipped with Rolls Royce Conway engines or three Boeing 707/320s equipped with Pratt & Whitney J–75, at a total estimated cost (including spare engines, initial spares, customer-finished equipment, flight simulator, import duty, delivery, and training expenses and contingencies) not exceeding Rs. 115 million is requested.

b. Authority is requested to issue a Letter of Intent to the Boeing Company for the purchase of the above aircraft at a cost ex-factory, excluding customer-finished and radio equipment, of $15,450,000, payable as follows:[1]

5% within 10 days of issuing the Letter of Intent...... $	772,500
28% in 12 quarterly installments terminating six months	
prior to delivery.................................	4,326,000
67% on delivery....................................	10,351,500
100%..	15,450,000

The above figures are based on aircraft equipped with Pratt & Whitney J–75 engines and are subject to a slight downward revision, and substitution of sterling for dollars, in respect of the engines if Rolls Royce Conway engines are purchased.

c. Sanction is requested of an advance by the Government during the current financial year of a sum of Rs. 8,806,000 made up as follows:

5% down payment................... $	772,500	Rs. 3,669,000
Three quarterly payments............	1,081,500	Rs. 5,137,000
Total requirement for 1956–57........	$1,854,000	Rs. 8,806,000

1. What criteria were used by Air-India in evaluating the purchase of jets? Were these criteria quantitative or qualitative in character? Should a more exact quantitative approach have been applied?
2. In evaluating the jets from the financial point of view, what measure did Air-India use: payback period, discounted rate of return, present value, or some other alternative? Was this the appropriate measure?
3. What attention was given to the cost of capital in the decision? Should more or less attention have been given to this factor?
4. What revisions in the capital budgeting procedures of Air-India might be appropriate?
5. At the time of this case, foreign exchange was in extremely short supply in India. In fact, one could call the situation a foreign exchange crisis. How is your analysis influenced by this fact?
6. Should Air-India have purchased the Boeing 707s as outlined in the proposal of June 9, 1956?

---

[1] $1.00 = Rs. 4.76 at the time of this case. It is simpler to use the rate $1.00 = Rs. 5.00; the resulting error is not large.

7. How would you evaluate Air-India procedures in dealing with large equipment purchases?

AMERICAN TELEPHONE AND
TELEGRAPH COMPANY*

The Federal Communications Commission has jurisdiction over interstate telephone services and rates. In this area it has been able to follow, for many years, a policy of regulation based on continuous surveillance. The commission has maintained continuing studies of extensive financial and operating data which it requires the Bell System companies to submit in monthly, annual, and special reports. Through its field offices located in New York City, St. Louis, and San Francisco, the commission's staff conducts on-the-spot investigations of the companies' books and associated records. The commission also keeps itself informed of the companies' plans for new constructions and financing, as well as of the commission staff and the Bell System views concerning the level of earnings required, by means of periodic informal meetings.

Following this process the commission has taken action to secure overall rate reductions where it thought such reductions warranted. Since 1934, numerous rate reductions have been made and one general rate increase has been allowed. Based on 1962 volumes of traffic, the net effect of the major rate changes during this period have resulted in savings to the public of over $1 billion annually.

The commission has not been committed, however, exclusively to informal procedures. In several instances where agreement could not be reached informally, the commission instituted formal rate reduction proceedings through show-cause orders. In each instance, this action led to a satisfactory resolution of the matter without the need to proceed with the hearings. The commission also has initiated formal hearings dealing with specific rates and services. At one time recently, there were 31 formal cases involving the Bell System before the commission.

The commission held a series of informal conferences between September 1962 and January 1963, concerning the level of earnings required from the interstate telephone operations of the Bell System. In addition to explaining its plans for new construction and financing, the company presented testimony supporting its view that an 8 percent return was both within the range of reasonableness and required to encourage the greatest development of its communications services at the lowest cost to the users over the long term. Conversely, an expert retained by the commission staff testified that a rate of return of 6.1 percent would be adequate.

---

* This case is based primarily on official FCC proceedings on September 19 and 20, and December 13, 1962, and January 4, 1963.

The cost of capital: Professor Friend's testimony

One of the company's expert witnesses, Professor Irwin Friend of the Wharton School of Finance and Commerce, testified that the cost of capital to the AT&T was more than 7.5 percent. Such a figure would cover the 3.9 percent of "embedded" debt cost and a 9.2 percent cost of equity, assuming a capital structure of 35 percent debt and 65 percent equity.

Professor Friend concentrated most of his analysis on the cost of equity. He rejected both past earnings-price ratios and past dividends-price ratios as measures of the cost of capital. These measures, he said, would apply only if investors were expecting no change in earnings, dividends, or market prices. The fact is that investors buy common stocks in the expectation of growth in earnings and dividends, so that a provision for growth must be included in the cost of capital.

Professor Friend presented a formula for the computation of the cost of equity capital. The formula is

$$i_e = g + \frac{E}{P}(1 + g)d$$

in which i_e is the cost of equity capital, g is the expected growth in earnings per share, E/P is the earnings-price ratio, and d is the expected dividend payout ratio. One assumption Dr. Friend made with respect to AT&T stock is that the investor expects the E/P ratio will be the same at the termination of his investment as at the beginning. Therefore he found that the cost of equity for AT&T is the sum of the expected growth rate in earnings plus the dividend-price ratio adjusted for growth.

Professor Friend stated as a fundamental that the price-earnings ratio used in the formula must be consistent with the growth rate. Exhibit 1 shows a relationship between growth rates and price-earnings ratios for a group of income stocks, growth stocks, and utility stocks. This demonstrates that a low growth rate is accompanied by a low price-earnings multiple (a high earnings-price ratio). It would be "improper to combine a high growth rate with a low price-earnings multiple or on the other hand a high price-earnings ratio with a low rate of growth."

Exhibit 2 provides some evidence on AT&T growth rates and price-earnings multiples. The period from 1946 to 1950 was atypical, being a period of depressed earnings and low interest rates. The price in 1947 seemingly was held up by the expectation of increased earnings; when the increased earnings did not materialize the price-earnings multiple declined.

The price-earnings multiple for the period 1950–58 averaged about 13.5 times. Earnings per share in this period increased about 4 percent per annum. In the period 1958–62 the growth rate in earnings per share was 5.5 percent, which goes far to explain the rise in the price-earnings multiple in that period. Professor Friend concluded from this analysis

Exhibit 1
Relationship between growth and price-earnings multiples, Moody's indexes°

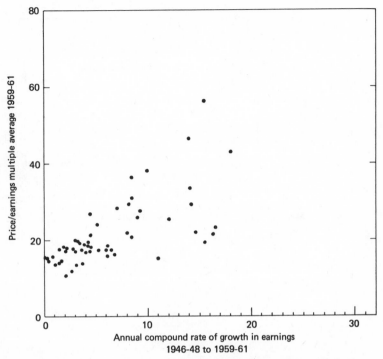

Price/earnings multiple average 1959-61

Annual compound rate of growth in earnings
1946-48 to 1959-61

* Moody's "20 Income Stocks, 20 Growth Stocks and 24 Utility Stocks."

that a 1962 investor would expect an average price-earnings multiple of 18 times and a growth rate of 5 percent for the foreseeable future. Even higher expected growth rates, he believed, might be justified on the basis of the postwar evidence.

Exhibit 3 shows Professor Friend's computation of the cost of equity capital. He assumed a 65 percent payout even though the recent AT&T payout had been somewhat below that figure. In the bottom half of the exhibit, he made an adjustment for the "underpricing" of the stock— that is, for the fact that the proceeds to the company on a sale of new stock would be 10 percent below the market price. The result was an estimated cost of equity capital of 9.2 percent.

Professor Friend used a cost of debt capital of 3.9 percent in his computation of the overall cost of capital. This estimate was low because it was well below the current costs of *new* debt. These are higher than the "embedded" costs which are weighted heavily by the low interest rates in the 1940s and early 1950s. A weighted average of the 9.2 percent cost of equity and the 3.9 percent cost of debt resulted in an overall cost of 7.4 percent. An adjustment for the low cost of debt and for the use of

Exhibit 2
AT&T stock: Earnings per share and price-earnings multiples

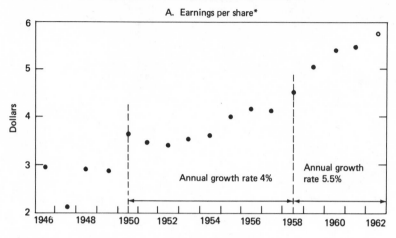

A. Earnings per share*

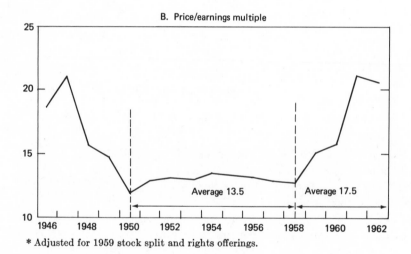

B. Price/earnings multiple

* Adjusted for 1959 stock split and rights offerings.

book-value weights instead of market-value weights would raise the estimate to over 7.5 percent.

Professor Friend denied that an increase in debt financing would lower the cost of capital. While it is true that debt carries a lower cost than equity, any attempt to increase the debt-equity ratio would bring an increase in investor risk, and thus in both the interest rate and cost of equity. The tax-exempt status of interest on debt would not result in a significant saving in cost.

Exhibit 3
Cost of AT&T common equity

Investors' capitalization rate
  Reasonable expectations for AT&T stock:
    Annual growth in earnings per share....... 5%
    Price-earnings multiple................... 18
    Dividend payout........................ 65%

$$\text{Capitalization rate} = 5\% + \frac{1.05 \times 65\%}{18} \text{ or } 8.8\%$$

Cost to company
  Investors' capitalization rate adjusted for difference
  between market price and proceeds to company on
  sale of new shares.
  Reasonable expectations for AT&T stock:
    Proceeds on new shares 10% below market price

$$\text{Cost} = 5\% + \frac{1.05 \times 65\%}{18 \times 90\%} \text{ or } 9.2\%$$

The cost of capital: Mr. Kosh's testimony

One of the FCC's consultants, Mr. Kosh, differed from Professor Friend in two major respects. First, he made use of recent earnings-price ratios with only a minor provision for growth. Second, he used a debt ratio of 50 percent on the grounds that the commission should use a theoretical "optimum" capital structure in its computations even though the actual ratio was 35 percent. In his opinion a 50 percent debt ratio was safe for the telephone company even under conditions of depression. The failure to increase the debt to that level meant a failure to take full advantage of the "leverage" principle. The result of his computations was a 6.1 percent overall cost of capital instead of over 7.5 percent which Dr. Friend found.

The comparable earnings test

Another AT&T argument for an 8 percent of return presented by Mr. J. J. Scanlon, a vice president of AT&T, was based on a comparison of equity earnings with a broad cross section of both regulated and unregulated companies. Exhibit 4 shows how these companies were selected.

They were the firms whose growth in both dividends and the book equity per share was greater than the increase in the Consumer Price Index, but did not exceed the growth in real GNP. The claim was that the long-term risk for AT&T is at least as great as the risk in these companies and that differences in short-term risks are equated by their differing capital structures. On this basis comparable rates of return on

Exhibit 4
Average increase, 1946–1960, in 225 manufacturing companies and 96
electrics (classified by growth in book equity and dividends per share)

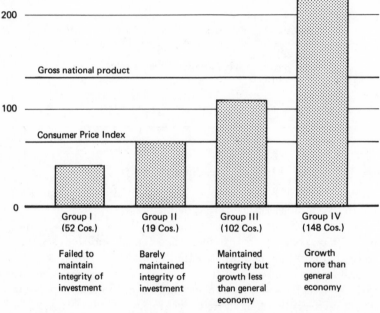

equity would be justified. Exhibits 4 and 5 show that the selected firms
earned an average of 10.4 to 12.5 percent on equity, leading to the conclusion that the Bell System requires equity earnings of at least 10.5
to 11 percent.

Professor James C. Bonbright of Columbia University, another consultant retained by the FCC, was critical of the comparable earnings test.
He admitted that the Bell System did face competition for many of its
services, but he noted that consumers had no choice but to use the Bell
System if they were to make telephone calls. He also argued that industrial companies are subject to greater risks and therefore did not
provide a sound basis for comparison.

Other considerations

The hearings on AT&T's earnings also covered several other issues.
Professor Bonbright was concerned with the ratio of market value to book

Exhibit 5
Average earnings on common equity, 1946–1960 (groups of
companies per Exhibit 4)

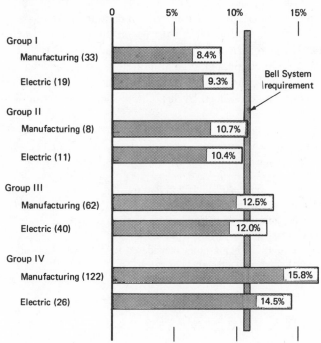

value of the AT&T stock. He would concede a rate of return which in
prosperity would allow the company a market value "well in excess of
book value." But when the market value reached a price double that
of book value, as was the case in 1962, he became skeptical.

Witnesses at the hearings also went into the effects of rate regulation
on the national economy. Dr. Paul W. McCracken of the University of
Michigan, who was formerly on the President's Council of Economic
Advisors, expressed fear that a reduction in the rate of return, with a
consequent reduction in the market value of AT&T stock, would have an
unsettling effect on the national economy. He, as well as Dr. Joseph
Kieper of New York University, claimed that an adequate return would
stimulate the AT&T construction and equipment program which would
help bolster the economy. The profitable companies, they claimed, were
the ones making the greatest contribution to economic growth. This
position would mean that the FCC should be concerned with much more
than the cost of capital. Professor Bonbright, however, maintained that
the FCC should confine itself mainly to the task of finding a rate of
return which would attract capital.

The record on the FCC proceedings was closed out on January 4, 1963.

It resulted in an announcement that interstate station-to-station toll rates would be reduced to a maximum of $1 coast to coast after 9:00 P.M. This reduction, offset in part by an increase in person-to-person rates which had gotten out of line with increasing labor costs, resulted in a net $30 million annual saving to the public and a cutback of about 0.3 percent in the return the company was earning. The FCC believed, however, that technological change and an increased market for telephone service would permit the company to maintain a level of earnings within the 7–8 percent range realized by it since the last rate reduction in 1959.

1. In your opinion what was the cost of capital to AT&T in 1962–63? Discuss.
2. What is the significance of Exhibit 1? What is its relevance in determining the cost of capital?
3. What is the relevance of Exhibit 2 in determining the cost of capital?
4. Develop the logic behind the computations in Exhibit 3.
5. Evaluate the comparable earnings test. In that connection evaluate Exhibits 4 and 5 as to pertinence in rate regulation.
6. Make a list of the other factors considered in this rate case and give your opinion on their significance and relevance.
7. Should the reduction of "after 9" long-distance rates have been instituted in 1963?

Part seven

Applications in public and nonprofit agencies

Chapter 15

Cost-effectiveness and benefit-cost analysis

Government has a major role in modern economic systems. Many people in business believe that the government "interferes" in the economy more than it should, but the interests and activities of business firms and public agencies are becoming ever more closely intertwined. The government is the regulator and rule maker for the conduct of business and, at the same time, a major customer for business and industrial outputs. Businesses supply most of the nonlabor inputs used in public sector production, but are in turn major demanders of public services. Clearly, the profit and nonprofit sectors of the economy are important to each other from the points of view of both supply and demand.

The importance of government agencies and nonprofit enterprises relative to the private sector has been growing rapidly. Nearly one fifth of the current labor force is employed in the public sector, and not-for-profit enterprises also have substantial numbers of workers. Many students will be employed in public and nonprofit organizations during part or all of their careers. Thus, there is need for attention to applications of managerial economics in the public sector.

The chapter begins by showing that the objectives of government agencies and nonprofit organizations are necessarily broader than those of profit-oriented firms. The chapter then follows the topics sequence of

639

preceding chapters, so as to proceed from a discussion of demand to analyses of production and costs in the public sector. Pricing decisions are considered at some length. Attention then turns to longer-run decisions involving investment. A discussion of the many (possibly conflicting) goals of public activities in a democratic society brings the chapter, and the book, to a close.

ROLE OF THE PUBLIC SECTOR
IN THE ECONOMY[1]

Externalities, public goods, and options

In general, a market economy uses resources efficiently. However intervention may be needed to oppose over- or under-allocations of resources to particular activities because of *externalities*.[2] Externalities are costs imposed upon, or benefits provided to, third parties as the result of production and consumption decisions. Examples of externalities are all around us. When a person decides to drive a poorly tuned auto using leaded fuel, he or she pollutes the air, possibly leading to health problems for others. Because the health costs of others are not borne by the driver, the effects may not be considered in the decision of whether or not to have the engine tuned. Similarly, when one person is immunized for polio, the probability that other nonimmunized persons will contract the disease is reduced. Since the person does not obtain the value of this benefit to others, it may not be a factor in deciding whether or not to get the vaccination.

The first of the above examples is a negative consumer externality (the decision maker imposes costs upon others), while the second example is a positive consumer externality (benefits are conferred upon others). Producers also create externalities. A firm that pollutes a river causes downstream users to have additional costs of cleaning the water before using. On the other hand, a firm that carries out research often produces benefits worth much more than the returns actually realized.

From the social welfare point of view, activities that yield external costs are overproduced and overconsumed because the producers and consumers take into account only the costs that they must bear. On the

---

[1] This section is a brief summary of certain aspects of the field of "public finance." For comprehensive treatments, see Richard A. Musgrave and Peggy B. Musgrave, *Public Finance in Theory and Practice,* 2d ed. (New York: McGraw-Hill, 1976); or John F. Due and Ann F. Friedlander, *Government Finance—Economics of the Public Sector* 6th ed. (Homewood, Ill.: Richard D. Irwin, Inc., 1977).

[2] Public intervention may also be needed to prevent inefficiencies resulting from noncompetitive behavior of firms. Regulation of monopoly is discussed in Chapter 12. Topics related to prevention and dissolution of monopoly (antitrust activity) are beyond the scope of this book.

other hand, activities that have external benefits are underproduced and underconsumed because the decision makers give no weight to the third-party gains from the activities. To attain a socially optimal level of an activity that has externalities, the third-party benefits or costs must somehow be reflected in the outcome for the decision maker. In other words, the government must deal with the externalities so that a socially desirable resource allocation is achieved. Taxes and subsidies are often used to "internalize" the external costs or benefits. For example, an additional tax on leaded gasoline may be an incentive for drivers to use unleaded fuel and thus to cut down on pollution. Or a subsidy on health care (free immunization) may be an incentive for citizens to protect against polio and thus to decrease the disease hazard for others.

In some activities, externalities are so great in relation to internal benefits and costs that the activities will be undertaken only by the government. Such activities are called *public goods.* Public goods are available to everyone in a given area and no one can be excluded for non-payment. The classic example of a public good is national defense. If one person is made safer because of the Minuteman missile, that does not in the least detract from any other person's welfare. Furthermore, the Pentagon could not deprive any person of the benefits if he or she refused to buy a share. City planning, pollution control, consumer product testing, and many other services have the characteristics of public goods. The taxing power of the government is necessary in paying for public goods because users (who realize that they cannot be individually excluded from benefits) will not make voluntary contributions equal to the value of the goods.

Finally, there are some public activities that have benefits even less direct than those from pollution control or national defense. Persons who do not visit Yellowstone Park, or ride the Bay Area Rapid Transit system, or swim in the Santa Barbara Channel may place some value on the knowledge that the facilities are available for possible future use. Nonusers may be willing to pay something for such *options* that are created and preserved by public actions.

How public agencies differ from private firms

Although there are many similarities between public agencies and private firms, there are several major differences that should be noted. *First, the constituency of the public agency is much larger than that of the business firm.* A private enterprise may either confer benefits or impose costs upon the general public, but its responsibilities to employees, customers, and stockholders must be given priority if the firm is to continue producing and investing. Interests of stockholders and the general public may diverge, as in the case of pollution-creating processes, but the pressure of competition usually does not allow a business firm to assume more social responsibility than the law requires. On the other hand, in the case of a public agency, the well-being of those indirectly helped or harmed by its activities may be as important as that of the direct users of the agency's services. For example, the highway department is as responsible to those whose lives are disrupted by highway construction as it is to potential travelers of the route. Decision making and investment analysis for government agencies should take into account and fully weigh the interests of all individuals and groups that will be affected.

A second peculiarity of public management is that many products and services are not sold directly for a price, and many others are priced at less than average cost. Those principles of pricing that are applicable to public agencies must be tailored somewhat to the public viewpoint. Furthermore, the guides to production and investment decisions that businesspersons obtain from market prices are not fully available to public managers.

Despite the above distinctions between private and public enterprise, both kinds of organizations can use profit as a test of efficiency in resource allocation. In public decisions, it is necessary to redefine the concept of profit, and it is perhaps useful to rename it "net social benefit." In order to maximize public profit, or net social benefit, a public service is expanded until decreasing marginal benefits become equal to marginal costs. The concept of social benefit is quite similar to that of private revenue—it is the value of agency output to the various beneficiaries. Owing to the public viewpoint, the concept of social cost embraces the value of all opportunities foregone by the constituent population as a result of the agency's activities.

Finally, we note that public decisions often involve equity considerations. That is, at times public decisions are made partially on the basis of *who* derives the benefits and *who* bears the costs, in addition to the determination of whether net social benefit is increased. Since equity appraisals involve subjective judgments, little can be said about them in the context of optimizing. Nevertheless, equity criteria will be examined after completing the discussions of benefit and cost estimation, pricing, and benefit-cost analysis.

ESTIMATING DEMANDS AND EVALUATING BENEFITS

Public sector activities in the modern economy are nearly as diverse as those of the private sector. Governments provide cradle-to-grave services ranging from prenatal medical advice to burial in public cemeteries, and they make and sell goods and services ranging from water to works of art. Estimating the demands for some public activities is very difficult. However, many functions performed by governments are similar to activities in the private sector, and the demands for these functions are analyzed by similar methods.

Demands for public services

The value of services provided by a public agency derives ultimately from citizen demands, which some agencies can determine in essentially the same ways used by private sellers. For example, the postal service, water departments, and agencies renting campsites could use the methods described in Chapters 3–5. These agencies provide services for fees assessed on a partial or full-cost, pay-as-you-go basis.

However, many government agencies produce nonpriced outputs. Demand for nonpriced outputs is a meaningful concept, but special methods are required in demand estimation. Basically, proxy variables must be substituted for prices of the service and its substitutes. Consider the example of outdoor recreation. A "free" recreation or park area actually has a "price" per visit in the form of extra costs (travel time, meals and lodging, vehicle operation, and so on) that must be borne by the user. The price would vary with the distance traveled by each prospective visitor, so that the rate of visits as a proportion of total population would tend to vary with distance from the park. Analysts have used this relationship to derive estimates of demand for outdoor recreation. The demand curves are constructed by relating visit rates of the population in each (distance) zone to estimated differences in cost.[3] The accuracy of such demand estimates depends upon proper estimation of all costs which would not have been incurred except for the visit to the park. In addition, just as prices of other goods and levels of income are important determinants of demands for privately produced goods, factors such as the availability of other parks and income variations within the region should be taken into account.

Marginal value versus total benefit estimation

A public agency manager may have great difficulty in estimating the entire demand function for one of the agency's services, especially if there are no charges for them or there are no good proxy variables that can be substituted for prices. However, it may still be practical to estimate the maximum amount users would be willing to pay for *additional* service. Note that this approach is framed in marginal terms.

---

[3] See Jack L. Knetsch and Robert K. Davis, "Comparison of Methods for Recreation Evaluation," in *Water Research,* ed. A. V. Kneese and Stephen C. Smith (Baltimore: Johns Hopkins Press, 1960).

For decisions involving small changes in the level of an *ongoing* activity, *marginal* valuations may be sufficient. The city water department would have to carry out a sophisticated analysis if the value of its total output were needed. On the other hand, the marginal value of additional water may be easy to estimate for most users, and this is the relevant value in decisions about additions to capacity of the system.

In the case of proposed new programs, evaluations of total benefits are needed. Such analyses may be quite difficult, but they are necessary if rational decisions are to be made.[4] Total benefit estimation is described below.

Enumerating benefits

The first step in evaluating a particular government program is to enumerate specific ways in which various groups are benefited, whether these are direct uses, externalities, options, or public goods. In this undertaking, the pitfalls to avoid are (1) counting benefits to some individuals or groups that are offset by costs imposed upon others, and (2) counting the same benefits twice.

Suppose the objective is to list the benefits of a new highway. The primary benefit is time and expenses saved by those who travel the new road, net of possible increases in costs to others who use only feeder roads which have become more congested. External benefits may accrue to travelers using parallel routes that have become less congested because of the diverting of traffic. These motorists may also place some value on the option of an alternate route.

There is no net benefit from those effects that simply alter resource or goods prices without changing physical production or consumption possibilities. For example, a new highway will improve the profitability of service stations, restaurants, motels, and the like along its route; however, much of this improvement is offset by reduced incomes to other facilities affected by traffic reductions along previously existing roads. A new highway will also increase values of adjacent land suited for facilities rendering services to travelers, but these increases are simply capitalizations (present values) of the potential additions to future income production on the sites. Listing both the current increases in land values and the current increases in incomes would be double counting.

It is sometimes difficult to make a clear distinction between benefits and costs. To do so, the agency must specify a *target population* for

---

[4] For an extensive discussion of benefit-cost analysis, see E. J. Mishan, *Cost—Benefit Analysis* (New York: Praeger Publishers, 1976). The topic is also discussed in Harley H. Hinrichs and Grahame M. Taylor, *Program Budgeting and Benefit-Cost Analysis* (Pacific Palisades, Calif.: Goodyear Publishing Co., 1969).

which the program is intended. Benefits often fall to persons outside the target group—construction contractors, for example—at the expense of those within it—the region's taxpayers. A similar point of view applies to increased employment, at possibly higher pay, of local construction workers. Their gains are also at the expense of the area's taxpayers. In both examples, the payoff from the program is the difference between the value of the services and the cost of producing them.

Ideal evaluation of benefits

Simple enumeration of benefit categories and their incidence is only a beginning. *Choice of the best level for a program and choice among competing programs require measurement of benefits, usually in terms of money.* The ideal measurement would be monetary value of total utility to all beneficiaries of a program. This value may be illustrated conceptually by means of Figure 15–1. Curve D represents demand of all beneficiaries for the output of a program—it indicates at every level of the program the marginal value of the program to beneficiaries. Now,

Figure 15–1
Consumers' surplus in comparison of programs

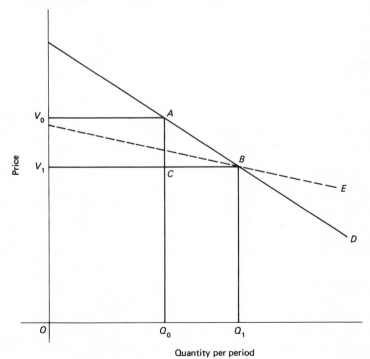

Quantity per period

suppose it is proposed to expand the program in a large "jump" from Q_0 to Q_1. The value of marginal units will fall from V_0 to V_1. Total monetary value of the expansion of services to the users is Q_0ABQ_1. However, if output is priced at V_1, revenue is less than the increase in monetary value of benefits provided (by the amount ABC). Area ABC is an increment in the total, called "consumers' surplus." Consumers surplus is the summation of differences of marginal valuations from price. Note that the price, OV_1, which just rations the increased output, is below the consumers' *marginal* evaluations of those quantities acquired in moving from Q_0 up to the greater output at Q_1.

To illustrate the implications of the consumer's surplus approach to benefit evaluation, suppose an analyst attempts to put a value on the use of a congested facility by measuring the amount (and value) of time that users will voluntarily sacrifice by waiting in line. Expansion of the facility by some sizable amount would reduce the waiting time "price" paid by all users. However, to value all output of the facility at the new lower "price" would be ignoring the fact that some users of the service would be willing to wait longer (pay a higher price) than they actually do.

Direct estimation techniques

Estimation of consumers' surplus may be impractical, since it requires estimation of the entire demand curve. Consumer expenditure (value of the *last* unit times all units) is much easier to estimate and will not be a serious underestimate of monetary value of benefits if demand is highly elastic or if the project adds only marginally to the amount of service available. Estimation of "expenditure" is easiest when the output of the project is an intermediate good used in production. For example, if one of the outputs of a dam is irrigation water that will be used to increase output of agricultural land, the value of the increased agricultural output is a good estimate of the value of the irrigation portion of the project.

Often the output of a public program is a capital good expected to yield a stream of benefits over a period of years. Such is the case with major construction projects, such as dams, roads, and rapid-transit rail systems. Benefits from such programs must be estimated over the expected lives of the capital goods created. In some programs, such as vocational training and rehabilitation of disabled workers, benefits are expected to extend over time spans beyond the program's life. The final product of such programs is the trainees' increased productivity (sold by the workers rather than by the government). The *discounted,* or present, value of the expected increase in the workers' future productivities is the appropriate measure of the value of such programs.

Indirect Estimation Techniques

External benefits, public goods, and unpriced direct benefits must be evaluated through indirect estimation of consumer demands. The three most common techniques of indirect estimation are: (1) to observe changes in prices of land (or other complementary goods) affected by the project; (2) to obtain prices paid for close private substitutes for the benefit in question; and (3) to estimate reductions in cost that are made possible by the project.

The demand for land is affected by external costs and benefits. For example, buyers may be willing to pay a premium to live near a neighborhood park. On the other hand, the value of land directly under the final approach to an airport is likely to be depressed. One indirect measure of the benefits or costs of a public program is the difference in land values between the affected properties and otherwise similar land not affected by the program.[5]

Prices of close private substitutes are sometimes available when a public project duplicates private facilities already operating in other locations. An example is electricity generated at a publicly owned dam. The value of the electricity can be estimated by using prices of privately produced power.

Reduced costs to direct beneficiaries or to society as a whole may be a large part, even all, of a program's output. Thus, a program to reduce school dropouts may do more than increase lifetime incomes of students; society also benefits from decreased costs of crime and welfare.[6] The most important benefit of a rapid-transit system is the reduced cost of commuting time.[7]

Each of these indirect estimation techniques can be illustrated by reference to Rothenberg's study of urban renewal projects.[8] The principal efficiency objective of urban renewal is to improve productivity of land in and around the renewal site. Assembly of a number of separately

---

[5] For discussions of the use of property values in indirect measurement of benefits of public programs, see Roy W. Bahl, Stephan P. Coclen, and Jeremy J. Warford, Land Value Increments as a Measure of the Net Benefits of Urban Water Supply Projects in Developing Countries: Theory and Measurement," *Government Spending and Land Values,* ed. C. Lowell Harriss (Madison: University of Wisconsin Press, 1973); or A. Myrick Freeman, "On Estimating Air Pollution Control Benefits from Land Value Studies," *The Journal of Environmental Economics and Management* 1 (1974).

[6] Burton A. Weisbrod, "Preventing High School Dropouts," in *Measuring Benefits of Government Investments,* ed. Robert Dorfman (Washington, D.C.: The Brookings Institution, 1965), pp. 117–71.

[7] For a discussion of valuation of travel time, see James R. Nelson, "The Value of Travel Time," in *Problems in Public Expenditure Analysis,* ed. Samuel B. Chase, Jr. (Washington, D.C.: The Brookings Institution, 1968), pp. 78–126.

[8] Jerome Rothenberg, *Economic Evaluation of Urban Renewal* (Washington, D.C.: The Brookings Institution, 1967).

owned parcels into one large tract allows a developer, public or private, to build better housing that is not exposed to the value-depressing effect of a surrounding slum district. Increased rentals (net of increased costs) are capitalized in higher land values for those sites that are sold to private interests for highest bids. Thus, increases in land values provide a dollar measure of part of the direct benefits of an urban renewal project.

A typical urban renewal project will also increase the attractiveness of real estate in adjoining neighborhoods. Hence, increases in market values of land surrounding the project provide partial measures of external benefits of the project. Another type of external benefit which may result is reduction in fire hazard to nearby neighborhoods. This benefit can be measured in the form of lower costs of fire protection services and lower insurance premiums—an example of a benefit measured as a reduction in associated costs.

Finally, there may be a problem of estimating the value of public housing built as part of the project, where this property is not sold at competitive market prices. If such housing does not constitute a large portion of the total supply in the community, its value may be estimated on the basis of values of nearby private housing with similar characteristics.

The above illustration does not give a complete accounting of benefits from urban renewal. Actual estimates of changes in values and costs due to a program and the identification of appropriate private substitutes for unpriced publicly provided benefits may require a great deal of ingenuity.

Problems in estimating benefits

Benefit estimation encounters several difficulties: (1) risk associated with project outcomes; (2) valuation of lives saved; and (3) measurement of intangibles. When project outcomes are uncertain, the best approach is to attach probabilities to the alternative outcomes, as discussed in earlier chapters in relation to the decision tree approach. The expected value of the project will then be a probability weighted average of the dollar values of net benefits of each of the possible outcomes.[9]

Transportation projects, health care projects, and other public activities may be expected to reduce the likelihood of accidental or premature death. Benefits of life saving cannot be estimated without estimates of the "value of life." One method of assigning value to life is based on ex-

---

[9] Uncertainties are prominent in John M. Vernon, "Benefits and Costs of Developing Advanced Nuclear Power Reactors," *Applied Economics* 1 (1969), pp. 1–16.

pected lifetime incomes of persons expected to live longer as a result of the project.[10]

Finally, some programs have benefits that defy monetary valuation. As examples, "increased beauty of the environment" or "increased prestige of the nation" are difficult to translate into monetary terms. In such cases, analysts often provide a list of intangible benefits to inform decision makers that these benefits do exist and should be considered.

PRODUCTION AND COSTS
IN THE PUBLIC SECTOR

Public sector production and cost can be analyzed in essentially the same ways used in the private sector.[11] However, it may be important to distinguish between the outlays for the project (dollar amounts that appear in the budget) and the project's true economic costs. Only the latter costs are relevant in benefit-cost analysis.

Project outlays

Estimates of program costs should take the form of projections of outlays for each year of the project's life on the basis of current market prices of inputs. General increases in input prices need not be considered, since they affect all alternatives alike, but changes in the relative prices of inputs should be taken into account.

True economic cost (social cost) may be substantially different from the explicit outlays. *Social cost is the opportunity cost of all resources used in the project.* Many social costs do not show up *in the budgets* of public agencies, since these agencies may use underpriced services of other agencies, use agency-owned lands and facilities without showing the corresponding costs of capital, and impose external costs upon other persons or groups.

Estimating true economic costs

As an example of the estimation of a project's relevant costs, consider an urban highway project. The immediate explicit costs are site acquisition, planning, and construction. Future explicit costs include operation and maintenance of the facilities over their estimated useful lives. If a portion of the right-of-way is already under government own-

---

[10] See Thomas C. Schelling, "The Life You Save May Be Your Own," in *Problems in Public Expenditure Analysis,* ed. Chase, pp. 127–76.

[11] For a discussion of productivity in the public sector, see John P. Ross and Jesse Burkhead, *Productivity in the Local Government Sector* (Lexington, Mass.: Lexington Books, 1974).

ership, the value of this land in its next most productive use is an opportunity cost.

The highway project may have external costs. Construction involves disruption of established travel patterns and dislocation of residents along the right-of-way. Moreover, to the extent that it encourages an increase in vehicle-miles of auto travel within the jurisdiction, there are future increases of air pollution and noise. Unless reimbursements of affected individuals is specifically required by law or by agency policy, external costs are not borne by the agency, but they are still relevant costs from the point of view of the welfare of a target population.

Project outlays that are based upon market prices of inputs may need to be adjusted for effects of unemployment, monopoly elements, government controls, price supports, or other conditions that cause market prices to diverge from marginal social costs of the resources. For example, consider the case in which some unemployed resources are expected to gain employment as a result of a project. The social cost of such resources is much less than their prices, since they would otherwise produce nothing. Note that adjustments for unemployment are appropriate only if the condition is expected to exist at the time that the resource is to be used. Project analysis usually concerns some future period, and it is probably not reasonable to assume that mass unemployment will persist year after year.

Monopoly prices and government-supported prices may overstate the opportunity cost of resources required by a project. Unfortunately, there are no reliable rules of thumb for making the necessary adjustments in such cases. Since the unadjusted market prices do represent marginal evaluation of those resources (at inefficient usage levels), they may be the best estimates available to the analyst.

An illustration of the need for careful handling of implicit cost is given by a study of graduate education in management in India.[12] From the student's point of view, the largest *private* cost of management education is the value of foregone earnings from postponement of full-time employment. Of course, his or her projected gross earnings would be reduced by indirect taxes, sales taxes, property taxes, and excise taxes to obtain the *net* private sacrifice. Under assumptions of competition in the labor market and full employment, the student's *gross* earnings represent *social* cost of the sacrifice of his or her contribution to production. On the other hand, if there is a pool of educated underemployed, as was found in Paul's study of India, there may be little social cost of the student's withdrawal from the labor force. In this case, a series of workers "move up" to better

[12] S. Paul, "An Application of Cost-Benefit Analysis to Management Education," in *Benefits, Cost and Policy Analysis* ed. W. A. Niskoven, et al. (Chicago: Aldine Publishing Company, 1973).

jobs, and most of these are about as productive as the person they replace.

PRICES, CHARGES, AND SUBSIDIES

Public agencies produce a wide variety of outputs, some of which might properly be termed *private goods*. These are goods which, in contrast to *public goods,* can be enjoyed independently and exclusively by individuals. That is, one person's use reduces the amount available to others but does not otherwise affect their well-being. Such goods can be divided and offered to individuals in varying amounts. Among such services commonly provided by governments are parking, water, recreation facilities, and limited-access highways. It is feasible for public agencies to impose direct charges for private goods.

Pricing of public services helps in the efficient rationing of scarce supplies. Demand for a private good that is provided free is likely to outrun the available supply. This is so because the good will be consumed up to the level at which marginal units are worth nothing to users, without regard to the additional cost of providing increased service. For example, on warm summer days there are never enough free public swimming pools. As a consequence, such facilities are usually rationed by *exclusion rules,* such as time limits or residence requirements, and/or by *queues.* More efficient *price rationing* of such goods can be achieved by using the rule that price should equal marginal cost.

Marginal-cost pricing

Marginal-cost pricing can be illustrated by the example of a congested highway. Variable costs of highway transportation include highway maintenance, traffic control, vehicle maintenance and operating costs, and the travel time, effort, discomfort, and safety hazard incurred by travelers. Most of these costs (per vehicle) increase as the traffic flow increases. A toll set equal to marginal cost (in place of the present system of gas taxes set at levels that cover average costs) would cause each user to compare the *value of benefits* from use of a congested highway with *all costs* of the addition to traffic, including those costs *imposed on others.* If the toll exceeds marginal benefit for a particular trip, then the trip will not be made (at least not by this route), thus reserving the highway for others who value their trips more highly. Hence, a system of tolls that vary with changes in traffic levels could potentially improve economic well-being of highway users.[13] This is the same concept of peak-load pricing that was discussed in Chapter 12.

---

[13] William Vickrey, "Pricing in Urban and Suburban Transport," *American Economic Review, Papers and Proceedings* (May 1963), pp. 452–65.

User charges do not just *ration scarce facilities;* they also *provide guides to decision about investment in additional capacity.* In the simplest case where expansions may be made in small increments and production exhibits constant returns to scale, expansion is justified whenever total revenues exceed total costs. In other words, positive net revenue is evidence that expansion will yield benefits in excess of additional costs. In the absence of user charges, there are no such direct measures of the benefits of expanded facilities.

A more general rule for expansion of a program that has direct user charges is that expansion should continue until long-run marginal cost equals demand price. An agency that wished to apply this rule would need to estimate marginal cost for a variety of program sizes and then estimate the number of users at a charge equal to marginal costs. If scale economies are present, the optimal solution would result in losses, so that the "profitability" test does not hold. Conversely, decreasing returns to scale imply that total charges would exceed costs even at optimum program size. These are the same problems of marginal cost pricing that were discussed in Chapter 12.

In some cases, it may be appropriate for an agency to deliberately charge less than marginal cost. Recall that many public services are of the type which have important external benefits to nonusers. Such nonusers might reasonably be said to have demands for (that is, place value upon) the services. A user charge that decreases the frequency of residential trash collection increases the unsightliness and health hazard that must be tolerated by those who are passing by. A charge on direct users which completely covers costs will result in an undersupply of services to the indirect users. Since indirect benefits accrue to taxpayers collectively (as public goods), subsidization of services to the fee-paying direct users by appropriations from general tax revenues can raise the total community well-being as compared to full-cost pricing.

Indirect charges

A number of public outputs have not normally carried direct charges, despite their basically private character, because of the *high cost of collecting* from users. This condition holds for most streets and highways and many recreation facilities. However, indirect methods of charging may be feasible. These may take the form of *licenses* or of *taxes on private goods that are complementary* with the public outputs. For example, hunting and fishing license fees can finance wildlife conservation programs; taxes on gasoline can pay for transportation facilities. Another example of an indirect price commonly used by local government is the basing of sewage charges on usage of water. This arrangement is reasonable to the extent that increased water consumption means greater output of sewage.

Since the tax is tied to use of the service, these "benefit levies" serve some rationing function as well as providing revenue. On the other hand, such charges do not follow the principle of marginal cost, since the user pays nothing for additional units of the associated government service. In particular, taxes on complementary goods do not ration efficiently if the public output is subject to peak-load congestion. For example, marginal costs of highway use fluctuate widely among locations and hours of the day. These differences cannot be reflected in the amount of gasoline tax, since gasoline purchase is largely independent of the time and place of highway use. Likewise, using water consumption as a basis for sewage charges does not differentiate between users. One user may be using large amounts of water to sprinkle lawns (with no resulting load on the sewer system) and another user may be washing clothes and dishes (which does impose load on the system).

Prices of "bads": Penalties

A type of government-administered "price" which has been receiving increased attention is the *penalty for damage to the environment.* Examples are proposed taxes on leaded gasoline and sulfurous fuels. These would be incentives to *reduce production of underpriced,* or unpriced, *"bads."* As another example, suppose the waste from a plant were tested periodically for concentration of a harmful chemical, and a charge equal to the value of damages were levied per unit of discharge of this effluent. A profit-maximizing firm would respond to this charge according to its cost of controlling the waste. Allen V. Kneese has shown the effect of this policy by means of Figure 15–2. Costs associated with waste disposal are minimized at Point *E* rather than at Point *D*, where the latter represents the level of waste disposal when use of the stream is free to the firm. The institution of the charge induces the firm to adopt socially optimal waste disposal methods, reducing but not eliminating pollution; note that further treatment would require resources (equipment, location changes, or processes) that outweigh in value the additional improvement.

Subsidies

In a similar way, *subsidies* may be used to encourage *increased production* of goods that are overpriced in private markets because the *suppliers cannot collect the value of externalities.* Higher education, low-income housing, and commuter railroads are among the goods which may

Figure 15–2
Industrial plant's response to effluent charges

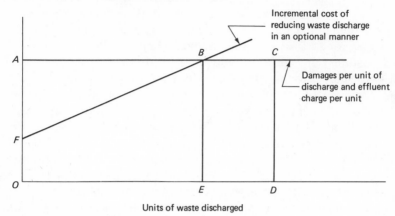

OD: Units of waste discharge if no charge levied on effluent.
OA: Damages per unit of waste discharge and effluent charge per unit.
OACD: Total damages associated with unrestricted waste discharge, i.e., no effluent charge levied.
OE: Reduction of waste discharge with effluent charge OA.
OFBE: Total cost of reducing effluent discharge to ED.
OFBCD: Total cost associated with waste disposal with ED waste discharge, i.e., residual damage costs plus cost of reducing discharge.
OABE: Total damages avoided.
ABF: Net reduction in waste disposal associated costs by reducing waste discharge by OE, i.e., OABE minus OFBE.

be produced privately and sold to direct users, but also provide significant benefits to others. One means to improve social welfare in such cases is to leave production in private hands, but to provide a public subsidy that will allow the private firm to set the price to direct users below the average cost.

Pricing and efficiency

Charges and subsidies will usually increase *efficiency of resource use* as compared to rationing by prohibitions, regulations, or other direct controls. Consider again the case of water pollution. The natural capacity of water to cleanse itself is an important resource. This resource can be overused, and it almost certainly will be if it is entirely free, but outright prohibition of its use would require some waste treatment with cost in excess of benefits. Cost of control varies widely among effluent-producing activities, and efficiency requires that any given level of water quality should be attained at the lowest possible total cost. Rules restricting the absolute quantity of effluent from each source do not take into consideration the varying costs of waste treatment. By contrast, effluent charges leave the choice of type and level of waste treatment to the polluting firm. As shown above, each firm would expand waste treatment up to the point where marginal treatment cost is just equal to the effluent charge. Any desired level of water quality can be achieved by this method depending upon the level of the effluent charge. The choices of the individual firms then minimize the total social cost of achieving any given level of water quality. Pricing in the public sector is no longer simply an academic topic. In order to receive federal construction grants, local sewer systems will be required to use rate structures that reflect the loads each of the users is imposing.[14] Although strict marginal cost pricing is not mandated, the prices must be tied to costs so as to come closer to the desired efficient allocations of resources.

Since we have been stressing the importance of the pricing mechanism in properly allocating resources, it is appropriate to review the situations under which charges are justifiable or questionable. The following list is by Professors John F. Due and Ann F. Friedlander.

Use of the pricing mechanism where possible instead of free distribution with financing by taxation is regarded as most justifiable when:

1. Benefits are primarily direct, so that charges will not cause significant loss of externalities.
2. Demand has some elasticity, so that the use of prices aids resource allocation and eliminates excessive utilization.
3. Charges do not result in inequities to lower-income groups, on the basis of accepted standards.
4. Costs of collection of charges are relatively low or alternate taxes measured by use can be employed.

Use of charges is more questionable when:

1. Externalities are significant and will be lost in part if charges are made.
2. Demand is perfectly inelastic, so that resource allocation is insensitive to the pricing system. Even so, charges may be regarded as warranted on equity grounds.
3. Equity standards require that the lower-income groups be assured of obtaining the services.
4. Collection costs are relatively high and alternative tax measures related to usage cannot be devised.[15]

---

[14] This is required by Section 204 of the Federal Water Pollution Control Act Amendments of 1972.

[15] Due and Friedlander, *Government Finance,* p. 101. For an excellent discussion of the economics of pricing services of public agencies, see Alice John Vandermeulen, "Reform of a State Fee Structure," *National Tax Journal* 17, no. 4 (1965), p. 394.

BENEFIT-COST AND COST-EFFECTIVENESS ANALYSES

Benefit-cost analysis is a set of techniques for comparing alternative programs or projects that are expected to yield returns over a period of years. To a considerable extent, benefit-cost studies follow the same principles of cost and return estimation that are used in private investment decisions. They are intended to provide for the public sector the kinds of guides to investment policy that are given to private firms by market prices and considerations of competition.

Competition can be *simulated* in decisions about public projects by the specification of a number of *alternative production techniques, levels of service, and combinations of output*. This list of alternatives will also probably include the possibility of no additional government program at all (the "status quo" alternative). The purpose of systematic analysis is not only to *justify government expenditure* to advance a certain objective, but also to find the *most efficient means* to that objective and to determine the *best level of service to provide*. *Comparisons among alternatives* may be largely *technical*, having to do with alternate types of equipment, or they may involve more fundamental questions of *priority* such as whether to build more job training centers or more research libraries.

Definition of the outputs or objectives of the project is the first necessary step in any benefit-cost analysis. These may be simple and obvious, as in the case of a bridge, or quite complex, as in the case of multiple-purpose water resources projects. In the latter case the outputs could be electric power, recreation, irrigation water, domestic and industrial water, flood control, and pollution control. Each of these outputs can be produced at different levels, but their production cannot be considered independently. In other cases, project objectives may be quite intangible. Consider the problem of defining "outputs" of a correctional institution.

After objectives are stated and feasible alternative means and program levels are formulated, the goal of benefit-cost analysis is to estimate net improvement in the well-being of the target population for each of the alternatives.

Discounting benefits and costs

In practice, most studies of this type deal with durable projects from which benefits and costs will accrue over a period of years. However, investment in intangibles that are expected to yield a stream of future benefits (for example, Head Start programs for preschool children or, more generally, any educational programs) can also be subjected to benefit-cost analysis. Any such investigation requires that evaluation of both costs and benefits take account of timing as well as absolute amounts of dollar magnitudes. The methods for dealing with time streams of costs and returns were discussed in Chapter 14. The same type of reasoning applies to government projects. For example, building a dam will require government financing which, either by raising resource prices or increasing taxes, will take resources away from other public investment, such as roads, or from private sector investment, such as factories. Since the time streams of costs and returns will be different for these competing alternatives, discounting is required so that the projects can be compared in terms of present values.

The appropriate rate of discount is the *estimated rate of return on alternative investment which must be foregone* in order to carry out the project under evaluation. The importance of correct choice of a discount rate may be shown by the following example.

Consider two potential government housing projects. The first, alternative A, would be built over two years at a level annual cost of $100,000 and is expected to produce benefits worth $30,000 per year beginning in year 3 and ending after ten years of use, whereupon it is replaced by a more productive land use. Alternative B would take three years to build at $100,000 per year, but would generate benefits of $30,000 per year for 20 years before it, too, becomes obsolete. The following table compares the net present values (NPV) for these two projects under three different discount rates.

Project	NPV discounted at 5%	NPV discounted at 7%	NPV discounted at 10%
A.....................	$25,383	$ 3,465	$—23,330
B.....................	29,661	—3,205	—62,474

Notice that the choice of the discount rate is crucial in determining (1) whether a public project is warranted as compared to private investment or other uses of public funds, and (2) whether long-term or short-term investments will be favored. At 10 percent, neither project is justified. At 7 percent, project A is justified but B is not. At 5 percent, both projects are justified, but B is preferable to A. *Increases in the discount rate simultaneously improve the relative position of shorter-term alternatives and disqualify a greater number of projects.*

Choosing the discount rate

Public agencies should use a discount rate which assures that public investments at the margin yield at least the opportunity rate of return on marginal private alternatives. The most common measures of "opportunity cost of capital" are the various market borrowing and lending rates. Which of these is most relevant to public investments? Actual government practice of recent years has favored using the rates which the governments must pay to borrow funds. Since public and private securities compete for the same lenders, these rates are related to private investment opportunities. However, a private investment that used the same resources would pay corporate income taxes; total social return is greater than the net private yield. In addition, the rate paid on government bonds is subsidized by granting personal income tax advantages to lenders. For these reasons, governments are able to borrow at rates that are well below marginal social return on private investments. Commercial rates, on the other hand, include the effects of financial risks that are relevant for investment by individual firms, but not for the expected return from all private investment taken together.

Considering these factors, suppose that corporations are paying 8 percent to obtain capital, using their optimal blend of debt and equity financing. Because of risk, a private firm might be willing to pay this rate to finance a project only if its expected return after taxes were substantially greater than the cost of capital. Corporate profits are taxed at approximately 50 percent in the United States, but (depending upon the proportion of debt finance) this tax is partially offset by deductibility of interest. For example, a before-tax return of 15 percent with a 50–50 ratio of 6 percent bonds to new equity would be an after-tax yield of 9 percent.[16] If firms regard this as sufficient return to offset risk, then the 15 percent *before-tax* return would represent the contribution of the marginal private investment to the value of national output. Using this as the discount rate for government investment decisions would equalize marginal returns in the public and private sectors.

Although the above approach yields a reasonable estimate of the cost of capital for the public sector, there is not a definitive method of obtaining such costs.[17] Actual benefit-cost studies often show benefits and costs under alternative discount rates, so that decision makers can see how sensitive the results are to changes in the rates.

Now suppose that benefit and cost streams are quantified as accurately as possible in dollar terms for each feasible alternative, and a discount rate is chosen. Estimated net benefits in each year may then be discounted to present values and a total discounted net benefit may be determined for each project.

In the simplest case, all projects under consideration would be independent of one another (in terms of the resources to be used or the out-

---

[16] An investment of $1 returns 15 cents in Year 1 and (with half of total capital obtained by borrowing) incurs an interest charge of 3 cents (6 percent on 50 cents). Taxable profit is therefore 12 cents and taxes are 6 cents, leaving a 9-cent profit after taxes.

[17] For discussions of the choice of discount rates, see Mishan, *Cost-Benefit Analysis,* op. cit.

comes expected) and funds would be available for all worthy projects. In this case, *all projects with net discounted benefits greater than zero should be undertaken.* This is equivalent to recommending adoption of any "lumpy" project whose internal rate of return exceeds the discount rate, or increasing size of any continuously variable project with marginal rate of return above discount rate. Under this criterion, if marginal private investments are yielding a 10-percent before-tax return, any public project (or incremental increase in a project) that promised a greater return would be adopted and revenues would be raised to finance it.

But real public agencies are seldom able to undertake every project and every expansion that they can justify on net benefit grounds. Usually the budgetary limitation will be expressed in *maximum dollars available* rather than as a *required rate of return.* These conditions complicate the choice process. A foolproof choice criterion can still be simply stated— approve that set of independent projects that maximizes discounted net benefits without exceeding the budget constraint. However, if the list of projects is long and the number of mutually exclusive sets is large, project ranking requires mathematical programming techniques.

Examples of benefit-cost studies

This section provides two examples of benefit-cost studies that show: (1) benefit-cost techniques can be used to determine whether investing in "human capital" is efficient, as well as in appraisals of tangible capital projects, and (2) the approach can be applied in an ex poste evaluation of old projects, as well as in decisions on whether or not to undertake new ones.

The first study is an analysis of benefits and costs of a rapid rail and bus transit system for the metropolitan Atlanta, Georgia, area.[18] "Quantifiable" and "nonquantifiable" benefits are listed in Table 15–1, and estimated values of the quantifiable benefits are shown in Table 15–2 under the assumptions that the value of time of commuters would average $2.75 per hour from 1971 through 2020 and that benefits of future periods should be discounted at 6 percent. The table shows that more than *one quarter* of the value of benefits is in the form of expected time saved by highway users making no direct use of the rapid transit system (an example of a project's external benefits). The second largest category of benefits is the expected decrease in costs of highway accidents due to reduced congestion. These examples show that estimation of indirect benefits often has a major role in a benefit-cost study.

Part A of Table 15–3 shows the sensitivity of estimated benefits to

---

[18] Development Research Associates, "Benefits to the Atlanta Metropolitan Area from the Proposed Regional Transportation Program" (Metropolitan Atlanta Rapid Transit Authority, 1971).

Table 15–1
Benefits of the proposed Atlanta MARTA system

Nonquantifiable benefits
    Facilitation of regional growth
    Retention and enhancement of existing urban areas
    Broadening educational opportunities
    Increasing the accessibility of cultural and recreational sites
    Reduction in emission of air pollutants
    Reduction of traffic accidents

Quantifiable benefits
    Time savings to "constant" transit users
    Benefits to motorists using transit (diverted auto drivers and riders)
        Time savings
        Operating cost savings
        Insurance savings
        Additional vehicle savings
        Parking cost savings
    Time savings to motorists not using transit (nondiverted auto
        drivers and riders)
    Benefits to the business community
        Time savings to the trucking industry
        Parking facility savings to suburban employers
    Other benefits
        Savings from termination of present bus system
        Highway accident savings

Source: Development Research Associates, "Benefits to the Atlanta Metropolitan Area from the Proposed Regional Transportation Program" (Metropolitan Atlanta Transit Authority, 1971), p. 2.

changes in prices (in this example, prices of time saved) and to changes in discount rates. A doubling of the discount rate reduces the value of benefits by more than half. Part B of Table 15–3 is the estimate of the 1971 present value of the projected future costs of the system, and Part C shows benefit-cost ratios resulting from various combinations of prices of time saved and discount rates. The ratios vary from 1.85 to 4.19.

The second example of a benefit-cost study is an analysis of investment in human capital—the Upward Bound program.[19] This program attempted to identify "high school students who would be unlikely to go on to college because of poverty or because of low perceptions of probable success associated with race or socioeconomic status."[20] The program, operated by the U.S. Office of Education, consisted of enrolling such students in local colleges during summers after their sophomore year in

---

[19] Walter I. Garms, "A Benefit-Cost Analysis of the Upward Bound Program," *Journal of Human Resources* 6 (Spring 1971), pp. 206–20.

[20] Ibid., p. 206.

Table 15–2
Monetary values of the quantifiable benefits of the proposed MARTA system
(cumulative benefits by 2020, discounted to constant 1971 dollars)

Constant transit commuters	$ 321,650,000
Diverted motorists	
Time savings	219,770,000
Operating cost savings	217,930,000
Insurance cost savings	22,540,000
Additional vehicle savings	160,170,000
Parking cost savings	103,840,000
Nondiverted commuters	1,052,990,000
Business community	
Time savings to trucking industry	685,040,000
Parking facilities savings to employers	7,990,000
Other benefits	
Termination of present bus system savings	58,000,000
Highway accident savings	745,410,000
Total	$3,595,330,000

Source: Development Research Associates, "Benefits to the Atlanta Metropolitan Area from the Proposed Regional Transportation Program," (Metropolitan Atlanta Rapid Transit Authority, 1971), p. 36.

high school, so as to introduce them "to skills and attitudes that are helpful in college and to remedy those subject matter areas in which the student is weak."[21] Stipends were paid to the participants.

The estimated internal benefits and costs (that is, benefits and costs to the participants in the program) are shown for two rates of discount in Table 15–4 for students of different sexes and races. The principal benefit was the expected increase in lifetime earnings after having attended college. It was not necessary to include foregone earnings as a cost since the benefits were estimated as of age 16. Estimated benefit-cost ratios for participants varied from 1.49 (nonwhite males and a 10 percent discount rate) to 10.18 (nonwhite females and a 5 percent discount rate).

The above analysis of Upward Bound is based on internal benefits and costs alone. Table 15–5 shows an analysis that also includes costs borne by persons who were not participants in the program. From the larger point of view, the program was not a clear-cut success. Although benefit-cost ratios greater than one were calculated using a 5 percent rate of discount, benefits were less than costs when both were discounted at 10 percent.

Cost-effectiveness analysis

Cost evaluation is usually considerably easier than evaluation of benefits, since inputs are more often subject to pricing in the market than

[21] Ibid.

Table 15–3
Benefit-cost analysis, proposed MARTA system

A. Total quantified benefits

Discount rate	Value of time in 1971 (in $ millions)		
	$2.25	*$2.75*	*$3.25*
4%	$5,496.48	$5,989.75	$6,555.62
6	3,305.44	3,595.33	3,885.23
8	2,105.43	2,286.37	2,467.30

B. 1971 Present value total costs

Discount rate	Present value (in $ millions)
4%	$1,566.0
6	1,325.0
8	1,139.0

C. Benefit-cost ratio under alternative assumptions

Discount rate	Value of commuter time		
	$2.25	*$2.75*	*$3.25*
4%	$3.51	$3.83	$4.19
6	2.50	2.71	2.93
8	1.85	2.01	2.18

Sources: Development Research Associates, "Benefits to the Atlanta Metropolitan Area from the Proposed Regional Transportation Program" (Metropolitan Atlanta Regional Transit Authority, 1971), pp. 36, 38, and 40.

are public outputs. It is sometimes feasible to make explicit dollar comparisons among alternative programs *only in terms of costs,* thus bypassing the difficult problems of benefit estimation. If the programs to be compared are *alternative ways of reaching the same objective,* this procedure obviously yields useful results. The alternative which has lowest cost is judged most effective. Notice also that both explicit and implicit *costs that are common to all alternatives can be disregarded* in cost-effectiveness analysis.

This type of approach is commonly used in highway planning. A variety of alternate routes between origin and destination may result in similar benefits and the major categories of benefits are time saving and safety improvements, both of which are difficult to evaluate in dollars. Common standards can be set in terms of average speeds, lives saved, and property damage avoided; comparison of alternatives can then be based only upon quantifiable costs.

Even in cases where performance specifications of alternatives are not identical, comparison of costs may be useful in clarifying the issues involved in choice. For example, an increase in average speed of two miles per hour may be shown to be attainable on Route A, which will cost $1 million more than alternate Route B. These values can be combined with

Table 15–4
Benefits and cost from the individual's viewpoint*

	White		Nonwhite	
	Male	*Female*	*Male*	*Female*
Discount rate 5 percent				
Benefits				
Lifetime income differentials				
(after taxes)†.........................	$5,209	$3,549	$3,943	$5,843
Upward Bound stipend‡..................	210	209	224	224
Scholarships and grants§.................	454	394	683	498
Total benefits.......................	$5,873	$4,152	$4,850	$6,565
Cost differentials‖				
Tuition#..............................	370	319	537	378
Extra living costs**.....................	260	225	379	267
Total costs..........................	$ 630	$ 544	$ 916	$ 645
Net benefits.............................	$5,243	$3,608	$3,934	$5,920
Discount rate 10 percent				
Benefits				
Lifetime income differentials				
(after taxes)†.........................	$ 770	$1,152	$ 354	$1,902
Upward Bound stipend‡..................	202	201	214	214
Scholarships and grants§..................	373	324	561	410
Total benefits.......................	$1,345	$1,677	$1,129	$2,526
Cost differentials‖				
Tuition#..............................	308	264	446	314
Extra living costs**.....................	215	185	312	220
Total costs..........................	$ 523	$ 449	$ 758	$ 534
Net benefits.............................	$ 822	$1,228	$ 371	$1,992

* All figures shown as present value at age 16, the approximate age at which a decision is made to include a student in Upward Bound.

† Differentials are calculated by multiplying the proportion of Upward Bound students in each educational category by the present value of lifetime income for that category, and summing over all four categories. The same is done for siblings, and the difference between those figures is the raw differential. The raw differential is reduced by 25 percent to allow for taxes paid, and the result is again reduced by 25 percent on the assumption that only 75 percent of income differentials are caused by education.

‡ Stipends averaged $45.36 per month during the summer and $5.60 per month during the school year. For the whole program, stipends ranged from $218 for white females to $233 for nonwhite females. Figures shown are present values of these amounts.

§ Scholarships and grants ranged from $739 to $793 per year for Upward Bound students and were assumed to be identical for siblings. Differentials shown arise because of differential rates of college attendance between Upward Bound students and siblings.

‖ Because present values are computed at age 16, the income series automatically shows foregone income as a reduction in benefits, and it is not included separately as a cost. This is also true of the reduced receipts of unemployment and welfare payments by educated individuals.

Based on average 1968–69 tuition of $602 for all U.S. institutions.

** Assumes an average of $425 per year in extra living cost while in college.

Source: Walter I. Garms, "A Benefit-Cost Analysis of the Upward Bound Program," *Journal of Human Resources* 6 (Spring 1971), p. 216.

Table 15–5
Benefits and costs from society's viewpoint*

	White		Nonwhite	
	Male	*Female*	*Male*	*Female*
Discount rate 5 percent				
Benefits				
Lifetime income differentials				
(before taxes)†..............	$7,020	$4,777	$5,491	$7,942
Cost differentials‡				
Upward Bound cost to the				
government§................	$1,811	$1,798	$1,922	$1,919
Upward Bound cost to colleges‖..	260	257	275	275
Cost of education#.............	1,057	872	1,424	1,028
Extra living costs**............	260	225	379	267
Total costs................	$3,388	$3,152	$4,000	$3,489
Net benefits....................	$3,632	$1,625	$1,491	$4,453
Discount rate 10 percent				
Benefits				
Lifetime income differentials				
(before taxes)†..............	$1,066	$1,560	$ 598	$2,609
Cost differentials‡				
Upward Bound cost to the				
government§................	$1,737	$1,724	$1,845	$1,842
Upward Bound cost to colleges‖..	249	247	264	264
Cost of education#.............	852	724	1,183	856
Extra living costs**............	215	185	312	220
Total costs................	$3,053	$2,880	$3,604	$3,182
Net benefits....................	—$1,987	—$1,320	—$3,006	—$ 573

* All figures are present values at age 16.

† Differentials are calculated as in Table 15–4, including the assumption that only 75 percent of differentials are caused by education, but excluding the reduction for taxes paid. The effect of decreased receipts of unemployment and welfare benefits by educated individuals has been removed because in the social context these are transfer payments.

‡ As in Table 15–4, foregone income is included in lifetime income differentials as a reduction in benefits.

§ Excludes cost of stipends paid students, which are transfer payments. Cost calculated from data furnished by OEO.

‖ Calculated from data furnished by OEO.

Based on total economic cost of education, estimated at $623 per pupil in high school and $1,470 per pupil in college.

** Extra living cost is estimated at $425 per year while in college.

Source: Walter I. Garms, "A Benefit-Cost Analysis of the Upward Bound Program," *Journal of Human Resources* 6 (Spring 1971), p. 219.

traffic projections to derive an estimate of the value that must be placed on each hour of time saved in order to justify the additional cost of Route A. An example of an especially useful type of cost-effectiveness analysis is comparison of costs of public operation of garbage collection with costs of contracting with a private firm. Outputs (benefits) of the two modes of operation are identical, so the relevant analysis is limited to the cost comparison. The method that costs the least is deemed to be "cost effective."

Note that cost-effectiveness analysis cannot indicate the efficient level of a particular program, nor is this technique useful in choosing among programs with dissimilar benefits. Nonetheless, because it requires less information than benefit-cost analysis and is less demanding of the time and expertise of agency personnel, it has become a regular part of the planning process in most federal agencies and in many states and localities.

Appraisal of benefit-cost analysis

Users of the benefit-cost approach should be aware of both the strengths and weaknesses of the technique.[22] Perhaps the most important strength of benefit-cost analysis is its firm basis in economic theory. It emanates from a consistent and well-defined set of principles. Secondly, the technique is systematic. Alternative projects are compared according to common assumptions about prices of benefits realized and inputs used. Finally, the emphasis upon measurement of outcomes tends to decrease the effects of preconceived notions and pure rhetoric upon the final decisions made.

While the strengths of the benefit-cost approach are impressive, the weaknesses lay the technique open to several criticisms. One line of criticism attacks benefit-cost analysis on the pragmatic grounds that it is difficult to carry out. Determination of shadow prices and appropriate discount rates, specification of target populations, the importance of "nonquantifiable" benefits, price adjustments needed when there is unemployment or noncompetitive market structure, and the handling of uncertainty about outcomes are not standardized practices. The examples earlier in this chapter showed that results of benefit-cost studies may be quite sensitive to the assumptions and judgments that the analyst makes about these matters. Some observers have suggested that a reasonably imaginative analyst can produce positive benefits for any project without violating generally accepted practices.

A second line of criticism is that benefit and cost estimates are solemnly totaled and compared regardless of what individuals or groups stand to gain and what persons are expected to bear the costs. For example, a recreation area accessible mainly to higher-income families and designed to accommodate their motorized campers may outrank neighborhood playgrounds in ghetto areas. This is the result of dollar evaluations of benefits that depend upon the purchasing power of the beneficiaries as well as their relative preferences among goods and services.

---

[22] More complete evaluations of benefit-cost analysis are provided in Jesse Burkhead and Jerry Miner, *Public Expenditure* (Chicago: Aldine Publishing Co., 1971), pp. 246–49; and Alan Williams, "Cost Benefit Analysis: Bastard Science? And/or Insidious Poison in the Body Politick?" *Journal of Political Economy* (August 1972), pp. 199–226.

For completeness, benefit-cost studies should always be accompanied by studies of the incidence of benefits and costs upon various groups of people.

Another line of criticism is that a target population which is not also the funding population has a very strong incentive to make the benefit-cost ratio look better than it actually is. For example, a local project which will be funded primarily from federal tax dollars can have large local benefits in relation to local costs even though the true overall benefit-cost ratio is negative. Local sponsors of a proposed project may exaggerate benefits and understate costs in order to establish a higher priority for federal funding.

A final criticism is that benefit-cost analysis is seldom applied to the problem of choosing the *best level* of programs. Choosing among *whole programs* on the basis of their benefit-cost ratios is based on comparisons of *averages*. It would be desirable to pay more attention to estimates of the *marginal* benefit-cost ratios for *incremental changes in program sizes*. *Planning-programming-budgeting*, or PPB, is an attempt to apply incremental analysis across the total expenditure plans of a governmental unit, with the various programs being scaled up or down as indicated by comparisons of benefit-cost estimates for incremental changes. *Zero-base budgeting* is PPB with the added feature that whole programs must be justified from the ground up (in addition to being evaluated for incremental changes in program size) with consideration being given to the possible elimination of programs.

MULTIPLE OBJECTIVES AND GROUP DECISIONS IN THE PUBLIC SECTOR

Most of this chapter's discussion of government decision making has dealt with the problems of increasing efficiency of resource use. Except for the brief consideration of intergroup equity in the preceding paragraph and in the first section of the chapter, we have been assuming that all parties to any decision regard efficiency as the primary goal. In reality, efficiency may not be the only, or even the most important, concern, and it may not be fully compatible with other objectives.

A full listing of objectives perceived by public agencies would include: (1) efficient allocation of resources; (2) equitable distribution of costs and benefits; (3) prosperity, growth, and stability of the overall economy; (4) economic development of particular regions or sectors of the economy; and (5) the country's relations with other nations. The last three of the above goals are particularly important in the decision making of federal agencies.

There is often conflict among the first two of the above goals.[23] For example, consider the decisions related to energy policy. From a pure efficiency point of view, it might be desirable to allow all energy prices to rise as supply and demand conditions change. Yet, such a policy would produce windfall gains for firms holding reserves of energy sources and would impose hardships upon consumers generally and upon low-income groups especially.

To understand how all five of the above goals enter into public decisions, consider the analysis of a federal program aimed at encouraging increased exploration for domestic sources of petroleum. A benefit-cost study would be aimed at answering whether federal dollars would generate more valuable benefits in this or some other use. However, even if net benefits are positive, some may object that benefits accrue narrowly to producers and marketers of oil and to large oil consumers at the widely distributed expense of typical taxpayers. In addition, many people will have an interest in the impact of the employment- and income-generating effects of the program. Still others will be interested in which regions of the country are helped most (and which, if any, are hurt). Finally, there will be concern for the effect of increased domestic oil capacity on national military preparedness, international political power, and the balance of international payments. Benefit-cost analysis alone is not suited to considering all these objectives at one time.

Conceptually, an optimal decision in the case of multiple goals requires that those goals be given explicit decision weights. Suppose, for example, that *efficiency* is measured in terms of net dollar benefits, *equity* in terms of the number of dollars transferred from those above the median family income to those below it, *regional development* as the dollar addition to the gross product of a region (e.g., the Southwest), and *international affairs impact* by net change in the domestic trade balance. If weights can be assigned according to the relative importance of each goal, and the weighted outcomes can be regarded as additive, it is possible to produce a single number with which to compare alternative programs. For example, one might have as the overall objective to maximize $0.4E + 0.3Q + 0.1R + 0.2I$, where E stands for efficiency, Q for equity, R for regional development, and I for international affairs as measured above.

A somewhat more sophisticated and realistic procedure for dealing with problems of this type is given by goal programming. *Goal programming* is an extension of linear programming which allows the setting of target minimum values for each goal, with relative priorities specified among them. For example, goals for a program might be to achieve $5

---

[23] For an interesting essay on the choice between efficiency and equity, see Arthur M. Okun, *Equality and Efficiency, The Big Tradeoff* (Washington, D.C.: The Brookings Institution, 1975).

million of priority net benefits, $2 million of redistribution, $1 million of regional development, and $2 million of improvement in the balance of payments. The priorities are then simply the relative importance of the targets in case they are not all simultaneously attainable. The advantage of this method is that the setting of *target values* may be easier or more politically feasible than explicit determination of *relative weights* of goals categories.

In the public agency, perhaps more so than in private business, the decision analyst must be aware that economic consequences will not entirely rule the final choice. The decision models described in this chapter handle economic variables imperfectly, and other variables, such as political costs, are not dealt with at all. Nevertheless, benefit-cost analysis and related techniques provide systematic organization of available economic information and some guide to the relative importance of information that is not yet at hand.

SUMMARY

In general, an economy in which actions of private firms are determined by self-interest as regulated by competitive markets will use resources efficiently. Intervention by public agencies may be needed to prevent inefficiencies resulting from noncompetitive behavior and from externalities. The chapter dealt only with cases of externalities.

Externalities are costs imposed upon or benefits provided to third parties as the result of private producer and consumer behavior. From the social welfare point of view, activities that have external costs are overproduced and overconsumed. Activities that have external benefits are underproduced and underconsumed.

Where externalities are small in relation to private costs and benefits, the activities may well be left to the private sector; the externalities can be offset by imposing taxes on activities that have external costs and by providing subsidies to those that have external benefits. However, a good or service cannot be profitably produced by the private sector if nonpayers can receive the same benefits as payers; if they are to be available, such goods and services must be produced by public or nonprofit agencies.

The constituency of a public agency is much larger than that of a private firm; decision making by a public agency should take into account the interests of all individuals and groups that will be affected. Estimation of the values of public agency outputs may be more difficult than for products and services of private firms, since many of these outputs are provided to users at zero prices or at prices well below average cost. Nevertheless, public agency managers should attempt to maximize public profit (net social benefit) by expanding public activities so long as the marginal value of social benefits is greater than the marginal social cost.

Steps in benefit estimation include: (1) enumeration of specific ways in which various groups are benefited; (2) estimation of monetary values of *total* tangible benefits (in the case of proposed *new* programs) or of *incremental* tangible benefits (in the case of evaluation of expansion or contraction of *ongoing* programs); and (3) enumeration of any intangible benefits, such as beautification or prestige. Direct estimation of monetary values can be carried out only for goods and services sold at prices reflecting their value in marginal applications. Indirect estimation techniques must be used for unpriced goods and services; these techniques include: (1) observation of changes in land values affected by public programs, (2) use of prices of close substitutes produced in the private sector, and (3) estimates of reductions in private cost resulting from the public programs.

Costs of public production are estimated in essentially the same ways as in the private sector. However, opportunity costs of resource services used by a public agency may be different from the explicit outlays in the agency's budget; the social cost of services of a monopoly-produced or government price-controlled resource may be well below prices paid by the agency—on the other hand, the agency may use some services of resources owned by the agency (or by other agencies) that have no budgeted agency cost but do have social opportunity costs.

Benefit-cost techniques are useful in analyzing public investment. The values of future benefits and costs are discounted, and the ratio of present value of benefit to present value of cost is formed. Marginal social opportunity costs of capital should be used in discounting. Assuming full employment and capacity production, the marginal social cost of capital is the marginal pretax return on total capital in the private sector. Marginal social cost of capital may be zero or close to zero in periods of considerable unemployment and excess capacity.

QUESTIONS

1. "An activity that has external costs will be overproduced and overconsumed, whereas an activity that yields external benefits will be underproduced and underconsumed." Explain. What can be done to bring activities that have externalities closer to their socially optimal levels?

2. What are the distinguishing or unique characteristics of pure public goods?

3. What is a target population? How is specification of the target population helpful in a cost-benefit analysis?

4. Explain the difference between consumers' surplus and consumers' expenditure. How do these two concepts fit into the ideal evaluation of benefits from a program or project?

5. What is social cost? In what ways might social cost vary from the budgeted outlays for a program or project?

6. How could you determine whether a particular public program should be expanded or cut back?

7. What do penalties and subsidies have in common?

8. How could you determine the discount rate (or rates) that should be used in calculating present values of a program's future benefits and costs?

9. List the strengths and weaknesses of benefit-cost analysis.

FURTHER READING

Davis, O. A., and Whinston, A. "The Economics of Urban Renewal." *Law and Contemporary Problems* 26, Winter 1961.

Fisher, G. H. "The World of Program Budgeting." *Long Range Planning*, September 1969.

Lee, Sang M. "Decision Analysis through Goal Programming." *Decision Sciences* 2, April 1971.

Maass, Arthur. "Benefit-Cost Analysis: Its Relevance for Public Decision Making." *Quarterly Journal of Economics* 80 (1966).

Mishan, Ezra J. "The Postwar Literature on Externalities: An Interpretative Essay." *Journal of Economic Literature*, March 1971.

Mishan, Ezra J. "Evaluation of Life and Limb: A Theoretical Approach." *Journal of Political Economy*, July–August 1971.

Newhouse, Joseph D. "Toward a Theory of Nonprofit Institutions: An Economic Model of A Hospital." *American Economic Review* 60, March 1970.

Prest, A. R., and Turvey, R. "Cost-Benefit Analysis: A Survey." *The Economic Journal*, December 1965.

Schelling, Thomas C. "On the Ecology of Micromotives." *The Public Interest* 25, Fall 1971.

Walters, A. A. "The Theory and Measurement of Private and Social Costs of Highway Congestion." *Econometrica* 29, October 1961.

<table>
<tr><td>

Cases for part seven

</td></tr>
</table>

The two cases in this section (I. The Public Sector and II. The Private Sector: Lanier Auto Parts) provide an opportunity to view the same problem—what to do with junk autos—from both the public agency and the private business points of view. Case II, dealing with the private sector, should be handled first, with case I being read to provide background. In case I, the analytic complications resulting from the larger constituency of public agencies and the fact that most of the benefits resulting from their activities are not sold to the users can be brought into sharp focus.

THE AUTO-WRECKING INDUSTRY

The auto-wrecking industry is comprised of approximately 15,600 small to medium-sized companies whose primary business is taking in damaged, junked, or abandoned motor vehicles, stripping them of useful parts, and selling those materials. Secondarily, they dispose of the scrap metal residue. The industry employs almost 100,000 workers, equivalent to the fabricated structural steel industry. However, 70 percent of the firms employ five or less people, 17 percent being one-person operations.

The auto-wrecking industry provides a highly valuable service. Were it not for the used auto parts made available in this manner, many older cars would have to be discarded once the manufacturer quit supplying new replacement parts. The total value of this operation is out of proportion with the junk yard image. For instance, in 1968, the auto-wrecking industry took in 9,033,000 automobiles and trucks. The average price was $334; the average resale value of the parts was $587 per vehicle, yielding an overall gross revenue of $5.3 billion. The accompanying table compares this figure with other industries' experience:

SIC code	Industry	1967 Value of shipments ($ millions)
3722....................	Aircraft engines and parts	$5,320
2834....................	Pharmaceutical preparations	4,743
2042....................	Prepared animal feeds	4,640
3522....................	Farm machinery and equipment	4,428
3651....................	Radio and TV receiving sets	3,929
	Auto wrecking/dismantling	5,296

Source: Except for auto-wrecking-dismantling industry estimates, all data are from *Census of Manufacturers, 1967, Summary Series, Preliminary Report*, Bureau of the Census, U.S. Department of Commerce, April 1969.

The average revenue for each of the 15,600 members of the industry was about $339,000.

Some other industry figures for 1968 point up some important considerations for the future of the industry. In that year, an estimated 8.4 million motor vehicles were abandoned or junked. However, more than 9.0 million autos were taken in by the industry. The 600,000 difference between these figures is the amount by which wreckers chewed into the backlog, as it were, of junked and abandoned autos. Estimates of the number of vehicles spread across the country range from 10 to 30 million. The sources of these vehicles are given below:

Source	Percent
Individuals..	38%
Auto and truck dealers, new/used..	26
Insurance companies...	21
State and local agencies...	12
Other..	3
Total...	100%

Source: *Automobile Disposal: A National Problem*, Bureau of Mines, Department of the Interior, Washington, D.C. 20240, 1967, p. 11.

Disposal of scrap and waste is the most pressing problem in the industry today. Although there would seem to be a ready market for automotive scrap iron and steel, certain economic factors work against profitable disposal. The auto hulk must be stripped, processed, and shipped to a point where the metal is salable. Processing in this case means the preparation of the auto hulk for use by the steel industry. This usually consists of rendering the metal into bales, slabs, or shreds so that it is easily handled or moved.

One of the more common methods of processing auto hulks is the use of a baler. The auto hulk is dropped in a compartment wherein hydraulic rams reduce it to a cube weighing approximately 1,200 pounds. This is the No. 2 bundle, the basic item in auto scrap. Even so, the No. 2 bundle is not especially desired by the steel industry as it is quite easy to contaminate the metal with nonferrous or even nonmetallic substances. The exact number of balers in operation is not known. However, a 1968 Business and Defense Services Administration report indicated that at least 293 companies had installed such equipment.

A piece of equipment which produces a more easily inspected product is the slab shear. The process begins by compressing the auto hulk into a rectangular block 2 feet by 2 feet by up to 20 feet. This "scrap log" is then automatically fed through a shear which slices and compresses the metal into pillow-shaped slabs. The pieces have very high density and are easily transported. The primary advantage is that it is easy to inspect the slabs for contaminants such as copper, zinc, chrome, stainless steel, rubber, plastic, and glass.

The machinery which poses the greatest promise for the wrecking industry is the scrap shredder. This piece of equipment chews up auto hulks into small-sized pieces, some at rates of up to 120 cars per hour. Some advantages of the method include the ability to magnetically separate the resulting scrap into ferrous and nonferrous metals and the ease of handling. However, such a machine represents a substantial investment. Prices start at about $500,000 for a small unit handling up to 100 tons per hour or more. Aside from price, the main disadvantage of the shredders is their appetite. They often can lay idle because of their efficiency and the costs of transporting hulks to the work site.

For all processing methods, the auto hulks must be stripped before they can be effectively processed. Stripping involves removing nonferrous metals. The cost may range from $3 to $5 per car, depending on wage rates and worker efficiency. A particularly difficult problem is removing the residual copper wire from the hulk. Copper in even very small quantities is a serious contaminant of steel and iron products. The average hulk weighs about 1,200 pounds of which maybe 4 pounds is copper wiring in mostly inaccessible places. Over half of this wire must be removed if the copper content of a baled or slabbed hulk is to have less than the 0.15 percent required by steel processors. This problem is less urgent when a shredder comes into play.

The process of stripping can be somewhat improved by burning the auto hulk. By incinerating the car body, various contaminants can be removed. Such might include rubber, plastic, paint, and upholstery. Incinerators may be of the pit, batch (or garage), or continuous operation type. The incinerator of the pit type is simply a covered cavity into which the hulk is placed to be burned. When the exhaust gases are caught and fed into an afterburner, the incinerator is termed a *small-batch* incinerator. Larger units, of the batch type, are more often of the garage type, resembling an oven, with an accompanying afterburner. The pit-

type incinerator has a capacity of 8–10 autos per day, the garage type
of 40–45. In addition, continuous-operation incinerators may achieve
rates of 50 autos per day. They operate by hauling bodies through a
tunnel on a continuous conveyor.

In 1970, however, because of stronger air pollution abatement regulations and uneconomical operating conditions, almost none of the pit- and
garage-type incinerators were in use. All of the continuous-operation
units were shut down at that time for similar reasons. Of particular importance for the larger units—of all types—was lack of utilization. It
would be necessary for a number of wreckers to use the same facility in
order to achieve an economical utilization of the equipment. However,
many members of the industry did not express a willingness to utilize
the incinerators available, mainly for economic reasons. One economically feasible alternative to incineration was open-air burning, but air
pollution abatement regulations have now removed this alternative from
practical consideration.

Another serious problem in disposing of scrap metal is the matter of
transport to the point of sale. The wrecker usually does not shred or
bale his own scrap. After stripping the hulk, he flattens the body for
shipment to a collection point where shredding or baling may take place.
Exhibit 1 indicates what the wrecker may have to pay to transport the
flattened hulks to a scrap salvage.
These figures indicate that freight costs can considerably eat into the
$6–$8 that the wrecker may receive for each hulk.

One of the major problems of the auto-wrecking industry is disposing
of the solid wastes left by the stripping operation. Of these materials,

Exhibit 1
Estimated cost of hauling flat auto scrap, reported rates for common carrier and private/
contract carrier for transport via truck of 35 flat scrap auto bodies (approximately 40,000
pounds)

Point of departure	Destination	Approximate distance (mi.)	Common carrier Total	Common carrier Ton/mile	Private/contract Total	Private/contract Ton/mile
1. Amarillo, Tex....	Pueblo, Colo.	340	—	—	$180.00	2.6¢
	Dallas, Tex.	350	—	—	180.00	2.6
	Eagle Pass, Tex.	550	—	—	240.00	2.2
2. Memphis, Tenn..	Nashville, Tenn.	207	$164.00	4.0¢	144.90	3.5
	Jackson, Miss.	214	168.00	3.9	149.80	3.5
	St. Louis, Mo.	286	196.00	3.4	200.20	3.5
3. Olathe, Kan.....	Kansas City, Kan.	15	75.00	25.0	50.00	16.7
4. Elizabeth, N.J...	Jersey City, N.J.	10	85.00	42.5	25.00	12.5
	Philadelphia, Pa.	60	135.00	11.3	55.00	4.6
	Newark, N.J.	6	45.00	37.5	12.00	10.0

Note: Some carriers may move 35–40 flat bodies per load.
Source: Cost information submitted by selected companies; ton-mile cost computed by BDSA.

tires are by far the largest single item. Over 100 million tires are consumed annually in the United States. However, there is currently no truly feasible way to either destroy them or recycle the material. For instance, the price paid per ton at Akron, Ohio, in 1970 was $12, about 12 cents for the average 20-pound passenger car tire. At Eastern collection points, prices were about $7 per ton. The cost of handling and shipping would result in the average wrecker's incurring a loss to dispose of tires. There is hardly an incentive to deliberately collect them. The outlook is even more harsh with respect to the other waste materials.

All things taken into consideration, the wrecker can expect to incur a loss from disposal of the parts of an automobile which are not salable as repair or replacement items. This fact is lamentable because the sheer bulk of some of these materials represents a substantial resource. For instance, Exhibit 2 indicates the market value of the various metals found in a junk automobile.

Exhibit 2
Market value of metals in junk automobile (as of January 1967)

Metal	*Weight*	*Price*	*Total value*
Steel.........................	1.28 tons	$35.00 (ton)	$44.80
Cast iron....................	0.2335 ton	$35.00 (ton)	8.17
Lead.........................	29 pounds	9.0¢ (lb.)	2.61
Zinc.........................	67 pounds	6.75¢ (lb.)	4.25
Copper.......................	31 pounds	30.0¢ (lb.)	9.30
Aluminum.....................	31 pounds	13.5¢ (lb.)	3.87
Gross value...............			73.27
Per ton...................			41.16

Source: *Bureau of Mines Research For Utilizing Automobile Scrap*, Karl C. Dean, Bureau of Mines, Department of the Interior, Washington, D.C., 20240, 1967.

However, the auto wrecker can realize only a portion of this value, primarily due to two factors. First, there is another operator in the supply chain between the wrecker (salvage yard operator) and the market (steel maker or foundry). The other reason is that the various metals are so contaminated by one another that the value of each is appreciably lessened.

I. THE PUBLIC SECTOR

Many state and local governments have an interest in the disposal of junked and abandoned automobiles. When an automobile is left on city streets in conspicuous, obnoxious, or hazardous places, local governments must often incur the costs of impounding and storing the vehicle until a public auction of the auto provides partial reimbursement. In rural areas,

Exhibit 3
The auto scrap process

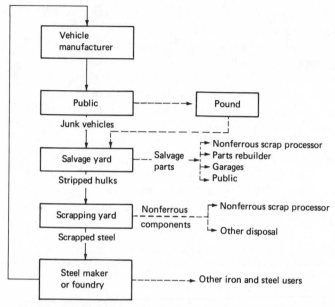

Source: "Copper Content in Vehicular Scrap," Ralph Stone and Company, Los Angeles, 1968, p. 41; study prepared for Bureau of Mines, Department of the Interior, Washington, D.C.

abandoned vehicles litter the countryside. The price available at most graveyards would not pay for the cost of hauling in the rotting hulks from remote rural areas.

These local governments also are concerned with the method of disposal. In the reclamation cycle, it is desirable to burn auto bodies to reduce the degree of contamination of the steel and iron to be recycled. Growing interest in ecological considerations has prompted passage of regulations all but forbidding this practice, however. At the same time, rapid disposal of existing hulks is desired in pursuit of better-looking communities. Therefore, state and local governments are asking wreckers to find a fast, clean method of processing junk autos.

To a somewhat lesser extent, the federal government is also interested in such a method. However, national interests are more concerned with the economic recycling of the scrap materials generated by the wrecking process. At present, only about 9 percent of all scrap consumed by the steel industry comes from discarded autos. The potential is much greater. There are an estimated 10–30 million junked automobiles scattered about the countryside which could prove to be a valuable source of iron and steel. However, at this time there is no incentive for a private agency to undertake the collection of the hulks.

The answer to many of the problems in this industry is the scrap shredder, many have said. The shredder would raise the value of scrap by more thoroughly separating ferrous and nonferrous metals. In conjunction with properly controlled incineration, more of the nonmetallic substances would also be removed without undue air pollution. Hence, the scrap salvager could afford to pay more for hulks, allowing the wrecker a wider margin. Hence, the wrecker could pay more for autos, prompting the recycling of more junked and abandoned vehicles.

Several things point to the idea that help will be needed in accomplishing the goals considered above. While the logic that the effect of higher prices will reach back to the beginning of the recycling channel is basically sound, some people feel that the differences will not be great enough to accomplish the total goal. An additional economic incentive would be needed to prompt collection of auto hulks for reprocessing. Additionally, the shredder equipment represents a substantial investment of money, up to several million dollars. These machines may have a capacity of 100 tons of scrap per hour. In order to be operated economically, the machines must be kept busy, so that a supply of up to 1,000 cars per day might be needed at a particularly large installation.

In 1970, there were 62 auto-shredder plants in operation in the United States, and seven more were under construction. They were dispersed geographically as presented in Exhibit 4. The capacity of the plants is described in Exhibit 5.

Exhibit 4
Location of auto-scrap shredder plants in the United States

Note: Locations are schematic only. Some symbols represent more than one installation.

Exhibit 5
Geographic distribution of auto-scrap shredder plants in the United States (status as of April 1969)

Division	Number of plants*	Estimated annual capacity (net, tons)	Percent of U.S. total
New England...................	4	205,000	5.0%
Middle Atlantic...............	7	480,000	11.5
East North Central............	19	1,470,000	35.4
West North Central...........	4	252,000	6.0
South Atlantic................	7	265,000	6.3
East South Central............	5	261,000	6.3
West South Central...........	6	198,000	4.7
Mountain.....................	7	350,000	8.4
Pacific.......................	10	685,000	16.4
Total....................	69	4,163,000	100.0%

* Operating, under construction, or definitely planned for 1969. Note: The number may include some plants also using other than auto scrap.

Source: BDSA estimates; based upon information from the Institute of Scrap Iron and Steel and auto-wrecking industry association.

Because of the discrepancies between capacity and location of scrap as presented in Exhibit 6, it has been proposed that the federal government partially subsidize the technical work necessary to build capacity for 7.5 million auto hulks annually, and to guarantee loans for the construction of the necessary plant.

1. How much additional shredder capacity is actually needed to bring capacity up to 7.5 million autos annually? What might it cost if an installation can operate 2,000 hours in a year? Where should the new capacity be distributed?
2. How might the government best encourage collection of abandoned autos? What are the economics of the situation? If auto disposal were subsidized by state and local government, what form should it take and to whom should it be given?

Exhibit 6
Comparison of auto-scrap shredder plant capacity with motor vehicles junked in 1968

Division	Percent of shredder capacity	Percent of vehicles junked in U.S.
New England.....................	5.0%	5.7%
Middle Atlantic..................	11.5	19.4
East North Central...............	35.4	24.3
West North Central..............	6.0	8.0
South Atlantic...................	6.3	13.9
East South Central...............	6.3	4.6
West South Central..............	4.7	9.6
Mountain........................	8.4	3.5
Pacific..........................	16.4	11.0
Total.......................	100.0%	100.0%

II. THE PRIVATE SECTOR: LANIER AUTO PARTS

A small group of people is interested in starting up an auto-wrecking business in a large southeastern metropolitan area. The team has decided to approach the situation on a different track. The common junk yard is a large open area in which rusting hulks lie about in various stages of dismemberment. The appearance of the yard alone brings about several problems, most notably unfavorable zoning restrictions. Additionally, the haphazard stacking and aisle making use the available space very inefficiently. The cost of urban land is high enough to make the average 8–10 acre graveyard a substantial investment. As the autos lie about in the open, the elements take their toll on otherwise salable parts.

Another major area of concern is junk yard management. Most salvage companies are run and controlled by the owner in a "seat of the pants" manner. He maintains all inventory in his head, often losing out on sales because he forgets where or if he has a requested part. Records of the businesses are often inadequate. Sometimes little more is kept than is needed to satisfy the Internal Revenue Service. In many yards, even required sales information does not get into the books, especially as "under the table" transactions occur.

The management team is considering a completely enclosed operation. Auto hulks would spend a minimum time under company control before being completely stripped of all desirable parts. The rest of the hulk would be disposed of immediately. Fortunately, the entrepreneurs plan to locate their facility in a city which has a scrap shredder. All stripped parts would be tagged and recorded immediately, being distributed to bins according to part type and auto model. The stripping operation would take place in one of four stripping bays equipped with a variety of power tools.

The advantages of the proposal are relatively evident. Since salable parts are kept indoors, the effect of the elements on them has been largely reduced. Also, the mechanics who strip the hulks need not work under inconvenient space, weather, or time conditions. The saving of space is equally important. Since the hulks will be stripped and disposed of promptly, there is no need for a large investment in property. Also, the unsightly appearance is avoided, and zoning laws become less strict, allowing the location of facilities in more desirable places.

Investigating the opportunity brought certain information to light which was necessary for evaluating the feasibility of the proposal. A small survey of area wreckers showed that the daily sales of a salvage operation varied from a low of $1,000 to a high of $2,500, the average being $1,900 per day. Of that figure, the average breakdown into retail (user) and wholesale (garage dealer) sales was about $500 to $1,400. However, the number of transactions was split evenly between the two categories. Fast-moving items included engines, front ends, hoods,

bumpers, fenders, and brake parts. Particularly slow items were wind-
shields, heater cores, AM radios, and bucket seats.

The investment group considered specializing in one particular make
of auto. To test this idea, they surveyed several auto dealerships and
garages that handled a particular make. The monthly average purchases
of these repair parts consumed from junk yards is summarized below:

	High	Low	Average
Mechanical parts	$ 800	$200	$ 500
Body parts	$1,500	$750	$1,000

Four of the ten shops interviewed kept regular accounts with at least one
yard. They averaged two. All remaining shops had dealings with at least
two different yards, the average being three. Eight of the ten shops responded favorably to dealing with a yard specializing in a particular
make. One dealt with such a yard already. Other estimates showed that
there was a potential market of $120,000 per month for used parts on the
particular make in question.

The management team planned to staff the operation in the following
manner. There was to be a manager, paid $250 per week, to oversee the
operation, bid on junk cars, set prices, and keep adequate records. Two
countermen would wait on customers. The manager would have to rely
heavily on these workers while acquainting himself with the workings of
the operation. Thus, these workers would have to be well experienced,
commanding a pay rate of $200 per week. Additional personnel would
include four car strippers whose skill would have to be equivalent to that
of a repair mechanic. These workers would expect a pay rate in the
range of $125–$150 per week. Finally, the staff would include a parts
person to clean, inspect, and maintain parts in the warehouse; and a
delivery person to deliver parts to customers. These employees would require salaries of $150 and $100 per week, respectively.

All operations were to take place indoors, in a building to be laid out
as in Appendix A. Outfitting the building would require the equipment
listed in Appendix B. The building, equipment, and other assets were to
be insured according to the following plan:

Type	Coverage	Annual premium
Fire, legal liability on building	$ 30,000	$ 201.00
Fire, extended coverage on contents		155.00
Workmens' compensation, employees' liability	100,000	220.00
Public (general) liability	100,000/300,000 BI 100,000 PD	382.00
Automobile liability, covering wrecker, delivery truck, and flat bed truck	100,000/300,000 BI 100,000 PD	1,012.00 $1,970.00

The building itself would be leased for a period of one or two years. Lease payments would be $12,000 annually.

The utility costs for this proposed operation would include not only the normal consumption of power and gas, but also an extensive communications network. The prospective junk dealers are considering tying into the various teletype networks which interconnect the yards throughout the Southeast. These facilities are used primarily to locate and price parts. The estimated power consumption would be $200 per month. Normal telephone service and Yellow Pages advertising would cost $150, while the teletype service would cost about $600 per month.

The operation start-up would require two and one-half months. During this initial period, the following cash outlays would have to be made:

Cost of equipment.....................	$15,850
Raw materials (100 cars)..............	50,000
Salaries (2½ months).................	20,700
Rent (2½ months)...................	2,500
Insurance (2½ months)..............	410
Utilities (2½ months)	
(except communications)............	500
License............................	250
Initial advertising....................	1,000
Total.........................	$91,210

The initial investors expect that little or no revenue would accrue during this period. Hence external sources of funds would have to be relied on for operating capital in the start-up period. The group found that it can raise only a small portion of the necessary capital. It expects to be able to borrow $60,000, payable over the next five years in monthly installments of $1,320.

After the original start-up period, sales are expected to be in the range of $1,000 per day at first, increasing to the industry average of $1,900 per day at the end of the first year of full operations. Cost of goods sold is anticipated to be one half of the sales value of the auto parts derived from each hulk.

Assets will be depreciated on a straight-line basis over a period of five years. Property taxes will be levied at about 2.0 percent of true value on fixed assets and inventories. An additional 6 percent of the payroll will have to be paid to the Social Security fund as required by law. Income taxes will be 40 percent of net income. The yard will operate five days a week.

1. Project the cash flows of the proposed operation for the start-up period and the first 12 months of full operations. Draw up a pro forma income statement and balance sheet as of the end of that period.

2. What are the advantages and disadvantages of specializing in one make of auto? Is it feasible to specialize? How much of the market would be necessary for the make of auto alluded to in the case?

3. What effect would the availability of the shredder have on operations and profitability? (If it were not available, how much more would it cost to dispose of hulks, etc.?)

Appendix A
Proposed utilization of warehouse space, area–22,500 sq. ft.

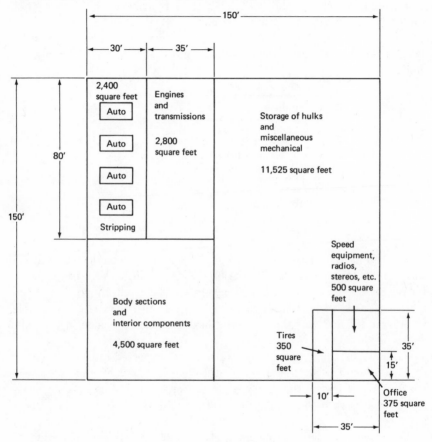

Appendix B
Costs of operating equipment

A.	Air compressor with distribution system	$ 1,000
B.	Parts washer (for cleaning small parts)	260
C.	Cutting torches: 2 @ $200	400
D.	Pneumatic impact wrenches with attachments: 4 @ $175	700
E.	Floor jacks (hydraulic, 1-ton capacity) 4 @ $150	600
F.	Jack stands: 20 @ $5	100
G.	Hydraulic crane (for removing motors)	1,000
H.	Steam cleaner (for cleaning large parts)	400
I.	Mechanics' tool sets, 2 @ $300	600
J.	Parts carts (for transporting parts between stripping area and storage area) 10 @ $100	1,000
K.	Material for storage bins and racks	2,000
L.	Cash register (for sales area)	150
M.	Tire machine (for dismounting saleable tires)	300
N.	Wrecker (used)	3,000
O.	Flat bed truck (for hauling off scrap) (used)	1,500
P.	Material for four (4) work benches for stripping area	100
Q.	Bench vices for stripping area: 4 @ $75	300
R.	Pneumatic chisel (with attachments)	200
S.	Puller set	150
T.	Bench grinder	100
U.	Hydraulic ram set (for forcing and bending metal)	130
V.	Creepers (for working under cars): 4 @ $15	60
W.	Electric saw (for removing body panels)	300
X.	Pickup truck (for delivering parts) (used)	1,500
	Total	$15,850

Appendix

12% PER PERIOD

Period	(1) Present value of $1	(2) Amount to which $1 will accumulate	Present value of $1 per period		Amount to which $1 per period will accumulate	
			(3) Received at end	(4) Received continuously	(5) Received continuously	(6) Received continuously
1	89286E 00	11200E 01	89286E 00	94542E 00	10000E 01	10589E 01
2	79719E 00	12544E 01	16901E 01	17895E 01	21200E 01	22448E 01
3	71178E 00	14049E 01	24018E 01	25432E 01	33744E 01	35730E 01
4	63552E 00	15735E 01	30373E 01	32161E 01	47793E 01	50607E 01
5	56743E 00	17623E 01	36048E 01	38170E 01	63528E 01	67268E 01
6	50663E 00	19738E 01	41114E 01	43534E 01	81152E 01	85929E 01
7	45235E-00	22107E 01	45638E 01	48324E 01	10089E 02	10683E 02
8	40388E-00	24760E 01	49676E 01	52601E 01	12300E 02	13024E 02
9	36061E-00	27731E 01	53282E 01	56419E 01	14776E 02	15645E 02
10	32197E-00	31058E 01	56502E 01	59828E 01	17549E 02	18582E 02
11	28748E-00	34786E 01	59377E 01	62872E 01	20655E 02	21870E 02
12	25668E-00	38960E 01	61944E 01	65590E 01	24133E 02	25554E 02
13	22917E-00	43635E 01	64235E 01	68017E 01	28029E 02	29679E 02
14	20462E-00	48871E 01	66282E 01	70183E 01	32393E 02	34299E 02
15	18270E-00	54736E 01	68109E 01	72118E 01	37280E 02	39474E 02
16	16312E-00	61304E 01	69740E 01	73845E 01	42753E 02	45270E 02
17	14564E-00	68660E 01	71196E 01	75387E 01	48884E 02	51761E 02
18	13004E-00	76900E 01	72497E 01	76764E 01	55750E 02	59032E 02
19	11611E-00	86128E 01	73658E 01	77994E 01	63440E 02	67174E 02
20	10367E-00	96463E 01	74694E 01	79091E 01	72052E 02	76294E 02
21	92560E-01	10804E 02	75620E 01	80072E 01	81699E 02	86508E 02
22	82643E-01	12100E 02	76446E 01	80947E 01	92503E 02	97948E 02
23	73788E-01	13552E 02	77184E 01	81728E 01	10460E 03	11076E 03
24	65882E-01	15179E 02	77843E 01	82426E 01	11816E 03	12511E 03
25	58823E-01	17000E 02	78431E 01	83048E 01	13333E 03	14118E 03
26	52521E-01	19040E 02	78957E 01	83605E 01	15033E 03	15918E 03
27	46894E-01	21325E 02	79426E 01	84101E 01	16937E 03	17934E 03
28	41869E-01	23884E 02	79844E 01	84544E 01	19070E 03	20192E 03
29	37383E-01	26750E 02	80218E 01	84940E 01	21458E 03	22721E 03
30	33378E-01	29960E 02	80552E 01	85294E 01	24133E 03	25554E 03

15% PER PERIOD

Period	(1) Present value of $1	(2) Amount to which $1 will accumulate	Present value of $1 per period		Amount to which $1 per period will accumulate	
			(3) Received at end	(4) Received continuously	(5) Received continuously	(6) Received continuously
1	86957E 00	11500E 01	86957E 00	93326E 00	10000E 01	10733E 01
2	75614E 00	13225E 01	16257E 01	17448E 01	21500E 01	23075E 01
3	65752E 00	15209E 01	22832E 01	24505E 01	34725E 01	37269E 01
4	57175E 00	17490E 01	28550E 01	30641E 01	49934E 01	53592E 01
5	49718E-00	20114E 01	33522E 01	35977E 01	67424E 01	72363E 01
6	43233E-00	23131E 01	37845E 01	40617E 01	87537E 01	93950E 01
7	37594E-00	26600E 01	41604E 01	44652E 01	11067E 02	11877E 02
8	32690E-00	30590E 01	44873E 01	48160E 01	13727E 02	14732E 02
9	28426E-00	35179E 01	47716E 01	51211E 01	16786E 02	18015E 02
10	24718E-00	40456E 01	50188E 01	53864E 01	20304E 02	21791E 02
11	21494E-00	46524E 01	52337E 01	56171E 01	24349E 02	26133E 02
12	18691E-00	53503E 01	54206E 01	58177E 01	29002E 02	31126E 02
13	16253E-00	61528E 01	55831E 01	59921E 01	34352E 02	36868E 02
14	14133E-00	70757E 01	57245E 01	61438E 01	40505E 02	43472E 02
15	12289E-00	81371E 01	58474E 01	62757E 01	47580E 02	51066E 02
16	10686E-00	93576E 01	59542E 01	63904E 01	55717E 02	59799E 02
17	92926E-01	10761E 02	60472E 01	64901E 01	65075E 02	69842E 02
18	80805E-01	12375E 02	61280E 01	65769E 01	75836E 02	81392E 02
19	70265E-01	14232E 02	61982E 01	66523E 01	88212E 02	94674E 02
20	61100E-01	16367E 02	62593E 01	67178E 01	10244E 03	10995E 03
21	53131E-01	18822E 02	63125E 01	67749E 01	11881E 03	12751E 03
22	46201E-01	21645E 02	63587E 01	68245E 01	13763E 03	14771E 03
23	40174E-01	24891E 02	63988E 01	68676E 01	15928E 03	17094E 03
24	34934E-01	28625E 02	64338E 01	69051E 01	18417E 03	19766E 03
25	30378E-01	32919E 02	64641E 01	69377E 01	21279E 03	22838E 03
26	26415E-01	37857E 02	64906E 01	69660E 01	24571E 03	26371E 03
27	22970E-01	43535E 02	65135E 01	69907E 01	28357E 03	30434E 03
28	19974E-01	50066E 02	65335E 01	70121E 01	32710E 03	35107E 03
29	17369E-01	57575E 02	65509E 01	70308E 01	37717E 03	40480E 03
30	15103E-01	66212E 02	65660E 01	70470E 01	43475E 03	46659E 03

18% PER PERIOD

Period	(1) Present value of $1	(2) Amount to which $1 will accumulate	Present value of $1 per period		Amount to which $1 per period will accumulate	
			(3) Received at end	(4) Received continuously	(5) Received continuously	(6) Received continuously
1	84746E 00	11800E 01	84746E 00	92163E 00	10000E 01	10875E 01
2	71818E 00	13924E 01	15656E 01	17027E 01	21800E 01	23708E 01
3	60863E 00	16430E 01	21743E 01	23646E 01	35724E 01	38851E 01
4	51579E 00	19388E 01	26901E 01	29255E 01	52154E 01	56719E 01
5	43711E-00	22878E 01	31272E 01	34009E 01	71542E 01	77803E 01
6	37043E-00	26996E 01	34976E 01	38037E 01	94420E 01	10268E 02
7	31393E-00	31855E 01	38115E 01	41451E 01	12142E 02	13204E 02
8	26604E-00	37589E 01	40776E 01	44344E 01	15327E 02	16668E 02
9	22546E-00	44355E 01	43030E 01	46796E 01	19086E 02	20756E 02
10	19106E-00	52338E 01	44941E 01	48874E 01	23521E 02	25580E 02
11	16192E-00	61759E 01	46560E 01	50635E 01	28755E 02	31272E 02
12	13722E-00	72876E 01	47932E 01	52127E 01	34931E 02	37988E 02
13	11629E-00	85994E 01	49095E 01	53392E 01	42219E 02	45914E 02
14	98549E-01	10147E 02	50081E 01	54464E 01	50818E 02	55266E 02
15	83516E-01	11974E 02	50916E 01	55372E 01	60965E 02	66301E 02
16	70776E-01	14129E 02	51624E 01	56142E 01	72939E 02	79323E 02
17	59980E-01	16672E 02	52223E 01	56794E 01	87068E 02	94688E 02
18	50830E-01	19673E 02	52732E 01	57347E 01	10374E 03	11282E 03
19	43077E-01	23214E 02	53162E 01	57815E 01	12341E 03	13421E 03
20	36506E-01	27393E 02	53527E 01	58212E 01	14663E 03	15946E 03
21	30937E-01	32324E 02	53837E 01	58549E 01	17402E 03	18925E 03
22	26218E-01	38142E 02	54099E 01	58834E 01	20634E 03	22440E 03
23	22218E-01	45008E 02	54321E 01	59075E 01	24449E 03	26588E 03
24	18829E-01	53109E 02	54509E 01	59280E 01	28949E 03	31483E 03
25	15957E-01	62669E 02	54669E 01	59454E 01	34260E 03	37259E 03
26	13523E-01	73949E 02	54804E 01	59601E 01	40527E 03	44074E 03
27	11460E-01	87260E 02	54919E 01	59725E 01	47922E 03	52116E 03
28	97119E-02	10297E 03	55016E 01	59831E 01	56648E 03	61606E 03
29	82304E-02	12150E 03	55098E 01	59920E 01	66945E 03	72804E 03
30	69749E-02	14337E 03	55168E 01	59996E 01	79095E 03	86017E 03

20% PER PERIOD

Period	(1) Present value of $1	(2) Amount to which $1 will accumulate	Present value of $1 per period		Amount to which $1 per period will accumulate	
			(3) Received at end	(4) Received continuously	(5) Received continuously	(6) Received continuously
1	83333E 00	12000E 01	83333E 00	91414E 00	10000E 01	10970E 01
2	69444E 00	14400E 01	15278E 01	16759E 01	22000E 01	24133E 01
3	57870E 00	17280E 01	21065E 01	23107E 01	36400E 01	39929E 01
4	48225E-00	20736E 01	25887E 01	28397E 01	53680E 01	58885E 01
5	40188E-00	24883E 01	29906E 01	32806E 01	74416E 01	81632E 01
6	33490E-00	29860E 01	33255E 01	36480E 01	99299E 01	10893E 02
7	27908E-00	35832E 01	36046E 01	39541E 01	12916E 02	14168E 02
8	23257E-00	42998E 01	38372E 01	42092E 01	16499E 02	18099E 02
9	19381E-00	51598E 01	40310E 01	44218E 01	20799E 02	22816E 02
10	16151E-00	61917E 01	41925E 01	45990E 01	25959E 02	28476E 02
11	13459E-00	74301E 01	43271E 01	47466E 01	32150E 02	35268E 02
12	11216E-00	89161E 01	44392E 01	48697E 01	39580E 02	43418E 02
13	93464E-01	10699E 02	45327E 01	49722E 01	48497E 02	53199E 02
14	77887E-01	12839E 02	46106E 01	50576E 01	59196E 02	64936E 02
15	64905E-01	15407E 02	46755E 01	51288E 01	72035E 02	79020E 02
16	54088E-01	18488E 02	47296E 01	51882E 01	87442E 02	95921E 02
17	45073E-01	22186E 02	47746E 01	52376E 01	10593E 03	11620E 03
18	37561E-01	26623E 02	48122E 01	52788E 01	12812E 03	14054E 03
19	31301E-01	31948E 02	48435E 01	53131E 01	15474E 03	16974E 03
20	26086E-01	38338E 02	48696E 01	53417E 01	18669E 03	20479E 03
21	21737E-01	46005E 02	48913E 01	53656E 01	22503E 03	24684E 03
22	18114E-01	55206E 02	49094E 01	53855E 01	27103E 03	29731E 03
23	15095E-01	66247E 02	49245E 01	54020E 01	32624E 03	35787E 03
24	12579E-01	79497E 02	49371E 01	54158E 01	39248E 03	43054E 03
25	10483E-01	95396E 02	49476E 01	54273E 01	47198E 03	51775E 03
26	87355E-02	11448E 03	49563E 01	54369E 01	56738E 03	62239E 03
27	72796E-02	13737E 03	49636E 01	54449E 01	68185E 03	74797E 03
28	60663E-02	16484E 03	49697E 01	54515E 01	81922E 03	89866E 03
29	50553E-02	19781E 03	49747E 01	54571E 01	98407E 03	10795E 04
30	42127E-02	23738E 03	49789E 01	54617E 01	11819E 04	12965E 04

Index of cases

Air-India (E) 618
American Telephone and Telegraph Company 629
The Auto-Wrecking Industry 671
   I. The Public Sector 675
   II. The Private Sector: Lanier Auto Parts 679
Avella, Inc. 613
Bausch and Lomb, Inc. 156
Birch Paper Company 534
Case Concrete Products 496
An Exercise in Business Conditions Analysis 151
Fall River Nursery 513
Finch Printing Company 598
Fulgrave Printing Company 507
International Harvester Company 501
M and H Company (B) 384
The Minerva Oxygen Vent Valve 392
Newville Branch of Ajax Cleaners (revised) 49
The Pricing of Automobiles 150
Randolph Stone Company 382
Sears, Roebuck and Company 505
Selected Decision-Making Rules and Practices 52
Sprague College Store 500
The State University Press (A) 148
The State University Press (B) 402
Steel Prices in 1962 519
Telephone Charges to Auxiliary Activities 517
Thomas Denton, Contractor 498
Utah Pie Company v. Continental Baking Co. (*et al.*) 525
Waldo, Smith, and Maxey 609
What Price Progress? 46
White Castle Trucking Co. 604

Index

A

Acceleration principle
  defined, 76
  empirical studies of, 78–80
Accounting costs
  contrasted with economic costs, 308–10
  limitations of, for decision making, 308–9
Air conditioners, as example of the demonstration effect, 81
Aircraft manufacturing, as example of
    application of decision tree approach to profitability analysis, 337–40
  learning curve, 335–37
  product life cycle, 334–35
Algebraic approach
  break-even analysis, 314–15
  economic order quantity, 362–65
  optimum output-sales, 323–25
  profit-volume analysis, 319–21
Almon, Clopper, Jr. (input-output technique), 559–60
Alternative products, 201–2, 478–79
Ansoff, H. I. (corporate strategy), 540
Arc elasticity, of quantity with respect to income, 67
  own price, 61
  price of other product, 67–68
Aspiration levels as organization goals, 11
Autocorrelation, effects of, 89
Automobiles, as example of study of demand for a durable good, 90–91
Average costs
  defined, 253
  relationship of, to total costs, 253–54
Average revenue, relationship of, to total and marginal revenue, 66

B

Bads, 168–69
Banking, as an example of
  demand forecasting for a firm, 144–46
  use of dummy variables in cost estimation, 290–92
Barriers to entry
  as basis of monopoly, 412–13
  in oligopoly, 421–22
  relationships of, to market structure, 409
Bay Area Rapid Transit (BART), as example of options to use, 641
Beckwith, Neil (applications of critical path method), 350–51
Behavioral equations in econometric models, 121
Behavioral theory of the firm, summary of, 11–12
Benefit-cost analysis
  appraisal of, 665–66
  choice of discount rate for, 657–59
  discounting benefits and costs in, 656–57
  examples of, 659–61
Benefits (in benefit-cost analysis)
  direct estimation of, 646
  enumeration of, 644–45
  evaluation of, 645–49
  indirect estimation of, 647–48
  problems in estimation of, 648–49
Bergfeld, A. J. (profit-volume analysis), 319
Bonbright, J. C. (public utility rates), 474–76
Book printing, as example of tradeoffs between production cost and inventory carrying cost, 354–55

Break-even analysis, 311–19
  algebraic approach to, 314–15
  appraisal of, 317–19
  constructing charts for, 315–16
  contribution form of, 314
  diagrams, 312, 316, 318
  scale of output axis in, 316–17
Broiler processing, as example of eco-
    nomic-engineering approach, 774–77
Buffer inventories, 356
Buildup approach in short-range fore-
    casting, 140–41
Burstein, M. L. (demand for durables),
    91–92
Buying power approach in short-range
    forecasting, 141

C

Capacity cost (in peak-load pricing),
    462–66
Capacity forecasting, 137–40
Capital budgeting
  under the condition of capital ration-
    ing, 592–93
  empirical studies of techniques used in,
    593
  involving mutually exclusive projects,
    583–85
  measuring project profitability in, 573–
    79
  an overview of, 570–71
  relationship of marginal resource cost
    to, 570
  relationship of marginal revenue prod-
    uct to, 570
  use of risk premiums in, 585–86
Capital rationing, 592–93
Cartter, A. M. (trends in demand for
    and supply of Ph.D.s), 563–65
Case method, 44–46
Cash flows
  defined, 571–72
  forecasting of, for a project, 571–73
  relationships of, to capital budgeting,
    570–71
Cement industry, as example of relation-
    ship of industry capacity to profit-
    ability), 139–40
Certainty equivalent (of a gamble), 431
Chisholm, R. K. (forecasting methods),
    131
Circular flow of national product, 98
Classification approach (to estimation of
    cost functions), 301–11
Cobb-Douglas production functions, 283
Coffee, as example of time series ap-
    proach to demand estimation, 86–89

Coincident indicators
  defined, 102
  list of, 103
Collusion in oligopolies, 425–26
Common costs, 34
Competences of the firm, 542
Compounding, 35
Computer system, as an example of use
    of systems analysis, 554–55
Computone Systems, Inc., 237–40
Consistency of the components of a
    GNP forecast, checks for, 119–20
Conspicuous consumption, 81
Constant marginal productivity
  defined, 170
  diagrams of, 171, 172, 177
  optimum use of an input that has,
    170–80
Constant marginal rate of product trans-
    formation, 198
Constituency of a public agency, 640–41
Constraints (restrictions) of an LP for-
    mulation, 204–5, 232
Consumer credit outstanding, relation-
    ship of, to demand, 143
Consumers' expectations of the future,
    use of, in forecasting, 106–7
Consumers' surplus, 646
Consumption
  as a component of a GNP model, 113
  sources of information about, 116–117
Continuative production, defined, 247–48
Continuous input substitutability at con-
    stant rates, 245–46
Contribution budget, use of, in decen-
    tralized control, 490
Contribution concept
  per unit of output, 29
  per unit of scarce resource used, 29–31
  relationship of
    to linear programming, 31–32
    to profit-volume analysis, 319–21
    to transfer pricing, 481–85
Contribution form of break-even anal-
    ysis, 314
Controllable costs, 305
Corporate strategy
  defined, 569
  example of formulation of, 561
  formulation of, 539–40
  objectives and goals of the firm in,
    540–42
  relationship of long-range forecasting
    to, 544
  relationship of, to capital budgeting,
    568–70
  selecting the business to be in, 542

Corporate taxes, effects of, upon
cash flows of projects, 571–73
social cost of capital, 657–59
Correlation (as a forecasting technique),
551
Cost classifications
common, 304
controllable, 305
direct, 305
escapable, 304
fixed, 302–3
implicit, 305
incremental, 303–4
inescapable, 304
marginal, 303–4
noncontrollable, 305
opportunity, 304
separable, 304
sunk, 303
variable, 302–3
Cost of capital
debt, 579–80
equity, 580
marginal, 581–82
relationship of, to inventory carrying
cost, 359
weighted average, 580–81
year-to-year changes in, 582–83
Cost-effectiveness analysis, 661–65
Costs of producing Ph.D.s, 562–63
Critical path method, 347–51
diagram of, 348
Cross elasticity, 66–68
Culliton, J. W. (make-or-buy decision),
37–38
Cultural trends, 544–46

D

Debt-equity ratio, 578
Decentralized control without profit centers, 490
Decision-tree analysis
adjustments for risk in, 430–34
applications of, to
capital budgeting decisions, 586–92
decisions whether or not to introduce products and how, 337–40
an oligopoly firm's pricing decision,
427–30
calculation of the mathematical expectation of payoff in, 339–40
handling decision-event-decision chains
in, 586–92
Decomposition of cash flows at
the discount rate, 577–78
the project's internal rate of return,
575–76
Decoupling inventories, 356

Decreasing marginal productivity
defined, 185–86
diagrams, 186, 187, 223
optimum use of an input that has,
185–96
Delphi method, 552
Demand
arithmetically linear model of, 58, 68–
71
constant elasticity model of, 58, 71–73
defined, 57–58
deliberate shifting of, 416–20
empirical studies of, 83–92
estimation of, 84–92
quantitative expressions of, 58–59
relationships of, to
incomes, 82
long-run and short-run perspectives,
77
population changes, 78
product improvements, 77
promotional activity, 78
psychological and sociological concepts, 80–83
Demand curves, 59
diagrams of
an arithmetically linear demand
curve, 69
a family of, 60
a log-linear demand curve, 72
kinked, 422–24
Demand equations
defined, 58–59
estimation of, 83–92
Demand estimation
for durable goods, 91–92
using cross-section (household consumption) data, 86–88
using experimental data, 84–86
models used in, 68–72, 82–84
using time-series (market) data, 88–89
Demand for Ph. D.s, 563–65
Demand for public services, 643
Demand schedules, 59
Demand shifting (deliberate), 416–20
Demographic trends, 547–48
Demonstration effect, 81
Depreciation
opportunity costs as basis for determining economic, 310
special problems of, in the classification approach to cost analysis,
309–10
Derived demand, 75–77
effects of attitudes and expectations
on, 76–77
relationship of acceleration principle
to, 76

De Salvia, D. N. (peak-load pricing), 467
Differential cost, 305
Differentiated oligopoly,
  defined, 421
  kinked demand under, 422–24
Differentiation of products, relationship of, to
  market structure, 408–9
  price discrimination, 456–59
Diffusion index, 103–4
Direct costs, 305
Direct requirements tables, 134–35
Direct user charges, 651–52
Discounting, 35, 574
  period-by-period with varying rates, 578–79
  relationship of, to capital budgeting, 571
Discrete input substitutability, 244–45
Discrete runs of production
  defined, 248
  diagrams
    choice of optimal rate of output, 347
    relationship of total costs to changes in volume and rate, 353, 357
    ways of changing output, 342
Discretionary buying power, 143
Diseconomies, of
  scale of plants, 258
  size of multiplant firms, 260
Due, J. F. (use of pricing by public agencies), 655
Dummy variables approach, 290–92
Durable goods, measuring costs of, 271–73

E

Earley, J. E. (pricing practices), 21, 443–44
Econometric models
  appraisal of, 125
  estimation of parameters of, 121
  examples of, 123–24
  simulation with, 121–22
  specification of, 121
  use of, in business conditions forecasting, 120–25
Economic order quantity, (EOQ), 358–59
  determination of, by
    algebraic approach, 362–65
    trial-and-error, 361–62
  graph of, 362
Economic profit
  calculation of, contrasted with use of incremental reasoning, 24–28
  contrast of, with accounting profit, 24

Economic substitutability of inputs
  diminishing marginal rates, 227
  isocost lines, 227–29
  least-cost combinations, 230
Economic-engineering approach (to estimation of cost functions), 265–77
Economies of scale of plants
  in banking, 290–92
  relationships of, to scale effects and input substitution effects, 250
  sources of, 256–58
  specialization as a source of, 256–57
  substitution of inputs as a source of, 258
  vertical integration as a source of, 258
Economies of size of multiplant firms, 258–60
Elasticity of demand, 60–62, 66–68
  arc elasticity, 61, 67, 68
  point elasticity, 61–62, 67, 68
Electric service, as example of price discrimination, 461–62
Envelope forecasting, 552–54
EOQ; see Economic order quantity
Equimarginal principle of resource allocation, 182–84, 191–96
  diagram, 194
Escapable costs, 304
Evans, M. K. (approaches to forecasting), 104, 107
Exclusion rules, 651
Expansion path
  contrasted with input-output function and scale line, 248–50
  defined, 240–41
  diagrams, 241, 249
  for increasing sales at a given price, 418–19
  relationship of, to
    long-run cost function, 255
    short-run cost function, 248–50
Expense, contrast of, with cost, 303
Exploratory approaches to technological forecasting, 551
Externalities, 640–41

F

Farming, as example of a product mix problem, 196–97
Feasible region (solution space), 206
  diagrams, 207, 236
  an optimum solution must be at a corner of the, 208, 235–37
Feast-and-famine industries, 66
Feed manufacturing, as example of application of linear programming to product mix problem, 231–39

Feed manufacturing—*Cont.*
statistical approach to estimation of cost functions, 287–90

Firm's demand, 129

Fixed cost
contrasted with variable cost, 302–3
relationship of, to total cost, 250–52

Flexibility
relationship of, to corporate strategy, 541
relationship of, to costs of the plant, 254–55

Forecasting demand in a specified market, for
consumers' goods, 141
producers' goods, 140–41

Forecasting the firm's share of demand in a specified market, 141–42

Forecasting general business conditions (GNP and its components), with
econometric models, 120–25
indicators, 101–4
partially specified GNP model, 108–120
surveys of attitudes and plans, 105–7
table listing sources of information useful in, 114–16

Forecasting industry capacity, 137–40

Forecasting an industry's demand, 129–137, 143–44

Forecasting a project's cash flows, 571–73

Full cost pricing, 434–35
in transfers of intermediate goods, 488–90

Functional fields of business, integration of with managerial economics, 7

G

Gas and electricity (as examples of price discrimination), 461–62

Gerstenfeld, Arthur (uses of technological forecasting), 555

Goal programming, 667–68

Governments' intentions
sources of information about, 115
use of, in forecasting, 105

Governments' spending
as a component of a GNP model, 109–10
sources of information about, 115

Graduate education, as example of divergence between private and social cost, 650–51

Grocery store, as example of cost classification approach, 306–7

Gross National Product
defined, 98–101
forecasting of (see forecasting general business conditions)

H

Hall, R. L. (pricing practices), 442–43

Haynes, W. W. (pricing in small firms), 21–23, 445

Helmer, Olaf (Delphi method), 552

Henderson, B. D. (proposed system of decentralized control), 490

Highway construction, as example of external benefits and costs, 649

Household consumption surveys, 86–88

Houthakker, H. S. (demand), 90–91

Huxley, Aldous (concepts of the future world), 546

I

Imitative (going-rate) pricing, 436

Implicit cost, 305

Income elasticity of demand, 66–67

Incremental cost
contrasted with marginal cost, 303–4
contrasted with sunk cost, 303
defined, 19

Incremental reasoning
contrasted with economic profit calculation, 24–28
contrasted with marginal analysis, 20–21
defined, 18–20
use of,
in forecasting cash flows of projects, 571–73
in decisions involving discrete input substitutions, 245
in decisions about input substitution, 241–43
in pricing, 436–38
in resource allocation, 190–91
in searching for the expansion path, 244

Indicators approach to forecasting, 101–4
diagram, 102
sources of information about indicators, 117
table listing indicators, 103

Indirect user charges, 652–53

Industry demand, 129

Inescapable costs, 304

Inferior goods, 66

Innovation as a source of profits, 9

Input-output approach to forecasting
appraisal of, 136–37
direct requirements tables, 134–35
input-output tables, 133–35
total requirements tables, 134–36

Input-output approach to forecasting—
Cont.
use of, in long-range forecasting, 558–60
use of, in short-range forecasting, 133–37
Input-output functions
with constant marginal productivity, 170–72
contrasted with scale lines and the expansion path, 248–50
relationship of, to short-run cost function, 248–50
with varying marginal productivity, 186–88
Internal rate of return, 574–76
Intuitive technological forecasts
Delphi method of, 552
scenario method of, 552
Inventory types or functions
buffer, 356
decoupling, 356
lot-size, 356
seasonal or anticipations, 356–57
Inventory-carrying costs, 359–60
Inventory investment
as a component of a GNP model, 111–12
sources of information about, 116
Isocontribution lines, 199–201
diagram, 201
Isocost lines, 227–29
diagrams, 228, 236
Isoquants, 223–25
diagrams, 224, 228

J–K

Jantsch, E. (technological forecasting), 551
Joint products
defined, 168
optimum output and pricing of, 476–77
Kahn, H. (scenario approaches to forecasting), 552
Kaplan, A. D. H. (pricing), 444–45
Katona, G. (consumer attitudes), 82–83
Kinked demand, 422–24
Klein, L. (econometric models of U.S. economy), 122–23
Kotler, P. (relationships of social and cultural trends to demands for products and services), 545–46

L

Labor costs, measurement of, 269–70
Lagging indicators
defined, 102
list of, 103

Law of variable proportions, 183
Leading indicators
defined, 101–2
list of, 103
Learning, relationship of, to use of models in decision making, 13–14
Learning curves
diagram, 336
effects of, on variable cost per unit, 335–38
learning rate, 335
relationship of, to proportion of work that is machine paced, 335–36
Learning rate, 335
Least-cost combinations of inputs, 229–30
Lewis, J. P. (forecasting methods), 104, 107–8
Life cycles of products, 331–32
Linear programming
application of, to least-cost formulation, 231–37
application of, to product-mix determination, 202–14
constraints (restrictions) in, 204–5
divisibility of activities assumption, 205
formulation of a tableau for, 203–6
graphic solution of, 206–10
objective functions used in, 204
relationships of, to basic economic concepts, 214
technological coefficients used in, 204–5
Long-run cost functions, 255–60
managerial uses of, 292–94
Long-run perspective, 33–34
of cost, 255–60
of production, 170
Lot-size inventories, 356
Luck, as a source of profits, 9

M

Macroeconomic theory, relationship of, to managerial economics, 5
Make-or-buy decisions, 37–38
Managerial economics
relationships of, to other branches of learning, 4–7
scope and method of, 3–16
usefulness of, 15–16
Marginal analysis, contrasted with incremental reasoning, 20–21
Marginal cost
contrasted with incremental cost, 303–4
defined, 252
relationship of, to
peak-load pricing, 462–66

Marginal cost—*Cont.*
  short run average costs, 252–53
  variations in rate of output, 268–69
Marginal cost of capital, 581–82
Marginal cost pricing, 472–73, 651–52
Marginal product
  constant marginal product, 172
  defined, 172
  varying marginal product, 184–85
Marginal rate of technical substitution, 225–26
Marginal resource cost, 174–75, 181–82, 570
Marginal revenue
  defined, 63
  relationship of, to
    average and total revenue, 66
    price and elasticity, 64
Marginal revenue product
  defined, 173, 178
  diagrams, 177, 180, 182, 184
  relationship of, to capital budgeting, 570–71
Market demand, 129
Market structure
  determinants of, 408–9
  relationships of firms demand to industry demand under various forms of, 73–75
  principle forms of, 409
Market potential, forecasting of, 140–41
Market share, forecasting of, 141–42
Materials costs, measurement of, 271
Measurement of costs of major inputs, 269–73
Meat products, as example of joint products pricing, 479–80
Microeconomic theory, relationship of, to managerial economics, 4–5
Models
  defined, 11–13
  of demand, 68–72, 82–84
  of production and cost, 281–83
Monopolistic competition
  choice of optimum output and pricing under, 413–15
  contrasted with other market structures, 409
  defined, 413–14
  diagrams, 414–15
Monopoly
  choice of optimum output and pricing under, 412–13
  contrasted with other market structures, 409
  defined, 412
  diagrams, 413
  as a source of profits, 9

Morphological analysis in technological forecasting, 552
Multicollinearity, 89, 284–85, 287–90
Multiple objectives in the public sector, 666–68
Multiple-product pricing
  alternative products, 478–79
  joint products in fixed proportions, 476–79
Multiplier, 118–119
Multistage approach to pricing, 440–41
Mutually exclusive projects, 583–85

N

National Bureau of Economic Research, 102–4
National income, 99–100
Net exports, as a component of a GNP model, 112
Net present value, 571, 576–77
Net social benefit, 642
New plant and equipment
  as a component of a GNP model, 110–11
  sources of information about, 115–16
New product profitability analysis, 332–40
Non-price competition in oligopolies, 426–27
Normative approach to technological forecasting, 551
Number of firms in an industry, relationship of, to market structure, 408

O

OBE (Office of Business Economics) model, 123–24
Objective functions, 204, 232
Oil industry, as example of transfer pricing problems, 490–91
Oligopoly
  collusion in, 425–26
  decision tree analysis of the marketing decisions of a firm in, 427–34
  defined, 420–22
  kinked demand and sticky prices in, 422–24
  non-price competition in, 426–27
  price leadership in, 424
  price wars in, 426
Ontological view of technological forecasting, 551
Operations research, relationship of, to managerial economics, 6–7
Opportunistic approach to business conditions analysis, 107–8

Opportunity cost
  as a basis for determining economic depreciation, 310
  contrasted with costs requiring no sacrifice, 304
  defined, 23–24
  relationship of, to benefit-cost analysis, 649–51
  relationship of, to capital budgeting, 573
  use of, in analyzing profitability of change in length of discrete run, 343–45
  use of, in analyzing profitability of change in rate of discrete run, 345–47
Options to use, 641
Ordering costs, 360–61
Orwell, George (views of the future), 546
Out-of-pocket costs, 305

P

Peak-load pricing, 462–70
  empirical studies of, 469–70
  general principles of, 462–64
  practical problems related to, 466–68
Pear packing, as example of economic engineering approach, 274–75
Penalties, 653
Penetration pricing, 340–41
Permanent income hypothesis, 82
Petroleum industry, as example of applications of linear programming, 215–16
Ph.D.s, trends
  in cost of producing, 562–63
  in demand, 563
  in supply, 564–65
Point elasticity, 61–62, 67, 68
Political trends, 546–47
Population changes, relationship to demand, 78, 143
Preference values, 431
Present value, 573–74
Price discrimination
  choosing pricing and output to maximize profit under, 456–57
    with marginal costs that differ among products, 458
  conditions necessary for, 458–59
  defined, 454–55
  examples of, 458–62
  nature of gains from, 455
  personal, or first-degree, form of, 459–60
  social and legal issues related to, 460–61

Price elasticity of demand
  arc, 61
  elastic demand defined, 65
  defined, 60
  inelastic demand defined, 64
  influences that determine, 65–66
  relationship to output and total revenue, 64–65
  relationship to price and marginal revenue, 63–64
  unitary demand defined, 64–65
Price leadership in oligopolies, 424–25
Price takers, 436
Price wars, 426
Pricing
  of alternative products, 478–79
  checklist for, 441–42
  empirical studies of, 442–45
  of joint products, 476–77
  under monopolistic competition, 413–15
  under monopoly, 412–13
  multistage approach to, 440–41
  under oligopoly, 420–27
  parties involved in, 439
  peak-load, 462–70
  under price discrimination, 454–61
  under pure competition, 409–11
  regulation of, of utilities, 470–73
  of transfers of an intermediate product, 480–81
  using incremental reasoning in, 436–38
  using shortcuts in, 434–36
Pricing goods and services produced by public agencies, 651–55
Pricing process
  checklist for, 441–42
  multistage approach, 440–41
  parties involved in, 439–40
Process flow in production, 266–67
Process ray, 247
Producers' expectations, use in forecasting, 105–6
Product life cycles, 331–32
  diagrams, 332, 341
Product line decisions, 39–40
Product-mix problem
  defined, 196–97
  optimum solution of, 201–2, 478–79
Production
  defined, 167–68
  inputs used in, 168
  outputs of, 168–69
  production functions, 169–70
  production processes, 168–69
Production possibility curves, 197–99
  diagrams, 198, 199
Production scheduling, 355–57

Production surface, 170–72, 186–87
  diagrams, 171, 223, 224, 282
Profit-volume analysis, 319–21
  diagram, 320
Profitability analysis of discrete production runs, 330–76
Profitability index, 578
Profits
  alternative theories of, 8–9
  as central concept in managerial economics, 7–11
  as objective in strategic planning, 540–41
Programmed fixed cost, 302
Psychological and sociological concepts of consumer behavior, 80–83
Public goods, 641
  contrasted with private goods, 651
Public sector, role of, in the economy, 640–42
Public utility rate regulation, 470–73
Pure competition
  choice of optimum output and sales under, 409–11
  contrasted with other market structures, 409
  defined, 409
  diagram, 410
Pure oligopoly
  contrasted with other market structures, 409
  defined, 420–21
  kinked demand and sticky prices, 422–24

Q–R

Quantity discounts, 365
Queues, as method of rationing, 651
Quinn, J. B. (technological forecasting), 551, 555
Rapid transit system, as example of benefit-cost analysis, 659–60
Rate of output
  analyzing profitability of changes in for continuative production, 311–26
  for discrete runs of production, 343–54
  ways of changing, 341–42
Relevant costs, 306
Replacement demand, 144
Residential construction, as component of GNP model, 111
  sources of information about, 116
Resource allocation
  limited input
    constant marginal revenue products in several uses, 175–78

Resource allocation—*Cont.*
  limited input—*Cont.*
    decreasing marginal revenue products, 182–85, 191–96
  unlimited input
    constant marginal revenue products, 173–74
    decreasing marginal revenue products, 179–85, 191–96
Resource forecasting, 556–58
Ridge lines, 227
Risk and uncertainty
  adjustments for, 430–34
  certainty equivalent, 431
  preference value, 431
  risk premium, 432
  as source of profits, 8–9
Rothenberg, Jerome (indirect estimation methods), 647–48

S

Safety stocks, 370–76
Saturation levels, relationship of, to demand, 143
Scale line, 248–50
Scenario writing, in technological forecasting, 552
Seasonal or anticipations inventories, 356–57
Selecting the business to be in, 542–43
Sensitivity analysis
  of economic order quantity solution, 365
  of linear programming solution, 211–14
Separable costs, 304
Serial correlation, 285–87
Setup costs, 366–67
Shepherd, W. G. (peak-load pricing), 469–70
Short list of economic indicators, 103
Short-run cost functions, 247–55
Short-run perspective on production, 169–70
Shortcuts in pricing, 434–36
  full-cost pricing, 434–35
  imitative pricing, 436
  suggested prices, 435–36
Simulation, use in decisions about numbers, sizes, and locations of plants, 293–94
Size and age distribution of stocks of goods, relation to demand, 43–44
Skimming pricing, 340–41
Social cost, 649–51
Social forecasting
  cultural trends, 544–46
  demographic trends, 547–48

Social forecasting—*Cont.*
  an example of, 548–60
  political trends, 546–47
Solomons, David (transfer pricing and measurement and control of divisional performance), 486, 490–91
Southwick, Lawrence, Jr. (trends in costs of producing Ph.D.s), 562–63
Spatial costs, adding to plant's internal costs, 275–77
Specialization as source of economies
  of scale of plants, 256–57
  of size of multiplant firms, 259
Stage of production, 266
Standby fixed costs, 303
Statistical approach to estimation of production and cost functions, 277–92
Statistical forecasts of industry demand, 130–33
Statistics, relation to managerial economics, 5
Status symbols, 81
Stigler, George J. (empirical tests of kinked demand theory), 443
Stockouts, 369–70
Stollsteimer, J. F. (model for choosing numbers, sizes, and locations of plants), 293–94
Suboptimization, 13
Subsidies, 653–54
Suggested prices, 435–36
Suits, D. B. (multiplier and accelerator effects), 114

Sunk costs, 303
Surveys, approach to business conditions analysis, 105–7

T

Target population, 644–45
Technical substitutability of inputs, 223–26, 244–47
Technological forecasting
  acceptance of, 555
  general approaches to, 551
  limitations of, 555
  techniques used in, 551–55
Teleological view of technological forecasting, 551
Theory of decision making, relationship to managerial economics, 5–6
Time perspective on decisions, 33–34, 77
Time value of money, 34–37
Total cost, 248, 251, 270
Total revenue, 64–65
Transfer pricing, 481–90
Turvey, Ralph (demand shifts for electric power), 468

U–W

Upward-bound program, as example of benefit-cost analysis, 660–61
User charges, 651–53
Variable cost, 250–52, 302–3
Vertical integration, 258, 260
Water supply, as example of price discrimination, 461

This book has been set in 10 and 9 point Modern #21, leaded 2 points. Part numbers and titles are 24 point Ultra Bodoni; chapter numbers and titles are 18 point Ultra Bodoni. The size of the type page is 27 by 45½ picas.